MUSIC AND MUSICIANS ON THE LONDON STAGE, 1695–1705

Performance in the Long Eighteenth Century: Studies in Theatre, Music, Dance

Series Editors

Jane Milling, University of Exeter, UK
Kathryn Lowerre, Michigan State University, USA

Focusing on performance culture during the long eighteenth century, this series offers studies of individuals, institutions, forms and trends in all types of cultural performance including theatre, opera, dance, musical performance, and diverse popular entertainments. It is a forum for interdisciplinary work, drawing the debates of historians, musicologists, literary scholars, dance, theatre and opera scholars into a creative symbiosis.

The editors welcome studies which are concerned with British, European, and early American cultural history. Studies that concern themselves with theoretical questions surrounding acts of performance during this period are also welcome.

Other titles in the series

*The Dramatic Works of Catherine the Great
Theatre and Politics in Eighteenth-Century Russia*
Lurana Donnels O'Malley

*The Incomparable Hester Santlow
A Dancer-Actress on the Georgian Stage*
Moira Goff

*Women Writing Music in Late Eighteenth-Century England
Social Harmony in Literature and Performance*
Leslie Ritchie

Music and Musicians on the London Stage, 1695–1705

KATHRYN LOWERRE
Michigan State University, USA

ASHGATE

© Kathryn Lowerre 2009

All rights reserved. No part of this publication may be reproduced, stored in a retrieval system or transmitted in any form or by any means, electronic, mechanical, photocopying, recording or otherwise without the prior permission of the publisher.

Kathryn Lowerre has asserted her right under the Copyright, Designs and Patents Act, 1988, to be identified as the author of this work.

Published by
Ashgate Publishing Limited
Wey Court East
Union Road
Farnham
Surrey, GU9 7PT
England

Ashgate Publishing Company
Suite 420
101 Cherry Street
Burlington
VT 05401-4405
USA

www.ashgate.com

British Library Cataloguing in Publication Data
Lowerre, Kathryn.
  Music and Musicians on the London Stage, 1695–1705. – (Performance in the Long Eighteenth Century: Studies in Theatre, Music, Dance)
  1. Drury Lane Theatre – History. 2. Lincoln's Inn Fields Theatre – History. 3. Music in the theater – England – London – History – 17th century. 4. Music in the theater – England – London – History – 18th century. I. Title II. Series.
  792'.09421'09032–dc22

Library of Congress Cataloging-in-Publication Data
Lowerre, Kathryn.
  Music and Musicians on the London Stage, 1695–1705 / Kathryn Lowerre.
     p.   cm. – (Performance in the Long Eighteenth Century)
  Includes bibliographical references and index.
  1. Musical theater – England – London – History – 17th century. 2. Musical theater – England – London – History – 18th century. 3. Lincoln's Inn Fields Theatre. 4. Drury Lane Theatre. I. Title.
  ML1731.8.L7L69 2009
  792.609421'09032–dc22   2009020285

ISBN 9780754666141

Printed and bound in Great Britain by
MPG Books Group, UK

For my mother, Nan Jamieson Lowerre,
who taught me to appreciate history
&
in memory of my father, George F. Lowerre,
who loved mathematics, music, and the theater.

Contents

List of Musical Illustrations	*ix*
List of Tables	*xi*
Acknowledgements	*xiii*
Abbreviations	*xv*

Prologue: Rival Crews: Music and Musicians in the London Theaters   1

PART I: THE PLACE AND FUNCTION OF MUSIC IN DRAMATIC PRODUCTIONS

1	Musical Approaches in Comedy	17
2	Musical Tragedies and Dramatick Operas	65

PART II: MUSIC AND MUSICIANS IN THEATRICAL COMPETITION

3	Initiation, 1695–1697	123
2	Competition, 1697–1700	195
5	Power Shift, 1700–1703	263
6	Realignment, 1703–1705	329

Epilogue	375
Appendix 1: Glossary of Musical Terms and Concepts	377
Appendix 2: Composers Active in the London Theaters, 1695–1705	383
Selected Bibliography	*393*
Index of Persons	*401*
Index of Productions	*407*

List of Musical Illustrations

1.1	John Eccles, "Restless in thought, disturb'd in mind" in *She Ventures and He Wins*. From Eccles, *A Collection of Songs for One, Two, or Three Voices* (London, 1704), pp. 2–3. By permission of the Folger Shakespeare Library.	33
1.2	J. Franck, "Go Home unhappy wretch and mourn" in *Love's Last Shift*. From *Thesaurus Musicus* book 5, pp. 8–10. By permission of the Folger Shakespeare Library.	38
1.3	G. Finger, "See, Vulcan, Jealousie appears!" in *The Loves of Mars and Venus*. From *Single Songs and Dialogues in the Musical Play of Mars & Venus*, pp. 17–8. By permission of the Folger Shakespeare Library.	49
2.1	R. Elford, "To thee, o gentle Sleep" in *Tamerlane*. By permission of the British Library [Shelfmark G.151 (144)].	75
2.2	J. Eccles, chaconne [treble and bass] in *Rinaldo and Armida*. From *Theater Musick* (Walsh, 1698), book 1 pp. 23–4. Courtesy of Durham Cathedral [Durham Cathedral Library Music Pr. C78].	110
3.1	J. Eccles, "Stretch'd in a dark and dismal grove" in *Pyrrhus, King of Epirus*. From *Deliciae Musicae* vol. 1 book 3, pp. 8–9. By permission of the Folger Shakespeare Library.	137
3.2	J. Eccles, "Let us revel and roar" in *The Lover's Luck*. From Eccles, *A Collection of Songs,* p. 160. By permission of the Folger Shakespeare Library.	149
3.3	D. Purcell, "Alas! When charming Sylvia's gone" in *The Spanish Wives*. By permission of the British Library [Shelfmark K.7.i.2 (38)].	162
3.4	R. Leveridge, "When Cloe, I your Charms survey" in *A Plot and No Plot*. By permission of the British Library [Shelfmark G.151 (176)].	184
4.1	J. Eccles, "All things seem deaf to my complaints" in *The Pretenders*. From Eccles, *A Collection of Songs,* pp. 15–6. By permission of the Folger Shakespeare Library.	218
4.2	J. Eccles, "Can Life be a blessing" from *Troilus and Cressida*. From Eccles, *A Collection of Songs*, p. 137. By permission of the Folger Shakespeare Library.	224

4.3	D. Purcell, "In a grove's forsaken shade" in *Amalasont, Queen of the Goths*. By permission of the British Library [Shelfmark Lbl K.7.i.2 (40)].	228
4.4	D. Purcell, "Morpheus, thou gentle God of soft Repose," in *Achilles*. By permission of the British Library [Shelfmark G.151 (105)].	246
5.1	J. Eccles, "Must then a faithful lover go" from *Acis and Galatea*. From Eccles, *A Collection of Songs*, pp. 86–7. By permission of the Folger Shakespeare Library.	281
5.2	Mr. Gillier, "For mighty Love's unerring Dart" in *The Ladies Visiting Day*. By permission of the British Library [Shelfmark K.7.i.2 (88)].	285
5.3	D. Purcell, "Tis done, tis done the pointed arrow's in my heart" in *The Humour of the Age*. By permission of the British Library [Shelfmark G.151 (159)].	288
5.4	D. Purcell, "Let not Love on me bestow" in *The Funeral*. By permission of the British Library [Shelfmark G.151 (90)].	298
5.5	J. Eccles, "Fie Amarillis, cease to Grieve" in *The Fickle Shepherdess*. From Eccles, *A Collection of Songs*, p. 42. By permission of the Folger Shakespeare Library.	320
6.1	J. Eccles, "In vain malicious Fate contrives" in *The Rival Brothers*. From the Library of Congress.	349
6.2	J. Wilford, "In vain I hope to find relief" from *The Libertine*. By permission of the British Library [Shelfmark K.7.i.2 (77)].	354
6.3	"Here are People and Sports" in *The Mountebank*. By permission of Olive Baldwin and Thelma Wilson, private collection.	364

List of Tables

2.1	Musical events in Oldmixon's *The Grove*	93
2.2	Musical events in Settle's *The Virgin Prophetess*	94
2.3	Comparison of musical scenes in *Phaeton* and *Rinaldo and Armida*	99
2.4	Pastoral entertainments in *Phaeton* and *Rinaldo and Armida*	105
3.1	Selected singers in each company, spring 1695 and 1695–97 seasons	127
3.2	New productions during the spring and summer of 1695	132
3.3	New productions during the 1695–96 season	140
3.4	New productions during the 1696–97 season	165
3.5	Musical entertainments in *The World in the Moon*	189
4.1	New productions during the 1697–98 season	204
4.2	New productions during the 1698–99 season	227
4.3	New productions during the 1699–1700 season	242
5.1	New productions during the 1700–1701 season	272
5.2	New productions during the 1701–1702 season	295
5.3	New productions during the 1702–1703 season	307
6.1	New productions during the 1703–1704 season	338
6.2	New productions during the 1704–1705 season	356

Acknowledgements

My profound thanks are due to Olive Baldwin and Thelma Wilson for their reading of this book in draft form, for their helpful comments, and for saving me from many biographical and bibliographical slips. I thank Jonathan Glixon for inviting me to talk about my work at the University of Kentucky, where several ideas in Chapter Two had their first public hearing. I also wish to thank Michael Burden for questions and conversations, Amanda Eubanks Winkler for our discussions of music and magic, and Tony Rooley for his indefatigable enthusiasm for John Eccles's music and Anne Bracegirdle's performances.

Like so many other projects related to the London theaters, my work has been made possible by the scholarship of Robert Hume, Judith Milhous, and Curtis Price. I appreciate their willingness to talk with me about my project in its early stages. My debt to many other scholars in dance, music, theater history, and related disciplines goes well beyond my footnotes.

This book would have been impossible without the assistance of library staff in many places including the Bodleian Library, British Library, Durham Cathedral Library, Fitzwilliam Museum Library, Folger Shakespeare Library, Harvard Theatre Collection, Houghton Library, Library of Congress, Royal College of Music, and the Michigan State University Library.

I received funding for portions of my research from the W. Jackson Bate/Douglas W. Bryant/American Society for Eighteenth-Century Studies Visiting Fellowship at Houghton Library, Harvard University; Michigan State University's Intramural Research Grants Program; and The Society for Theatre Research.

Many thanks to former colleagues at Michigan State University, with special thanks to Joe Lonstein. At Ashgate, I thank Ann Donahue, Jane Milling and the anonymous readers who provided comments. Finally, I thank my far-flung family and friends.

Abbreviations

In referring to productions, I identify the place of performance and year of premiere, for example *Love for Love* (LIF, 1695). Using original editions, I refer to act and page number.

Abbreviations: General

Apology	*An Apology for the Life of Mr. Colley Cibber*, ed. Robert W. Lowe
DL	Drury Lane Theater
DG	Dorset Garden Theater
D&M	Cyrus Lawrence Day and Eleanore Boswell Murrie, *English Song-Books, 1651–1702*. Numerical references are to the index of songs, unless otherwise specified.
DNB	*Dictionary of National Biography* (2004)
Hunter	David Hunter, *Opera and Song Books Published in England, 1703–1726*. References are to entry (song number).
M&H *London Stage*	Judith Milhous and Robert D. Hume, *The London Stage, 1660–1800*, Part 2: 1700–1729, vol. 1, 1700–1711. [July 2001]
LIF	Lincoln's Inn Fields Theater
Music Productions LIF	Kathryn Lowerre, *Music in the Productions at London's Lincoln's Inn Fields Theater, 1695–1705*
PC	Patent Company
Theatrical Documents	Milhous and Hume, *A Register of English Theatrical Documents, 1660–1737*
Thomas Betterton	Judith Milhous, *Thomas Betterton and the Management of Lincoln's Inn Fields, 1695–1708*
State Affairs	Narcissus Luttrell, *A Brief Historical Relation of State Affairs, 1678–1714*
UC	United Company

Abbreviations: Library Sigla

Unless otherwise indicated, all abbreviations are for collections in England (prefix GB)

Cfm	Fitzwilliam Museum, Cambridge
Ckc	Rowe Music Library, King's College, Cambridge
DFo	Folger Shakespeare Library, Washington DC, USA
DLC	Library of Congress, Washington DC, USA
DRc	Durham Cathedral Library, Durham
Lbl	British Library, London
Lcm	Royal College of Music, London
Lgc	Gresham College Collection, Guildhall Library, London
Ob	Bodleian Library, Oxford
Obh	Harding Collection, Bodleian Library, Oxford
Obt	St. Michael's College, Tenbury Collection, Bodleian Library, Oxford
Och	Christchurch College, Oxford
MH-H	Houghton Library, Harvard University, Cambridge MA, USA

Prologue
Rival Crews: Music and Musicians in the London Theaters

> Let *Musick* try its Pow'r in ev'ry Breast.
> Musick, that tune's the Floods, make's Desarts gay,
> And woo's all Nature in the tendrest way.
> Whose subtlest Magick acts on ev'ry Part,
> But makes its quickest Passage to the Heart.
> Musick, whose mighty Pow'r alone can boast,
> It most delights us, when it Wounds us most.
> …
> Thrice happy *Artists*! Who alone have found
> The utmost Force and Energy of *Sound*.[1]

In England at the turn of the eighteenth century, music's power and potential perils lay in its ability to move human passions, and bodies with them. Its associations with magic, power and love made it an essential element of theater, although there were both practical and philosophical concerns about its proper use.

Active contemporary debates about music and the extraordinary variety of printed materials (textual and musical) produced after the lapsing of the Licensing Act in 1695 make the 1695–1705 decade key to our understanding both of seventeenth-century musical traditions and the development of eighteenth-century ones. While this decade has been studied from a theatrical perspective, this is the first attempt to look comprehensively at the repertoire, its creators and its performers from a musical point of view.[2] The inclusion of both topical and chronological chapters is designed to maintain the benefits but avoid the limitations

---

[1] "A Prologue Spoken to the Ladies before the Musick Act, at the Publick Commencement at Cambridge, On Tuesday the 5th of July 1698," in Pierre Danchin, *Prologues and Epilogues of the Restoration*, Part III: 1691–1700, vol. 5, no. 512, p. 522, lines 40–46, 49–50.

[2] Several recent dissertations have done valuable work on specific composers, performers, and types, including Mark Humphreys, "Daniel Purcell: A Biography and Thematic Catalogue" (D.Phil., New College, Oxford, 2004); Matthew Roberson, "Of Priests, Fiends, Fops, and Fools: John Bowman's Song Performances on the London Stage, 1677–1701" (Ph.D., Florida State University, 2006); and Timothy L. Neufeldt, "The Social and Political Aspects of the Pastoral Mode in Musico-dramatic Works, London, 1695–1728" (Ph.D., University of Toronto, 2006).

of either a purely chronological approach or one focused on genres. This structure emphasizes performance choices made over time and facilitates the making of connections and comparisons.

From 1682 until 1695 there was only one licensed theatrical company operating in London. In 1695 a group of actors broke away to create a new company at Lincoln's Inn Fields, where senior actors were in charge and considerations related to artistic quality were apparently given more precedence than at the Patent Company,[3] managed on a business model with notorious emphasis on the bottom line. The role played by music and musicians in the resulting theatrical competition is significant.

As commercial theaters, the need to combat successes at "the other house" and mount new shows at their own led each theater company to experiment with a wide variety of different kinds of musical productions and entr'acte music. Regular newspaper documentation of performances begins, revealing the persistence of seventeenth-century musical repertoire and conventions alongside the adoption of new models.

At the turn of the eighteenth century, the London theaters were engaged in an elaborate balancing act: offering audiences both generic familiarity and novelty. If new productions were too formulaic, they might not please. If they were too experimental, they also ran the risk of a quick dismissal. Audiences enjoyed moments within productions which operated on multiple levels—rewarding and challenging an audience's theatrical knowledge, from the general (a favorite actress's usual character type) to the privileged (who wrote an anonymous prologue or song).[4] Many of the most successful productions involved substantial amounts of music.

Both companies employed a common tradition of musical practices. Music is an essential part of many of the most public events (triumphs, spectacles) and private moments (love scenes, "discovery" scenes) represented on stage. Like the control of the visual (the gaze), control of the *aural*, of what an audience on and offstage was hearing and how they heard it, is part of the essential dynamic of power and representation. Young musical women steal the show with their musical skills in song and dance (sometimes in breeches), while the older women depicted as usurping power often stage-manage the music as well: think of Lady Wishfort's dance entertainment in William Congreve's *The Way of the World* or the masque ordered by the incestuous queen Berengaria in *The Fatal Discovery*, attributed to

---

[3] The terms 'Patent Company' and 'Drury Lane company' are used interchangeably, although the company also performed at the Dorset Garden theater on occasion.

[4] Peter Holland made a similar observation in his *The Ornament of Action: Text and Performance in Restoration Comedy* (Cambridge, 1979). "The real audience was 'informed', made up of regular visitors to the playhouse, an audience that would recognise the changes that a playwright might make in an established mode. When they entered the theatre, they had a set of preconceptions, of patterns, of predictions that the playwrights [and performers] could fulfil or frustrate" (p. 18).

George Powell. Similarly, tyrannical male rulers manipulate musical activities to their own ends.

The competing actors and managers of the two companies were just one of the many rivalries active during this decade, for reasons both commercial and artistic. Publishers of music and plays were also in direct competition, and even the network of composers and musicians, usually assumed to have been politely collegial, appear to have existed as separate groups with limited intermingling. The Patent Company boasted "the organists": mostly students of John Blow's associated with the Chapel Royal, like Henry Purcell, Jeremiah Clarke, William Croft, and Daniel Purcell, occasionally featuring music from Blow himself. In contrast, Lincoln's Inn Fields seems to have been the haven of string players associated with the court instrumental ensemble (His/Her Majesty's Musick), including violinists John Eccles and John Lenton. Careful examination of the evidence from concert programs and published dedications suggests the musicians and composers active in the theaters were divided into "rival crews," like other theatrical personnel.[5]

At the same time, there appears to have been a gradual change from music-only concerts supplementing performance in theaters—see, for example, Robert Roades's benefit on 29 March 1699, "a Consort, all new Music, ... There being no Play at either House"[6]—to competing directly with the theaters. York Buildings and other concert venues begin mounting concerts even on play nights, for example the concert performance of Henry Purcell's Yorkshire Feast Song set against a revival of Ben Jonson's comedy *Volpone* at Drury Lane on 18 June 1701.[7] In the 1700s, concerts even take over theatrical spaces, as in the "Subscription Musick" concert series, which included musical-theatrical works, masques and plays as well as independent instrumental and vocal numbers. Throughout the decade, concert series and theater performances shared composers and musicians. Indeed, composer John Weldon's successful "Consort of Vocal and Instrumental Musick" seems to have helped him get his foot in the door at the theater and at court.

Along with the proliferation of concert series came an increasing number of musical publications and an assortment of theatrical experiments. These experiments sought to link music and drama in ways which, although they bore a family resemblance to past productions, attempted to gratify the tastes of an increasingly diverse and fickle audience—one familiar with Italian violin sonatas by Arcangelo Corelli, French ballet airs by Jean-Baptiste Lully, and Henry Purcell's dramatick operas, as well as street-ballads and the musical drolls at Bartholomew Fair.

---

[5] For a complete listing, see the table "Composers Active in the London Theaters, 1695–1705" in the Appendix.

[6] William Van Lennep, ed., *The London Stage 1660–1800*, Part 1: 1660–1700, p. 509.

[7] Judith Milhous and Robert D. Hume, new version of *The London Stage: 1660–1800*, Part 2: 1700–1729, p. 32.

Since Curtis Price's study of Purcell as a theater composer (*Henry Purcell and the London Stage*) and Roger Fiske's groundbreaking *English Theatre Music in the Eighteenth Century* there have been a number of studies investigating particular works and performers, particularly in relation to Purcell. However, the overall context of music in the theater has not been presented. Some aspects of music in earlier seventeenth-century English theater have been reconsidered in the light of new theoretical perspectives, for example, Amanda Eubanks Winkler's work on gender and genre.[8] Yet even insightful recent works on the theater of this period by scholars in English and theater history often fail to take into account the music which played a significant part in creating and staging dramatic representations.

In covering the productions staged during these seasons, I address a wide range of works from the canonical to the barely noticed.[9] I say little in the following pages about many worthy plays, since they contain relatively little music, or employ music in utterly conventional ways. Other productions, given short shrift by critics and scholars, receive considerably more attention due to their extensive use of music. Productions which do not conform to the conventions of Aristotle, as understood in the eighteenth century, or to the conventions of good taste (in either their century or ours) could still be highly effective and successful theatrical productions.

Writing on such subjects requires one to deal with what Curtis Price has called "a nasty tangle of mutables—actors, theatres, public taste, foreign influences, and political circumstances."[10] Because I hope this work will be of use to scholars in more than one discipline, I have included brief notes and explanations of several things music or theater historians who specialize in this period will already know well. For those whose training is outside of music, I have included a glossary of music-related terms in historical context.[11] Following investigations into the uses of music in comic and tragic productions, the second section of the book recounts the theatrical history of this fascinating period from a musical point of view. An understanding of how music was used *then* serves to illuminate musical-theatrical practices of later periods and as a point of departure for reading, staging, and viewing these plays today.

---

[8] Amanda Eubanks Winkler, *O Let Us Howle Some Heavy Note: Music for Witches, the Melancholic, and the Mad on the Seventeenth-Century English Stage* (Bloomington, 2006).

[9] I admit not having read all of the extant scholarship on canonical plays such as the comedies of Congreve or Farquhar—to name just two authors—but hope I have benefited from what I have read. Likewise, many plays produced during these seasons were based on, adapted from, or otherwise indebted to earlier plays; however, this aspect is only mentioned where significant for musical reasons.

[10] Curtis Alexander Price, *Henry Purcell and the London Stage* (Cambridge, 1984), p. 27.

[11] Many musical terms, like symphony, may be familiar but do not mean the same thing c.1695–1705 as they come to mean later.

My original study of music at the Lincoln's Inn Fields Theater, my dissertation, was intended in some respects as a musical companion piece to Judith Milhous's *Thomas Betterton and the Management of Lincoln's Inn Fields, 1695–1708*. This book takes a wider perspective by including musicians and productions at the Drury Lane and Dorset Garden theaters as well as chapters focused on certain kinds of productions. Increasing familiarity with the full repertoire has enabled me to amend many ideas about theatrical works that I discussed previously.

The continuous processes of production resulted in a variety of types of music. In the creation, performance, and reception of each piece composers, performers, playwrights, and audiences all played a part. Scholars of theater music need to realize that they are investigating the intersection of a host of different ideas and concerns about their work, from the most elementary (What is music doing here? Who would sing this?) to the highly complex (How will this music relate to other music this audience is accustomed to hearing and how will that affect their perception of the play?). The "post-Purcell" decade provides unprecedentedly rich material for investigating such intersections at work in the London theaters during this period of instability and rivalry. These productions are interesting as documents of the theatrical procedures of their time, as models for reading the music in other plays, and as sources for modern revival and performance.

Materials and Evidence

Considerable material is available for all types of musical works from this period, from virtuosic songs to much-copied sets of act music. However, new manuscripts continue to surface, even from a much-studied composer like Henry Purcell.

In reconstructing productions I have drawn on a variety of sources. For the texts I have relied principally on the first printed editions, although the printed play text is not necessarily an any more exact representation of what was said and done onstage than printed music is of what was performed.[12] Like printed music, printed plays often seem temptingly complete and specific, but the relationship between text and performance is that of architect's blueprint to fully constructed and landscaped structure. We have considerable evidence of changes made in the process of rehearsal and performance, from bawdy or blasphemous ad-libbing to extensive cuts. Excisions and other changes often pass silently in print, only occasionally indicated by authors like Pierre Motteux, although they were always complained about.

---

[12] Printers were not always working from a clean copy of the play, and errors are common. Playwrights also might revise their work prior to submitting it for publication (if printed, as most were, about a month after the first performance). Conversely, play texts might be submitted in a pre-performance version and not reflect changes made as the play was in preparation. This is often evident in song lyrics.

Music for these productions comes from many different manuscripts and printed formats. Little if any of the now extant manuscript music was actually used in the theater, although many of the sets of instrumental music survive in partbooks. These clearly were played from, possibly at musical evenings ("music meetings") like those held by musical enthusiast Thomas Britton, to whom one of the manuscripts, GB-Lbl Add. MS 24889, is supposed to have belonged.[13] For the printed music I have relied most on the weekly and monthly periodicals, collections, and anthologies of John Walsh and his competitors, supplemented with the single songsheets engraved by Thomas Cross. The surviving music further emphasizes the limitations of the printed text as a guide to the staged production, as song texts clearly associated with a play may be printed at the beginning or end of the play rather than in their "correct" position within the work, or left out altogether. Some texts were printed but not set to music, others were apparently set to music but never printed.

When examining the musical evidence from this period, both its richness and its limitations are soon apparent. Full scores, as for Gottfried Finger's *The Virgin Prophetess*, are not always available. Even scores that appear comprehensive are, on close examination, less than complete and may have been copied long after the original performances. The Tenbury score for Henry Purcell's *Dido and Aeneas* is only the most famous example of this. Working on dramatick operas and plays with music generally requires archival research and reconstruction from a variety of sources: manuscript, dances printed in one source, act tunes in another, songs and musical dialogues in a third or fourth.

For those willing to delve, it is possible to find a great deal of information about songs and instrumental music performed in these plays and other productions. For instrumental music, Curtis Price's *Music in the Restoration Theatre* remains the place to begin, although his 1979 catalogue has been supplemented by subsequent findings, such as the manuscript music bound with Purcell's *Ayres for the Theatre* in the Newberry Library in Chicago. Scholars and musicians now have the advantage of David Hunter's *Opera and Song Books published in England, 1703–1726* to supplement Cyrus L. Day and Eleanore Boswell Murrie's venerable *English Song-Books 1651–1702*, while Olive Baldwin and Thelma Wilson's facsimile edition of John Walsh's *The Monthly Mask of Vocal Music* is a recent and invaluable addition for theater songs from the first decade of the eighteenth century.

Published song collections are key sources; however, the record is incomplete without the single songsheets that document songs written for plays by composers or singers. There are still incompletely explored collections of "Ballads," "Songs," and "miscellaneous instrumental music" which may turn up in small local libraries as well as large national ones—and even quite racy theater music is often hiding in cathedral libraries (as at Durham Cathedral, England). The seventeenth- and eighteenth-century music lovers' practice of purchasing or copying individual

---

[13] Britton was known as 'the musical Small-Coal man' for his business and his musical interests. See Curtis Price, "The Small-Coal Cult," *Musical Times* 119 (1978): 1032–34.

favorite songs and tunes, which were later bound together, means that miscellaneous collections are far more common than volumes which contain full scores or even voice-continuo versions of all the musical numbers from a particular play or opera. The sheer volume and variety of music and musical sources permits the hope that some of the "not extant" songs or instrumental pieces described in plays and dramatick operas will be found in an incompletely cataloged collection—someday.

Background: The United Company, 1682–1695

Shortly after the restoration of 1660, Charles II granted patents to William Davenant and Thomas Killigrew to establish public theaters and theater companies. For the next two decades, the King's Company and the Duke's Company (named after Charles and his brother James) competed with each other and a host of more temporary entertainments provided by visiting troupes from the Continent, strolling companies of players at fairs, puppet shows, and so on. In 1682, due to falling revenues, retirements, and the destruction of one company's theater, the King's and Duke's companies were combined. For the next 13 years London had only one official theater company, the United Company.

The leading actor of the Duke's Company, Thomas Betterton, helped engineer the union, which was advantageous for veteran actors and playwrights but closed off opportunities for new writers and actors. With only one full-time licensed company acting, and the entire repertoire of stock plays open to them, they tended to stick with established successes.[14] The lavishly staged dramatick operas from this period were generally conservative in their authors, drawing on established masters such as Dryden, Fletcher, and Shakespeare, and leading players (Betterton).

Despite political upheaval, the United Company flourished in the 1680s. However, by 1694 complicated financial and legal tangles regarding shareholding left the United Company under the management of Sir Thomas Skipwith and Christopher Rich. Their high-handed executive decisions provoked a group of senior actors, headed by Betterton, to present a formal list of grievances to the Lord Chamberlain.[15] As manager of the King's Household, the Lord Chamberlain continued to exercise authority over the acting companies, as he had earlier when the companies were more obviously dependent upon noble and royal patronage.

---

[14] See Judith Milhous's *Thomas Betterton and the Management of Lincoln's Inn Fields, 1695–1708* (Carbondale, Illinois, 1979), pp. 40–41.

[15] For an enlightening discussion of finances and legal issues in the "Actors' Rebellion of 1694–1695," see Milhous, ibid., pp. 51–79.

With backing from the Lord Chamberlain (the Earl of Dorset and a friend of Betterton), the group of "rebel" actors obtained a license to act.[16] The Lord Chamberlain's license of 25 March 1695 stated:

> In pursuance of His Majesties Pleasure and Command, ... I doe hereby give and grant full power Licence and Authority unto Thomas Betterton, Elizabeth Barry Anne Bracegirdle [further list of names] ..., His Majesties sworne servants and Comoedians in Ordinary, and the major Part of them, their Agents and Servants, from time to time, in any convenient Place or Places, to Act & represent, all and all manner of Comedyes & Tragedyes, Playes Interludes, & Opera's, and to perform all other Theatricall and musicall Entertaynments of what kind soever, ... allwayes under my Government and Regulation.[17]

In the years to come, the Lincoln's Inn Fields company would take full advantage of its license to perform "musicall Entertaynments of what kind soever" often in direct competition with the dramatick operas and other musical productions staged by its rivals.

For the purposes of the present study, the contemporary texts briefly cited in the *Register of English Theatrical Documents* sketch out the important elements in the overall picture. Once licensed, the new company quickly wrote up a sharers' agreement.[18] However, Sir Thomas Skipwith at Drury Lane was still signing contracts with actors on 10 April.[19] On 16 April 1695 the Lord Chamberlain forbade actors signed at Lincoln's Inn Fields to change companies, but in July he needed to issue a more lengthy and explicit "Order forbidding actor transfers and enticement of personnel."[20]

This injunction was of limited utility. At various points during the following decade, each of the two companies took in (or seduced away) performers from the other house. Some talented but difficult individuals, like George Powell and Thomas Dogget, moved back and forth multiple times.

Individual performers and their modes of performance were very important to the creation and reception of the works being examined here. Contemporary audiences were interested in favored performers and in "points": set speeches and gestures detached from the action of the play and directed at the audience.[21] It can

---

[16] "What the actors received was not a 'patent' but a 'license' to perform. It was valid only at the pleasure of the monarch, but in contravening the patent monopolies it set an important precedent," ibid., p. 68.

[17] P.R.O. LC 7/3, printed in full in Milhous, *Thomas Betterton*, p. 67.

[18] Judith Milhous and Robert D. Hume, eds, *A Register of English Theatrical Documents 1660-1737* (2 vols, Carbondale, Illinois, 1991), vol. 1, nos. 1499, 1500.

[19] *Theatrical Documents*, nos. 1502, 1503.

[20] Ibid., nos. 1505, 1514.

[21] See, for example, Lisa Freeman, *Character's Theater: Genre and Identity on the Eighteenth-Century English Stage* (Philadelphia, 2002), pp. 28–32.

be argued that much nineteenth- and twentieth-century discomfort with the plays of the period arises from internalization of later codes of theatrical evaluation, emphasizing coherent character, "realism," and the unfolding of development in character or plot over time. Instead, audiences were accustomed to non-continuous productions and theatrical experiences.

Because actors played such "points" they were particularly vulnerable to competition from alternative "points," including musical ones such as songs, which might function in some of the same ways.[22] During this decade, playwrights, managers, and performers had to negotiate a complex network of audience expectations for an evening's entertainment, including certain types of characters performed by specific actors and certain kinds of performance "moments": comic or tragic, spoken or musical, which, properly delivered, could result in a successful evening and, for a new production, a successful run.

Music and Musical Conventions in the London Theaters

By the 1680s, plays in London theaters were expected to begin with instrumental music: usually two pairs of tunes or airs, called the first and second music. These pieces provided some amusement for the audience, who had to arrive early in the days when most seats were not reserved, and warning for the audience and possibly for the actors that the play would begin shortly.[23] Music-loving audience members could even attend the opening music, then leave and have their money refunded.

In addition to this preliminary music, each play would have an overture or curtain tune as well as a set of shorter tunes played between the acts. The overture followed the spoken prologue and generally accompanied the rise of the curtain. However, the distinction between "overture" and "curtain tune" is not rigid, and some musical productions apparently had both. Typically, overtures are longer and more elaborate, nearly always in "French overture" form. In contrast, curtain tunes are simple, distinguished from act tunes only by their greater length. In theater music sources from the turn of the century it is sometimes difficult to distinguish between the preliminary first and second music, and the act tunes which followed. In collections presumably intended for other kinds of music-making—concert or home performance rather than theatrical use—the overture was often copied first and the short pieces which follow are not clearly divided into pairs or groups.

Comedian Richard Estcourt's humorous dedication of his comedy *The Fair Example* to Christopher Rich, manager of the Patent Company, includes a brief

---

[22] While Freeman explicitly makes the comparison between speeches and opera arias, there are examples closer at hand, within the plays themselves.

[23] For roughly contemporary descriptions of this practice, and examples of modifications or exceptions to it, see Curtis A. Price, *Music in the Restoration Theatre* (Ann Arbor, 1979), pp. 51–8.

rundown of the music to be expected. In it, Estcourt promises not to "trouble" Rich with the proper components of playmaking, which are "as familiar to you as the Play-House Tunes. The first is an Air, the second a Chacone, and the third an Overture, commonly called the Courtain Tune, the rest Act-Tunes."[24] Indeed, the popularity of the chaconne, a triple-meter dance and variation form, is easy to see in the sets of theater music published by John Walsh.[25]

Much like the evening's entertainment as a whole, the chaconne offered a familiar structure with variety in each repetition. Musical connoisseurs could compare a new chaconne with those of past masters, like Henry Purcell, or France's Jean-Baptiste Lully. The less musical could enjoy the pleasantly recurring musical patterns (or converse with their neighbors). This is assuming, of course, that the chaconne was not also choreographed and danced.[26]

The relationship between the instrumental music heard within the course of a production and the drama varied considerably. How much individual composers knew about the plays for which they were asked to provide music—beyond the basics of title and genre, and texts for any songs required—probably depended on their relationship (if any) with the author and on the author's status. Presumably company composers would have been allowed to attend read-throughs and rehearsals, although all of the composers who worked in the theaters also had other professional commitments to attend.[27]

In his discussion of the function of act tunes in Henry Purcell's works, scholar Roger Savage notes "the connection of act-tunes with the ends of the acts preceding them is the crucial thing, since it seems quite often to have been a matter of act-mood at that point determining act-tune" and one can often, as Savage does, make a plausible case for a tune continuing the mood of the act it followed.[28] However, as Savage acknowledges, there is little direct evidence of this with the exception of author-critic John Dennis's comments on his own 1698 *Rinaldo and Armida*, in which he draws attention to the deliberate, close connection between the act tunes

---

[24] Estcourt, *The Fair Example; or, The Modish Citizens* (London, 1706), unpaginated. Also cited in Price, *Music in the Restoration Theatre*, p. 53.

[25] Chaconnes have a practical aspect, since they're constructed of sections, with the possibility of indefinite repeats or a quick conclusion once the audience assembles and the actors are ready.

[26] At LIF the tragedy *The Villain* was advertised with a chaconne performed by Mrs. Elford in June 1703 and at DL *The History and Fall of Caius Marius* was advertised "With a new Chaconne composed by Monsieur Cherrier, and perform'd by him and 6 others" in February 1704. See M&H *London Stage* pp. 105–6, 146.

[27] See the table of composers in the Appendix. All composers active in the theaters performed on one or more instruments (or as vocalists), many had additional positions at court or a religious institution, virtually all taught private pupils and served as their own agents, managing their publications and concert appearances.

[28] Roger Savage, "The Theatre Music," in Michael Burden, ed., *The Purcell Companion* (Portland, Oregon, 1994), pp. 311–83 (p. 331).

and the drama.[29] Indeed, Dennis's insistence on this as a special aspect of his work with composer John Eccles suggests this close connection was not common.

The correspondence between songs and the scenes in which they appear also varies from production to production. It was fairly common for plays to include songs written by poets other than the playwright: their mentors, colleagues, or friends. Did it matter? Consider the case of poet-playwright William Congreve, who contributed several songs, prologues, and epilogues to plays by other authors, yet ensured the songs within his plays are always his own. The relationship between his songs and the characters and action of his plays, suggestive but rarely obvious, has intrigued audiences and scholars ever since.

Generic love or ritual lyrics—sometimes intimately tied into the play and its characters, at others seeming wildly inappropriate—attracted non-professional writers as well, those desirous to display their wit and learning. However, the majority of the vocal numbers heard onstage were written by and for professionals, working within well-established poetic and performance conventions.

"The Musick": Instrumental Musicians

Theatrical documents from this period rarely mention musicians by name and it is more difficult to trace the theatrical career of a modestly successful instrumental musician than a comparable actor or singer. The instrumentalists were simply "the musick," a flexible group usually paid by the night or by the week from a lump sum given to the house's master of music. While no complete listing of musicians who played in the London theaters from 1695 to 1705 has been recovered, later documents, along with the evidence of the play texts and surviving music itself, provide some general information.

In the late seventeenth century, the term "musick" could mean either players or the pieces they performed, and the spelling varies. I use "musick" with a "k" to indicate groups of performers, like the King's Private Musick or the musick (instrumentalists) who played at the theater. The "first and second music," performed before the overture each night, sometimes written "first and second musick" in contemporary sources, have been given throughout in modern spelling, which preserves the distinction between "music" (pieces being played) and "the musick" (the performers).

The physical placement of musicians when not onstage, whether in a side box, gallery, or down in front, remains an area of uncertainty, since our knowledge of the physical set-up within the theaters, particularly Lincoln's Inn Fields, is very limited. Complaints about inattentive musicians disrespectfully wearing their hats certainly suggest that they were within audience view,[30] and not withdrawn into a

---

[29] John Dennis, *The Musical Entertainments in the Tragedy of Rinaldo and Armida* (London, 1699).

[30] Milhous and Hume, *Theatrical Documents*, no. 1605.

music room or behind the scenes, although the Dorset Garden theater was equipped with a "music box" above the stage.[31] As with many other practical performance issues, the placement of the musicians doubtless varied according to the needs of a given production.

The surviving instrumental music for productions from 1695 to 1705 makes it clear that a four-part ensemble of strings with first and second treble, tenor (viola) and bass parts was typically employed.[32] However, the number of players on each line is hardly ever indicated. Certainly string players outnumbered the other instrumentalists, making up a large proportion of the overall ensemble, and "fiddlers" were often called on to appear onstage.[33]

Trumpets and drums were available for martial entertainments and battle scenes, but probably only one or two of each, except for special occasions. Flutes (recorders) were on hand for pastoral and romantic musical scenes, often in pairs. Other woodwinds such as the oboe and bassoon or serpent were called for more rarely, and performers presumably doubled on these instruments.[34] A couple of early Patent Company productions actually call for a harpsichord onstage, and its usefulness as a continuo instrument probably outweighed its practical difficulties in positioning and tuning. Plucked-string instruments, most likely theorbos (more rarely a guitar or lute), would also have been used to provide continuo support.[35] It has been suggested that both harpsichord and theorbos were reserved for accompanying voices,[36] however, some sets of act music do include figures

---

[31] See Frans Muller's reconstruction of the theater in "Flying Dragons and Dancing Chairs at Dorset Garden: Staging *Dioclesian*," *Theatre Notebook* 47/2 (1993): 80–95.

[32] In his 1701 dramatick opera *The Virgin Prophetess*, Finger writes for five-part strings, but this is unusual. Some passages in larger works are for three parts, which may indicate solo sections.

[33] As Price emphasizes, the "fiddlers" might include bass viols, and do more than play dance tunes. "Restoration Stage Fiddlers and Their Music," *Early Music* 7/3 (1979): 315–22.

[34] For more on instrumental ensembles, see John Spitzer and Neal Zaslaw, *The Birth of the Orchestra: History of an Institution, 1650–1815* (Oxford, 2004), chapter 8, "The Orchestra in England"; and Peter Holman, "Purcell's Orchestra," *Musical Times* 137 (1996): 17–23.

[35] Roger North writes admiringly of the use of pandoras (bandoras) as continuo instruments: "being a sort of double guitarres strung with wires, and of those the bases double and twisted, and struck with a quill, strangely inriched those vulgar consorts [theatrical music], which now for want of a mixture of the arpeggio appear beggarly... a better and more sonorous effect in the mixture, then ... harpsichords." *Roger North's* The Musicall Grammarian 1728, eds Mary Chan and Jamie C. Kassler (Cambridge, 1990), p. 213.

[36] Judith Milhous and Curtis A. Price, "Harpsichords in the London Theatres, 1697–1715," *Early Music* 18 (1990): 38–46. Peter Holman mentions the description in Thomas Shadwell's *The Tempest* (1674) of "the Band of 24 Violins, with the Harpsicals and Theorbo's which accompany the Voices" in "Purcell's Orchestra," p. 23.

(indicating chords to be played) over the bass line,[37] so the use of such continuo instruments in purely instrumental pieces written for the theater during this decade cannot be ruled out.

According to a written plan for reuniting the Lincoln's Inn Fields company with the Patent Company in 1703, twenty musicians are needed for a full instrumental ensemble, but no specifics are given. For a twenty-member musick, Peter Holman has proposed "two trumpets, timpani, two oboes/recorder, bassoon and two theorbo players (Eccles would presumably have played the harpsichord himself), … [and] 12 strings, which of course is the same size as the orchestras of the 1660s and 1670s, when the Twenty-Four Violins [King Charles II's court ensemble], divided into two, was working regularly in London's two theatres."[38]

Similar, but more detailed, plans for instrumental music at the theater in the Haymarket from 1707 to 1708 call for thirty musicians, about twenty of them string players, including William Corbett, a violinist who composed music for Lincoln's Inn Fields, and James Paisible, who performed and composed for the Patent Company.[39] Like nearly all composers of the period, those who wrote for the rival theaters were professional performers as well, and probably formed the core of the company's musick. Individual composers, instrumental soloists, and singers will be discussed in greater detail in the "Musical Assets" sections of the chronological chapters.

Conclusion

During these initial seasons of competition, each company had to build its performance roster and reputation anew. The Lincoln's Inn Fields company began with the advantage of experienced, popular actors and actor-singers, as well as several strong professional vocalists. John Eccles and other members of the court instrumental ensemble, the King's Private Musick, composed for them, while among their authors they could boast both talents like William Congreve and facile librettists like Pierre Motteux. Christopher Rich, the manager of the remaining Patent Company, held leases on both the Drury Lane and Dorset Garden theaters. These were larger venues that housed a treasured store of sets, costumes, and music. If his actors were generally young and scrappy, his singers were young and talented. He also had a firm musical base in the Purcells, supported by other Chapel Royal composers including John Blow. Although Lincoln's

---

[37] See, for example, *A New Set of Tunes in four Parts, In the Governour of Cyprus Acted at the New Theater, and Composed by Thomas Deane of Worcester* (London, 1703). Engraved by Thomas Cross, it includes figured bass. Walsh occasionally prints bass figures in his series *Harmonia Anglicana*, as in Finger's music for *Love Makes a Man*.

[38] Holman, "Purcell's Orchestra," p. 22.

[39] Judith Milhous and Robert D. Hume, eds, *Vice Chamberlain Coke's Theatrical Papers, 1706-1715* (Carbondale Illinois, 1982), documents 17, 18 and 22.

Inn Fields acquired significant performance resources and aristocratic support, neither company truly had the upper hand. The stage was set for a long-running competition between houses, with increased opportunities for authors, actors, composers and musicians.

PART I
The Place and Function of Music in Dramatic Productions

Chapter One
Musical Approaches in Comedy

Comedies were the most common type of new productions in the theaters during the 1695–1705 decade and had the highest proportion of musical numbers, outside of explicitly musical works like masques and dramatick operas. They were integral to the success of both companies, particularly during the early seasons. William Congreve's *Love for Love* was the first play staged at Lincoln's Inn Fields, and a triumph for the new company. A few months later, Colley Cibber's *Love's Last Shift* did much to save the Patent Company's 1695–96 season. Each became a regular part of its respective company's repertoire during the following decade.

Musical Conventions in Comic Plays at the Turn of the Century

Scholars have advanced varied arguments regarding the changes in comedy during the 1695–1705 decade. While several analytic and descriptive labels have been applied: reform, sentimental, humane, and so on, the songs and other musical entertainments featured in comic productions are bawdy and sentimental by turns, and comedies from 1705 are as likely as those from 1695 to include titillating references to sex and plenty of broad humor. Comedies without musical events are virtually unthinkable in contemporary practice—only three play texts out of over ninety comedies and farces from this decade fail to indicate some type of music performed within the play—but the published texts vary enormously in their specificity about the music included.

In his 1728 *Musicall Grammarian*, lawyer and essayist Roger North tried to systematically divide the practice of music by 'intent': "1. Solitary, 2. Sociall, 3. Ecclesiasticall, and 4. Theatricall." After describing the felicities of solemn, choral church music, North turns to theater music, which he divides into two parts: "first Comick, and the other, Opera." Dramatick opera and musical tragedy are addressed in Chapter Two.

North, who lived for the most part in London between 1670 and 1700, identifies comic music by its performance and structure, as well as its effect on the body.

> I mean the comon entertainment and interludes of plays, which in former times were dispersed abroad by the name of playhouse tunes; and of this sort is all our comon musick at feasts and celebrated rejoycings. There is not much to be observed of these, but onely that they are chiefly compounded of melody, and pulsation or time. The consort is not much heeded, and if the melody is ayery, or what they call pretty, the ground may be of a comon style, and the more

vulgar, the better. And all the force of these consorts lyes in the upper part, to which all the rest and even the base sometimes is subservient. Therefore it is to litle purpose to crowd in accords by inner parts, for if they could have any melody care is taken, by doubling the superior, to drowne them; and the best accomplishment is by number and nois[e] ... this sort of popular [theatrical] musick is most apt for driving away thinking, and letting in dancing; and the former of these [being] dispatched, all people's members are apt to assume the other, and almost sencelessly to move one way or other, keeping the time as the pulses of the musick, wherein consists the cheif efficacy, incites.[1]

North's description of popular theater music of the comic sort focuses on these elements: the musical interest is in the melody and pulse, with the tune in the highest voice or instrument in the group ("consort"), the bass line ("ground") is often simple and even "vulgar," while the accompanying instruments flesh out the sound. Most ominously, this type of music encourages the audience to stop thinking and to move their bodies to the rhythm of the music, which has the strongest effect on its auditors. With a little updating, North could be talking about genres of Western popular music nearly three hundred years in his future.

Vocal Music and Instrumental Music in Comedies

The following section covers the types of songs, dances, and instrumental music commonly found in comedies, briefly outlining their essential characteristics and providing examples from contemporary productions revealing the ways in which such music was used. More detailed discussion of specific comedies appears in later sections.

Song Types

The majority of musical events indicated in the printed play texts are songs. They are also one of the most common types of surviving music not indicated in the printed text (see, for example, Farquhar's *Love and a Bottle*, PC 1699), or only indicated generally ('songs and dances here'). In many cases the musical setting of a specific song can be matched to its lyrics and positioning within the play. In other cases the placement of a song may depend on the association of its song type with a characteristic scene or situation. Songs may be reflective, pastoral, mad songs, 'witty' songs or parodies of the more serious types, ballad-style songs (often topical or patriotic, rustic, or "Scotch"), drinking songs, or serenades.

By this categorization, reflective songs are those which depict an emotional or interior state. They are usually set in a more elaborate musical style and sung by a professional singer, rather than an actor-singer. These are the types of songs

---

[1] Chan and Kassler, *Roger North's* The Musicall Grammarian *1728*, pp. 215–16.

often 'ventriloquized' by a companion or servant for a high-status man or woman,[2] reinforcing their heightened dramatic focus. "Restless in thought," from *She Ventures and He Wins* (LIF, 1695, discussed later in this chapter) is an excellent example of this type.

Pastoral songs cover a lot of territory, depending on the strictness of the definition. As with other kinds of texts, the pastoral at this period is probably best understood as encompassing a broad continuum marked by themes, names, language, and intertextual references. As Timothy Neufeldt has noted, the later eighteenth-century clichés of 'pastoral' style in music (for example, Handel's "Pastoral Symphony" in *Messiah*) are not clearly established in English music during this decade.[3] Witty songs about sexual politics and preferences which throw in a single reference to a "nymph" or mention the name "Amintor" are obviously several steps away from ones that explicitly reference a pastoral world or are sung by pastoral characters. The "pastoral entertainment" with music is one area of overlap between comic and tragic productions. Another is the mad song.

Mad songs, in their lyrics and overall structure, much resemble the mad rants often found at the end of tragedies, spoken as characters are dying. They exhibit grandiose, usually mythological delusions, extreme changes in mood and syntax, and recurrent images of flying, burning, or drowning. Composers set them to music in short, contrasting sections that reflect the moods and images of the text, as in Henry Purcell's famous song "From silent shades," commonly given the title "Bess of Bedlam."

There are relatively few outright mad songs in comedies during this period, when compared to the number of songs overall, although they are among the most memorable. Actor-singers Anne Bracegirdle and John Bowman's most famous mad songs were originally performed in the second part of Thomas Durfey's *Don Quixote* (PC, 1694). However, *Don Quixote* is an exceptional case and not a straightforward comedy, written by an author whose earlier comedies were unusually musical.[4] Another exceptional case is George Powell's *Imposture Defeated* (PC, 1697), another highly musical and generically unstable work. Pastorals like *The Fickle Shepherdess* (LIF, 1703) and masques like *Acis and Galatea* (LIF, 1701) and *Hercules* (LIF, 1697) also include mad songs. While some reflective songs resemble mad songs in their use of short contrasting sections and depictions of varying emotional states, the delusional and mythological references are missing.

---

[2] See Amanda Eubanks Winkler, *O Let Us Howle Some Heavy Note*, for discussion of several earlier seventeenth-century examples of this practice.

[3] See Neufeldt, "The Social and Political Aspects of the Pastoral Mode in Musico-dramatic Works," pp. 12–13, 21.

[4] Durfey's comedy *The Richmond Heiress* famously featured a mad dialogue by Henry Purcell, performed by professional singers, and a mock-mad dialogue by Dogget and Bracegirdle, in character. See Curtis Alexander Price, *Henry Purcell and the London Stage* (Cambridge, 1984), pp. 164–8.

Ballad-style songs are typically performed by lower-status characters, or as entertainments by characters pretending to a status they do not merit. Ballads are strophic, using the same melody for each verse of text, and narrative. When printed they often lack a bass line, and may have been performed without one. While ballad quotations are a familiar feature in earlier seventeenth-century plays (*Hamlet* being only the most famous example), in comedies from this decade performances of entirely new ballad-style songs are most often indicated. Durfey is particularly fond of introducing ballad-like songs into his comedies. These stage ballads could travel from the theater into the street, as did John Eccles's "A Soldier and a Sailor," (*Love for Love*, LIF, 1695).[5]

Drinking songs, performed either by male characters or to entertain men, range from solo to the communal, with any number of voices. Like ballads, they are typically strophic with a simple tune, singable by an untrained voice, and are printed either without a bass line or with the most rudimentary (North's "vulgar") one. They appear frequently as quotations (see below) sung by one or two characters as they enter or exit, quickly telegraphing their condition. Drinking songs are also the most likely type of music within a play to be borrowed from pre-existing repertoire, as Joseph Harris does in *The City Bride* (LIF, 1696) when a group of sailors sing "Here's a health to jolly Bacchus" (27), published five years earlier.

Songs for two voices are of two types, either two-part songs, in which the two voices share the same text and essentially the same music, and musical dialogues, where the two voices represent different characters or points of view and usually sing together only at the end of the piece. Two-part songs often feature the voices imitating one another, in ways which can be simple or elaborate. They are written on a range of topics, from love, "I tell thee Charmion," (*Love for Love*, LIF, 1695) to drinking and fox hunting, "Away, ye brave fox-hunting race," (*The Bath; or, the Western Lass*, PC, 1701). The range of musical styles and level of vocal training required varies, whereas in the musical dialogue settings are fairly consistent, with—as Roger North deplored—very regular rhythms.

Musical Dialogues

The musical dialogue, typically comic or erotic even when performed in a tragedy, represents a practical English answer to the problem of narration in singing. The dialogues are not Italian or French-style recitative, for they feature regular meter and a clear tune, rather than irregular patterns following the text accent. The simple musical settings are practical, since the humor and interest of the exchanges relies on the audience's comprehension of the words, and the performers acting out the miniature drama (texts often include or imply specific actions and gestures). Their

---

[5] For this and other examples of theatrical tunes which became broadside ballads, see Claude M. Simpson, *The British Broadside Ballad and Its Music* (New Brunswick, New Jersey, 1966).

tunefulness made them accessible to general audiences and to performance by actor-singers. Sometimes used as act dividers (see *The Cornish Comedy*, PC, 1696), musical dialogues were popular additions to an evening's entertainment, although their presence in play texts becomes less frequent after the first three seasons of the decade.[6] Like the practice of ballad singing, musical dialogues from the turn of the eighteenth century can be linked to earlier performance traditions through stage jigs, "brief farces sung and accompanied by dancing" which would often follow the performance of a play during the late sixteenth and early seventeenth centuries.[7]

Musical dialogues generally feature stock sexual situations (man in pursuit of woman or girl, more rarely the reverse) typically treated with broad humor, though some pastoral dialogues, while still erotic, are more elegant in their diction.[8] A very popular subtype of the male–female dialogues is that where the 'woman' is actually a man in drag, sending up women's fears and their motivations (love/lust/drink), as in *Massaniello* and *The Island Princess* (both PC, 1699).[9]

An unusual example of a cross-dressing dialogue with women comes from Elkanah Settle's comic dramatick opera *The World in the Moon* (III, 22), where Cynthia's train of attendants summon "airy Forms" to please her:

> Two BEAU's arise from under the Stage; to whom enter
> Two Young Ladies, and dance.

> Dialogue between Mrs. *Cross* and Mrs. *Lucas*
> *Mrs. Cross.* Oh dear, sweet Sir, you look so gay,
>   So fair; you steal my Heart away:
>   That Mien, that Shape, that Face, that Air—
> *Mrs. Lucas.* What does the Creature say?
> *Cross.* In those sweet Eyes such Charms I see
>   . . . .
>   Oh turn but one kind Look on me,
>   My racking Pains to view;

---

[6] This may be due in part to Letitia Cross's leaving the PC. See Chapters Three and Four.

[7] See Charles Read Baskervill, *The Elizabethan Jig and Related Song Drama* (Chicago, 1929), p. 3. Unlike jigs, musical dialogues were not typically the final entertainment of the evening, and usually had new music composed for them, rather than employing familiar tunes.

[8] Baskervill notes the popularity of broadside ballads employing dialogue, and links some late seventeenth-century stage dialogues to earlier jigs with similar themes. *The Elizabethan Jig*, chapter 5, "The Aftermath of the Jig" and chapter 6, particularly pp. 205–10.

[9] While the last well-known female impersonator in serious drama, Edward Kynaston, was playing only mature male roles by the 1690s, male comedians still appeared in drag in comedies such as Richard Steele's *The Funeral* (PC, 1700).

> *Lucas.* No, foolish, pratling Thing, you see,
>   I have something else to do.
> *Cross.* Then cannot you love?
> *Lucas.* No, no; not I.
> *Cross.* This too unkind Requital:
>   Ah Cruel! Can you see me die?
> *Lucas.* I care not, stop my Vital.[10] …

The tables are turned in the second half of the dialogue, as Lucas's beau becomes intrigued, and Cross says the final line above back at him. The beau's line, "Stap my vitals," quotes a characteristic phrase of Cibber's, when playing Sir Novelty Fashion in his comedy *Love's Last Shift* (PC, 1696), thus referring to both a popular show and the popular comic performer. Anne Bracegirdle also sang in male costume in character in Pierre Motteux's masque, *Acis and Galatea* (LIF, 1701).

Sex is the subject of many musical dialogues, almost to the point of obsession. Like 'smutty' prologues, they have been commented on with distaste by later scholars and by contemporaries, as in *A Comparison Between the Two Stages*, where the critics complain about the "greensickness" dialogue, "How long, my Flavia, shall your Swain," (II, 18–9) in *The Generous Conqueror* (PC, 1701). Curtis Price has written acerbically about the "girl and boy" dialogues popular in the 1690s, calling one a "pornographic dialogue for children."[11] Such dialogues do force the consideration of some key questions. Are they to some degree explained by an eighteenth-century view of children as simply smaller adults? Is it considered healthy and normal for the pubescent (or pre-pubescent) to express sexual desire? And if perhaps the youth-to-youth dialogues are understandable, are the old-to-young more disturbing? At the time, cross-generational interest was treated as aberrant, as in Motteux's musical dialogue "Hold good Mr. Fumble, Fy! What do you mean,/ To court my Grand Daughter? She's scarce yet fifteen" (*The Island Princess*, PC, 1699).[12] However, there were a number of duets performed by a young, teenaged Letitia Cross or Mary Anne Campion and a fully adult male: common, seemingly acceptable, and quite popular with their original audiences.

Among theatrical composers, John Eccles was an especially prolific creator of musical dialogues. In the preface to his comedy *Love's a Jest* (discussed further, below), Pierre Motteux particularly thanks Eccles, who "not only set my three dialogues to most charming Notes, but humour'd the Words to Admiration."[13] One might compare Eccles's success in this genre to the pieces Gershwin and similarly

---

[10] Settle, *The World in the Moon* (London, 1697), p. 22.

[11] Price, *Henry Purcell and the London Stage*, p. 78.

[12] Motteux, *The Island Princess* (London, 1699), p. 44. However, the grandmother's rebuke is immediately undercut by the interest she takes in a youth. At the end of the four-part dialogue, everyone gets an age-appropriate partner.

[13] Motteux, *Love's a Jest* (London, 1696), unpaginated.

successful song pluggers created for Tin Pan Alley. Great technical skill and a sophisticated harmonic vocabulary were not required, but a good ear for a tune, an awareness of the words, and a strong sense of popular taste were essential.

While there are some dialogues written for three or four voices, trios or quartets which are not dialogues are quite rare in comic productions, and I am aware of only one, Eccles's "Wine does wonders ev'ry day," attributed to two 'lost' plays,[14] which could also be classified as a sophisticated drinking song. Choruses, and solos alternating with chorus (a common type of musical event in tragedy), are virtually unheard of in comedies except within an inserted masque, unless the generic definition is expanded to include pastoral works like Oldmixon's *Amintas* (PC, 1698) and *The Fickle Shepherdess* (LIF, 1703), where ancient Greek practice offered a model.

Although songs from comedies were frequently printed, the versions published for amateur musicians did not always include all of the music. As previously mentioned, some songs were published with the vocal line alone. Most were printed with voice and continuo parts. The songs composed by John Eccles for Nicholas Rowe's comedy *The Biter* (LIF, 1704, discussed below) were published in unusually complete form, with their instrumental symphonies and 'returnells' (Italian *ritornelli*). Similar pieces from earlier productions, like "Fair Belinda's youthful charms" from *She Ventures and He Wins*, survive in manuscript complete with three-part symphonies which the printed songs lack. Many more songs may have been performed with symphonies and ritornelli that did not fit in the limited space of a single songsheet and were presumably of little interest to buyers who did not have a theater band at home to play the instrumental parts. These are often lost to modern scholars and performers when no manuscript music survives.

Dancing Songs

Regular, moderately paced triple-meter minuet songs are the most frequently noted type of dance songs. Based on one of the most familiar types of formal dancing, from French models, they appear regularly in the 1690s, usually associated with amorous scenes. Examples can be found in comedies ranging from early Durfey through Farquhar's comedies featuring Sir Harry Wildair. In *The Constant Couple* (PC, 1699) Sir Harry's nonsense syllables and dancing may hark back to Act II of Durfey's comedy *Love for Money; or, The Boarding School* (PC, 1691), where the music master Semibreve attempts to teach girls to sing while the dancing master Coupée sings and dances a minuet with one of his students, with physical instructions that would serve for more than one kind of 'dancing': "Make your Honour Misse, tholl loll loll."[15] These kinds of nonsense syllables at the end of

---

[14] Attributed in different songsheet publications to both *The Morose Reformer* and *Justice Buisy; or, The Gentleman Quack* (both LIF, c.1699–1700).

[15] Durfey's song also appeared as a broadside, in various adaptations. See Simpson, *The British Broadside Ballad*, pp. 479–80.

each line turn up frequently in Harry Wildair's dialogue, and (with some variation) in many other male characters', gentle and otherwise.

The association holds for other types of productions as well: in the prologue to Thomas Durfey's dramatick opera *Cinthia and Endimion*, Zephirus sings "Night, dear Promoter of Lovers Felicity" to a "Minuit T[une]," while in Dryden's *King Arthur*, the song "How happy the Lover/ How easie his Chain" performed by "Nymphs and Sylvans," one of the seductive pleasures that tempt Arthur from his quest in Act IV (31), was intended to be a minuet song, as noted in Dryden's text (Purcell wrote a massive passacaglia instead). In Pierre Motteux's comic masque *The Loves of Mars and Venus* (LIF, 1696), discussed below, elaborate choreographies were performed while choruses sang at the end of the prologue and of each act.

Dance Types

Dances within comedies included both dances performed by the cast and those by professional dancers, whose appearances are increasingly well documented during the latter part of the 1695–1705 decade. These two categories could and did overlap, as in the case of the dancing actresses Margaret Bicknell, Letitia Cross, Mary Anne Campion, Jane Lucas, Mrs Prince, and Elizabeth Willis.[16] All six also sang—Cross and Campion most proficiently.

There were several different theatrical dance types executed by professionals. These included Mimick (imitating a character or profession like a sailor), Antick (usually rustic or savage characters like satyrs or foresters), and Figure (abstractly choreographed) dances.[17] "Grotesque" dances featured unnatural characters like witches and also *commedia dell'arte* characters like Harlequin and Scaramouche.[18] These are more often mentioned in farces, like Mountfort's *Dr. Faustus* (revived LIF, 1697). They were also performed commonly as entr'acte entertainment or additions to the evening's bill.

The more formal, or 'grave' and elevated types of dances included minuets, chaconnes, and sarabandes, with minuets being the simplest and most accessible of these. An onstage minuet, performed in character, features prominently in Farquhar's *The Inconstant* (PC, 1702). Chaconnes, as noted in my introduction, may have been danced with the lengthy first and second musick pieces written in this form, and are later advertised as special attractions. Dances in different national characters such as Spanish, Dutch, or Scotch were a feature of masques

---

[16] Probably the most famous example of a dancer-actress from the following decades was Hester Santlow. See Moira Goff, *The Incomparable Hester Santlow: A Dancer-Actress on the Georgian Stage* (Aldershot, 2007).

[17] See Moira Goff, "'*Actions, Manners*, and *Passions*': Entr'acte Dancing on the London Stage, 1700–1737," *Early Music* 26/2 (1998): 213–28.

[18] See Jennifer's Thorpe's essay on Harlequin and Scaramouche dancing in London, in *Stages 'Adorn'd with ev'ry Grace'* (Ashgate, forthcoming).

and entertainments, and Farquhar ends his first comedy with an entertainment of Irish dancing "in Fingallion costume" (*Love and a Bottle*, PC, 1699). English dancing included the communal country dances often performed at the end of a comedy.

Entertainments, Masques and Masquerades

Any of these types of vocal music and dances, together with instrumental numbers, might form a part of multi-sectional events variously labeled entertainment, masque, or masquerade. Elaborate masques, with allegorical or mythological characters, are actually not that common among the comedies of 1695–1705. The more general 'entertainments' or 'diversions' which include at least two or three songs and dances are the most flexible larger-scale combination. They range from the apparently fully documented (listing music performed, performers, text authors, and composers) to the vague "Songs and Dances here." Masquerades, in which play characters appear in costume and dance, are infrequent among comedies from this decade, although two from the 1695–96 season at Drury Lane include such scenes.

Other Instrumental Music

Purely instrumental pieces are less common than dance music, far less common than the various types of vocal music, and usually found in conjunction with them. This is a clear distinction from masques, tragedies, and dramatick operas, where instrumental music more often is used alone, at the opening of a scene ("discovery") or to set a mood ("soft music" or "melancholy music"), practices discussed in Chapter Two. Instrumental music is typically found in scenes of serenading or processions, at banquets, or in concert scenes. Serenades, which may include vocal as well as instrumental music, can be straightforwardly romantic or played for laughs, as in *Feign'd Friendship* (LIF, 1699), when the heroine (disguised) leads fiddlers and torchbearers in a daylight serenade, to the other characters' astonishment, or when a serenading spark winds up drenched with water (*A Cure for Jealousie*, LIF, also 1699). In concert scenes the music performed often mocks fashionable musical tastes and pretensions, as in *Love's Last Shift* (PC, 1696), where Sir Novelty Fashion has the musick play a trumpet sonata in St James's Park (III, 45) or the concert scene with "sonato" at the end of the second act of *Love Without Interest* (PC, 1699).

Act Music

As noted in the introduction, the relation of first and second music, overture, and especially the act tunes to plays from this decade varies. There are some plausible connections to be made in Congreve's *Love for Love*, where the rustic "Scotch" act tune which follows the end of Act III can be heard as a continuation of the musical mood established by Sailor Ben's ballad and the sailors' dance. If not pressed too strongly, similar associations between the instrumental music and dramatic situations might be made for the other act tunes, such as the quick playful piece following the end of Act II as Tattle chases Miss Prue off the stage. However, Gottfried Finger's choice of a jig for the fourth and final act tune probably had more to do with the convention of ending a suite of pieces with a lively dance number than it had to do with anything in Congreve's play.

The music for many comedies was written by multiple composers. The most common division of labor was to have act tunes and songs by different hands. Musical connections in the form of key relationships sometimes exist between the instrumental music and songs, suggesting a degree of coordination among composers, though this is hardly universal. Choice of key also reflects practical aspects, such as keys in which particular performers' voices or particular instruments sounded well and keys associated with particular moods or topics (love, triumph).[19]

Topical References, Musical Humor, and Quotation

One of the most frequent and elusive elements of comedies from this decade relies on making connections between the printed text and other texts, performance practices, and the musical world of London. As noted in the chronological chapters, prologues and epilogues often satirize Italian singers, the musical extravagances of opera, French and Italian dancing, the fashionable concerts at York Buildings and Richmond Wells, and other musical follies. Pierre Danchin's work on prologues and epilogues has made many of these previously arcane references clear, and biographical work on performers has cleared up other mysteries.

What appear to be referential performance cues in the printed play texts can be just as hard to interpret. In Durfey's minuet song, "Make your Honour, Miss, tholl loll loll" in *Love for Money*, originally performed by John Bowman as Coupée (21), the singer uses syllables which may indicate rhythm to extend the line. This is similar to solmization, the practice of assigning musical pitches to syllables, which is also frequently referenced and mocked.

Such nonsense syllables imply humming or singing Durfey's minuet song or something like it.[20] Many characters played by Robert Wilks have such syllables cued, as does a non-Wilks character in *Love at First Sight* (LIF, 1704). The anonymous author of *A Comparison Between the Two Stages* says dismissively of Wilks that he could not keep still onstage, but "like the Pendulum of a Clock, perpetually shuffling from one side to t'other; that affected levity in his Heels

---

[19] See Glossary.
[20] See Simpson, *The British Broadside Ballad and Its Music*, regarding versions of this song in circulation, including a popular broadside and a 'male adaptation,' pp. 480–81.

renders him as Antick as *Griffin* [another actor] is Stiff and Formal."[21] The nonsense syllables in his part may indicate movement as much as sound, even when no movement cue is printed.

Fortunately, many quotations and performance indications are more explicit. Curtis Price has observed that Durfey loved to insert references to his previous comedies in his later ones, and provides examples from *The Richmond Heiress*.[22] However, most authors and actors draw on a general stock of recognizable popular songs (including some of Durfey's), as in Mary Pix's *The Innocent Mistress* (LIF, 1697), when John Bowman's character, wooing a foolish young lady, quotes a song originally sung by comedian Thomas Dogget in drag ("Fie, what mean I foolish maid"), and quite enchants her.[23] Aside from the potential audience pleasure in recognition and anticipation of the lines to come once they've recognized the song quotation and placed it in relation to the current scene, there is also a practical element to this practice: no new songs need be written (or learned).[24]

In comedies such as Thomas Baker's *Tunbridge Walks* (PC, 1703) such quotations could create a sense of mastery and continuity, as they remind the audience of past productions by the actors or company they are watching onstage. Alternatively, in *The Female Wits* (PC, 1696) the author quotes lines from Delarivier Manley's recent tragedy *The Lost Lover* to mock both her and it.

An interesting example from early in the decade can be found in Motteux's epilogue to *Neglected Virtue* (PC, 1696). Although *Neglected Virtue* was a tragedy, the comedian Jo Haynes is using the device of musical quotation for comic effect.

> OUR Poet made me mad, and I dare say,
> You're all as mad, if you don't like his Play.
> Some are Horn-mad, and some are Bible-mad;
> Some mad to write damn'd Plays, and that's damn'd bad.
> In short, 'tis a mad World; for now I spy
> A Hundred here, at least, as mad as I.
> Thick Plot, thin House, I can't forbear to cry.
> This Fasting time is like to mortifie us;
> Three times a Week, at least, you'll not come nigh us:
> Pray do by t'other House, as you do by us.
>   *'Twas Pride hot as Hell*
>   Taught 'em first to rebell.   [*Sings.*

---

[21]   *A Comparison Between the Two Stages*, p. 140.

[22]   Price, *Henry Purcell and the London Stage*, pp. 164–8.

[23]   Pix, *The Innocent Mistress* (London, 1697), p. 14. The song comes from John Crowne's *The Married Beau* (UC, 1694).

[24]   For more on the use of quotation in contemporary comedies, see "'Quotation is the Sincerest Form of …?': Signature Songs as Intertheatrical References," in Kathryn Lowerre, *Stages 'Adorn'd with ev'ry Grace'* (Ashgate, forthcoming).

I'll sing no more; I caught this Hoarseness, I'm afraid,
Dancing at Drapers-Hall last Masquerade.
. . . .
See that Spark yonder Ogle th' Orange Wench.
What think you of the Invasion by the French?
What's here? on every Woman's Head I spy   [*Starts.*
The Whore of Babylon's Mitred-dress three Stories high.
See, see, she's here! see 'tis the very same,
Her Face a Picture, her Commode the Frame.
[recto] What long-curl'd Main that pouder'd Thing annoys!
All you patched Maidens, and old bearded Boys,
Off, off, off with these vain fantastick Toys.   [*Sings, throws off his Perriwig, &c.*
   Abstain from Vanities, and vicious Ways,   [*Cants.*
Among the Congregation spend your Days.
Young Women, shun all Sports, but our Religious Plays.[25]

The italicized phrases are lines from Anne Bracegirdle's famous mad song "I burn, I burn, my brain consumes to ashes," originally performed in Durfey's *Don Quixote*. For this type of comic musical quotation to work, audiences must both recognize the words and melody and associate them with a particular performer and his or her performance.

Stock Comedies: Etherege's *Man of Mode*

As an example of continuity with earlier decades of the century, I briefly consider one of the most famous Restoration comedies, George Etherege's *The Man of Mode* (1676), which was regularly revived during the 1695–1705 period.[26] The intrigues of the play center around an engaging rake, Dorimant, who has been working his way through the ladies of London; when we meet him he is busying tying up loose ends with one mistress and has already become involved with another. He meets his match in a witty young lady, Harriet, who, despite her interest, has few illusions about him, and the remainder of the play involves their negotiations with each other and maneuvers to outwit those, including Harriet's mother, who oppose the match.

The play is filled with references to music making, songs, and dances too many to enumerate here, such as Dorimant's exit, singing in Act I (29). Music is part of the fabric of the fashionable and not-so-fashionable London society depicted,

---

[25] *Neglected Virtue; or, The Unhappy Conqueror* (London, 1696), unpaginated, italics reversed.

[26] Edition used, *The Man of Mode,* ed. W.B. Carnochan, Regents Restoration Drama Series (Lincoln, Nebraska, 1966).

from courtly masquerades to the orange women calling their wares around the playhouse.

During the third act, Harriet asks her maid, Busy, to sing "When first Amintas charmed my heart," ostensibly to make her stop giving advice. The song, which Harriet has "lov'd so well ever since you saw Mr Dorimant"—is a warning about loving not wisely but too well, couched in pastoral garb. In addition to providing some insight into Harriet's feelings, it provides a brief pause in the spate of rapid dialogue.

The fourth act opens with dancing at Lady Townley's. Dorimant, under an assumed name, flatters Harriet's old-fashioned mother by deploring the way "All people mingle nowadays"—though it is precisely this mingling which gives Dorimant and Harriet a chance to meet and talk in some privacy. Music helps create a new space, one where decisions must be made (and the possibilities are greater). Later in the scene most of the male characters indulge in a late-night drinking song. Music also opens the door to satire, as in the second scene Sir Fopling Flutter performs a silly "French" dance with some hired assistance, and performs a song of his own making, "How charming Phillis is, how fair!" set to "a pretty new tune." Its comical conclusion parodies the sentimental song with the gap between Sir Fopling's emotional language and his actions: "I sigh, I languish now,/ And love will not let me rest;/ I drive about the Park and bow ..." (IV, ii, 130–32), a sure cure for any distracted lover!

In the fifth act, Harriet's maid Busy is called upon to sing—and once again the song reveals Harriet's thoughts. Dialogue between one of the other ladies and Busy reveals that the pastoral song "As Amoret with Phillis sat" was written by Dorimant—and that Harriet has asked her maid to sing it for her "a dozen times a day." The song, and following discussion, put an end to Harriet and Dorimant's verbal dueling.

Comedies typically end with a concluding dance to re-establish social order and metaphorical harmony. This is especially important to *The Man of Mode*, since Etherege does not neatly tie up his hero and heroine in matrimony. Harriet agrees to retire to the country with her mother and Dorimant, if his faith passes the test, will join her there.

Both of the songs Busy performs for Harriet were originally set by Nicholas Staggins, Master of the King's Musick.[27] John Eccles wrote two songs for a production of *The Man of Mode* at some point during the 1695–1705 decade. However, neither Eccles song takes its text from the play, and it is uncertain whether they replaced songs from Etherege's text, were added to it, or simply sung before or between acts.[28] Between 1706 and 1709, singer-composer Littleton Ramondon published new settings of all three of Etherege's song lyrics in Walsh's *Monthly Mask of Vocal Musick*. Although the title lines for Ramondon's songs state

---

[27] See D&M 196 and 3716.

[28] See D&M 518 and 3196. The ascription to *The Man of Mode* for D&M 518 comes from a single songsheet engraved by Thomas Cross

simply that they were performed in the theater and not specifically in Etherege's play, *The Man of Mode*'s standing as a stock play and frequent revivals make their performance in a production of the comedy most likely.

Musical Comedies for the Rival Companies, 1695–96

Several of the new productions staged during the first season relied extensively on song and dance. However, these productions demonstrate variety in the placement and proportion of different kinds of musical numbers and in the relationship between musical and textual messages.

Lincoln's Inn Fields' She Ventures and He Wins

She Ventures and He Wins, by a young lady (pen name "Ariadne") contains charming examples of typical comedy song types. Often mentioned as part of the "great year" of women dramatists, its music—most of which was never published—has generally been overlooked or misinterpreted.[29]

The musical numbers in *She Ventures and He Wins* clearly match conventional song and scene types, yet they are involved in other sets of conventions as well. All of Eccles's songs are about love, but the messages they encode are not those implied by the speeches of Ariadne's adventurous heroine and her thoughtful brother, who refuses to try to control her or force her into a suitable marriage.

The play opens with the entrance of Charlot (Anne Bracegirdle) and her cousin Juliana, dressed as men. Charlot has not only appropriated the freedom of movement and language permitted by her male disguise but plans to appropriate the male prerogative of selecting a lover and possible future husband (Lovewell).

The first two songs in the play are conventional antitheses: a serenade describing the qualities of a fictional desirable woman, requested publicly from hired musicians by two gentlemen; and a lament about the torments of a secret, unrequited love, requested privately from a personal servant by Juliana. Light and tuneful, the first song, "Fair Belinda's youthful charms," was performed by John Bowman playing Sir Charles.[30]

---

[29] Both "Fair Belinda's youthful charms" (D&M 931) and "Restless in thought, disturbed in mind" (D&M 2800) appeared as a single songsheets. "Fair Belinda" was also included in *Deliciae Musicae* and "Restless" in Eccles's *Collection of Songs*. "Fair Belinda" and "Oft have you told me that you loved" can be found in GB-Lbl Add. MS 29378, along with the final duet, "Look down great Hymen."

[30] This attribution comes from a songsheet in the Guildhall Library, London. In the play text, Sir Charles orders the musicians "let's have the song," which presumably refers to their playing the symphony and accompanying him. The songsheet does not advertise the production title, possibly due to the play's cool reception.

In addition to substituting "Fair Belinda" for "Young Celinda," there are other minor emendations in the sung lyric from that given in the play text (below). The song begins with a short symphony in G minor for two treble instruments (violins) in sweet-sounding thirds over an unfigured bass. The upper instruments drop out as the voice enters.

> Young *Celinda*'s youthful Charms,
>   Fills the admiring Town with wonder;
> The stubbornst Heart, her Eyes alarms,
>   And makes them to her Power surrender.
> Face, and Shape, and Wit so rare!
>   Heavens Master-piece she was design'd:
> A graceful Mien, and such an Air,
>   Nothing excells it but her Mind.
> Tho' Women envy, Men admire;
> Her Eyes, in all, do Love inspire.[31]

Eccles's song is simple and graceful, the text setting is largely syllabic, with no repetition of lines or words until the final phrase "her eyes do Love in all inspire." Repeating "Love" the singer finally reaches his highest note (G), completing the ascending line begun in the first setting of the phrase.

After the first song, as she and Juliana enter, Charlot insists "I told you 'twas but your fancy; I was sure no music, nor no one else but my brother would enter here, and he is not at home" (II, 14). She is wrong, but the implication is clear. Juliana, the more romantic lady, heard music where Charlot heard none. At the end of Juliana's song, when the singer laments that she is "Enslaved to love, and love in vain," Charlot brusquely replies "That's your own fault." She has no need of songs like Juliana's, for "where'er I loved, I'd tell him so, and break that useless piece of modesty, imposed by custom, and gives so many of us the pip" (II, 13).

The simple tunefulness of the "symphony song" Sir Charles orders contrasts sharply with the highly personal and emotional idiom of the song Juliana requests Betty (Mary Hodgson) to sing for her.

> Restless in Thoughts, disturb'd in Mind,
>   Short Sleep's deep Sighs: Ah much, I fear,
> The inevitable Time assign'd,
>   By Fate, to Love's approaching near.
> When the dear Object present is,
>   My flutt'ring Soul is all on fire:
> His sight's a Heaven of Happiness;
>   And, if he stays, I can't retire.
> Tell me, some one, in Love well read,
>   If these be Symptoms of that Pain.

---

[31] Ariadne, *She Ventures and He Wins* (London, 1695), pp. 13–14.

> Alas, I fear, my Heart is fled,
> Enslav'd to Love, and Love in vain.[32]

Eccles's setting begins with a pair of melismas over a sustained G in the bass (Figure 1.1). The detailed bass figures given for the other held-note passages in the continuo line make the absence of figures in the initial six measures noteworthy, and reinforce the harmonic stasis. Even the melismas on "Restless," despite their busy motion, inevitably return to the note they started on, and the last quartet of sixteenth notes is the same as the first. This rootedness fits the lyric, as the speaker can't escape: she is "fated" to love, her heart is "enslav'd," and she is physically unable to leave whenever he's near. Even in the setting of "disturb'd," which opens up more musical space (moving towards B-flat) most of the harmonic motion occurs over a dominant pedal.

Like mad songs, Juliana's lament is constructed of several short, contrasting sections. After the striking opening passage, Eccles writes short imitative exchanges between singer and continuo, and obsessive repetition at different pitch levels of single words—"no," a particularly popular one in contemporary songs, is used here.[33] The final section in cut time is almost jaunty, until the solemnity of the written-out second ending provides a last sharp contrast, heavy with futility ("in vain").

A more complicated antagonism between the musical messages and the characters' speech and actions appears at the end of the third act. The musical dialogue "Oft have you told me that you lov'd," sung by a man and a woman, is requested by Lovewell as entertainment during the private supper celebrating their secret marriage. By this time, Charlot has revealed that she is a woman, but not that she is Sir Charles's sister and an heiress.

It follows the typical dialogue pattern, a series of exchanges followed by a brief chorus. Although the female speaker is initially reluctant, she eventually surrenders in exchange for a promise of faithfulness and joins the man in a chorus predicting a succession of pleasure-filled days and nights "till together we Die,/ And in each others Arms to *Elizium* will fly."[34] Eccles's setting employs a series of characteristically lively tunes but his musical choices also shape the message conveyed. Where the text outlines the terms of the woman's surrender, Eccles emphasizes it, repeating her final solo line, "My heart and my freedom I'll give up to you," and even having her echo the man's final couplet before joining in the ecstatic chorus. Immediately afterward, Charlot gives her new husband money and leaves. There is no hint of her response to the music.

The final musical event in *She Ventures and He Wins*, following a reconciling dance, is the duet to Hymen sung at the end of Act V. The text consists of three

---

[32] Ariadne, *She Ventures and He Wins*, pp. 15–16.

[33] Eccles inserts "no" into line 8 "And, if he stays, I can't [no, no, no, I can't] retire," and repeats the inserted portion multiple times.

[34] Ariadne, *She Ventures and He Wins*, p. 25.

Figure 1.1   John Eccles, "Restless in thought, disturb'd in mind" in *She Ventures and He Wins*. From Eccles, *A Collection of Songs for One, Two, or Three Voices* (London, 1704), pp. 2–3.

Figure 1.1   Concluded

rhymed couplets, perhaps an allusion to the three sets of lovers about to be united.

> Look down great *Hymen* from Above,
> These Pairs preserve in Peace and Love.
> May never Jars their Joys molest,
> But still a sweet and Halcyon rest
> Upon their mutual Bliss attend,
> And ev'ry Hour new Pleasures send.[35]

Eccles's musical choices here are straightforward. He writes a descending melody for the opening lines, and places extensive melismas on "pleasures" and other suggestive words. Musically, the duet emphasizes imitation between countertenor and bass, presumably featuring the company's professional singers. Despite the vocal display, the duet itself is harmonically simple although Eccles chooses an unusual key (C minor), which marks a definite departure from the others, all centered on G.

In addition to these more elevated pieces, Ariadne includes a song and dance for "devils" (vintner's assistants in disguise) at the beginning of Act III as part of the farcical subplot involving Squire Wouldbe (Thomas Dogget), who wants to sleep with Urania, his neighbor Freeman's wife. No music survives for "Say, Brother Divell" and the devils' dance, which were presumably broadly comic, like the devils in William Mountfort's farce *Dr. Faustus* (LIF revival, 1697).

Among the serious characters Sir Charles is active only in music—in the serenade and the dance at the end. This further accentuates his unusual passivity, and his diametric opposition to Charlot, who controls in everything else, but rejects or ignores all music until the last act. In the final lines, Charlot follows Sir Charles's lead for the first time and is incorporated into the inevitable dance. The traditional balance of power has reasserted itself.

Cibber's Love's Last Shift *and Behn's* The Younger Brother *at Drury Lane*

In his first comedy Cibber follows a different model for the use of music. Rather than spread throughout the play, musical events are concentrated in a few scenes, particularly in the masque at the end.

The trumpet sonata in St James's Park in Act III has already been mentioned as an example of contemporary taste and musical pretensions,[36] of which Sir Novelty Fashion has more than a few. The rakish song written by Daniel Purcell for Letitia Cross to sing, probably in Act IV as Loveless waits for his assignation

---

[35] Ibid., p. 44.
[36] See also Peter Holman, "The Trumpet Sonata in England," *Early Music* 4 (1976): 424–9.

with Amanda, is of a type quite unknown in *She Ventures and He Wins*, though having plenty of precedent elsewhere.

> What ungratefull Devil moves you,
> Come my Friend ye truth declare
> You Love Sylvia, Sylvia Loves you:
> Why then will you wedd the Fair.
> Marriage joyning does dissever,
> But Love freeing joyns for Life
> Wou'd you Love the Nymph for ever,
> Never let her be your Wife.[37]

As a song sung to entertain Loveless while Amanda prepares to act the part of a loose woman, it would fit very well—and audience members, knowing the characters' true relationship, could enjoy the added irony. This was obviously a popular song, as it was printed numerous times,[38] and the pithy closing couplet returns in several later productions as a quotation.

The Act V masque, for which no musical score survives, presents the allegorical characters of Fame, Reason, Love, Honour, and Marriage, "attended with a CHORUS."[39] As previously mentioned in this chapter, the chorus is indeed unusual in a comedy, and worth its weight in capitals.

Love, presumably played by Letitia Cross based on the surviving music (below), is seated on a throne, acclaimed by Fame and the chorus. When attacked by Reason ("Cease, cease fond Fools your Empty Noise") Love quickly dispatches his claims ("In Spight of Reason; Love shall live and reign"). A martial symphony announces Honour's entrance, Honour who, like Mars, opposes love to action. The entrance of Marriage "with his Yoke" brings a new litany of complaints: the promised eternal happiness and "raptures in the bridal-bed" are gone (102).

> *Marriage.*   Long since alas! the airy Vision's fled,
>   And I with wandring Flames my Passion feed.
>   O! tell me pow'rful God\Where shall I find
>   My former Peace of Mind!
> *Love.*   Where first I promis'd thee a happy Life,
>   There thou shalt find it in a Vertuous Wife.[40]

---

[37] D&M 3668, text from Motteux's periodical *The Gentleman's Journal* (no longer in publication in 1696).

[38] Day and Murrie list several songbooks in which it was printed, and Thomas Cross engraved it as a single songsheet. Olive Baldwin and Thelma Wilson also note its appearance in contemporary music manuscripts (personal communication).

[39] Cibber, *Love's Last Shift* (London, 1696), p. 101.

[40] Ibid., p. 102, italics reversed.

Only the music for the final section of the masque, by émigré composer Johann Wolfgang Franck,[41] was printed.

> *Love, & Fame.* Go Home unhappy wretch and mourn
> For all thy Guilty Passion past,
> There thou shalt those Joys return,
> Which shall for ever, ever last.[42]

The opening section of Franck's C major duet (Figure 1.2) contains an interesting moment as the singers repeat "and mourn," carefully marked "Slow." Franck keeps moving the music's center, with a chain of shifting harmonies. He also marks the repetition of "all thy guilty passion" both "Loud" and "Very Slow" as the singers come to a cadence in G, setting up the sweetly diatonic second section "Then thou shall find those Joys return/ Which shall for ever last." Audience members need not be music masters to absorb the import of the text, the way Franck sets it. The masque concludes with a reprise of the opening chorus, "Hail! Hail! Victorious Love!"

Given the roster of singers available, the part of Honour, whose solo air follows "A Martial Symphony" and mentions trumpet, was probably sung by John Freeman, while Reason and Marriage were probably played by lower-voiced males, possibly basses Thomas Edwards and Richard Leveridge. Following the masque, Loveless professes himself completely converted to virtuous love—Amanda's acquisition of a fortune and estate while he was away certainly do not hurt.

Although Cibber's success inspired imitators (Vanbrugh's use of music in *The Relapse* closely follows Cibber), the Patent Company mounted musically integrated comedies as well. Aphra Behn's *The Younger Brother*, prepared for the stage by Charles Gildon, contains a scattering of musical events throughout, like *She Ventures and He Wins*, but with even more cast involvement. Rather than a formal masque, her comedy employs the looser "masquerade," with characters participating rather than providing an audience. Such masquerades presumably took best advantage of the stock of costumes kept by the Patent Company after the 1695 split.

Derek Hughes reads Behn's comedy *The Younger Brother* as a 'transformation' of Wycherley's *The Plain Dealer*, and by extension *Twelfth Night*,[43] and notes the charms of the scheming Mirtilla, who nearly outwits everyone, managing to marry rich, become the mistress of a prince, and somehow keep at least a small portion of the affection honest George Marteen (the title character) felt for her before the play began.

---

[41] Franck previously worked in Italy and Germany, composing operas for Hamburg's Gansemarkt Theater. Resident in England for over two decades, he had published numerous songs and run his own concert series.
[42] Cibber, *Love's Last Shift*, p. 103.
[43] Hughes, *English Drama 1660–1700* (Oxford, 1996), pp. 391–3.

Figure 1.2   J. Franck, "Go Home unhappy wretch and mourn" in *Love's Last Shift*. From *Thesaurus Musicus* book 5, pp. 8–10

Figure 1.2   Continued

Figure 1.2   Concluded

Several musical events are associated with the elder brother, Sir Merlin Marteen (William Penkethman). According to the printed text, he enters singing "What Life can compare with the Jolly Town Rake's" (7–8). This is Motteux's lyric, set by Daniel Purcell, and the only song from *The Younger Brother* known to survive.[44] The printed music, however, assigns it to Edwards. The spoken dialogue and action make it clear Penkethman's character is not the bold figure as he claims, but more acting a part, as he seeks to entice his wealthy cousin Sir Morgan into a properly rakish London life. Sir Morgan first appears badly hung over, and apparently Sir Merlin thinks a dance routine will help ("Here the Dance, representing Rake-hells Constable watch &c." Act I, 11), which is performed with Morgan's mother and Merlin's father as an audience. The cousins later interrupt the masquerade in Act III by entering drunk, singing, and by the end of the act they really have been seized by the constables.

Dancing is an important part of the masquerades at the beginning of Act III and the end of Act V, and marks the progression of the relationship between Mirtilla and the Prince. In Act III, they dance "the Spanish Dance" while conversing (26), and in Act V their entrance among the other couples, leaving Mirtilla's husband Sir Morgan unpartnered, gives an unmistakable sign of their relationship (52). Another significant dance occurs at the end of Act IV, when George Marteen (played by George Powell), cured of his love for Mirtilla, executes "a Dance of Country Lovers, where Passion is sincere" (43). If he dances this with his new love Teresia (actress-singer Diana Temple), the pastoral dance is both sincere and insincere at the same time, as Marteen is pretending to court the older Lady Youthly in order to gain access to the younger. Lady Youthly's dancing talents are not neglected either: she dances with George's father, Sir Rowland, during the masquerade, and takes part in the final dance at the very end of the play.

The vigorous Sir Rowland also attempts to court Teresia, with a short song, "Tho the young prize *Cupid's* Fire/ 'Tis more val[u]'d by the Old" (Act II, 23), while parallel songs, performed for Mirtilla and the Prince in Acts II and IV, expound the charms of irresistible women ("Delia" and "Charmion"— both presumably stand-ins for Mirtilla). The fact that Gildon wrote both lyrics suggests that this symmetry is not coincidental. The remaining vocal number is a musical dialogue which the text explains is sung "in the Masque, at the beginning of the third Act" (23). From the concluding lyrics, the dialogue "Time and Place you see conspire" must have been sung by the young Letitia Cross and one of the adult male singers (Edwards again, or Leveridge):

> *She.* Let me dye now, you'r grown a strange sort of a man
> To force a young Maid, let her do what she can;
> I fear now I blush to think what we're doing,
> And is this the End of all you Men's wooing?
> *He.* At this pleasure all Aim, both Godly and Sinners,

---

[44] D&M 3649. It also appeared as a Cross songsheet, Lbl G.315 (song 88).

And none of 'em blush for't but poor young beginners.
In pleasure both Sexes, all Ages agree,
And those that take most, most happy will be.
Chorus. In pleasure both Sexes, &c.[45]

Given contemporary enthusiasm for musical dialogues, it is surprising that it does not seem to have been published.

Motteux's Experiments with Music and Comedy

Among the various comic productions from the first seasons of competition, some of the most highly musical are the work of Pierre Motteux. Motteux, whose advocacy of opera is well known, drew on French and Italian models for his musical-dramatic works and, from 1705, worked as a libretto adapter for some of the first Italian-style, all-sung operas performed in London.

The following discussion addresses three of Motteux's early efforts: *Love's a Jest*, *The Loves of Mars and Venus* and *The Novelty*. Motteux's printed texts are particularly valuable as a guide to productions because he documents the musical forces and the costuming and choreography of the dances (or at least, what he intended) in greater detail than many authors.

Motteux's *Love's a Jest* calls for multiple musical events in every act. This lavish use of music allows Motteux to show off most, if not all, of the actor-singers, professional singers, and dancers at Lincoln's Inn Fields in the spring of 1696. It is of interest both for the variety of the music and the way the musical events are integrated and balanced.

Motteux opens the first act of *Love's a Jest* with a song, "Slaves to London, I'll deceive you," which serves a clear dramatic function by establishing the location of the country-house comedy—a pleasant escape for a London audience in June. After Sam Gaymood sings the opening line he breaks off, commenting "E'gad I've as good a voice as most Composers!"[46] Upon request, his servant takes over, caroling conventional criticisms of London and extolling the "Quiet harmless Country Pleasure" that can be found away from the metropolis.[47]

---

[45] Behn, *The Younger Brother; or, The Amorous Jilt* (London, 1696), p. 24.

[46] Doubtless an inside joke. Roger North comments "it hath been a misfortune, that most of our great masters of musick have wanted good voices, whereby it is become proverbiall to say any one sings like an organist." *Roger North's* The Musicall Grammarian 1728, Chan and Kassler, p. 125. Colley Cibber similarly comments on "great Composers of Musick, who cannot sing," *An Apology for the Life of Mr. Colley Cibber*, ed. Robert W. Lowe (2 vols, London, 1889), vol. 1, p. 113.

[47] Two contemporary settings of "Slaves to London" survive: one by Bernard Martin Berenclow, a very minor composer, in songsheets issued by Thomas Cross and Daniel Wright, and "A Song in the Comical Mistakes sung by Mr. Lee" engraved by Cross and

The song "Shou'd I not lead a happy life" and the following dialogue are two of the musical entertainments ordered by Sir Thomas Gaymood, owner of the country house where the courting and eventual pairing of four sets of lovers takes place. Sir Thomas is as lavish with his entertainments as with food and drink, although his hospitality is not to everyone's taste.

When Squire Illbred and Sir Topewell Clownish enter Gaymood's hall, already tipsy, they make "antic gestures" at the dancers who are performing, identifying themselves as boors before they even open their mouths. Nearly every line Sir Topewell speaks sounds like a paraphrase of a drinking song. When Sir Thomas instructs his household to follow the dancing with a short "Scotch" song and the other listeners comment politely, Sir Topewell exclaims "Odsooks one merry Drinking Catch is worth a hundred on't" (18). His host then promises something more to his taste.

The new entertainment begins with a solo by comic bass John Reading, who enters carrying a bottle, complaining that enjoying the good things in life always results in his bottle getting empty and his wife full (pregnant) and wishing it worked the other way around. Another male singer then enters in drag as the very pregnant wife and begins scolding her husband for drinking ("Still at your Pot, you Drunken Sot?"). Eventually, through example and experience, the wife is made to appreciate the pleasures of drinking, and they are reconciled in a final chorus. However bald the words and threadbare the dramatic excuse, Eccles's setting of the text is reliably funny, and it puts a heavy responsibility on the instrumentalists as well as the comic skills of the singers, with active bass lines and quick imitation between voices and continuo.

Where Ariadne offered serious songs in courtly language and Cibber an allegorical masque, Motteux incorporated topical references and created characters in his musical dialogues, rather than the generic 'man' and 'woman.' While John Reading was never assigned straight acting roles, he did play Hercules in Motteux's masque (discussed below) and must have made an entertaining musical drunk.[48]

Sir Topewell likes the drunken dialogue so well he throws the singers a couple of shillings, but the reactions of the other characters are not given. This creates some ambiguity about the effect of the entertainment. If Sir Thomas is pandering to the tastes of Sir Topewell, isn't Motteux equally pandering to the tastes of the audience? London audiences are presumably sophisticated enough to know that the singers are feigning drunkenness and pretending to be a smith and his wife, but Sir Topewell believes that they are exactly what they appear to be and invites them

---

attributed to "Mr. Clarke" in a handwritten addition to GB-Lbl G. 315 (song 111). Some modern sources state it was by Jeremiah Clarke, but this is unproven. Berenclow sometimes reset lyrics from recent theater hits, including "Ophelia's Air, her Mein, her Face," from *Love Makes a Man* (PC, 1700). The simple song for Lee may have been used in 1696.

[48] See, for example, "Let us revell and roar," in Thomas Dilke's *The Lover's Luck* (LIF, 1695), discussed in Chapter Three.

to come and drink at his house, another classic trope of comedy—the untutored spectator who can't distinguish between acting and reality.

Unlike the drunken dialogue, the musical dialogue sung in character by actor-singers Anne Bracegirdle (Christina) and John Bowman (Mr Airy) near the beginning of Act IV, "Hark you, Madam, can't I move you," does not resolve the dramatic opposition at the end of the piece. Although there is a closing chorus, the two singers continue to assert contradictory statements, as any resolution between them before the last act would be premature.[49]

The attraction Airy feels for Christina is expressed foppishly in the spoken dialogue, and rakishly in the text of the musical dialogue. In the extravagant play-acting Airy does prior to the musical performance, the stage directions repeatedly instruct him to hum a song, and it seems likely Bowman performed snatches of music from some of his singing fop roles.[50] When Christina remarks "I suppose you've a Mind I should ask you to Sing?" Airy's reply, "Why the Devil don't you then? Gad, I fancy you are as fond of being ask'd as I. Why, you sing almost as well as I do. Come, let's sing the last Dialogue our Master set," (41) depends on knowledge of the actors for its humor. As amply demonstrated elsewhere, Motteux is not interested in maintaining an illusion of a separate reality onstage. Any experienced audience member would know that Eccles was the company's music-master and Bracegirdle and Bowman the leading actor-singers of the time.[51]

There are several notable musical and dramatic moments in the dialogue. Instead of the courtly approach used in romantic or sentimental songs—everyone admires *you*—the dialogue singers assure each other "everyone admires *me*." Airy's first passage is full of leaping bravado to suit the text: "Ha'n't I told you twice I love you?/ come then, kiss me, or I'm gone" (42). In the following sections Eccles writes jaunty melismas (emphasizing the "ogling" and "sighing" of the beaux who pursue Christina) and musically sets up a carefully choreographed slap as Christina interrupts Airy's vocal line and silences him for two whole measures.[52] Following the dialogue, Airy (in his own character) attempts to make love to Christina, but she rebuffs him by waking their "audience," Sam Gaymood, who has fallen asleep (another inside joke?) during the performance.

Near the end of the play, while calling for the final dialogue between "a little Boy and Girl" beginning "Pretty Miss, let's talk together," Sam Gaymood chides Airy for becoming too serious and calls for singers from the playhouse to teach him to "make Love in Jest still." However, during the musical dialogue, which Eccles

---

[49] Compare with the dialogue sung by Jacinta and Wildblood in Dryden's *An Evening's Love* (Bridges Street, 1668). Unlike Dryden's play, both actors and the characters they play are consummate performers.

[50] Perhaps Goosandelo, from Dilke's *The Lover's Luck* (LIF, 1695) or Lord Froth, from Congreve's *The Double Dealer* (UC, 1693).

[51] Some similar points are made by Curtis Price in *Music in the Restoration Theatre*, p. 2.

[52] Bracegirdle was famous for resisting sexual overtures both onstage and off.

sets with an easy tunefulness, the little boy and girl fall into the same vein as their elders and express a rather mature appreciation of the pleasures of marriage.[53]

In addition to the dialogues, *Love's a Jest* provides examples of two other song types. The first is the "Scotch" song by Christina's music-master which precedes the drunken dialogue in the Act II musical entertainment and the second, the rondeau "Mortals, learn your lives to measure" performed before the two noble lovers in Act IV.

Like Eccles's musical dialogues, composer Samuel Akeroyde's "Scotch" song promptly appeared in a new volume of the song collection *Deliciae Musicae*, where the text has four verses in mock-Scots dialect as the singer seeks her lover in London, and includes a suitably patriotic allusion to William III's military campaign against France.[54] Although the song is far from the best example of either "Scotch" songs or Akeroyde's songwriting, it provides the excuse for another inside joke. After soprano Mary Hodgson sings Akeroyde's piece, the character played by her husband, John Hodgson, is asked how he liked it ("extremely, Madam.").

Motteux's lyrics for a more courtly type of song, the very French rondeau, proclaim a *carpe diem* philosophy, appropriate to the changing feelings of the reformed rake Railmore and bluestocking Lady Single, its onstage audience. The song opens with its regularly repeated refrain "Mortals, learn your lives to measure/ Not by length of Time, but Pleasure." Eccles's musical setting is pretty, if relentlessly regular and thus not a particularly good example of his flair for text setting.[55]

Motteux never neglects dancing, and in *Love's a Jest* there are three dance scenes, one preceding the "Scotch" song in the dinner-time musical entertainment in Act II, a country dance by Doll Hoyden and other rustics in Act III, and an antic dance by Squire Illbred in Act V. However there is one dance publication. In *The Dancing Master II* (1698), the "Scotch" song has become a country dance. While some song tunes were used for dancing onstage, when a dance followed a song or chorus, in this case, *The Dancing Master* does not advertise the tune and choreography "as danc'd in the play," and I am inclined to think the printed dance an example of the appropriation (by dancing master, editor, or both) of a popular tune for a new use.

The final aspect of Motteux's comedy worth noting is his extensive use of quotation. Light-hearted musical references to old chestnuts and recent productions can be found in many other contemporary comedies. However,

---

[53] This juvenile dialogue, probably performed by Jemmy Laroche and Lucretia Bradshaw, was definitely designed to compete with the popular boy–girl duets between Letitia Cross and Jemmy Bowen at DL.

[54] Motteux, *Love's a Jest*, p. 18. Only the first two verses were printed in the play text.

[55] Eccles included the rondeau and the first two dialogues in his 1704 *Collection of Songs*. All three dialogues were also copied into GB-Lbl Add. MS 29378. In contrast with the vocal music, the instrumental music for *Love's a Jest* has not been positively identified.

Motteux's quotations are particularly plentiful and specific, doubtless due to his well-known interest in music.[56] Near the end of the first act, as Airy flirts with the countrified ingenue Kitty, he attempts to kiss her. Kitty responds by quoting the coy refusal "No, no, no, no, no, no kissing at all" from the haymakers' musical dialogue "Now the Maids and the Men," presumably continuing to sing until Airy succeeds. Motteux clearly expected his audience to recognize the fragment of Henry Purcell's popular piece and enjoy its appropriateness.[57] Characters in *Love's a Jest* also quote from old standards like the Roger de Coverley, or the drinking song "The little house under the hill," and popular tunes from recent publications like the "New Vagaries," Eccles's song "So well Corinna likes the joy" from Granville's *The She-Gallants* (LIF, 1695), and Daniel Purcell's "What ungrateful devil moves you" from *Love's Last Shift* (PC, 1696).

Love's a Jest launched Motteux's career as a playwright and gave Eccles a chance to display his mastery of musical comedy. Their dialogues are, as Motteux points out in his preface, the musical highlights of the play. Like Purcell's "Now the maids and the men," Eccles's dialogues "Hark you Madam, can't I move you" and "Shou'd I not lead a happy life" would take on independent life, becoming featured entr'acte entertainments in seasons when *Love's a Jest* was no longer revived.[58]

The comic musical dialogue was also a major part of Motteux's next production, the decidedly anti-heroic *The Loves of Mars and Venus*, a "Musical Play or Masque" performed with Edward Ravenscroft's farce *The Anatomist, or the Sham Doctor* at Lincoln's Inn Fields in November 1696. Music for the masque was written by John Eccles and Gottfried Finger, and was one of their most successful collaborations. Compositional duties were divided by section, with Eccles setting the first and second acts and Finger setting the prologue and final act. Although no score has been recovered, several of the songs as well as a libretto were printed.[59]

The Loves of Mars and Venus, "Entertainment odd and new," was Lincoln's Inn Fields's answer to Drury Lane's operas, as the prologue, spoken by Thomas Betterton, states:

---

[56] Motteux's magazine, *The Gentleman's Journal* (1692–94), contains songs and essays on music (particularly opera) in nearly every issue.

[57] In its original version, Purcell's dialogue was sung by the soprano Mrs Ayliff (Mopsa) and the bass John Reading (Coridon). For the 1693 revival, Purcell transposed the dialogue, and John Pate sang the part of Mopsa in drag. While there is no record of a full revival of *The Fairy Queen* after 1693, both versions of the song were published, and all three singers were at LIF in 1695.

[58] As in the 27 July 1704 revival of *The Maid in the Mill* at LIF. M&H *London Stage*, p. 175.

[59] As often occurs, there are some discrepancies between the lyrics and performers given in the published songbook, compared with the printed libretto.

We've in our Show the First of Cuckolds too:
And what we call a Masque some will allow
To be an Op'ra, as the World goes now,
So is your poysoning Quack miscall'd a Doctor,
And your worst Mimick calls himself an Actor.
So your dull Scribbler (to our Cost we know it)
Writes a damn'd Play, and is misnam'd a Poet.
Once Song and Dance cou'd buoy up want of Thinking,
But now those Bladders can't prevent its Sinking:
Plays grow so heavy, that those helps are vain;
Three times they rise, and never rise again.[60]

The Loves of Mars and Venus is not really a "masque within a play"—it is an equal partner with *The Anatomist*. Its action is as ongoing and extensive as the play's is, and it is at least equal in performance duration. While *The Anatomist* is given 'framing' lines, the masque pretends to peer behind the whole theatrical illusion, as the prologue is set on the stage at Lincoln's Inn Fields and the final act of the masque concludes the evening's combined entertainment.

After a fully orchestrated overture (the libretto describes "The Overture: A Symphony of Trumpets, Kettle-Drums, Violins and Hautbois"), *The Loves of Mars and Venus* begins with a musical prologue performed by a few of the appropriate muses, "Scene the *New Theatre*." The first song, "Come all, with moving Songs prepare," is particularly worth mentioning, as Finger's vocal music is not always this charming. Set by Finger and sung by Mary Hodgson, it consists of a series of lovely trumpet-like calls over sustained bass. It is followed by a series of short songs for the three graces. In the libretto, Motteux calls for different instruments to play the ritornelli, contrasting flutes (recorders) and violins.

Mary Hodgson's singing also opens the first act, with Eccles's song "To meet her Mars, the Queen of Love/ Comes here adorn'd with all her Charms." After some byplay with a mirror as the vain Venus prepares to see her lover, Cupid enters to announce Mars's imminent arrival from his travels in "the lovely *British Isle*" (7). Here Motteux works in a few compliments to English beauties and some suggestive comments on the "freedom" of English marriages. The final couplet of the scene is a bit of a non-sequitur: "Happy Isle! and happier far/ If thou knew'st no other War!" (7) but presumably refers to Mars and particularly to the contemporary conflict on the Continent.

In addition to some languishing airs for Bracegirdle and Bowman as the adulterous lovers ("My Mars!/ My Venus!/ Oh!"), Eccles provided the music for a raucously comic dialogue between Vulcan and Venus; a fully worked out musical

---

[60] Motteux, *The Loves of Mars and Venus: A Play Set to Music* (London, 1696). A play which lasted (or rose) for three nights earned an author's benefit on the third night. Evidence suggests Motteux's work was considerably more successful, and it was revived during later seasons.

scene with extensive solos, two choruses and plenty of implied choreography. Vulcan particularly calls attention to all the fashionable accoutrements Venus toyed with earlier: her make-up, her clothing, and her elaborate hair-dressing and headdress.

> *Vul.* Thou Plague of my Life,
> Thou Devil, thou Wife!
> Come, tell me, why did you
> Dress so like a Crack? you know I forbad you.
> Why d'you Patch thus and prink?
> What, you're Painted I think!
> Why this Head six foot high?
> S'Blood and Fire, who am I?
> *Ven.* My Fool; for what else can that Property be
> That's ugly, and old, and ill-natur'd, like Thee?
> I'll dress when I please, nay I'll Cuckold Thee too:
> What else have young Wives with such Husbands to do?
> *Vul.* If ever you dare,
> I'll make the World know what a Strumpet you are.
> *Ven.* Nay, what do I care?
> You'll make the World know what a Cuckold you are.
>   *Both at the same time in a scolding manner.*
> *Vul.* I'll make the World know what a Strumpet you are.
> *Ven.* I'll make the World know what a Cuckold you are.
>   *Ritornel.*
> *Vul.* Join, and curse the Tye with me,
> That confines us to one Bed!
> *Ven.* Thus at least we'll once agree;
> Curs'd be he that made us wed!
>   [Vulcan *repeats that Verse three times with Venus.*[61]

In the dance that follows, Motteux indicates that the Cyclops and their wives "frown, jolt, and threaten each other" and "the Women make Horns at the Men" all of which could easily be incorporated into the dialogue. Given a lively performance by Bracegirdle and Reading, this doubtless brought the house down.

Once Mars and Venus come together in Act II, there are some close calls—at one point Gallus has to convince Vulcan that Venus's wrapping her arms around Mars was merely to measure him for armor—and as Act III opens, Vulcan is determined to be a fool no longer. Finger's song for Mary Hodgson as the allegorical figure "Jealousie," who incites Vulcan to action, is quite effective and has been called one of his finest songs (Figure 1.3). Although more often admired for his instrumental writing, Finger gives this song the potential for a hissing and

---

[61] Motteux, *Loves of Mars and Venus*, pp. 8–9.

Musical Approaches in Comedy 49

Figure 1.3 G. Finger, "See, Vulcan, Jealousie appears!" in *The Loves of Mars and Venus*. From *Single Songs and Dialogues in the Musical Play of Mars & Venus*, pp. 17–8.

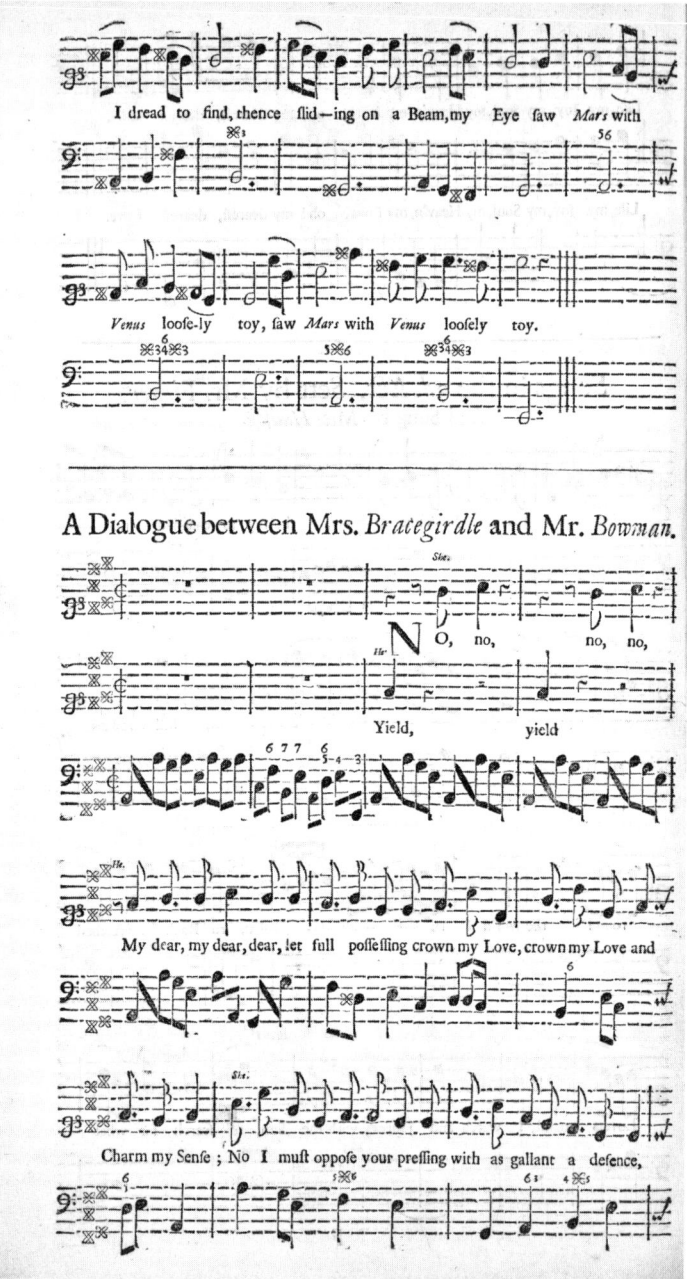

Figure 1.3 Concluded

sinister power in striking contrast to the generally merry (or mad) music. Among Finger's other published English songs are some written for Hodgson to sing in concert performances in Charles Street or at York Buildings. He doubtless knew the soprano's vocal and dramatic abilities well.[62]

Like Motteux's later masques, detailed dance sequences are built into the structure of *The Loves of Mars and Venus*; the prologue and each act ends with a dance.[63] As in the cast list, where Motteux notes that the part of Mars's henchman, Gallus, was "design'd for Mr. *Dogget*," the description of the first dance outlines what was to have been performed

> While the Grand Chorus is performing; there is an Entry of Dancing-masters, teaching their Scholars, and making Love to 'em: and a Harlequin mimicking 'em with a She-Harlequin, which expresses the business of the Prologue. This Dance cannot be perform'd, the Master who made it being sick. Another Entry is danc'd instead.[64]

The first and second acts each end with a dance by Vulcan's Cyclops, first with their wives and then the male Cyclops alone, singing, dancing, and striking their anvils, which as Motteux admits in his preface, has its precedents in Shadwell's *Psyche* and earlier French and Italian opera.[65] The final grand dance pits the followers of Mars, with shields and scimitars, against those of Cupid, with their bows and arrows.

Motteux's work designs to instruct as well as delight, despite the prologue's references to the production's "lightness." The final message of the Motteux masque is one of reconciliation and forgiveness, of spouses who will respect and like each other, if they cannot love, thanks to Cupid's intercession:

> Thus all unequal Unions break.
> Thus *Hymen* without Love is weak.
> But I'll exert my Pow'r anew,
> Make *Vulcan* kind, and *Venus* true.
> Her Gratitude will soon Improve,
> And Friendship shall resemble Love.[66]

---

[62] See for example, "My Suit will be over, my Fire will decline" (D&M 2284) or "She that wou'd gain a faithful Lover" (D&M 2901).

[63] For a general discussion of dance within the masque tradition particularly in dramatick operas, see Michael Burden, "Aspects of Purcell's Operas," p. 15.

[64] Motteux, *The Loves of Mars and Venus*, p. 4.

[65] Ibid., unpaginated.

[66] Ibid., p. 26.

The message is reinforced in the epilogue, "Learn of *Vulcan* to forgive;/ or else, egad, few Plays or Wives will live."[67] Once freed from Vulcan's golden net, in which the guilty lovers were trapped, Mars is shipped out to spend his time more profitably, fighting. Following a varied musical entertainment, both comic and sexy, Motteux concludes with a message to his audiences promoting both domestic tranquility at home and martial valor abroad (fighting Louis XIV), rather than the round of sexual intrigues.

Curiously, the anonymous author of *A Comparison between the Two Stages* attacks Durfey's *Cinthia and Endimion*—"notwithstanding the vain and conceited Title-page, 'tis good for nothing within: He's the very Antipodes to all the Poets, Antient and Modern: Other Poets treat the Deities civilly, but Mr. *Durfey* makes the Gods Bullies, and Jilts of the chastest Goddesses" (1702, 29)—but spares Motteux's, one character commenting merely "I remember the success of that was owing to the Musick" (31). Of course, a mocking attitude towards the Greek gods is hardly original to Motteux and Durfey, and can be seen in Dryden's *Amphitryon*, a popular song-filled comedy from the early 1690s, which featured many of the Lincoln's Inn Fields actors and singers, particularly John Bowman.[68]

A masque featuring classical characters was also a significant part of Motteux's *The Novelty; or, Ev'ry Act a Play* which shortly followed *The Loves of Mars and Venus* in spring 1697. Like Motteux's previous spring offering, *Love's a Jest*, *The Novelty* was marketed as light entertainment for those lingering in London in June on their way out of town for the summer. As the title indicates, each of the five acts is a different kind of dramatic entertainment: pastoral, comedy (French), masque, tragedy, and farce (Italian).

In his preface to *The Novelty*, Motteux is again attempting to educate the English public about Continental entertainments (as he did in *The Gentlemen's Journal*), telling his readers:

> I was put on this bold Attempt, being hinder'd from giving you a better Play, which, waiting its Turn, cannot appear till next Winter. Most of the best Actors being engaged on other Plays, I could not expect they would study mine. This made me think of something that might be got up by the by.
>
> I writ the masque of *Hercules*, and Mr. *Eccles* having set it with his usual Success, and yet more masterly than my *Mars* and *Venus*, if possible, I prevail'd with the ingenious Mr. *J. Oldmixon* to give me a short *Pastoral*, while I scribbl'd over a *Farce* after the *Italian* Manner, and an Imitation of part of a diverting *French* Comedy of one Act. (for such Plays are very common in Foreign Parts.) Then I wanted nothing but a Tragedy to have something of every kind. But, as I said already, the best Tragedians were engaged …

---

[67] Ibid., unpaginated, italics reversed.

[68] *Amphitryon* is known to have been revived by both companies in 1705. See Chapter Six.

At last I bethought my self of one already studied, called *The Unnatural Brother* ... [excerpting] the most moving Part of the Story into the Compass of one Act, with some Additions; ...

All this was done in a very short time, the warm Season threatening me with your Absence.[69]

Clearly Motteux wanted to have something new in front of audiences for the spring season. He claims he created *The Novelty* because "most of the best Actors" were involved with other plays. What is most surprising about the cast is the absence of Anne Bracegirdle and John Bowman, the best-known and admired actor-singers, and Mary Hodgson, the most commonly featured professional singer. Instead, Elizabeth Bowman sings in both the pastoral *Thyrsis* and the masque *Hercules*, and she acted in a supporting role in *The Unnatural Brother*. Many performers were double cast, and two others were also triple cast. However, Bowman is the only performer from *Hercules* featured in other acts.

Most of the singers and singing actors who took part in the masque of *Hercules* were familiar from Motteux's *The Loves of Mars and Venus* and the season's earlier comedies. Singing actress Elizabeth Willis (Hercules's wife, Dejanira) was a recent acquisition for the Lincoln's Inn Fields company. She would later become a frequent featured singer, nearly always in comic roles. John Reading (Hercules) and Jemmy Laroche (their son) had played Vulcan and Cupid in Motteux's earlier masque.

Unfortunately it is not possible to judge Motteux's enthusiastic (and politic) assertion that Eccles's music for the new masque was "even more masterly" than that for *The Loves of Mars and Venus*, since only a single song survives. He further notes that he has "not altogether kept close to the Story of Hercules" (preface), although some of the most famous domestic events of the hero's life are enacted. The masque opens with "A Symphony with Trumpets, Kettle-Drums, Hautboys, &c." welcoming Hercules to the Lydian court. He immediately falls in love with the queen, Omphale (Elizabeth Bowman), and offers to try to satisfy any wish of hers. Omphale replies "All you Men, when Love is new,/ Promise much, but little do." She asks him to learn to spin, providing the excuse for a dance by two women and men (and two spinning wheels) in which "they turn the Wheels with diverse Postures, and Motions" (27). Hercules does not prove much good at spinning and is beaten by Omphale's women.

At this point Dejanira enters with her two children and accosts him angrily. The song which follows, "Hee, oh! pray Father," is the only extant music for the masque.[70] It is another one of Motteux's little boy and girl dialogues, like "Pretty Miss, let's talk together" from *Love's a Jest*. However, in *Hercules* the boy and

---

[69] Motteux, *The Novelty. Every Act a Play. Being A Short Pastoral, Comedy, Masque, Tragedy, and Farce after the* Italian *manner* (London, 1697), unpaginated.

[70] A single songsheet was engraved by Cross. A copy can be found at the Guildhall Library, and another in the Library of Congress, Hunter 5 (323).

girl (Laroche and Lucretia Bradshaw) are calling their father Hercules home to comfort their mother, who "cannot lye alone." Extremely short and simple, the dialogue lacks—at least, in the printed songsheet—even the customary closing chorus. Following the dialogue, Hercules tries to leave but agrees to put on the shirt Dejanira has made for him. Meanwhile, "One of Hercules's Children dances for joy that her Father is putting on the Shirt, which *Dejanira* has been told will restore her his Love" (29). The shirt has been dipped in the poisoned blood of the centaur Nessus, and, following classical tradition, will prove no love charm, but an instrument of revenge.

As soon as his family leaves him, the poison in the shirt begins to work, causing Hercules agonizing physical pain—a wonderful opportunity for a mad song. At the end "A Poetical Heaven appears in Perspective, and a Fire under it," and Hercules promptly casts himself into the fire, in order that his spirit may ascend to glory. The Lydian attendants, who were, stage directions tell us, "frightened away by his Rant, return towards the End of his Rapture; and when 'tis over, begin the following grand *Chorus*" (30).

As in *The Loves of Mars and Venus*, Motteux depicts his classical characters in very human terms and is careful to include a variety of musical numbers and dances, including one of his famous dialogues. Again, it is unfortunate that the popularity and commercial viability of the musical dialogues (all printed) were not matched by Eccles's other songs from the masques, which have not yet been recovered.

Another song by Eccles, "Her Eyes are like the morning bright," survives from the first part of *The Novelty*, Oldmixon's pastoral *Thyrsis*. The pastoral features the usual shepherds and shepherdesses and a wicked satyr disporting themselves in an Arcadian setting. The dialogue is principally composed of long eclogues from each character and is, as Motteux states in his preface, not intended to be "dramatic." While there is some soft music (recorders) to lull Thyrsis asleep after a despairing speech in the middle of the playlet and a dance to conclude, "Her Eyes are like the morning bright" (and its following chorus) is the only vocal music indicated in the text.

Sung by Elizabeth Bowman, the song is a graceful setting of a consciously simple love-lyric, the familiar catalog of the beloved's beauties "… Her Cheeks like Roses fair,/ Her Breasts like Water'd Lillies White,/ Like Silk her flowing Hair …"[71] Musically, Eccles's dance-like song can seem a little too ingenuous and repetitive. However, an instrumental introduction for two recorders gives it more substance, while the minor key has a plaintive charm. "Her Eyes are like the morning bright" was popular, printed both in Eccles's 1704 *Collection of Songs* (in the full version with the symphony of "flutes") and as a songsheet, with voice and continuo only.

The song is followed by further musical celebrations, a chorus "With gentle steps let's beat the ground" and a "Dance of Clowns [country bumpkins] and

---

[71] Motteux, *The Novelty*, p. 9.

Shepherds," after which the happy cast "Exeunt with Music" (9). This short work prefigures Oldmixon's full-length pastoral *Amyntas* (PC, 1698) and Motteux's more rustic and robust *Acis and Galatea* (LIF, 1701).

The final section of *The Novelty*, the farce *Natural Magic*, includes scenes parodying the incantation scenes, songs and dances of infernal spirits found in tragedies and dramatick operas, as well as a number of *commedia dell'arte* routines in which a performer imitates a monkey, or a chair. The plot is also based on *commedia* material: the old miser Pantalone must be frightened into relinquishing money and property he has stolen from his former friend's son Cynthio and his niece Isabella, who want to marry.

The farce features the company's dancing master, dancer-choreographer Joseph Sorin, as Pasquarel, Cynthio's man. For his part in the plot to frighten Pantalone, Pasquarel "jumps up and down, chatters, scratches himself, and does many pleasant Tricks, like a Monkey" in one scene (44), later sliding up and down a ladder, then in the next scene pretends to be a chair (Pantalone sits on him) and untunes the old man's guitar as he tries to play it before walking on his hands, which frightens the old man offstage (45). A "ghost" and "devil" further appear to haunt Pantalone, before the most elaborate part of the ruse, in which Cynthio appears "like an Infernal Deity" and calls on "Spirits of Earth and Fire" in rhyme (51). Although Motteux's lines do not indicate they were sung, presumably they were at least intoned to match similar scenes of summoning. Two men dressed as devils appear and help make away with Pantalone's chests of treasure. The devils reappear for a final scene of judgement, with Mezzetin the clown dressed as Minos and the other characters in robes and masks. This thoroughly reforms the old miser.

Motteux notes in his preface:

> You have here the Farce as 'twas Acted the first day; the latter part being left out afterwards; some few of the Audience having been offended at it, but more at the length of the Act. I have seen most of the things that were mislik'd, much applauded when Acted by *Harlequin* and *Scaramouch*. But it must be own'd, that many fooleries pleas'd when grac'd by those incomparable Mimics which may not suit with the Genius of our Stage.[72]

Given the popularity of *Dr. Faustus*, and the various Harlequin and Scaramouche dances briefly alluded to in advertising and accounts of other performances, it is hard to identify what audiences may have objected to. Certainly there would be an extreme contrast between Sorin's antics and the serious acting of Thomas Betterton and Elizabeth Barry in the mini-tragedy just preceding, but such variety is precisely what Motteux's preface promised—and his show delivered.

These three musical works by Motteux not only showcase the talents of the Lincoln's Inn Fields performers he wrote for, they also demonstrate Motteux's

---

[72] Motteux, *The Novelty*, unpaginated, italics reversed.

mastery of a comprehensive repertoire of comic musical numbers. Even when he miscalculates, as with the *commedia dell'arte* performances in *The Novelty*, Motteux may simply be running ahead of popular taste, as he did with his endorsement of all-sung opera in the 1690s. The enormous popularity of Harlequin and Scaramouche dances in the early eighteenth century certainly validates his choice to end his medley with them.

Musical Comedy during the Final Seasons of Competition

Comedies from the seasons which followed *The Novelty* make use of the comic musical components outlined above in various combinations. Two musical comedies from the final seasons of competition, Nicholas Rowe's *The Biter* and Richard Steele's *The Lying Lover*, both make extensive use of music, much of it surviving and enabling reconstruction of musical elements in the original production. Despite their authors' past successes, top-notch casts and composers, neither *The Biter* nor *The Lying Lover* was the hit it was expected to be. Considered in the context of past musical standards, these are productions that should have succeeded, but largely did not.

Both comedies place emphasis on the telling of tall tales, either 'biting' like Rowe's annoying Squire Pinch, or romancing, as Steele's hero Bookwit does. Amid all the various examples of 'biting' in Rowe's play, it is possible that some allusion to the manager of the other house is meant. Colley Cibber characterizes Christopher Rich as a 'biter' in his *Apology*.[73] Although there is a clear difference in social status and intent between Pinch's 'bites' and Bookwit's tales, the similarities are suggestive. Pinch seeks to instantly discomfort those taken in by his 'biting,' while with Bookwit, sometimes it takes a good long while for the other characters to see through his elaborately scripted romances.

Rowe's The Biter

The Biter, a farce in three acts, was Nicholas Rowe's sole venture into comedy and has been little regarded by theater or music historians. Set in Croydon, it featured Thomas Betterton as the rich merchant Sir Timothy Tallapoy, John Verbruggen as his nephew Clerimont (in predictable financial straits), and Anne Bracegirdle as the witty heroine Mariana, secretly married to Clerimont but pursued by his uncle. The singing actor George Pack portrayed Pinch, "a biting Squire," the title character. A city solicitor and his very common wife, her soldier cousin, various servants, and two whores provided local color for Croydon and the scenes set at Croydon Fair.

As for the title, 'biting' someone means pulling his or her leg with a more-or-less plausible lie, and Pinch does not do it in a friendly fashion. If the other 'bites,'

---

[73] *Apology*, vol. 1, p. 252.

it is the modern equivalent of someone 'falling for it'—and to be bitten may imply stupidity or naïveté, as well as amusing and increasing the self-importance of the biter. Aside from the 'biting' the most striking thing about the play is Betterton's character, the eccentric Sir Timothy Tallapoy, and the form his eccentricity takes.

During his years in the East Indies, Sir Timothy has 'gone native,' and he has attempted to recreate a Chinese style of living at his present home in Croydon, with predictably awkward results. The other characters display a great deal of disdain for the merchant's behavior and his entire community agrees (on this if on nothing else) how ridiculous it is for Sir Timothy to imitate non-English customs.[74] On one level, the exoticized Sir Timothy is still a variation on the country squire character, as the humor arises from the contrast between how he behaves and the 'normal' way the rest of civilized London does. Sir Timothy, played by the dignified Betterton, has his good qualities. He refuses to put up with the mean-spirited importunities of Squire Pinch and eventually locks Pinch up, refusing to believe that any son of an old friend could be so abominable.[75]

Four songs from the play were published in Walsh's *Monthly Mask of Vocal Music*; three of them specially featured (and advertised) for the December 1704 issue. In addition, some of the instrumental music written by John Lenton survives in the Filmer Collection at Yale. Unfortunately, the 'Biter tunes' seem to have been saved only because they were copied on the same sheet as another set of pieces, and they are incomplete.[76]

Of Eccles's four songs for *The Biter*, only one is incorporated into the action of the play, Motteux style: Bracegirdle's musical dialogue. The dialogue "Iris I have long in vain" was sung by Bracegirdle and Pack (Mariana and Pinch) during the second act of the play. Two of the other songs, "Chloe blush't and frown'd and swore," sung by Mr Cook, and "Silly Swain give o'er thy wooing," sung by John Davis, were apparently performed on empty stages at the ends of the first and second acts. The fourth song, "Maenis underneath this shade," sung by Mary Hodgson, does not appear in the play text and may have been performed before or after the farce. In terms of company practices, it is significant that Eccles writes

---

[74] Anticipating marrying Mariana, Sir Timothy proposes to "engender a Male Off-spring, who shall drink nothing but the Divine Liquor Tea, and eat nothing but Oriental Rice, and be brought up after the Institutions of the most excellent *Confucius*." Nicholas Rowe, *The Biter* (London, 1705), pp. 21–2.

[75] In the second act, Sir Timothy refers to him forthrightly (and accurately) as a "Son of a Bitch" (p. 24) and dismisses him. When Pinch continues to torment, Sir Timothy beats the younger man "round the stage" (p. 25), action with which anyone not extremely dedicated to non-violence would sympathize.

[76] Filmer MS 12 is a set of three rather dog-eared sheets. Due to the difference in complexity of parts and resulting spacing the first treble part contains only four typical dance tunes, while the second treble includes the overture as well, and the bass both the overture and two subsequent tunes, possibly a minuet and jig. For complete transcriptions of the first four tunes, see *Music Productions LIF*, Appendix B.

a song for each of Lincoln's Inn Fields' professional singers, the "regulars" of entr'acte entertainment from 1703 to 1705: Cook, Davis, and Hodgson.

The Act II dialogue referred to by characters in the comedy as the "Biting Song" is of course a ditty written by Squire Pinch. As in several of Bracegirdle's earlier dialogues, the text seems to refer to the actress's celebrated chastity:

> *Thyrsis* Iris, I have long in vain,
>   Been your Slave, and worn your Clog;
> 'Tis but just I shou'd complain,
>   Since you use me like a Dog.
> *Iris* Faithful Lovers are but few;
>   Cou'd I trust, I wou'd trust you:
> Of all your Sex I am afraid,
>   And therefore vow to die a Maid.
> *Thyrsis* Die a Maid! So young, so pretty!
>   I'll be true, by all that's good:
> Die a Maid! I'll swear 'tis pity.
> *Iris* Bite! Thyrsis, did you think I wou'd?
> But since you will be mine alone,
>   Here kiss the Book and swear:
> The Wedding Ring shall make us one.
> *Thyrsis* Bite! Iris, now I think all's fair.
> *Chorus* Bite! Thyrsis [/Iris], now I think all's fair,
>   And well we may agree,
> Since thus we love upon the square,
>   And Biters both are we.[77]

Poetry is not Squire Pinch's strong suit.[78]

Eccles's setting is disappointing in many respects, when compared with the settings of earlier Motteux dialogues. The features are familiar ones—but the execution is often rather clumsy. In both text and music it is suggestively like a parody of the conventional pastoral dialogue, and the awkwardness of the opening sections for Squire Pinch may be intended as a reflection upon the skills of the onstage 'composer.'

The symphony, opening exchange, and ritornello are all rooted in F major, which makes the shift to F minor at Bracegirdle's second statement even more striking. Eccles's setting of the text beginning "But since you will be mine alone" is in a plaintive, affected style, with a jagged melisma on "mine" and plenty of passing sevenths (momentary dissonances) between the voice and bass, it contrasts sharply with the almost universal consonances and syllabic setting of the previous

---

[77] Rowe, *The Biter*, pp. 32–3.

[78] But the prize for worst poem penned by a character in a LIF comedy should go to Goosandelo in *The Lover's Luck* (1695) for his "Rich Mines of Hot Love are rooted here."

sections. As with most theatrical musical dialogues, the cues for gestures are numerous, here allowing Bracegirdle to parody her own acting in tragic roles.

The dialogue raises an interesting question—certainly Squire Pinch is a self-proclaimed biter, and proud of it. But is Mariana a biter too? She certainly deceives and turns the tables on a succession of the other characters, including Squire Pinch and Sir Timothy. Yet her motives are not a desire to cause confusion and raise her own status.

Mariana's sense of humor is established in Act I, when she reports her "adventures" at the fair to Lady Stale and Mrs Clever. When Pinch arrives towards the end of the act, he has not yet seen his intended bride (daughter of Sir Timothy), but he finds Mariana very attractive. However, the song performed at the close of Act I is curiously at odds with the conversation preceding it. After turning aside a succession of clownish compliments, Mariana makes Pinch swear to be her servant for the remainder of the day. The song concludes the act.

> *Chloe* blush'd, and frown'd, and swore,
>   And push'd me rudely from her;
> I call'd her perjur'd, faithless Whore
>   To talk to me of Honour.
> But when I rose, and wou'd be gone,
>   She cry'd, nay, whither go ye;
> Young *Damon* stay, now we're alone,
>   Do what you will with *Chloe*.[79]

Eccles's setting employs a lively disjunct melody, with wide leaps, the text setting simple and syllabic. No word or phrase repeats until the final line, "Do what you will with Chloe." The four-part symphony frames the song in an equally straightforward manner. No spoken dialogue explicitly relates to the theme of the song. It is not mentioned or witnessed by any of the characters, all offstage. At this point in the play, Pinch believes he has successfully commenced an *amour*, and although Mariana is amusing herself, she is not being faithless to Clerimont.

"Silly Swain give o'er thy wooing," the song performed by John Davis at the end of Act II, also employs a four-part symphony and a "Ritornell." The text is disillusioned with love, but in a different vein, concluding:

> Prove the Nymph and taste her Treasure,
> Tell me then, when full of Pleasure,
> What dull thing thou can'st discover,
> Duller than a happy Lover.
> *Silly, silly Swain give over, &c.* [80]

---

[79] Ibid., pp. 16–17, song text only.
[80] Ibid., pp. 45–6.

The opening phrase "Silly Swain give o'er thy wooing" is set to notes from the pentatonic scale, inflecting it with a folk-like character.

"Maenis underneath this shade," the song for Mary Hodgson, employs the most frequent alternation between voice and instrumental ensemble, as Eccles begins with a short symphony and then alternates her phrases with brief ritornelli

Maenis underneath this shade to Aminta told his pain

Here the Coy the Cruell Maid
Kill'd him with her Cold Disdain.
Here pity, pity me he cry'd,
Here she frown'd and here he dy'd.

The setting is simple, with a fondness for two-note slurs and cute touches like the "Scotch" snaps on "coy" and "cruel." This overblown quasi-pastoral might have been sung before or after the play, or between the acts.[81]

Although *The Biter* included musical elements that had been surefire draws in past seasons, like a racy musical dialogue in character for Bracegirdle, the other songs are detached from the action of the play and feel flat in comparison with Eccles's earlier pieces. One of the most intriguing missed opportunities occurs near the end of the second act, when we learn from the dialogue that Sir Timothy "has made a *Chinese* Song upon you [Mariana], ... singing it to an Oriental Kettle-Drum."[82] What would the theater's "Chinese" music have sounded like? Exotic settings accompanied by very English music were common in tragedies, but rarely seen in contemporary comedies. The idea of a love song with percussion accompaniment simply emphasizes the ridiculous aspect of Sir Timothy's courtship.

In place of the generic songs for Cook, Davis, and Hodgson, Rowe might have done better to incorporate a Chinese musical entertainment by Sir Timothy, though Eccles's efforts would risk comparison with Henry Purcell's magnificent (and utterly un-Chinese) music for the Chinese Man and Woman in the final act of the Shakespearean dramatick opera *The Fairy Queen*. However, *The Biter* remains unremittingly 'homely,' with no flights of fantasy or musical exoticism.

Steele's The Lying Lover

Richard Steele's *The Lying Lover* follows his earlier comedies in its extensive incorporation of music within the dramatic action, like the comedies of earlier seasons by Behn and Motteux. There is music called for in every act except the first. In it, Young Bookwit, the 'lying lover' (romance spinner, tall-tale teller)

---

[81] The other possibility is that the ascription to *The Biter* was a mistake and that Eccles wrote this song for another production from this season.

[82] Rowe, *The Biter*, p. 43. Contemporary audiences would know that Betterton *never* sang.

portrayed by Robert Wilks, spends several minutes describing an elaborate and entirely imaginary musical entertainment he hosted on the river the previous night. Bookwit's description of his evening is both a fascinating picture of such events and our first extended introduction to Bookwit's talent for romancing, or more bluntly, lying, though he prefers to think of it as "Wit, ... Fable, Allegory, Fiction, Hyperbole, or be it what you call it" (14).

> I took five Barges, and the fairest kept for my Company; the other four I fill'd with Musick of all sorts, and of all sorts the best; in the first were Fiddles, in the next Theorbo, Lutes, and Voices.
> Flutes and such Pastoral Instruments I'th'third.
> Loud Musick from the fourth did pierce the Air;
> Each Consort vy'd by turns;
> Which with most Melody shou'd charm our Ears.
> The fifth the largest of 'em all was neatly hung,
> Not with dull Tapistry, but with green Boughs,
> Curiously interlac'd to let in Air,
> And every Branch with Jessemins, and Orange, Posies deckt.
> In this the Feast was kept.
> Hither with five other Ladies I led her, whose Beauty alone governs my Destiny. Supper was serv'd up straight; ... 'tis enough I tell you this delicious Feast was of six Courses, twelve Dishes to a Course.[83]

Bookwit continues describing the gala, including role playing (with Penelope as Ceres, receiving offerings from Bookwit) and magnificent fireworks, followed by dancing until dawn (12–13). Concerts with dancing afterwards were a regular feature of the London season and particularly of the summer spas, like Richmond Wells, and Colley Cibber's father-in-law, Matthias Shore, owned a musical pleasure barge. Fireworks, as at a royal event or civic celebration, just add to the magnificence of Bookwit's imaginary entertainment.

In Acts II and III, Steele creates the opportunity for double performances of his songs, as he did in his earlier comedy *The Funeral*. "Thou soft Machine that do'st her Hand obey," supposedly written about Penelope, is read and then sung with a spinet while, according to the text, the serenading song "Venus has left her Grecian Isles" is sung first by hired musicians and then by Young Bookwit himself. To these songs, set by William Croft and Daniel Purcell, Steele adds an outright drinking song by Leveridge in Act IV, "Since the Day of poor Man." Like the songs for Rowe's *The Biter*, all three were published in Walsh's *Monthly Mask of Vocal Music*.[84]

---

[83] Steele, *The Lying Lover; or, The Ladies Friendship. A Comedy.* (London, 1704), pp. 11–12.

[84] Once again, the printed play text, which indicates that Wilks sang the song himself, does not match Walsh's songsheet, which states "Set and Sung by Mr Leveridge." However,

When Bookwit (Wilks) arranges a serenade for the lovely Victoria, accompanied by his friend Latine (Cibber), he does it in his usual over-the-top manner with musicians, chairmen, torches, etc.:

> *Lat.* But you know I love Musick immoderately.—How do you dispose your Entertainment, let 'em begin—
> *Book.* Well, give me but leave.—The Fiddles will certainly attract the Ladies, I mean the Nymphs who have Grotto's round this enchanted Forest. —In the first place, you Intelligences that move this Vehicle.—How the Fellows stare!
> *Chair.* Good your Honour, speak to us in English.—
> *Book.* Why then you Chairmen, —wherever I move you are to follow me. —For I mean to strut, shine through the Dusk of the Evening, and look as like a lazy Town Fool as I can to charm 'em—
> *Lat.* Well, but the Musick—
> *Book.* But remember, ye Sons of *Phoebus*, Brethren of the String, and Lyre; that is to say, ye Fidlers. —Let me have a Flourish as I now direct. — When I lift up my Cane, let it be Martial. — If I but throw my self just forward on it, or but raise it smoothly. —Sigh all for Love to shew, as I think fit, —That I wou'd die, or fight for her you see me bow to—Well then strike up—
>
> SONG, by Mr. *Leveridge*
>
> Venus has left her Grecian Isles,
> With all her gaudy Train
> Of little Loves, soft Cares and Smiles
> In my larger Breast to reign.
> Ye tender Herds and list'ning Deer,
> Forget your Food, forget your Fear,
> The bright Victoria will be here.
> The Savages about me throng,
> Mov'd with the Passion of my Song,
> And think Victoria stays too long.
>
> *Book.* There's for you, *Jack*; is not that like a fine Gentleman that writes for his own Diversion?
> *Lat.* And no bodies else.[85]

Daniel Purcell's setting creates contrasting musical sections out of each verse, with a sighing "tender" motif for the second, and a lively dotted rhythm gesture for "bright Victoria." Fortunately for Latine's patience, the ladies soon arrive and are entertained, but entirely unsubdued, by Bookwit's elaborate production values.

Act V has the usual complement of music and dancing, ending with another song performed "By Mr. Leveridge": "The rolling Years the Joys restore,/ Which

---

Walsh apparently did not publish the song until July 1707, and Leveridge presumably took over singing it as entr'acte music by that time. The other two songs were printed in 1704.

[85] Steele, *The Lying Lover*, pp. 35–6, numbering of song verses cut.

happy happy Britain knew/ When in a Female Age before/ Beauty the Sword of Justice drew." In addition to his song, Croft also composed the incidental music, including a lengthy and impressive chaconne, presumably part of the first and second music.

Both Steele and later critics have attributed poor audience response to the comedy to the fifth act. In it Bookwit, thinking he has killed a friend (another major character) in a duel, is revealed lying on a couch asleep (no 'soft music' is cued, but it would be entirely appropriate). When wakened by his friend Latine, Bookwit is subject to agonies of remorse, in his usual flowery language. The scene makes a not-so-comic parallel with the opening of the final act in Rowe's recent tragedy *The Fair Penitent* (LIF, 1703). Here Steele is breaking the operational code of comedy (no one dies except rich old uncles, offstage), which certainly would account for some of the contemporary audience's distaste. Yet as a modern reader, it is hard to take Cibber's character seriously, and contemporary audiences may have had a similar problem. Latine's overblown speeches in earlier acts make it very hard to hear his lines without humor, though the potentially comedic aspects of this scene could have been unintentional, as Steele insists he wanted to convince his audiences of the evils of dueling.

Conclusion

The typical comedy from this decade included both vocal and instrumental music, most often in the form of solo songs, musical dialogues, and dances. Both houses worked within a shared set of conventions and traditions regarding the use of music in comic productions, and over the course of the decade shared the services of the most musical comedy authors, Durfey and Motteux. However, each house's authors, performers and composers helped shape the ways in which music was used during this decade. While both houses made extensive use of musical dialogues, both 'straight' and in drag, many were tailored to their performers: for example, compare the sexually suggestive ones performed by Letitia Cross at Drury Lane, by various composers, with the comic and teasing but less explicit ones featuring Anne Bracegirdle, composed by Eccles. Both houses had Thomas Dogget—somctimes—and roles with appropriate songs and dances were tailored to him. Lincoln's Inn Fields had John Bowman, with his long history of musical roles in comedies as a singing fop,[86] while Drury Lane had comedians Penkethman and Bullock, good for comic songs and dancing. In the latter part of the decade, they gained enormously from the mobile and musical Robert Wilks as leading man.

---

[86] For Bowman's earlier roles, see Matthew Roberson, "Of Priests, Fiends, Fops, and Fools: John Bowman's Song Performances on the London Stage, 1677–1701" (Ph.D. Diss., Florida State University, 2006).

Professional singers and dancers also contributed an enormous variety of performances to comic productions, from the musically elaborate and (at least momentarily) serious to the simplest. In some cases, these performances were simply dropped into the show, but in many works they play an important role.

Structurally speaking, Patent Company comedies were more likely to have a masque in the final act, like *Love's Last Shift*, than those at Lincoln's Inn Fields. Both houses used dances and 'entertainments' equally often.[87] Although we know from surviving printed music that both houses often employed musical dialogues, it is at Lincoln's Inn Fields that they are far more likely to appear in the printed play text. As we have seen, they are also more likely to be connected to the action of the play, and the influence of house composer John Eccles, whose dialogues were particularly admired, may account for this. Among the Patent Company composers, Leveridge and Jeremiah Clarke regularly contributed songs to comedies. Like musical dialogues, these pieces were often excerpted and performed with later works or in concert. Regarding Leveridge's song in *The Lying Lover*, Baldwin and Wilson comment "The play flopped but the song lasted well"—equally applicable to many songs from this decade.[88] Such flexibility and detachability is more common to musical numbers written for comedies, although as we shall see in the following chapter, comic numbers and independent star turns for featured performers were part of dramatick opera and tragedies as well.

---

[87] Seven out of ten masques in printed comedies from this decade (11 comedies, counting *The Novelty*) were at DL. Both houses made extensive use of masques in tragedies and dramatick operas. See Chapter Two.

[88] *The Monthly Mask of Vocal Music, 1702–1711*, facsimile, ed. Olive Baldwin and Thelma Wilson (Aldershot, 2007), notes for no. 188.

Chapter Two
Musical Tragedies and Dramatick Operas

Conventions Regarding the Use of Music in Tragedies

Several tragedies from the 1695–1705 decade entirely avoid music within the play. However, critic-authors like John Dennis, Charles Gildon, and John Oldmixon could use the example of the ancient Greeks, either imbibed directly from classical texts or via France, to justify the inclusion of music and attempt to rehabilitate its use in tragic drama. In his 1693 *Short View of Tragedy* Thomas Rhymer had insisted inclusion of the chorus was essential, but purely Grecian choruses were not widely accepted or put into practice in the 1690s, either as act dividers or within the acts. Shakespeare, Middleton, Beaumont, and Fletcher provided models from the English tradition for the use of other types of music, particularly songs.

Dennis's thinking on the uses of music underwent some development between his 1693 *The Impartial Critick*, written in response to Rhymer, and his 1698 tragedy, *Rinaldo and Armida*. In 1693 Dennis writes "it is in vain to think of setting up a Chorus upon the *English* Stage, because it succeeded at *Athens*; or to think of expelling *Love* from our Theatres, because it was rarely in *Grecian Tragedies*."[1] Choral music was usually limited to one or two scenes within the drama, but most modern tragedies of the 1690s, like other types of plays, had instrumental music played between the acts.

Roger Savage has suggested Dennis must have been uneasy that although act tunes serve a practical function in the structure and performance of tragedies, "they are not in themselves part of the drama's essential Aristotelian unity, not wholly under the dramatist's control, and hence only haphazardly relevant, if relevant at all, to a play's ethos and pathos."[2] It is this lack of connection and integration between the music and the drama that *Rinaldo and Armida* attempts to rectify, and Dennis is quite specific about the effect he intended to achieve. This fascinating production will be discussed in the context of contemporary works later in this chapter.

A Comparison Between the Two Stages has little to say about the role of act tunes in tragedy or comedy, though its speakers find much to criticize in specific

---

[1] *The Critical Works of John Dennis*, ed. Edward Niles Hooker (Baltimore, 1939), vol. 1, p. 13.

[2] Roger Savage, "'Even the music between the acts…'—John Dennis, Johann Adolph Scheibe and the rethinking of incidental music, 1698/1738," in *Books and Bibliography… Essays in Commemoration of Don McKenzie*, ed. John Thomson (Wellington, 1998), pp. 141–59 (p. 146).

types of musical 'ornaments' (French dancing, Italian singing), musical numbers, and productions. As for music within the dramatic action, the entire practice is called into question:

> —sometimes a Song or a Dance may be admitted into a Play without offending our Reason: I won't say it is at any time necessary, for some of our best Tragedies have neither: But perhaps it may be done without offence, sometimes to alleviate the attention of the Audience, to give the Actors time and respite, but always with the regard to the *Scene*; for by no means must it be made a business independent of that:[3]

In this passage, the critic Sullen gives reasons and rationales for music that would work equally well for comedies. However, as he continues, he makes an argument against vocal numbers which will be very familiar to anyone who has read much criticism of all-sung opera, either eighteenth century or more recent: the time that it takes to sing a response (solo or ensemble) while the action of the drama is suspended.

> In this particular our *Operas* are highly criminal, the Musick in 'em is for the most part an absurd Impertinence; for instance, How ridiculous is it in that Scene in *The Prophetess* [*Dioclesian*, music by Henry Purcell] where the great Action of the *Drama* stops, and the chief Officers of the Army stand still with their Swords drawn to hear a Fellow Sing—*Let the Soldiers rejoice*—'faith in my mind 'tis as unreasonable as if a Man shou'd call for a Pipe of Tobacco just when the Priest and his Bride are waiting for him at the Altar.[4]

While no musical insertion in a contemporary tragedy is quite that egregious, drinking songs do appear and, in Durfey's bloody *Famous History of the Rise and Fall of Massaniello* (PC, 1699), comical musical dialogues and dances occur with some regularity.[5]

Several of the Patent Company's dramatick operas, like *Brutus of Alba* (PC, 1696), make virtually no attempt at dramatic integration of their musical numbers.

---

[3] Anonymous, *A Comparison Between the Two Stages, With an Examen of* The Generous Conqueror *and Some Critical Remarks on* The Funeral ... (London, 1702), p. 50.

[4] Ibid., p. 51.

[5] I follow Robert Hume and Derek Hughes in assigning *Massaniello* to the general category of tragedy, though the title page reads *The Famous History of the Rise and Fall of Massaniello*. Two other 'tragical' history plays performed around this time are Cibber's *Tragical History of King Richard III* and Otway's *History and Fall of Caius Marius*.

The Examples are innumerable, no *Opera* is without 'em, tho' perhaps these may find a better excuse for 'em than Tragedies, because the Musick in these is the chief Entertainments; but for all that, I see no reason why the *Drama*, by much the nobler part, nay the Parent of the other, shou'd be made a Bawd to set off the musick; and I'm directly of Opinion, that even in *Operas* the Musick and the rest of the pageantry is a Vice wherever 'tis improperly plac'd, that is, where the *Scene* does not easily, and without force seem to require it.[6]

The anonymous critic is concerned with dramatic verisimilitude in both dramatick operas and tragedy. Many musical events in tragedies are given cover by the need to celebrate the victories of their noble heroes (or tyrannical villains), or to amuse them when they are not out conquering kingdoms. As in comedies, conquering the 'fair sex' also seems to require music.

Comments regarding the absurdity of unnecessary music patched onto existing scenes are fairly common, as are those about the impossibility of adequately balancing both musical and dramatic interest. In this respect, essayist Roger North and the anonymous author of *A Comparison* would agree.

As previously mentioned, North divides 'Theatricall Musick' into 'Comick' and 'Opera,' although (writing in 1728) he primarily considers the later Italian-language operas under the latter term. His term "semi-opera" for productions like Henry Purcell's reflects his opinion that such works were attempts, in a culinary metaphor, to serve two dishes (music and dramatic poetry) at once, to audiences who had a taste for one or the other but could not equally enjoy them both.[7] Clearly contemporary audiences were not all of North's mind.

As musicologist Michael Burden has observed, in any reasonable review of productions from 1690 through the first decade of the eighteenth century, "what is clearly shown is that dramatick opera as a genre straddled 1695, and that Purcell's death did not inhibit the production of such works, whatever we may think of the quality of the product … It suggests further that public demand was not lacking."[8] Burden's table of dramatick operas and extravaganzas shows clusters of musical works in the 1696–97 season (*Brutus of Alba, Cinthia and Endimion, The World in the Moon*) and the 1698–99 season (*Rinaldo and Armida, The Island Princess*).

---

[6] Sullen goes on to blame the music, "this blemish of the Stage," on the fashionable fancy for things Italian: "They are all Idolaters of Musick, an effeminate Nation, not relishing the more masculine Pleasures; their *Theatres* are meer Musick meetings, and the little hodge-podge, which is their *Drama*, is little better than a continu'd Song, without action, incident, or variety." *A Comparison Between the Two Stages*, pp. 51–2.

[7] Roger North, *Memoires of Musick*, in *Roger North on Music*, ed. John Wilson (London, 1959), pp. 353–4.

[8] Michael Burden, "Aspects of Purcell's Operas," in Michael Burden, ed., *Henry Purcell's Operas: The Complete Texts* (Oxford, 2000), pp. 3–27, p. 5. Burden also suggests that Henry Purcell might have "had a monopoly on the genre."

Other musical works could be added to these clusters, though they have a more tenuous link to dramatick opera. In 1696 Motteux's musical play *The Loves of Mars and Venus* offers a comic counterpart to the mythological productions at Drury Lane and Dorset Garden. In 1698 and 1699, however, the emphasis was on tragedy rather than comedy, and the pertinent contemporary productions are works like Charles Gildon's *Phaeton* and Durfey's *Massaniello*, which both make extensive use of music. Such works, like Dennis's *Rinaldo and Armida*, find themselves occupying generic space where these two types of productions overlap.

Instrumental and Vocal Music in Tragedies and Serious Dramas

Examining the use of music in tragedies and other serious works, it quickly becomes clear that the situation is largely reversed from that of comedies. Tragedies are much more likely to have instrumental music passages setting the mood of a scene, though they also make fairly frequent use of solo song. A common musical insertion rarely seen in comedies is the grand set-piece featuring soloists and chorus, often set in a temple, with an invocation or hymn by its votaries. Since this elaborate ensemble music was not printed for domestic consumption, like solo songs and sets of act tunes, it rarely survives except in manuscript. As a result the study of music for such works relies on a more limited number of sources. For many tragedies no music is known to survive, though indicated in some detail in the printed play.

The following remarks are based on examination of the texts of sixty-two tragedies and other 'serious plays' performed during the 1695–1705 decade, including John Dennis's *Rinaldo and Armida*. Ten of them call for no music of any kind within the play text, a far greater proportion (one in six) than found in comedies and farces, where only three (one in thirty) lack any indication of musical events. The positioning of musical events within tragedies and serious plays also differs from comedies in several respects. The most likely place to find a musical event in a comedy is, predictably enough, at the end of the fifth act (due to the final dances), followed by the middle section of Acts II, III, or IV. In tragedies, the most common placement of musical events occurs at or near the beginning of Acts III (often a concert scene) and IV, though the beginning and middle of Act II are also common sites for music. In both types of productions, the middle of Act V very rarely includes music, presumably for practical reasons regarding plot resolution, while the middle of Act III, one of the most common places to find music in a comedy, is one of the least likely places to find music in other types of plays—with interesting implications for dramatic structure and pacing.[9]

---

[9] I refer to the general position of music within an act (beginning, middle, end) for comparison rather than using scene designations, because printed plays often employ scene designations haphazardly, while conventions employed by modern editors vary.

When it comes to establishing a basic template for the use of music in tragedies and serious plays, the combination of the high proportion of tragedies without music, taken together with several highly musical tragedies (particularly productions from 1695–96, 1698 and 1699), makes any average of the number and type of musical events misleading. Tragedies with an 'average' number of musical events are not all that common. However, some general statements can be made about the types of music used and their placement within these parameters.

Instrumental Music

Purely instrumental music unrelated to dancing appears to be a more prominent part of serious plays than of comic ones. In tragedies, it is fairly common to have either "soft," "solemn," or "martial/warlike" music indicated before or during scenes where it matches or molds the mood, a practice inherited from earlier seventeenth-century tragedy and similar to the practice of underscoring in popular film. Sometimes the music is performed by an ensemble accounted for in the dialogue, either onstage or just off, like the serenade heard in Motteux's *Beauty in Distress* (LIF, 1698).[10] In other cases, the music, like the act tunes, simply happens, without any explanation provided.

Instrumental music which is unaccounted for within the narrative (non-diegetic music, in film terms) is frequently used in specific types of scenes, particularly the discovery scene. In such scenes the curtain rises or scene draws open to reveal a new tableau, often centered around a recumbent figure, who is most likely to be female. The first act opening of Congreve's tragedy *The Mourning Bride* (LIF, 1697) provides a classic (and oft misquoted) example of such a discovery scene. It both conveys the power of music, with suitable classical references to the story of Orpheus and Platonic ideas about music's powers, and yet also asserts even this is not enough to assuage Almeria's grief. Thus Congreve's tragedy begins by celebrating the power of music and undercutting it at the same time, manifesting an ambivalence towards music discernable in many contemporary tragedies.

A Room of State.
The Curtain rising slowly to soft Musick, discovers *Almeria* in Mourning, *Leonora* waiting in Mourning.
After the Musick, *Almeria* rises from her Chair, and comes forward.

    Alm.   Musick has Charms to sooth a savage Breast,
To soften Rocks, or bend a knotted Oak.
I've read, that things inanimate have mov'd,
And as with living Souls, have been inform'd,
By Magick Numbers, and persuasive Sound.
What then am I? Am I more senseless grown

---

[10] [Pierre] Motteux, *Beauty in Distress. A Tragedy* (London, 1698), p. 36.

Than Trees, or Flint? O Force of constant Woe!
'Tis not in Harmony to calm my Griefs.[11]

The initial impact of this scene is made through the senses of sight and hearing, as the audience is given a span of time to observe Almeria (Anne Bracegirdle) and hear the music before she speaks. Jean Marsden has written about the emphasis in many contemporary tragedies on spectatorship, focusing the audience's gaze like that of the male characters on a female object, but it is worth noting the additional stretch of performance time indicated by the use of music in such scenes.[12] The ability of music to alter perception of time—at its most prosaic level, to maintain interest in a fixed scene—is regularly employed to draw out the audience's attention.

The discovery scene, with its static positioning of a main character and invitation to gaze, is similar to the sleep scene, and sometimes scenes combine both types, as the curtain rises to reveal a sleeping figure, as in Jane Wiseman's *Antiochus the Great*, where "Scene draws, and Discovers *Ormades* [young, handsome actor Barton Booth] Lying on a Couch; *Philotas* sitting by him, soft Musick Playing."[13] The music for such slumber scenes may be inspired in part by "sommeil" scenes in seventeenth-century French *tragédies lyriques* by Philippe Quinault and Jean-Baptiste Lully, like *Armide* (Paris, 1685), in which beautiful music is heard as Renaud (Tasso's Rinaldo) sleeps.

The "soft musick" used in most discovery and sleep scenes is also called for in scenes of seduction or attempted seduction. A fine example occurs in Cibber's *Xerxes*, where the sound of soft music alerts both the heroine Tamira (Elizabeth Barry) and the audience that Xerxes is coming, and that he intends a very intimate interview.

> *Tam.* What can this Musick mean?—Address'd to me?   [*Soft Musick*
> Good Heav'n! the King![14]

Tamira may well ask what the music means, as its full significance can only be understood through a combination of factors, where its sound (soft rather than solemn or martial) allows only a partial decoding. Cibber's Xerxes is already established as an abuser and manipulator of music for his own ends, with a faked triumphant processional in the first act (discussed below). Although this is one of many cases in which no music is known to survive, contemporary examples give a

---

[11] William Congreve, *The Mourning Bride, A Tragedy* (London, 1697), p. 1.

[12] Jean I. Marsden, *Fatal Desire: Women, Sexuality, and the English Stage, 1660–1720* (Ithaca, New York, 2006), pp. 70–9.

[13] Jane Wiseman, *Antiochus the Great: or, The Fatal Relapse, a Tragedy* (London, 1702), performed at LIF. Marsden includes this as an example of a male figure as the focus of a discovery scene. Marsden, *Fatal Desire*, p. 127 note.

[14] Colley Cibber. *Xerxes. A Tragedy* (London, 1699), p. 34.

good idea of what constitutes "soft musick": scored simply for strings and perhaps flutes (recorders), in a moderate or slow tempo.

The other types of instrumental music within tragedies also feature characteristic instruments and other qualities. Trumpets, oboes, and drums and bright major keys are associated with military triumphs, while a specific drum pattern and softer brass (trumpets or sackbuts) in a minor mode indicate a dead (funeral) march, as in the anonymous *Neglected Virtue* (PC, 1696) and John Banks's *Cyrus the Great* (LIF, 1695).[15] "Solemn musick," typically associated with religious rites including funerals, is a little harder to assign specific instruments or musical gestures, although it too might include drums and trumpets, as in *The Faithful Bride of Granada* (PC, 1702),[16] as well as flutes and oboes, or the everyday string ensemble, played at a slow tempo.

When not bent on seduction or rapine,[17] the appearances of kings are more often marked by a "Symphony of Warlike Musick," which, like "soft musick," often serves a practical function, covering the time needed to get the monarch and his entourage onstage. As with soft music, the triumphal music may be authentic or inauthentic, as in the first act of Cibber's *Xerxes*, where the tyrant hires slaves, elephants, and presumably musicians to stage a triumph after resounding defeat. The "Martial Symphony" performed (well or ill) simply highlights the theatrical falseness of Xerxes's pomp (5).

Unlike "soft musick," which is found in both comic and tragic plays, and martial music which occasionally appears in comedies (either straight or parodied), "Solemn musick" is only explicitly called for in serious dramas and tragedies.[18] It is often heard either preceding or as part of a scene set in a temple, with elaborate visual effects and music. An example can be found in Nicholas Rowe's first tragedy *The Ambitious Step-mother*, in which solemn music is heard at the end of Act III, scene i, prefiguring the scene change to the temple of the Sun, where, after more instrumental music, a choral hymn is performed.[19] Similarly, solemn music for the elaborate ritual procession in Charles Gildon's *The Roman Bride's Revenge* is first

---

[15] Anonymous, *Neglected Virtue; or, The Unhappy Conqueror* (London, 1696), p. 42. John Banks, *Cyrus the Great; or, The Tragedy of Love* (London, 1696), p. 57. It would be interesting to know whether these plays used funeral music written for the recently deceased queen, just as Purcell's prelude was reused in a revival of Shadwell's *The Libertine*. See Bruce Wood, "The First Performance of Purcell's Funeral Music for Queen Mary," in Burden, ed., *Performing the Music of Henry Purcell*, pp. 61–81.

[16] Anonymous, *The Faithful Bride of Granada. A Play* (London, 1704)

[17] Unspecified music covers the offstage rape of Julia by Caligula in John Crowne, *Caligula. A Tragedy* (London, 1698), p. 34. Possibly modeled on a similar scene with a masque in Rochester's *Valentian*.

[18] The sole exception is "a Solemn Dance, expressing despairing Love" in Act Two of the first part of Durfey's *Don Quixote*.

[19] Nicholas Rowe, *The Ambitious Step-mother. A Tragedy* (London, 1701), pp. 38–9.

heard at a distance under dialogue, as coming from the temple at the back of the scene, and then heard again as the procession passes across the stage.[20]

Act Music

The instrumental music performed before the tragedy and between the acts is often the only music which survives, usually due to publication in suites for the amateur music market, John Walsh's *Harmonia Anglicana* series. Beyond its basic components—the overture and six to eight shorter pieces, sometimes in dance forms—such instrumental music defies easy categorization. Uncertainty about the order of act tunes, save in manuscript copies where the function of the pieces is indicated ("1st Musick" etc.), complicates any attempt to assign significance to particular modes, meters and melodies and relate them to the action of the drama.

In considering sets of act music, there is wide variance between tragedies accompanied by reused material, like Henry Purcell's act music for *The Rival Sisters* (PC, 1695) or John Barrett's suite for *The Generous Conqueror* (PC, 1702), which were assembled from pre-existing pieces,[21] and tragedies like Dennis's *Rinaldo and Armida*, for which all of Eccles's music was newly composed and, Dennis tells us, intimately connected to the drama. Most examples can be found between the two extremes. Curtis Price has suggested that some of the act tunes for Southerne's *Oroonoko* can be connected to the mood and events of the previous act, particularly the slow lament air which follows the end of Act IV when Oroonoko and his wife Imoinda are brutally separated.[22] For sets of tunes which survive, like those in Walsh's *Harmonia Anglicana*, without any express order, selections can certainly be arranged to suit the dramatic context.

The act music for Nicholas Rowe's tragedy *Tamerlane*, composed by John Lenton in C (major and minor) and published by Walsh without ascriptions, is an interesting case. First of all, the first piece printed (always the overture) is marked "symphony." It does not follow the conventional French overture pattern of the other theater overtures. Instead, it begins in triple meter and changes meter no fewer than four times (rather than once, or at most, twice), as the dancing triple meter is broken by march-like sections in cut time. This unusual musical structure could be intended to reflect the action of play, soft passages interspersed with martial valor.[23]

---

[20] Charles Gildon, *The Roman Bride's Revenge. A Tragedy* (London, 1697), pp. 1, 4.

[21] For *The Rival Sisters* see Price, *Henry Purcell and the London Stage*, pp. 77–8. Purcell reused an overture from a court ode and the sources for the other tunes are "not trustworthy." Previously printed sources for Barrett's music are listed in Price's *Music in the Restoration Theatre*, p. 172.

[22] Price, *Henry Purcell and the London Stage*, p. 81.

[23] While in Walsh's set of act tunes the symphony takes the place of the overture, it is possible that in the play it was performed in Act I, sc. 2, when a "Symphony of Warlike

The first act tune is a "Trumpett Round O," or a trumpet tune (with its characteristic leaping fourths) in the form of a rondeau, an unusual combination. The trumpet tune continues the action of the previous scene, in which the general, Axalla, is called away from his beloved Selima by the sound of trumpets. The act tune also serves well as an introduction to the opening of Act II, which takes place in Tamerlane's army camp. The act tunes which follow also suggest an unusually direct correlation between the action of the play and the type of tune. A slow air follows the end of Act II, when the tragic couple Moneses and Arpasia separate, momentarily resigned to their miserable fates, mutually tormented by Bajazet's marriage-rape of Arpasia.

In contrast, at the conclusion of Act III, Tamerlane bids Moneses rouse himself once again to martial endeavor:

> ... the warlike Trumpet's loud Alarms
> To virtuous Acts excite, and manly Arms;
> The Coward Boy [Cupid] avows his abject Fear,
> On silken Wings Sublime he cuts the Air,
> Scar'd at the noble Noise, and Thunder of the War.

The act tune that follows is a march. Of course the use of mood music to awaken martial valor within scenes is another familiar topos, strikingly illustrated in Cibber's *Xerxes* (where the trumpets, for once, fail to work). The fourth act ends with Bajazet's schemes and is followed by another of Lenton's slow airs in C minor. The final act opens with Arpasia's dark musings ("Sure 'tis a Horror, more than Darkness brings,/ That sits upon the Night; Fate is abroad"). The reference to darkness parallels the dialogue at the end of the second act, which was also followed by a slow air.

Such direct correlation between types of act tunes and the mood and dialogue of the acts they separate is rare. The other music for the play (a song by Richard Elford) is in the same key as the act tunes, additional evidence suggesting care was taken to make *Tamerlane* and its music a coherent whole. However, this degree of musical-dramatic integration is certainly not evident in the majority of tragedies.

Vocal Music: Solo, Duet, and Ensemble

Like comedies, tragedies incorporate solo songs in a variety of types, often overlapping: reflective, pastoral, mad, witty or parodic, and ballad-type songs, even drinking songs. Songs used as serenades are also found. As Robert Gale Noyes states in his classic article "Conventions of Song in Restoration Tragedy," authors in the later seventeenth century "were not inventing but following conventions

---

Music" is played in Tamerlane's tent. Apparently an experiment, it was not repeated by Lenton.

well known" in their use of vocal music in tragedies, both "more operatic" and less.[24]

Returning to Rowe's *Tamerlane*, a scene from Act IV provides an excellent example of a 'discovery' scene with song instead of instrumental music, as the scene draws to reveal the much-abused princess Arpasia asleep on a couch. The text which follows is "A Song to Sleep. By a Lady."[25]

> To Thee, oh! gentle Sleep, alone
>   Is owing all our Peace,
> By Thee our Joys are heighten'd shown,
>   By Thee our Sorrows cease.
> The Nymph, whose Hand, by Fraud, or Force,
>   Some Tyrant has possess'd,
> By Thee, obtaining a Divorce,
>   In her own Choice, is blest.
> Oh! stay; *Arpasia* bids thee stay,
>   The sadly weeping Fair
> Conjures Thee, not to lose in Day
>   The Object of her Care.
> To grasp whose pleasing Form she sought,
>   That Motion chac'd her Sleep
> Thus by our selves, are oftenest wrought
>   The Griefs, for which we weep.

Afterwards, waking, Arpasia rises and speaks a sad soliloquy ("Oh! Death! thou gentle end of human Sorrows").

"To Thee, oh! gentle Sleep, alone," set to music by singer-composer Richard Elford, became a very popular song.[26] Sung not by Elford, but by Mary Hodgson, it opens in C minor (the key of the act tunes) with a declamatory gesture and a section in free arioso which is more dramatically effective than the very regular triple-meter music which follows (Figure 2.1). Although tuneful, it would be difficult to convey the sense of anguish the text demands until the final line, "The Griefs for which we weep." Elford sets "Griefs" to an ascending chromatic line, and the music indicates that this affecting final phrase is to be immediately repeated.

---

[24] Robert Gale Noyes, "Conventions of Song in Restoration Tragedy," *PMLA* 53 (1938): 162–88, 164.

[25] Nicholas Rowe, *Tamerlane. A Tragedy*, second edition (London, 1703), p. 44.

[26] See Hunter 5 (191). The song was reset in the later eighteenth century by organist Jonathan Martin and sung by famous tenor John Beard in revivals, then widely disseminated in popular prints. Rowe's poem was even made into a three-part glee (an a cappella vocal piece) and appeared in John Arnold's *The Essex Harmony: Being an entire new collection of the most celebrated Songs, Catches, Canzonets, Canons and Glees*, vol. 2 (London, 1777), p. 4.

Figure 2.1   R. Elford, "To thee, o gentle Sleep" in *Tamerlane*

While mad speeches and rants are common in tragedies, particularly in the final acts, the singing of mad songs is rare, despite the example of Shakespeare's Ophelia.[27] Instead, mad songs are found in comedies and pastorals, like *Acis and Galatea* (LIF, 1701). One exceptional example is the lovesick Lausaria's mad song "Oh! Take him gently from the pile" performed by Anne Bracegirdle in *Cyrus the Great* (LIF, 1695), a tour de force displaying extreme shifts in mood and music. This type of vocal writing is not repeated in later tragedies staged by either company. One can speculate about the reasons.

Tragedies and serious dramas do include songs sung in the dramatic context of madness, such as the songs performed onstage for the distracted Alonzo in *The Rival Sisters* (PC, 1695). However, these are not mad songs, but coherent lyrics reflecting a specific emotional state or situations (see, for example, "Celia has a thousand charms"), even though they are sung for characters who are mad. Later in Gould's tragedy, when Letitia Cross's character goes mad, one might expect a mad song from the popular actress-singer, but Gould (and Henry Purcell) do not provide one.

Another favorite song type, musical dialogues, are less common in tragedies, but they are far from absent. Many examples come from the Patent Company's 1695–96 season or from the 1698–99 season. As noted previously, the speakers in *A Comparison Between the Two Stages* were acid in their criticism of the vaguely pastoral and romantic dialogue "How long, my Flavia, shall your Swain" in Higgons's *The Generous Conqueror* (PC, 1701).

In most cases, these dialogues are more elevated in tone than many of those in comedies, though there are still examples of lascivious boy–girl duets in Pix's *Ibrahim* (PC, 1696) and Wiseman's *Antiochus the Great* (LIF, 1701), and Durfey uses broadly comic dialogues in both parts of his *Massaniello* (PC, 1699). In *Massaniello* the dialogues between fishwives and "a town sharper and his hostess" are obviously intended to illustrate the crass tastes of Massaniello's wife, Blowzabella. However, it is certain that Durfey also recalled the success of similar dialogues featuring the singers John Pate and Richard Leveridge in Motteux's *The Island Princess* earlier that year.

Among the other 'low' musical numbers more common in comedies, drinking songs can be found in the anonymous tragicomedy *Timoleon* (PC, 1697), Centlivre's tragedy *The Perjur'd Husband* (PC, 1700), Boyle's tragedy *Altemira* (LIF, 1701) and, most notably, the drinking catch in Powell's *Bonduca* (PC, 1695). It is considerably more common in tragedies and dramatick operas to place drinking songs in classical guise as songs for Bacchus and his followers within a formal entertainment, as was done in William Philips's *The Revengeful Queen* (PC, 1698), discussed below.

Musical numbers which involve soloists and chorus in alternation are another type of vocal number for multiple singers frequently found in tragedy and

---

[27] Noyes lists only a few, much earlier, examples (none later than 1683), citing Bracegirdle's as the last. "Conventions of Song," pp. 186–7.

dramatick opera. They rarely occur in other types of productions, and when they do, solos with chorus generally appear in pastorals or as part of a pastoral interlude. In tragedies and serious plays they are most often associated with rituals and/or the supernatural. Their musical settings usually involve elaborate solo lines, with verses assigned to each soloist or fragmented across several singers' parts. While solos may be assigned to as many as five or six singers, smaller numbers (three or four) or a single soloist are more common. The choral sections, typically in four parts, often resemble contemporary church anthems in a range of forms and styles, though they rarely use elaborate choral counterpoint. In the first act of his dramatick opera *The World in the Moon* (PC, 1697), Elkanah Settle boasted a grand chorus of twenty voices,[28] and other dramatick opera ensembles may have been near this size. However, in tragedies and other productions, as in later Italian opera, the chorus was probably just the soloists, with a few added singers for volume and gravitas. The funeral scene quoted below mentions six priests and two women, suggesting two singers to a part in a typical four-part texture (soprano–alto/countertenor–tenor–bass).

The most common and memorable use of large-scale musical numbers during this decade occurs in temple scenes, with priests as soloists and chorus, though they are significantly less common than instrumental music. As the emperor Caligula comments in Crowne's 1698 tragedy, "Priests sing, and make an Opera of their Prayers."[29] Noyes lists several examples of songs used in religious ceremonies and in scenes of sacrifice, including Richard Norton's *Pausanias* (PC, 1696), Charles Hopkins's *Boadicea* (LIF, 1697) and Dennis's *Iphigenia* (LIF, 1699).[30] Occasionally, instead of priest-soloists alternating with chorus, the ceremonial music takes the form of a choral hymn, as in Mary Pix's *The Double Distress* (LIF, 1701).

Scenes of incantation, sorcery, and witchcraft often overlap with the scenes of ritual and sacrifice, as the depiction of "pagan" ritual and superstition combines both elements. For example, in Act III of *The Unnatural Mother, The Scene in the Kingdom of Siam* (LIF, 1697) the title character, Callapia, appears at the funeral of her husband. The music performed by the Siamese priests and women combines religious ritual with magical incantation:

> Scene draws, discovers the Body of *Pechai* laid on a Pile of Wood, *Callapia* dress'd in White, seated at the feet of *Pechai's* Body, with a Garland of Flowers on her Head; *Sennorat, Munzuffer, Cemat* at a distance, *Bebbemeah* and *Chousera* in mourning Veils, six Priests, and two Women. Two Priests and two Women sing the

---

[28] Elkanah Settle, *The World in the Moon. An Opera* (London, 1697), p. 7.
[29] Crowne, *Caligula*, p. 9.
[30] Noyes, "Conventions of Song," p. 179.

> following Song.
> *1st Priest*   Hence, you infernal Spirits, come not near
> This sacred Pile ...[31]

Such scenes may in some cases reflect anti-Catholic propaganda in addition to a more general depiction of foreign, misguided, or evil practices.[32] The potential for contemporary reading (or misreading) is particularly powerful in the depictions of kings who attempt or fail to listen to and obey instructions from supernatural sources.

Music for magic is more often found in the earlier heroic plays, like John Dryden's *The Indian Queen*,[33] and is used to spectacular effect in the dramatick opera versions of them performed during the 1695–1705 decade. In works like *Brutus of Alba* all the music derives from magic, while of *Rinaldo and Armida*, Noyes asserts, "Dennis's tragedy approaches dangerously near to opera, which readily accepts the conventions of the supernatural."[34] This dangerous consanguinity is discussed later in the chapter.

In straight tragedies from this decade, scenes of musical magic are relatively rare, aside from the occasional ghost, and all are from plays written before 1700.[35] In John Banks's *Cyrus the Great* (LIF, 1695) four witches (both male and female singers) perform a necromantic ritual to empower the dead to prophesy for them, each adding their own sorcerous aids ("Mummy with Cats Blood," "A Feather from the Phoenix Wing" etc.).[36] As in similar scenes in *Macbeth*, the prophecy is not ultimately favorable to the king who hears it. Solos with chorus also appear occasionally as part of the multi-sectional entertainments and masques presented to entertain rulers and their courts, discussed below.

Dancing Songs and Dances

Like musical dialogues, dances are infrequent in tragedies when compared with comedies, and occur most often in productions written before 1700. When they are included, dances are usually entertainment for the characters onstage, rather than participatory. Typically part of banqueting or other social scenes like masquerades, the dances are often pastoral, like the dance of shepherds and nymphs in *The Rival*

---

[31] Anonymous, *The Unnatural Mother, The Scene in the Kingdom of Siam* (London, 1697), pp. 22–3, italics reversed.

[32] For several examples and discussion, see Eubanks Winkler, *O Let Us Howle Some Heavy Note*, pp. 48–54.

[33] See Steven E. Plank, "'And Now about the Cauldron Sing': Music and the Supernatural on the Restoration Stage," *Early Music* 18 (1990): 392–407.

[34] Noyes, "Conventions of Song," p. 181.

[35] See Trotter's *Agnes de Castro* (PC, 1695) and Walker's *Victorious Love* (PC, 1698). Both ghosts are accompanied by a song, and appear in Act IV.

[36] Banks, *Cyrus the Great*, p. 5.

Brothers (LIF, 1704), or exotic, like the dances "after the Indian manner" in *The Unnatural Mother* (LIF, 1698).

In contemporary dramatick operas, dances are often associated with magic or the supernatural, such as the numerous dances in *Brutus of Alba* (PC, 1696), which are all entertainments arranged by an infernal magician. In contrast, the dances in tragic works may involve pastoral or exotic figures but remain within the human world of the play. Exceptions are the dance of wizards in *Cyrus the Great* (LIF, 1695) and revivals of Shadwell's *The Lancashire Witches* and *Macbeth*.[37] Occasionally dances are part of ritual ceremonies or celebrations, as in Mary Pix's *The Double Distress* (LIF, 1701), in which the Act III temple scene includes "Hymn to *Apollo*. Solemn Musick. Antick Dances. After which the High Priest speaks."[38]

While both parts of Durfey's *The Rise and Fall of Massaniello* contain a great deal of music, dancing is particularly prominent in the second part, which includes both comic dancing at a ball in Act II and serious dancing (a sarabande) by the deposed aristocrats in Act III. In Act V dancing is an important part of the gruesome final masque, in which the fisherman and fishwife wind up dancing with Death.

Entertainments, Masques, and Masquerades

Approximately one quarter of the dances and vocal music in tragedies can be found in multi-part events labeled "entertainment," "masque," or "masquerade." Typically performed at a banquet or in a court setting, such entertainments may be classical (featuring the deities), allegorical (with characters like Love, Peace, Plenty, etc.), pastoral, or miscellaneous. While they often serve some of the same functions in tragedy as in comedy, providing entertainment for the characters onstage, a change of pace for the theater audience, and a demonstration of the powers and interests of the characters promoting them, such entertainments in tragedies are more likely to have a specific and often sinister connection with the action of the play.

The bloody masque in Elkanah Settle's *The Empress of Morocco* (DG, 1673) is probably the most famous Restoration example, and the players' show in *Hamlet* the best known from the seventeenth century. Masques are performed in Thomas Scott's *The Unhappy Kindness* (PC, 1696), Ravenscroft's *The Italian Husband* (LIF, 1697), the anonymous *The Fatal Discovery* (PC, 1698), Gildon's *Phaeton* (PC, 1698), Durfey's *Massaniello* (PC, 1699), and Cibber's *Xerxes* (LIF, 1699). In *The Italian Husband* and *Phaeton*, masques including the goddess Juno provide classical commentary and warnings about marriages in the process of going horribly (and fatally) wrong, while in the fifth act masque in *Massaniello*, as in *The Empress of Morocco*, the masque leads directly to murder.

---

[37] See Plank, "'And Now about the Cauldron Sing'" and Eubanks Winkler, *O Let Us Howle Some Heavy Note*, for discussion of this musical tradition.

[38] Mary Pix, *The Double Distress. A Tragedy* (London, 1701), p. 36.

In *The Unhappy Kindness* and *The Fatal Discovery*, the masque text is not given in the printed play, and the dialogue provides little information about what was seen and heard. This suggests that the play's author did not write the masque text and opens up the possibility that a popular masque from another production was used. Admittedly, documentation of this practice is only found in later seasons, once regular advertisements appear. For example, an unspecified masque by Henry Purcell was advertised with revivals of Beaumont and Fletcher's *The Maid's Tragedy* in February 1704.[39]

The "Musick" in Act III of William Philips's *The Revengeful Queen* (PC, 1698) is not called a masque, but includes songs and choruses by the gods Mars and Bacchus as well as a troop of virgins defending love. Another example in which the title "masque" is not used but seems appropriate occurs in the third act of *Rinaldo and Armida*, where Cupid and Venus sing airs, followed by choruses, and Cupid's followers dance.

In tragedies from 1695 to 1705, entertainments of music and dancing vary. Like the masques, they may be minutely described in the printed text, as in *The Italian Husband*, or simply indicated, as in *Caligula* (PC, 1698), where Caligula attempts to divert himself with an unspecified entertainment until the cries from outside become too loud, the rebels enter the palace and kill him. Interestingly, the two tragedies which include masquerade entertainments with dancing date from after 1700, Susannah Centlivre's *The Perjur'd Husband* (PC, 1700) and Jane Wiseman's *Antiochus the Great* (LIF, 1701), but, with the exception of a wedding entertainment in Rowe's *The Fair Penitent* (LIF, 1703), masques and extended musical entertainments are completely absent from the printed texts of new tragedies performed after 1700, although the occasional combination of song and dance or instrumental music and vocal music still appears, as in Joseph Trapp's *Abra Mule* (LIF, 1704).

Topical References, Musical Humor, and Quotation

When it comes to the topical references and musical quotations employed in comedy, tragedies are more sinned against than sinning, more often quoted than quoting. Witty dialogue is not usually a component of contemporary tragedy, and the game of recognition played with the audience in comedy is dissonant with the other modes of viewing and listening which tragedy and dramatick opera demand.

Contemporary references in serious plays are general, and go no farther than the inescapable impression that many "ancient" Persian/Roman/Babylonian musical entertainments, with their Italian singers and musical dialogues, sounded much

---

[39] See M&H *London Stage*, pp. 144, 147. Similarly, the masque of Bacchus and Cupid composed by Henry Purcell for Shadwell's version of *Timon of Athens* with a revival of the comedy *Love's Contrivance* (DL, April 1704). Ibid., p. 164.

like contemporary London. The visual representation, through sets and costuming, of the long ago and far away was often equally anachronistic.

Even when performers moved from comedy to tragedy, like Robert Wilks, Anne Bracegirdle, or Elizabeth Bowman, in tragedies they more often watch and listen (or weep) than sing and dance. This is not to say there are no comic numbers in serious plays, but even Noyes can find few examples in the entire corpus of Restoration tragedy.[40] In Durfey's *Massaniello* several numbers are funny but also, as Price and Noyes have argued, make points pertinent to the drama. On the practical side, they employed singers and some of the actor-singers who would usually have no roles in serious plays.

Stock Tragedies: Nathaniel Lee's *The Rival Queens*

It would be difficult to overemphasize how familiar and influential Nathaniel Lee's *The Rival Queens* was within the theatrical community (professionals, patrons, audience members) during the decade from 1695 to 1705. The third, fourth, and fifth editions of the tragedy were printed in 1699, 1702, and 1704, and despite scanty performance records for the decade, evidence shows it was regularly revived.[41] Lee's tragedy was frequently quoted and mocked in contemporary comedies and prologues. Examples include George Powell's mean-spirited imitation of Thomas Betterton playing Alexander in the prologue to *The Fatal Discovery* (PC, 1698), George Farquhar's Sir Harry Wildair mocking Alexander in the runaway comic success *The Constant Couple* (PC, 1698), and Catharine Trotter's Beaumine employing an overwrought line of Lee's to comic effect in *Love at a Loss* (PC, 1700).[42]

Nathaniel Lee's tragedies frequently make substantial use of music, and his 1680 tragedy *Theodosius* is known as the first dramatic work for which composer Henry Purcell created music. The musical passages indicated in the printed text of Lee's *The Rival Queens* occur in Acts II, IV, and V. The first scene of Act II combines simple martial music with elaborate special effects, a portent of things to come.

---

[40] Noyes, "Conventions of Song," 169.

[41] Cibber recalls "there was no one Tragedy, for many Years, more in favour with the Town than *Alexander.*" He attributes its success to the performers, especially Betterton. Cibber, *Apology*, vol. 1, p. 106.

[42] See Act V, sc. 1, pp. 94–7 in Farquhar's comedy, where Wildair imagines Angelica is "just come flush from reading the *Rival Queens*" and quotes a line. In Act II *Love at a Loss*, the witty Miranda entertains Beaumine with "a Song made by a Heroick Lover of mine," inspiring him to mock ecstasy and quotation: "What shall I say to work upon thy Soul!" a line spoken by Alexander to Statira. *Love at a Loss; or, Most Votes Carry It. A Comedy* (London, 1701), p. 21.

> Noise of Trumpets sounding far off.
> The Scene draws, and discovers a Battle of Crows, or Ravens in the Air; an Eagle and a Dragon meet and fight; the Eagle drops down with all the rest of the Birds, and the Dragon flies away. Souldiers walk off shaking their Heads. The Conspirators come forward.[43]

After the conspirators recount the horrible omens they have seen, trumpets sound again for Alexander's entrance.

Music is explicitly indicated again in a conventional banquet scene in Act IV, where the martial music of Act II is supplanted by more exotic entertainments.

> The Scene draws, *Alexander* is seen standing on a Throne, with all his Commanders about him, holding Goblets in their Hands.
> *Alex.*   To our Immortal Health, and our fair Queen's;
> All drink it deep, and while it flies about,
> *Mars* and *Bellona* joyn to make us Musick.
> A hundred Bulls be offer'd to the Sun,
> White as his Beams—Speak the big voice of War,
> Beat all our Drums, and blow our Silver Trumpets,
> 'Till we provoke the Gods to act our pleasure
> In bowls of *Nectar* and replaying Thunder.   [*Sound while they drink.*[44]

During the feast, the old soldier Clytus, who knew Alexander's father, refuses to wear a Persian robe or flatter the 'boy' by suggesting Jupiter Ammon was his father. After their exchange, "Here follows an Entertainment of *Indian* Singers and Dancers: The Musick flourishes" (IV, 40). Clytus urges a toast to Philip:

> *Clyt.*   This to his memory.
> Sound all the Trumpets there.
> *Alex.*   They shall not sound
> Till the King drinks—by *Mars* I cannot take
> A moments rest for all my years of Blood,
> But one or other will oppose my pleasure.
> Sure I was form'd for War, eternal War;
> All, all are *Alexander*'s Enemies;
> Which I cou'd tame—yes, the Rebellious world
> Shou'd feel my wrath—But let the Sports go on.
>   *The* Indians *Dance.*[45]

---

[43]   Nathaniel Lee, *The Rival Queens; or, The Death of Alexander the Great*, third edition (London, 1699), p. 12.

[44]   Lee, *The Rival Queens*, pp. 38–9.

[45]   Ibid., p. 41.

When Clytus continues to refuse to offer adulation and reminds the king of some of his less noble deeds, Alexander, drunk, angry, and suspicious, kills him with a javelin. Filled with remorse, he is lying next to the corpse when news is brought that his first wife, Roxana, and her slaves threaten the safety of his beloved second wife, Statira.

From the beginning of the tragedy, Lee associates Statira with music, and this quality as well as her softness made the role (originally played by Elizabeth Boutell) very suitable to Anne Bracegirdle, who played the role with Betterton as her Alexander and Elizabeth Barry as her rival. In the opening scene, as Statira remembers Alexander, she recalls how she "Laid him all night upon my panting Bosom,/ Lull'd like a Child, and hush'd him with my Songs" (I, 9).

At the conclusion of Act III, Alexander instructs:

> All Revel out the day, 'tis my Command;
> Gay as the *Persian* God our self will stand,
> With a Crown'd Goblet in our lifted hand.
> Young *Ammon* and *Statira* shall go round,
> While antick Measures beat the burden'd ground,
> And to the vaulted Skies our Clangors sound.[46]

The opening of Act V combines several types of scene with which music is associated: music for discoveries, music accompanying a sleeping figure, and music for supernatural occurrences.

Statira is discover'd sleeping in the Bower of *Semiramis*. The Spirits of Queen *Statira* her
   Mother, and *Darius*, appear standing on each side of her, with Daggers, threatning her.
                              They Sing.
   Dar.   Is Innocence so void of cares,
   That it can undisturbed sleep,
   Amidst the noise of horrid Wars,
   That makes Immortal Spirits weep?
   Stat.   No boding Crows, nor Ravens come,
   To warn her of approaching doom?
   Dar.   She walks, as she dreams, in a Garden of flowers,
   And her hands are employ'd in the beautiful Bowers:
   She dreams of the man that is far from the Grove,
   And all her soft Fancy still runs on her Love.
   Stat.   She nods o're the Brooks that run purling along,
   And the Nightingales lull her more fast with a Song.
   Dar.   But see the sad end which the Gods have decreed.
   Stat.   This Ponyard's thy Fate.
   Dar.   My Daughter must bleed.

---

[46] Ibid., p. 32.

> *Chor.* Awake then, Statira, awake, for alas you must dye:
> Ere an hour be past, you must breath [*sic*] out your last.
> *Dar.* And be such another as I.
> *Stat.* As I.
> *Chor.* And be such another as I.[47]

Lee crafts this musical insertion by bringing together images from earlier in the play, both the flock of crows or ravens in Act II, and the blissful Persian bower. Similar scenes, featuring parental ghosts addressing their child musically, are found in later tragedies like William Walker's *Victorious Love* (PC, 1698) and Dennis's *Rinaldo and Armida*.

Statira is enmeshed in a romantic fantasy, unaware of acts of state—or the need for self-preservation. She then speaks a soliloquy. No stage directions indicate her rising, but presumably she comes forward, so she can 'retire' when Roxana enters with her slaves (and her dagger).

True to tragic convention, Alexander enters after Roxana has stabbed her rival, but before Statira dies.

> O she is gone! the talking Soul is mute!
> She's hush'd, no voice, no Musick now is heard?
> The Bower of Beauty is more still than Death;
> The Roses fade, and the melodious Bird
> That wak'd their sweets, has left 'em now for ever.[48]

Alexander soon dies by poison, and has a last mad scene. His remaining companions promise to avenge him.

Although no music appears to survive from the 1677 premiere, the 'operatized' version with music by Gottfried Finger and Daniel Purcell is discussed in Chapter Five.[49] The principal musical events in Lee's play are those in Acts IV and V. *The Rival Queens* lacks music in Act III, where tragedies in the 1695–1705 decade were likely to include it. Although it does not serve as a structural template, Lee's *The Rival Queens* can be considered an influential middle way within the inherited tradition of tragedies, between Thomas Otway's *Venice Preserv'd; or, A Plot Discover'd*, with its single instance of "Soft Musick" for its overwrought heroine in Act V, versus the much-revised version of *Macbeth*: the classic musical tragedy, with its supernatural songs and dances.

---

[47] Ibid., p. 46.

[48] Ibid., p. 50.

[49] A single song, "Phillis talk not more of Passion," was printed as "A SONG set by Mr. Dan: Purcll in Alexander the Great" (Hunter 5 [148]). It may have been performed with the play, though it is a poor fit with any scene except the banquet. The song text had been set very differently by Henry Purcell (D&M 2689) and appeared in a 1685 anthology.

The Employment of Music in Tragedies after 1695

Noyes observed many years ago that "after the dissolution of the union of the patent companies in 1695 the rivalry of the houses at Drury Lane and Lincoln's Inn Fields in producing lavish *divertissements* exerted noticeable effect on the writing of tragedy."[50] The first full season, 1695–96 saw eleven tragedies produced by the two companies, many with extended musical entertainments.[51] The Patent Company works (including *Bonduca* and *The Indian Queen*) have received more musicological attention, being the final productions to which Henry Purcell contributed, though two equally lavish in their use of music were staged at Lincoln's Inn Fields.

Expectations regarding music in tragedies after the first season of competition are grumpily articulated in author Edward Filmer's complaints. In the preface to his unsuccessful tragedy *The Unnatural Brother* (LIF, 1697) Filmer writes:

> Foreseeing part of what has since happened, and meerly to gratifie the Rabble, after I had finished this Play, I added a Comical part to it. Wherein, so there were but a smart kind of a hurry and confusion, with a Song or two at the end—*His nam plebecula gaudet*. I thought it would pass well enough. But the Comedy being altogether independent from the Tragedy, and the whole appearing something too long the first time it was acted, I easily consented to have it all left out, and so threw my self wholly on the Men of sense for my Judges. *Verum Equitis quoque jam migravit ab aure voluptas Omnis, ad incertos oculos & gaudia vana.*
>
> For, to my cost, I find that even our men of Sense, have been so long entertained with the gaudy, glaring splendour of our Operas, that nothing now can please their eyes, but what dazel's 'em: And that their ears have, of late, been so well belabour'd with Drums, Kettle-Drums, Trumpets, and Hautboys, that they are almost become deaf to Sense, or any thing else, convey'd to 'em in a less Noise, than those their darling Consorts generally are.[52]

Filmer's sneers about "Drums, Kettle-Drums, Trumpets, and Hautboys," a martial catalogue of instruments, may be aimed at Thomas Dilke's decision to include Eccles's "Triumphal Ode" in Lincoln's Inn Fields' last production, the comedy *The City Lady*, but it also reads as a more general anti-music attack, in reaction to both the dramatick operas *The Indian Queen* and *Brutus of Alba*, and the heavily musical tragedies performed during the past year and a half.

These musical tragedies, many more successful than Filmer's, included *Bonduca*, *The Rival Sisters*, and *The Roman Bride's Revenge* at Drury Lane and *Cyrus the Great* and *The Royal Mischief* at Lincoln's Inn Fields. All included

---

[50] Noyes, "Conventions of Song," p. 174.
[51] See Chapter Three. Only one, *Philaster*, did not indicate any musical events within the play.
[52] Filmer, *The Unnatural Brother* (London, 1697), p. 2.

several musical numbers (minimum five) performed in at least three discrete musical scenes, often with elaborate scenery. Filmer's rant remained timely for the following two seasons as well, in which *Phaeton, The Revengeful Queen, Victorious Love*, and the massively musical *Massaniello* at Drury Lane competed for audiences against *The Italian Husband, The Unnatural Mother, Rinaldo and Armida*, and *Xerxes* at Lincoln's Inn Fields.

An examination of the tragedies and dramatick opera productions for the first seasons reveals an interesting alternation between seasons when either type predominated. During seasons in which several new tragedies appeared, there are relatively few dramatick operas or other largely musical works (lengthy independent masques or "plays set to musick"). Seasons in which multiple dramatick operas were staged have fewer tragedies. Of course there is a purely practical aspect to this: the resources required in terms of sets, costumes, and casting were heavy for both types of productions, while the dramatick operas also needed machines, more spectacular and individuated sets, and even more in the way of music and performers, including dancers who rarely made up part of a tragedy.

Among the musical tragedies of the later 1690s Edward Ravenscroft's *The Italian Husband* stands out for its experimental design (three acts) and extensive use of music, noted by Robert Hume as "a striking reminder that serious use could be made of music if dramatists wanted to take the trouble."[53] Like librettists for dramatick opera, the poet in Ravenscroft's printed prelude describes self as having kept the "talk" in the tragedy to the minimum needed by the action, which allows room for the musical entertainments.[54]

The first act entertainment, appropriately enough for a duke and duchess living in retirement in a country house, presents the various pleasures and privations of life in country, city, and court. The performers include "Singers and Dancers. Shepherds, Shepherdesses, a Court Lady and a Citizens Daughter." Before the debate commences, however, the first musical number is a jubilant anniversary song, "Joy to the youthful happy pair" (3).

The songs which make up the remainder of the celebration alternate between praise and scorn of country life, court life, and city life, though a final critical song against city living does not appear in the text. The two shepherdesses who sing the praises of the country and criticize the court have more material to work with, but it is the citizen's daughter who gets the last word. A nod to the London audiences, perhaps, but the song says matter-of-factly that wealthy citizens acquire their money through usury and extortion. It is an odd place to end a celebration.

As the second act opens, the guilty and remorseful duchess is presented "in black, lying on Carpets, her hair loose, leaning on a Deaths head, a Book in her

---

[53] Robert D. Hume, "Opera in London, 1695–1705," in Shirley Strum Kenny, ed., *British Theatre and the Other Arts, 1660–1800* (Washington: Folger Books, 1984), pp. 67–91 (p. 80).

[54] Edward Ravenscroft, *The Italian Husband. A Tragedy* (London, 1698), unpaginated

hand, and the Picture of a *Magdalen* over her Oratory" (15). In the previous scene, her husband discovered her tryst with a former lover, and as the second act develops, she becomes increasingly delusional. When she calls for a song "to lull my troubled thoughts asleep," someone performs a pastoral rondeau, with the refrain "Nymphs that are now in your prime,/ Make, O make good use of time"(22). Stoddard Lincoln suggested this was either highly inappropriate or diabolically cruel, since the Duchess's current miserable state comes of doing just that—seizing a chance for pleasure.[55] However "good use of time," though suggesting a *carpe diem* phrase, is ambiguous. A musical setting would reveal much about Eccles's sense of the lyric and its original performance.

The masque of *Ixion*, like Motteux's *Hercules* (LIF, 1697), is a classical miniature, requiring fantastic scenery (a "Poetical Hell," to match *Hercules*'s "Poetical Heaven") and machinery similar to that employed by the Patent Company (peacocks for Juno, a descending eagle for Jupiter). Arriving in heaven as a messenger, Ixion dares to approach Juno, the goddess of marriage and wife to the most infamous philanderer of legend. He sings "a light ayre" which begins rakishly, "What a fool is a Wife to lye pining at home,/ When to pleasures abroad the false Husband is gone?" (29). Juno evades him and he is consigned to dreadful torments by the divine couple. The scene changes to hell, and Ixion is broken upon the wheel by a chorus of devils and furies. This counterpoints the action of Ravenscroft's drama. Although the duke has pretended to forgive both his wife and her lover (and the duchess, unlike Juno, reciprocated her lover's advances), he has been preparing a horrible revenge.[56]

Considered as part of the late 1690s repertoire, *The Italian Husband* is significant both for the amount of music included and its level of integration with the dramatic action.[57] All of the surviving music, Eccles's attention-grabbing overture and act tunes, employs keys built on the B-flat triad (B-flat major, D minor, F major and minor). Without the vocal music, it is impossible to know how the overall key structure may have worked, but it seems likely that, as in Eccles's later opera *Semele*, there was one.

Dramatick Opera and the Question of Genre

In his introductory essay for the Oxford edition of Henry Purcell's opera texts, Michael Burden includes a table of dramatick operas. All were published as "An

---

[55] Lincoln, "John Eccles: The Last of a Tradition," p. 212.
[56] See Hughes, *English Drama, 1660–1700*, pp. 438–9, for an insightful consideration of Ravenscroft's tragedy in relation to contemporary thinking on religion, law, and male privilege.
[57] The second tune in the second music, a country dance, was very popular. Under other names ("A new French dance call'd the Zar of Moscow") it appears in numerous contemporary publications. See Price, *Music in the Restoration Theatre*, p. 185.

opera," "A Dramatick Opera," or "A New Opera," with the exception of Dennis's *Rinaldo and Armida*. In a similar table surveying the wider repertoire of English operas, Robert Hume includes many additional works, including several published with the designation "tragedy" on the title page: Shadwell's *Psyche*, Davenant's *Circe*, Powell's *Bonduca*, and Granville's *The British Enchanters*.[58] However, even Hume does not expand the list as far as his own definition would allow: "The term usually means little more than a dramatic work of any genre in whose performance music and scenery figure prominently."[59]

Contemporary sources are neither clear nor consistent on the subject of English operas. Following are three well-known late seventeenth-century descriptions of opera and dramatick opera from librettists closely involved with many of the most popular and influential productions of the 1690s.

Poet and dramatist John Dryden writes in his preface to *King Arthur; or, The British Worthy* (UC, 1691):

> the Numbers of Poetry and Vocal Musick, are sometimes so contrary, that in many places I have been oblig'd to cramp my Verses, and make them rugged to the Reader, that they may be harmonious to the Hearer. Of which I have no Reason to repent me, because these sorts of Entertainment are principally design'd for the Ear and Eye; and therefore in Reason my Art on this occasion, ought to be subservient to his.[60]

Dryden's emphasis on dramatick opera as a matter of sight and sound is bluntly seconded by the practical prompter John Downes, who emphasizes the new scenes, machines, costumes, and French dances when describing *Psyche* and the music when describing *Circe*.[61] The librettist's apologia for "rough" poetry is a familiar one, and Motteux would later pen many variations on it.

The anonymous preface to *The Fairy Queen* (UC, 1692) emphasizes the French connection, particularly the lavish machine plays which inspired the

---

[58] Robert D. Hume, "The Politics of Opera in Late Seventeenth-Century London," *Cambridge Opera Journal* 10 (1998): 15–43.

[59] Ibid., p. 16. Dryden scholar James Anderson Winn has also written about the continuity between heroic plays, dramatick opera, and Italian opera. He leaps over a great deal, passing from Dryden to Handel, specifically works from the 1695–1705 decade, but it is a welcome call for scholars to continue working across disciplines. "Heroic Song: A Proposal for a Revised History of English Theater and Opera, 1656–1711," *Eighteenth-Century Studies* 30 (1996): 113–37.

[60] Burden, *Henry Purcell's Operas: The Complete Texts*, p. 273. In his preface to *Albion and Albanius* (UC, 1685), Dryden refers to the revised *Tempest* as a mixture of tragedy and opera, including supernatural action, stage effects, and musical numbers, but not sung throughout.

[61] John Downes, *Roscius Anglicanus*, eds Judith Milhous and Robert D. Hume (London, 1987), pp. 75, 77.

construction of the Dorset Garden theater, probably designed by Betterton after a trip to Paris.[62]

> That France borrow'd what she has from Italy, is evident from the *Andromede* and *Toison D'or*, of Monsieur *Corneille*, which are the first in the kind they ever had, on their publick Theaters; they being not perfect *Opera*'s, but Tragedies, with Singing, Dancing, and Machines interwoven with 'em, after the manner of an Opera. They gave 'em a tast first, to … Judge whether in time they would be able to digest an entire *Opera*.[63]

The author then touts Davenant's *The Siege of Rhodes* as "a perfect *Opera*: there being this difference only between an *Opera* and a Tragedy; that the one is a Story sung with proper Action, the other spoken." It did not include machines or dancing, though it did boast elaborate scenery. However, the assertion that opera is 'sung tragedy' is an interesting one, as *The Fairy Queen* is far from tragic.

Pierre Motteux frequently discussed musical and dramatic matters in his short-lived periodical *The Gentleman's Journal*, where, before the premiere of *The Fairy Queen* in 1692, he wrote:

> We shall have speedily a New Opera, wherein something very surprising is promised us; Mr. *Purcel* who joyns to the Delicacy and Beauty of the *Italian* way, the Graces and Gayety of the *French*, composes the Music, as he hath done for the *Prophetess*, and the last Opera call'd King *Arthur,* which hath been plaid several times the last Month. Other Nations bestow the name of Opera only on such Plays whereof every word is sung. But experience hath taught us that our English genius will not rellish that perpetual Singing. I dare not accuse the Language for being over-charged with Consonants, which may take off the beauties of the Recitative part, tho in several other Countries I have seen their *Opera*'s still Crowded every time, tho long and almost all Recitative. It is true that their *Trio*'s, Chorus's, lively Songs and *Recits* with *Accompaniments* of Instruments, Symphony's, Machines, and excellent Dances makes the rest be born with …

The emphasis on vocal ensembles and dancing in the operas of "several other Countries" suggests that Motteux's operatic model is French. However, Motteux insists that the English audience requires satisfaction in sense as well as sound.

> But our English Gentlemen, when their Ear is satisfy'd, are desirous to have their mind pleas'd, and Music and Dancing industriously intermix'd with Comedy or

---

[62] See Judith Milhous, "The Multimedia Spectacular on the Restoration Stage," in Shirley Strum Kenny, ed., *British Theatre and the Other Arts, 1660–1800* (Washington, 1984), pp. 41–66.

[63] Burden, *Henry Purcell's Operas: The Complete Texts*, pp. 347–8.

Tragedy ... the Audience is no less attentive to some extraordinary Scenes of passion or mirth, than to ... the most ravishing part of the Musical Performance. But had those Scenes, tho never so well wrought up, been sung, they would have lost most of their beauty. All this however doth not lessen the Power of Music, for its Charms Command our attention when used in their place, and the admirable Consorts we have in *Charles-street,* and *York buildings,* are an undeniable proof of it. But this shows that what is unnatural, as are Plays altogether sung, will soon make one uneasy, which Comedy or Tragedy can never do unless they be bad.

Where Edward Filmer sneers at the consorts in York Buildings and Charles Street—venues providing regular subsidiary employment to theater singers, musicians, and composers—Motteux celebrates them as music empowered in its proper place. Yet the question of music's proper place in the theater is left unanswered, despite the condemnation of "Plays altogether sung." Ironically, Motteux later penned the very popular "Play Set to Musick," *The Loves of Mars and Venus* (LIF, 1696).

In the following section, Motteux emphasizes the "excellent Trebles" (castrati) as well as the elements lacking in the Venetian operas, areas where the French and English are presumably superior: in machines, decorations and clothes, acting, and illumination.[64] Indeed, special effects involving lighting, as noted by Michael Burden and Roger Savage, are an important part of the spectacular transformation scenes of dramatick opera.[65]

All three contemporary commentators demonstrate an awareness of continental traditions and a strong sense both of national artistic pride and of theatrical expediency. What they do not provide is a clear picture of the essential features of the genre.

Returning to the 1695–1705 decade, the question remains: What did "opera" mean specifically in the 1690s? What is essential, besides a substantial proportion of music? Machines? Magic? A final masque? Comparison of *The Indian Queen* with *Bonduca,* distinguished by their title pages and in contemporary comment, offers one avenue towards enlightenment. It is possible to see the 1695 *Bonduca,* "With a New Entertainment of MUSICK" important enough to be announced on the title page, as having taken a step towards operadom but not reaching it.[66] Aside from the complex musical scene in the temple during the third act, *Bonduca*'s music is limited to two isolated vocal numbers, a drinking song for soldiers in Act

---

[64] Pierre Motteux, *The Gentleman's Journal, Or The Monthly Miscellany. By Way of Letter To A Gentleman in the Country. Consisting of News, History, Philosophy, Poetry, Musick, Translations, &c.* (London, January 1692), pp. 4–5.

[65] See Burden, "Aspects of Opera," 11–13.

[66] The rather confused relationship between the text and music suggests that *Bonduca*'s musical development may have been halted by practical considerations. See Chapter Three.

II and a swansong for a doomed princess (Letitia Cross) in Act V, which would certainly not distinguish it among other contemporary tragedies.[67]

The Indian Queen, "As it is now Compos'd into an Opera" as the collection of songs published in November 1695 proudly announces,[68] provides a close contemporary example of an opera, and a very popular one. Yet due to uncertainties about its structure, particularly the placement of several musical events, it is not an easy guide to follow. The musical elements in *The Indian Queen* display no innovations: a masque for Fame and Envy, a dance by Indians, songs by a conjuror and the representative god he conjures up, songs by "aerial spirits," a melancholy song, temple scene with priest soloist and chorus (set in the golden temple of the Sun, that cliché of tragedy and set design), and final masque of Hymen and Cupid. However, while there may be less music, less dancing, and fewer spectacular sets and special effects than in *King Arthur* or *The Fairy Queen*, these elements are all present, and not in *Bonduca*.

Unless, as Andrew Pinnock believes, the masque of Fame and Envy placed in Act II was misplaced from the third act, where it arguably makes a better dramatic fit,[69] there was no music within the action of the play (following the sung prologue) until the beginning of the third act. This would also make the third act heavily saturated with music, including both the masque and all of the magic-related numbers. The suggestion has been made that the masque might have been moved to correct this imbalance, perhaps during early revivals, at which time Daniel Purcell's final masque of Hymen and Cupid may also have been added.

The conclusion to *The Indian Queen* contains a prime example of the dramatic disjuncture that the anonymous author of *A Comparison* so objected to, juxtaposing two suicides with the final masque of Hymen. The masque in *The Indian Queen* can also be directly compared with the final masque of "Love in every Age" in *The Island Princess*, which somewhat more appropriately follows the rescue of Armusia and Quisara from the evil Governor and the return to cordial relations between the king of Tidore and the Portuguese. A marriage masque also concludes *The Fairy Queen*, but the path to the final triumph of Montezuma in *The Indian Queen* has involved a lot more collateral damage than that of Oberon.

Following *The Indian Queen*, a sung prologue becomes typical of productions staged by the Patent Company in the 1690s that proudly claimed the title "opera." These range from the satirical patter song by Leveridge in *The Island Princess*

---

[67] Robert Etheridge Moore suggested that there might (and should) have been music for Bonduca's funeral, following "a very clear musical cue." *Henry Purcell and the Restoration Theatre* (Cambridge, Mass., 1961), p. 154.

[68] Henry Purcell, *The Songs in the Indian Queen: As it is now Compos'd into an Opera* (London, 1695). See also D&M Bibliography, no. 137.

[69] The placement is based on the manuscript GB-Lbl Add. MS 31449, source A, the primary 'complete' manuscript. See Andrew Pinnock, "Play into Opera: Purcell's *The Indian Queen*," *Early Music* 18/1 (1990): 3–21. Also see Purcell, *Works*, vol. 19 *The Indian Queen*, eds Margaret Laurie and Andrew Pinnock (London, 1994).

to the elaborate multi-sectional prologue to Durfey's *Cinthia and Endimion*, with singers representing classical characters. The prologue to *The World in the Moon*, set by Jeremiah Clarke, is equally complex, though the singers are given no names. The "slipshod" *Brutus of Alba* is the exception, having been printed with a recycled prologue, and a completely inappropriate one at that.

In his 1984 study, Curtis Price includes works he categorizes as revivals, including (controversially) *The Indian Queen*, under the designation "Tragic Extravaganzas" rather than operas.[70] While Price is concerned with works containing music by Henry Purcell, he notes that "about the turn of the century, several genuine tragic semi-operas were produced" and lists them in a footnote: *Rinaldo and Armida, The Grove, The Rival Queens [Alexander the Great]*, and *The Virgin Prophetess*.[71] The interesting questions left unanswered in this brief mention are, of course, why this cluster of "genuine tragic semi-operas" appeared c.1698–1701 and how they might be connected with other contemporary works, like Durfey's *Massaniello*, about which Price has written admiringly elsewhere.[72] Like *The Indian Queen*, *Massaniello* contains much music and supernatural intervention although it makes limited use of special effects, sets, and machines. It even follows the template of earlier dramatick operas, with musical events most heavily concentrated in Acts II and V.

Two dramatick operas with music by Daniel Purcell and Gottfried Finger, performed in 1700 and 1701, provide a snapshot to compare with the examples from 1695. Both are called operas on their title pages, and both are newly written scripts rather than adaptations, though indebted to past works.

As with every dramatick opera production, the surviving sources are not completely consistent, although *The Grove* is well documented, with a printed libretto, full manuscript score, and numerous printed songs. The musical components and their placement in *The Grove* are shown in Table 2.1. Some revision took place within the Act III masque, where a second musical dialogue between a satyr and a nymph, "I've courted thee long," has been inserted, and some of the exchange between hunters and shepherds indicated in Oldmixon's text excised.[73] This brings the masque closer to the masque of Pan and Syrinx from Act III of Durfey's *Cinthia and Endimion* (PC, 1696) which also includes a musical dialogue between a nymph and a satyr. Oldmixon stated in his preface that the last

---

[70] See Price, *Henry Purcell and the London Stage*, "The Tragic Extravaganzas," pp. 97–143. His categorization has been challenged by Andrew Pinnock: "No one at the time found it necessary to ... invent a new name to describe it ('tragic extravaganza') when 'opera' served perfectly well." Pinnock, "Play into Opera," p. 7.

[71] Price, *Henry Purcell and the London Stage*, p. 97.

[72] Curtis A. Price, "Music as Drama," in Robert D. Hume, ed., *The London Theatre World, 1660–1800* (Carbondale, 1980), pp. 210–35.

[73] See GB-Lcm 988. For instrumental concordances and a listing of songs in D&M, see Price, *Music in the Restoration Theatre*, p. 175.

three acts marked a shift from pastoral to tragedy, and this shift can be seen in the changing musical entertainments listed in the table.[74]

Table 2.1 Musical events in Oldmixon's *The Grove*

Act	Placement	Description	Page
I	End	Song: "In Vain you tell me Love is sweet" [sung by Mrs. Erwin in place of Diana Temple as Phylante]	6
	End	Entertainment of Shepherds and Shepherdesses: "Come all away" [soloists & dancing chorus]	7
II	Beginning	Song by a shepherdess: "To Hill and Dale I tell my Care"	9
	End	[Music of the country versus the court]: "Ye Birds, who in our Forests sing"/ "Cease your Amorous Pipes and Flutes" [symphony, soloists, trumpet sonata, soloists and chorus]	14–15
III	Beginning	[Masque of Fame, Pan, & Ceres]: "Thro wondring Worlds I *Caesar*'s worth proclaim" [trumpet sonata, solos, symphony, chorus, musical dialogues, duet]	16–18
IV	Beginning	[Entertainment for Phylante with Shepherdess, Shepherd, Cupid, Ghost of Orpheus]: "Underneath a Gloomy Shade" [solos, duets, chorus]	27–8
V	End	[Masque of Cupid and Hymen with Priests of Love]: "Appear, old Hymen, from thy Cell" [solos, trio, grand chorus]	45–6

Multiple sources present a remarkably consistent composite picture of *The Virgin Prophetess*, particularly when the separately printed *Musical Entertainments* are read in conjunction with the musical scores (Table 2.2). Like *The Cornish Comedy* (PC, 1696), *The Virgin Prophetess* provides evidence of the continued practice of singing specific pieces between the acts, even in a production like a dramatick opera already well supplied with music.

---

[74] John Oldmixon, *The Grove; or, Love's Paradice. An Opera* (London, 1700), unpaginated.

Table 2.2 Musical events in Settle's *The Virgin Prophetess*

Act	Placement	Description	Page
I	End	The Triumph of Paris: "War, War and Battle, rage no more" [soloists & chorus]	6
	Between the acts	Dialogue between a Child and her Mother: "Hark. Hark, hark where am I?" [from *Musical Entertainments*, not printed in text]	—
II	Middle	Procession Song in the Temple of Diana: "Thou Goddess all celestial bright" [soloists & chorus]	12
III	End	[Entertainment by Paris for Helen] Symphony, Cupid's Song: "See here my Quiver, see my Darts" [solo]	22–3
		Chorus: "To Love we'll sing, great Love to thee"	23
		Dialogue between a Mother and a Daughter: "I Charge ye Daughter, once agen,/To fly those dangerous things call'd Men"	23–4
		Dance [not printed in text]	—
IV	Beginning	Song of Flora and her Nymphs: "Flora calls, where, where's my Train" [soloists & chorus] Dance of shepherds	25–6
	Middle	A Song by Spirits: "Hold, hold, yet hold, mad Boy/ Stop, stop the Fate of Troy"	27
	Middle	Instrumental music, dance of furies	28
V	Middle	Bacchanal song: "Come, come let us sing, and merrily troll" [solo & chorus]	38
		Bacchanalian dialogue: "Dull Fool I defie thee" [not printed in text]	—
		Grand Chorus/Chaconne: "Our Foes are run"	39

A few basic consistencies between Oldmixon and Settle's works are worth reiterating. Both include musical events in every act, and both reshuffle familiar tropes: pastoral entertainments, songs by spirits, and the appearance of Cupid and other gods via machines. Furies and ghosts make musical appearances in Act IV. Major musical events are linked with spectacular transformations in *The Virgin Prophetess* generated by the prophetess-sorceress Cassandra, and with simpler scene changes in *The Grove*, as in Act I, where "The Front Scene open and discovers a Circle of Seven Pillars adorn'd with Garlands of Flowers" (7) or Act V "Scene the Temple of Love" (45), which manages to combine marriage masque with temple scene. As previously noted, Settle's opera, like his earlier *The World in the Moon*, makes full use of the scenic possibilities and a wide range of special effects, from golden statues turning black with the thunder of divine disapproval (13) to Cassandra's magic, "the whole Garden being in a moment vanish'd, and the Prospect fill'd up with a view of Heav'n, in which the whole Hierarchy of the Heathen Gods, with all their several Chariots, Palaces in the Airs, &c." (27), and the elaborate entertainments staged by Paris for Helen in doomed Troy, with four sets of scenes revealing the blue and silver palace of Cupid and the god sitting in glory, "This Machine now filling the whole House, and reaching 24 Foot high, making so many Visto's of Pallace-Work" (22).[75]

Both productions include a major musical interlude in the final act, following earlier precedent: *The Grove* a nuptial masque and *The Virgin Prophetess* an entertainment with a grand chaconne. The varied placement—at the end of the act in *The Grove* and the middle, prior to the flaming catastrophe, in *The Virgin Prophetess*—reflects the conclusion of each drama. Unlike *The Indian Queen*, after Helen has thrown herself into the fires consuming Troy, the only celebration is a short, nasty speech from Menelaus, while music heard earlier in the act is the Trojans prematurely celebrating their 'victory.' In contrast, *The Grove* is one example of a dramatick opera which ends with music, rather than a final tag of spoken dialogue.

Like *The Indian Queen* or *The Island Princess*, both productions also seek to combine serious music with the popular comic dialogue. This is particularly apparent in *The Virgin Prophetess*, even though the dialogues are missing from the musical scores, and may not have been written by Settle or composed by Finger. The Bacchanalian dialogue inserted in Act V, if not written by Motteux, blatantly plagiarizes his popular dialogue from the recent operatic adaptation of Fletcher's *The Mad Lover* (LIF, 1701), "Proud Women I scorn you/ brisk Wine's my delight," printed in the anthology *Mercurius Musicus*. The pretext of both songs is the same as earlier drinking dialogues, like that in *Love's a Jest* (LIF, 1696), but in this case images and rhymes match exactly, often with simple word substitution. As the music is not known to survive, further comparison is not possible. The nymph–satyr dialogue and the reaper–binder dialogues in *The Grove* obviously draw on past dialogues as models, but are more original. What remains clear in both productions is the attempt to meet, mimic, or overshadow successful productions at the other house, as well as matching past triumphs at home, through competitive elements large and small, including the musical numbers.

As Judith Milhous has observed, "Once launched ... the operas fed into one another. Juno's peacocks and Apollo's sun chariot from *Albion and Albanius*

---

[75] Cupid's palace is reminiscent of the palaces of Flora, Pomona, Bacchus, and the Sun in the Act V masque in *Dioclesian* (UC, 1691).

reappear five years later in *The Prophetess*" and continue even after that.[76] Naturally, this recycling included other elements beyond the machines. *The Virgin Prophetess* ends in a fiery conflagration very similar to the one which ended the stage representation of another powerful sorceress, Davenant's Circe, in the 1670s.

Dramatick Opera and Musical Tragedy in 1698: *Rinaldo and Armida* and *Phaeton*

To analyze the relationship between dramatick opera and tragedy at the end of the century, I examine productions which premiered in the spring and autumn of 1698, Charles Gildon's *Phaeton*, with music by Daniel Purcell, and John Dennis's *Rinaldo and Armida*, with music by John Eccles. Both works were termed tragedies on their title pages, yet contained substantial amounts of music and made modest use of the spectacle, machines, and dancing commonly associated with operas. In describing and defending their musical tragedies both Dennis and Gildon specifically refer to the French *tragédies lyriques* of Lully and Quinault in their prefaces and prologues as well as alluding to the productions of the classical theater of Greece as models for the interaction of spoken drama and music in their works, particularly through the use of chorus. One has commonly been referred to by contemporaries, and by later scholars, as an opera, the other has not.

I previously argued, like the author of *A Comparison Between the Two Stages*, that Dennis's *Rinaldo and Armida* represented the Lincoln's Inn Fields company's first attempt to stage a fully fledged dramatick opera.[77] Like many works from the late seventeenth-century stage, it rests uneasily between rigid genre distinctions and it is far from alone in the fertile ground between musical tragedy or 'tragic extravaganza' and dramatick opera.

Dennis consistently called his work a tragedy, and, as a true tragedy, it lacks the concluding comic or celebratory masque of Henry Purcell's better-known dramatick operas, or indeed of its Drury Lane competitor, *The Island Princess*, although there may have been a substantial amount of other music in the final act. Rather than being an isolated production, *Rinaldo and Armida* takes part in a more general blurring of distinctions between tragedy and dramatick opera. A cluster of tragedies with musical events in the fifth act occurs in the 1697–98 and 1698–99 seasons, from *Caligula* to *Massaniello*. In Gildon's *Phaeton* this final musical insertion is an elaborate wedding invocation for priest-soloists and chorus in a familiar site, "the Temple of the Sun," where similar musical forces had assembled to sacrifice Montezuma before Zempoalla in *The Indian Queen*.

Gildon's earlier tragedy, *The Roman Bride's Revenge* (PC, 1696), also made good use of music in its first and fourth acts, including a striking ritual procession

---

[76] Milhous, "The Multimedia Spectacular on the Restoration Stage," p. 61.
[77] *Music Productions LIF*, p. 365.

followed by a temple scene, and a persecutory serenade (see Chapter Three). In *Phaeton*, Gildon complicates the action with substantially mixed characters. Rather than the noble bride and tyrant emperor, we have an abandoned wife-sorceress and a wavering hero, for whom the enticements of a new love combined with the Egyptian crown are too powerful to resist. Gildon justifies this by an appeal to personal emotional experience,[78] and to the classical precedent of "the Divine *Euripedes*," in the desire to represent varying passions.[79]

Derek Hughes describes Gildon's work, which combines Quinault's *Phaéton* with Euripides' *Medea* as "providing yet more evidence of the dwindling status of artistic unity. The resulting product is distinctly slapdash, and almost the only unifying element (apart from condemnation of the 'Arbitrary Pow'r' of man over woman, III, p. 14) is emphasis on the plight of the stranger."[80] However, the other unifying aspect of the work is its emphasis on music. Hughes suggests that Dennis's *Iphigenia* (LIF, 1699) may have been influenced by Gildon's *Phaeton*, but the more closely contemporary *Rinaldo and Armida* also shows signs of consanguinity, and Dennis must have been aware of both Gildon's musical tragedy and John Oldmixon's pastoral *Amintas* when preparing his 1698 tragedy.

In his preface, Gildon untangles his confusing intermingling of the myth of Phaeton, son of Apollo, reinterpreted for French opera, and Euripedes' tragedy, in which the hero Jason—after using Medea to get the Golden Fleece and forcing her to flee her country—abandons her and their children to marry another princess. Naturally Medea, forerunner of many a passionate sorceress in later opera, does not take this well. Gildon explains:

> Before it was my good Fortune to meet with the *Medea* of EURIPIDES, I drew the Plot of an *Opera* according to my propos'd Model from some hints of the French Opera of *Phaeton*;
>
> ...
>
> The *Antients* to dismiss their Audience with that *Pleasure* and *Profit* they design'd them by their Plays, scarce ever extended their *Tragedies* to above half the Lengths of ours: For, by obliging the Mind to a too long Attention, they thought they shou'd make it grow dull, and tyr'd, ... Tho' the Diversion indeed

---

[78] "I had *Nature*, and *certain Experience*, not any *Dogmatical* Notions ... For a *Generous*, and an *Amorous* Man, when he passes from his *first Love*, to a *new Affair*, does not immediately loose all his former Tyes; but doubts a great while, which he loves best ... and may very well mistake the Effects of *Use* and *Gratitude*, for the Sentiments of *Love*, ... any young Man, in *Phaeton*'s Circumstance, wou'd have the same Sentiments ... so might that *Passion* he thought he had for *Lybia*, owe its greatest share to Ambition." Charles Gildon, *Phaeton; or, The Fatal Divorce. A Tragedy* (London, 1698), unpaginated

[79] For example, in Act III, where Althea displays "grief, despair, rage, dissimulation, and resentment." Gildon, *Phaeton*, unpaginated.

[80] Hughes, *English Drama, 1660–1700*, p. 442.

was something lengthen'd by the singing of their *Chorus*, which answers the Musick I have brought in in Mine.

...

The Music was so admirable, that the best Judges tell me [...] that there is the true *Purcellian Air* through the whole: that tho' it be so very different in the several Acts, it is every where Excellent; and that Mr. *Daniel Purcells* Composition in this Play is a certain Proof, that as long as he lives Mr. *Henry Purcel* will never die; or our *English* harmony give place to any of our Neighbours.[81]

Gildon further details some changes he made to the characters of Jason (now Phaeton) and Medea (now Althea). Noting that English audiences might find Medea's slaughter of her children too extreme, he has Althea simply contemplate it, much as librettist Felice Romani has Norma contemplate harming her children in Bellini's opera over a century later. In Gildon's version, the fate of Phaeton—plummeting to earth after mishandling his father, Apollo's, chariot of the sun and scorching the land beneath him—is part of Althea/Medea's final mad rant. Like all mad characters in contemporary plays and songs, Althea has fantastically grandiose visions: Phaeton's fiery chariot is but one among many.

Gildon's tragedy opens in Egypt, where Althea/Medea and Phaeton remember their meeting and her rescue of Phaeton from prison in Samos after a bloody battle. We also learn in an aside that Phaeton has since fallen in love again with the princess Lybia—and that marrying her would secure the Egyptian throne. Althea has prepared a lengthy and lavish entertainment of shepherds and shepherdesses (Table 2.3).

---

[81] Gildon, *Phaeton*, unpaginated.

Table 2.3 Comparison of musical scenes in *Phaeton* and *Rinaldo and Armida*

Act	*Phaeton*	***Rinaldo and Armida***
I	Pastoral entertainment of nymphs & shepherds to amuse Phaeton (solos + chorus, dances) G major/D major/G minor/G major [*printed pieces only*]	Song by spirits of the air, as Armida's castle appears Spirits disguised as nymphs & shepherds to mislead the knights Carlo & Ubaldo (solos + chorus) B-flat major/G minor/G major
II	*No music indicated in printed play*	Spirits as ghosts of Rinaldo's parents and opponents to terrify Rinaldo (symphony, duet, chorus and dance) E minor/A minor Fame's Trumpet and voices "Rinaldo, in the Enchanted Grove" (song) [*music lost*]
III	[*Masque*] The gods Juno, Hymen, Nemesis and their attendants express their dismay at Phaeton's actions (solos + chorus, dancing) E minor [*printed song for Juno*]/?	[*Masque*] Spirits as Venus, Cupid & attendants to seduce Rinaldo (symphonies, solos, duet, chorus, grand chaconne) D minor/G minor
IV	Song with a symphony, to comfort Althea [*music lost*]	Infernal Spirits come to avenge Armida (symphony, solos, choruses) F major/D minor/F major/C minor/G minor/C minor
V	Priests of Isis, celebrating the wedding of Phaeton and Lybia (solos + chorus) [*music lost*]	A Spirit (solo song) "Ah wretched Queen, give o'er" C minor Final tableau of heroes & heroines in the clouds, which Armida (and Rinaldo eventually) will join [*music lost*][a]

Note: [a] This final musical tableau may have included "Behold in what glorious condition/ Thou once shalt Armida enjoy," a charming air for Mary Hodgson. Dennis's 1699 text mentions no music for the tableau, while GB-Lbl Add. MS 29378 contains no music for the last act at all. The song for Hodgson was printed in A major, a key not used in any previous acts, and the text certainly refers to the final scene. For further discussion and a transcription of the piece, see *Music Productions LIF*, pp. 422–5.

In the second act, Phaeton's mother Clymene, now married to the King of Egypt, Merops, seeks out Phaeton's friend Epaphus's help in detaching her son from Althea, the "cunning Samian songstress," (7) but Epaphus's technique consists of rudely insulting Althea, and Clymene has to intervene. When the two young men are reconciled, Epaphus lets it slip that Phaeton is "Son of the All-Seeing Sun" and thus should by rights "mount ... to th'topmost spoak of Fortune" (11). The joint attractions of Lybia and the Egyptian crown finally persuade Phaeton to listen while Epaphus and Clymene slander Althea and he agrees to send Althea away. Note that in the second act, where Althea is absent, music is absent too.

At the opening of the third act Althea is understandably despondent, sitting alone with her women in an arbor when the gods descend in front of them. After a masque of Juno, Hymen, and Nemesis, which is felt ("strange sounds") but not seen by Althea and her companions onstage, the princess is visited by the ghost of her father, who calls out to her for revenge on the Egyptians. In Act IV, a long and painful scene between Althea and Phaeton is followed by Althea's attempt to compose herself with some music. At the end of the song, Phaeton returns when summoned by Althea's servant to bid his lover and children farewell. Althea, plotting vengeance, begs him to let them stay in Egypt and offers to present a magic robe and crown (gifts from Juno) to Lybia. During the elaborate temple ceremony in Act V, the robe and crown take effect, poisoning Lybia and her father. Althea confronts Phaeton a final time: he faints, she stabs herself. Her children have been killed by an angry Egyptian mob, and Althea goes extravagantly mad in a rant of two full pages before dying. Epaphus gets to speak the final lines, and presumably inherits Egypt, since everyone else with any claim to it is dead. Bloody as it is, *Phaeton* does not break dramatic bounds with tragedies of the period, though the opening scene provides a pastoral entertainment of a magnitude which dwarfs the usual 'dialogue plus dance.'

As Gildon does in *Phaeton*, Dennis plays on a wide range of standard musical interludes, here all fed by Armida's sorcery. As author and critic, Dennis is well aware of theatrical convention and precedent, from Sophocles to Dryden, and of his contemporaries' efforts, both *Phaeton* and Oldmixon's recent adaptation from Tasso, *Amintas*. Like many prologues, that for *Rinaldo and Armida* shows considerable concern about the work's immediate reception. Characteristically, Dennis both reveals (some of) his sources and criticizes them, making the prologue "a sort of Preface."

> The *Prologue*'s so entirely new to Day,
> It nere can serve for any other Play.
> Then all you Sparks who have to *Paris* Rid,
> And there heard *Lullys* Musical *Armide*;
> And Ye too, who at home have *Tasso* read,
> This in precaution to you must be said;
> *Armida*'s Picture we from *Tasso* Drew,
> And yet it may Resembling seem to few;
> For here you see no soft bewitching Dame,
> ....
> ... such enervate Strains,
> The Tragick Muse with Majesty disdains.

> The great *Torquato*'s Heroine shall appear,
> But Proud, Fierce, Stormy, terribly severe,
> . . . .
> To change *Rinaldo*'s manners, we had ground,
> Who in the *Italian* is unequal found.
> At first he Burns with fierce ambition's fire,
> Anon he Dotes like any feeble Squire,
> . . . .
> In a Just Play such Heroes nere have part,
> For all that offends Nature, offends Art.[82]

In the printed preface, a lengthy essay, Dennis is more concerned with defending his tragedy against criticism, with the aid of Horace and Sophocles, than with the musical delights of Lully's *Armide*. His insistence that his work was not an opera is reflected in the few comments he reserves for production matters. About the actual staging of his work, Dennis insists:

> As the Action is Great, the Characters are Illustrious, and the Scene is extraordinary. All the Objects that appear to the Agents are almost intirely new; ev'ry thing they see in Nature, being wonderful, and surprising; ev'ry thing that they see in Art, being Terrible, and Astonishing. . . .
> The Action is not only Regular in the Mechanism, (the Incidents falling without any restraint into the narrow compass of the Representation) but Decent too, I hope, in the Conduct of it; and (to the Reserve of the Machines to which the necessity of the Subject oblig'd me) reasonable.

According to Dennis, the spectacular effects involved were only those "required" by the grandeur of the narrative; he did not create a 'machine play' or gaudy dramatick opera like *Brutus of Alba*. He also emphasizes that the tragedy was not staged with a worn-out assortment of previous costumes and sets, as the Patent Company's earlier dramatick operas had been.[83]

Dennis returns to the question of tragedy versus opera in yet another preface, written for *The Musical Entertainments in Rinaldo and Armida*, the booklet published, like similar ones for *The Loves of Mars and Venus* and *The Virgin Prophetess*, to allow the audience to follow the words written for the vocal numbers. Available at the theater, this type of publication was a direct conduit to

---

[82] Dennis, *Rinaldo and Armida*, unpaginated.

[83] Dennis, *Rinaldo and Armida* (London, 1699), unpaginated. The emphasis on the newness of the "Objects" presented certainly refers to new sets, props, and costumes. Although the scene types were conventional, they probably had a new "Enchanted Palace" in Act I. The "Poetical Heaven in perspective" from the masque *Hercules* (LIF, 1697) may have returned as the heavenly scene in Act V.

the audience (or its program-purchasing members) as they prepared to experience the production.

> Though the Tragedy of *Rinaldo* and *Armida*, of which the following Lines are a Part, has gone in the World under the Name of an *Opera*; yet is neither the Dramatical Part of it, like the Drama of our usual *Opera*'s, nor the Musical part of it like that which is Sung and Play'd in those Entertainments: For all the Musick in this Play, even the Musick between the Acts, is part of the Tragedy, and for that Reason the Musick is always Pathetick. ...The Design therefore of Musick, as well as Painting and Poetry, being to entertain the Imagination agreeably, nothing in Musick can be extreamly Fine but what is extreamly Moving: And Experience has confirm'd me in this Opinion, by so much fine Musick as I heard in *Italy*, both in their Churches and Theatres. Now as nothing can be very Pleasing but what is very Moving, so nothing that is very Moving can be Moving long ...
>
> In the following Lines, therefore, I design'd not only to move Passion, but as many Passions as I could successively without doing violence to my subject, ... How clearly, how fully, and how admirably Mr. Eccles has expressed these Passions I leave to the World to Judge, which has loudly on this Occasion, done justice to his Merit, even before the Play has been Acted.[84]

Dennis provides what he promises, with a different passion depicted in the music for each act. The first act shows a rescue party as the Frankish knights Carlo and Ubaldo, guided by the Christian muse-magician Urania, come to retrieve Rinaldo from Armida's enchanted isle. First they must resist the pastoral temptations posed by spirits disguised as nymphs and shepherds.[85] In the second act, Armida begins looking for ways to tie Rinaldo more firmly to her, as his heroic soul is not completely satisfied with the amorous delights she offers. The musical entertainments in Acts II and III are her attempts to influence him through magic, which are both foiled, the first by the sound of Fame's trumpet and the second (the vision of Venus and Cupid) dispersed by Ubaldo waving Urania's magic wand. Rinaldo agrees to leave the enchanted island, and Phenissa summons Armida's dark spirits for revenge, which provides the musical centerpiece for Act IV. Rinaldo comes to take leave of Armida and she stabs herself. In Act V Phenissa's treachery with the underworld is revealed. Armida stabs her and quickly converts

---

[84] Dennis, *The Musical Entertainments in the Tragedy of Rinaldo and Armida*, in C.H. Wilkinson, ed., *Theatre Miscellany: Six Pieces connected with the Seventeenth-Century Stage* (Oxford, 1953), pp. 97–116 (pp. 105–6).

[85] An insightful discussion of this scene and the musical techniques Eccles uses to set Dennis's verses can be found in Timothy Neufeldt, "The Social and Political Aspects of the Pastoral Mode in Musico-dramatic Works; London, 1695–1728," (Ph.D. Diss., University of Toronto, 2006), pp. 88–95.

to Christianity. Urania, who summons the final vision of heroes and heroines, promises that Armida and Rinaldo will eventually be united.

In both *Phaeton* and *Rinaldo and Armida*, as shown in Table 2.3, the first musical numbers within the drama are composed into extended pastoral entertainments, while masques featuring classical characters are found in Act III. In both cases, the authors' prefaces emphasize the desire to depict variety of passions, and musical scenes are designed to reflect a variety of emotional states with a corresponding variety of musical settings. In Eccles's setting the idyllic pastoral and erotic entertainments (Acts I and III) are made up of tonally stable components and are in the same or closely related keys (G major/minor, B-flat major, D minor). The music for the scenes of supernatural portents (Acts II and IV), particularly in Act IV, shows a much greater tendency to modulate and is, with the exception of a few touches of G and D minor, in different keys from the pastoral entertainments. Eccles and Purcell appear to be working within a shared set of conventions for key, making use of G minor and major in their pastoral entertainments and E minor for more threatening or ominous music.[86]

Unlike Gildon's *Phaeton*, nearly all of the music for Dennis's work survives.[87] GB-Lbl Add. MS 29378 preserves the music for each of the musical interludes in Acts I–IV in full score. Seven dances were printed in John Walsh's anthology *Theater Musick* as "from ye Opera of Armida," and the fifth-act song "Ah Queen! ah wretched Queen give o'er" appeared in the January 1699 *Mercurius Musicus* and later in Eccles's *Collection*. However, songs from *Rinaldo and Armida* show little contemporary circulation except for the pastoral ditty "The jolly, jolly breeze," which was both parodied and frequently reprinted.[88]

Compared with the multiple musical sources for *Rinaldo and Armida*, the surviving music for *Phaeton* is scanty. However, it is easier to assign singers to Gildon's tragedy than to *Rinaldo and Armida*, despite the lack of a full score, because John Heptinstall promptly published a collection of songs from *Phaeton*.[89] Such collections were commonly produced for dramatick operas and occasionally for other types of works (*Bonduca, Don Quixote, The Loves of Mars and Venus, Massaniello*), and the absence of one for *Rinaldo and Armida* is surprising. The title page of the song collection typically makes the genre of the production clear:

---

[86] There is some resemblance to Henry Purcell's usage of keys, described by Curtis Price in "Meanings of Keys in the Theatre Music," but the connection between G minor and death is not primary in Daniel Purcell and Eccles's works. *Henry Purcell and the London Stage*, pp. 21–6.

[87] Only missing its overture and act tunes, plus an occasional lyric and music for the final discovery. For the music, see Steven Plank's edition of *Rinaldo and Armida*, in Eccles's Collected Works (A-R Editions, forthcoming).

[88] "The jolly, jolly breeze" appeared in *Twelve New Songs* (London, 1699) and many editions of *Pills to Purge Melancholy*, as well as Eccles's 1704 *Collection* (p. 23) and several songsheets.

[89] See D&M Bibliography, no. 168.

tragedy (*Bonduca*), musical play (*The Loves of Mars and Venus*) or "a new opera" (*Brutus of Alba, The World in the Moon*). In the case of *Phaeton*, the title page gives the full title of the production but no clue to *Phaeton*'s genre.

Heptinstall's collection includes many of the pieces from the Act I entertainment of nymphs and shepherds. It comes as no surprise that these pieces were sung by a full complement of Patent Company singers, including some of the best voices in London at the time, sopranos Jemmy Bowen and Mary Anne Campion, tenor-countertenors John Freeman and John Pate. Another song collection, Henry Playford's *The Alamode Musician*, provides a setting of the song for Juno, "O Hymen, must I always see," in the masque of the third act, sung by soprano Mary Lindsey.[90]

An extended pastoral entertainment also opened the first act of Ravenscroft's tragedy *The Italian Husband* (LIF, 1697). The consistency of audience interest in this mode as part of a larger entertainment is reflected in the continued popularity of *Dioclesian*, with its massive Act V pastoral masque, incorporating Cupid, Bacchus, Flora, and other classical deities along with the nymphs, fauns, satyrs, shepherds, and shepherdesses.[91] Both Purcell and Eccles mix livelier airs ("Fond shepherd, prithee cease" for Pate, with its two accompanying violins, is particularly good) with languishing minuet songs ("Sorrow ever from us flies" and the less successful "Let ev'ry Shepherd bring his Lass") and choruses. Eccles's trio and the constant "ritournelles" separating the airs highlight their debt to the works of Lully, while Purcell's ensembles, both musical dialogues, emphasize the English tradition.

As Table 2.4 reveals, the more extensive entertainment is found in Gildon's tragedy, not Dennis's operatic production. Both emphasize the erotic side of the pastoral mode, with barely a passing reference to pastoral occupations and no explicit reference to the contrast between country and court, key features of the pastoral entertainments in *The Grove* and *The Virgin Prophetess*. They also employ courtly, polished language with no hint of rustic dialogue, even when the mood is humorous, as in the boy–girl dialogue in *Phaeton*. Both entertainments place their primary emphasis on pleasure, but in *Phaeton* the focus is on the individuals involved in its pursuit and, in *Rinaldo and Armida*, on the place itself.

---

[90] See GB-Lbl G. 91, song 6.
[91] Masque text and notes provided in Burden, ed., *Henry Purcell's Operas*, pp. 241–7.

Table 2.4 Pastoral entertainments in *Phaeton* and *Rinaldo and Armida*

Phaeton		*Rinaldo and Armida*	
Singers	**Text**	**Singers**	**Text**
	[Symphony]		[Overture]
1st Shepherd [Freeman] & chorus	"Come, come, all ye Shepherds, come come all away"	Shepherd	"Welcome to these Lovely Plains"
2nd Shepherd [Magnus] & Chorus	"Let every Shepherd bring his Lass"	Nymph	"Welcome to these blissful Shades"
3rd Shepherd	"Ye smiling Graces, come inspire"	[Trio, 2 Nymphs & Shepherd]	"Here we feel no want nor Care"
Chorus	Chorus and Dance again	[2nd] Shepherd	"Sorrow ever from us flies,"
Boy and Girl [Bowen & Campion]	Musical Dialogue: "Life is but a little span"	Nymph	"If any thing like Sorrow's seen"
1st Shepherd and Shepherdess	Musical Dialogue: "Come, gentle Phyllis, we'll softly retire"	Chorus	"All about us and above/Gaiety and Love inspires;"
2nd Shepherd	"Cruel *Daphne* do not fly me"	Shepherd [Gouge]	"The Jolly Breeze"
3rd Shepherd [Pate] & Chorus	"Fond Shepherd prithee cease to wooe her"	Nymph	"All around Venereal Turtles/Cooing, Billing…"
4th Shepherd [Bowen]	"To passive years resign your pining"		[Country Dance?][a]
Chorus	"When to sighing and groans you pervert the brisk joy"		

Phaeton		Rinaldo and Armida
[2nd] Shepherdess & Chorus	"Can you, can you, will you leave me?"	
2nd Shepherd	"Enough of delays, my passion to raise"	
Chorus	"Resistance and yielding well temper'd, still prove/ The best Sauce to the surfeiting Banquet of love."	

Note: [a] I suggest that the G major country dance printed in Walsh's *Theater Musick* could have been used in this scene.

In *Rinaldo and Armida*, the pastorally garbed spirits are the first line of defense for Armida's enchanted castle. In Canto XV of Torquato Tasso's *Gerusalemme Liberata*, the weary, hungry knights Carlo and Ubaldo are tempted by two naked nymphs playing in a pool with a rich banquet set beside it, but Dryden had already used the scene in *King Arthur* (the "two daughters of this aged stream" who attempt to seduce Arthur in Act IV). Aside from their opening "Welcomes" the singers do not address their spectators. The nymphs and shepherds remain abstract and anonymous, without names or relationships, always speaking in the plural ("we"). They endlessly emphasize the collective pleasures of the place, a space initially defined in the negative, by what is absent from it: want, care, sorrow. This is characteristic of descriptions of Elysium from ancient Greek texts, additional evidence (if any were needed) of Dennis's classical bent.

In contrast, the pastoral entertainment in *Phaeton* is designed by human agency for a specific viewer, Phaeton himself. Althea proposes that she and the restless Phaeton "banish all anxious thoughts" and "drown in Music" (3) as a way of celebrating their shared history (it's the anniversary of the day they first met) and diverting him. Like Xerxes' soft music or the Roman emperor's serenade in Gildon's earlier tragedy, this is music performed with a purpose which shapes the nature of both sound and sense, one of the ways in which Althea continues to woo Phaeton.

Unlike entertainments in some productions, Gildon's (Althea's) pastoral interlude is more than a string of separate songs and dances. Carefully labeled in the text, the pairings off of pastoral characters complete a catalogue of situations, and a dramatic arc for which Gildon even includes blocking (motion across the stage, pulling by the sleeve, directing the gaze). Following the two dialogues, the other shepherds attempt to persuade the second shepherd that to pursue without winning is to "pervert" pleasure and "sin against youth,"[92] while the shepherdess Daphne retorts that "resistance makes [love] lasting." The couple are reconciled by the final chorus (although whether on his terms or hers is left ambiguous). At the entertainment's conclusion, Althea finds herself in a false position, due to gender, a situation for which the pastoral world of the entertainment does not prepare her. In the world of the play, it is she, no shepherd, who pursues a reluctant lover.

In contrast, Armida's spirits claim that no one is baulked of their pleasure. The air "The Jolly, Jolly Breeze," performed by Mr Gouge, is a description of the *locus amoenus*, redolent of seductive scents, and was the single hit song out of the entire production.

> The Jolly Breeze,
> That comes whistling through the Trees,
> From all the blissful Region brings
> Perfumes upon its spicy Wings,
> With its wanton motion curling.
>   The Crystal Rills,
>   Which down the Hills
> Run o'er golden Gravel purling.[93]

Eccles sets this as an Italianate air constructed of short sequences and ornamented with satisfyingly active text depiction for all "motion" words in both voice and continuo.[94]

Within the entertainment Eccles has established a musical pattern of solo–solo–ensemble, twice repeated, in which the final two airs set up the expectation of a chorus or group number, and the lack of a conventional final grand chorus fits the dramatic context, as the spirits do not complete their musical spell. A dance may have been inserted here, as this scene conspicuously lacks the dances found in most pastoral musical interludes. The country dance printed by Walsh both matches the key of the last airs sung, and would provide a satisfying visual image as Urania scatters the spirits with her wand.

Although provided with tuneful and tender music by Purcell and Eccles, for the sake of the plot both entertainments must fail their prescribed purpose within the drama. Armida's spirits are dispersed and the rescue party continues on. The nymphs and shepherds remind Phaeton of his other love, Lybia. In the end, it is Althea's spoken pleading, not her magnificent musical entertainment, which

---

[92] A very similar exchange takes place in Handel's masque *Acis & Galatea*, with poetry by John Gay and others.

[93] Dennis, *Rinaldo and Armida*, p. 7.

[94] For a transcription of this air and further discussion see *Music Productions LIF*, 377–82. Neufeldt also examines this entertainment, including several musical examples in "The Social and Political Aspects of the Pastoral Mode," pp. 88–95. Note, however, that the trio is SSB, not STB, with the upper voices in sweet-sounding thirds.

sways him back to her side temporarily. However, she does not follow the precepts of the pastoral entertainment, insisting her love is absolute "in Act, in Word, in Thought" (5); she has been an "Easie love," offering no resistance. What are the onstage and offstage audiences to learn from this?

The second pair of entertainments which correspond between the two productions are the Act III masque-type entertainments featuring Roman deities who appear in their emblematic machines, trailed by attendants. In Act III of *Rinaldo and Armida*, the temptations of pleasure are more explicit than ever, as Armida has her spirits impersonate Venus and Cupid. Like the dream sequence in Act II, the masque is designed for a single spectator, Rinaldo, but ultimately proves no more persuasive. As one of Armida's supernatural advisors explains, the impersonators are aerial spirits, better able to combat the empyreal forces, including Armida's nemesis Fame, than the "Gloomy Powers" of Hell: "And they, ... with Enchanting Voices,/ To Pleasure may seduce *Rinaldo*'s Soul" (19). At Armida's command, the spirits take the form of the "Gods whom *Greece* ador'd," attended by Loves and Graces.

The play text gives no stage directions for this scene besides noting a "Symphony of Flutes." However, according to *The Musical Entertainments*, "Venus is discover'd reclin'd on a Couch, with her Attendants of Loves about her; and singing in soft complaining Notes."[95]

> *Ven.*   *Cupid*, come to the Relief
> Of thy Mother's piercing Grief;
> Hither quickly, *Cupid* fly;
> With thee bring thy keenest Dart,
> To subdue a Rebel Heart,
> Thou art Scorn'd as well as I.

The chorus echoes and elaborates Venus's sentiments in a simple musical setting.

Eccles saves the more active lines for the airs for Cupid, the irresistible force in the scene, in contrast to Dennis's languid Venus. Cupid promptly descends and promises, "I'll make that Mortal know,/ That none too Great for Love can grow" (26). Alluding to his power over Jove and Pluto (echoed by the chorus), Cupid gives orders to his amatory troops:

> [But let us cease our soaring strains
> Love Conquers Most when he complains][96]
> Now quickly thro' th'Enchanted Grove,
> Let all my nimble Brethren Rove.

---

[95] Wilkinson, *Theatre Miscellany*, p. 112.

[96] These two lines, set as recitative, seem to have been left out of Dennis's 1699 printed edition of the libretto, but appear in GB-Lbl Add. MS 29378.

This passage shows Eccles moving from recitative into song with an easy grace.

Immediately following Cupid's air, at the center of the musical scene is a G minor chaconne (Figure 2.2), probably inspired by the grand G minor passacaglia, "How happy the Lover," in Act IV of *King Arthur*. In additional evidence of Eccles's concern for continuity, the rhythms and ground bass of a chaconne were employed for Cupid earlier in the scene, where Eccles used a chaconne-like "symphony" in D minor for Cupid's descent.[97] In the full score, Eccles divides the ground between the bass and tenor lines, with virtuosic divisions for the first violin and recorder alternately.

Although the other dances in G minor printed by Walsh would make sense inserted here in the Act III masque,[98] in the manuscript, the end of the chaconne leads directly into the introduction to Venus's next air.[99] If the British Library manuscript is, as I have previously suggested, a score for a concert performance of the musical entertainments, this would make sense. The chaconne is the most complex and beautiful of the dances Eccles wrote for *Rinaldo and Armida* and would have been missed. However, the other dances, while charmingly French, are relatively brief, and might well be cut. At some point after their publication, an enterprising hand at Drury Lane apparently added them to the rival company's stock of incidental music.[100]

As singers' names are not given in the manuscript, and none of these airs appears to have been published, it is not known for certain who performed the roles of Venus and Cupid. It has usually been assumed that Venus was played by Anne Bracegirdle. However, Bracegirdle may have appeared instead as Cupid, a role she portrayed in *Cyrus the Great* (LIF, 1695), complete with bow and arrow. Re-examining the score from the Act III entertainment reveals that the vocal range for both roles is identical.[101] Although Venus's airs open and close the scene, there

---

[97] The chaconne proper has been copied into GB-Lbl Add. MS 29378 in six parts: four part strings plus two flutes (recorders). It is transcribed in appendix B of *Music Productions LIF*.

[98] The dances for Dennis's work: a country dance, minuet, lengthy chaconne, and a pair each of rigadouns and paspes are listed, with concordances, in Price's *Music in the Restoration Theatre*, pp. 217–18.

[99] See GB-Lbl Add. MS 29378, f. 31.

[100] Several dances from *Rinaldo and Armida* are included in GB-Lcm MS 1172, which contains instrumental music from DL productions, all in G minor. See *Instrumental Music for London Theatres, 1690–1699*, a facsimile edition of GB-Lcm MS 1172, intro. Curtis Price (Withyham, 1987), xv–xvi. The dances from *Rinaldo and Armida* have only the bass and treble lines, leaving the inner parts blank—suggesting the copyist only had access to Walsh's publication.

[101] Cupid may have been played by Jemmy Laroche, as in *The Loves of Mars and Venus*, but there is no evidence he was still with the company, or a boy soprano, in 1698–99.

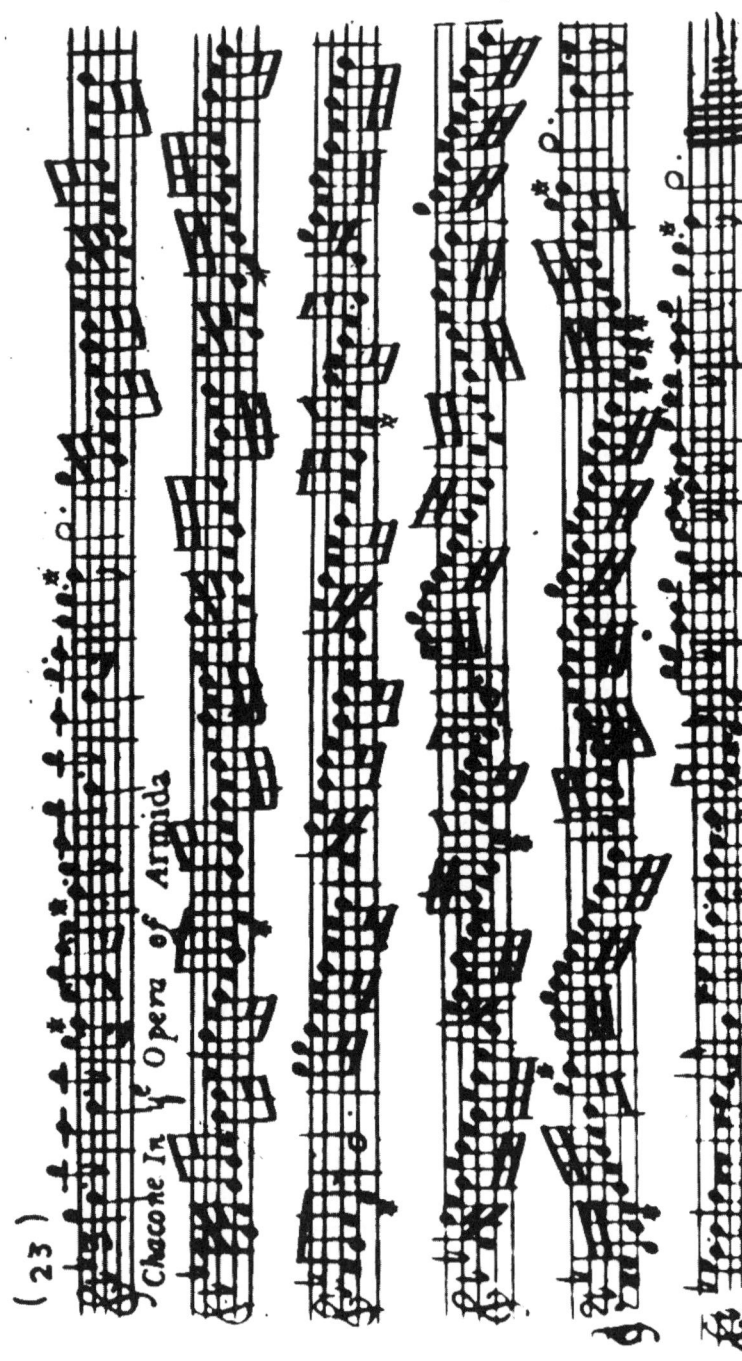

Figure 2.2 J. Eccles, chaconne [treble and bass] in *Rinaldo and Armida*. From *Theater Musick* (Walsh, 1698), book 1, pp. 23–4

Figure 2.2 Concluded

is actually more music for Cupid than Venus, and the music for Cupid's more active airs is not beyond Bracegirdle's ability.[102]

Casting Bracegirdle as Cupid may help clarify a confusing comment on *Rinaldo and Armida* in *A Comparison between the Two Stages*, when the character Sullen remarks: "The Jolly—Jolly breeze—came whistling thro'—all the Town, and not a Fop but ran to see the Celebrated Virgin [Bracegirdle] in a Machine; there she shin'd in a full Zodiack, the brightest Constellation there."[103] The suggestion that Bracegirdle may have appeared in the opera's final heavenly tableau is plausible,[104] but does not preclude Bracegirdle's playing the part of Cupid as well—her appearance as two different characters in different entertainments is documented in the later dramatick opera *The Mad Lover*—and I suspect the fops would have been more excited to see Bracegirdle "flying down," the most characteristic use of machines, than simply appearing as a scene opens.

The masque ends with Venus's injunction to the elements, echoed by her attendants: "Let Earth, and Air, and Flood, and Fire,/ And ev'ry thing around conspire/ To breath forth soft and sweet Desire." The airy spirits of pleasure are dispersed by Carlo, waving Urania's wand, which the guide gives to him ("tis Heav'ns High will that I Retire,/ And the remaining Task consign to you"), and Rinaldo wakes in angry confusion from his voluptuous swoon. Rinaldo, as a knight, must be rescued from female enchantment by his fellow knights, and not a beneficent female magic user.

In Act III of *Phaeton*, the gods are also angry over the behavior of a male mortal, although here they seek to influence Althea, rather than Phaeton, as she sits in an arbor "in a very melancholy posture" (13). Gildon's briefer masque presents three divine characters: Juno, Hymen, and Nemesis, each entering with their trains. Juno and Hymen, appropriately, descend from above and, after expressing their anger (Hymen: "These crimes unpunish'd must not go") in solo airs, summon Nemesis in chorus. When summoned, Nemesis and her train of Furies address Althea with predictably grim advice:

> *Nemesis.*   Grieve, grieve no more, nor sigh in vain.
> Revenge alone can ease your pain.
> Revenge affords a sure Relief,
> While Love alas promotes your Grief.
> *Chorus.*   At the hiss of their Snakes let that passion retire,
> That more noble revenge that Bosom may fire.
>   In this Chorus they dance and shake their Snakes over or
>   towards *Althea*, then descend—

---

[102] Actress Charlotte Butler portrayed Cupid in the original production of *King Arthur*, a production Dennis and Eccles clearly had in mind.

[103] *A Comparison Between the Two Stages*, p. 36.

[104] See Staring B. Wells's edition of *A Comparison between the Two Stages*, p. 142, notes to lines 25 and 29–30.

> *Juno* and *Hymen* with their Train ascend, and then
> *Merope* and *Cassiope* come forward.[105]

Following Gildon's masque, Althea's attendants are uneasy, though they have heard only "Strange sounds." Unlike them, Althea seems to be directly influenced by the goddesses' exchange—she does seek a horrible revenge. Although not seen by mortal eyes, the power of the goddesses affects their human object, though the classical setting perhaps accounts for their greater effectiveness. Unlike Armida's Venus and Cupid, these are apparently "real" goddesses.

Like Gildon, Dennis also makes use of a chorus of dancing, hissing furies in his production, a trope familiar through stock productions like Lee's *Oedipus Dioclesian*, recently borrowed for *Brutus of Alba*, and soon to reappear in Durfey's *Massaniello*. In Act II Armida summons "Spirits or Dreams … in the shapes of *Bertoldo* and *Sophia*, parents to *Rinaldo*; and of some that *Rinaldo* had slain in Battel" (16). However familiar the ghosts-of-parents scene may be as a dramatic convention, it is more disturbing than Armida's other efforts: having her spirits impersonate Rinaldo's parents is a personalized deception.

Eccles takes care to have these spirits sound nothing like the earlier ones, singing in a starkly declamatory fashion suitable to their ominous words. Like Statira, Rinaldo is wrapped in an amatory dream from which his 'parents' seek to wake him—but no more effectively than Statira's parents do.[106]

> *Bert.*   Rowze all thy Faculties my Son,
> . . . .
> No longer let thy Fancy run
> After that Aiery Phantom Fame;
> But Love *Armida* …
> . . . .
> *Soph.*   Ah! see around the Raving Hosts
>   Of purple Ghosts;
> Whose Blood thou hast in Battle spilt,
>   With fearful Guilt.
> Who, unless aw'd by her Commanding Pow'r,
> Would, ah, this Moment, tear thee and devour!
> *Bert.*   How they advance with whirling Brands,
> All flaming in their threatning Hands!
> And as they go their dreadful Round,
>   Revenge, Revenge Resound![107]

---

[105] Gildon, *Phaeton*, p. 13.

[106] A similar scene can be found in Davenant's *Circe*; the sorceress has Orestes haunted by spirits from the god of Sleep, and he hallucinates the ghost of his mother Clytemnestra.

[107] Dennis, *Rinaldo and Armida*, pp. 16–18.

As usual, Eccles flexibly follows the shifts in speech patterns with his music, opening up expressive ornamentation where the text suggests it and differentiating Bertoldo and Sophia musically. Amidst the horrific imagery, the promise is clear: if Rinaldo will love Armida (the music shifts momentarily to C major) all may yet be well.[108] The following chorus, "For Revenge, for Revenge, to *Armida* we call," is a triple-meter dance in A minor, far too reminiscent of happy shepherds. The "astonishing Horrors" doubtless depended on the dancing spirits with their "whirling Brands." To Armida's shock and anger, Rinaldo "smiles at all their Threats," and the spirits vanish as Fame's trumpet sounds (18).

The music of Act IV in *Rinaldo and Armida* and that leading into it has received the most scholarly attention for its special instrumental effects and some contemporary controversy.[109] A lead spirit summons "Ye Spirits that dwell in Earth, Fire, and Air," to avenge Armida's betrayal: "Hither, hither, hither, Hurry all to her Aid,"[110] with conventionally rapid repetitions of "hurry" and "hither." The chorus which follows is more complex than earlier ones, including sweeping melismas for "With *Vengeance* laden we *fly*." Sections for leader and chorus continue alternately, summoning "Fiends that are lurking in Graves" and "Pow'rs who govern the Air."[111] For the chorus of aerial spirits, "Hark how they blow!" Eccles mimics the rushing winds with constant motion in sixteenth-notes alternating between the violins and basses, through which the chorus trumpets, a passage which Dennis claims was particularly admired.[112]

Dennis's reference to Eccles's "borrowing" from *King Arthur* (UC, 1691) and his vehement defense of the composer must refer to the fourth chorus in Act IV of *Rinaldo and Armida*, in which the malevolent aerial spirits "shake/ At the dire Confusion we make." The music indicates that they shake in their singing as well.[113] Eccles's chromaticism in this passage, with its emphasis on and return to a dissonant (diminished) chord built over F-sharp (on the word "dire"), is richly ominous in the context of the straightforward F major of the preceding passages.

---

[108] For more on this scene, including excerpts from the dialogue and chorus-dance, see *Music Productions LIF*, pp. 394–9.

[109] At the end of Act III, Urania warns: "the Furies Arm,/ Th'Infernal Trumpet thro'the Abiss profound,/ Horribly rumbles …" During her speech, stage directions instruct "The Serpent and Basses" to play "softly under the Stage," and then "the Musick plays out," full force. Dennis, *Rinaldo and Armida*, p. 33.

[110] Ibid., p. 36.

[111] Bowman may well have sung the similar "Ye blust'ring brethren of the skies" as Aeolus in the fifth act of *King Arthur*. Price, *Henry Purcell and the London Stage*, p. 313.

[112] Wilkinson, *Theatre Miscellany*, p. 106.

[113] Like Lully's "shivering chorus" in *Isis* (1677), there are wavy lines written over the musical notes. Their exact meaning is not agreed upon, but may indicate a change in articulation and thus in sound, suitable to shivering and shaking. See Lionel Sawkins, "*Trembleurs* and Cold People: How Should They Shiver?" in Burden, ed., *Performing the Music of Henry Purcell*, pp. 243–64.

A later passage between the lead spirit and his brethren moves to C minor for a fiendish jig. A series of call-and-response exchanges between him, the instruments, and the chorus, which is full of special sound effects: "clinking of Chains," "Howls of the Damn'd," screams, roars, and a "Serpentine Hiss" (37–8). The finale of the entertainment features all the racing strings, thunder, and full choral singing of the previous segments:

> *Spir.* Let *Lucifer*'s Thunder now answer to this,
> And Bellow alternately thro' the Abyss.
> [indication in GB-Lbl Add. MS 29378: "Play all"]
> *Cho.* 'Tis done, and 'tis past our pow'r to know,
> Whither this be Chaos or no?[114]

Eccles follows Dennis's description in the rushing exchanges between violins and bass, punctuated with thunderclaps and choral interjections. If too organized for true chaos, it is a highly effective musical scene. Yet the infernal spirits thunder in vain.

In comparison, in Act IV of *Phaeton*, Gildon continues the work of rehabilitating the audience's sympathy for Althea/Medea by including a song sung to cure her melancholy.

> How happy wou'd poor Woman be,
>   From the Cares of Love still free,
> Did not false Mans deluding Arts
>   Rob us of our Peace and Hearts.
> With Tears and Oaths the Cheat maintain
> Till we poor helpless women love again,
> And wound ourselves, alas! to cure their pain.
> But then, ah! then! how soon they change!
> . . . .
> Ah! seal my Heart! ye chaster Pow'rs,
> Against their cunning Art,
> And of my Lifes succeeding Hours,
> Ah! give to Love no Part.[115]

There may be some irony in referring to Althea/Medea as a "poor helpless woman." The song is profoundly clichéd, from the opening lines to its concluding prayer to avoid Love henceforth, but the seriousness of Gildon's lyric and its applicability to the dramatic situation can be usefully compared with the

---

[114] Dennis, *Rinaldo and Armida*, p. 38.
[115] Gildon, *Phaeton*, p. 23.

incongruously comic marriage dialogue sung in Act IV of Motteux's *The Island Princess*, when the music is for a lovesick hero languishing in an orange grove.[116]

The fatal events of Act V do not prevent Gildon and Dennis from adding more music to their productions. In the case of *Phaeton*, the music is that of a conventional temple scene with two priest-soloists and chorus, "O! sacrid *Isis*! and *Apollo* hear!"[117] Yet the ceremony is merely the backdrop for Althea/Medea's final desperate act of poisoning her rival, who is seen being led up to the altar as Althea (disguised) soliloquizes and pulls Phaeton aside to confront him.

While the final music in *Phaeton* is a fruitless hymeneal prayer, that of Dennis's tragedy remains supernatural. At the end of the previous act, Armida had been unable to stab Rinaldo and instead turned the dagger on herself, which keeps Rinaldo by her side as he works to save her life. As the fifth act opens Rinaldo is surprisingly happy, and as in Tasso, observes "Thou hast renounc'd thy Faith, renounc'd thy Art,/ And thy Wound is not Mortal" (47). When he leaves to seek his friends, the situation once again reverses. A spirit rises from under the stage to sing Eccles's "Ah Queen! ah wretched Queen give o're." Despite her own experience in conjuring false spirits, Armida believes Phenissa when she claims Rinaldo has left forever, and stabs her for "concealing" it. When Armida hears Rinaldo returning with Urania and the knights to the darkened stage, she holds off death a moment to both "upbraid him" and "forgive him."[118] Surveying the scene, Urania promises Rinaldo that because of Armida's repentance, though she is dying, after death they will "reign united" over the celestial heroes and heroines revealed above.

In both *Phaeton* and *Rinaldo and Armida*, the music is powerfully linked to the female protagonist. Although neither Armida nor Althea/Medea sing in character, per the conventions of dramatick opera, nearly all of the music in both productions is directly connected to them. In the case of Armida, the musicians and singers onstage are spirits she has conjured up, and they function as extensions of her will. Even when she is absent, they obey her wishes (as they understand them) and reflect her moods. Thus nearly all the music in the first four acts of *Rinaldo and Armida* is overtly part of Armida's magic. Although Gildon greatly downplays his heroine's sorcerous past, his Althea/Medea is the one who organizes the pastoral entertainment in Act I and the one whom the gods come to sing to in sympathy with her situation in Act III. In addition, she's the one who calls for music when severely depressed by Phaeton's faithlessness in Act IV. Again, in both cases, as their power over circumstances wanes, they also lose control over the music, and the musical events in Act V assert the hegemony of other forces, diabolical and heavenly in *Rinaldo and Armida* or of the Egyptian gods and fate in *Phaeton*.

---

[116] The dialogue is "Hold, John, e're you leave me," sung by Leveridge and Pate (in drag). Pierre Motteux, *The Island Princess, or The Generous Portuguese. Made into an Opera* (London, 1699), pp. 21–2.

[117] The solo for Pate as second priest, "Look down bright God of day," is the only music which survives.

[118] Dennis, *Rinaldo and Armida*, p. 51.

So where does the tipping point between musical tragedy and dramatick opera lie? In naming *Rinaldo and Armida* a tragic dramatick opera I am on firm ground with Dennis's contemporaries and my own. *Phaeton* is more problematic. Other tragedies include examples of musical numbers like those described: pastoral entertainments, masques, melancholy songs, and temple scenes, but not in such profusion. While *Phaeton* does not fit Burden's schema for dramatick opera, lacking a big second act masque, new and/or elaborate sets, or any spectacular transformation scenes, it is provided with machines, dances, and elaborate costumes, together with a substantial amount of music.

Far more than *Bonduca*, *Phaeton* approaches opera, with its grand pastoral entertainment, masque and temple scene. In *Phaeton* the relative brevity of the spoken text versus the length of the musical sequences, and their importance both within the production and in publication (Heptinstall's book of songs), together with the invocation of the French *tragédie lyrique* by Gildon are all significant. The addition of a single magical musical scene with spirits summoned by Althea/Medea as she returns to her sorceress roots (like Armida or Circe) would swing the balance.

Conclusion: Dramatick Opera and Musical Tragedy

In one section from *The Gentleman's Journal*, Motteux provides "A Description of the Kingdom of Poetry." It begins:

> The Kingdom of *Poetry* is large and well peopled, it borders on one side on that of *Painting*, and on the other on that of *Music*: It is divided into high and low, like several other Countries. *High Poetry* is inhabited by a sort of grave sowre-look'd melancholy People, who speak a language which is to the other Provinces as *Welsh* to the *English*. The tops of all the Trees in *High Poetry* shoot into the Clouds. Their Horses out-run the Wind. The Men are generally Heroes by profession, … As for the Women, if they have never so little beauty, there is no comparison between them and the Sun. The Metropolis of this Province is call'd Epic Poem, 'tis built on a sandy and ungrateful Soil, which hardly any take the pains to cultivate.

A later passage turns to opera:

> In the same Province is a fine gaudy inchanted Castle, called *Opera*. It was first contriv'd by an *Italian* Magician; from *Italy* it went into *France*, and is now remov'd to another place, after its tedious Travels … Some Conjurers bring there, by their Art, the Sun, Moon, and Stars from their Orbs; Heaven and Hell, Land and Sea, and all the Fry of Heathen Gods attend their motion, and sing and dance very lovingly together: for those that live there are everlasting Singers, whether in joy or sorrow, and often, like Swans, sing best at their death. They

have reform'd this tiresome way lately, and intermixing the language of Tragedy with their agreeable Musick and surprizing Show, are very entertaining.[119]

Motteux is writing in 1692, and thus probably thinking of *King Arthur*. However, his words resonate with the situation some five years later. After the more broadly comic and fantastic operas of 1696 and 1697—Settle's *The World in the Moon*, Durfey's *Cinthia and Endimion*, and Powell's *Brutus of Alba*—some playwrights, particularly those like Gildon and Dennis with the greatest pretensions to literature and scholarship, were once again striving to unite tragedy with "agreeable Musick and surprizing Show."[120]

A contemporary producer, author, and composer team attempting to codify a recipe for success in musical tragedy or dramatick opera at the turn of the century would have to untangle the usual web of factors contributing to success or failure. Box office behavior, then as now, was not entirely consistent. In *A Comparison Between the Two Stages*, the character Ramble suggests:

> The Town, not being able to furnish out two good Audiences every Day; chang'd their Inclinations for the two Houses, as they found 'emselves inclin'd to Comedy or Tragedy: If they desired a Tragedy, they went to *Lincolns-Inn-Fields*; if to Comedy, they flockt to *Drury-lane*; which was the reason that several Days but one House Acted; but by this variety of Humour in the Town, they shared pretty equally the Profit.[121]

Since we do not have a complete list of revivals at either theater from the early years of the decade, this remains a contemporary's impression, rather than documented fact. From a musical standpoint, the evidence is more equivocal. Strong tragedy with integrated music often did well, as *Rinaldo and Armida* did. But polyglot works like *The Island Princess*, assembled under constrained circumstances, sometimes did even better. Each house tried both the integrated musical tragedy and the tragedy with popular types of musical extras—and many variations.

For musicologists coming from the study of operatic traditions, a key question remains: How much of the interest in creating new dramatick operas can be attributed to the theaters' composers? Was there a desire to write a complete (or substantially complete) set of music rather than piecemeal songs and instrumental pieces? Authors of plays regularly made public statements about their work in

---

[119] Motteux, "The Kindom of Poetry," in *The Gentleman's Journal*, January 1692, p. 17.

[120] I have argued elsewhere that Dennis's concerns regarding his musical tragedy can be read in the context of stage reform, a hot topic in 1698–99. See Kathryn Lowerre, "Dramatick Opera and Theatrical Reform: Dennis's *Rinaldo and Armida* and Motteux's *The Island Princess*," *Theatre Notebook* 59 (2005): 23–40.

[121] *A Comparison between the Two Stages*, p. 14.

prefaces and prologues, however suspect and stilted those sources are. Composers very rarely did so. Presumably a complete opera would potentially be worth more money, and would also confer more prestige on the composer. Before their eyes, Eccles and his contemporaries had the model of Henry Purcell as a master composer, one to whom they were constantly being compared.

Rather like movie moguls today, the difficulty for managers was in programming for widely varying public tastes, including navigating the interactive divide between critical and popular approbation. The "variety of passions" Dennis and Gildon sought to portray in their tragedies, including the musical scenes, was only a partial success, while the notoriously "motley assortment" of musical numbers in the final masque of *King Arthur* continued to hold the stage. In preparing a new musical production at the turn of the century, some things were better bets than others: popular stars, great scenes and special effects, a sensational story line, and Motteux's help with the script—but they were always a gamble.

PART II
Music and Musicians in Theatrical Competition

Chapter Three
Initiation, 1695–1697

The first seasons of competition featured many new musical productions as well as changes and additions to the musical personnel of the United Company, now divided into rival bands.

Context

Both artists and audiences were significantly affected by events outside the theaters. These generally fall into one of three categories: political and military events, attempts at censorship, and legal troubles relating to theft, bankruptcy, or nuisance complaints.

In December 1694, England had lost its queen, Mary II, who followed Stuart tradition by patronizing the arts—albeit with some moral reservations about the theater. Henry Purcell's odes for her birthdays, including "Celebrate this Festival" and "Come Ye Sons of Art" are probably her best-known musical legacies. Her widowed husband William III had less time for, and interest in, the performing arts.

In spring 1695 William was still at war with Louis XIV, and there was public discontent around taxation, coinage, and the war itself, including a few noisy demonstrations in support of the deposed king, James II, and his son. These events were echoed on both stages and in at least one case, directly participated in by theater performers.

On 20 June two of the Lincoln's Inn Fields company's singers, John Pate and John Reading, were among those arrested for taking part in a suspected Jacobite riot.[1] According to historian Narcissus Luttrell, on 10 June,

> being the birthday of the pretended prince of Wales, several Jacobites mett in several places, and particularly at the Dogg Tavern in Drury Lane, where with kettle drums, trumpets, &c. they caroused, and having a bonfire near that place, would have forced some of the spectators to have drunk the said princes health, which they refusing, occasioned a tumult, upon which the mob gathering, entered the tavern, where they did much damage, and putt the Jacobites to flight.[2]

---

[1] *Theatrical Documents*, no. 1508.

[2] Narcissus Luttrell, *A Brief Historical Relation of State Affairs from September 1678 to April 1714* (6 vols, Oxford, 1857), vol. 3, pp. 483–4.

Ten days later Luttrell notes that Reading and Pate were "displaced ... from their places in the new play house for being in the late Jacobite ryot."³ At trial in July, several men were found guilty; others were acquitted.⁴ Neither singer was charged—they could have argued they were simply there to perform.

During these events William III was away campaigning in Flanders. He visited London in October 1695, but was soon off again on "a progresse into the North"⁵ and did not return until the second week in November, when the city celebrated his successful campaign and the taking of the city of Namur. Although William did not patronize the theaters like his uncle, Charles II, his absences eliminated the possibility of well-paid performances at court, and took potential theater patrons and audience members out of town.

The political situation remained unsettled. Exchanges between Jacobites in Britain and the court of deposed king James II near Paris culminated in another attempt at revolution. The discovery of a plot against William III's life was announced in late February 1696.⁶ On 11 March trials began for conspiracy to commit regicide, ending in a January 1697 execution.⁷ William's military involvement on the Continent continued, although peace negotiations progressed throughout the early months of 1697.

The theater companies and the playwrights who wrote for them were officially part of the royal household (however detached from it in actual operation) and thus under the supervision of the Lord Chamberlain. In January 1696 the Lord Chamberlain issued a familiar order instructing both companies to submit scripts to Charles Killigrew, the Master of the Revels, for licensing,⁸ the traditional form of censorship. They complied, but this would be a source of contention during later seasons, when actors were charged with profanity and blasphemy in performing licensed plays. Although some charges probably involved racy ad-libbing, the actors justifiably felt that if a play text had passed review they should be able to speak its lines. It also could not have escaped anyone that enforcement of the edicts against profanity and blasphemy, like the Master of the Revels' review, was far from consistent.

The rival theater companies also found themselves facing practical problems beyond the competition for performers, playwrights, and audiences. These included

---

³ Ibid., vol. 3, p. 487.

⁴ Ibid., vol. 3, pp. 494–5. For more on the riot and events which followed, see Jane Garrett, *The Triumphs of Providence: The Assassination Plot, 1696* (Cambridge, 1980).

⁵ John Evelyn, *The Diary of John Evelyn,* ed. E.S. de Beer (London, 1955), vol. 5, p. 220.

⁶ Ibid., vol. 5, pp. 231–2. James II was to wait at Calais with a French army to take advantage of the confusion following the murder. Discovery of the plot and invasion threat made William (temporarily) more popular.

⁷ On 28 January Sir John Fenwick, acquitted in the earlier Dog Tavern riot, was beheaded.

⁸ *Theatrical Documents*, no. 1523.

theft of expensive costumes and petty charges against individual personnel, usually for debt.⁹ On 6 July 1695 the new playhouse in Lincoln's Inn Fields was denounced as a public nuisance by the Grand Jury of Middlesex, the first of many such complaints during the following decade.¹⁰

The issue of licensing arose again at the end of the 1696–97 season, when the newly appointed Lord Chamberlain, the Earl of Sunderland, responded to complaints that "many of the new Plays Acted by both Companys ... are scandalously lew'd and Prophane, and Contain Reflections against his Majesty's Government," reminding both companies that they needed to submit new scripts for review.¹¹ It is easier to see lewdness and profanity in spring 1697 productions than "reflections against his Majesty's government"; however, both John Vanbrugh's *The Provok'd Wife* and Thomas Durfey's *The Intrigues at Versailles* included sexually suggestive and potentially political songs.

Musical Assets

This section briefly surveys some of the practical elements of onstage music. While *The London Stage* lists personnel known at each theater for each season, the following account emphasizes the major musical assets held by each company. These range from high-profile actor-singers, professional singers, dancers, and composers to less obvious assets such as collections of manuscript music and playwrights or librettists who created productions in which music figured prominently.

Actor-singers

During the initial seasons of competition, the Lincoln's Inn Fields company not only had the superior actors, including Thomas Betterton and Elizabeth Barry, but the best of the actor-singers in Anne Bracegirdle and Thomas Dogget, and John and Elizabeth Bowman. Actor-singers were often the favorites of audience members, who were not as enthusiastic about professional singers or the more

---

⁹ Milhous and Hume, *Theatrical Documents*, nos. 1507, 1528, 1531, 1532, 1534, 1536. More serious was an assault charge, never brought to court, against Colley Cibber by actress Jane Lucas. See Helene Koon, *Colley Cibber: A Biography* (Lexington, 1986), p. 34.

¹⁰ Milhous and Hume comment, "Like sports stadiums today, theatres were noisy at night, created parking problems and traffic jams for local residents, and brought undesirables into respectable residential neighborhoods." For the full petition see "New Documents about the London Theatre 1685–1711," *Harvard Library Bulletin* 36 (1988): 248–74 (pp. 260–61).

¹¹ *Theatrical Documents*, no. 1556.

elaborate music written for them. They could perform in character and were often featured in comedies and masques.

The juvenile Letitia Cross ("Miss Cross," "the Girl") quickly became the Patent Company's most potent attraction in this category, appearing in a variety of productions: comic, tragic, and operatic. Younger and of less chaste repute than Bracegirdle, she often performed with the professional singers in songs and dialogues when not part of a play's cast.

In April 1696 Thomas Dogget, a key part of comic productions at Lincoln's Inn Fields, signed articles at Drury Lane. This was apparently the result of protracted negotiation, in defiance of the Lord Chamberlain's edicts.[12] The following autumn the Lincoln's Inn Fields company was still struggling to fill roles designed for him (such as Gallus in Motteux's *The Loves of Mars and Venus*). Many of his parts, like Sailor Ben in *Love for Love*, depended on a multi-talented actor who could not only be very funny but also dance and put over a song.

Susanna Mountfort Verbruggen, a popular comedienne who shone in comic musical numbers and would have been welcome at Lincoln's Inn Fields, remained at Drury Lane when her actor husband changed companies. Instead, Lincoln's Inn Fields acquired a useful actress-singer, Elizabeth Willis. After appearing in *Brutus of Alba* and *Aesop* at Drury Lane Willis moved to Lincoln's Inn Fields by April 1697, when she appeared in *The Provok'd Wife*. She played a variety of supporting roles every season thereafter. Her best-known songs were simple comic ones, but some of the musical material written for her by composer John Eccles suggests she could handle more complex pieces when needed.

Singers

There were talented vocalists of all types available, from soprano to bass, many of them known from the substantial research Olive Baldwin and Thelma Wilson have done on singers who worked with Henry Purcell.[13] It has often been said that Henry Purcell was left without high-caliber singers when the United Company split. As seen in Table 3.1, many of the most experienced singers went with Betterton, but the Patent Company still boasted a varied ensemble, including veteran vocalist John Freeman.[14]

---

[12] *Theatrical Documents*, nos. 1526–1527. In October 1696 the Lord Chamberlain issued another order against transfers (no. 1539), although he allowed Dogget's transfer to and actor John Verbruggen's transfer from DL. Changes between companies—actual or threatened, perhaps as part of salary negotiations—remained numerous enough that he issued yet another order in May 1697 (no. 1555).

[13] See "Purcell's Stage Singers," in *Performing the Music of Henry Purcell*, Burden, pp. 105–29 and individual DNB entries.

[14] Not the same person as the actor John Freeman at LIF.

Table 3.1 Selected singers in each company, spring 1695 and 1695–97 seasons

Name	Voice Type	PC	LIF
Mrs. Ayliff	*Soprano*		1695, 1695–96
Jemmy Bowen, 'the Boy'	*Treble*	1695, 1695–97	
Mary Anne Campion	*Soprano*	1696–97	
John Church	*Tenor*	1695, 1696–97	
Katherine Cibber	*Soprano*	1695–97	
Mr. Curco [variants]	*Baritone*		1695–96
Thomas Edwards	*Bass*	1695–97	
John Freeman	*Tenor–Countertenor*[a]	1695, 1695–97	
Mary Hodgson [Hudson][b]	*Soprano*		1695–97
Jemmy La Roche, 'the Boy'	*Treble*		1695–97
Richard Leveridge[c]	*Bass*	1695–97	
Mary Lindsey	*Soprano*	1696–97	
John Pate	*Tenor–Countertenor*	1696–1697	1695
John Reading	*Bass*		1695, 1695–97

*Note*s:

[a] Both Freeman and Pate have usually been referred to as countertenors; however, as Baldwin and Wilson note, the range they apparently sang in would be comfortable for a high light tenor. Pieces they sang were copied and printed in both G clef (treble, presumably performed down an octave) and C clef (alto).

[b] Hudson and Hodgson, freely intermingled in cast lists and songbooks, are variant spellings for a single singer's name. Mary's husband, actor John Hodgson, appears similarly.

[c] A "Mrs Leveridge" sang in *The Royal Mischief* (LIF, Spring 1696), according to both the play text and a printed songsheet. Scholars (myself included) have followed the 1706 anthology *Wit and Mirth* in 'correcting' this to Richard Leveridge. However, Baldwin and Wilson make a convincing case that there was a Mrs. Leveridge, possibly a relative. Personal communication.

Each company had a boy soprano, Jemmy Bowen at Drury Lane and Jemmy La Roche at Lincoln's Inn Fields, as well as an array of adult male singers. Although Pate and Reading were dismissed in June 1695, Reading was soon back at Lincoln's Inn Fields, singing in *The Lover's Luck* in December. Pate seems to have left the Lincoln's Inn Fields company. He began singing for the Patent Company in autumn 1696. His whereabouts during the 1695–96 season are uncertain,[15] although some music written for 1695–96 productions at Lincoln's Inn Fields may have been intended for him.

Another trained singer, the exquisite soprano Mrs Ayliff, would also leave Lincoln's Inn Fields sometime during the 1696–97 season.[16] Most of the women singers remained with their companies, though the careers of some, like Letitia Cross's, would have interesting hiatuses.[17]

Composers

For their vocal and instrumental music, both companies had an assortment of competent composers to draw upon, although the central figures were clearly Henry Purcell and John Eccles. Composers associated with the two companies during these years generally split along lines of association. The organists, many of them students of John Blow and associated with the Chapel Royal, were with the Patent Company: Henry and Daniel Purcell, Thomas Morgan, Raphael Courteville, and Jeremiah Clarke. The string players, many of them violinists associated with the King's Private Musick, went to Lincoln's Inn Fields, including John Eccles, John Lenton, and Thomas Tollett.[18]

James Paisible (recorder, bass viol) and Gottfried Finger (bass viol) were foreign-born and had played in Charles II and James II's Private Musick and in James II's Catholic Chapel. Finger would later switch companies, but he began firmly in the Lincoln's Inn Fields camp, while Paisible consistently worked for the Patent Company. Italian harpsichordist Giovanni Baptista Draghi was another very senior member of the old court music who apparently supported Lincoln's Inn Fields. Although he is only known to have written one piece performed there, this was probably due to age and ill-health.

Henry Purcell, the 'English Orpheus,' was widely acknowledged as the leading composer of his time. In his 1710 *Life of Mr. Thomas Betterton*, Charles Gildon emphasizes that Purcell's music "supported a Company of young raw Actors, against the best and most favour'd of that Time, and transported the Town for several Years together, as they do yet all true Lovers of Music," specifically mentioning pieces from the dramatick operas *The Indian Queen* and *King Arthur*,

---

[15] Baldwin and Wilson suggest he may have made a trip to the Continent (as he later did) or worked privately for a wealthy family.

[16] She was rumored to be a kept woman, enabling her early retirement.

[17] See Judith Milhous and Robert D. Hume, "Theatrical Politics at Drury Lane: New Light on Letitia Cross, Jane Rogers, and Anne Oldfield," *Bulletin of Research in the Humanities* 85 (1982): 412–29.

[18] See the table of composers in the Appendix.

the first composed for and the second frequently revived by the Patent Company.[19] Both the quality and the amount of music he wrote for Patent Company productions have drawn the attention of most musical scholarship. However, Daniel Purcell and John Eccles were well-respected and definite assets. Perhaps the best indicator of their status is the care authors like Motteux, Dilke, Dennis, and Oldmixon took to thank them in their prefaces and epistles.

In addition to composers, the Patent Company retained a valuable library of theatrical music, paralleling its superior stock of stages, sets, and costumes. Its library included scores for all of Henry Purcell's dramatick operas, which it used on a regular basis. The value placed on such music as property can be seen in the substantial reward offered for return of the missing score for Purcell's *The Fairy Queen* in 1701.[20] The manuscript GB-Lcm 1172 illustrates the range of instrumental pieces the company had to draw upon (in addition to Purcell's music),[21] from newly composed tunes to favorite opera airs by French composer Jean-Baptiste Lully and pieces attributed to Italian violin virtuoso Arcangelo Corelli.

Dancers

Information about the professional dancers active during these seasons is sadly scarce. Considerably more is known about performers from later seasons, whose appearances were advertised in the newspapers.

Thomas Betterton's contract with Joseph Sorin as dancing master at Lincoln's Inn Fields has been preserved.[22] During these seasons presumably Sorin was not only appearing onstage himself but also coaching and choreographing the other professional dancers, as well as the actors who could dance in character. Sorin took the speaking role of Pasquarel in a short farce,[23] but is usually absent from play texts. Among the other dance professionals were Joseph Prince and Thomas Bray, whose publication *Country Dances* (London, 1699) documents some of the music and choreography which may have been used in the theaters.[24]

Scholars have often assumed that a very senior dancer-choreographer, Josias Priest, served as dancing master for the Patent Company, just as he had for the United Company. However, significant questions have been raised about his

---

[19] Gildon, *The Life of Mr. Thomas Betterton* (London, 1710), p. 167.

[20] See *Theatrical Documents*, no. 1671 for the advertisement. The PC offered 20 guineas for it.

[21] Available in a facsimile edition, *Instrumental Music for London Theatres, 1690–1699*, intro. Curtis Price (Withyham, 1987).

[22] *Theatrical Documents*, no. 1535.

[23] Motteux's *Natural Magic*, part of *The Novelty*. Like many *commedia dell'arte*-based characters, Pasquarel requires acrobatic talents.

[24] Unique copy in the Vaughan Williams Memorial Library, Cecil Sharp House (GB-Lcs 3620), modern edition edited by Christine Helwig and Marshall Barron. Unfortunately, many dances provide only the tune and name of the choreographer.

identity.[25] Priest apparently designed dances for Purcell's earlier dramatick operas, *Dioclesian*, *King Arthur*, and *The Fairy Queen*,[26] while dances from the later dramatick opera *The Island Princess* (PC, 1699) and at least one piece from *The Indian Queen* (PC, 1695) are attributed to him.[27]

Among the actors, George Powell danced, and several comedies require him to dance in character, sometimes with minor actress-singer Diana Temple. Actress-singer Jane Lucas was particularly known for her dancing (featured in *The Female Wits*) and the better-known Letitia Cross could also oblige. At Lincoln's Inn Fields, the versatile Dogget was good for comic dancing, and many comedians (of both genders) could cut capers when required.

Playwrights and Librettists

The rival companies competed for authors. They staged a tug of war over Sir John Vanbrugh, whose plays were split between them. After the success of Colley Cibber's first comedy at Drury Lane, Lincoln's Inn Fields attempted to secure his new play. In response, Christopher Rich made a contract with Cibber, ensuring right of first refusal for any plays as long as the actor remained with the Patent Company.[28] Congreve had a similar agreement to provide plays for Lincoln's Inn Fields. In addition, Drury Lane had actor George Powell, who as an author-adapter-director favored productions with "a whole train of Fiddles, Dance and Song"[29] resulting in works such as *Bonduca* and *Brutus of Alba*.

Among the authors whose works were largely musical, the Patent Company had the service of the very experienced Thomas Durfey and Elkanah Settle, while Lincoln's Inn Fields engaged Huguenot émigré Pierre Motteux for several productions. Durfey and Settle represented an older generation of poets, Durfey famous for his quick rhymes and colloquial comedies whereas Settle's best-known works were tragedies and public spectacles.[30] Motteux was an enthusiast for opera and opéra-ballet in Italian, French, and English forms.

---

[25] If Joseph, Josiah, and Josias Priest were indeed the same person, then he performed and choreographed dances for the public theaters from 1667, contributed to the court masque *Calisto* (1675) and later ran a boarding school with his wife where Purcell's *Dido and Aeneas* was performed in 1689. For more about the activities of various Priests, see Jennifer Thorp's "Dance in Late 17th-century London: Priestly Muddles," *Early Music* 26/2 (1998): 198–210.

[26] See Richard Semmens, "Dancing and Dance Music in Purcell's Operas," in *Performing the Music of Henry Purcell*, Burden, pp. 180–96.

[27] Included in Bray's *Country Dances*.

[28] *Theatrical Documents*, no. 1540.

[29] Powell, *Imposture Defeated; or, A Trick to Cheat the Devil* (London, 1698), prologue lines 7–9.

[30] Settle's designs set the stage for several civic events. The pageants Settle designed for the Lord Mayor's inauguration in 1698 were described and illustrated in *Glory's*

The divisions among authors were far from fixed. Even when their plays were performed at one house, some poets wrote verses for productions performed at the rival theater, for example, Motteux's rondeau "Man is for the Woman Made" (remembered today for Henry Purcell's musical setting) in Thomas Scott's *The Mock Marriage* (PC, 1695) or Congreve's epilogue for Thomas Southerne's *Oroonoko* (PC, 1695).

Opening Gambits: The Spring and Summer of 1695

The theater into which the veteran actors moved in the spring of 1695 was appreciably smaller than the one at Drury Lane, where the United Company performed regularly, or Dorset Garden, where their dramatick operas were staged. Lincoln's Inn Fields had been the site of one of the earliest Restoration theaters but had recently been serving as an indoor tennis court.[31] In addition to building renovation, new stage properties were required. At a minimum the basic capacity for moveable scenery and new flats or backdrops would have to be prepared, and machines which allowed for rising and sinking from the stage engineered. References to rising from beneath the stage are found from the very first season, in *Pyrrhus, King of Epirus*; however, the more complex machines needed to descend (in chariot or cloud) do not appear until slightly later, and may not have been available initially.

New Productions

The first new production of 1695, William Congreve's *Love for Love*, opened at the 'new' playhouse at the end of April. Although it was written for the United Company, Congreve managed to transfer his comedy to Lincoln's Inn Fields, ensuring that his friend Anne Bracegirdle, who created all of his heroines, would continue to do so. It ran for thirteen nights, an impressive number when any play that lasted past the third-night author's benefit was considered successful.[32] The comedy's enormous popularity is reflected in the many surviving copies of the songs, dances, and incidental music composed by John Eccles and Gottfried Finger.[33] One song in particular, "A Soldier and a Sailor," sung in character by Dogget, is ubiquitous in manuscripts, appeared as a ballad sheet, and prompted

---

Resurrection; Being The Triumphs of London Revived (London, 1698).

[31] For estimated dimensions of the three theaters, see Edward A. Langhans, "The Theatres," in Hume, ed., *The London Theatre World*, pp. 35–65.

[32] Congreve's *The Old Batchelor* ran for 14 nights in 1693. *London Stage*, vol. 1, p. 419. On benefit nights the authors, actors, or other personnel specified received the night's profit (after expenses).

[33] For a more detailed account of the music, including transcriptions, see *Music Productions LIF*, pp. 71–99. For a musical discussion of *Love for Love* in comparison with

numerous parodies.[34] *Love for Love*'s triumph both assured the company's immediate survival and set a standard for future productions.

The evidence suggests that the Patent Company struggled to counter *Love for Love* with a new production of its own, and mounted mostly stock plays during this abbreviated season. The operatic version of the Howard–Dryden tragedy *The Indian Queen*, with music by Henry and Daniel Purcell, premiered later in the spring.

Since initial performance dates for most new plays are conjectural, I have not attempted to give precise dates for productions in Table 3.2 or similar tables beyond their calendar season (Autumn–Winter–Spring–Summer). However, their relative positions indicate premieres which were in close competition. The tables are meant as a guide to the discussion, and additional information about dating can be found in the text and footnotes. The genres assigned are those given on the printed title pages. Genres supplied by me, when no printed text exists or no genre is given, are in brackets.[35]

Table 3.2 New productions during the spring and summer of 1695

	New works by the Patent Company		New works at Lincoln's Inn Fields	
SPRING[a]	*The Indian Queen*	[Dramatick Opera]	*Love for Love*	Comedy
SUMMER			*Pyrrhus, King of Epirus*	Tragedy

Note: [a] For convenience, the calendar seasons are each assumed to be three months long (autumn = September, October, November, etc.).

The Lincoln's Inn Fields company staged its first production, Congreve's comedy *Love for Love*, with great care, and Congreve dedicated the first edition to the Lord Chamberlain. Featuring familiar actors and character types, Congreve's

---

The Way of the World, see Kathryn Lowerre, "Music and Meaning in Congreve's *The Way of the World*," *Restoration and Eighteenth-Century Theatre Research* 15/1 (2000): 24–52.

[34] See Simpson, *The British Broadside Ballad*, pp. 670–71.

[35] Numerous distinctions could be made within the broad categories used here. One essential difference: in tragedies a sympathetic, virtuous character might die, whereas in comedy this would never be allowed. As Critick comments in *A Comparison between the Two Stages*, in comedy "All *Ideas* of distress are to be banish'd, and our Lives only to be represented, with the Humours, Vices, and Vicissitudes of 'em; but our Deaths not be mention'd, not so much as by Similitude" (p. 165).

deft manipulation of audience expectations made for effective theater, as did the musical contributions by Eccles (songs) and Finger (song and act tunes).

In Act III scene 3 the witty lovers, Angelica (Bracegirdle) and Valentine, share the stage for the first time together with the manipulative rake Mr Scandal, and Mr Tattle (John Bowman), an empty-headed beau.

When Scandal calls to attendants for "the first song in the last new play," it is both a theatrical cliché and a demonstration of Scandal's personal power. The lyrics reinforce his contemptuous view of society.

> A Nymph and a Swain to Apollo once pray'd,
> The Swain had been Jilted, the Nymph been Betray'd;
> Their Intent was to try if this Oracle knew
> E're a Nymph that was Chaste, or a Swain that was True.
> Apollo was mute, and had like t'have been pos'd,
> But sagely at length he this Secret disclos'd:
> He alone won't Betray in whom none will Confide,
> And the Nymph may be Chaste that has never been Try'd.[36]

Eccles's musical setting of "A nymph and a swain" (performed by John Pate) repeats words and phrases as well as entire sections, extending eight short lines into a substantial song. Its simplicity keeps the focus on Congreve's lyrics.

Eccles's second song, the ballad "A Soldier and a Sailor," sung in character by Dogget at the end of Act III, is even simpler. Eccles repeats the tail-rhyme lines, while both the rolling 6/4 meter of the music and the poetic form reinforce the humor. Like other songs for Dogget, it was doubtless designed to be acted with gestures.

> A Souldier and a Sailor,
> A Tinker and a Tailor,
> Had once a doubtful strife, Sir,
> To make a Maid a Wife, Sir,
>   Whose name was Buxom Joan.
> For now the time was ended,
> When she no more intended,
> To lick her Lips at Men, Sir,
> And gnaw the Sheets in vain, Sir,
>   And lie o'Nights alone …[37]

Ben's song describes a sailor's successful wooing, but the contrast between his rough-hewn performance and the urbane lady he seeks to woo (Mrs Frail),

---

[36] Congreve, *Love for Love: A Comedy* (London, 1695), p. 39.
[37] Ibid., p. 53.

plays up their comical incompatibility. He then treats Mrs Frail and her friends to a dance of sailors,[38] emphasizing the first real point of closure.

The song in the fourth act, "I tell thee Charmion," emphasizes the contrast between the hero Valentine and his younger brother, Sailor Ben. Although the performers (Pate and Reading) are not mentioned in the play, this is a serious song for professional singers.[39] Valentine invokes one of the conventions of stage madness and melancholy, wherein the afflicted needed to be soothed by song, as part of a ruse to manipulate his father and win a declaration of love from Angelica. Characters in Congreve's comedy—Valentine, Scandal, Ben—stage their musical events to show something, to get something, or to prove something.

The final musical event in *Love for Love* is the reconciling, celebratory dance that closes the last scene of Act V.[40] Behind the scenes, there was much to celebrate: strong performances by favored actors, enhanced by the music of Eccles and Finger, and assisted by the vocal powers of Pate, had successfully launched their new company.

Their rivals struck out in a different direction with the dramatick opera *The Indian Queen*. Based on the play by Sir Robert Howard and John Dryden but significantly adapted with extensive musical interpolations, it premiered at the Dorset Garden theater, where the grand sets and stage apparatus from earlier operatic productions (under Betterton's direction) could be used.

Many questions still remain—the jigsaw puzzle of pieces for *Love for Love* looks simple next to the tangled nest of sources for *The Indian Queen*.[41] Older plays of all types were regularly revived with new music in a process of continuous adaptation, although in many cases the musical evidence from a revival is a single published song. Given contemporary theatrical practices, it is possible that the revamped *Indian Queen* got a trial run during the late spring of 1695 without its concluding masque, and that the masque was subsequently added during the autumn run, both to suit audience expectations for an "opera" and for the added draw of something new.

The Indian Queen includes examples of several conventional types of musical scene: the incantation scene with singing spirits, an evocation of the monarch's

---

[38] The hornpipes in the preliminary music should not be read as a reference to Sailor Ben. See glossary.

[39] Singers' names appear in the fifth book of John Heptinstall's *Thesaurus Musicus: Being a Collection of the Newest Songs Performed At His Majesties Theatres; and at the Consort in Viller-Street in York-buildings* (London, 1696). See D&M 1603.

[40] I believe that the characters performed the dance for couples from Henry Playford's *The Dancing Master: Second Part* (London 1698), titled "Love for Love: Danc'd in the Play."

[41] Recent scholarship and contentious issues are deftly handled by Julia K. Wood in her essay and commentary on the libretto in Burden, ed., *Henry Purcell's Operas*, pp. 411–27. For complete information on the musical sources, see Margaret Laurie and Andrew Pinnock's edition in Purcell's *Works*, vol. 19 (1994).

glory and triumph, the temple scene with choruses of priests. It opens with a sung rather than spoken prologue featuring John Freeman and Jemmy Bowen, a musical novelty that would be employed several times during the following decade.

The first major musical event is an extended scene celebrating the usurping Mexican monarch Zempoalla, sung by Fame and Envy with their followers. The incantation scene opens with the famous invocation by the conjurer Ismeron, beginning "You twice ten hundred deities" and continuing "By the croaking of the toad."[42] There are also two lovely songs, including the favorite "I attempt from Love's sickness to fly in vain" (sung by Letitia Cross), duets, choruses of spirits, and several pieces of instrumental music, some not linked to any specific scene.

The final musical scene, save the masque of Hymen, is set in the "Temple of the Sun" as the priests prepare to sacrifice Montezuma with the Incan leader and his daughter Orazia. The music begins and ends with full chorus, while exchanges between the gruffly declamatory high priest (Leveridge) and his followers comprise the middle section. Henry Purcell ends the scene in the appropriately unsettling key of F minor:

> All dismal sounds thus on these Off'rings wait,
> Your pow'r shown by their untimely Fate;
> While by such various Fates we learn to know,
> There's nothing to be trusted here below.

As so often happens, the elaborate musical ritual invoked for Zempoalla proves useless, and the tables are quickly turned, leaving Montezuma in power and united with Orazia, while Zempoalla, having lost her throne, her love rejected, kills herself.

The concluding masque, with music by Daniel Purcell, represents another mode of musical-dramatic interplay. The masque begins by alternating the serious music of Hymen (Leveridge again) with a cynical dialogue between sophisticated spouses and a comic dialogue between rustic spouses (in 6/4 time). Cupid is called upon and his solo, accompanied conventionally enough by paired recorders, is succeeded by one for one of his followers, with trumpet, and then for two as a duet. The final grand chorus, "Let loud Renown with all her thousand Tongues,/ Repeat no Name but his in her immortal Songs," harkens back to the evocation of Fame for Zempoalla in Act II, both textually and musically. Like *Love for Love*, *The Indian Queen* included all the musical elements of its genre, though it lacked the star performers originally intended to act and sing many of its roles.

---

[42] This piece was performed for decades by Richard Leveridge and printed many times. However, a bass part copied for Leveridge (GB-Ob Tenbury MS 1278) contains only solo parts for the High Priest and Hymen, not the Conjurer, suggesting he may not have sung it in the initial production. The 1695 songbook (apparently printed without consulting Purcell) contains the music for songs performed by Freeman (several), Bowen, Cross, and Church but only the lyrics for the bass solos.

For the summer season, the only new play known is the tragedy *Pyrrhus, King of Epirus*, by Congreve's protégé Charles Hopkins. As the premiere date for *The Indian Queen* remains uncertain, it is possible that *Pyrrhus* was in direct competition with the dramatick opera. In *Pyrrhus* audiences would find a new tragedy which, while lacking the elaborate sets, machinery, and variety of musical numbers in *The Indian Queen*, featured the company's most powerful veteran actors and its professional singers.

Two musical numbers by Eccles were part of *Pyrrhus* and appear in the text.[43] The first is a martial showstopper of a duet, "Hark the big drums, how they beat to battle," in which Eccles makes full use of the conventional military instruments, including an attention-grabbing eight measure prelude for the kettledrums alone. The vocalists were probably Pate and Reading, as in the duet from *Love for Love*.

Within the play, this duet follows a speech by Pyrrhus exhorting his soldiers to vengeance for his fallen son. The first two quatrains of poetry describe the battle (shouts, clashing armor, and so on) and the last two its aftermath. Eccles reflects this division in theme by setting the first two verses in D major, with an opening symphony and recurring instrumental passages with trumpets and drums. He combines these with exuberant vocal melismas on the resounding vowels of "loud," "shout," and "raging." The second section is in the parallel minor key, with the warlike instruments replaced by violins, evoking a more restrained and somber mood, appropriate to the third quatrain: "Hundreds fall, and Thousands yield … Fate Triumphant through the Field … bestrides the Slain" (5). Eccles's text setting is essentially syllabic, the texture sparse. There is no final flourish of instruments, nothing except repetition indicates an ending.

A fourth verse printed in the play text returns to a martial and triumphant state of mind, ending "Death quickly ends the vanquish'd Wretches,/ And Laurel crowns the Conquerors." However Pyrrhus's string of victories is about to come to an end, and this may account for the absence of the final verse. It is fate that triumphs, not man, after all.[44] This is just one instance in which a musical setting reshapes the printed lyric, with dramatic implications.

The contrasting lament sung by Mary Hodgson in the fifth act, "Stretched in a dark and dismal grove," seems inserted to cover a scene change.[45] The lyric laments the irreconcilable demands of love and honor, and the final section of Eccles's E minor setting (Figure 3.1) employs a striking ground bass in arpeggiated triads built over a descending tetrachord, the 'lament bass' of Italian music famously

---

[43] D&M 1754, indexed under *Pyrrhus, King of Epirus* is actually a song Durfey wrote using a tune from *Pyrrhus*. Durfey's contrafacta are legion.

[44] The overall quality of GB-Lbl Add. MS 29378 makes it unlikely that the musical setting here is simply incomplete.

[45] See Charles Hopkins, *Pyrrhus King of Epirus* (London, 1695), p. 42. This practice may have occurred more frequently than is recorded. For additional examples, see Price, *Music in the Restoration Theatre*, pp. 14–15. For more on Eccles's musical settings in *Pyrrhus*, including transcriptions, see *Music Productions LIF*, pp. 141–53.

Figure 3.1   J. Eccles, "Stretch'd in a dark and dismal grove" in *Pyrrhus, King of Epirus*. From *Deliciae Musicae* vol. 1 book 3, pp. 8–9

Figure 3.1   Concluded

anglicized in Henry Purcell's *Dido and Aeneas*.[46] Although no one is onstage while the song is sung and it seems separate from the dramatic action, it gives more weight to the queen's point of view, preparing the way for a soliloquy in which she vows to die in battle with her husband.

Another late summer production, possibly an afterpiece to Hopkins's work or performances of a stock play, was Eccles's setting of Pierre Motteux's ode "The Taking of Namur," for soloists and chorus. On 31 August the Lord Justices issued a public proclamation ordering a Thanksgiving "for the successe in taking the town and castle of Namur, to be observed .... here in London."[47] Motteux's poem is predictably fulsome in praising William III's prowess.[48]

Spring 1695: Revivals

There was no official division of existing plays between the two companies, as had been done during Charles II's reign. Any existing play was fair game, and the practice of mounting competitive productions in imitation of the rival house appears from the beginning.[49]

Both companies had a few weeks to plan their 1695 spring season, and presumably the actor-managers at Lincoln's Inn Fields revived works in which they had been successful.[50] Most Patent Company actors had few past roles to draw on. Judith Milhous's list of possible productions includes three Shakespearean dramas mentioned by Colley Cibber in his *Apology* (*Hamlet*, *Julius Caesar*, *Othello*), and the Shakespeare–Shadwell *Tempest*. A song for Letitia Cross by Henry Purcell, "Dear pretty youth," suggests its revival this spring or the following fall.[51] Congreve's earlier comedy *The Old Batchelor* was performed by Patent Company actors imitating the actors at Lincoln's Inn Fields, and from the evidence of an early songsheet, the company may have staged Dryden's *The Conquest of Granada* to compete with a rival production at the other house.[52]

Aphra Behn's *Abdelazer; or, The Moor's Revenge* is the sole revival confirmed at Drury Lane. Musical evidence consists of a set of act tunes and the rondeau "Lucinda is bewitching fair" by Henry Purcell, sung by 'the boy' Jemmy Bowen, and printed in the fourth book of *Thesaurus Musicus*, which also featured songs

---

[46] In Dido's aria "When I am laid in earth."

[47] Luttrell, *State Affairs,* vol. 3, pp. 518–19.

[48] Eccles's music has not been found. Musical celebrations of a later diplomatic victory, the 1697 Peace of Ryswick, are discussed in Chapter Four.

[49] See Milhous, *Thomas Betterton*, p. 71.

[50] Milhous suggests revivals of Dryden's *Troilus and Cressida* and *Tyrannick Love*, and possibly *The Conquest of Granada* during the spring of 1695. *Thomas Betterton*, p. 100.

[51] D&M 821. Also found as a Thomas Cross songsheet.

[52] The song, a musical dialogue, is discussed further with the production of *Oroonoko*, following.

from *Love for Love*.⁵³ Printed songs in datable anthologies are essential evidence of revivals, but the evidence from instrumental music is less conclusive until later seasons, when John Walsh began publishing sets of act music.

Comic Turns and All Manner of Shows: The 1695–96 Season

New Productions

Lincoln's Inn Fields opened brilliantly, yet both houses struggled during their first full season of competition. While the Patent Company attempted more new productions (shown in Table 3.3), among them only *Oroonoko* and *Love's Last Shift* were major successes.

Table 3.3 New productions during the 1695–96 season

	New works by the Patent Company		New works at Lincoln's Inn Fields	
AUTUMN	*The Mock Marriage*	Comedy	*She Ventures and He Wins*	Comedy
	Bonduca	Tragedy		
	The Rival Sisters	Tragedy		
	Don Quixote, Part III	Comedy		
	Oroonoko	Tragedy		
WINTER			*The Lover's Luck*	Comedy
			Cyrus the Great	Tragedy
	Agnes de Castro	Tragedy	*The She-Gallants*	Comedy
	Love's Last Shift	Comedy		

---

⁵³ This songbook reflects the interrupted 1694–95 season, having relatively few songs from theatrical productions (more are from concert venues, or list no venue), when compared with the third book—virtually all theater songs.

	New works by the Patent Company		**New works at Lincoln's Inn Fields**	
WINTER/ SPRING	*The Younger Brother*	Comedy		
	Philaster	Tragi-comedy		
SPRING	*Neglected Virtue*	Tragedy	*The City Bride*	Comedy
	The Lost Lover	Comedy		
	Pausanias	Tragedy	*The Husband His Own Cuckold*	Comedy
			The Country-Wake	Comedy
			The Royal Mischief	Tragedy
SUMMER	*Ibrahim, The Thirteenth Emperor of the Turks*	Tragedy		
	The Cornish Comedy	Comedy	*Love's a Jest*	Comedy
	The Unhappy Kindness	Tragedy		
	The Spanish Wives	Comedy		

At Lincoln's Inn Fields, following the presumed premiere of *Pyrrhus* in August, pride of place was given to a new comedy, *She Ventures and He Wins*. Written by "Ariadne," it had the backing of leading actress Elizabeth Barry. John Eccles, their top composer, wrote all the songs, and Anne Bracegirdle took the lead as the independent Charlot, who spends much of the play disguised as a man. Despite their combined efforts, the comedy was not a success.

Like most of the comedies staged this season, it included a number of musical events, including several songs (discussed in Chapter One). As in *Love for Love*, although featured, Bracegirdle does not sing in character. Instead, her heroine Charlot is directly or indirectly responsible for most of the music heard, including an Act I serenade, a witty dialogue about love, and a vocally elaborate duet invoking Hymen's blessing on the inevitable marriages.

The Patent Company also opened with a comedy by a new author, Thomas Scott's *The Mock Marriage; or, The Woman Wears the Breeches*, which was modestly successful. For the musical numbers, Scott had the assistance of Durfey and Motteux, who wrote lyrics for the solo songs in Acts II and IV, and a serenade scene with instrumental music and a song ("'Twas within a furlong of *Edinbrough* Town") in Act III.[54] All three songs are simple and comic, performed by "the musick" (Letitia Cross) or minor characters.[55] The setting of Durfey's "Scotch" song became very popular, and is one of relatively few "Scotch" songs from the period to employ the "Scotch snap" so frequently found in later music. This distinctive rhythmic gesture also appears in the act tune, which would have been played after Act IV. Henry Purcell probably composed all of the songs,[56] while Thomas Morgan provided the act music and perhaps other music as well.[57] Scott's comedy concludes with the cast plus an unspecified number of dancers, all in masquerade, a move which let the Patent Company employ its wealth of costumes— though it can't have helped audiences keep track of the convoluted plot.[58]

For the remainder of the autumn months, while Lincoln's Inn Fields presumably staged more revivals, the company at Drury Lane quickly brought out fresh tragedies and two musical works: George Powell's hasty rewrite of a stock play by Fletcher, *Bonduca; or, The British Worthy*, and the third part of Durfey's comic extravaganza, *Don Quixote*.

On its title page, *Bonduca* was advertised as "With a New Entertainment of MUSICK, Vocal and Instrumental/ Never Printed or Acted before." In the play text, the two major musical events are an Act III temple scene with priests and chorus "Hear us, Great Ruguith, hear our Prayers," followed by the martial duet and chorus "To Arms, to Arms: Your Ensigns strait display" (lead-in to "Britains, Strike Home"), and a solemn song for the doomed princess Bonvica (Letitia Cross) in Act V, before her death, both by Henry Purcell. Cross performed "Oh! Lead me to some peaceful Gloom" in character, accompanied by the appropriately "antique" lute.

Manuscript music for the temple scene includes far more of the dialogue than indicated, creating a grand musical structure. Many lines printed as spoken by Powell, playing the British general Caratach, were actually sung. The lines "Sing, sing ye Druids,/ All your Voices Raise ..." become a mesmerizing duet for two

---

[54] See D&M 2168, 2479, and 3500.

[55] The play text states that Mrs Knight (Lady Barter) sings "O How you Protest, and solemnly Lye," an error repeated in the first publication of the song, but dialogue indicates that Mrs Clark (as Lady Barter's maid) performs it.

[56] "Man is for the Woman Made" is definitely by Purcell, "'Twas within a furlong" probably by Purcell, and "O how you protest" was later attributed to him.

[57] The set of act tunes includes ten pieces rather than the usual nine (GB-Lbl Add. MS 35043, ff. 45v–46v). See Price, *Music in the Restoration Theatre*, pp. 201–2 for concordances.

[58] Although no clear cues are given, the dialogue implies dancing and hints about the costumes.

priestesses, echoed by the chorus. "Divine Andate! President of War ..." becomes a stirring recitative. Curtis Price has written admiringly of Purcell's counterpoint, harmonic language, and the "unity" of the score.[59] The music for such temple scenes often does not survive, but invocation scenes in other works, sometimes uninspired-looking on the page, probably received similarly expansive musical treatment.

From published songsheets we know that the duet "To Arms, to Arms: Your Ensigns strait display" was sung by tenor-countertenor John Freeman, known for 'trumpet songs' and martial music,[60] and by bass Thomas Edwards. The remaining vocal parts could easily be cast from the company. The catch "Jack, thou'rt a toper," sung by soldiers in Act II, provides a snatch of low comedy, a mix more often seen in Patent Company productions than at Lincoln's Inn Fields.

Robert Gould's tragedy *The Rival Sisters; or, The Violence of Love* contains many more separate musical events than *Bonduca*, with music in every act except the last, in which far too many murders and mad monologues are taking place. Two sisters (Catalina and Berinthia) love the same man, Antonio. He loves one sister, but their father has arranged for him to marry the other. Their brother becomes engaged to Antonio's sister, after Antonio influences her to reject her faithful suitor, Alonzo.

Henry Purcell composed all of the surviving solo songs and act music; the songs were published promptly in the contemporary anthology *Deliciae Musicae*.[61] In addition, John Blow made one of his rare contributions to the company with the musical dialogue "To me y'ave made a thousand vows," printed in his song collection *Amphion Anglicus*. Perhaps out of deference to his dedicatee, Princess Anne, Blow's setting makes extensive changes to the lyrics. Rather than a dialogue between a shepherd and shepherdess, it is "a Dialogue between a Man and his Wife" and "the naked Pleasure of the Bed" (17) becomes "the pleasures of the Nuptial Bed."[62] As Price noted, to the typical soprano–bass dialogue Blow adds a passage for two sopranos about the futility of wives' complaining.[63] The chorus, however, returns to the typical male–female format and urges resignation: "Time,

---

[59] Price, *Henry Purcell and the London Stage*, pp. 117–24.

[60] Baldwin and Wilson, "Purcell's Stage Singers," p. 116. Freeman would sing trumpet songs in several later PC productions.

[61] See D&M 511, 1416, and 3145. D&M 3430 (Blow's dialogue) was printed separately in *Amphion Anglicus*.

[62] Blow, *Amphion Anglicus* (London, 1700), p. 137. In the dedication, Blow insists "I will make no Apology ... thô [my songs] are generally conversant about Love-Affairs; since the divertisements and delights of those softer Affections, when conceiv'd in pure Thoughts, and cloathed with innocent Expressions, have been always allowed in all Wise and Good-natur'd Polite Nations."

[63] Price suggests the added singer represents Catalina, *Henry Purcell and the London Stage*, p. 77.

Reason, or Change, at last, will relieve."[64] Blow's setting is relentlessly regular in its meter (triple) and key center (F), but typically tuneful. Unfortunately there is no music for the "Antick by Forresters, with other Dancing" (17) which preceded the dialogue, all part of a pastoral entertainment ordered by Antonio's future brother-in-law, Sebastian, to entertain his friend and Antonio's prospective wife, Alphanta.

The solo songs occur in familiar contexts. As Catalina muses over her hopeless love for Antonio in Act I, she asks one of her women to sing "Not tho' I know he fondly lies/ Prest in my Rival's Arms" (8) about similarly single-minded devotion, concluding: "Did you the Shepherd see, / You'd either perish in the Flame,/ Or cease from warning me!" No musical setting appears to have survived. Other songs are performed as Alonzo, rejected by Alphanta (Letitia Cross), calls for music to soothe him (Act II), or to make her understand what she's done (Act III).

Both songs for Alonzo were sung by 'the Boy,' Jemmy Bowen. The first, the well-known "Celia has a thousand charms," belongs to the long-established seventeenth-century convention of the masculine "ventriloquized lament."[65] Quintessentially Purcellian, it juxtaposes a lavishly ornamented declamatory opening with a lilting second section.[66] The second song for the boy, describing a jilt, "Fair, and soft, and gay, and young,/ All Charm! She plaid, she danc'd, she sung!" (25, also a fair description of Miss Cross) was not set by Purcell, though an anonymous setting was published some time later under the heading "The Inconstant."

The song for the servants, "Take not a woman's anger ill," sung by old Gerardo to the maid Ansilva, was performed by Richard Leveridge, not the actor. Its casual misogyny mirrors Alonzo's wild statements. Another song for Letitia Cross, "How happy is she that early her Passion begins," blithely advocates "warming" before one's teens, yet Purcell's musical setting (relentlessly G minor) seems to question its message. It is hard to imagine its place within the play unless it was sung during Alphanta's final scene in Act V, amid the sudden switches in mood typical of mad rants and mad songs.

For all their lavish use of music, neither *The Rival Sisters* nor the Patent Company's next production was successful. In bringing the third part of Thomas Durfey's popular musical comedy *Don Quixote* to the stage at Dorset Garden, Rich's Patent Company was operating under insurmountable obstacles. Nearly all of the original performers (William Bowen, Anne Bracegirdle, John Bowman) had gone to the rival company, and Durfey had already used up most of the Spanish Knight's adventures that readily translated to the stage.

Curtis Price discusses all three parts of the trilogy, the first two in which Henry Purcell and John Eccles largely shared the song composition, and the

---

[64] Blow, *Amphion Anglicus*, p. 144.

[65] Winkler, *O Let Us Howle Some Heavy Note*, p. 138.

[66] For more on this song and its reputation among eighteenth-century music historians, see Price, *Henry Purcell and the London Stage,* pp. 75–6.

patchwork third part, which contained music by Purcell, Raphael Courteville, Thomas Morgan, and Samuel Akeroyde.[67] The most memorable elements of the third part were doubtless comedienne Susanna Verbruggen's portrayal of "Mary the Buxom," singing the bawdy ballad "The Old Wife she sent to the Miller her Daughter"; the onstage puppet show, "design'd to be Acted by Children," in Act IV; and the mad song "From rosy bowers" performed by Letitia Cross, "the last Song that Mr. Purcell Sett, it being in his Sickness."

Following an illness of some duration, Henry Purcell died on 21 November 1695 and was buried in Westminster Abbey, where he had served as organist. The service included the funeral music he had written the previous year for Queen Mary II. Purcell's reputation extended far beyond the theater world, but the dedicatory poems which prefaced the first book of his posthumous *Orpheus Britannicus* show how he was valued by major figures in it. The poems include a lamentation by Nahum Tate (set by Daniel Purcell), odes by Dryden (set by Blow) and a Cambridge fellow (set by Finger, and sung at York Buildings). During December, a pastoral ode mourning Purcell's death, "Come, Come Along for a Dance and a Song," set to music by Clarke, was performed at Drury Lane by four of the company's leading singers: Jemmy Bowen, Letitia Cross, John Freeman, and Richard Leveridge.[68]

The Patent Company had lost its most prolific and acclaimed composer. However, Purcell had written a few pieces for plays that premiered after his death, and collections of his theater music and songs were published during the following years. Many of his works continued to be revived, reprinted, and performed regularly, including his songs for *Oroonoko*.

Thomas Southerne's tragedy *Oroonoko*, set, like Aphra Behn's novel, in Surinam, combines a serious plot about a slave revolt led by African prince Oroonoko and the attempts of the governor to kill him and rape his wife, Imoinda, with a lighter plot about two sisters (one posing as male) who have come to find rich colonial husbands. A single musical scene appears in the text in the middle of Act III, when Oroonoko and the governor are with Blanford, virtuous owner of a plantation.

In previous scenes Oroonoko has described the loss of his wife, Imoinda, and we have seen the governor pressure the beautiful slave Clemene for sex. Imoinda and Clemene are, of course, the same person.

> *Blan.* The Men are all in love with fair *Clemene*
> As much as you are: and the Women hate her,
> From an instinct of natural jealousie.

---

[67] Price, *Henry Purcell and the London Stage*, pp. 207–22. A facsimile edition of the music for all three parts appeared in *Music for London Entertainment 1660–1800*, Series A vol. 2.

[68] In GB-Lbl Add. MS 30934. See Baldwin and Wilson, "Purcell's Stage Singers," p. 105.

>   They sing, and dance, and try their little tricks
>   To entertain her, and divert her sadness.
>   May be she is among 'em: shall we see? [*Exeunt.*
>   *The Scene drawn shews the Slaves, Men, Women, and Children upon the Ground, some rise and dance, others sing the following Songs.*
>   A SONG. [By an unknown hand.]
>   Sett by Mr. *Courtevill*, and sung by the Boy to *Miss Cross.*
>   I.
>   A Lass there lives upon the Green,
>   Cou'd I her Picture draw;
>   A brighter Nymph was never seen,
>   That looks, and reigns a little Queen,
>   And keeps the Swains in awe.
>   ...
>   A SONG, by Mr. *Cheek*.
>   Sett by Mr. *Courtevill*, and sung by Mr. *Leveridge*.
>   I.
>   Bright Cynthia's Pow'r divinely great,
>   What Heart is not obeying?
>   A thousand Cupids on her wait,
>   And in her Eyes are playing.
>   ...
>   *During the Entertainment,* The Governour, Blanford, Stanmore, Oroonoko, *enter as Spectators; that ended,* Captain, Driver, Jack Stanmore, *and several Planters enter with their Swords drawn.* [*A Bell rings.*[69]

A few things are worth noting. Blanchard, Oroonoko, and the governor are all spectators at an entertainment not meant for them, but the 'natural' expression of the male slaves' love and concern for Clemene.[70] The singers named are both men, matching Blanchard's statement that it is the male slaves who seek to cheer her. The entertainment is emphatically pastoral, rather than exotic. This musical interlude is quickly followed by an attempt by a band of Indians to seize the slaves. Fighting them off allows Oroonoko to display his heroic propensities before a tender recognition scene with Imoinda/Clemene.

Both songs survive, as does a full set of act music by James Paisible. The first, sung by Jemmy Bowen, bears a strong family resemblance to one he performed in *The Rival Sisters*. The second, "*Cynthia*'s Power divinely great," shows off Leveridge's range and flexibility. The other surviving vocal music for the play is a musical dialogue for Bowen and Cross, "Celemene, pray tell me," another faux-

---

[69] Southerne, *Oroonoko: A Tragedy* (London, 1696), pp. 27–30.
[70] Price's summation, "In an attempt to lift her [Clemene's] spirits, the governor orders some slaves to perform a proto-minstrel show" is not accurate. *Henry Purcell and the London Stage*, p. 79.

naïve boy–girl duet, set by Henry Purcell. Price suggests it was also sung in Act III and demonstrates the governor's crassness (as the Courteville songs do not). However there is another possibility.

In *The Cornish Comedy* a similar duet is printed before the play text as having been sung between the acts. This duet may have been used in the same way. The fact that it was also printed by Thomas Cross as "A Dialogue in the Second Part of the Conquest of Granada"[71] further suggests that it was an entr'acte entertainment, possibly performed with both Southerne and Dryden's plays. When Letitia Cross was not part of the cast, it was important to include her in the evening's entertainment.

The first-known new play at Lincoln's Inn Fields after the unsuccessful *She Ventures and He Wins* is a December effort, Thomas Dilke's comedy *The Lover's Luck*, which ran for eight nights. The play is a quick-paced froth of mistaken identities, with some digs at gentlemen of minimal talent who aspire to be poets. It contains a country bumpkin role tailored to Dogget and a witty heroine (Bracegirdle) who overcomes her guardians' schemes to marry her loyal lover, Colonel Bellair (Betterton).

Many of the songs for *The Lover's Luck* were published in contemporary anthologies and in Eccles's retrospective *Collection*.[72] Sadly, the pastoral entertainment for the final act,[73] a musical dialogue between Mary Hodgson and John Reading, "Come Thyrsis, come," and a dance by two shepherdesses, is lost, although the dialogue was valued enough to be revived at Queen Anne's birthday celebration in 1704.[74] While pastoral interludes were a well-established convention, this one was likely a competitive response to the audience-pleasing pastoral entertainments in the last three productions at Drury Lane.

John Bowman's role as Goosandelo parallels his earlier role of Mr Tattle in *Love for Love*. In Act II he performs one of his own works ("but the loose droppings of my pen").

> Rich Mines of Hot Love are rooted here,
> Flashes of Flames in my Eyes appear;
>   When swift as the Sun,
>   To the Arms of Thetis I run,

---

[71] See GB-Lbl K.7.i.2 (song 13).

[72] Goosandelo's song in Act II, "Rich Mines of Hot Love are rooted here," appeared in *Deliciae Musicae*, vol. 2 book 1 (London, 1696), D&M bibliography 149. "Full of the God I feel my raging Soul" and "Let us Revel and Roar," the songs in Acts III and IV, both appeared in *Thesaurus Musicus*, book 5 (London, 1696), D&M bibliography 154.

[73] Included in Timothy Neufeldt's discussion of contemporary "pastoral inserts" as an ironic juxtaposition of "natural, pastoral" love in the face of a male-dominated, property-obsessed society. Neufeldt, "Social and Political Aspects of the Pastoral Mode," pp. 36–9.

[74] For the evening's program, featuring performers from both houses, see M&H *London Stage*, pp. 145–6.

> To seize on my bliss,
> In the parts where it is:
> Oh! you know, you know, you know where.

Colonel Bellair gets a song of his own in Act III, "Full of the God I feel my raging Soul," set by Eccles and sung by an attendant, which unfortunately is not much of an improvement over Goosandelo's.

A very different sort of male music making is represented in the lusty two-part song "Let us Revel and Roar" in Act IV, which brings the exuberance of the drinking song into the "refined" musical atmosphere established earlier.

> Let us Revel and Roar, the whole World is our Store;
>   Nay the Gods shall club to our Pleasure,
> When we wallow all Night, in an unknown Delight
>   Aurora discovers the Treasure.
> Let us never repine, whilst brisk Wenches and Wine,
>   Make the Brims of our Lives run over,
> Leave the *How* and the *What* to the Politick Sot,
>   And the *When* to the Fool of a Lover.
> Thus free from all Cares of Taxes and Wars,
>   We know not the Name of *Dull Sorrow*;
> Ev'ry Purse is our Prey, which we spend in a Day,
>   And the Devil take Care for tomorrow.

Eccles has fun with the word "Roar" (Figure 3.2), which, when delivered by two full-powered basses (Reading and Curco) with sufficient swagger would make this musical moment a show-stopper.

The choreography for the final dance, executed by professional dancers rather than the actors portraying the happy lovers, may reflect Betterton's well-known inability to dance. No dance music is known, but the act tunes and overture, composed by Thomas Tollett, can be found in more than one source. One manuscript clearly labels the music by function: "first act tune," etc.[75] Such specificity is, unfortunately, not common.

Also in December, the Lincoln's Inn Fields company produced John Banks's *Cyrus the Great; or, The Tragedy of Love*, originally written and rejected over a decade earlier. Prompter John Downes includes *Cyrus the Great* as one of the "Principal new Plays" of the decade,[76] but it did not last long onstage.[77]

Much of the music for *Cyrus the Great* survives only in GB-Lbl Add. MS 29378, where it follows songs from *She Ventures and He Wins*. The first major musical event is a four-part musical dialogue for a band of Chaldean sorcerors (soprano,

---

[75] See GB-Lbl Add. MS 24889, ff. 10–11.
[76] Downes, *Roscius Anglicanus*, p. 92.
[77] Due at least in part to the death of an actor in a major role.

Figure 3.2 J. Eccles, "Let us revel and roar" in *The Lover's Luck*. From Eccles, *A Collection of Songs*, p. 160

alto/countertenor, and baritone), who have come to practice necromancy over the corpse-strewn battlefield in the first scene of Act I. The dialogue is followed by a dance of wizards and a four-part chorus accompanied by strings.[78] Their music is similar to the music Eccles wrote for the witches in *Macbeth* (following) and to the musical scene in the third act of Dryden and Lee's stock tragedy *Oedipus, King of Thebes*, revived at both theaters.

The witches' invocations are followed by another martial piece, "Hark the Trumpets and the Drums," which uses the same instrumental forces as *Pyrrhus*'s "Hark the big Drums, they beat to battle."[79] Again there is a complete change of mood in the second section, in D minor with only continuo accompanying the voice ("The Royal Captive now appears") urging pity for the captive princess Panthea. As in *Pyrrhus*, the play text does not agree with the musical setting, which lacks a triumphant chorus at the end.

The third musical scene in the tragedy is for Bracegirdle. As Princess Lausaria, she has revealed her unrequited love for Cyrus and it has driven "her Sence ... out of Tune" (42). She enters dressed as Cupid, with bow and arrows, and wounds Cyrus before being led away.

"Oh! Take him gently from the pile" begins with an ornamented recitative in D minor, imagining Cyrus's funeral pyre, followed by a brief spoken exchange with her father. It concludes with a rousing 6/4 air:

> I'm Arm'd and declare for a Vigorous War,
> By my Bow and my Quiver I swear,
> Not a Rebel to Love will I Spare, ...

This musical mad scene was probably added to the play in 1695 to capitalize on the popularity of Bracegirdle's mad songs, particularly her recent triumph, "I burn, I burn, my brain consumes to ashes" (also by Eccles), in *The Second Part of Don Quixote*. "Oh! take him gently from the pile," survives both in print (*Deliciae Musicae*) and in manuscript with the ensemble pieces. The other music indicated is a "Dead March" in Act V (57). Like trumpet fanfares, this was probably a stock piece rather than newly composed.

George Granville's *The She-Gallants* is the last new play known at Lincoln's Inn Fields in 1695. Downes remembers it as "Extraordinary Witty, and well Acted; but offending the Ears of some Ladies."[80] As in *She Ventures and He Wins*, Bracegirdle appeared in breeches, and Eccles composed all of the songs, including

---

[78] In the play text, the dance precedes the "Witches SONG," but the score indicates that the dance (no music provided) follows the musical dialogue and precedes the chorus. John Banks, *Cyrus the Great: or, the Tragedy of Love* (London, 1696), p. 5.

[79] The vocal line is written in treble clef, and the high continuo line (which would create crossings if sung by a tenor) suggests it was written for a soprano, probably Mrs Ayliff.

[80] Downes, *Roscius Anglicanus*, p. 94.

"While Phyllis does drink" and the suggestive "So well Corinna likes the Joy," sung by young Jemmy Laroche. Gottfried Finger wrote the lively overture and act tunes, which survive in several sources.[81]

For the final musical event in Granville's comedy, the lyric "While Phyllis does drink," sung in Act IV, Eccles composed a lively jig.[82] The combination of two of the most popular song topics (love and wine) and a rollicking tune ensured its popularity. Later published as "Whilst Phillis is Drinking," it survives in nearly as many copies as "A Soldier and a Sailor."[83]

"So well Corinna likes the joy" requires more vocal agility and employs more sophisticated musical effects (suspensions, seventh chords).

> So well *Corinna* likes the Joy,
>   She Vows, she'll never more be Coy.
> She Drinks Eternal Draughts of Pleasure,
>   Eternal Draughts do not suffice;
>   Ah! Give me, give me more, she Cryes,
>   'Tis all too little Measure.[84]

The printed song does not set the second stanza, but the quatrain could easily be fitted to the opening eight bars, ending with the singer insatiably repeating "'Ah! Give me more, …/ Tis all too little Measure."

Framed by two dances, "So well *Corinna* likes the joy" is the second part of an entertainment arranged by Angelica (Bracegirdle) in male disguise and performed before the aging coquette Lady Dorimen, her niece Lucinda (who has replaced Angelica in Bellamour's affections), and Philabel, Lucinda's lover.

In the middle of Act III, Angelica is busy insinuating herself into Lady Dorimen's household to prevent Lucinda and Bellamour's marriage. The song and dances are preceded by the dialogue "Delia, how long must I despair." As "Thirsis," Angelica, acknowledged author of the dialogue, questions Delia's fickleness. Delia explains that she "esteems" both Thirsis and Strephon but is "moved" by and will marry only his rival. This is remarkably similar to what Bellamour says in Act II when questioned by Angelica (in disguise) about his feelings for her.[85]

Around this time, Drury Lane tried to entice audiences with two additional serious plays. Unlike those mounted earlier, both were abstemious in their use of music. Veteran playwright Elkanah Settle's reworking of an old John Fletcher favorite, the tragicomedy *Philaster; or, Love Lies A Bleeding*, calls for no music

---

[81] See Price, *Music in the Restoration Theatre*, pp. 221–2.

[82] The song can be found in Eccles's 1704 *Collection* (74) and in *Deliciae Musicae*, vol. 2, book 1 (1696), p. 14.

[83] Similarly, it also became part of the broader musical culture, appearing (in slightly varied form) without attribution to author, play, or composer.

[84] George Granville, *The She-Gallants* (London, 1695), p. 41.

[85] Ibid., pp. 20–21.

within the printed play at all. Its initial performance date is uncertain; the prologue asks for the audience's indulgence as the young players develop.

Agnes de Castro was the first play by Catharine Trotter, taking advantage of 1695's doubled theatrical opportunities. In Trotter's tragedy, the heroine Agnes is threatened and finally overcome by the machinations of an engagingly wicked brother–sister pair, Alvaro and Elvira. The inconsistent king of Portugal is tyrannical at the beginning and philosophical in the end, after nearly everyone is dead. The only music is an unspecified song preceding the appearance of the ghost of murdered princess Constantia to her murderer, Elvira, in the middle of Act IV: "I've heard soft Musick charms a troubled Mind/ Luls [*sic*] Cares asleep, and calms the roughest Passions;/ Who waits there? Sing me some mournful Song. [*After a Song the Ghost of the Princess rises*."[86] Like Lady Macbeth, once the deed is done, Elvira's psyche begins disintegrating. She moves from self-justifying ploys to obsessed consideration of her appearance, then into an increasingly incoherent monologue.

Of the three new comedies staged at Lincoln's Inn Fields, only *The Lover's Luck* had a modest success. Drury Lane turned from new tragedies, among which only *Oroonoko* had prospered, to new comedies. Colley Cibber's *Love's Last Shift* proved nearly as great a success for them as *Love for Love* had been for their rivals.

Colley Cibber's *Love's Last Shift; or, The Fool in Fashion*, has been characterized as catering to audience tastes for both sex and sentiment. The musical events, discussed in more detail in Chapter One, occur in the last three acts. In Act III the 'fool' of the title, the fop Sir Novelty Fashion (Cibber himself), desires to have a trumpet sonata played in St James's Park (45). In Act IV, an unspecified song is sung as the virtuous Amanda, posing as a free-living lady, prepares to seduce her long-absent husband, Loveless (who believes her dead). Finally, in Act V, Amanda arranges for a masque of Fame, Love, Reason, Marriage, and Honor to be performed: "a little Musick, the Subject perhaps not improper to this Occasion!"(101).

As he did for many productions this season, James Paisible supplied instrumental music, though no trumpet sonata.[87] Daniel Purcell wrote a teasing, rakish song for Letitia Cross to sing, concluding: "Wou'd you Love the Nymph for ever,/ Never let her be your Wife."[88] Of the masque music, only the final duet for Fame (Jemmy Bowen) and Love/Cupid (Cross) was published in John Heptinstall's *Thesaurus*

---

[86] Catharine Trotter, *Agnes de Castro* (London, 1696), p. 34. Jean Marsden notes the relative absence of "sexual spectacle" (*Fatal Desire*, p. 117) and argues that the usual sensationalism appears only in scenes with the villainess Elvira. That Elvira is also the only character with a musical scene supports Marsden's argument.

[87] See Price, *Music in the Restoration Theatre*, p. 196, for sources and concordances.

[88] D&M 3668, "What ungratefull Devil moves you," text from Motteux's periodical *The Gentleman's Journal*.

Musicus,[89] the sole piece known to have been composed for either company by senior émigré composer Johann Wolfgang Franck.[90]

After *Love's Last Shift*'s surprisingly successful opening run, it became a stock play. It was succeeded onstage by two more comedies *The Younger Brother* and *The Lost Lover*, neither of which made as strong a showing.

Having scored a hit with Southerne's adaptation of Behn's novel *Oroonoko*, and revived her tragedy *Abdelazer*, the Patent Company tried Charles Gildon's reworking of Behn's posthumous comedy *The Younger Brother*. Gildon attributed its failure to factions raised against it, but the prologue demonstrates the usual competitive anxiety: "As Rivals ... both strive which shall gain the Lady's Love, / So we for your Affections daily Vie ..."[91] Musically speaking, the model for the comedy is more Durfey than Cibber—every act is interlaced with musical numbers. These include a dialogue for Cross in an Act III masquerade scene and a significant number of dances by actors in character (see Chapter One). Motteux, who contributed a song to the play, may also have been influential.

Delarivier Manley's first play, the comedy *The Lost Lover; or, The Jealous Husband*, is not as lavish in its use of music as Behn's, but the musical events are effectively integrated into the plot. Many are associated with Lady Young-Love, "an Old Vain Conceited Woman" who considers herself engaged to the rake Wilmore. The first song occurs in a scene between her daughter Marina and their family friend (her secret rival) Belira, who asks her page for "the last new Song," "Ah Dangerous Swain, tell me no more" (4), which transparently reveals the situation and Belira's feelings about Wilmore.

In the second act, Wilmore arranges for "Musick and Dancing after Supper" (11). The results are shown at the beginning of Act IV, when Lady Young-Love and all her guests enjoy the "Song and Entertainment of Dancing" (23) and Wilmore slips out with Marina. The only surviving song, Daniel Purcell's "If you Men like Turtles would not stray,/ then we might be as kind as they," sung by Cross, was probably performed here.[92] Afterwards, the fop Sir Amorous, fresh from his Continental tour, asks Lady Young-Love to dance a courante or minuet, but she puts him off, saying "if I share the Dance, I shall lose the entire prospect of your

---

[89] D&M 1141. Day and Murrie err in stating it was not printed in the play. Price repeats the error (*Music in the Restoration Theatre*, p. 196). Viator and Burling err in the opposite direction, stating that all the songs were printed in *Thesaurus Musicus* (*The Plays of Colley Cibber*, vol. 1, p. 37).

[90] Baldwin and Wilson speculate that Franck may have coached soprano Mrs Ayliff ("Purcell's Stage Singers," 114), but there is no evidence he composed anything for her to sing at LIF.

[91] Behn, *The Younger Brother; or, The Amorous Jilt. A Comedy* (London, 1696), unpaginated.

[92] Copy in GB-Ob Harding Mus. G. 332 (song 7), engraved by Thomas Cross. 'Turtles' are the dove rather than the reptilian sort. Cross also spoke the epilogue.

Person" (24) and insists Belira dance with him, preventing Belira from going to find Wilmore.

The final song is performed between the first and second scenes, "To Love and all its Sweets adieu," followed by the entrance of Sir Amorous, who despairs of convincing Lady Young-Love of his passion. Once she sees Wilmore with her daughter, Sir Amorous succeeds, and a final dance is implied by the dialogue. Belira is not married off, but swears she will have vengeance and tries (offstage) to stab her rival before decamping in a chair (alas, a chariot drawn by dragons was not a comic option).

In March, the actor Hildebrand Horden brought another tragedy to the stage by at Drury Lane. In *Neglected Virtue; or, The Unhappy Conqueror*, the anonymous author seems to have a collection of specific sets in mind as well as a great fund of dramatic clichés. In the middle of Act II there is a court celebration: "The King [of Parthia] sitting on a Throne; the Queen and Princess [Alinda] by him. On each side the Throne, *Memnon, Castillio, Lysander*, Singers in Warlike Habits, A Symphony of Warlike Musick, and then a Song./ After the Song, the King, &c. rises" (13); and in the middle of Act V, "The Drums beat a dead March; and Trumpets sound without" (42). Act music by James Paisible survives;[93] both the "warlike song" and the dead march could have used music from the company archives. Although there is no evidence Letitia Cross sang in the play, she both appears in breeches and pretends to be mad, two practices that usually went over well with (male) audiences.

The extant song by Daniel Purcell, "Olinda turne, turne, turne & though thy eys; should pierce me through ye heart,"[94] sung by 'the Boy' would make no sense as the warlike song in Act II. However, assuming "Olinda" is a misspelling of the name of the heroine, it could easily find a place in Act IV (30–3), when the lovesick King of Media watches Alinda in the palace gardens, and Alinda's father tries to bully her into accepting him.

More significant for future productions than the play itself is the epilogue Pierre Motteux wrote for comedian Jo Haynes, quoted in Chapter One. In it Haynes mockingly sings quotations from Anne Bracegirdle's signature mad song "I burn, I burn" (*Don Quixote* II, UC, 1694), alluding to the 'rebel' actors at Lincoln's Inn Fields and the vanity of (French-inspired) fashion.[95] Whether the impetus for quoting Anne Bracegirdle's song was initially Haynes's or Motteux's, improvised or scripted—parodic singing becomes a significant element in later Patent Company shows.

The tragedy *Pausanias, The Betrayer of His Country*, attributed to Richard Norton, is one of the hardest productions to date. Although its publication was not

---

[93] It includes the first and second music in B-flat major and an overture and three act tunes in D major. In GB-Lbl Add. MS 35043 these are followed by a short piece in C major, marked "Very Slow" and "Symph[ony]" which may have been used in Act II.

[94] GB-Lbl G. 304 (song 114).

[95] For an excerpt of Motteux's epilogue and further discussion, see Chapter One.

advertised until May 1696, it contains two vocal numbers by Henry Purcell, who had died in November 1695, plus a choral temple scene by Daniel Purcell.[96] Henry Purcell's music is heard in Act III, when the Persian courtesan Pandora, mistress of Sparta's regent, Pausanias, attempts to seduce or blackmail his handsome protégé Argilius, threatening to reveal Pausanias's traitorous negotiations with the Persian Empire. As Price noted, Henry Purcell's songs establish the eroticism of Pandora's interests. Presumably "Sweeter than Roses" was entrusted to Letitia Cross to sing, and she may have also taken the soprano part in the enticing duet "My dearest, my fairest" which follows.[97]

By Act V Pausanias's treachery has been uncovered and his iron-willed mother has thwarted his plans. Daniel Purcell's music for the scene in Neptune's temple is set in C minor throughout. The "Solemn Musick" Norton indicates begins with a "very slow" symphony, followed by alternating passages for the High Priest (a baritone, perhaps Leveridge) and chorus.[98] Curiously, the manuscript copy of Daniel Purcell's setting leaves out a quatrain Norton indicated as sung by the High Priest and a second priest, "Glory attend each filling Sail,/ May Sailors Courage never fail,/ Let the merry Victors go/ Destroy the treacherous Foe" (39). Instead, the High Priest alone sings "Encrease our Trafick, and our gain,/ On equal Terms, we never fear,/ We will be Masters every where./ And Triumph ore the Main" in a swinging triple meter, repeated by the chorus—these are maritime sentiments surely not meant to be limited to ancient Sparta. In the end, Pausanias stabs Argilius and his mother stabs Pandora. She then orders her traitorous son walled up alive in the temple.

Among the spring comedies at Lincoln's Inn Fields, *The Husband His Own Cuckold* was John Dryden Jr's attempt to emulate his famous father.[99] Musical evidence suggests it was performed early in the spring, as Dogget's name appears in a manuscript copy of a musical dialogue sung in character.[100] Dogget signed with the Patent Company in April, and, aside from *The Country-Wake*, he is not known to have appeared in any spring productions at Lincoln's Inn Fields. He is conspicuously absent from Motteux's *Love's a Jest* in June.

---

[96] Daniel later dedicated his collection of songs from *Brutus of Alba* to Norton, who had a private theater at his country home and invited leading London actors to perform there. Norton may have hosted John Oldmixon while he worked on *The Grove* (PC, 1700). An inventory taken after Norton's death included "A parcell of Musick & play Books." See R. Jordan, "Richard Norton and the Theatre at Southwick," *Theatre Notebook* 38 (1984): 105–15.

[97] See Price, *Henry Purcell and the London Stage*, pp. 81–4.

[98] In Ob MS Tenbury 1175, pp. 71–9.

[99] Congreve wrote the prologue, with flattering reference to Dryden Jr.'s illustrious father (though not going so far as to compare the two).

[100] *The London Stage* lists it as the first play at LIF in 1696. Milhous and Hume hypothesize a premiere early in June. See "Dating Play Premières from Publication Data, 1660–1700," *Harvard Library Bulletin* 25 (1974): 374–405 (pp. 399–400).

Compared with other comedies, Dryden's play is sparing in its use of music, having only two songs, a solo for Mrs Ayliff, "Help, help ye Pow'rs Divine," and a dialogue, "Why so Coy, and so Strange?" both set by Eccles.[101] In Act I the lovesick Lady Crossit asks her maid to call someone to perform her favorite song (its uninspired lyrics by Sir Robert Howard, the play's dedicatee).[102]

> Help, help ye Pow'rs Divine,
> For sure from you this Lightning came,
> That from his Eyes shot thorough mine,
> Down to my Heart a subtile flame.
>
> I try to get free, but always in vain,
> For as fast as I fly, I fly with my pain.
> There's nothing my Love and my Life can divide,
> For equally both to my Heart-strings are ty'd.[103]

The audience has just learned that Lady Crossit has fallen in love with the foppish Doctor Lorman. Her plan to spend an evening with him is discovered by her husband. Her husband's impersonation of the doctor—a slight variation on the traditional bed trick—forms one of the main strands of the plot. Lady Crossit loves the song, evocatively set by Eccles, since it implies that she is helpless before her own passion, excusing her doing what she likes.[104]

After a series of domestic intrigues between two married couples and the marriage of two new couples, everyone is onstage for the finale. The scheming rake Feewell enters costumed "like Hymen" and announces the arrival of the new couples, their advent preceded by "Soft Musick." After this mock-masque, four Gypsies enter and tell fortunes. The final event in this dramatic miscellany is a dialogue performed by Mr and Mrs Lurch (at odds throughout the play), a performance which another character observes "may be a means to make a thorough Reconciliation" (56).

The Lurches' dialogue, "Why so Coy, and so Strange?" survives in both manuscript and print. Sung by Bracegirdle and Dogget, it was doubtless inspired by the success of their dialogue in Durfey's *The Richmond Heiress* (UC, 1693). The final lines propose an open marriage:

---

[101] For sources, see *Music Productions LIF*, Appendix C, Catalog of Songs.

[102] Howard was author of *The Committee* and a contributor (with Dryden senior) to *The Indian Queen*. He supported the LIF company. The attribution is in Eccles's 1704 *Collection* (p. 82).

[103] John Dryden Jr., *The Husband His Own Cuckold* (London, 1696), p. 9.

[104] For more about this song and a transcription, see *Music Productions LIF*, pp. 56–60.

> *He.* What's past, we'll forget,
> *She.* What's to come, ne'er enquire,
> *Both.* But take surest Advice of present Desire.

Eccles's setting is simple and syllabic, and a petite reprise reiterates the final line, to make sure no one in the audience misses the point. This musical conclusion undercuts the mended fidelity of Lady Crossit and her husband and casts a sardonic shadow on the recent nuptials. In playing a musical role, Bracegirdle's wit is once again more evident than her chastity.[105]

The other musical event of interest in *The Husband His Own Cuckold*, a performance requested by the provincial squire Sir Timothy Shallow in Act IV, evokes earlier performance traditions. Describing country hospitality (including "a Barrel of special Ale"), Sir Timothy claims "all the while *John Slouch*, the best Piper in the North of *England*, plays to us; and afterwards every one trips off a Jigg cleverly away" (42). Shallow calls in his servant Johnny Thump, who asks if the musicians can play "John Stoaks his Jigg," presumably a venerable tune like Kemp's Jig,[106] recalling the Shakespearean clown Will Kemp and the jigs of his day, comic routines ('playlets') sung, danced, and acted, using ballad tunes.[107] The only other reference to someone performing a jig in works from this decade is in Mary Pix's farce *The Spanish Wives*, which premiered at Drury Lane that same summer.[108] The character performing it is disguised as a country man, and again there is the intriguing possibility that his dancing included other aspects of earlier jig performance.

Despite the Dryden reputation and the best performers, the play was not a success. In composing the instrumental music Finger could not resist making a musical joke, alluding to the main action of the play with a "Cuckoe" air. The act

---

[105] The cast list was not printed, so Elizabeth Howe does not include this play (in which Bracegirdle's character does not commit adultery but tries to) in her analysis of Bracegirdle's roles. Peter Holland discusses two earlier comedies by Durfey and Southerne in which Bracegirdle portrayed unchaste characters in *The Ornament of Action*, pp. 148–9 and 153–6.

[106] Also known as "Nutmegs and Ginger." See Ross W. Duffin, *Shakespeare's Songbook* (New York, 2004), pp. 277–8. Most jig tunes carried multiple names.

[107] While many named pieces ("Hayn's Jig," etc.) appear in Playford's *Dancing Master*, "John Stoakes" is not among them. If the name refers to the subject and not a performer, the piece may refer to colorful sea captain John Stoakes (c.1610–55) whose reputed adventures in the Mediterranean, Africa, and the West Indies could easily supply material for a short ballad farce.

[108] "Hidewell: If your Lordship pleases, being in this Dress, I will aim at a Jigg, I danc'd thus once in a Masquerade. [*A Jigg by Hidewell.*] Mary Pix, *The Spanish Wives. A Farce* (London, 1696), p. 19.

tunes seem to have been more popular than the play itself, surviving in several concordances.[109]

March 1696 saw the Lincoln's Inn Fields debut of *The City Bride; or, the Merry Cuckold* by actor Joseph Harris. The comedy, featuring John and Elizabeth Bowman, included a patchwork of music by various composers. The play opens with a wedding feast in the City, where the guests are treated to a variety of entertainments: instrumental music by Finger, a song by Eccles ("Many I've lik'd" sung by young Jemmy Laroche), and a dance. In Act III a "Dialogue set by Seignior Baptist" (Giovanni Baptista Draghi), probably sung by the professional singers, is called for to cheer the onstage company. The scene ends with a previously printed drinking song, "Here's a health to jolly Bacchus," performed by a bunch of visiting sailors around a punch bowl,[110] and a dance of the sailors and their wives, forming a nautical entertainment very similar to the end of the third act in *Love for Love*.

The fourth act closes with another dialogue, "Faith and Troth I love thee dearly,"[111] composed by Eccles. The usual love-debate is couched in nautical terms suitable to ship-master Compasse and his former and future wife (Anne Perrin), who sings that she will not "venture out to sea" with him until she's sure of good weather (36–7).[112]

Thomas Dogget's comedy *The Country-Wake* premiered in April, but unlike Cibber's, it was not a success.[113] In the bitter epistle dedicatory, Dogget snarls that it "suffer'd in the Acting. By the Industrious Care of whom, was so visible to the Audience, I shall spare any further Reflexion."[114] Since Barry spoke the prologue, Betterton the epilogue, and Eccles wrote the songs, Dogget could not claim his play was neglected. Six pieces of music survive, two songs (one a four-voice comic dialogue) and four dances, but placing them within the printed text is difficult, suggesting last-minute revisions and lack of coordination among the artists involved.[115]

In April or early May the Lincoln's Inn Fields company premiered Delarivier Manley's *The Royal Mischief*, full of the "plumes, trappings, and extravagance"

---

[109] Price, *Music in the Restoration Theatre*, pp. 179–80.

[110] The song, D&M 1357, first appeared in Playford's 1691 *Apollo's Banquet* (the final piece in the book).

[111] The musical dialogue is assigned to *The City Lady* (performed nine months later) in GB-Lbl Add. MS 29378 but belongs to *The City Bride*.

[112] The text suggests that Perrin sings the song with "Neighbour Luff" rather than her (ex-)husband (actor John Freeman). While the play includes a final chorus critical of "Priestly Knavery", Eccles does not appear to have set it.

[113] If, as Milhous suggests, the play was performed to keep Dogget at LIF, it proved equally unsuccessful. See Milhous, *Thomas Betterton*, pp. 84–5. Despite his popularity and devotion to his craft, Dogget was difficult.

[114] Dogget, *The Country-Wake: A Comedy* (London, 1696), unpaginated.

[115] For discussion of the musical numbers see *Music Productions LIF*, pp. 51–5.

that Dogget loathed.¹¹⁶ Manley had not been pleased with the Patent Company's treatment and removed her play after it began rehearsals. At Lincoln's Inn Fields, with a top cast, it ran for a respectable six nights, but of the music, only a song survives.¹¹⁷

Rather than musical evocations of battle or temple ritual, *The Royal Mischief* contains a song about longing for love, "Unguarded lies the wishing maid," and an ode to peace. The Act III song, set by Eccles, seems to exist merely to create a division between scenes. In Act IV "The sweets of peace succeed our toils of war," "Set by Mr. Finger, and sung by Mrs. Hudson,"¹¹⁸ Manley carefully describes the accompanying spectacle: "The curtain flies up to the sound of flutes and hautboys, and discovers the River Phasis, several little gilded boats, with music in them, a walk of trees the length of the house, lights fixed in crystal candlesticks to the branches, several persons in the walk, as in attention."¹¹⁹

In a competitive response to Manley's play, the Patent Company mounted Mary Pix's *Ibrahim, The Thirteenth Emperor of the Turks*, launching her career. Both Pix and Manley's tragedies are discussed by Jean Marsden as contrasting examples of she-tragedy, emphasizing (respectively) the spectacle of female suffering and the seductive representation of female desire.¹²⁰ Like Manley's play, Pix's has been noted for its vibrant villainess. Another interesting element is the casting of Susanna Verbruggen as chief of the Eunuchs. Western fascination with this 'exotic' surgical practice and its results was particularly linked to music, through the castrato singers of Italian courts, chapels, and opera.¹²¹

In Pix's play, the typical Act III music performed for the momentarily melancholy sultan includes both a soothing (ego-building) song, "Imperial Sultan, Hail" ("Prepared by the Italian Masters") and a dialogue by Durfey in which Jemmy Bowen plays "an Eunuch Boy" and Cross "a Virgin," who rebuffs the boy, telling him "Boast not thy Musick, for I fear/ That Singing Gift has cost thee dear" (17). Printed in Henry Playford's 1696 *Deliciæ Musicæ*, Daniel Purcell's

---

¹¹⁶ Cibber, *Apology*, ed. Lowe, vol. 1, p. 229.

¹¹⁷ Eccles's song "Unguarded lies the wishing maid" is D&M 3520. A songsheet exists in a bound volume (containing an equally rare songsheet from *She Ventures and He Wins*) in GB-Lgc.

¹¹⁸ Mary Hodgson also sang as an emissary of peace in Motteux's *Europe's Revels for the Peace of Ryswick* (LIF, 1697).

¹¹⁹ Price cites this passage in his subsection "Music for Discoveries," *Music in the Restoration Theatre*, p. 9.

¹²⁰ Marsden, *Fatal Desire*, pp. 107–10 and 120–6.

¹²¹ Castrato singers were not new to 1690s London. Richard Luckett describes castrati in the "Italian Musick" at Charles II's court in the 1660s. However, they do not seem to have appeared in public theaters until later. "Exotic but rational entertainments: the English dramatick operas," in Marie Axton and Raymond Williams, eds, *English Drama Forms and Development* (Cambridge, 1977), pp. 123–41 (p. 127). The famous castrato Siface visited James II's court in 1687.

setting establishes the couple's incompatibility with contrasting meters. The final chorus is only four measures long, befitting a pair who cannot be conventionally united. However incongruous a modern reader finds the comic dialogue, it further emphasizes the titillating distance between East and West. The following autumn, *The Female Wits* not only included recognizable caricatures of Pix and Manley, but emphasized a dialogue by Letitia Cross as an essential element in any Drury Lane production.

The songs from the next new production at Lincoln's Inn Fields, *Love's a Jest*, were specially featured in *Deliciæ Musicæ*.[122] Motteux's comedy premiered in June, just before the gentry's summer excursions to their estates, and used a country setting. Having written songs, odes, and epilogues for both companies, Motteux filled his comedy with musical numbers set by different composers. It contains three musical dialogues set by Eccles, including one featuring Bracegirdle and Bowman (discussed in Chapter One).

Downes comments that the play "succeeded well, being well Acted, and got the Company Reputation and Money."[123] In his preface Motteux defends himself against detractors at some length, but concludes by thanking Eccles for his dialogues and insisting "we need not fear Music shou'd decline, while we have so fine a Genius to support and raise it."[124] Motteux's allusion to the possible "decline" of music refers to Henry Purcell's recent death, one of the most significant musical changes during the first season of competition.

Drury Lane continued mounting new productions well into the summer months. Thomas Scott's second play for Drury Lane, the tragedy *The Unhappy Kindness; or, A Fruitless Revenge*, is another adaptation of a Fletcher play. The prologue speaks to the loss of audience in summer, but also confirms the important part music played in attracting them: "Where are those Friends, that did in numerous throngs/ Crowd to our Musick, and applaud our Songs?"[125]

Scott's printed text is cagy about exactly what was performed, and no surviving music is known. In the middle of Act II there is "A Warlike Shout within. The Scene draws and discovers a Royal Throne on which the King places himself, then Valerio enters in a Triumphal manner, being ushered in with a Song" (13). At the end of the act, "Scene draws and discovers the Court seated for the Masque, that ended the King speaks" (19). It is not clear when the scene shuts during the spoken dialogue which separates the two openings, or how much of the masque (perhaps from another production) is assumed to have been performed.

---

[122] The songs from *Love's a Jest* were puffed on the title page of *Deliciae Musicae*, vol. 2, book 2 (D&M Bibliography 150), in the same way the first book promised "Additional Musick to the *Indian Queen*, | by Mr. *Daniel Purcell*."

[123] Downes, *Roscius Anglicanus*, p. 93.

[124] Motteux, *Love's a Jest* (London, 1696), unpaginated.

[125] Thomas Scott, *The Unhappy Kindness; or, A Fruitless Revenge* (London, 1697), prologue, lines 3–4.

Perhaps in imitation of the country comedies at Lincoln's Inn Fields, Drury Lane also staged *The Cornish Comedy*. This anonymous play is interesting for what precedes it—a fulsome dedication to Christopher Rich by Powell—and its record of a performance practice that may have been more widely employed. It includes the text of a lengthy musical dialogue, "If *Cloris* please," attributed to Jo Haynes, who also spoke the prologue. Set by Jeremiah Clarke, who provided all the extant music for the play, we are told it was performed between Acts II and III and Acts III and IV, though only music for the second section, sung by Letitia Cross and Jemmy Bowen, appears to have survived.[126] What is most striking about it is its continuous storyline, which would require audiences to remember two sets of characters and incidents (the play's and the dialogue's) during the braided presentation.[127]

Within the play text, Leveridge sings Clarke's "When Maids live to Thirty, yet never repented" to the lovesick hero Manley at the very beginning of Act II, which probably explains why the musical dialogue occurs between the later acts. Manley is far from the rake that Leveridge's song, with its jaunty couplets about the impossibility of faithfulness, would suggest: "When all *Europe*'s at Peace, and all *England* contented, ... When an old Face shall please as well as a new;/ Wives, Husbands, and Lovers, will ever be true" (8), though Manley later pretends to have "debauched" his beloved so her father will permit their marriage. A blustering militia captain's entrance shortly thereafter is the excuse for "A Posture Dance in imitation of Soldiers Exercise" (11) and no more is heard about music until an unspecified song and dance are performed by 'the Musick' in Act V, celebrating the marriages of the various characters. It is not clear why this comedy and Pix's farce were both performed at Dorset Garden, when, unlike *Don Quixote* or *The Indian Queen*, there is no evidence that they required elaborate sets, scenery or machines.

Mary Pix's farce *The Spanish Wives* is a far cry from her earlier tragedy, but was another respectable success. Although the printed play is often vague about what was performed, Pix manages to fit a substantial amount of music into three acts. In addition to the musical numbers, the merry old Governor of Barcelona bursts into snatches of song at every opportunity. No cast list was printed, but it appears Susanna Verbruggen played the governor's sprightly lady, who "staggers but does not fall" and is reconciled with her husband.

The first music within the play is an entertainment arranged by the English colonel Peregrine, who has been serenading the governor's lady. The song Peregrine selects, "Alas! When Charming *Sylvia*'s gone" as set by Daniel Purcell and sung by Bowen (Figure 3.3), moves from cataloging the singer's reactions to Sylvia to

---

[126] See GB-Ob Mus.2.c.76 (song 1): "A Dialogue between Mr James Bowen & Mrs Cross in the Cornish Comedy Set to Musick by Mr Clarke and exactly engrav'd by Tho: Cross."

[127] Scholars of opera will recall Pergolesi's intermezzo *La Serva Padrona* (and works like it) which were used in a similar way.

162   Music and Musicians on the London Stage, 1695–1705

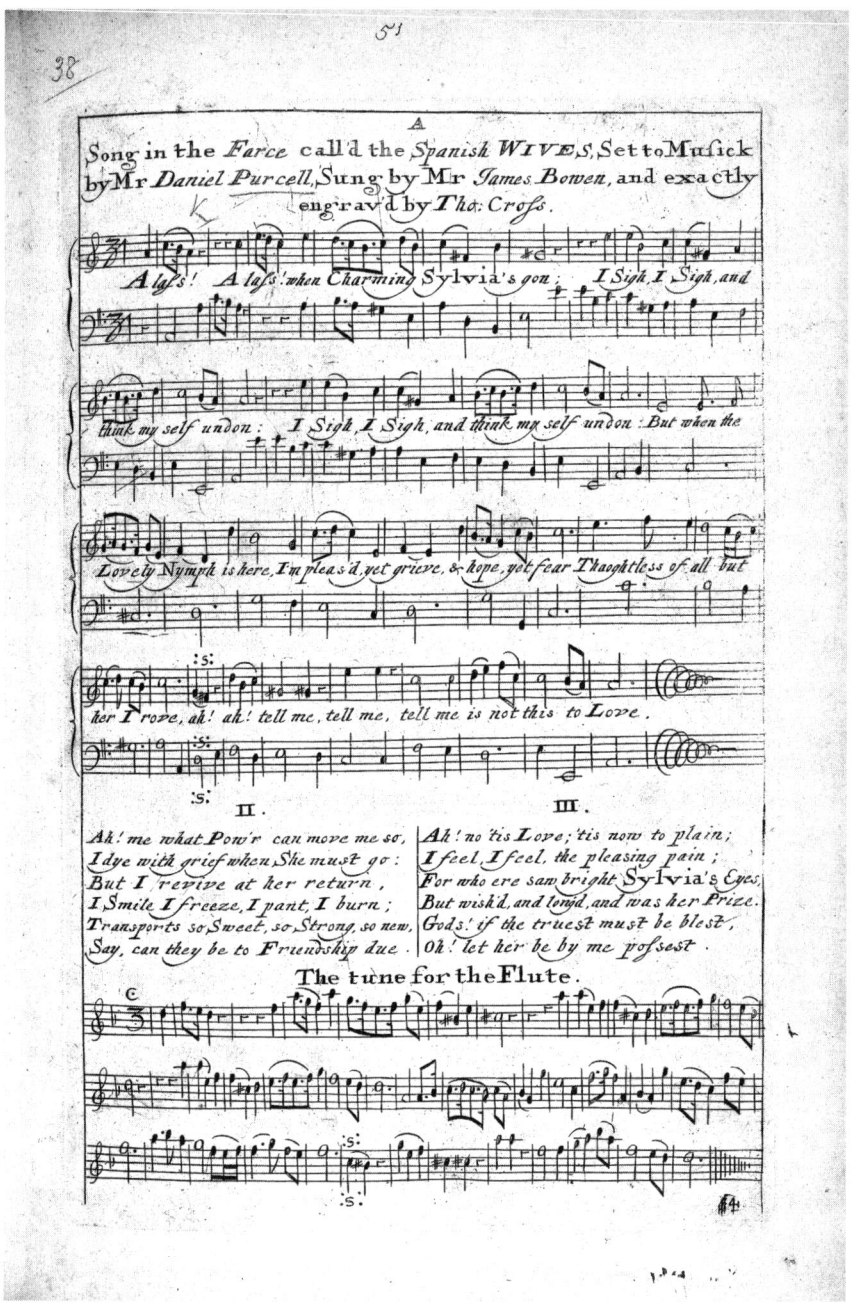

Figure 3.3   D. Purcell, "Alas! When charming Sylvia's gone" in *The Spanish Wives*

end with his hopes for future possession, with seductive slurs on "I sigh," "I dye," and "I feel." At the song's conclusion, the colonel and the governor's lady dance together. Afterwards the governor calls for more songs and dances, but despite the freedom he allows his wife, he makes sure he's the one sitting next to her.

The second act reveals the misery of Elenora, locked up by her stereotypically Spanish husband—the song she wants to hear begins "Be gone, be gone, thou Hagg despair" (13). Later in the act, Peregrine again provides musical entertainment, this time for Camillus, a Roman count who loves Elenora. This entertainment is a musical dialogue, "Fairest Nymph that ever bless'd our Shore," between Leveridge, representing a Spaniard, and Cross, an English lady (19–20). The Spaniard is forced to give up when he realizes that she must be allowed her 'English' freedom to go out alone and flirt with beaux. In addition to unspecified dances, there is also the "jigg" performed by the count's servant. While the earlier songs have implications for the dramatic action, in the final act Pix simply indicates celebratory "Songs and Dances" (48), easily changed for subsequent performances.

1695–96 Season: Revivals

After the closing of the Lincoln's Inn Fields theater in September, "the last new play Not taking," no performances are known prior to the premiere of Dilke's comedy *The Lover's Luck* in December. For economic reasons it is inconceivable that the company remained inactive for three months and it presumably mounted more revivals, perhaps challenging the Patent Company's Shakespeare productions with its own.[128] George Etherege's comedy *The Comical Revenge; or, Love in a Tub* was revived at one of the theaters in December, but the playgoer didn't bother to note which.[129] No musical evidence confirms the supposition that the Lincoln's Inn Fields company revived Dryden and Lee's *Oedipus, King of Thebes* in July 1696.[130]

There is musical evidence for other revivals around this time. A song set by William Williams and sung by Mary Hodgson suggests a revival of the comedy *The Generous Enemies*, recently reprinted.[131] A set of act tunes by John Lenton, who composed solely for Lincoln's Inn Fields during later seasons, is ascribed in GB-Lbl Add. 24889 to "The Moor of Venice" (*Othello, Moor of Venice*) and in GB-Lcm 1144 to "Venice preserv'd," Thomas Otway's 1682 tragedy, which was

---

[128] See Milhous, *Thomas Betterton* (pp. 100–101) and Cibber's *Apology*, "Shakespear was defac'd, and tortur'd in every signal Character ... at our first setting out, with what rude Confidence, those Habits, which Actors of real Merit had left behind them, were worn by giddy Pretenders that so vulgarly disgrac'd them!" (vol. 1, p. 202).

[129] *London Stage*, vol. 1, p. 466.

[130] Ibid., p. 463. Music by Henry Purcell for an earlier revival survives, but there is no evidence of new act tunes or song settings composed for LIF.

[131] D&M 3256, "Unjustly Phillis you accuse your slave," in the fifth book of *Thesaurus Musicus*.

reprinted in 1696. As both works were favorite vehicles for Betterton and Barry, the music suggests a revival of at least one of these plays during the 1695–96 season. Another set of tunes, and a line in the prologue to *Bonduca*, suggest a revival of Roger Boyle's *Mustapha, Son of Solyman the Magnificent*.[132]

At Drury Lane, either Sir Charles Sedley's *Anthony and Cleopatra* or John Dryden's *All for Love* was probably revived.[133] A compilation of instrumental music from the mid-1690s whose datable contents are roughly chronological suggests revivals of other stock plays: Durfey's *The Virtuous Wife*, John Lacy's *Monsieur Raggou; or, The Old Troop*, and Dryden's *The Spanish Fryar*, performances not otherwise confirmed. All three were probably mounted at Drury Lane, given the composers who wrote the music: Jeremiah Clarke, Thomas Morgan, and Robert King.[134] In addition, the Patent Company is known to have revived *The Indian Queen* in April, establishing its practice of premiering or reviving a dramatick opera in the spring, a pattern in future seasons.

Masques, Operas and Miscellanies: The 1696–97 Season

New Productions

Both companies emphasized comedies in 1696–97, most with extensive musical scenes. It appears the Patent Company was first to begin regular fall performances, opening with a comedy (Table 3.4). *The Female Wits* mocks the "lady poets," particularly Delarivier Manley, who had taken her tragedy away from Drury Lane the previous spring. The Patent Company also made the most of their musical and stage assets, producing three dramatick operas.

---

[132] In GB-Lbl Add. MS 24889, mentioned in my prologue (former property of the "musical small-coal man" Thomas Britton). The act music for "The Moor of Venice" attributed to Lenton is followed by a set for "Mustapha," another set by Tollett, and Tollett's music for *The Lover's Luck* (LIF December 1695), suggesting that this series of act tunes represents LIF revivals in 1695.

[133] *London Stage*, vol. 1, p. 450. Also see Price's introduction to the facsimile edition of GB-Lcm 1172, published in the series *Music for London Entertainment, 1660–1800*.

[134] See GB-Lbl Add. MS 35043, ff. 37–41v, where they follow a set of music for *Bonduca*.

Table 3.4 New productions during the 1696–97 season

	New works by the Patent Company		**New works at Lincoln's Inn Fields**	
AUTUMN	The Female Wits	Comedy		
	Brutus of Alba	Dramatick Opera		
	The Roman Bride's Revenge	Tragedy	The Anatomist + The Loves of Mars and Venus	Comedy, Masque
	The Relapse	Comedy		
WINTER	Aesop	Comedy	The City Lady	Comedy
	Cinthia and Endimion	Dramatick Opera		
	Woman's Wit	Comedy	The Unnatural Brother	Tragedy
	Timoleon [?]	Tragi-comedy		
	The Triumphs of Virtue	Tragi-comedy	The Mourning Bride	Tragedy
SPRING	Aesop, Part II	[afterpiece]		
			The Provok'd Wife	Comedy
	A Plot and No Plot	Comedy	Intrigues at Versailles	Comedy
	The Sham Lawyer	Comedy		
SUMMER	The World in the Moon	Dramatick Opera	The Novelty	Pastoral, Comedy, Masque, Tragedy & Farce
			The Innocent Mistress	Comedy

The second full season at Lincoln's Inn Fields seems to have been a scramble. Despite the modest successes of the previous season's serious plays, only two are known: William Congreve's *The Mourning Bride*, providing pathos onstage and profit at the box office, and Edward Filmer's unsuccessful *The Unnatural Brother*. Although several new comedies appeared, none matched the success of *Love for Love*. However, Motteux, one of its most industrious authors, prepared two unusual works, *The Novelty* and *The Loves of Mars and Venus*, combining disparate dramatic elements with plenty of music.

In addition to the reasonably full schedule of new productions shown above, several songs and sets of act tunes give production titles that cannot be connected with an existing play. Three of these musical 'lost' plays, all comic, are tentatively assigned to this season: *The Match at Bedlam* and *The Surpriz'd Lovers* at Lincoln's Inn Fields, and Thomas Durfey's *A Wife for Any Man* at Drury Lane. Eccles wrote the songs for the Lincoln's Inn Fields productions, engraved by Thomas Cross. Anne Perrin sang the racy "Amintor's warmth declines you say/ make use of him some other way" in *The Match at Bedlam* and John Bowman "When first I saw her charming Face" in *The Surpriz'd Lovers*. Durfey's *A Wife for Any Man* left its mark with two songs performed by Letitia Cross and a set of act tunes by Jeremiah Clarke.[135]

Drury Lane's autumn productions showcased every available musical asset. Like George Villiers's *The Rehearsal*, *The Female Wits* pretends to show life behind the scenes, as the Patent Company prepares the 'opera' of the poetess Marsilia (Delarivier Manley).[136] Her colleagues Mrs Wellfed (Mary Pix)—who followed Manley to Lincoln's Inn Fields this season—and Calista (Catharine Trotter) also attend.

Letitia Cross plays both a character in Marsilia's play and herself. When Mrs Wellfed asks to hear her "New Dialogue" while they wait for Marsilia, they call for Leveridge and the two sing (17). The dialogue is not specified, though "Fairest Nymph that ever bless'd our Shore" from *The Spanish Wives* (PC, August 1696) is a distinct possibility.

The next musical number is also by a performer, Jane Lucas, playing herself. Although there is no record of the "Scotch" song "By Moonlight on the Green" being printed before c.1700, it was Lucas's signature song. Part of its refrain (italicized below) is misquoted by the fatuous Praiseall (Cibber) when he suggests summoning her:

---

[135] The songs for Cross are D&M 831 and 2449. Although the second was not published until 1699 there is a consensus that the play premiered earlier and revived in 1699. The act tunes by Clarke are in GB-Lbl Add. MS 35043, ff. 71–2. For concordances see Price, *Music in the Restoration Theatre*, p. 233.

[136] Marsilia notes that operas typically "take care of the Songish part" and neglect the play. To be different, she has done the reverse. *The Female Wits* (London, 1704), p. 29.

> Oh how she trypt it,
> Skipt it, leapt it, Whist it, friskt it,
> Whirld it, twirled it, Swimming, Springing, Starting;
> So quick the tune to Nick,
> *With a heave, and a toss, and a Jerk at Parting.*[137]

Doubtless performed with a wink, the song describes a pretty lass who dances so energetically she wears her would-be suitor out. When Praiseall calls, Lucas enters and obliges with her most recent dance. Additional dances from the 'opera' occur in the second and third acts, one by Letitia Cross (38), a grotesque dance by women, "because it should differ from t'other House" as Marsilia explains (46–7), and a dance upon all fours for "the emperor's wedding day" (64), during which the dancers revolt, and stand up. There is a final dance, "practising for the next new Play" before George Powell joins the remaining gentleman-observer for dinner.

The other musical events are an "Italian Song" performed by Pate (46), and an unspecified song (64). Pate's piece, which Marsilia claims as "my own," completely melts Lord Whiffle (another hanger-on), as Italian music is wont to do.[138] The final "Song" may be William Corbett's "The Eagle ev'ry night Prometheus spares," also sung by Cross, as the songsheet states it was performed in *The Female Wits*.[139]

Numerous scenes make fun of Manley's melodramatic plotting and language. One passage is particularly apt in mocking the improbabilities of opera.[140]

> *Fastin.*   They fly! they fly! sound Trumpets, Sound! Let *Clemene*'s Musick joyn[.] confine my Father to yon distant Tower: I'll not see him 'till I have punish'd the Adultress: Set wide the Gates, and let *Clemenes* know she's Mistress here.
> *Lady Loveall* [his mother-in-law, also Clemene]   Where is he; Let me fly and bind his Wounds up with my Hair, lull him upon my own Bosom, and sing him into softest ease.
>   To Feat, and Revels dedicate the Day.
>   Let the old Misers stores be all expos'd and made the Soldiers Prey!
> D'ye hear, let the Butler dye, least he tell Tales.[141]

---

[137] "A Scotch SONG Sung by *Mrs. Lucas* at the Theater," GB-Lbl G.151 (song 20). D&M 449, Hunter 5 (21). Lucas and Cibber do not appear to have played a similarly friendly scene together after the events of summer 1697 (see note 9, this chapter).

[138] Pate visited Italy in 1697–98. The song might have been acquired on an earlier, undocumented trip or through working with an Italian musician in England.

[139] See Hunter 5 (355).

[140] There are also the well-known references in the text to Dryden and Purcell's *King Arthur*, "the Songish Part" and "the Pudding and Dumpling Song" ("Your Hay it is Mow'd"). See Price, *Henry Purcell and the London Stage*, pp. 314–15.

[141] *The Female Wits*, p. 53.

The actual opera performed subsequently, *Brutus of Alba*, brought to the stage by Powell and Verbruggen, is very nearly as ridiculous as Marsilia's. It reads like a compendium of types of musical scenes, dance routines, and spectacular sets, slapped together to cover the widest range of tastes.

Despite its inconsistencies as a text,[142] *Brutus of Alba* provides plenty of evidence of the "exuberant display" of scenic magic and special effects that Milhous has argued are essential to the Dorset Garden dramatick operas, from the 1670s to the more recent *Dioclesian*, *The Fairy Queen*, and *King Arthur*.[143] Indeed, *Brutus of Alba* is infamous for recycling specific scenes and effects from earlier shows, such as the prospect of the Thames and Juno's chariot of peacocks from *Albion and Albanius*.[144] Even the prologue printed with it was borrowed from an earlier production, as Pierre Danchin notes.[145]

In *Brutus* the "airy spirits" Angello and Seraphino work with the gods and allegorical characters (Augusta, Thamesis) to promote Brutus, his son Locrinus, and Albion while opposing the wiles of Arsaracus, who wants the crown and Locrinus's intended bride. Arsaracus is aided by the diabolical magician Coreb, who can call on the devil and Pluto. Most of the dances are Coreb's, and thus diabolical, either furies frolicking in hell (8) or the entertainments he summons to amuse his two bumpkinish recruits, with windmills, witches, Harlequins, and Scaramouches.[146]

While the dance sequences are at least clearly laid out, fully half of the songs printed in Daniel Purcell's *The Single Songs, With the Dialogue, Sung in the New Opera, Call'd Brutus of Alba* (London, 1697) do not appear in the printed text. This is far more of a discrepancy than that in Powell's earlier adaptation, *Bonduca*. Of the three dialogues printed in the text, only the most generic, "Why dost thou fly me, pretty Maid?" between an old man (Edwards) and a girl (Cross) had its music published. The "Dialogue between a *Triton* and a *Nayad*" in which the male singer is "Charm'd with those green Tresses, bright Scales, and blue Eyes" (17) and the dialogue for Cupid, Vulcan, Mars, and Venus, "The God of Love, with all his Train/ Shall wait great *Albion* o'er the Main" (42–3), are missing.

The published songs not in the text are equally generic. Two rakish ones were written by Jo Haynes, "I Courted and Writte shew'd my Love and my Witt," sung by tenor John Church, and "How happy am I the fair Sex can defy," sung

---

[142] For example, on page 13 Amarante and Arsaracus suddenly become "Joanna" and "Richard."

[143] Milhous, "The Multimedia Spectacular on the Restoration Stage."

[144] Several of the special effects and scenic transformations are discussed by Burden in "Aspects of Purcell's Operas."

[145] Pierre Danchin, ed., *The Prologues and Epilogues of the Restoration, 1660–1700*, Part III vol. 6, 324.

[146] *Brutus of Alba; or, Augusta's Triumph* (London, 1697), pp. 22, 31. Burden comments on the connection between these dances and magic in "Aspects of Purcell's Operas," pp. 22–3.

by Leveridge. The others also focus on inconstancy, like Letitia Cross's "Cease *Cynthia*, cease your fruitless tears."[147] Only two songs in the collection are from the opera's serious mythological masques: "Great [Bright] Queen of *Hymen*'s hallowed fires" (Elizabeth Willis) and "If Mortals laugh and sing, 'tis time we Gods take wing" (John Freeman), both in Act III.[148]

Looking at the work structurally, it becomes apparent that in Acts I, III, and IV there is a 'good' entertainment, usually a masque, opposed to an infernal one arranged by Coreb. In Act V, Albion has triumphed and it's all good. However, in Act II, which is slightly shorter than the others, Coreb produces an atypically beneficent, mythological, and aquatic transformation to soothe Arsaracus, with a fountain, dancing statues, and triton-naiad dialogue (16–17). It is the only musical sequence in the act. The crux of the spoken dialogue has to do with Amarante and Locrinus's constancy towards each other—Coreb's magic will be used in the following act to make the princess appear faithless.

Might the miscellaneous songs Daniel Purcell prints, and the out-of-place ones in Act V have been part of an entertainment of inconstancy in Act II? This could be performed either for Arsaracus or for Locrinus, to influence his thinking and make him more susceptible to suspicion. With only fragments to work from, this must remain a tentative hypothesis, but the production cannot have been as random as the surviving printed evidence makes it seem. The different typeface and complete lack of connection between the dialogue for Cross and Edwards and Freeman's "'Tis vain you tell me I am deceiv'd" in relation to the masque of Fame and the deities which concludes the fifth act suggests that these were written on loose sheets which simply happened to be at the end when the whole mess was given to the printer. Barring the discovery of a score for the opera, it is virtually impossible to ascertain what was heard when.

Drury Lane also had a new tragedy, Charles Gildon's *The Roman Bride's Revenge*. The opening scene, "A Grove, at the end of it, a Magnificent Temple: Solemn Musick is heard at a Distance" (1), leads to a sacred procession of priests and augurs with an ensemble of "Heautboys, Flutes, and Trumpets" (4) and, when the scene opens, into the temple. There a choral invocation is sung as the valiant general Martian and his beloved Portia begin their nuptial rites with fire and water. The rites are interrupted by Emperor Galienus, who wants Portia for himself. Naturally, his empress and Martian are furious, and various intrigues unfold.

At the beginning of Act IV, Portia, thinking she's about to escape from court, is seated at her window and forced instead to hear a serenade. Richard Leveridge's song, "If Caelia you had Youth at Will,"[149] urges the listener to take advantage

---

[147] See D&M 488, 1206, 1409, 1508, 1694, 1986, 3402, 3921, 3928.

[148] Although the title line for the first song is correct that Mrs Willis sings her piece in Act III, Freeman's song is also in the third act, not the fifth. Freeman's other song, "'Tis vain you tell me I am deceiv'd," did appear in the fifth act.

[149] Olive Baldwin and Thelma Wilson believe this to be the first song Leveridge composed for the theater. *Richard Leveridge: The Complete Songs (with the music in*

of her current opportunities, in terms reminiscent of Robert Herrick's "Gather ye rosebuds" (even to some of the rhymes). As a *carpe diem* ditty, Leveridge's setting is pleasant, but the song is grotesquely insulting for an imprisoned woman trying to fend off an imperial rapist. Escape plans foiled, Portia decides on "divine revenge," enacted in Act V.

In the final scene the emperor calls for triumphant music for his wedding, but there is no indication that music actually sounds (silence would be ominous, but so would be the right music). Portia spikes the sacred bowl with poison, both drink and die after extended mad rants, Martian stabs himself, and Portia's brother takes over Rome. The combination of a 'light' song or dialogue in one scene with solemn ceremonial music in another is a common pattern in contemporary tragedies, though critics often objected.

In November 1696, the Lincoln's Inn Fields company staged one of the most interesting musical works from this period; Ravenscroft's farce *The Anatomist* presented in alternation with Motteux's masque or "Play Set to MUSIC," *The Loves of Mars and Venus*.[150] Motteux's libretto for the masque, which was set by Eccles and Finger, includes comic dialogues for Mars, Venus, Cupid, and Vulcan which cast the dialogue for the same deities at the end of *Brutus of Alba* in the shade. *Mars and Venus* was so successful that the collapse of the Patent Company was briefly rumored.[151]

The cast list offers an unusually full view of the vocal resources available at Lincoln's Inn Fields in 1696. Anne Bracegirdle appears as a coquettishly seductive goddess of love.[152] Bass John Reading is cast as the gruff Vulcan, in opposition to the light baritone (and pleasing figure) of John Bowman as Mars. The cast list also assigns multiple roles to Mrs Ayliff, Mary Hodgson, and Anne Perrin as Muses and Graces. After the part of Gallus, "Mars's pimp," played by Mr Lee, is printed "design'd for Mr. Dogget," not something any other actor wants written after his part. A line in the epilogue refers both to Dogget and to William III's attempts to unite the rest of Europe in opposition to Louis XIV: "our League its neighbouring Foes defies;/ Tho they brib'd lately one of our Allies." For more on this important production, see Chapter One.

Macbeth*)* (London, 1997), p. xiii. No sources for the instrumental music are known.

[150] Scholars have found various ways of referring to Motteux's music-laden short dramatic works. Motteux himself, aware of the genre tangle, generally is quite "modern" (eighteenth-century) in his use of the term masque for self-contained narratives featuring classical characters and a clear plot, set to music throughout.

[151] The pertinent passage from a letter appears in *The London Stage*, vol. 1, p. 470, and listed in *Theatrical Documents*, no. 1545.

[152] In her Appendix I to *The First English Actresses*, "Major actresses and their roles in new plays," Elizabeth Howe characterizes Venus in *The Loves of Mars and Venus* (and Congreve's *Judgment of Paris*) as "a young girl" (p. 182), which "signifies a virginal and virtuous young heroine" (p. 178). Motteux's Venus is neither virginal nor virtuous.

Vanbrugh's fall comedy *The Relapse; or, Virtue in Danger* is linked to Cibber's *Love's Last Shift* not only by plot and characters, but in its overall design and inclusion of music, limited to a single Act IV song and a masque at the end (this time there is no trumpet sonata for Sir Novelty). *The Relapse* is also of interest for its printed wordbook,[153] which provides texts for the song and the masque of Hymen and Cupid, and demonstrates that such audience guides were created for productions besides dramatick operas.

The song in *The Relapse*, "I Smile at Love, and all its Arts," occurs in a scene between Amanda, the faithful wife Loveless is once again straying from, and her widowed cousin Berinthia, the direction in which he's straying. This is a typical dramatic setting for a song about love, but aside from a generalized warning about the pains love can cause, it is neither requested nor commented on by the characters, as Berinthia proceeds to tease Amanda about the interest she's evoked in another man.

The concluding masque, like the play, suits Vanbrugh's darker themes. Instead of Fame, Honour, and Love, as in Cibber's play, Vanbrugh's masque is a debate between Cupid and Hymen, as the chorus calls "For change, W'are for change, to what ever it be" (103). Vanbrugh's god of marriage not only admits that marriage doesn't make people chaste, but suggests it is easier to tempt married women. No one in the cast save Sir Tunbelly Clumsy, who organized it, makes any comment and Sir Tunbelly simply calls it "fine." Since he is about to storm out, having been tricked in the marriage of his daughter, this is not a ringing endorsement.

A song set by Leveridge, "When Lovesick Mars ye God of War," may have been substituted for the Act IV song or sung between the acts. Since the performer was Elizabeth Willis, who left the Patent Company by autumn 1697, it was presumably performed during this season.[154] Two songs by Jeremiah Clarke also exist. The first, "Was it a Dream or did I hear the Goddess at whose feet I lye," was performed by Mary Lindsey and appears, like Leveridge's song, to date from the initial run.[155] The second, "Long has Pastora rul'd the Plain," sung by Mary Anne Campion, was probably written later. The published act tunes by Daniel Purcell definitely date from a revival about ten years after the premiere. A manuscript set of tunes by John Barrett, "ye 2d pt. to the fool in Fashion," may date from the premiere, and marks the earliest contribution to theater music by a young composer who would become a significant part of the musical scene in later seasons.[156]

---

[153] GB-Lbl 806.K.16 (68).

[154] Not in D&M, see Hunter 5 (214). Precisely dating the songsheets Walsh's customers made personal collected volumes from is difficult, but the heading "Sung by Mrs. Willis in the Second part of ye Foole in fashion" suggests that it was printed when Cibber's play was well known, but Vanbrugh's was not.

[155] Single copy in GB-Ob Mus. 1. C. 73 (24).

[156] Barrett began publishing songs in 1699, and wrote act tunes for *The Pilgrim* (PC, 1700).

In December 1696 Lincoln's Inn Fields finished the year with Dilke's second comedy, *The City Lady*, which was even more musical than its predecessor, though not equally successful. It includes a lot of singing in character, but curiously lacks a song for John Bowman, whose character spends most of the play pretending to be a German count.[157]

The City Lady features the usual tangled plot, with an unusually large number of characters, including an "essence-seller" and "intelligencer." Barry plays Lady Grumble, a merchant's wife, whose acquisition of wealth and title has made her unbearably pretentious; the heroines are her niece Lucinda (Elizabeth Bowman) and her niece's companion, Formosa (Mrs Prince).[158]

The second act opens in a garden, where Lucinda and Formosa are discussing Lucinda's unacknowledged lover, just returned from abroad. Lucinda asserts that men are by nature inconstant; Formosa counters that women may change too, and blessings balance out the evils. The heroines continue their debate in contrasting songs.[159]

> *Luc.* I know our disputes might be Eternal on this subject, and therefore let's sit down on this Bank, and I'll sing you a Song. (*sings.*)
>   SONG.
> Love is an empty airy Name,
>   A word in course and fashion;
> 'Tis something worse creates the Flame,
>   And Mony moves the Passion.
>
> Then *Cælia* don't expose your Charms,
>   And lavish all your Beauty;
> Who'd ever lye within those Arms,
>   Where all is thought but Duty?[160]

Eccles sets the two stanzas in contrasting meters; indicating a modified repeat of the first section, beginning at "'tis something worse." As in his songs for Anne Bracegirdle the opening lines contain moderately challenging melismas on "empty" and "course," but the performer only needs to sing them once—the

---

[157] Price's note on *The City Lady* (*Music in the Restoration Theatre*, pp. 247–8) is misleading. The individuals who sing in character were singing actors, and more music survives.

[158] Dilke may have hoped that Bracegirdle and Bowman would portray his singing heroines.

[159] The poetic statement and its (mocking) answer participate in a classic literary tradition, including Christopher Marlowe's *The Passionate Shepherd to his Love* ("Come live with me and be my love") and Sir Walter Raleigh's *Nymph's Reply*. A contemporary example of the paired-song format can be found in Southerne's *The Fate of Capua* (LIF, 1700).

[160] Thomas Dilke, *The City Lady; or, Folly Reclaimd* (London, 1697), p. 11.

remainder of the piece is simpler. In the opening section the continuo line picks up the characteristic dotted rhythms of "empty" from the voice and echoes them under "name" and "a word," musically reinforcing the link.

To this critique, Formosa can offer only the *carpe diem* philosophy espoused by unnumbered male characters, concluding "Cælia don't the Miser play,/ And starve in height of Plenty;/ The Fruit that now looks fresh and gay,/ Will fade at One and twenty" (12). In contrast to the serious C minor of "Love is an empty airy Name," Eccles's setting of "All Beauty were a foolish Toy" is in the same bright G major as Finger's act tunes,[161] and similarly emphasizes triadic motives.[162]

The next solo song is performed in the middle of Act IV by Cicely the Cook-Maid (Anne Perrin) for an admiring audience of servants. Cicely's ballad, "There lately was a maiden fair," survives in several sources.[163] Like "A Soldier and a Sailor"—even to the repeated "sirs" at the end of each third line—the song narrates an unromantic encounter between lower-class characters. Her song is differentiated both textually and musically from the songs of the ladies above stairs. While the heroines' songs debate "Celia's" wisest course of action, the ballad singer deals in absolutes. Childishly naïve, she believes one man instantly and, when deceived, resolves to leave the city and never trust men again.

The male characters are decidedly unmusical, save for Lady Grumble's son Pedanty, whom she intends should marry Lucinda. In Act V Pedanty performs a "Song that I made upon my Laundress at Oxford" (44), including several mock-scholarly and collegiate references, asserting his physical (rather than mental) prowess. Like Cicely's ballad, "Fine Laundry Nell" is composed of short lines in colloquial language, forming a simple narrative. Lady Grumble is shocked to discover Pedanty singing this while "rumpling" Lucinda's maid, but, as the audience has seen, even Oxford cannot give her son the "quality" she desires.

The grandest musical event occurs in Act III. A variation on the banquet scene, here Lady Grumble acts as hostess to the German "Count Dunder" (Lucinda's lover).[164]

> Scene opens, and the Company goes in to a Banquet, flourish of Trumpets as they lead up: During the Banquet an Entertainment of Music, Singing and Dancing.
> **Ode Triumphal**.

---

[161] Finger's music survives in several sources. See Price, *Music in the Restoration Theatre*, pp. 154–5.

[162] In Eccles's 1704 *Collection*, the singer is given as Mary Hodgson. Possibly Mrs Prince found Eccles's song beyond her.

[163] Durfey's *Wit and Mirth; or, Pills to Purge Melancholy* (London, 1700), with both tune and song text (unusual) in *The Second Part of the Dancing Master* (London, 1698), and in a songsheet in GB-Obh, which names the performer. The music is attributed to Eccles.

[164] It is curious Dilke did not write a song for Bowman, or a dialogue for the Bowmans to sing together.

> Give to the Warrior loud and lasting Praise,
> May bounteous Blessings crown his Days;
> Reach forth the Laurel, and adorn his Brow,
> While Crowds around his Royal Person bow ...

Whatever patriotic mood the ode invokes is shattered instantly as two town sparks enter and begin a drunken dialogue. The ode's serious martial theme does not fit the often slapstick humor of the rest of the play, as Dilke admits in his dedication:

> I very well know that the Ode in the third Act seems to be introduc'd something unseasonably. It was made and set long since, in hopes of having it perform'd before the King, at his return from *Flanders*; and the Music being so finely compos'd by Mr. *John Eccles*, I was loath it shou'd be wholly lost to the Town.[165]

Like the earlier "Taking of Namur," none of the music composed by Eccles is known to survive, although thanks to Dilke we know both the composer and its original intent. This is far from the only example of such recycling—Daniel Purcell reused his welcome song in *Cinthia and Endimion* (see below), and later his birthday music for Princess Anne and a chorus from a St Cecilia Ode.[166]

Another new comedy from Drury Lane, *Aesop*, attributed to Vanbrugh, premiered in December. A revision of a French comedy, in it the title character (Cibber) offers rhyming versions of his wise fables and counsels his fellow men. He pretends to want to marry a young woman, but instead shows her father that she should marry her age-appropriate suitor. Vanbrugh features the company's comedians, writing plum roles for Dogget as a heavy father and Jo Haynes as a country bumpkin, while Penkethman is triple cast (tradesman, country gentleman, herald). Both Haynes and Dogget sing snatches of song in character, in Dogget's case, "Lillibulero."

All the formal musical events are crowded into Act V, when a "Troop of Musicians, Dancers, &c." enter (66) to celebrate the mock wedding. The musical conventional turns into burlesque when "The Trumpets sound a Melancholly Air till *Aesope* appears [dressed as a beau, with entourage]; and then the Violins and Hautbois strike up a *Lancshire Hornpipe*" (68). The trumpets flourish as Aesop, at the last minute, joins the young lovers' hands before the priest.

A surviving song, "Shou'd I once change my Heart," once again set by Leveridge, and sung by Letitia Cross,[167] is not found in the play text but matches

---

[165] William returned from Flanders in October 1696, after six months' absence.

[166] In *The Grove* (PC, 1700) and *Alexander the Great* (PC, 1701). See Chapters Four and Five.

[167] See Hunter 5 (164) and Baldwin and Wilson, *Richard Leveridge: Complete Songs*, Song 103 and notes.

the rational philosophy of the play overall. The singer hopes to choose a husband "endow'd with the Charms of the Mind" rather than "outward perfections," one who is sincere, faithful, and financially secure.

Spurred by the resounding success of the original *Aesop*, the Patent Company presented *Aesop Part II* in the spring. As printed, it runs to only sixteen pages: enough for an afterpiece or add-on to the original. In it, the author satirizes the unreasonable demands of the Lincoln's Inn Fields actors. No music is called for.

The Lincoln's Inn Fields company's first new production in 1697 was Edward Filmer's dismal tragedy *The Unnatural Brother*. A duet by Eccles, "For you who are rid by the fury Love"[168] (advocating alcohol as remedy), does not appear in the play, but it could have been performed between the acts. The preface suggests that comic and musical elements were added to and then deleted from the production during rehearsals.[169] In its printed form, *The Unnatural Brother* is free of music and unremittingly gloomy, featuring poisoned gloves, attempted rape, and an Othello-like husband.[170]

Thomas Durfey's *Cinthia and Endimion; or, The Loves of the Deities*, Drury Lane's new "Dramatick Opera" (1) was produced after Motteux's *The Loves of Mars and Venus*, and probably accepted by Christopher Rich in hopes of matching the success of Motteux's work. As in Dilke's *The Lover's Luck*, music originally written to welcome King William home from Flanders was put to theatrical use, here as the final musical entertainment in *Cinthia and Endimion*.[171]

According to the title page, the opera had been intended "to be Acted at Court, before the late Queen" and it has been suggested that the relatively modest scenery, machines, and special effects are due to its original venue. The court masque tradition, dating back to Ben Jonson, is also evident in the "Antimask of Nations, of Arabs, Indians, Moors, with Noisy Instruments in their Hands" in Act IV (42) and in the "grand Dance of Gods and Goddesses" (48), which was presumably intended to end the masque in its original form, prior to the addition of Daniel Purcell's ode.

Durfey provides a key, explaining the characters are "morally fashioning the Vertues and Vices of Human Nature," with Cinthia, "Representing Greatness and Honour, attack'd by natural Frailty and Wavering Passion," opposed by Syrinx, "Representing Singular Passion, Treachery, and Envy." Motteux had placed a brief "Explanation of the Fable of *Mars* and *Venus*" at the end of his masque, labeling Venus "libidinous Pleasure" and Vulcan "the Fire of Lust" (29–30), but

---

[168] Eccles, *Collection*, pp. 153–4 and GB-Lbl Add. MS 29378 ff. 177v-178v. No singers' names are given.

[169] For more on Filmer's comments about music and his tragedy, see Chapter Two.

[170] No actors' names are given in the 1697 edition. Some can be surmised from the condensed version performed as part of *The Novelty* in June.

[171] The connection between the two was first made by Olive Baldwin and Thelma Wilson in "The Music for Durfey's *Cinthia and Endimion*," *Theatre Notebook* 41/2 (1987): 70–4.

a modest acquaintance with the classical deities would suffice. In Durfey's case, although Apollo as "Wit and Love" and Psyche as "Innocent Vertue, o'ercome by insinuation" could be understood via mythology, the other characters would be more difficult to intuit. Jupiter's meaning is given only as a prudent dash, and there is no explanation provided for the comical shepherd Collin (Thomas Dogget), or the other musical characters, although in the elaborate sung prologue, Durfey indicates that Saturnia represents Night (as the stage darkens).[172]

As in most major musical productions for the Patent Company, the task of composition was shared among composers. The prologue was set to music by Daniel Purcell and survives in a single manuscript copy, with solos for Saturnia (alto),[173] Merope (one of the Pleiades, soprano) and Cupid's minion Zephyrus (treble, probably Jemmy Bowen).[174] From songsheets engraved by Thomas Cross, we know Diana Temple portrayed Amphitrite in the masque of Neptune in Act II (8–10), set by Jeremiah Clarke, and Mary Lindsey sang "The poor Endimion lov'd too well" in Act IV, again by Purcell.[175] Presumably Richard Leveridge sang in the antimasque in Act V, as he set the druid's bass solo "Black and Gloomy as the Grave."

The other surviving printed songs are the comic ones from Act III: Collin Clout's (Dogget's) "'Twas when the sheep were shearing" and Daniel Purcell's setting of a dialogue between a nymph and a satyr, "Last Night when *Phoebus* went to Bed," which Timothy Neufeldt notes was reused in Durfey's comic opera *The Wonders in the Sun* (1706).[176] The positioning of the comic relief numbers in Act III was no doubt deliberate. Given the usual musical casting, Letitia Cross may have sung in the flirtatious dialogue between a nymph and a satyr (III, 24–5) and the amorous one between Zephyrus and Iris (V, 44).

The other surviving music, Purcell's welcome ode "The loud tongu'd War," becomes the final entertainment, a "SONG, in Two Parts, between *Mars* and *Minerva*" (48). Baldwin and Wilson comment on the use of tenor-countertenor John Freeman, whose name is marked in the score,[177] suggesting "the Roman goddess of wisdom, could have been seen as a martial figure, suitable to be

---

[172] For comments on the lighting and other visual stage effects in this and contemporary works, see Burden, "Aspects of Purcell's Operas," pp. 10–13.

[173] It is possible that John Freeman sang Saturnia, as the range is quite low, identical to his part in the final entertainment. No known female singers could cover it. Though Mary Lindsey's part in *Arsinoe* (PC, 1705) is similar, during the 1690s her parts are all in the soprano range.

[174] GB-Ob Tenbury MS 1175, pp. 59–69.

[175] Both can be found in GB-Obh, in G.82 (13) and G.333 (10).

[176] See Neufeldt, "The Social and Political Aspects of the Pastoral Mode," pp. 28–36, for a discussion of this scene and the music. The satyr in the dialogue is atypical in his willingness to be 'beautified.' However, Durfey has also included some more traditional satyrs, whom Collin and his fellows fight to rescue Flora.

[177] Lbl Add. MS 30934, ff. 94–104, alto line marked "Mr Freeman" on 96v.

sung by a countertenor, or perhaps Daniel Purcell, in his eagerness to exploit Freeman—a specialist in songs with trumpet—chose to write the piece for two masculine deities."[178] Two aspects of the text suggest that the first hypothesis may be right. Earlier in the opera, the shepherd Collin is railing against the gods, calling "*Bacchus* a Sott, *Mars* a Bully, *Mercury* a Thief, and *Cupid* a Pimp: ... *Juno*'s an envious Scold, *Cynthia*'s an inconstant Jilt, *Pallas* an Hermaphrodite" (17). Unlike the other divinities named, Pallas/Minerva does not appear in the opera until the final song. Once costumed with the appropriate attributes, Minerva could simply stand and sing. The bass singing Mars was presumably Leveridge, and Purcell's music would end the evening in rousing style, with trumpets and kettledrums.

Another winter production, *Timoleon; or, The Revolution*, is an old-fashioned tragicomedy, and may not have been staged. The anonymous author's preface makes an explicit connection between the hero Timoleon and King William III as "Dethroners of Tyrants, and the Restorers of Liberty" who have overcome nefarious assassination attempts. Musical events include a "Song of Triumph" performed before Timoleon in Act II, which resembles the triumphal odes written for William: "Sing, sing his Praise, Heroick Acts rehearse,/ His Deeds repeat in Everlasting Verse" (18). In Act IV an unspecified drinking song is performed by "two Plebians," who put some of the comedy into tragicomedy (51). In the final act, Timoleon is reconciled with Leonora, daughter of the tyrant he defeated (another blatant parallel). A dance of shepherds and shepherdesses marks the couple's transition to a pastoral life, leaving the people to govern themselves.

Cibber's second comedy, *Woman's Wit; or, The Lady in Fashion*, was probably acted at Drury Lane in February. It was not successful, which Cibber attributes at least in part to the pre-performance history:

> [D]uring the time of my Writing the two first Acts, I was entertain'd in the New Theatre, and of course prepar'd my Characters to the taste of those Actors ... In the middle of my Writing the Third Act, ... I return'd again to the Theatre Royal, and was then forc'd ... to confine the Business of my Persons to the Capacity of different people, and not to miss the Advantage of Mr. *Dogget*'s Excellent Action; I prepar'd a low Character, which [...] I knew from him cou'd not fail of Diverting ... I was forc'd to Write to the Mouths of those I knew wou'd speak as well as they cou'd ... Every one did their best, and I thank 'em.[179]

There is an interesting musical scene in Act III, obviously designed by Cibber to display the talents of his wife, Katherine (playing Olivia),[180] but no Act V masque or

---

[178] Baldwin and Wilson, "The Music for Durfey's *Cinthia and Endimion*," p. 73.

[179] Colley Cibber, *Woman's Wit; or, The Lady in Fashion. A Comedy* (London, 1697), unpaginated, italics reversed.

[180] Before marrying Cibber, Katherine Shore (from a family of musicians) apparently took lessons from master Henry Purcell. See Baldwin and Wilson, "Purcell's Stage Singers," p. 113.

song for Dogget. The 'lesson' Katharine Cibber plays during the 'women's music' scene is not specified (one of Henry Purcell's would be appropriate). However, the song she sings "Tell me, Bellinda, prithee do," survives, in an energetic setting by Richard Leveridge,[181] as does a set of act tunes by William, Lord Byron.[182]

The play also provides an early example of Cibber quoting a specific song in character to make a point—something he and other authors would do to a greater degree in later plays. In Act II Cibber's character turns the tables on the jilt Leonora by singing a phrase from "Take not a Woman's Anger Ill," the misogynistic rondeau from *The Rival Sisters* (PC, 1695). Purcell's song seems to have been a popular one for quoting, both for the memorable tune and the sentiment expressed, "if one won't, another will."

The only play known to have been acted at Lincoln's Inn Fields in February and March 1697 was Congreve's tragedy *The Mourning Bride*. Like *Love for Love* in 1695,[183] it was a great success and ran for thirteen nights. In his prologue, Congreve states that he intended to "please and move"—audiences found Queen Zara (Barry) and Princess Almeria (Bracegirdle) extremely moving. No songs are called for, although the text contains scenes with instrumental music in both soft and martial moods, as an aural backdrop for a soliloquy by Princess Almeria and to announce the triumphal return of her father. Finger provided the overture and act tunes, which survive in a few sources.[184]

Around the same time the Patent Company staged another tragicomedy, *The Triumphs of Virtue*, which may have suffered from direct competition with *The Mourning Bride*. The work of an anonymous author, it reframes elements of *Measure for Measure*, with a protofeminist twist. The virtuous and talented Bellamira, earning her living as companion to Isidora (Letitia Cross), agrees to appear to be the Duke of Naples's mistress, but only to awaken her wastrel brother's sense of honor and responsibility.

Bellamira is directly or indirectly responsible for all of the music, little of which appears to have survived. In Act II Bellamira is shown with Isidora, who "plays upon the Spinette, and sings" (matching the scene for Katherine Cibber in *Woman's Wit*). The song she performs, "So bright young Celia's Charms, you'd swear," questions the role of the well-born maiden: "We Dress, we Plume, we Dance, we

---

[181] It was engraved by Thomas Cross (GB-Lbl K.7.i.2, song 67) and published in Leveridge's *A New Book of Songs* by Walsh in 1697. See Baldwin and Wilson, *Richard Leveridge: Complete Songs*, song 5.

[182] Treble part only, GB-Lbl Add. MS 35043, ff. 85–6. See Price, *Music in the Restoration Theatre*, p. 235 for the few concordances.

[183] Congreve's comedy was acted at court in honor of the Princess Anne's birthday on 6 March 1697. *The London Stage*, vol. 1, p. 474.

[184] Price, *Music in the Restoration Theatre*, p. 203. The first and second music can also be found at the Newberry Library, Chicago, bound with Henry Purcell's *Ayres for the Theatre*. For the act tunes in GB-Lcm MS 1172 see the facsimile edition, *Instrumental Music for London Theatres, 1690–1699*.

Play,/ And all to give our Souls away" (17). Isidora then begs her governess to perform, but Bellamira (Jane Rogers, less musically gifted) declines.

In Act III Bellamira uses her new influence with the enraptured duke to arrange a musical entertainment for the court, a symphony and a dance, followed by the song "What is Beauty? what is Youth?" set, we are told, "by the fam'd Musitian/ To the great Cardinal of *Alba*" (27–8). Instead of the usual martial, bibulous, or seductive entertainments found in Act III court scenes, Bellamira's dialogue asserts that true beauty is found in virtue.

Amidst all the virtue, the final song is comic relief. Dogget, as Bellamira's servant Massetto, has been looking forward to guarding the Duke's wine cellar. Well fortified, he offers "I'le sing you a Song of my Mistris so pretty,/ A Lady so frolick and gay …" (36–7).[185] With material like this, Dogget couldn't miss.

In April the Lincoln's Inn Fields company staged Sir John Vanbrugh's *The Provok'd Wife*, a moderate but very welcome success at its premiere. According to Cibber, the Lord Chamberlain (reputedly an admirer of Bracegirdle's) asked Vanbrugh to give the play to Lincoln's Inn Fields.[186] Barry portrayed the much-provoked wife of the title (Lady Brute) and Bracegirdle her witty, pretty niece Bellinda.

Elizabeth Bowman played the most musical character, Lady Fancyfull, a female version of her husband's singing fop roles. An inveterate lover of music, particularly of her own voice and her own verses, Lady Fancyfull is directly responsible for the first three songs. The first arrives by post as she converses with her French maid (Elizabeth Willis). Lady Fancyfull goes into raptures and calls for a servant, Mrs Pipe (Mary Hodgson), to sing it: "Fly, fly, you happy Shepherds, fly,/ Avoid *Philira*'s Charms;/ The rigour of her heart denies/ The Heaven that's in her Arms." (9). The tired conceits of the quasi-pastoral poetry (fire and ice, etc.) are imitated in the complete predictability of the musical material. Eccles apparently did not set the second verse, in which the admiring poet mocks Philira, granted beauty but denied bliss.[187]

The second and third songs are performed during a visit from Lady Fancyfull's singing master, Mr Treble (John Bowman). Treble brings a new setting for a dialogue his patroness wrote, revealing Lady Fancyfull's monstrous vanity:

> MAN: Ah, lovely nymph, the world's on fire;
> Veil, veil those cruel eyes.
> WOMAN: The world may then in flames expire,
> And boast that so it dies.
> MAN: But when all mortals are destroyed,

---

[185] D&M 1636, printed in Durfey's *Wit & Mirth* (London, 1700).
[186] Cibber, *Apology*, ed. Lowe, vol. 1, pp. 217–18.
[187] It appeared in Eccles's *Collection* and survives as a songsheet. The words to the second verse do not easily fit the music, but even if it was sung, Lady Fancyfull is incapable of hearing anything but a compliment.

Who then shall sing your praise?
WOMAN: Those who are fit to be employed:
The gods shall altars raise.[188]

The play text mentions only Treble, and later dialogue makes it clear that Lady Fancyfull will not sing, due to her "cold." Mrs Pipe, who sings the next song, may have taken the woman's part, but a more comic option would be to have Bowman sing both, as he did in "Delia tired Strephon with her Flame," a song from a later comedy by Pix, in which he mimicks an old woman (probably in falsetto).[189]

Treble also brings a new song, "Not an angel dwells above,/ Half so fair as her I love," which ends with the resolution to stop loving if the beloved remains unkind (23). Lady Fancyfull instantly assumes it was written by Heartfree, who briefly attempted to "reform" her of her affectations in the first act.

Treble changes the subject, and continues to compliment her in an exchange that must have amused contemporary audiences, knowing the Bowmans' offstage relationship:

> TREBLE: ... I know nobody sings so near a cherubin as your ladyship.
> LADY FANCYFULL: What I do, I owe chiefly to your skill and care, Mr Treble. People do flatter me, indeed, that I have a voice, and a *je ne sais quoi* in the conduct of it, that will make music of anything. And truly, I begin to believe so, ... in the Park (for I often walk late in the Park, Mr Treble), a whim took me to sing 'Chevy Chase', and—would you believe it—next morning I had three copies of verses and six *billets-doux* at my levee upon it.[190]
> TREBLE: And without all dispute you deserved as many more, madam. Are there any further commands for your ladyship's humble servant?
> LADY FANCYFULL: Nothing more at this time, Mr Treble. But I shall expect you here every morning for this month, to sing my little matter there to me. I'll reward you for your pains.
> TREBLE: O Lord, madam—
> LADY FANCYFULL: Good morrow, sweet Mr Treble.[191]

Despite her plans—a month of musical drudgery for Mr Treble—Lady Fancyfull's musical interests fade when she learns that Heartfree has fallen in love with Bellinda. All her energies are subsequently devoted to separating them.

---

[188] Vanbrugh, *The Provok'd Wife: A Comedy* (London, 1697), p. 22.

[189] If Cibber's account is correct and Vanbrugh's play was originally intended for DL, Mr Treble may have been designed for Cibber.

[190] "Chevy Chase" is an old, old ballad—mocking Lady Fancyfull's musical pretensions.

[191] Vanbrugh, *The Provok'd Wife*, p. 24.

The following song in Act III, "What a pother of late," is enthusiastically performed during their late-night revelry by Lord Rake with Sir John Brute and company. It praises drinking, mocks the state and religion, and concludes:

No saucy remorse
Intrudes in my course,
   Nor impertinent notions of evil;
So there's claret in store,
In peace I've my whore,
   And in peace I jog on to the devil.[192]

Throughout the play, Vanbrugh makes the music organic to its setting, whether music lesson or male social gathering. Lady Fancyfull's passion for songs written by or for her is an important element in her characterization, while Lord Rake's song (his own composition) quickly conveys the licentious camaraderie Sir John prefers to his home life.

The last song, inserted near the end of Act V, is requested by Lady Brute's would-be lover, Constant. It serves the convention of music at the end of a comedy, but "When yielding first to Damon's flame" seems designed to break up couples rather than bring them together. The speaker becomes intimate with her Damon, but "Too greedy of his Prey,/ My Shepherd's flame alas Expir'd/ Before the Verge of Day." Damon's only advice to his mortified lover: "Wou'd you my Flame renew,/ Alas you must retreat like me;/ I'm lost if you pursue" (78). The setting by Eccles makes the most of boy soprano Jemmy Laroche's vocal dexterity; as published, the song's tessitura sits quite high, and requires the singer to ascend an octave and a fifth (a wide range) in little more than a measure.

Significantly, this is a "song by a new-married lady," which may pose a warning to the soon-to-be-wed. Delivering no happy endings, it reflects the unsettled state of Christian, social, and sexual morality at the end of the play, a function similar to the cynical masque of Hymen and Cupid in Vanbrugh's earlier comedy, *The Relapse*.

The run of new comedies continued in May with Thomas Durfey's *The Intrigues at Versailles; or, A Jilt in All Humours*. Durfey may have offered his play to Lincoln's Inn Fields at the request of his dedicatee, playwright and wit Sir Charles Sedley, or because of the disappointing reception of his *Cinthia and Endimion*. Durfey's *Intrigues* makes fun of fashionable French foppery and is liberally laced with musical numbers.[193]

Durfey's dialogue is often racy, and the entire comedy is built on a network of illicit affairs. Bracegirdle's character, the Duchess de Sanserre, falls from grace with a handsome young Englishman, Guillamour. The affair is eventually betrayed

---

[192] John Vanbrugh, *The Provok'd Wife; A Comedy* (London, 1697), pp. 37–8.
[193] The prologue, "As in intrigues of love we find it true," was reprinted in Durfey's popular anthology *Wit & Mirth; or, Pills to Purge Melancholy*. Day and Murrie mistakenly list it as a song (D&M 222), but it was never set to music.

to her elderly, autocratic husband by the vengeful jilt Vandosme. The Bowmans play a cross-dressing pair: he in disguise to avoid the ill-consequences of a duel, and she to escape a foolish older spouse, the Count de Brissac.

Durfey uses a variety of music to keep scenes from falling into seriousness—with marriages and royal edicts at issue, and several dangerous weapons onstage—both to prevent the discovery of intrigue and to highlight it. In Act II, the jealous Duke de Sanserre waits in the garden, disguised in his wife's nightclothes and carrying a pistol. He hopes to catch her in a tryst with Guillamour. Instead two rustics enter and sing ("squall") a rude ballad until he drives them away, getting caught in his undignified disguise (18).[194] Later in the same scene, the Bowmans perform (cross-dressed) for the assembled company. The play text indicates a song and a dance, then prints the verses for a musical dialogue. The dialogue text, beginning "The World is full of hurry" seems to refer to the peace between France and England (still under negotiation) as well as love intrigues.[195]

The next musical event is an entertainment ordered by Vandosme as part of her attempt to seduce Guillamour. The song "Ye pretty birds that chirp and sing," titled "Love's Rapture" in the play text, appeared later in *Wit and Mirth*, but without the music, credited to William Croft. Beginning with pastoral and Platonic celebrations of love, the final section of the poem concludes with more explicit sentiments.[196]

The only surviving music, the colorful "Dialogue between two Sleepy Chairmen Waiting at a Tavern Door,"[197] is an entertainment staged by Englishman Sir Blunder Busses in order to amuse Vandosme during Act IV. Sir Blunder's chief characteristic is his penchant for calling everyone by rude names, which, combined with his well-filled wallet, Vandosme finds strangely charming—even drinking beer and retiring with him.

While "Hey hoe, hey hoe," satirically narrates the dangerous pranks of a stereotypical rake-about-town, it includes pointed references to current military and political situations,[198] in contrast with the more common male–female dialogues. Eccles apparently did not set the final couplet of Durfey's text, concluding triumphantly with the chairmen's patriotic resolution to join the army and "Pimp no more" rather than the sorry end of Lord Rantipoll's evening: "Whilst they [whores he picked up], like two Bitches, and he a third Brute,/ Feel the Constable's

---

[194] The ballad, "There was Andrew and Susan, Rebecca and Will," can be found at GB-Lbl.

[195] The second quatrain reads: "Religion and Ambition/ Make us in poor Condition,/ Till for our sad Division/ A General Peace Attone." Durfey, *The Intrigues At Versailles* (London, 1697), p. 23.

[196] Durfey, *Intrigues at Versailles*, p. 29.

[197] In GB-Lbl Add. MS 29378 (ff. 183–187v) and printed in Eccles's 1704 *Collection*.

[198] Land taxes, capitation (a poll tax) and military service were all issues of intense public interest in the spring of 1697. Durfey published various dialogues on topical subjects.

Clutches, or trudge home a foot," recalling Sir John Brute's revels in *The Provok'd Wife*.[199] Naturally, the abusive, hard-drinking Lord Rantipoll patronizes the Theatre Royal at Drury Lane, not Lincoln's Inn Fields. Durfey's comedy ends with a "Song against Cuckold-making" (unspecified) and dance ordered by the Count de Brissac, and his wife's vow of future fidelity.

Drury Lane offered two new May comedies, John Dennis's *A Plot and No Plot* and James Drake's *The Sham Lawyer*. Both included a high proportion of London professionals (bankers, lawyers, curates, sextons, solicitors, even prostitutes and actors) and a limited number of gentlemen and ladies. Neither was particularly successful.

Dennis explains he intended to write a farce, and the cast features two crossdressed roles, Bullock as a bawd, and Maria Allinson as a young beau (as in *The Relapse*). All of the music in *A Plot and No Plot* is light hearted, beginning with the comical love song young Bull calls for in Act III to demonstrate his love for the bawd's daughter, Friskit:

> When Cloe, I your Charms survey,
> My wandring Senses run away.
> My trembling Heart goes pit a pat,
> Can you not guess what I'd be at?
> Sometimes in gentle Sighs I move
> The Air, with softest Breeze of Love.
> Sometimes like Gun of largest Bore,
> I vent my Sighs with dismal Roar:
> Disorder'd, know not what I do,
> And all my Dear, for Love of you.[200]

Set by Leveridge, the first section of the song stays within conventional bounds, if apt to self-parody in the melismas adorning "wandring" and "run" (Figure 3.4). In the setting of the second part of Thomas Cheek's poem, the "roar" of the gun and chromatic notes on "disorder'd" are purely comic.

As the actor Baldernoe, pretending to be a French nobleman, Penkethman makes a grand entrance in Act IV "in a Chair, Singing and whimsically drest. Three or four Fiddles, before, and five or six persons dancing by the sides" (54), a marker of the French (or would-be French). Baldernoe also calls for a minuet as "officers" come to search Bull's house for contraband and requests the drinking song and dance at the end of Act IV after Bull junior and his lady friends have been hauled away under suspicion of plotting with the French. In the end, old Bull the merchant is cured of his penchant for international affairs, his nephew and

---

[199] Durfey, *Intrigues at Versailles*, pp. 41–2. For complete text and music, see *Music Productions LIF*, pp. 191–4 and 731–41. A lively performance can be heard on The Consort of Musicke's CD *The Mantle of Orpheus* (Musica Oscura/Columns Classics, 1995).

[200] Dennis, *A Plot and No Plot* (London, 1697), pp. 40–1.

Figure 3.4 R. Leveridge, "When Cloe, I your Charms survey" in *A Plot and No Plot*

virtuous young ward (who apparently need no music) are united, and Friskit and her mother are sent packing.

Drake made no secret of his opinion of the Patent Company's production of his play, *The Sham-Lawyer: Or The Lucky Extravagant. As it was Damnably Acted at the Theatre-Royal in Drury Lane*. Many lines are marked as cut, no music is known to survive. The prologue also takes aim at fellow-playwrights and childish audiences: "Instead of Manly sense, and strong writ Plays,/ They bring you *Harlequin* and *Opera*'s."[201]

Three songs are indicated, first the courtly "Why was not Wit with Beauty joyn'd?" (II, 18) when an old lawyer asks his wife, Florella, to entertain his new student, not realizing that the 'student' is her lover. The second is a hypocritical drinking song sung by a curate and a sexton: they find revelation at night in the bottle (III, 34–5). The third song, "In vain Melissa we defend/ Our selves against your conqu'ring Eyes," seems simply dropped in at the beginning of Act IV (35–6).

In June, Lincoln's Inn Fields segued into the summer season with Motteux's theatrical experiment *The Novelty*, consisting of five single-act entertainments, and finished with Mary Pix's first work for Lincoln's Inn Fields, the comedy *The Innocent Mistress*. Both included several songs and were modest successes.

Pierre Motteux's *The Novelty; or Ev'ry Act a Play* cleverly recycled existing material (acts from a French comedy and Filmer's *Unnatural Brother*), combining it with new elements: the masque *Hercules*, set by Eccles; Oldmixon's miniature pastoral, *Thyrsis*; and the farce *Natural Magic*, "after the Italian manner" (also derivative). The surviving songs by Eccles are a lovely pastoral melody for Elizabeth Bowman with accompanying flutes, and a salacious boy–girl duet.[202] This production is discussed in further detail in Chapter One.

Pix's first comedy, *The Spanish Wives* (PC, 1696), was full of songs, dances, and other musical entertainments, and for her Lincoln's Inn Fields debut Pix had the support of Motteux, who provided the prologue and epilogue. However, musically *The Innocent Mistress* is quite average, including just three songs: two for solo voice and one musical dialogue. There is no final dance indicated, although an unspecified dance is performed between songs in the musical entertainment in Act III. Additional dances probably were performed, as the prologue makes reference to several novel entertainments of dancing.

In a complete reversal of Vanbrugh's *The Provok'd Wife*, Pix's Sir Charles Beauclair is a much-provoked husband. The first song falls in Act II, as the designing sharper Spendall (John Bowman) sings "a song of his own" to amuse ill-bred Lady Beauclair and her daughter Peggy, narrating the adventures of a

---

[201] Drake, *The Sham Lawyer; or, The Lucky Extravagant* (London, 1697), lines 15–16, italics reversed.

[202] "Her Eyes are like the Morning Bright," D&M 1341 and "Hee, oh! Pray Father come with my Mother," Hunter 5 (323), engraved by Thomas Cross.

shepherdess who slips out to meet her swain. After five and a half verses, she is (like *The She-Gallants'* Corinna) quite a different girl:

> ... panting, dying with Delight,
> She Blest the kind transporting Night,
>   And Curst approaching Day.[203]

The suggestive text meets with uncomprehending approval from Lady Beauclair and Peggy, who know they are supposed to appreciate poetry and music.[204] A true love of music is something the courtly lovers Sir Charles and Bellinda share.

Stage directions instruct Lady Beauclair and Peggy to "imitate his Gestures" while Spendall sings: visual representation of their places in polite society. They are imitating what they do not understand and consequently doing it badly—a clever manipulator like Spendall can do what he likes with them.

The songs that follow are both part of a musical entertainment at the India House.[205] The first song, to a text by Pix, "When I languish'd, and wish'd you wou'd something bestow," was sung by Mary Hodgson. The speaker teases her would-be lover with mock innocence, reinforced by Eccles's simple triple-meter air, concluding, "Tho' I practice a thousand false Doctrines on you,/ I shall still have enough for the next." (21–2)

In contrast, the dialogue, "How long must I the Hours employ," directly addresses the situation of the platonic lovers Sir Charles and Bellinda, though in terms they are too refined to employ themselves: "How long must I the hours employ/ To see, be lov'd, yet ne'er enjoy?" (22). The singers resolve to love on (chastely) and enjoy the pain. Although performers are not specified, Eccles's music suggests that they were professional singers.[206]

The quality of the instrumental music, like that of the songs, varies.[207] Francis Forcer's French-style overture in C major is very pretty. His use of paired subject and countersubject (as in his overture for *Boadicea*) differentiates his overtures from those of the other theater composers, who used a single theme in all four parts.

---

[203] Mary Pix, *The Innocent Mistress* (London, 1697), pp. 14–15.

[204] A later musical setting by Galliard exists, but the only contemporary setting located appears anonymously in GB-Och Music MS 363. The manuscript contains pieces from *Bonduca*, *Abdelazer*, *The Fairy Queen*, and *The Indian Queen*, and is dated 1703 on the flyleaf.

[205] Goods from East India merchants could be seen and purchased at the India House. A concert was held at "the Great India House" (in Pall Mall) on 28 February 1704. M&H *London Stage*, 213.

[206] See GB-Lbl Add. MS 29378, ff. 190–3.

[207] The act tunes copied in Yale's Filmer MS 9 are in multiple keys, possibly recycled. The number of tunes (eight) suggests that one is missing. See *Music Productions LIF*, pp. 224–7.

The Patent Company also experimented with music and comedy, but with less success. Although Robert Hume called *The World in the Moon* "the one interesting operatic piece from these years"[208] it was not considered so by contemporary audiences. The Dorset Garden theater had been used during the spring months for revivals of old dramatick operas (*Psyche*, *The Tempest*, *Dioclesian*) and the recent *Indian Queen*. However, Settle's dedication to Christopher Rich famously emphasizes his opera's difference from recent productions:

> The model of the Scenes of this Play, are something of an Original: I am sure I have removed a long Heap of Rubbish, and thrown away all our old *French* Lumber, our Clouds of Clouts, and set the Theatrical Paintings at a much fairer Light. And therefore am an humble Suppliant to the Generous Audience ...
> For as I dare confidently averr [*sic*], the Prospect of this Stage will put all the old Rags out of Countenance ...[209]

In light of what we know about its failure, Settle's hopeful statement "if Industry, Labour, and Expence, can deserve a Smile, it stands high for a Favourite" prompts a rueful smile.

Scholars have debated why Rich put time and money into such a production, suggesting his desire to outdo Betterton's past successful dramatick operas and his reaction to criticism after the failure of *Brutus of Alba* and *Cinthia and Endimion*, one with shoddy, reused scenery and the other with little in the way of elaborate scenic effects.[210] While these probably were part of Rich's decision-making process, I wonder if the success of *The Female Wits* the previous autumn also influenced his willingness to gamble on Settle's show.[211]

Both productions include contemporary comic scenes set in the theater, with favorite performers playing themselves, in alternation with the rehearsal of an 'opera.' Certainly Settle's opera is far more musically and scenically elaborate and far less ridiculous than 'Marsilia's.' Yet the basic formula of the works is similar: Settle took care to include not one but two musical dialogues for Letitia Cross and Richard Leveridge, a cross-dressed dialogue (sung by Cross with Jane Lucas), characteristic pieces for Freeman and Leveridge, and at least two pieces for 'the girl' (probably Mary Anne Campion).

In Settle's opera, however, unlike *The Female Wits*, the most foolish character is an obnoxious young country bumpkin, Tom, who is persuaded by two gentlemen of the town that what he sees on stage is real, and 'Cynthia' loves him. Aided by

---

[208] Hume, *The Development of English Drama*, p. 428.
[209] Settle, *The World in the Moon; an Opera* (London, 1697), unpaginated, italics reversed.
[210] See Milhous, *Thomas Betterton*, pp. 94–5.
[211] The anonymous author even has Marsilia make the end of her opera "the World in the Moon" (*Female Wits*, p. 63). Settle's show-within-a-show is supposed to be *The New World in the Moon*.

comedian Jo Haynes (famous for practical jokes), by Act IV Tom finds himself in an "Imperial Bed" of crimson silk and gold, waiting for his queen. Instead the bed drops under the stage, and he is last heard crying for help (26). In the slightly more serious plot, the crafty Jacintha manipulates her father and an old alderman, Fondlove. She arranges for the performance of a marriage masque in Act IV, with a 'heating' dialogue between Leveridge and Cross as lusty groom and reluctant bride, and persuades Fondlove into trying to steal her away at midnight. Fondlove's attempt is ludicrously foiled, and in his subsequent embarrassment he relinquishes his claims so she can marry her beloved Worthy. Fondlove even makes Worthy his heir.

The scenes and lighting effects (both dark and bright), as described in Settle's text, must have been striking. Even the prologue displayed new paintings. Compared with the tired orange groves and flat palaces of earlier shows, the description of the palace of Cynthia in the clouds in Act II (14) is marvelous enough, but Settle placed the most elaborate scene effects in Acts I and V. In Act I,

> The Flat-Scene draws, and discovers Three grand Arches of Clouds extending to the Roof of the House, terminated with a Prospect of Cloud-work, all fill'd with the Figures of Fames and *Cupids;* a Circular part of the back Clouds rolls softly away, and gradually discovers a Silver Moon, near fourteen Feet Diameter: After which, the Silver Moon wanes off by degrees, and discovers the World within, consisting of Four grand Circles of Clouds, illustrated with *Cupids*, &c. Twelve golden Chariots are seen riding in the Clouds, fill'd with Twelve Children, representing the Twelve Celestial Signs. The Third Arch intirely rolling away, leaves the full Prospect terminating with a large Lanschape of Woods, Waters, Towns, &c. Enter *Cynthia's* Train; being Twenty Singers, and other Retinue.[212]

The size of the final scene is even more astonishing, as the terraces of Cynthia's Bower cover "Eight several Stages mounted one above another," their decoration including paintings of "Heroick History" and sixteen gold statues, with marble steps ascending through the middle to a height (Settle tells us) of twenty-four feet (42).

The large number of singers called for in Settle's text (twenty) is not reflected in the music. The printed songs and play text identify eight soloists, but the surviving choruses never divide into more than the standard four parts. As the soloists are predominantly high voices, additional singers would need to provide support for Leveridge on bass and sing the tenor part.[213] Settle reveals less about the dancers, but the dance of four swans and five green men (much like *The Fairy Queen*) at the end of the Act I entertainment and the "Dance of Eight Figures" at the court of Cynthia in Act II indicate a similarly grand number of dancers.

---

[212] Settle, *The World in the Moon; An Opera* (London, 1697), pp. 6–7.

[213] These singers probably included Edwards and Church, who were singing for DL this season.

Musical responsibilities within the opera were divided between Jeremiah Clarke and Daniel Purcell (Table 3.5). A late eighteenth-century copy of the score for three sections (Prologue, Acts I and IV) survives,[214] as well as competing collections of songs, published by John Heptinstall for Henry Playford, and by John Walsh. Much of the surviving music is charming, and all of it adequate to Settle's requirements and suited to the performers. But even with stunning new scenery and Miss Cross in every act, Settle's opera did not win approval or even come close to recouping its costs. The June premiere may be blamed in part, since those wealthy or noble enough to have country estates or to travel generally departed for the summer. Settle seems to have seriously misjudged audience tastes, although it is difficult from the evidence we have to see exactly how. In *A Comparison Between the Two Stages* in 1701–1702, Settle's opera wasn't even accorded a mention, although Durfey's *Cinthia and Endimion* was panned for its pretensions.[215]

Table 3.5 Musical entertainments in *The World in the Moon*

Position	**Description**	**Composer**	**Pages**
Prologue	*Prologue to Beauty*	Jeremiah Clarke	unpag.
Act I (End)	*The World in the Moon*	Clarke	6–7
Act II (near End)	*Entertainment at the Court of Cynthia*	Daniel Purcell	14–15
Act III (Middle)	*Entrance of Cynthia's Train, Revels*	Purcell	21–2
Act IV (Beginning, near End)	*Song* *Nuptial Entertainment*	Purcell Purcell [Clarke in mss.]	27 32–4
Act V (End)	*Cynthia's Bower, Pastoral Entertainment*	Purcell	42–3

All in all, it was a disheartening end to the season for the Patent Company. Motteux's thrifty generic experiment *The Novelty* worked with audiences, at least up to a point, and Settle's extravagant experiment did not.

---

[214] See GB-Lbl Add. MS 31813 ff. 99–126.

[215] *Comparison Between the Two Stages*, pp. 29–30.

Season of 1696–97: Revivals

Although many stock plays were doubtless performed this season, again there is little specific evidence. The first production *The London Stage* lists for the Lincoln's Inn Fields company is a revival of Fletcher's comedy *To Rule a Wife and Have a Wife*. No music is known for this revival, but, as in most of the Beaumont and Fletcher canon, there are several opportunities for music making, and it was probably revived by the Patent Company as well.[216] The Lincoln's Inn Fields company would certainly have revived the previous season's great success, *Love for Love*, performed at court on 6 February.[217]

The 1697 printing of William Mountfort's farce *The Life and Death of Dr. Faustus* suggests it was performed in March at Lincoln's Inn Fields, when a farce was shown there. The title page reads: "The Life and Death of Doctor Faustus, Made into a Farce. // By Mr. Mountford. // With the Humours of Harlequin and Scaramouche: As they were several times Acted ... at the Queens Theatre in Dorset Garden. // Newly Revived, At the Theatre in Lincolns Inn Fields, With Songs and Dances Between the Acts."

Mountfort's play is significant for its dance sequences, broad comedy, and special effects, putting productions like *The Cornish Comedy*, *The Loves of Mars and Venus*, and *Brutus of Alba* in context. To stage *Dr. Faustus*, Lincoln's Inn Fields must have had the machines needed for "good and bad angels flying down" or "a devil rises in thunder and lightning." Indeed, the special effects are often better described than the music. What music was performed between the acts is not indicated. The *commedia dell'arte* characters and their performers (likely including dancing master Sorin) get much more time onstage than Faust does, and may have helped inspire Motteux's Italian farce in *The Novelty*.

During the winter of 1696–97 the Patent Company revived its previous season's successes, *Oroonoko* and *Love's Last Shift*, and they were probably revived at other times as well. As always, the company revived plays by Dryden and Shadwell: Dryden's *Don Sebastian* and *Marriage a la Mode*; Shadwell's *The Lancashire Witches*, *The Libertine*, and *Timon of Athens*. They turned to dramatick operas during the spring months: *Dioclesian* and *The Indian Queen* at Dorset Garden in March, *Psyche* in April, *The Tempest* in May. *The Indian Queen* returned in June.[218]

Musical evidence for other Patent Company revivals includes songs by Jeremiah Clarke for Durfey's comedies *Madam Fickle* and *The Fond Husband*, probably performed this season. Both were engraved as single sheets by Thomas

---

[216] A song from a UC revival, "There's not a swain on the plain" (D&M 3251), exists.

[217] For Princess Anne's birthday. *London Stage*, vol. 1, p. 474.

[218] *London Stage*, vol. 1, p. 480. It is assigned to DL, but Dorset Garden seems more likely.

Cross and appear in a Royal College of Music volume assembled c.1695–97.[219] Clarke's song for *Madam Fickle*, "So sweet the charms of Love," was sung by Jane Lucas. Elizabeth Willis, whose career at Drury Lane was quite short, performed a "Scotch" song in *The Fond Husband*, "The bonny grey ey'd morn." Often reprinted, its first appearance in a song collection was October 1697. Act tunes by William Gorton for Fletcher's *The Humorous Lieutenant* support publication data suggesting a summer revival.[220]

The final revival I propose for this season is also based on musical evidence. The cast of singers given in John Eccles's manuscript music for a production of the Shakespeare–Middleton–Davenant *Macbeth* suggests a 1697 date.[221] The cast includes Elizabeth Willis and Mr Lee, together with John Bowman (as Hecate), Mary Hodgson and John Wiltshire, but does not include Mrs Ayliff, or John Freeman and Richard Leveridge, who would presumably have been included in a United Company performance.

The cast closely resembles that for *Europe's Revels for the Peace of Ryswick* (LIF, autumn 1697), and *Macbeth* may have been performed in spring or autumn 1697, as a counter to Drury Lane's dramatick operas, both revivals and new productions. This dating would make sense of some shared traits between Eccles's music for *Macbeth* and that for his *Rinaldo and Armida*, performed the following season. Both make use of special instrumentation (the bass serpent), articulation markings, and more elaborate imitative choral music than Eccles generally wrote for theater works, qualities noted by Amanda Eubanks Winkler in her recent edition.[222]

Eccles's *Macbeth* witches sing vocal counterpoint far more elaborate than the witches' chorus in *Cyrus the Great*, music similar to a welcome ode or choral anthem. Since the witches' music is not a true celebration, but a mocking or perverted shadow of such music, their performance might have reflected this with a change in vocal quality (nasal, cackling). This seems particularly likely, given the many actor-singers involved.[223]

Because performance records are so limited for the 1690s, we have no way of judging how often Eccles's music for *Macbeth* may have been performed, but it surely inspired Richard Leveridge's later setting for Drury Lane (see Chapter

---

[219] GB-Lcm II.J.32 contains both song collections and single sheets. The single songs from premieres (*Aesop*, *Cinthia and Endimion*, *The City Lady*, etc.) and datable events (the Duke of Gloucester's investiture) are from 1696, with two exceptions.

[220] *London Stage*, vol. 1, p. 482. Act tunes can be found in Lcm MS 1172, ff. 23–25v.

[221] The debate over dating (late 1694 versus 1695–96) is summarized by Amanda Eubanks Winkler in *Music for Macbeth* (Middleton, Wisconsin, 2004), p. viii.

[222] Winkler, *Music for Macbeth*, ix–x.

[223] In her book, Winkler addresses the question of 'natural' versus falsetto singing by male witches in earlier plays, but reaches no firm conclusion. *O Let Us Howle Some Heavy Note*, pp. 22–3.

Five), the music which audiences would associate with Shakespeare's tragedy well into the nineteenth century.

Conclusion

Like *Love for Love*, *The Indian Queen* was an attempt to maintain and extend the theatrical and musical strengths of the United Company, particularly the music of Henry Purcell. The conventional uses of music in both productions were imitated, extended, and revised in subsequent seasons' productions, reflecting both the changing musical resources of each house and audience responses to such offerings.

Productions at both houses from the first full season show the range of future productions, but are well within previously established genres. Musical and dramatic experimentation would follow once the companies had established themselves— and when the classics of Restoration theater ceased to draw sufficient supporters. It is unfortunate that so little evidence of revivals remains, but the season is rich in music for premieres. No future season had so many new productions, or so large a proportion of the music survive for future study and performance.

Lincoln's Inn Fields worked around limitations in theater space, machines, and scenery, but John Eccles and his colleagues rose to the occasion, providing songs of all types for the trained soloists and singing actors available, and a steady stream of instrumental works. Although Eccles may have been equally prolific in later seasons, it is hard not to have our ideas about the use of music in the Lincoln's Inn Fields theater influenced by the fact that so much more music survives in full score from 1695–96. Our understanding of music for the Patent Company during this first season is equally influenced by the presence of Henry Purcell, whose music is readily available, recorded, and analyzed in a way his contemporaries' music has not been, although this is changing.[224]

During their second season both companies were busy developing their own coterie of playwrights to provide new productions. Where the first season at Lincoln's Inn Fields had offered a broad variety, the second season concentrated on comedies. Unfortunately none proved the solid success that *Love for Love* had been. Motteux's musical experiments, particularly *The Novelty* and *The Loves of Mars and Venus*, did well, and *The Provok'd Wife* and *The Innocent Mistress* provided modest returns.

In his prologue for *The Innocent Mistress*, Motteux comments on the state of the competing companies at the end of the 1696–97 season, with references to the recent offerings at both houses:

---

[224] Publications and performances featuring music by Eccles, Clarke, Daniel Purcell and their contemporaries have increased during the past two decades. In 2008 the Purcell Society announced a new Purcell Companion Series. The first volumes of Eccles's *Collected Works* are forthcoming from A-R Editions.

> This season with what Arts both Houses strive,
> By your kind presence, to be kept alive!
> W'have still new things, or old ones we revive;
> We plot, and strive to bring them first o'th'Stage,
> . . . .
> W'have scaling Monkies, and w'have dancing Swans,
> To match our nimble cap'ring Chairs and Stands:
> There's Opera's with, and here without Machines:
> Here, Scenes well wrought, and there, well painted Scenes;
> Castles and Men i'th'Air, the *World i'th'Moon*,
> Where you, like Swallows fly, but soon y'are gone.[225]

Motteux's prologue emphasizes the usual distinction between the two theaters—Lincoln's Inn Fields with limited facilities but better actors—and the competition for scarce audiences, which prompted constant changes in repertoire and the increasing inclusion of various novelties, both musical and miscellaneous.

The prologue to Congreve's *Mourning Bride* similarly expresses concern about the state of the theater: "The Time has been when Plays were not so plenty,/ And a less Number New, would well content ye" (lines 1–2). Congreve might well worry about the short lifespans of many recent plays, including several by his protégés. He was already behind on his contract with Lincoln's Inn Fields to provide a new one every year.

The Patent Company prospered better than might have been expected, its comic hits *Love's Last Shift*, *Aesop*, and *The Relapse* becoming perennial crowd pleasers, while *Oroonoko* satisfied the taste for heroism, tragedy, and sentiment. Their musical experiments, like Powell's *Cornish Comedy* and the comic dramatick opera *The World in the Moon*, were less successful. However, certain individual numbers, like musical dialogues featuring Letitia Cross, were always popular. Both companies knew the value of good musical material and of the performers (Bracegirdle, Cross, Freeman, Pate) who could make it connect with their audiences.

---

[225] Pix, *The Innocent Mistress*, lines 1–4, 9–14, italics reversed.

Chapter Four
Competition, 1697–1700

Productions from the final seasons of the 1690s display an increasing polarity between intensely musical works, both serious and comic, and those which limit or eliminate musical numbers. Advertisements for musical attractions and star performers at concert and court venues illustrate the intersection of artists and audience tastes across the broad canvas of London's musical life.

Context

In the spring and summer of 1697 William III's successful military campaign and peace negotiations with Louis XIV prompted mass celebrations. News of the treaty reached London in September, sparking the first official festivities. When William finally returned in November, additional celebrations were held.

William III rode from Greenwich "in great splendor, ... attended by the privy council, the great officers of the household, nobility, bishops, judges, &c." The parade through the city of London included notables from court and city, with the usual drummers and trumpet players.[1] A Thanksgiving Day was proclaimed, and it was announced that the king would appear at St Paul's, "where the doctors of musick, singing men, &c. are to attend to perform all the ceremonies, &c."[2] Instead, William attended services at Whitehall, dined at St James's, and watched an extravagant fireworks display in the evening.[3]

Theater musicians associated with the Chapel Royal and the King's Private Musick took part in these events.[4] In addition to such official royal welcomes and triumphs with all of London as an audience, there were many smaller-scale celebrations held at the universities and in the theaters.[5]

---

[1] Luttrell, *State Affairs*, vol. 4, pp. 306–7.

[2] Ibid., vol. 4, p. 308.

[3] Supposedly £10,000 worth. Ibid., vol. 4, pp. 313–14.

[4] John Blow wrote a choral anthem, "I was glad when they said unto me" for the peace and the opening of St Paul's Cathedral, while GB-Lbl Add. MS 35043 includes "Mr Lentons Tunes Playd before ye King at his Returne," ff. 106v–107.

[5] See, for example, organist Vaughan Richardson's "Entertainment of New Musick composed on the Peace" advertised in February 1698 at York Buildings. At Oxford, composer John Weldon, soon to become a significant factor in London theater music, composed an ode (GB-Cfm MS 120, pp. 60–95).

During the previous year, attitudes toward the continuing war varied. While both theater companies found it politic to emphasize the glories of peace and profusely thank the monarch for providing them, a satirist writing in the spring of 1697 insisted: "Hadst thou an interest, war would never cease;/ But we have felt enough to wish for peace."[6] Complaints about taxation were common and can be found in the texts of contemporary plays and even in musical dialogues, as seen in *The Intrigues at Versailles* (LIF, spring 1697).

Among the other domestic issues William faced were organized attempts to eradicate blasphemy, profaneness, and immorality. William's public proclamations were one thing, and many authors and actors paid at least lip service to the king's stated desire to reform the theater.[7] However, the playwrights and performers of London reacted strongly to a wholesale attack from Jeremy Collier, Jacobite clergyman and non-juror.[8] In March 1698, Collier published his (in)famous work *A Short View of the Immorality and Prophaneness of the English Stage*, attacking noted playwrights like John Dryden (Shakespeare, by Collier's standards, is indefensible) and quoting liberally from the Church Fathers and classical authorities.

In a section of chapter six, Collier turns his attention to music and dance. He is willing to concede that the dancing seen on the London stage might not be quite as lewd as the Roman *pantomimi*; however,

> 'Twere to be wish'd that either the *Plays* were better, or the *Musick* worse. I'm sorry to see *Art* so meanly Prostituted: Atheism ought to have nothing Charming in its *Retinue*. 'Tis a great Pity *Debauchery* should have the Assistance of a fine Hand, to whet the Appetite, and play it down.
>
> Now granting the *Play-House-Musick* not vitious in the Composition, yet the design of it is to refresh the *Ideas* of the *Action*, to keep *Time* with the *Poem*, and be true to the *Subject*. For this Reason among others the *Tunes* are generally Airy and Galliardizing: They are contriv'd on purpose to excite a sportive Humour, and spread a Gaity upon the Spirits. To banish all Gravity and Scruple, and lay Thinking and Reflection asleep. This sort of Musick warms the Passions, and unlocks the Fancy, and makes it open to Pleasure like a Flower to the Sun. It helps a Luscious Sentence to slide, drowns the Discords of *Atheism*, and keeps off the Aversions of Conscience. It throws a Man off his Guard, makes way for an ill Impression, and is most Commodiously planted to do Mischief. A Lewd

---

[6] *Poems on Affairs of State*, vol. 5, p. 504.

[7] See Motteux's panegyric prologue to *Europe's Revels* (1697) "Taught by the Vertuous Ruler of our Isle,/ The Stage, Reform'd, has learnt a Chaster Style./ Ev'n with the Pious, 'twill at last be fam'd,/ For Vertue cherisht, and from Vice reclaim'd:/ Such Deeds in Peace, will prove the Monarch's care,/ Who, Boldly Wise, reform'd the Coyn in War" (lines 37–42). William's currency reform provided revenue for his campaigns and was not popular.

[8] Non-jurors refused to take the oath of allegiance to William and Mary.

Play with good Musick is like a Loadstone *Arm'd*, it draws much stronger than before.[9]

The Loves of Mars and Venus could serve as a recent example, and most of the comedies at either playhouse could be made to fit, depending on how strictly one defines "lewdness" and "good music." Like Roger North (see Chapter One), Collier is highly suspicious of music as a physical, sensual pleasure.

Using classical pronouncements about the power of music in different modes to awaken different passions, Collier puts them into very seventeenth-century terms. Those who govern, he suggests, should restrict access to music:

> Now why should it be in the power of a few mercenary Hands to play People out of their Senses, to run away with their Understandings, and wind their Passions about their Fingers as they list? Musick is almost as dangerous as Gunpowder; And it may be it requires looking after no less than the *Press*, or the *Mint*. 'Tis possible a Publick Regulation might not be amiss. No less a Philosopher than *Plato* seems to be of this Opinion. He is clearly for keeping up the old grave, and solemn way of *Playing* ... He does not stick to affirm, that to extend the *Science*, and alter the *Notes*, is the way to have the *Laws* repeal'd and to unsettle the *Constitution* ...

Earlier, Collier fails to condemn all the instrumental music heard in the theaters, being unwilling "to Censure at Uncertainties" though he seems to be in favor of old-fashioned viol consorts rather than modern Italianate ensembles (using violins), who play chromatic music, with "altered" notes not in the mode.

If instrumental music gets a partial pass, vocal music bears the brunt of his criticism:

> If the *English Stage* is more reserv'd than the *Roman* ... If they have any advantage in their *Instrumental* Musick, they loose it in their *Vocal*. Their *Songs* are often rampantly Lewd, and Irreligious to a flaming Excess ... the very *Spirit* and *Essence* of Vice drawn off strong scented, and thrown into a little Compass.[10]

It is not hard to imagine which songs Collier was thinking of, as several of Durfey and Motteux's lyrics come to mind. Durfey's *Don Quixote* gets an entire section to itself in the fifth chapter of Collier's *magnum opus*, with considerable criticism of the song-texts, although Durfey's recent racy comedy *The Intrigues at Versailles* escapes without comment.[11]

---

[9] Jeremy Collier, *A Short View of the Immorality and Prophaneness of the English Stage: A Critical Edition*, ed. Benjamin Hellinger (New York, 1987), pp. 331–3.
[10] Ibid., pp. 333–4.
[11] Ibid., pp. 239–54.

Collier specifically refers to "a Drunken Atheistical Catch" in *The Provok'd Wife* (April 1697). This is Lord Rake's song in Act III, "What a pother of late," in which the singer boasts "religion ne'er dares to disturb me" and concludes: "in peace I jog on to the devil."[12] As various playwrights pointed out, what would you have a rake sing during a drinking scene? Collier's answer would be to have neither rake nor drinking scene; he would also do away with another audience favorite, the mad song. In one of his many warnings to the players Collier admonishes: "Because there is a Space between Blasphemy and Vengeance ... Let them retreat in time, ... Before they come to that place, where Madness will have no Musick, nor Blasphemy any diversion."[13]

Collier's work provoked responses from Congreve, Dennis, Gildon, and other playwrights and critics—as well as many amusing prologues and epilogues. Some authors, like Motteux, put the responsibility back on the consumers of plays to moderate their own consumption of theatrical fare.[14] As is clear from the Lord Chamberlain's orders, several powerful people had already decided to clean up the stage, and they were not alone. Robert Hume identifies no fewer than six distinct, albeit overlapping, groups operating in the 1690s with "overt objections to the current state of English drama."[15] These included reformist playwrights and critics, the Societies for the Reformation of Manners and abolitionist individuals, grand juries and the informers who reported performance infractions.

In May 1698 the Grand Jury of Middlesex made yet another pronouncement against the theaters, objecting to the language used in Congreve's *The Double Dealer* and Durfey's *The Comical History of Don Quixote*, key targets of Collier's, and to the presence of women in masks, as leading to "debauchery & immorality."[16]

The following February, the theaters received another remonstrance from the Lord Chamberlain, citing the usual issues:

> Severall new Plays have lately been Acted, containing expressions contrary to Religion and good manners ... the Actors do often neglect to leave out Such prophane expressions, as he has struck out. These are therefore to signify his

---

[12] Vanbrugh, *The Provok'd Wife*, p. 55. See Chapter Three.

[13] Collier, *A Short View of the Immorality and Prophaneness of the English Stage*, p. 112.

[14] See Motteux's tragedy *Beauty in Distress* (London, 1698), printed with a "Discourse of the Lawfulness & Unlawfulness of Plays, Lately written in French by the Learned Father Caffaro, Divinity-Professor at Paris. Sent in a Letter to the Author By a Divine of the Church of England."

[15] Hume, "Jeremy Collier and the Future of the London Theater in 1698," *Studies in Philology* 96/4 (1999): 480–511 (p. 487). Hume points out that Collier is strangely silent regarding the person who should have been enforcing moral standards, Charles Killigrew, the Master of the Revels.

[16] *Theatrical Documents*, nos. 1585–1588.

Majesties Pleasure, that you do not hereafter presume to Act any thing, in any new play, which the Master of the Revells shall think fitt to be left out ...[17]

Citing complaints, the Lord Chamberlain also ordered that the musicians cease wearing their hats in the theater and onstage.[18]

Predictably, the Grand Jury of Middlesex continued to harass the actors, objecting (again) to Vanbrugh's *The Provok'd Wife* in October 1699,[19] opposing the posting of theatrical bills advertising plays, and objecting to the existence of playhouses in any shape or form.[20] In addition, during the 1699–1700 and 1700–1701 seasons, plays and "Musick-booths" were forbidden at Bartholomew Fair. The fair was a favorite venue and welcome source of funds during the summer season for many comic actor-singers, including Thomas Dogget, William Penkethman, and Elizabeth Willis.[21] The reason given was the tendency of such entertainments to promote immorality and idleness.

Musical Assets

During this period, many new productions were designed to go head to head with offerings at the rival theater. While Lincoln's Inn Fields continued to have the best actors, the disadvantages of self-rule, including limited funds and interpersonal squabbling, and the limitations of the theater itself hampered their efforts. In contrast, the Patent Company added to its attractions with new actors, singers, and composers.

Actor-singers

Cast lists at Lincoln's Inn Fields stayed relatively stable, the Bowmans and Bracegirdle continuing in their usual lines, with the addition of Thomas Dogget when available. They were assisted by Mrs Prince and Elizabeth Willis, both of whom could also dance, making them excellent utility players. Mrs Willis's switch from the Patent Company in 1697 was a definite win for the actors' troupe.

Funny men who could make (or mock) music were also to be found at Drury Lane: in addition to Colley Cibber, both William Penkethman and William Bullock

---

[17] Excerpt from *Theatrical Documents*, no. 1603.

[18] Ibid., no. 1605.

[19] Ibid., no. 1618. Presumably this was at LIF, where the play premiered.

[20] Milhous and Hume provide evidence that the Court of Aldermen supported the Grand Jury, ordering "all possible measures be taken to discourage attendance at plays" and instructing constables to "apprehend ... anyone presuming to post playbills." *Theatrical Documents*, no. 1638

[21] *Theatrical Documents*, nos. 1639, 1645, 1648, 1650, 1667 and 1668. The ban was repeated during the following seasons. *Theatrical Documents* nos. 1701–1703, 1733.

were frequently called on to sing and dance. Young leading man Robert Wilks, returned from Ireland, could really carry a tune, and cut suitable capers with his co-stars. Singer Letitia Cross took an increasing number of roles in comic and serious plays, principally variations on "youthful object of desire," though her career was about to be interrupted. Diana Temple, who had sung in character during earlier seasons, continued to act, but songs for her characters were apparently covered by others.[22] A new player, Maria Allinson, could also sing in character, while Mary Lindsey and Jane Lucas developed both comic and musical lines, supplemented in Lucas's case with dancing.

Singers

Drury Lane made the most of its vocal assets during these seasons, using tenor-countertenors John Freeman and John Pate frequently in its dramatick operas, comedies and tragedies, and in entr'acte performances. Having made at least one trip to Italy in 1697–98,[23] Pate could not only sing virtuosic Italian-style pieces but sing in Italian as well, evidenced by the aria "Pastorella che trà le selvei" printed in the 1699 *Mercurius Musicus* as "Perform'd at the *Theatre* Royal; By Mr. Pate with great Applause."

In his letter to the reader, printed with the libretto for the dramatick opera *The Island Princess* (PC, 1698), Pierre Motteux explicitly thanks Pate for his "admirable Performance [in various musical numbers, both straight and in drag], which, with Mr. Leveridge's, gives life to the whole Entertainment."[24] As singer and as composer, Leveridge was a double asset to Drury Lane, and his departure for Ireland before the 1699–1700 season meant "for want of him we han't one Opera play'd this Winter; tho' [Daniel] Purcell has set one New One and Fingar another."[25] Among the women, the Patent Company would lose Letitia Cross to amorous pursuits,[26] and gain Mary Anne Campion, equally young and attractive, and vocally trainable. Campion would sing a Cross-like musical dialogue with Bowen in *Phaeton* (spring 1698). During these seasons James 'Jemmy' Bowen seems to have been in transition from boy treble to (young) adult tenor. His songs in *Phaeton* lie in alto-countertenor range, but the 'boy' roles in *The Island Princess*

---

[22] She may have lost her voice (no surprise, given the often haphazard vocal training of young women at the time), or the music-master and audiences at DL their patience.

[23] Evidence regarding Pate's trip(s) to Italy and much else appears in Olive Baldwin and Thelma Wilson, "Purcell's Stage Singers," in Burden, ed., *Performing the Music of Henry Purcell*.

[24] Motteux, *The Island Princess, or the Generous Portuguese, Made into an Opera* (London, 1699), unpaginated.

[25] See Vanbrugh's letter 25 December 1699, excerpted in *The London Stage*, vol. 1, p. 521. Vanbrugh attributes Leveridge's absence to debt.

[26] See Baldwin and Wilson, "Purcell's Stage Singers," p. 125.

(February 1699), including another dialogue with Campion, were taken by "Mr. Magnus's boy," the pupil of another theater singer.[27]

In April 1699 Drury Lane countered Lincoln's Inn Fields' high-profile French dancer Jean Balon with a singer, "Signior Clementine," a castrato from the court ensemble of the Elector of Bavaria. During the previous months Drury Lane advertised the Italian (and English) singing of Signior Fideli, previously heard at concerts in York Buildings.[28] Like Balon, Clementine was only in London for a short time and commanded fees the local talent might well envy.[29] His success doubtless paved the way for another expensive castrato singer, Francisco, "the Emperors Crooked Eunuch," in December 1699.[30]

The roster of singers at Lincoln's Inn Fields was diminished by the loss of Mrs Ayliff, although they continued to rely on Mary Hodgson, Anne Perrin, and bass John Wiltshire. His fellow bass, John Reading, seems to have disappeared from theatrical life around this time.

Dancers

There is evidence that both Thomas Bray and Josias Priest continued to choreograph dances for their respective theaters during these seasons. The best-documented examples come from major musical works like *Europe's Revels for the Peace of Ryswick* (LIF, 1697) and *The Island Princess* (PC, 1698),[31] though they doubtless contributed to many less prominent productions as well.

During these seasons both houses began importing foreign stars for limited engagements. As prompter John Downes recalls in 1708:

> In the space of Ten Years past, Mr. *Betterton* to gratify the desires and Fancies of the Nobility and Gentry; procur'd from Abroad the best Dancers and Singers, as, Monsieur *L'Abbe,* Madam *Sublini,* Monsieur *Balon, Margarita Delpine, Maria Gallia* and divers others; who being Exorbitantly Expensive, produc'd small Profit to him and his Company, but vast Gain to themselves;[32]

---

[27] Mr Magnus and his wife sang at DL from 1697 until about 1700. Little is known about them.

[28] *London Stage* vol. 1, pp. 507, 508, 510.

[29] *Theatrical Documents*, no. 1611 gives the newspaper report heralding his appearance. The speakers in *A Comparison between the Two Stages* (pp. 49–50) mock "the Ladies" and their fondness for him.

[30] Letter from Vanbrugh, excerpted in *The London Stage*, vol. 1, p. 521. Although Vanbrugh talks about personalities at both theaters, the use of 'we' and 'they' suggests that Francisco also sang at DL.

[31] See Bray, *Country Dances* (1699). Regarding Josias/Joseph Priest, see Chapter Three.

[32] Downes, *Roscius Anglicanus*, pp. 96–7.

Among the imports listed by Downes, the dancers were the first to arrive.[33] L'Abbé was the first to come to Lincoln's Inn Fields, and there is musical evidence of his performance there. *The Second Part of the Dancing Master* includes "A New *Spanish* Entrey, and Sarabrand Danced by Mounsieur L'*Abbe* before His Majesty at *Kensington*, and at the Theatre in *Little Lincolnes-Inn-Fields*, with great Applause."[34] In their notes on Downes, Milhous and Hume observe that L'Abbé's performances before William III and "at the Play-house" were reported in the *Post-Boy*, a London newspaper (issue dated 13–17 May 1698).[35]

The 1698–99 season was also notable for the arrival in April of another French dancer, Monsieur Jean Balon of the Paris Opéra, of whom critic Sullen, in *A Comparison Between the Stages*, remarks "the Town ran mad to see him, and the prizes [*sic*] were rais'd to an extravagant degree to bear the extravagant rate they allow'd him."[36] Luttrell notes that Balon only stayed five weeks, names a noble patron (Lord Cholmley), and confirms the generous terms on which Balon appeared.[37]

At the end of the season in June a popular English dancer, Susanna Evans, announced through her father her intention to leave the company, perhaps in search of greener pastures.[38] Evans remained at Lincoln's Inn Fields, but would be dead by December 1699. While there is little documentary evidence of her performances, Vanbrugh clearly believed in her popularity and importance to the company.[39]

Composers

Company rosters reveal some significant shifts among the composing staff during the 1697–1700 seasons. Gottfried Finger left Lincoln's Inn Fields, probably at the end of the 1696–97 season, and when he returned to London, he went to work at Drury Lane. The last known Lincoln's Inn Fields production with Finger's music was Congreve's *The Mourning Bride* in the early spring. Francis Forcer, who had been composing sporadically for the theater since the 1670s, seems to have been

---

[33] For discussion of de l'Epine and Gallia, who began singing during the 1702–1703 season, see Chapter Five.

[34] *The Second Part of the Dancing Master*, printed for H. Playford (London, 1698), pp. 47–8.

[35] *Roscius Anglicanus*, p. 96 (note 339).

[36] *A Comparison Between the Two Stages*, p. 49.

[37] Luttrell, *State Affairs*, vol. 4, pp. 502–3.

[38] *Theatrical Documents*, no. 1614.

[39] "She's much lamented by the Towne as well as the House, who can't well bare her loss; Matters running very low with 'em," Vanbrugh letter previously quoted, *The London Stage*, vol. 1, p. 521.

a temporary replacement.[40] During the autumn of 1697 Forcer wrote tunes for *Boadicea* and *The Innocent Mistress*. In early 1698, sets of act tunes for *Heroick Love* and *The Pretenders* are the first firmly attributed to Lincoln's Inn Fields productions written by violinist-composer John Lenton, another member of the King's Private Musick.

Like the aging actors, it seems that Eccles and the musical members of the Lincoln's Inn Fields company largely failed to develop a crop of younger talents. After Finger left the company, who besides Eccles could score an opera? Certainly not Lenton, who wrote a few songs, but very weak ones. Rather than encouraging new composers, Lincoln's Inn Fields appears to have been drawing on the previous generation with Forcer and Solomon Eccles (John's uncle), another instrumentalist in the King's Private Musick, who had contributed music to plays from the 1670s and 1680s. Samuel Akeroyde, older than Eccles, also wrote occasional songs for Lincoln's Inn Fields but maintained ties at Drury Lane as well. Lincoln's Inn Fields had already lost Thomas Tollett, who had written tunes for *The Lover's Luck* (1695).

The company at Lincoln's Inn Fields may have had copies of the music Henry Purcell wrote for some of the 1690s productions it staged, such as Congreve's earlier comedies. The full scores of his major stage works seem to have remained at the Drury Lane theater or in the hands of those who were friendly with Rich and the Patent Company. However, between 1697 and 1700 more and more of Purcell's songs and act music were published, making them accessible to all musicians, professional and amateur.

Of course, the Patent Company did not need to rely on pre-existing music. Where the music for Lincoln's Inn Fields was in the hands of Eccles and Lenton, plus a scattering of older composers, Drury Lane could boast Jeremiah Clarke, Gottfried Finger (by 1699), Richard Leveridge (though periodically absent), and Daniel Purcell. Despite the loss of Henry Purcell, it seemed to be gaining the upper hand among composers. Although it also lost Thomas Morgan, he had contributed to relatively few productions: *The Mock-Marriage* (1695), *The Younger Brother* (1696), *Imposture Defeated* (1697), an entertainment for the Peace of Ryswick (1697), and possibly revivals of *Psyche* and *The Maiden Queen*. Raphael Courteville also seems to have stopped writing regularly for Patent Company productions, although he continued to publish songs. Nevertheless its four principal composers, particularly the three Britons, were relatively young and very active.

Librettists

Reviewing the musical successes of the first three seasons of competition, it is not surprising that the Patent Company appears to have made an effort to acquire

---

[40] Like several PC composers, Forcer trained as a chorister and organist. The oft-repeated assertion that he (like his son) was involved in managing the musical spa at Sadler's Wells seems to be mistaken. See *DNB* vol. 20, p. 316.

the services of Pierre Motteux, whose comedy *Love's a Jest* had done well, and whose musical play *The Loves of Mars and Venus* had done even better. Although Motteux's letter to the reader expresses surprise at the success of his dramatick opera adaptation of *The Island Princess* (PC, 1699), surely this is what they expected. Durfey switched companies for *The Intrigues at Versailles*, a comedy, but returned to the Patent Company for his musical tragedy *Massaniello* (1699). On the 'classical' and scholarly side, Lincoln's Inn Fields staged works by John Dennis and the Patent Company works by his friend John Oldmixon, including tragedy, pastoral and opera.

When John Dryden died in May 1700, the London stage lost its most distinguished living author. Despite his early support of Lincoln's Inn Fields, Dryden's last theatrical work, *The Secular Masque*, was written for the Patent Company, and set to music by its composers.

Patriotic Ploys: The 1697–98 Season

New Productions

Capitalizing on its acting assets, Lincoln's Inn Fields opened the 1697–98 season with a series of new tragedies that were quickly imitated at Drury Lane (Table 4.1). Several of these productions involved extensive and elaborate musical scenes (discussed in more depth in Chapter Two).

Table 4.1 New productions during the 1697–98 season

	New works for the Patent Company		**New works at Lincoln's Inn Fields**	
AUTUMN	*Imposture Defeated*	Comedy	*The Unnatural Mother*	Tragedy
			Boadicea, Queen of Britain	Tragedy
			The Italian Husband	Tragedy
	[*Celebration of the Peace*]	[Masque]	*Europe's Revels*	Entertainment
			The Deceiver Deceived	Comedy
WINTER			*Heroick Love*	Tragedy
	The Country House	Comedy		

	New works for the Patent Company		New works at Lincoln's Inn Fields	
SPRING	*The Fatal Discovery*	Tragedy		
	Caligula	Tragedy	*The Pretenders*	Comedy
	Phaeton	Tragedy		
			Beauty in Distress	Tragedy
			The Fatal Friendship	Tragedy
SUMMER	*The Campaigners*	Comedy		
	Victorious Love	Tragedy		
	The Revengeful Queen	Tragedy	*Queen Catharine*	Tragedy

In addition, this season witnessed a nasty feud between actor-playwright George Powell and author Mary Pix. Pix's farce *The Spanish Wives* had been moderately successful, but when Powell plagiarized the new comedy she had submitted for consideration at Drury Lane and mounted a production under his own name, Pix went over to Lincoln's Inn Fields, where all her subsequent plays were performed.

Given the situation, it made sense for Powell to get his play out quickly. In September Drury Lane staged *Imposture Defeated*: a smorgasbord of loosely connected scenes, with masques in Acts I (Lovers in the Elysian Fields), III (Fame versus Bacchus and his pastoral followers), and V (separately titled, *Endimion, The Man in the Moon*). All the surviving vocal music was set by Thomas Morgan.

The comic equivalent of *Brutus of Alba*, in *Imposture Defeated* Powell employs the 'everything but the kitchen sink' approach, complete with numerous spectacular transformations and musical events. Acts II and IV, containing no formal musical numbers, are enlivened by old Guzman, who is constantly singing snatches of ballads and drinking songs as he stumbles through the subplot.

The first set of musical numbers occurs in Act I, after the spirit Artan decides to show the young rake Hernando (Powell) all he can do, in the interest of obtaining Hernando's soul—reminiscent of both Pix's play and Mountfort's *Dr. Faustus*, revived at Lincoln's Inn Fields the previous year. A transformation scene offers a prospect of the Elysian Fields, complete with orange and cypress trees. The play text indicates that a man and woman sing "How calm *Elisa* are these Groves"— Morgan's songsheet gives the performer as Mary Lindsey, with a countertenor (perhaps Pate) joining her for the lilting chorus "In these sweet *Elesian* Groves." The following musical numbers (not extant) are a dialogue between a persecuted wife and jealous husband ("As I watch'd you in Life, I'll watch you in Death"), a mad song from a demented lover, and "a Dance between a Lawyer, and a Poor Clyent, a Courtier and a Lame Soldier, a Userer [sic] and a Prodigal, a Physician and a Fool" (5–7). These are interspersed with symphonies, and a final song from the first two happy lovers leads to the grand chorus. Hernando is suitably impressed and plans to return to Venice to face his creditors and enemies with Artan's help.

The masques in Acts III and V are entertainments presented at the court of the Duke of Venice, Hernando's uncle. For the Act III masque, only a song by Morgan for Mary Lindsey ("A Shepherdess") survives, "Happy we who free from Love," sung with a suitably pastoral symphony of two flutes, usually warbling together in sweet thirds. The other numbers include a symphony of trumpets and solo for Fame (likely John Freeman), one for Bacchus, contrasting dances by "Clowns and Country Maids" and "Shepherds and Shepherdesses," a comical dialogue between two shepherdesses, and a final solo for Fame and grand chorus. This masque is of particular interest as Powell includes specifics about the blocking: "*Fame* comes Down from the top of the Stage to the front and Sings" (26) and "Enter on one side *Corydon*, ... on the other several Nymphs ... and in the middle *Bacchus*" (27).

Earlier in Act V, Hernando casts off his dependence on Artan and thwarts the spirit's attempt to drag him to hell (complete with thunder, lightning, fiery images) and the excuse for the final masque of Endimion is celebration of his wedding with the Duke's daughter Marcella. From Morgan's published songs, we know that Letitia Cross sang the role of Cupid, Katherine Cibber was Endimion, and Margaret Mills, Cynthia.

In the opening ensemble Endimion's fellow shepherds watch him sleep and mock him. When they leave Cupid (Cross) descends, singing one of Morgan's loveliest airs, "Sleep Shepherd Sleep, till thou Wak'st in Joy." Endimion wakes to join in procession with Cynthia and a "Train of Stars" (perhaps recycled from the operatic *Cinthia and Endimion*); their happiness is reiterated by the grand chorus. Powell claims in his preface that the production ran for five nights, but there is no evidence it was revived.

The new production opening the autumn season at Lincoln's Inn Fields, *The Unnatural Mother*, was an exotic spectacle of a tragedy written, like *She Ventures and He Wins*, by an anonymous young lady. Set in Siam, it provided a choice villainess role for Elizabeth Barry and called for an extensive amount of solo and choral vocal music.[41] As in the Dryden-Purcell dramatick opera *King Arthur*, there is a singing spirit essential to the plot, and as in so many tragedies, a grand musical set piece (a temple funeral) in Act III.

When consulted by a prophet, the (genderless) spirit descends to tell the hero "You fly from what you seek," (8) in Act I. The spirit returns at the end of Act IV to clear up mysterious events, first speaking from under the stage, then ascending to

---

[41] None of the music is known to survive. It was probably not composed by Eccles, since none of it was copied into GB-Lbl Add. MS 29378 with his other music from the early seasons at LIF.

guide the hero back to wisdom. In the middle of Act V there is another conventional musical scene in which a lovelorn lady (Bebbemeah) asks her maid to sing for her. Since this is the last act, the hero, finally convinced that Bebbemeah is innocent of the dreadful things she has been accused of,[42] promptly enters, and they are reconciled.

The Act V song takes place in the country, where Bebbemeah has been exiled, as does the dance "after the Indian manner" in Act IV.[43] These events, unlike earlier ones, do not advance the plot. In pastoral fashion, the country is not only the place of exile (and rustic clowns) but also the space where there is time for music and dancing. When compared with the Patent Company's *Imposture Defeated*, *The Unnatural Mother* demonstrates that the Lincoln's Inn Fields theater, if not equipped for elaborate transformation scenes, did have the usual machines for ascending and descending.

Charles Hopkins's *Boadicea, Queen of Britain* was playing at Lincoln's Inn Fields by October,[44] although it may have premiered earlier.[45] The nationalistic plot (British queen casting off foreign usurpers) may have been intended to uplift, but there are still plenty of gory horrors. In this dramatic effort, dedicated to Congreve, Hopkins wisely gives Barry and Bracegirdle more time onstage than in *Pyrrhus*.

The overture and act tunes for *Boadicea* were written by Francis Forcer, and are known from only one source.[46] Forcer's overture demonstrates an unexpected application of counterpoint ("learned" music), making the first section of the overture a miniature fugue, with subject and countersubject stated in each of the four voices and the subject restated in stretto at the end of the section.[47] After

---

[42] In the middle of Act III, "Scene draws, discovers Bebbemeah asleep on a Couch, with a Black Slave in her Arms." This is a set-up—both are drugged. Barry's villainess enters with the hero and kills the slave with a dagger (her usual problem-solving method). When Bebbemeah wakes, covered in blood, no one believes her protestations of innocence. See Jean Marsden (*Fatal Desire*, pp. 72–3) for an insightful reading of this scene in the context of she-tragedy.

[43] There is a similar dance at the end of Act III of Manley's *The Royal Mischief*, "Performed by Indians" (26). It would be wonderful to locate music or choreography for these "Indian" pieces.

[44] Elizabeth Barry wrote "this day we entertain the Dutchess of Portsmouth with the Tragedy of Boadicea," *Theatrical Documents*, no. 1568.

[45] See Milhous and Hume's commentary in their edition of Downes's *Roscius Anglicanus*, p. 93 note 320. They cite a hypothesis of Price's (based on the Filmer 9 manuscript at Yale) that *Boadicea* was first performed between *Love for Love* (April 1695) and *The City Lady* (December 1696). I am not certain we can trust Filmer MS 9 to be chronological, as many sets of act tunes do not give a production title.

[46] Also from Filmer MS 9. The tunes and overture are in G minor and apparently copied in performance order.

[47] See *Music Productions LIF*, pp. 270–2.

this unusual opening, the second section is the conventional triple-meter imitative texture.

Within the play there is only one musical scene, singing druids sacrificing at the temple in Act IV, "Prepare our Altar, make it clean," no setting known. While the second druid describes a human sacrifice of blood in some detail, there are no stage instructions. At the end of the song "an Eagle flies into the Temple, and flutters awhile about the Flame of the Sacrifice; at last falls in, and is burnt," doubtless providing some tense moments for the stagehands. Drury Lane's *Bonduca* (1695) featured a similar scene of sacrifice and augury in Act III.[48]

November was a busy month for new productions at Lincoln's Inn Fields, but information from Drury Lane is sketchier. The Lincoln's Inn Fields company staged *Europe's Revels for the Peace of Ryswick*, a topical musical entertainment by Motteux; a tragedy, *The Italian Husband*, by Edward Ravenscroft; and a comedy, *The Deceiver Deceived*, by Mary Pix. House composer John Eccles was responsible for all extant music from these three productions. The manuscript score for *Europe's Revels* is attributed entirely to him;[49] he provided the overture, act tunes, and possibly the vocal music for *The Italian Husband*; and he wrote two musical dialogues for *The Deceiver Deceiv'd*.

Celebrating the Peace of Ryswick

Important military and diplomatic events on the Continent received their full share of attention from both theaters. Productions celebrating the Peace of Ryswick included Jeremiah Clarke's ode "Tell the World Great Caesars come" ("composed by Mr. Jer. Clarke upon the Peace of Reswick and performed at Drury Lane playhouse"), another Drury Lane production with music by Thomas Morgan in which singers portrayed classical deities, and the well-documented Motteux–Eccles collaboration, *Europe's Revels for the Peace of Ryswick*.

Clarke's ode was a concert-style piece, but the printed songs from Thomas Morgan's 1697 *Collection of New Songs* were obviously part of a staged dramatic production.[50] Morgan's songs "in the Musick of the Generall Peace" were printed in a specific order, beginning with "Great Jove look down and pity the distrest," sung by Mary Lindsey. The second song, "What wou'd Europa whose shrill cryes," was sung by Leveridge as "Jupiter descends on his Eagle." The third song, "Rebellious Discord 'tis in Vain" is titled "Love Sung by Ms. Cross." The song lyrics suggest a dramatic arc including at least four characters: Europa (Lindsey), Jupiter (Leveridge), 'Rebellious Discord' (possibly Freeman), and Love (Cross), who resolves the conflict.

---

[48] See Price, *Henry Purcell*, pp. 120–21.

[49] In GB-Lbl Add. MS 29378.

[50] D&M 1200, 2788, and 3673. Day and Murrie assigned these songs to *Europe's Revels*, but they have no place in Motteux's libretto and were all performed by PC singers.

[Love]   Rebellious Discord tis in Vain
My Pow'r shall all thy heat restrain,
As out of Chaos Once this mighty Orb did move,
Rais'd by my Charms the Beautious work of Love.
So from a second Chaos Ile restore
The labring world more happy then before
The Son's of Brittain shall to Plough Sheres now,
Convert their Swords, nor Shall they Plough
With Warlike Ships the trembling main,
But strive with forreigne Stores t'encrease Domestick Gaine.

Intended for the London theater audience and not for court, the language of Love's triumph is interestingly mercantile.

The first two songs and the beginning of "Rebellious Discord" are all set in D minor, while the second section of Love's song, beginning "So from a Second Chaos," is set in D major, which would presumably lead into a triumphal concluding chorus. All three open with a declamatory gesture and quickly gain momentum through short sequences. Their brevity suggests that there were several other components to the entertainment. A fourth song by William Williams, "Haste, haste ye Britains," may be from a separate celebration, but is sufficiently generic that it cannot be ruled out of the Patent Company production without more evidence.[51]

The classical allusions of the Patent Company production, and the high seriousness of the other surviving entertainments for the peace, contrast with the lightheartedness of Motteux's work, *Europe's Revels*. As a Huguenot, Motteux had personal reasons to be thankful,[52] but theatrical considerations certainly played a large part in his design. Within the cast of characters, national stereotypes run rampant, with a whisky-laden Irish soldier, English "clowns" (simple countrymen) and their lasses, an affected French couple and an Italian mountebank. These characters perform a series of comic songs, framed by two dance sequences (an entry of nations and a grenadiers' exercise) and enclosed by large-scale musical numbers for chorus, soloists, and orchestra. In the opening and closing numbers, singer Mary Hodgson portrays the Messenger of Peace, contrasting solemn poetry and music reminiscent of a court ode to the actor-singers' broad comedy. In addition to Hodgson and bass John Wiltshire, the cast featured Elizabeth Willis and the Bowmans.

---

[51] The song is said to have been sung by "Mr Lee." Michael Lee sang and acted at LIF but he had a brother at DL, and the song is not identified as a theatrical performance, suggesting a concert or private venue.

[52] In his dedication Motteux complains "I have been condemn'd to Drudge on Laborious Trifles, and Till the barren Fields of Poetry ... being Depriv'd of a handsome Patrimony in *France* before the War, and since that of the small Correspondence I had there." *Europe's Revels* [iii].

The question of performance location(s) for the Motteux–Eccles entertainment is a vexed one. The libretto title page states that the "Musical Interlude"[53] was "Performed at the Theatre in Little Lincolns-Inn-Fields," but it also includes "Words for a single Song on the Kings Return. Design'd for a Private Performance," printed at the end.[54] Given its length, *Europe's Revels* was presumably presented with another work.

In the dialogue between a soldier and a country lass, "Come girls, let's be merry; the War's at an end," Motteux makes light work of a real problem: settling returning soldiers back into the fabric of peacetime society. He depicts the promise of peace in the return and transformation of the soldier into the familiar lover.

> *A Country Lass.*
> Come Girls, let's be merry; the War's at an end;
> We all shall get Husbands: The times now will mend:
> . . . .
> *Enter a Soldier, who runs and kisses her.*
> Dear Joany,
> My Hony.
> What hast thou forgot me? O—How the Wench Stares!
> I'm Thomas the Thresher, just come from the Wars.
> I'm still thy Sweet-heart; and by Cannons and Morttars,
> I'le take thee by Storm; and I'll beat up thy Quarters.
> . . . .
> *She.* Go, I hate you, I vow,
> You look, and you talk like a Gentleman now:
>   Come, off with this Geer,
> And d'on the Reparel, that once you did wear.
> . . . .
> *He.* Well since the War's over, my Brav'ry shall down,
> Off goes the brave Soldier, on goes the plain Clown.
> *[He pulls off his Red Coat, Throws down his Arms and his Wig, and appears, in a Moment, drest like a Country Fellow; she leers on him all the while; and then at last runs and kisses him.*
> *She.* Oh now how I like thee! Oh now I'm thy own!
> . . . .
> *Both Merrily.*

---

[53] On their title pages, Motteux refers to *Europe's Revels* and *Britain's Happiness* (1704), musical celebrations with a small amount of spoken dialogue and minimal plot, as "interludes." Like earlier court masques, these interludes make no sense without reference to the reigning monarch.

[54] This song, "Come, let us revel, drink, and sing," does not appear in the manuscript score, nor was it printed. The "private performance" Motteux aimed at may not have occurred.

> Thus now we agree,
> Let all do like me, She, Like thee,
> To keep their Necks free.
> Leave threshing of Jackets, and get 'em all Wives;
> Then thresh in their Barns, with a thump, thump, thump;
> Then thresh in their Barns, and lead all merry Lives.

Set to a swinging compound meter, the musical dialogue emphasizes certain phrases of the text. "I'm Thomas the thresher" is presented in a steadily ascending line of quarter-notes, suggesting determination, while Joany's repeated exclamation of dismay, "You look and you talk like a *gen*tleman now," contains an abrupt leap upwards emphasizing her shock.

Along with the broad country humor and tuneful music, there are significant implications. Is the countryman John's transformation back into a happy civilian a reflection of contemporary English attitudes towards William III's desire to maintain a standing army after the signing of the peace? One could also read a message for returning soldiers, as Thomas must relinquish his red coat, which masks his "true" identity, and return to his proper peacetime state before being rewarded by Joany.

This central section of the entertainment consists largely of musical dialogues, a favored form for Motteux. In the first dialogue between an English Lady and a French Officer, Eccles has taken care to musically distinguish the Frenchman, whose garbled Franglais is set in stiffly misaccented recitative, from the gay duple-meter melody of the English Lady. There is no reconciliation for this pair, musically, and in the manuscript score there is a direct segue from the dialogue's final lines into "Hub, ub ub, booh," a song for an Irish soldier.[55] Comparing the score with Motteux's libretto reveals that a part for a French Woman was cut, as was the reconciling chorus emphasizing the pleasures of home over "Foreign Charms" (6). A dialogue for the English Lady and English Officer (the Bowmans) was also excised.[56]

The musical highlights of the piece are the opening and concluding solos and ensembles, with John Bowman's call to arms, "Arm, Britons! Hark! how from afar/ Alarming Drums and Trumpets call to War," and the airs for Mary Hodgson as the messenger of Peace, whose appearance effects a musical transformation. The change from "a Warlike Symphony, an Alarm with Trumpets and Drums" to "softer Notes, with accompaniments of Flutes" is an entirely conventional one, but Eccles's music is a delightful realization of the convention. Graceful flourishes on "tunes" and "harmonious" change to more emphatic music as the messenger of Peace describes the English king: "Who can like *Neptune* calm the Seas,/ And bless, like *Jove*, his very Foes."

---

[55] See GB-Lbl Add. MS 29378, f.128.

[56] There are many possible explanations for the cuts, but given the absence of both Mrs Ayliff and Anne Perrin, perhaps LIF was temporarily short of singers.

Motteux clearly considered the dances, including the entry of nations with Dutch, English, French and Spanish couples, an important part of the overall production. There is more surviving musical evidence for these dances than is usual, although choreography is not available for most of them.[57] The "grenadiers exercise" which precedes the final triumphal chorus may be a reference to the grenadiers who led William III's procession into London, but such dances were also a favorite comic device, witness the "Posture-Dance in imitation of Soldiers Exercise" in Act II of *The Cornish Comedy* (PC, 1696).

In addition to the more familiar national stereotypes embodied in the French and Irish characters, the figure of the Savoyard with the Raree-Show (a peep show, cabinet-sized, with multiple niches) probably alludes to the Duke of Savoy, who had been an ally of William's before breaking to deal separately with Louis XIV.[58]

> Here be d'*Inglish* and *French* to eatch oder most civil,
> Shaka Hand, and be Friends, and hug like de Deevel
>   O Rareeshow, &c.
> Here be de Savoyards a trudgin tro France,
> To sweep a de Shimny, to sing and to dance.
>   O Rareeshow, &c.
> Here be de Great Turk, and de Great King of no Land;
> And dere be some gallop from Hungary and Poland.
>   O Rareeshow, &c.
> Here's de brave English Beau for de Packet Bot tarries,
> To go make his Campaign, with his Taylor at Paris,
>   O Rareeshow, &c.

The stage directions instruct the singer to come onstage with his show and to turn the crank (moving the figures in the niches) with every chorus. According to Motteux's text, the Savoyard begins and ends his performance with a "Savoyard Ditty," beginning "Quand la cigala canta" to a simple tune.

The Raree-show song, the Irish's soldier's mock lament "Hub, ub, booh," and the dialogue for the country lovers were among the most popular portions of the entertainment, appearing in print shortly after the production opened.[59]

---

[57] For more on the dances and Motteux's libretto, see Kathryn Lowerre, "A *ballet des nations* for English audiences: *Europe's revels for the peace of Ryswick* (1697)," *Early Music* 25 (2007): 419–34.

[58] See Tom Brown's vindictive *Satyr upon the French King* (October 1697), where he imagines Louis XIV forced to become a barber-surgeon and Savoy to travel with a raree-show. *Poems on Affairs of State,* vol. 6, pp. 10–11.

[59] D&M 640, 1474, and 2519. "The Raree Show" also appeared as an illustrated broadside, with the performer displaying his apparatus. An example from the British

The Savoyard's song, "O Raree Show," would have a long afterlife and inspire numerous parodies.[60]

Productions later in the 1697–98 season were also highly musical. Edward Ravenscroft's tragedy *The Italian Husband*, like his comedy *The Anatomist*, includes a masque, *Ixion*, but in *The Italian Husband* the masque is directly connected to the plot. Ravenscroft's tragedy has only three acts, which he anticipated would evoke criticism. To counteract this he wrote a preliminary dialogue between a poet, a critic, and a traveler, contending that subject and characters, not the number of acts, determine genre. The poet states:

> many Plays of late are all talk and no business; others have some business, but so much talk, that the business is almost lost ... and the Plays lag ... to avoid this, I have now laid the business so close, that every Scene may seem necessary to carry on the design ... I confine my self to three Acts, which gives me also opportunity to introduce some Musical Entertainments, and those seeming natural to the Play; which few Poets have yet observ'd.[61]

These "natural-seeming" entertainments are a public celebration of the anniversary of the wedding of Frederico, Duke of Radiano and his duchess Alouisa at the beginning of Act I, a song sung privately to soothe the guilty and distracted Duchess in Act II, and the masque of *Ixion* staged by the Duke as part of a grisly revenge banquet at the beginning of Act III. For more on this tragedy, see Chapter Two.

Pix's comedy *The Deceiver Deceiv'd* also features an Italian setting. The prologue is predictably acerbic on the subject of the Patent Company's *Imposture Defeated*:

> With Powderle-Pimp of Dance, Machine and Song,
> They'll spin ye out short Nonsense four hours long:
> With Fountains, Groves, Bombast and airy Fancies
> Larded with *Cynthias*, little Loves and Dances:
> Which put together, makes it hard to say,
> If Poet, Painter, or Fidler made the Play.[62]

Compared with Powell's exceedingly musical version of much the same material, *The Deceiver Deceiv'd* has only an average number of musical events, concentrated in two entertainments in Acts IV and V.

Museum is reproduced in the DNB entry for the original performer, James 'Jemmy' Laroche, vol. 32, pp. 583–4.

[60] See Simpson, *British Broadside Ballad*, pp. 538–9.
[61] Edward Ravenscroft, *The Italian Husband* (London, 1697), unpaginated.
[62] Mary Pix, *The Deceiver Deceiv'd* (London, 1698), unpaginated.

The Deceiver Deceiv'd contains two musical dialogues, printed at the front of the play text and penned by the best-known dialogue authors, Durfey and Motteux. The first, "When vill Stella kind and *tendre/* Recompense *Fidele amour*," was published in *Wit and Mirth*. It appears in an entertainment at the beginning of Act IV in which the foolish French beau and would-be author Count Insulls sings with the heroine, Ariana, in yet another Bracegirdle–Bowman comic dialogue. The play text also calls for unspecified songs and a dance by the flirtatious Lucinda (Mrs Prince) and a French beau (27). Lucinda's guardian, the scheming Lady Temptyouth, explicitly connects the illegitimately born Lucinda's musical graces with manipulation (22).

The second dialogue, "Why do I sigh and languish so," sung by "a Boy and a Girl, and an Old Man," appears in truncated form in Eccles's 1704 *Collection*, where it is attributed to *The Italian Husband*.[63] The place of the dialogue is not indicated, but given its celebration of marriage, presumably it precedes the dance at the play's end.[64] Once the virtuous couples have been paired off, Lady Temptyouth, having married Lucinda off, calls for "the Musick I ordered ... that we may conclude our Joys with a Dance" (47).

Lincoln's Inn Fields was apparently first to mount a new production in January 1698, a tragedy by George Granville which "mightily pleas'd the Court and City."[65] Dryden's poem, "To Mr. Granville, on his Excellent Tragedy, call'd HEROICK LOVE," is full of praise for the author, but harshly condemns the actors and the theaters. After all the panegyrics about the Lincoln's Inn Fields actors, Dryden's commentary ("Not ill they Acted ... Like Ancient *Rome*, Majestick in decay") comes as a shock, though he is brutally dismissive of the Patent Company's efforts as well. Dryden would continue to contribute poems to new productions, but his disaffection with Lincoln's Inn Fields is clear. His last theatrical work, *The Secular Masque* (April 1700), would be written for Drury Lane.

Lenton's act tunes for *Heroick Love*, all in the heroic key of D major, can be found in Filmer MS 9.[66] An ode of Abraham Cowley's, "I'll sing of heroes and of kings," was published as sung in *Heroick Love* and may have been performed between the acts.[67] If it was inserted in the play, it probably was sung for the love-sick Agamemnon (Cowley's poem proclaims "The Strings will Sound of nought but Love"). Achilles calls for music in Act IV: "Till every Valley eccho̊es back, *Rejoice*,"[68] but the only music indicated is the usual flourish of trumpets.

---

[63] Eccles's plaintive setting of the solo section for the girl is a simple triple-meter air.

[64] The text of the final chorus reads: "'Tis Time you should Wed, if already you long;/ We're quickly too Old, but we're never too Young."

[65] Downes, *Roscius Anglicanus*, p. 93.

[66] The overture and five of the tunes for *Heroick Love* in Filmer MS 9 are missing the bass part as well as tenor. See Price, *Music in the Restoration Theatre,* p. 177. The first and second music are in the relative minor.

[67] Day and Murrie list three earlier settings, D&M 1635.

[68] Granville, *Heroick Love* (London, 1698), p. 46.

Drury Lane mounted Vanbrugh's farce *The Country House*, a far different production from Granville's or those staged earlier in the season. Another translation from the French, *The Country House* was a two-act work which must have been performed with a main piece, but performance records are of no assistance, and no music is known for it.

In contrast, during the following months the Patent Company staged a series of tragedies employing considerable amounts of music, although little has been recovered. First, in February, the anonymous tragedy *The Fatal Discovery; or, Love in Ruines* appeared, complete with an unremittingly nasty preface by Powell, attacking Dryden and Granville. In performance, Powell spoke an often-quoted prologue mocking Betterton's performance in *The Rival Queens*.[69]

The printed text for *The Fatal Discovery* calls for a masque with dancing in Act II, organized by the incestuous mother, Berengaria, to celebrate the return of the absent son to whom she secretly bore a daughter fifteen years previously. To perfect the tragedy, the son immediately falls in love with his child. If the masque hinted at the tangled sexual sins of its patron or its onstage audience (like Ravenscroft's *Ixion*), the play text gives no indication, and no music is known. Perhaps the masque of Endimion from Powell's previous 'managed' production, *Imposture Defeated*, was reused, or another from a less recent work.

The Patent Company followed *The Fatal Discovery* with an equally lurid tragedy, *Caligula*, by John Crowne. The printed play text lacks detail about some of the musical events, though there are many. In *Caligula* music is once again purely a pleasure for the corrupt. While being petitioned for clemency, Caligula bids his general, Valerius, sing the petitions, adding "Priests sing, and make an Opera of their Prayers" (9). They surely do on the London stage, and in the second act, there is just such a scene. Rather than appearing in a temple, the priests process "carrying a golden Image of the Emperor, attended by Consuls and Senate" while singing his praises (17). The imperial misuse of music takes another turn in Act IV as Caligula accompanies the offstage rape of the virtuous, married Julia (one of his many crimes) with music: "Does she love noise? Then let my musick play" (34).

In the end, music cannot soothe the emperor or quell the coming bloody insurrection:

> *Cal.* ... Let Musick try, with sweet inchanting sounds
> To calm my stormy thoughts, to lull my care.
> Musick charm'd Hell and all the furies there.
> *[After a short Entertainment of Musick and Dancing; Shrieks and noises are heard from behind the Scenes.*[70]

---

[69] For example, "Wou'd it not any Ladies' Anger move/ To see a Child of sixty five make Love./ Oh! My Statira! Oh, my angry dear (Grunting like B[etterton]." *The Fatal Discovery; or, Love in Ruines* (London, 1698), unpaginated. Music in this stock tragedy is discussed in Chapter Two.

[70] Crowne, *Caligula. A Tragedy* (London, 1698), p. 48.

The only surviving music for *Caligula* appears to be two songs. One, by Daniel Purcell, "Beneath the Covert of a Grove" was sung by 'the Boy' and may have been performed during this final entertainment.[71] The other song, composed by Leveridge, was sung by Mary Lindsey at a performance attended by Princess Anne.[72] Overall, the princess's support appears to have been fairly evenly divided between the two theaters.[73]

The song for the princess, "Tho' over all Mankind," with violin obbligato, divides into the usual contrasting sections:

> Tho' over all Mankind beside my Conquering beauty Reignes,
> From him I Love, when I meet disdain,
> A killing damp comes ore my pride
> I'm fair & young in Vain,
> No, let him wander where he will,
> I shall have youth & beauty still:
> I shall have beauty, that can charme a Jove,
> And no fault but Constant Love.
> From my arms then let him fly,
> Shall I languish pine & dye;
> No, no, no not I.

The text is cheerful, and hard to imagine amusing Caligula, though it seems appropriate to amuse Princess Anne (Leveridge repeats the end of the first line several times for emphasis).

In March, amidst the run of tragedies, Lincoln's Inn Fields staged another Thomas Dilke comedy, *The Pretenders; or, The Town Unmask'd*. Like his earlier comedies, it was a showcase for the comic and musical talents of the Bowmans. Every character, with the exception of the virtuous Ophelia (Elizabeth Bowman) and Sir Bellamour Blunt, a "Country Gentleman of good sense," is pretending to *be* something they are not or to *have* something they do not. Lord Wealthy pretends he has no money and Lord Courtipoll pretends he has influence. Minx, kept by Courtipoll, pretends to be a naïve country girl while the hypocritical landlady Sweetny pretends to "Piety and Devotion." Vainthroat, "a loose talkative

---

[71] Not in D&M. Copy examined, GB-Lgc vol. 313 (song 25).

[72] Leveridge's song appeared as the first piece in his *Second Book of Songs* (London, 1699) and in a songsheet engraved by Thomas Cross (copy examined, Lbl K.7.i.2, song 66).

[73] She apparently attended performances of Pix's *Ibrahim* (PC, 1696) and Ravenscroft's *The Anatomist* (LIF, 1696). *Love for Love* was acted at court to celebrate her birthday in 1697. Congreve's *The Mourning Bride* (LIF, 1697) and Trotter's *The Fatal Friendship* (LIF, 1698) were both dedicated to her. She later requested a performance of the dramatick opera *The Island Princess* (PC, 1699).

Gentleman" (John Bowman), is not said to be pretending to anything, but he may be past pretence.[74]

The first song, "The Riddle of Nature,/ Is a Female Creature" is performed by Vainthroat at the beginning of Act II for Ophelia (who challenges his misogyny) and Sweetny (14). No setting is known. The next musical events, a song and dance, occur in the middle of Act III, as Vainlove strives to amuse the melancholy Sir Bellamour. The song begins, predictably enough, "Let never dull sorrow our joys invade,/ But for ever let's follow the toping trade" (24). Vainthroat's song suggests masculine revelry, but it is strictly a drinking song, without the bawdy or blasphemy of songs from *The Provok'd Wife* or *The Intrigues at Versailles*. The dance presumably continued the merrymaking.

Near the beginning of Act IV, Vainthroat sees Sir Bellamour again and "sings in a Ballad tone": "But see where walks the doughty Knight,/ Who all in doleful guise,/ Metes out the time of sable night/ With Tears dropt from his Eyes" referring to the melancholy Don Quixote, immortalized by Cervantes and recently dramatized by Durfey. Vainthroat's mocking allusions continue in the spoken dialogue (31).

Although the characters played by the Bowmans are not a couple, they are well matched in performance:

> *Oph.* This might be a proper Scene for some of the idle Romantick Stories we meet withal in Novels—As when Olimpia, lying under the constraint of severe Parents ... takes her Lute, and steals gently forth into the Garden, where, having burthen'd the ambient Air with pressing sighs, and long complain to the regardless Plants, at length the lovely Nymph warbles out some soft and killing words made of her absent Swain *Celadon*, conceal'd in an adjacent Arbour, surpriz'd with the unlookt for harmony, rushes out of his melancholy covert, flings himself at the feet of his charming Goddess, and there expires in the highest Transport of an amorous passion.
> (*She speaks this slightingly, as ridiculing the matter.*)
> *Nibs.* And would not this, Madam, look very prettily, were it to be performed in reality ...
> *Oph.* I will not deny you a Song, Nibs, but I believe the story as you call it, is like to begin and end with it.
>   SONG.
> All things seem deaf to my complaints,
>   In vain I roam the Groves along.
> Hear me ye Loves departed Saints,
>   That to Elizyan shades are gone.
> If to my faithful Celadon I prove not true,
> Let it be both our dooms never to come to you.
>   Sir Bellamour *rushes hastily from the Arbour, and flings himself at the Feet of* Ophelia.[75]

---

[74] Thomas Dilke, *The Pretenders; or, the Town Unmaskt* (London, 1698), unpaginated.

[75] Ibid., p. 35.

Figure 4.1　J. Eccles, "All things seem deaf to my complaints" in *The Pretenders*. From Eccles, *A Collection of Songs*, pp. 15–16

Figure 4.1 Concluded

Ophelia, understandably startled, "shreiks out," but when she has regained her composure continues to tease her plain-spoken lover.

Playing up Ophelia's sense of the ridiculous, Eccles sets "deaf" to melismas of a height and length—and presumably, volume—that ensure a listener would have to be deaf to miss the heroine's singing. The jaunty triple-meter of the first section (see Figure 4.1) is followed by straight quarter-notes in a contrasting section, "If to my faithful Celadon I prove not true." In the end, the portentous sound of the final line of poetry is undercut by the relentlessly regular dance rhythms of Eccles's music.

The act tunes and overture for Dilke's comedy were composed by Lenton, and while selected tunes were published and copied, the only complete set of music is in manuscript.[76] An air and jig from the preliminary music were printed in Playford's anthology *Apollo's Banquet*, described as "Danc'd by Mr. Eaglesfield at the Theatre," but it is not clear whether they were used as dances in the original production or, since the comedy did not become a stock play, if its act tunes were later used for other purposes.[77]

Charles Gildon's musical tragedy *Phaeton; or, The Fatal Divorce* premiered at Drury Lane some time early in the spring, and has a confirmed performance in mid-May. Like other Patent Company tragedies from this season, *Phaeton* has musical events in nearly every act. These include an extended pastoral divertissement in Act I featuring songs and dialogues performed by John Pate, James 'Jemmy' Bowen, Mary Anne Campion, John Freeman, and Mr Magnus, and a classical masque in Act III with Mary Lindsey as Juno, descending to confront Hymen and Nemesis (ascending), each with her train of attendants. The songs from *Phaeton* appeared in a separate songbook, like Walsh's for *The World in the Moon* (PC, 1697), *Brutus of Alba* (PC, 1696) and *The Loves of Mars and Venus* (LIF, 1696) but this time printed by John Heptinstall. The printed songs all come from the first act entertainment, except "Look down bright God of day," sung in the fifth act by John Pate as part of a temple ceremony. The other surviving song, Mary Lindsey's "O Hymen! Must we always see," from Act III appeared in Henry Playford's *The A'Lamode Musician*.

In his preface, Gildon explains his curious combination of elements from Philippe Quinault's *tragédie lyrique*, *Phaéton* with Euripedes's *Medea* and addresses some of Collier's criticisms of the stage. Gildon praises the actors, particularly Frances Knight as Althea (Phaeton's beloved, then abandoned, revenge-seeking wife) but notes "the *Music* was so admirable, that the best Judges tell me ... that there is a

---

[76] The source, again, is Yale's Filmer MS 9, in which the performance order is clear. The act tunes are suitably light-hearted: a "Scotch" tune, a hornpipe, a lively triple-meter air, and jig.

[77] Concordances from Price, *Theater Music*, p. 213. However, the piece which begins the set in *Apollo's Banquet*, no. 14, "This Entry and the two following Ayres, Danc'd by Mr. Eaglesfield at the Theatre," is not one of Lenton's, suggesting that someone (Eaglesfield, Lenton, or one of the theater managers) was recycling.

true *Purcellian Air* through the whole: that tho' it be so very different in the several Acts, it is every where Excellent; and that Mr. *Daniel Purcells* Composition in this Play is a certain Proof, that as long as he lives Mr. *Henry Purcel* will never die."[78] The music for *Phaeton* is discussed further in Chapter Two. Although the Patent Company offered no new dramatick opera this season, it continued reviving past successes like the Purcell–Dryden *King Arthur*, and its singers and musicians were kept busy enough with these musical tragedies.

The later spring months, April and May, each saw a new tragedy appear at Lincoln's Inn Fields: first, Motteux's *Beauty in Distress*, then Catharine Trotter's *The Fatal Friendship*. Neither was a great success, although Princess Anne apparently supported both (especially Trotter's play). Unlike *Caligula* or *Phaeton*, both restrict their use of music, including only a single scene with a "symphony" of instrumental music (a serenade, a celebratory concert). No act tunes or incidental music of any sort are known to have survived for them.[79]

The Patent Company responded to these new spring productions with three of its own, another comedy by Thomas Durfey, *The Campaigners; or, The Pleasant Adventures at Brussels*, and two tragedies by first-time authors, William Philips's *The Revengeful Queen* and William Walker's *Victorious Love* (less tragic than many). All three productions make generous use of music, and the contrast between the tragedies and those at Lincoln's Inn Fields is striking.

Published together with his response to Collier, Durfey's *The Campaigners* seems an old-fashioned comedy: the hero has weathered a bout of smallpox, the heroine had a baby out of wedlock (by the hero). The play shows many typical 'Durfeyisms,' including songs in every act and dances in the last three. The song "New reformation begins thro' the nation" borrows its tune from Henry Purcell's minuet for Durfey's earlier comedy, *The Virtuous Wife* (1679). Appropriately, it is performed with a dance during a drinking scene in Act IV (40–41).

Like *The Intrigues at Versailles* (LIF, 1697), *The Campaigners* is set on the Continent. Writing for Drury Lane, Durfey uses Colley Cibber's 'line' as a mock-Frenchman; he is cast as a ridiculous Marquis and performs the epilogue in character: "Me vill to please you do one odor ting,/ Not dance en Francois, but en Francois sing,/ Such time, sush graces, and such Raree-shew,/ Dat you sall tinke you are at *Fontainebleau*."[80] Performance directions indicate that Cibber "Mimicks the *French* Singers here," referring to the consort of the "best Voices lately come from France" heard in concert at York Buildings.[81] Equally ridiculous

---

[78] Gildon, *Phaeton; or, The Fatal Divorce* (London, 1698), unpaginated.

[79] For more on these tragedies and the details of the musical scenes, see *Music Productions LIF*, pp. 288–91.

[80] Durfey, *The Campaigners: or, The Pleasant Adventures at Brussels* (London, 1698), unpaginated, italics reversed.

[81] The French consort was advertised for 31 March 1698. Other concerts at this time touted "Signior Rampany, an Italian Musician belonging to the Prince of Vaudemont." *London Stage*, vol. 1, p. 493.

is Mary Lindsey's song in Act II, "My dear Cockadoodle, my Jewel, my Joy," which she sings in character as "An Affected, Tattling Nurse"—a far cry from her serious songs as Juno (*Phaeton*) or to entertain Princess Anne (*Caligula*).

Heptinstall printed three songs for *The Campaigners* in the songbook for *Phaeton*. Three songs also survive as engraved single sheets by Thomas Cross— the nurse's song for Mary Lindsey and two featuring youthful performers: "the new Boy" singing the virtuosic "Phillis has such charming Graces" by Daniel Purcell and Mary Anne Campion performing Clarke's Scotch song, "Jockey was a dowdy Lad" (Act III, also in the *Phaeton* songbook). The music for the Act V entertainment is not described but it may have included "*Phillis* has such charming Graces" or "*Cloris* for once take my advice," both attributed to *The Campaigners* but not printed in the text.

William Philips's *The Revengeful Queen* did not find favor with London audiences, though Philips (an Irishman) was patronized by the Duke of Ormond. In Philips's tragedy Queen Rosamund decides to revenge her father, slain by the present king (her husband Alboino) with the help of the "Rich, Dissembling, Cowardly" Almachild. Something of a ladies' man, Almachild both sings in character at the end of Act I, "No more, *Aminta*, say you love,"[82] and is sung to, "Oh Love how mighty are thy Joys!" when he retires with Rosamund in Act V.

The second song is clearly Rosamund's doing, not Almachild's, as it concludes "that I ever might partake/ Of such transporting Bliss,/ I wou'd in t'other World awake,/ As I expire in this" (41). If music and her love are not enough to cure Almachild's guilt over murdering her husband, Rosamund has a poisoned goblet ready for him (he forces her to drink from it too).

The major musical scene occurs in Act III, as King Alboino celebrates military victory with a masque of Mars and Bacchus, plus a "Troop of Virgins" who hold out for love (17–19). Bacchus triumphs in the end, but drinking leads directly to Alboino's downfall and murder, and his general, Aistolfus, snarls, "I hate these low effeminating Sounds;/ Such Musick which softens while it pleases:/ I'd hear none but the lofty *Phrygian* Airs" (19). As in Crowne's *Caligula*, Philips's tragedy presents music being misused for frivolous and sinister ends.

Another effort by a gentleman new to playwriting, William Walker's *Victorious Love*, was obviously designed for Letitia Cross to play the heroine, Zaraida. Walker's preface insists that "had it been Exposed in Winter, and in the Favourite House, I had succeeded," and that he was blamed for the venue and censured for acting in his own play.[83]

After a "Warlike Dance" and "Warlike Musick" for the Emperor of Tombus in Act I, Walker includes two conventional song scenes in Acts II and IV. The first, featuring Zaraida (a shipwrecked European orphan desired by virtually every male character), combines two classic situations: the grove scene and the "reclining

---

[82] D&M 171, published in Nicola Matteis's 1699 *A Collection of new Songs*, second book.

[83] Walker, *Victorious Love: A Tragedy* (London, 1698), unpaginated.

woman on a couch." Where most heroines listen as the song is sung, Zaraida rises and sings "*Myrtillo* Dead, and I a Slave!/ What Sorrow can suffice?" Walker apparently did not receive help from friends or colleagues in penning the song lyrics, which is regrettable.

The powers of music are less benign in the wild incantation scene, "Arise ye Fiends of Hell," in Act III. When summoned, both 'celestial' and 'infernal' spirits ascend and descend to incite the emperor to murder and rape, in long solos and choruses of execrable poetry, followed by dancing. The singing spirits are reminiscent of *King Arthur* and the aerial spirits of Act III of the operatic *Indian Queen*, but rather than providing supernatural insight, they have been co-opted by evil priests and are merely their mouthpieces.

The song in Act IV, "Ease with soft Sleep your weary Eyes," is sung from offstage by John Freeman as a benevolent spirit of some sort, though presumably *not* the ghost of Zaraida's mother, seen hovering over Zaraida's couch when the scene opens (à la *The Rival Queens*). Walker created his heroine for an actress known better for her vocal ability (and beauty) than her acting, and he uses music extensively. Yet he thanks no composers for their efforts and no music survives.

Mary Pix's *Queen Catharine; or, the Ruines of Love* was another summer effort, but blessed with a strong cast. In Pix's version of English history, Queen Catharine is the heroic figure, while Owen Tudor is simply a noble love-interest. Music appears only at the beginning of Act V, when "The Trumpets play an overture of Victory" (39); no surviving pieces are associated with it.

The one remaining new production possibly performed at Drury Lane during this season or early in the next is John Oldmixon's pastoral *Amintas*, based on Torquato Tasso. *Amintas* attempted to make an entire production out of pastoral revels, which in previous seasons had typically been confined to masques and entertainments, or even single songs. Oldmixon admits his work was not a success, that the "simple Action, tender Passions, and innocent Sentiments" were not pleasing to his audience, and that he was not particularly good at managing the staging. Like other Patent Company authors, he defends the actors: "I question if any other Company would have done it better."[84]

Amintas is self-consciously classical, using the chorus as a speaking role, while a musical chorus concludes each act except the last. Only one piece of vocal music appears to have survived, a song by Daniel Purcell, "Cupid make your Virgins tender," taken from the chorus and solos concluding Act III. Purcell's song was popular enough to appear both in *Mercurius Musicus* (March 1699) and in single songsheets (by both Walsh and Thomas Cross), but no printed version names the production—surely no selling point. However lacking in audience appeal, *Amintas* was printed with an admiring prologue from John Dennis, who would turn to Tasso himself for his next theater work, *Rinaldo and Armida*, in November.

---

[84] Oldmixon, *Amintas, A Pastoral Acted at the Theatre Royal* (London, 1698), unpaginated.

Figure 4.2 J. Eccles, "Can Life be a blessing" from *Troilus and Cressida*. From Eccles, A Collection of Songs, p. 137

Revivals, 1697–98

In October Lincoln's Inn Fields revived Howard's comedy *The Committee; or, The Faithful Irishman* and Dryden's tragedy *Troilus and Cressida*, both strong stock plays, and by authors it was politic to keep happy. For *Troilus and Cressida*, it had key members of the original cast. John Eccles wrote songs for both.

"Can life be a blessing," the "Song with a Symphony" published in Eccles's 1704 *Collection*, was probably written for a Lincoln's Inn Fields production, as so many of the other songs in the *Collection* were. Sung in Act III by hired musicians, the song is ordered by Pandarus to serenade the lovers he has brought together.

> Musick, and then Song: during which *Pandarus* listens.
> 1.
> Can life be a blessing,
> Or worth the possessing,
> Can life be a blessing if love were away?
> Ah no! though our love all night keep us waking,
> And though he torment us with cares all the day,
> Yet he sweetens he sweetens our pains in the taking,
> There's a hour at the last, there's an hour to repay.
> 2.
> In every possessing,
> The ravishing blessing,
> In every possessing the fruit of our pain,
> Poor lovers forget long ages of anguish,
> Whate're they have suffer'd and done to obtain;
> 'Tis a pleasure, a pleasure to sigh and to languish,
> When we hope, when we hope to be happy again.

It is a charming example of what Collier calls the "Airy and Galliardizing" triple-meter song (see Figure 4.2), although Collier would doubtless object to the lyrics and the scene in which they were heard. Eccles's setting gives no hint of "torment" or "anguish," but emphasizes the happy moment. Like several of Eccles's other songs, "Can life be a blessing" is brief but beautifully balanced and eminently singable.

The only other production known to have been revived at Lincoln's Inn Fields this season was Beaumont and Fletcher's *The Maid's Tragedy*. An anonymous song, "Gentle Night, befriend a Lover," appeared in the music periodical *Mercurius Musicus* for August 1699, and may have been performed at this time or during an undocumented revival the following season.[85] A song by Raphael Courteville

---

[85] Some tunes "for ye Maid's Tragedy" by Louis Grabu were copied into GB-Lcm 1144 with sets of act music from the 1690s by Finger, Lenton, Tollett, and the Purcells,

published in 1698,[86] "Sung in Orensebe [*Aureng Zebe*]" by Mary Hodgson, provides a tantalizing hint that the Dryden play may also have been revived at Lincoln's Inn Fields, and suggests Raphael Courteville may have written songs for Lincoln's Inn Fields as well as for Drury Lane.

Records for revivals at Drury Lane are more substantial. In autumn several comedies were revived, first old favorites from United Company days and then a more recent success, Vanbrugh's *The Relapse*. At the height of the winter months and into early spring Drury Lane mounted dramatick opera revivals, all with music by Henry Purcell: *Dioclesian*, *The Indian Queen*, and *King Arthur* (at least three times). In addition to its longevity in revivals, the influence of Dryden and Purcell's opera on musical practices in new productions at Drury Lane cannot be overstated.

Known summer revivals at Drury Lane are a mixed bag: one classic comedy (Wycherley's *The Plain Dealer*), one recent tragedy (Southerne's *Oroonoko*), and a possible dramatick opera (*The Tempest*). Of the other 'probable' plays listed in *The London Stage*, the musical evidence supports two. Songs by Daniel Purcell from *The Taming of the Shrew* (Lacy's adaptation, *Sauny the Scot*) including the popular "Scotch" song "'Twas in the month of May Jo," were printed in 1699.[87] Thomas Morgan's act music for Dryden's tragicomedy *Secret Love; or, The Maiden Queen*, written c.1695–97, suggests a revival at Drury Lane.

Musical Extravagance: The 1698–99 Season

New Productions

Although far fewer premieres are known during this season, once again patterns of competitive emulation emerge, as each company attempted to model a new work on one of the other's recent successes, eager to capitalize on any evidence of a successful match with audience tastes. A particularly well-known example of such theatrical one-upmanship concerns Dennis's *Rinaldo and Armida* and Motteux's dramatick opera version of Fletcher's *The Island Princess*. The competition during this season was described by a contemporary as "the great Turn which seem'd to decide the Fates of *Rome* and *Carthage*."[88] The success of *Rinaldo and Armida*, with its careful integration of plot, dialogue, staging, and music, was subsequently overshadowed by the flashy charms of *The Island Princess*, which became a stock entertainment and added to the Patent Company's useful repertory of dramatick operas.

---

suggesting that they were reused during this later period. Lcm 1144 includes music from productions by both companies.

[86] See D&M 531. *The London Stage* lists *Aureng Zebe; or, The Great Mogul* as a possible revival in 1698–99 (vol. 1, p. 502).

[87] *London Stage* vol. 1, p. 485. See also Hunter 5 (193).

[88] *A Comparison Between the Two Stages*, pp. 33–4.

As in 1697–98, several of the new plays produced during this season were of the 'blockbuster' type: large-scale extravaganzas that required extensive resources in costumes, sets, stage machines, and new music. The short list of new offerings (Table 4.2) may reflect the extra time and money needed for rehearsal, machines, and costumes for their spectacular new productions, or that both companies had to some extent cleared the backlog of completed plays and eager new playwrights which existed in 1695. The addition of the 'lost' plays *Amalasont, Queen of the Goths; or, Vice Destroys Itself* (PC), *Justice Buisy; or, The Gentleman Quack* (LIF), and *The Young Coquet* (PC) would also help to fill out the season. Oldmixon's pastoral *Amintas* may have been performed earlier in the summer or during Drury Lane's strikingly premiere-less autumn.

Table 4.2 New productions during the 1698–99 season

	New works for the Patent Company		New works at Lincoln's Inn Fields	
AUTUMN			*Rinaldo and Armida*	Tragedy
WINTER	*Love and a Bottle*	Comedy		
SPRING	*The Island Princess*	Dramatick Opera	*Xerxes*	Tragedy
			Love's a Lottery with Love and Riches Reconcil'd	[Farce] + Masque
	Love without Interest	Comedy	*The Princess of Parma*	Tragedy
	The Famous History of the Rise and Fall of Massaniello	Tragedy	*Feign'd Friendship*	Comedy
SUMMER			*False Friend*	Tragedy

Both Walsh and Cross published songs from *Amalasont* and *Justice Buisy* arguing a fair degree of popularity, at least for the music. Appropriately enough, the songs from *Amalasont* are the defiant "Hence ye Curst infernal Train" sung by Mary Lindsey, and a lament, "In a Grove's forsaken Shade" sung by Mrs Erwin.[89] Both were set by Daniel Purcell. Erwin's song begins with a dramatic declamatory arioso (see Figure 4.3) followed by a triple-meter air depicting the "raging fever" and flames of love.

---

[89] See Hunter 5 (103, 324).

Figure 4.3   D. Purcell, "In a grove's forsaken shade" in *Amalasont, Queen of the Goths*

For *Justice Buisy*, seven songs survive, five of them for Anne Bracegirdle; all were composed by Eccles. Little is known about Crowne's comedy beyond prompter John Downes's comments in *Roscius Anglicanus*, where he admits it "prov'd not a living Play" but notes Bracegirdle's "Potent and Magnetick Charm in performing a Song in't."[90] The song referred to by Downes, "I'll hurry, hurry thee hence," was reprinted elsewhere; however, a set of songsheets engraved by Thomas Cross and preserved in the Halliwell-Phillips collection includes three for Bracegirdle that are apparently unique.[91] The first is a typical 'airy' song for a witty heroine.

> No, no ev'ry Morning my Beauties renew;
> where ever I go, I have Lovers enough
> I dress and I dance; and I laugh and I Sing;
> am lovely and lively, and gay as the Spring:
> I visit, I game, and I cast away Care:
> Mind Lovers no more, than the Birds of the Air.

However the four short pieces which follow suggest a multi-sectional mad song scene, like that of Lyonel in Durfey's *A Fool's Preferment; or, The Three Dukes of Dunstable* (UC, 1688).

> My Lover has an inconstant Mind;
> he varies oftner than the Wind:
> My Beauties slighted Steal away,
> and in their flourishing Bloom decay;
> From Life no pleasure I receive,
> I breath to Sigh, and live to grieve.
>   Till now I supress'd the Fire in my Breast,
> it lay hid like a Lamp in an Urn:
> Retir'd and alone, I vented my Moan;
> & till now I let none see me Mourn;
> But now I am Mad, and without any Shame;
> I boldly confess my raging Flame.
>   E'er since you came into my Sight,
> I've wasted many a day and night;
> in sighing and in weeping
> & till thou art mine, can have no delight;
> and then shall loose all my Fortune by't;
> I think I shall pay for my peeping.
>   I'll hurry, hurry thee hence, with such Violence:

---

[90] Downes, *Roscius Anglicanus*, p. 94.

[91] Halliwell-Phillips Ballad Collection, Chetham's Library, Manchester. The collection also includes a copy of "Hence ye Curst infernal Train."

> The Lightning from my Chariot-wheels, and my Horses heels,
> shall make the Pavement shine:
> If any Man stops my furious Race;
> ye Stones in the Street, shall fly in his Face:
> As Nature does in mine.

All five of Bracegirdle's songs are closely related, in either G minor or G major, supporting the idea of a grand musical mad scene, whereas the pieces for other performers are in varied keys.

The lively masculine trio "Wine does Wonder ev'ry Day" for Gouge, Spalding, and Curco was also popular and survives in many collections. However, Walsh songsheets assign it and the other solo song, "You Ladies, who are young and gay,"[92] to *The Morose Reformer*, an otherwise unknown play. Both songs are generic and could easily have been used in more than one production.

The only Lincoln's Inn Fields production confirmed for the autumn of 1698 was the John Dennis–John Eccles tragedy *Rinaldo and Armida*. Dennis's tragedy draws on a range of Continental sources, including Torquato Tasso's epic poem and the final *tragédie lyrique* by Philippe Quinault and Jean-Baptiste Lully, *Armide* (1685), which was still regularly performed in Paris in the 1690s. Dennis explains in his preface and prologue how he reshaped the hero Rinaldo to embody English heroism; he likewise rehabilitates the beautiful and sorcerous Armida, transferring the most malevolent actions to her woman Phenissa. Unlike Powell or Walker's rather cut-rate demons (*Imposture Defeated, Victorious Love*), Armida's infernal spirits are genuinely frightening. They speak a quasi-Miltonic language, which is impressive, and Eccles provides music to match.

Although labeled a tragedy on its title page, *Rinaldo and Armida* makes extensive use of music in every act. Virtually all of the music is part of Armida's magic, including an extended pastoral entertainment in the first act and a delightful masque for Cupid in the third act, which almost certainly featured Anne Bracegirdle as the god of love. *Rinaldo and Armida* conspicuously lacks the comic relief of bawdy musical dialogues or 'rustic' songs, like those in *King Arthur* or later Patent Company dramatick operas.[93] A prime example of the generic overlap between tragedy and dramatick opera, like *Phaeton* (PC, 1698), *Rinaldo and Armida* is discussed in greater detail in Chapter Two.

Rather than a dramatick opera or musical tragedy, the Patent Company offered George Farquhar's first comedy, *Love and a Bottle*. It was not met with much enthusiasm; fortunately Farquhar persevered. A potpourri of familiar characters and intrigues, built around the adventures of the wild Irish gentleman Roebuck, it featured the comedians Bullock as Mockmode the would-be beau, Jo Haynes as

---

[92] "You Ladies" was performed by Mrs Haynes (according to Cross) and/or Mary Hodgson (according to Walsh).

[93] See Kathryn Lowerre, "Dramatick Opera and Theatrical Reform: Dennis's *Rinaldo and Armida* and Motteux's *The Island Princess*," *Theatre Notebook* 59 (2005): 23–40.

Rigadoon the dancing master, and Penkethman as a comic servant, all musical. On the female side, both Maria Allinson (in love with Roebuck, disguised as a page) and Margaret Mills (Roebuck's whore) appear to have sung in character. However, the songs printed as sung in the play and those actually included in the printed text do not overlap.

Musical events within the play include a dancing lesson like Durfey's (*Love for Money*), only without the flirtation: "Enter *Rigadoon* the Dancing-Master, leading in *Mockmode* by both hands, as teaching him the Minuet; he sings, and *Mockmode* dances awkwardly; *Club* follows" (II, 15–6). Act III is not neglected; here Leanthe sings "How bless'd are Lovers in disguise!" to Roebuck, though he fails to appreciate the topicality of the text or penetrate her page's costume (27). Although the play text says the song was set by "Mr. Richardson" (presumably Vaughan Richardson), it does not seem to have been printed.[94] The remaining musical events are a drinking song tossed off by Roebuck in Act III, scene ii "France ne're will comply/ Till he Claret run dry" and a final "Irish Entertainment" at the conclusion of Act V, with "three Men and three Women, dress'd after the *Fingallion* fashion," (64) reflecting the penchant for dances displaying different national characters. Later advertisements at both theaters promise various Irish dances, such as the "Irish Humour" and "Irish Trot."[95]

In addition, there are three published songs composed by Richard Leveridge, which do not appear in the text. In her edition of Farquhar's plays, Shirley Strum Kenny has done an admirable job in assigning probable places for the songs, bawdy rustic ones for Penkethman ("Early in the Dawning of a Winters Morn") and Margaret Mills ("On Sunday after Mass/ Dormett and his Lass") and a more 'elevated' flirtatious one for Maria Allnison, "When Cupid from his Mother fled." All three were printed as a set by Walsh, with the women's songs also engraved by Cross.

Drury Lane's direct competitive response to the Dennis–Eccles musical tragedy *Rinaldo and Armida* was *The Island Princess*, based, like *Dioclesian*, on an early seventeenth-century tragedy written by John Fletcher. The production incorporated music (some pre-existing) from Drury Lane's three principal composers: Daniel Purcell, Jeremiah Clarke, and Richard Leveridge, and probably music by Robert King, Thomas Morgan, and William Williams as well.[96] Motteux's adaptation

---

[94] Shirley Strum Kenny states that the song was printed in Richardson's *A Collection of New Songs, for One, Two, and Three Voices* (London, 1701). However the copy I viewed did not include it. Although the collection is in Day and Murrie's bibliography there is no entry for the song. *The Works of George Farquhar*, vol. 1, p. 589.

[95] See, for example, *London Stage*, vol. 1, pp. 530–1, M&H *London Stage* pp. 65, 81, 88, 89, 106 etc.

[96] For a comprehensive discussion of attribution problems regarding the music, see Price and Hume's introduction to the facsimile edition of *The Island Princess*, p. xix. The edition (of GB-Lbl Add. MS 15318) includes contemporary printed material (songs and a first edition of the libretto).

provides for a variety of musical entertainments (often sexually suggestive), concluding with a "Musical Interlude" (often referred to as a masque) in the final act, "The Four Seasons; or, Love in Ev'ry Age." After an opening sung by Richard Leveridge as "the Genius of the Stage" and John Freeman as Apollo, the interlude consists of a series of dances and dialogues: a precocious boy and girl (Magnus's Boy and Mary Anne Campion) representing Spring, a country maid and a town spark (Mary Lindsey and Richard Leveridge) for Summer, a "Lusty Strapping Middle-ag'd Widow" (Pate in drag) with a drunken Officer (Leveridge again) representing Autumn, and finally, as Winter, an old man and woman (Mr Crossfield and Lindsey again), chasing the boy and girl but settling for each other. It concludes with a grand chorus, "Hail, God of Desire!" Performed by audience favorites, the dialogues were particularly popular in print and excerpted for use as entr'acte entertainments.

The other music for the production included a sung prologue and epilogue, as well as music in every act except the first. A pastoral celebration in Act II contains solos for all the principal male singers, plus Mary Lindsey, whose "The Jolly Swains,/ that were roving o're the Plains" was an unmistakable verbal parody of "The jolly, jolly breeze" in *Rinaldo and Armida.* Act III contains but a single song, "Lovely Charmer, dearest Creature," sung to amuse the princess Quisara. Although the printed text suggests Quisara's woman sings the song (17), one of the numerous songsheets (Cross) says it was Magnus's Boy again.[97] Act IV opens with a disconcertingly comic dialogue between a clown and his wife, "Hold John e're you leave me," sung by Leveridge and Pate in drag, while the hero, Armusia, is "lying on a bank in a Grove of Orange-Trees" (21).

The fourth act ends with a musical incantation scene, set by Daniel Purcell, concluding with "The Enthusiastick Song" composed and performed by Leveridge. The incantation scene includes solos for each of the prominent male professional singers: Bowen, Freeman, and Pate, plus symphonies and a chorus, likely modeled, as Price and Hume suggest, on Henry Purcell's music for *The Indian Queen.*[98] Pate's verse "Rouse ye Gods of the Main," with its racing sixteenth notes and obbligato trumpet, was printed separately and seems to have been quite popular, though nothing to match the enthusiasm engendered by Leveridge's solo as the "Old *Bramin*" possessed by the spirit of prophecy. In his song, he foresees invasion and ruin, followed by vengeance on the blasphemers (the Christian Armusia and his fellow Portuguese, and the converted Quisara) and the eventual restoration of peace. It is on just such 'points' of performance that productions became successes.

In February Lincoln's Inn Fields staged Colley Cibber's new tragedy *Xerxes*, previously rejected by the Patent Company. Although *Rinaldo and Armida* lost ground to *The Island Princess*, it must have seemed possible audiences could be drawn back by a new, elaborately staged musical tragedy, but *Xerxes* was not a

---

[97] See GB-Lbl K.7.i.2 (song 34).
[98] Price and Hume, *The Island Princess*, p. xviii.

success. After the dynamic musical visions conjured up by Armida's magic, those in *Xerxes* often seem grafted on for little dramatic purpose.[99]

The title character is among the most unattractive emperors ever to grace the stage. Returning from crushing military defeats, he has hired slaves and baggage to look like a procession of captives and booty. The "Triumphal Song" is furnished by a character called "Poet," who writes "madrigals, songs, whims, and knick-knacks" which please the vulgar. Having become laureate by dint of excessive flattery,[100] he actively choreographs the spectacle, a parody of a welcome ode:

> POET: … it shall be sung, and Gloriously,
> When I give the Word; I love to have 'em
> Wait a little, it makes em take
> The more notice of me—Now sound, ye Slaves!
> That all the World may Hear—my Words.
> CLEONTES: Prepare, the King approaches.
> *The Chorus being rang'd on each side the Stage, Enter* Loyalty, Love, Peace, *and* Plenty.
> *After a Martial Symphony,* Loyalty *Sings.*
> *Loyalty.*
> Prepare, blest Sons of Art, prepare
> To Raise the Thundring Voice of War:
> Sing! sing! and sound the Hero's Fame,
> Let Warlike Notes, his Warlike Deed Proclaim.
> *Chorus.* Sing, sing &c. …
> *Enter Trumpets sounding, a Train of Captive Kings and Princes, Women and Children, several Nobles bearing Palms, Soldiers with Spoils and Trophies: Then* Xerxes *Advances.*[101]

Following the false pageant, to the disgust of his noble and imprudently plain-spoken generals, Xerxes resolves to devote himself to pleasure.

---

[99] No direct comparison of the settings of such unequal materials is possible, as no music seems to survive.

[100] Among Cibber's contemporaries, both Durfey and Motteux wrote singable "knick-knacks" and produced their fair share of masques and triumphal odes. The poet laureate in 1699 was Nahum Tate, best known among music historians for the text of Purcell's *Dido and Aeneas* and among theater historians for his version of *King Lear*. But any connection to Tate would draw a parallel between Xerxes and William III—both inaccurate and dangerous.

[101] Cibber, *Xerxes. A Tragedy* (London, 1699), pp. 5–6.

The masque of pleasures which follows in the next act strongly suggests Motteux either as author or as model in its treatment of the deities, the description of the stage action, and the verses themselves.[102]

> *While a Symphony is Playing,* Luxury *arises sleeping on a Bed of Roses, and* Mercury *Enters to him.*
> Mercury.   Awake, soft Luxury, awake
> ....
> Now Feast thy Senses, and Receive
> The sweetest Joy, the Gods can give.
> Awake, &c.
> *The Scene Drawing, discovers several Deities, Attended by their several Pleasures:* Cupid *Advances.*
> Cupid.
> ... wanton Cupid comes to prove,
> Life has no Joy like Lawless Love.[103]

Mars, Hymen, and Indifference (who opposes Hymen) present their cases but are all unsuccessful. Finally Venus ("steal a Mistress, Break all Ties/ That would confine your Love to Rules") wins Luxury over, and the masque concludes with a dance of pleasures. The company at Lincoln's Inn Fields made the most of its machines and scenes—the bed of roses returns in several later productions.

During the subsequent dialogue, one of the generals attempts to recall Xerxes to an appropriately martial frame of mind with trumpets (onstage) and military displays (off) but is imprisoned for his "treason." The sole female character is the long-suffering Tamira, wife of the general Artabanus, Presumably the popular singing actresses would have been featured in the musical interludes. After the first two acts, each with an extended musical entertainment, the third act is without music; a plot to overthrow Xerxes is discovered, and after considerable violence Artabanus is taken and Tamira tortured.

Further musical events take place in the fourth act. The first is an incantation scene in which Xerxes consults the magi he previously spurned. Naturally their predictions are not encouraging. Blusteringly undaunted by the supernatural, in the following scene Xerxes again attempts to seduce Tamira, despite her torture and her husband's imprisonment, and arranges for suitable "Soft Musick" to be played. The final act is filled with vengeful crowds who steal Tamira's child, a duel to the death between Xerxes and Artabanus, and Tamira's suicide. Unlike *The Island Princess*, there is no hint of a happy ending—or a comical, erotic masque to conclude the evening's entertainment.

---

[102] The placement of this masque in the second act is not typical of previous tragedies at LIF. However, second act entertainments in "serious" plays are quite frequent in the UC repertoire and in Purcell's dramatick operas.

[103] Ibid., p. 13.

In March Lincoln's Inn Fields tried another tack, mounting actor Joseph Harris's new topical farce *Love's a Lottery, and a Woman the Prize*,[104] presented "With a new Masque, call'd Love and Riches Reconcil'd." Compared with Harris's earlier comedy *The City Bride* (March 1696), *Love's a Lottery* shows little sign of the reform promised by its prologue. The masque resembles Motteux's, a burlesque of classical divinities, and may represent an attempt to recreate the success of *The Loves of Mars and Venus*. Like Motteux, the author of the masque gives fairly complete stage directions and descriptions for the various types of music and dances, but unfortunately includes nothing about the composers or performers involved.

The masque occurs quite conventionally near the end of the final act. It begins with a heated exchange between Plutus ("attended by Empire, Labour, and Industry") and Cupid ("attended by the Graces"). Momus is called in to moderate and appears attended by Hymen, Hebe, Peace, and Reason, and preceded by a symphony of oboes. He promises to "hear both sides,/ And then to Judge as Reason guides" but he hears only from one before deciding: the central portion of the masque consists of solos by each of the Graces, a duet by Hebe and Hymen, and a chorus of Cupid's followers, alternating with varied dance numbers. As a compromise, Momus gives the day to wealth and the night to love, and the masque ends with a chorus and dance. While Cupid and his followers have more say in the masque, the final lines spoken by the farce characters give more weight to Plutus. The hero, Clitander, observes unromantically, "when all's done, 'tis Money binds our Love" and his scheming servant Trickwell gets the last word: "There's nothing like dancing to the Musick of Gold" (40).

No cast list was printed, but Samuel Akeroyde's song, "Loving and Belov'd again," published in the January 1699 *Mercurius Musicus*, reveals that Elizabeth Willis played Isbell, the heroine's quick-witted maid. To divert her mistress in Act II, Isbell offers to sing "a new Song of my own making," a change from the usual scenes in which female servants sing the songs their mistresses request, and foolish gentlemen sing songs they've created. Harris draws attention to this novelty, as Isbell explains "Female Poets [like Pix and Trotter] are now in Fashion" (11). The protofeminist lyric compares daughters under a father's control to slaves, and argues that "Nature" allows free choice of mate. Akeroyde's setting suggests that Elizabeth Willis was musically capable of more than the simple songs she often performed.

Drury Lane's counter to Harris's effort was *Love without Interest; or, The Man Too Hard for the Master*. Milhous and Hume conclude that comedian William Penkethman, who spoke the epilogue and signed the "whimsical" dedication, did not write it, but simply promoted it, without great success.[105] No music survives.

---

[104] A recent entertainment, "The Wheel of Fortune" (DG, October 1698), combined a lottery drawing with prologue, epilogue, and instrumental music. DL actresses portrayed the allegorical figures Fortune and Justice (*London Stage* vol. 1, p. 504).

[105] Milhous and Hume, "Attribution Problems in English Drama," 23 (no. 41).

Although called a comedy on its title page, and boasting the required five acts, the play is farcical: a compendium of clichés, including clichés about inserting songs and dances. Old Sir Fickle engages musicians to play before dinner for his nieces and other guests, featuring a "Sonato," a song, "She that marries an Old Man, let this be her Care," and "A Dance. By Mr. Essex and Mrs. Temple," all of which Fickle's hungry servant Jonathan (Penkethman) bitterly objects to, being anxious for his food. Act III concludes with a dance, presumably by Jenny (Elizabeth Wilkins) the nieces' maid, inspired by the mock madness of the lovers. In Act V, one heroine calls a singer to "sing the Song my Sister made t'other Day" (33), a serious piece urging the lover to hope.

The anonymous author does not forget to work in a reference to *The Island Princess*, as Sir Fickle quotes a line, "you'll kill me with Kindness, as the Song says in the new Opera," (17) from the end of the bawdy dialogue between a lusty widow (Pate) and drunken Officer (Leveridge). The musical dialogue in *Love without Interest* is of a more serious sort. Supposedly composed by one of the heroes, Trulove, "Why so cruel to your Lover?" ends with the male speaker swearing he loves the woman's mind and virtue rather than her transitory beauty. A final dance follows.

Like many 1698 productions, the three new spring 1699 productions at Lincoln's Inn Fields illustrate some of the theater world's reactions to Collier's *Short View* and similar anti-theatrical tracts. Although the "gratuitous" use of music in triumphs, entertainments, and conversation scenes has been eliminated, marking a sharp change from earlier productions, certain stock situations (the serenade, the sleep scene, the love scene) were still included and presumably provided with suitable music, though none survives.

The first of these three plays, Henry Smith's *The Princess of Parma*, was a staid, morally correct tragedy. Music is confined to the usual trumpet calls and some unspecified "soft musick" in Act IV while the virtuous Princess Almira rests on a couch in the palace. As she sleeps, she is nearly stabbed by her rival, but is saved by the sudden appearance of her lover.

Its epilogue, written by Motteux and spoken by Bracegirdle, beginning "I Dreamt, this House, for want of due Support,/ Once more, was turn'd into a Tennis-Court," has often been quoted for its reflections on the current state of affairs.

> Stage Wars were ceas'd, both Houses shrunk to One,
> And all Expensive Foreigners were gone.
> ....
> No Sum was given, fam'd Monsieurs to Engage,
> To leave the French to flutter on our Stage.
> Nor wou'd the House, to Bribe you to New Fancies,
> Give ten times Thirty Pounds for Thirty Dances.
> Five Hundred Guineas were not given this Season,
> To Please your Ears and Mortifie our Reason.
> Nor were the Fair so fond of Musick grown

To be Diverted with the Voice Alone.[106]

The speaker refers of course to the dancers l'Abbé and Balon, and singers like Signior Clementine.

There could be no greater contrast between Smith's chaste and essentially music-free tragedy and Durfey's *Famous History of the Rise and Fall of Massaniello*, in two parts, performed at Drury Lane during May. The story of a Neapolitan fisherman who becomes a rebel leader, ruler and tyrant before being overthrown and executed, *Massaniello* is a tragic extravaganza of completely different mould than Dennis's *Rinaldo and Armida*, though it shares with Dennis and Cibber's tragedies an unusually frequent and varied use of music. Repeated performances of *The Island Princess* in March and April led up to the premiere, which both made good use of a very popular show and whetted audience appetites for more music and spectacle.

The prologue to the first part of *Massaniello*, spoken by William Penkethman, mocks the popularity of music, but also attempts to negotiate between audience tastes and Drury Lane's offerings:

> I must declare our Patentees are Mad;
> They've known my Comick Humour all along,
> And yet this Morning sent me here—a Song,
> A nimble dapper Dancing-Master too,
> And bids me chuse, for nothing else will do.
> Mad, Mad, stark Mad. Let's see, *Sol la, me, sol.*   [*Sings.*
> Zooks, how like Midnight Skreeker shall I howl;
> For can they ever think I will comply—
> I Dance, I Sing;* they'd as good bid me Fly,   [*Capers awkwerdly.*
> For as to th' first, my English bulk's not made,
> I want an Air for *Monsieur's* Capring Trade:
> And for the next, —
> If they expect, I'll be a Capon for't,
> I'd have 'em know, my Salary's too short;
> ....
> At Price so dear, we purchase Voices Killing,
> They're Laughing at us, when we think 'em Trilling.
> Oh, what vast Sums, since our late Vein of Plotting,
> Have both our Houses paid, for Quavering and Cutting.
> ....
> But since our Poet is resolv'd to day,
> Once more to entertain you with a Play,
> A famous Story, and known lately True,

---

[106] Henry Smith, *The Princess of Parma* (London, 1699), epilogue lines 3–11, 16–23.

>Mixt with good Humour, and good Musick too,
>Which there is in it, give the Devil his due ...[107]

Aside from Penkethman's concerns about becoming one of the *castrati*, most of this is familiar territory: in fact, Penkethman and his fellow comedians had well-developed Molièresque routines depicting the awkward or uncouth being taught to dance and sing.

Both parts of *Massaniello* use similar types of music in similar ways.[108] Although the order of the types used changes, the overall structural placement Durfey employs also remains consistent. Both productions hold their musical numbers until the second act, and begin with religious music, the magical intercession of the city's patron saint, St Genaro, in Part I, and the priests' invocation to the saint in Part II. In each case, there is a trumpet song set by Daniel Purcell, sung in the first part by Pate and in the second by John Freeman. They even end with extended melismas on the same word, "wond'rous."

Banqueting scenes are another shared site for music making, and display the 'low' tastes of Massaniello and, more particularly, his wife Blowzabella, whose name suggests a reference to Durfey's musical dialogue "Blowzabella my bouncing doxie," a contrafactum of "The *Italian* Pastorella" sung by Pate.[109] In Part I, the banquets fall in Act IV and V. The first is fairly simple, featuring Leveridge's "Fisherman's Song" and an unspecified song and dance. In Act V, Blowzabella is anxious to dress and entertain like an aristocrat, but displays her crudity at every turn. The serious atmosphere of the martial symphony (trumpets, oboes, drums) that accompanies her husband's entrance (43) is dispelled by the spoken dialogue and by the "comical Entertainment of Singing and Dancing," including an abusive "Dialogue between two Fish-Wives," Pate and Leveridge, this time *both* in drag (44–5).

In Part II of the tragedy, Blowzabella is hosting a ball in Act II, with "a Comical Entertainment of Mimicking Dancing at a Ball with Clowns, Morrice-Dancers and Tumblers mixt, and several Humorous Songs and Dialogues" (18). The opening dialogue "Whilst wretched Fools sneak up and down," between a 'town sharper' and the landlady to whom he owes money, is reminiscent of the old saw about "fa la la" being inserted into madrigals wherever the text got too suggestive. When Leveridge offers to pay his hostess "With charming sweet *sol fa*" he is not planning on singing for his supper.

---

[107] Thomas Durfey, *The Famous History of the Rise and Fall of Massaniello. In Two Parts* (London, 1700), unpaginated. Lines 1–15, 27–30, 44–48, italics reversed.

[108] Although both Hume (*Development*, pp. 456–7) and Price ("Music as Drama," pp. 225–8) have written admiringly about *Massaniello*, musically speaking, it reads like the tragic version of Durfey's *Don Quixote*.

[109] See "The *Pastoral*, Perform'd at the *Theatre* Royal; By Mr. *Pate* with great Applause." *Mercurius Musicus* July 1699, pp. 138–51.

Although both parts of *Massaniello* have extensive music in Act V, in Part II, rather than comedy, the musical entertainment is instrumental to the working out of the tragedy. Blowzabella is the guest of some of the "true" court ladies who have arranged to take their revenge through a masque for her and her fellow fishwives. A transparent allegory, featuring a fisherman and his wife, Pride (a pimp), who dresses them in "tawdry" finery, Rebellion with a train of furies, Death, a hangman, and the Devil, the masque opens and closes with dancing and miming, while the centerpiece is a bravura solo for Pate, "From Burning Caves the dreadful'st part of Hell," and laughing chorus of furies. Blowzabella is predictably slow on the uptake, and a servant has to explain who each character is. When Death, the Devil, and the hangman come to take Blowzabella and her servants away, they resist, but in vain. The final scene of *Massaniello* displays their corpses with that of Massaniello, who had been shot in the previous scene.[110]

In Part II Durfey raises the already high level of musical interpolation by adding events to Act III, a sarabande for the nobility (25), and a song for Saint Genaro (26), as well as the Act IV scene in which the maiden Fellicia (Mary Anne Campion) attempts to distract or dissuade Pedro from raping her (34–5). Once again, Leveridge played many musical roles, including St Genaro, whose "Song of Comfort" in Act III, "Weep no more, no longer sigh and groan," set by Samuel Akeroyde, exploits Leveridge's more than two-octave range. It is truly from a different world than the short simple tunes Akeroyde wrote for Mary Anne Campion to sing—though her songs seem to have been more widely disseminated.

Both John Playford and John Walsh issued competing collections of songs from *Massaniello*, and Thomas Cross engraved several as individual sheets.[111] Although *Massaniello* included many of the same types of musical numbers as *The Island Princess*, including "The Fisherman's Song" set and sung by Leveridge, a trumpet song for Freeman—"Glory our martial Paradice"—and bawdy dialogues for Leveridge and Pate in drag, these popular (printed, quoted) excerpts do not seem to have raised the popularity of the production as a whole.

In May, Lincoln's Inn Fields premiered *Feign'd Friendship; or, The Mad Reformer*. Like the anonymous author, the cast is unknown. Musical elements in the plot include a "mad" daylight serenade by the heroine Eugenia in disguise as a young gentleman, complete with fiddlers and linkboys. By imitating and exaggerating all of his whims, Eugenia plans to reform her friend Lord Frolicksome into a suitable lover. As in *The She-Gallants*, this manipulation of conventional

---

[110] The inspiration for the masque as instrument of murder may have been Settle's *The Empress of Morocco* (1673), also discussed by Price in "Music as Drama." It would be revived at DL in August 1701 "with the original Mask set to new Musick" (M&H *London Stage*, p. 33) and several times in 1704.

[111] See Day and Murrie, *English Song-Books*, bibliography nos. 177–179. No copy of the Walsh is known to survive. The Playford songbook can be found in the Harding Collection at Oxford. Some individual songs were not printed in collections, and thus do not appear in Day and Murrie, but can be found at the British Library.

aristocratic male music making as a public event is one of the important elements in Eugenia's plan overall and in the creation and maintenance of her masculine disguise.

At the end of the play, the sharper Squeezum enters disguised as a Bailiff, with "four dancing Masters like his Followers,"[112] to take away the villain of the piece, Mr Richley. Presumably the dancing masters' costume, posture, and manner of walking indicated to the audience what they 'really' were. The typical final dance follows.

Also from May 1699, the tragedy *The False Friend; or, The Fate of Disobedience* was another work from the prolific pen of Mary Pix. Like *The Princess of Parma*, *The False Friend* contains a single musical scene. Music is not mentioned as the scene draws in Act III to reveal the heroine Lovisa (Bracegirdle) asleep on a couch, but Pix does insert a song in the very next scene—and again a couch is involved. When the stage opens, it discovers the French nobleman Brisac, and Adellaida, a Sardinian noblewoman, sitting together listening to the music, and possibly 'making love' in dumb show. Despite national enmity the couple have fallen in love, with predictably disastrous results. Musically it is also worth noting the corrupt Lady Appamia's instructions to her Indian slave to prepare an entertainment for Lovisa ("let the *Italian* Eunuch Sing; and softest Musick turn her Griefs," [33]), although the audience apparently never hears it.

Revivals, 1698–99

Drury Lane's autumn revivals were stock plays, *Oedipus* again, Fletcher's *The Little Thief*, and Lee's *The Rival Queens; or, The Death of Alexander the Great*. A song "set by Mr. Dan: Purcll [sic] in *Alexander the Great*" and published by Walsh may come from this or a later revival at Drury Lane, before the play was converted into a dramatick opera with music in 1701. It is hard to imagine where "Phillis talk not more of Passion" might be inserted into Lee's text, but it may have been sung between the acts.[113]

The first production known to have been staged at Lincoln's Inn Fields in January 1699 was also a revival of *The Rival Queens*. Whether revivals of the tragedy at both houses ever overlapped in direct competition is unknown. According to a letter of Elizabeth Barry's,[114] *The Rival Queens* was performed to entertain a bridal party, an odd choice perhaps, but one which allowed the senior actors to shine. In March, they revived Congreve's comedy *The Double Dealer*. As no new music for the production is known, the music written by Henry Purcell for the original production in 1694 may have been used. As theater historians have

---

[112] *Feign'd Friendship; or, The Mad Reformer* (London, 1699), p. 45.

[113] Henry Purcell had set the same text, quite differently, in *The Theatre of Musick* II (London, 1685). For Daniel's version, see Hunter 5 (148). Price lists instrumental music for the play in his *Music in the Restoration Theatre*, but it is from the later opera production.

[114] Quoted in *The London Stage* vol.1, p. 507.

frequently noted, by 1699 Congreve was already behind on his contract to write new plays for Lincoln's Inn Fields.

Musical evidence of revivals includes several songs by Eccles published in Playford's periodical *Mercurius Musicus*: from Thomas Porter's *The Villain*, "Find me a lonely Cave"[115] (sung by Mary Hodgson, April 1699) and from Etherege's *Man of Mode*, "Celia with mournful pleasure hears" (Hodgson, May) and "That you alone my heart possess" (Mr Gouge, June).[116] Samuel Tuke's venerable Spanish comedy *The Adventures of Five Hours* may also have been revived.[117] A musical dialogue with poetry by Congreve and set by Eccles, "I lov'd [love] and am belov'd again," can be found with other music for the 1695–99 seasons in GB-Lbl Add. MS 29378.

In January the Patent Company reprised two very different shows from its first full season, the musical tragedy *Bonduca*, source of Henry Purcell's perennial hit "Britons Strike Home," and Mary Pix's good-natured, heavily musical comedy *The Spanish Wives*. Since Pix was now writing for Lincoln's Inn Fields, this could be seen as deliberately competitive and even ill-natured, like running revivals of Congreve's earlier comedies against his new productions.

Changing Times: The 1699–1700 Season

Reconstruction of the music for productions from the turn of the century becomes increasingly complicated, as many more revivals are known to have been staged than premieres. Contemporary music can be linked to about two-thirds of known productions, including revivals, but whether it is music from a specific season is sometimes uncertain. While Henry Purcell's music was certainly revived, it is not clear whether other music from United Company productions would have been reused at Drury Lane or available to the Lincoln's Inn Fields company.

New Productions

Although Vanbrugh complained in December that the absence of Leveridge meant no new operas, Oldmixon's *The Grove* and, to a lesser extent, Dryden's *Secular Masque* helped redress the balance for the Patent Company. There appear to have been no correspondingly musical productions at Lincoln's Inn Fields (Table 4.3). Only one 'lost' play is associated with this season, the farce *Women Will Have*

---

[115] Song also included in Eccles's 1704 *Collection*. A tune copied into GB-Lbl Add. MS 38189 was probably used for the dance in Act IV, but it cannot be confirmed for this revival. Price, *Music in the Restoration Theatre*, p. 231.

[116] Gouge, according to the Walsh songsheet and Eccles's 1704 *Collection*. Songsheets by Cross give the singer's name as both Gouge and "Mr. Fowell," probably a minor singer who also performed this song.

[117] *London Stage* vol.1, p. 502.

Their Wills, known from two songs, both by Eccles, "Bellinda's pretty pleasing Form" sung by Mr Gouge and "Love is a God, whose charming Sway" sung by Mr Knapp, performed at Lincoln's Inn Fields.

Table 4.3 New productions during the 1699–1700 season

	New works for the Patent Company		**New works at Lincoln's Inn Fields**	
AUTUMN			*Friendship Improv'd*	Tragedy
	The Constant Couple	Comedy		
WINTER			*A Cure for Jealousie*	Comedy
	Achilles; or, Iphigenia in Aulis	Tragedy	*Iphigenia*	Tragedy
			The Generous Choice	Comedy
	King Richard III	Tragedy	*Measure for Measure*	Tragicomedy
	The Grove	Dramatick Opera		
SPRING			*The Way of the World*	Comedy
	The Reform'd Wife	Comedy	*The Beau Defeated*	Comedy
			The Fate of Capua	Tragedy
	The Pilgrim with \ *The Secular Masque*	Comedy + Masque		
SUMMER	*Courtship a la Mode*	Comedy		

In autumn 1699 nothing is known of the productions at Lincoln's Inn Fields until November, when Charles Hopkins's *Friendship Improv'd; or, The Female Warriour* premiered with Bracegirdle in the title role. Hopkins's heroine Locris, disguised at birth by her mother, grows up thinking and acting as the warrior son desired by her father, a usurping tyrant.[118] Locris becomes shieldmate to her father's general, son of the former king and the true heir. When her female nature is revealed, their friendship is improved a great deal. In the midst of an insurrection they neatly solve the succession crisis by marrying. This heroic romance had its appeal in 1699 as England faced a new century and a divided royal succession, with the exiled James II and his son on one hand and Princess Anne and her son on the other.

No music is called for within the play except martial drums and trumpets. However, the production is of interest for the overture and act tunes, written by veteran composer Solomon Eccles. The incidental music for *The Female Warrior* (so called in all the music manuscripts) is his only known contribution to a Lincoln's Inn Fields production.[119]

Farquhar's second comedy, *The Constant Couple; or, A Trip to the Jubilee*, offers a first look at the amusingly rakish song-quoting hero type that Robert Wilks would develop in subsequent seasons. While Farquhar's play was a huge success, and important for the Patent Company, the comedy was not particularly musical.[120] It included only a single song by Daniel Purcell, "Thus Damon knock't at Celia's door," in Act IV and unspecified "Singing and Dancing" (presumably including the published "Country Dance") at the end of Act V. When Farquhar revised the play, he added new theatrical business to the confrontation scene between Sir Harry, Angelica, and her mother at the beginning of Act V. Among other additions, Sir Harry apparently improvises a snatch of suggestive song, "Behold the Goldfinches, tall al de rall/ And a Man of my Inches …," to a "Modish Minuet," which leaves one wondering, after Durfey's *Love for Money*, if any references to dancing a minuet can be taken at face value.

According to the play text the song "Damon knock't," printed as "The Serenading Song," is sung to the jilt, Lady Lurewell, by Sir Harry Wildair (Wilks). However, songsheets indicate it was sung by a professional singer: Pate

---

[118] The woman-in-disguise-as-a-soldier was also a popular motif in many contemporary ballads. Dianne Dugaw lists several examples from the 1690s in *Warrior Women and Popular Balladry, 1650–1850* (Cambridge, 1989), pp. 48–9.

[119] Eccles's act tunes for Hopkins's play can be found in Yale's Filmer MS 9, and in the manuscript additions to Purcell's *Ayres for the Theatre* at the Newberry Library. For more on Solomon Eccles's music, see *Music Productions LIF*, pp. 438–40. Sets of act tunes composed by the elder Eccles during the 1680s also survive.

[120] I do not consider Sir Harry's snatches of song, probably quotations, as full musical events, and I disagree with Shirley Strum Kenny (Farquhar, *Works* vol. 1, pp. 120–1) about "Come bring us Wine in Plenty." A contrafactum using a tune from *The Trip to the Jubilee* is evidence of its popularity, but there is no reason to believe it was performed during the play any more than the numerous contrafacta of Henry Purcell tunes were performed with *Bonduca*.

or Freeman.¹²¹ To complicate matters, there is a closely contemporary songsheet with a different setting by Leveridge used for performances at the Smock-Alley Theater in Dublin during Leveridge's stay there.

Anonymous tunes from the play were published in three contemporary instrumental music anthologies, but no complete set of act music is known.¹²² Walsh specifically advertises the *Jubilee* tunes on the title page of his *The Third Book of Theater Musick* (London, 1700) "*Being A Collection* of the newest *Aires* for the *Violin* with ye *Trumpett-Tunes, Scotch-Tunes, & French-Dances*, made for ye *Play-houses* Particularly those in ye new *Opera* [*The Grove*], likewise in *Ephigenia*, & ye *Trip to the Jubilee*, with severall new Cibells …," additional evidence (if any was needed) of the play's popularity. The two previous books of *Theater Musick* featured tunes from *Rinaldo and Armida* and *The Island Princess*.¹²³

John Dennis's starkly classical tragedy *Iphigenia* premiered at Lincoln's Inn Fields in December. In the allegorical prologue the Genius of England (John Verbruggen, who often played heroic roles) rises "to a Warlike Symphony" and speaks for the muse of tragedy:

> Oh is my *Brittain* faln to that degree,
> As for effeminate Arts t'abandon me?
> I left the enslav'd *Italian* with disdain,
> And servile *Gallia*, and dejected *Spain*:
> Grew proud to be confind to *Brittain*'s shore,
> Where Godlike Liberty had fix'd before;
> ....
> Here Song and Dance, and ev'ry Trifle reigns,
> And leaves no room for my exalted strains.
> Those Arts now rule that soften'd foreign Braves,
> And sunk the Southern Nations into Slaves.
> ....
> Oh what wou'd my magnanimous *Henry* say,
> Or *Edward*'s soul returning to the day;
> To see a Bearded more than Female throng
> Dissolv'd and dying by an Eunuchs Song.
> To give you wholesome true severe delight,
> With me the Tragick Muse returns to night.¹²⁴

---

¹²¹ The December 1699 *Mercurius Musicus* indicates the singer was Pate, Thomas Cross's songsheets say Freeman.

¹²² See Price, *Music in the Restoration Theatre*, pp. 156–7.

¹²³ Unique copies of these important theater music sources are housed (incongruously) in the Durham Cathedral Library.

¹²⁴ Dennis, *Iphigenia. A Tragedy* (London, 1700), unpaginated. Prologue lines 23–8, 34–7, and 43–8.

In Dennis's prologue the overabundant "trifles" of song and dance on the stage are objectionable enough, but the "Eunuchs Song," causing even Englishmen to be "soften'd" and "dissolv'd," presents the greatest danger to English masculinity. The previous spring, Penkethman's prologue to *Massaniello* had expressed similar sentiments, but in the comic mode—audiences went to hear castrato singers perform at Drury Lane (spring and winter, 1699).[125]

Iphigenia's sole large-scale musical scene is set in the temple of Diana, with chorus, but the score for this is lost. Price lists scattered tunes, probably from the act music, in various anthologies.[126] Since the Patent Company staged *Achilles; or Iphigenia in Aulis* (translated from Racine) during the same season, perhaps even the same month, tunes identified simply by "Iphigenia" (such as "Slow Aire in Iphigenia") cannot be confidently assigned to either house.[127]

Boyer's tragedy also features a musical temple scene, with an "Invocation to Diana" at the end of Act V. The play text suggests a series of solos followed by a chorus. The vocal music is preceded by a symphony, played while "an Altar is rais'd near the Sea Shore" on which the Grecian princess is to be sacrificed (45). Through the goddess's intercession, Iphigenia is spared at the last moment. The only other music in Boyer's play is a song sung at the beginning of the fourth act to console the jealous, scheming Princess Eriphile, captive to the Greeks.

Daniel Purcell sets "Morpheus, thou gentle God of soft Repose," in short contrasting sections like a mad song (Figure 4.4). Indeed, despite the calming influence of the god being invoked, the final stanza is anything but:

> I rage, I rave, I burn, my Soul's o' fire;
> Tortur'd with wild despair, and fierce desire
> My *Strephon*'s loss, I cannot, will not bear,
> I'll be reveng'd, and more than Woman dare.
> Death, only Death can now my Thoughts employ,
> I must my Rival, or my self destroy.[128]

The song is a showpiece for Mrs Erwin, who had several significant songs written for her during this season.

---

[125] See Musical Assets, this chapter. Dennis's anxieties about the effeminating effects of Italian music are strongly reiterated in his 1709 "Essay on Operas after the Italian Manner."

[126] Price, *Music in the Restoration Theatre*, pp. 182–3.

[127] In the third book of Walsh's *Theater Musick* (London, 1700), p. 9, where it shares a page with "A Country Dance in the way of the World."

[128] Boyer, *Achilles; or, Iphigenia in Aulis. A Tragedy* (London, 1700), p. 45, italics reversed.

Figure 4.4   D. Purcell, "Morpheus, thou gentle God of soft Repose," in *Achilles*

Figure 4.4   Concluded

Also performed in December, John Corey's comedy *A Cure for Jealousie* has no extant music, although the text indicates three songs. The cast includes familiar types: two pairs of lovers, a heavy father, a penny-pinching guardian and his unhappy wife, an officer returned from the wars (a son in disguise), and a beau. The first song, "Happy was man e're cheated Sence," is sung in Act II by a "woman of the town," to entertain the young men, Loveday, Wildish, and Colonel Blunt, while they're drinking at the Rose Tavern. The second song is sung in Act III by Wildish; it too ends in praise of drink ("Let the Politick Sot").

The final song occurs near the end of Act IV, when the beau Sparkish (probably John Bowman) decides to serenade Arabella, wife of the miserly old Scrapeall, with a concert of violins. His description of his intentions and motivation is worth quoting.

> 'Gad I don't know which to me is the greater satisfaction, making the Wife amorous, or the Husband Jealous— ... Now have I a Song which I design to sing purposely to increase both—come tune your Instruments—this is the Window—No sooner will she hear my most Melodious Voice, but she will be all o're Transports, Ecstasy, and Rapture.—'Gad, she'll go nigh to Cuckold him in Imagination, tho' in his Arms.[129]

Most serenaders are romantic, or pretending to be so. Sparkish's joy is in imagining not only what he believes Arabella is imagining but in provoking Scrapeall. Whom is he serenading after all? Like *Feign'd Friendship*, it's a parody of serenading, but in a very different humor.

Immediately following his speech, Sparkish begins singing, accompanied by the fiddlers. The song text he has penned is very topical, as he is serenading the young wife of an old man. The text itself is not ridiculous, although it may have been given an extravagantly clumsy or pretentious musical setting. The speaker calls "Heark, fair One, heark 'tis Musick's Voice," ending with more prosaic instructions to abandon the "Sleeping Drone" and "let him Snore alone." But Sparkish misjudges his audience; Scrapeall wakes and has the servants douse him with water. The final act concludes with a hasty untangling of plot complications and the union of the two young couples.

In February Lincoln's Inn Fields combined the works of the Bard of Avon with the English Orpheus, presenting Henry Purcell's *Dido and Aeneas* as a series of musical entertainments between the acts of Charles Gildon's revision of Shakespeare, *Measure for Measure; or, Beauty the Best Advocate*. Although most previous scholars have expressed distaste at the combination, Derek Hughes finds "the two tales of betrayal and forbidden love mirroring and reversing each other in a variety of striking and satisfying ways."[130]

---

[129] Corey, *A Cure for Jealousie* (London, 1701), pp. 41–2
[130] Hughes, *English Drama*, pp. 432–3.

Scholarly debate continues over where, when, and how Henry Purcell's famous masque-or-opera *Dido and Aeneas* was originally performed, and the exact circumstances surrounding its first appearance on the London stage remain somewhat mysterious as well. Curtis Price has observed that "the Theatre Royal repeatedly revived all Purcell's major stage works except *The Fairy Queen*, the score of which was lost ... [b]ut ... *Dido and Aeneas* was nowhere to be seen, a sign that the theatre did not possess a copy."[131] Purcell's music does not reappear in the scanty annals of the Lincoln's Inn Fields company until June 1703, when two of Purcell's solo songs were performed during a revival of the stock comedy *The Villain*.[132] This followed several revivals of plays at Drury Lane with Henry Purcell's music.

The Lincoln's Inn Fields company did not thrive in the early months of 1700. The preface to *Measure for Measure* reinforces the generally held notion that the Lincoln's Inn Fields company was a critical success but not a popular one: "In vain you said, you did their Farce despise;/ Wit won the Bays, but Farce the Golden Prize." Some of the lines which follow are particularly interesting from a musical perspective, with their usual slighting reference to the "ornaments" of music, dance, and scenery, and to the booths at the Smithfield fairgrounds. References to the fairs are almost always derogatory, and usually aimed at the other house: the allusion to "our Booth" is unusual, and it is difficult to judge the tone.

> Let neither Dance, nor Musick be forgot,
> Nor Scenes, no matter for the Sense, or Plot.
> Such things we own in Shakespears days might do;
> But then his Audience did not Judge like you.
> ....
> Study the Smithfield-Bards ... with care;
> Like those Write Non-Sense, and like these, you'll fare.
> By this you may, the Towns Resentment sooth;
> Or, you must Starve, and we shut up our Booth.
> ....
> No more than this, We, for our Selves, need Say,
> 'Tis *Purcel*'s Musick, and 'tis *Shakespears* Play.

Milhous presents convincing evidence that the company was not doing well, due to a combination of selfishness, laziness, and the lack of strong management.[133] Betterton must have enjoyed speaking the prologue to *Love for Love* more than this one.

The production itself, and Purcell's music for it, have been discussed at length by generations of Purcell scholars. Margaret Laurie presents the evidence of libretto

---

[131] Price, *Henry Purcell and the London Stage*, p. 234.
[132] M&H, *London Stage*, pp. 105–6.
[133] Milhous, *Thomas Betterton*, pp. 114–15.

and the two manuscript scores and argues that the Tenbury manuscript may be based on the performance at Lincoln's Inn Fields in 1704,[134] while Curtis Price comments extensively, from the Purcell angle, on the 1700 production of *Dido and Aeneas* with *Measure for Measure*. Some remaining questions about the relationship of the printed libretto to the Tenbury score are tackled by Andrew Pinnock in "'From Rosy Bowers': Coming to Purcell the Bibliographical Way."[135]

The only published songs from this production were Purcell's: a solo version of "Fear no danger" appeared in a contemporary songsheet combined rather incongruously with a catch for three voices, as did "Come away, fellow sailors," which, the title line informs us, was sung by bass John Wiltshire.[136] "Pursue thy conquest love," Belinda's air, had been published earlier in Purcell's posthumous songbook *Orpheus Britannicus*. The act tunes for *Measure for Measure* were composed by John Eccles and survive, like those for *The Way of the World*, in a single manuscript source at the Newberry Library.[137] These are, for the most part, brief and unexciting, though the final tune, "A new Scotch Ground," is an extended piece, probably used in the first or second music.[138]

Unfortunately the setting for "Direct me, friends what Choice to make," a dialogue between Aeneas and two mysterious friends which occurs during the interlude in Act II of Gildon's play, does not survive. The text was added by Gildon, and probably set by Eccles. The choice, variously phrased, is between love and empire. After the usual oppositional exchanges, all three characters conclude in chorus "Love without Empire Triffling is and Vain,/ And Empire without Love a Pompous Pain." They exit together as the Sorceress and witches enter.[139]

The cast list for *Measure for Measure* calls for both Bracegirdle and Elizabeth Bowman in speaking roles.[140] Presumably there was the usual separation between musical and dramatic casts. Aeneas may have been John Bowman (absent from in *Measure for Measure*) or singer Mr Gouge. Dido was almost certainly Mary

---

[134] A. Margaret Laurie, "Allegory, Sources, and Early Performance History," in Henry Purcell, *Dido and Aeneas: An Opera*, ed. Curtis Price (New York and London, 1986), pp. 42–58.

[135] In Burden, ed., *Henry Purcell's Operas: The Complete Texts*, pp. 41–93.

[136] First noted by Curtis Price and Irena Cholij, "Dido's Bass Sorceress," *Musical Times* 127 (1986): 615–18.

[137] They can be found in manuscript leaves bound with a copy of Henry Purcell's *A Collection of Ayres, compos'd for the Theatre, and upon other Occasions* (London, 1697). The additions include titled sets of act music by Eccles, Finger, Barrett, Lenton, Clarke, and Daniel Purcell, and other instrumental pieces.

[138] For more on the instrumental music from *Measure for Measure* and its relation to *Dido and Aeneas*, see *Music Productions LIF*, pp. 504–12, particularly p. 508.

[139] Charles Gildon, *Measure for Measure* (London, 1700), pp. 14–15.

[140] Although the idea of Bracegirdle as Dido is tempting, it is impossible for her to play both Dido and Isabella, as Isabella watches part of the performance (Gildon, *Measure for Measure*, p. 26).

Hodgson. John Wiltshire apparently played the Sorceress, just as Bowman and Leveridge played Hecate in the musical versions of *Macbeth*.

Casting the final entertainment, with its classical deities, rustics, and morris dancers, is problematic. Since no music survives, matching voice types to performers is impossible; one can only note similarities with earlier productions. Casts for *The Loves of Mars and Venus*, *Europe's Revels*, and *Acis and Galatea* provide several examples of singers' 'ypes' which fit the musical numbers, suggesting Elizabeth Willis and Wiltshire for the funny country dialogue, with Bowman and Hodgson for the gods of war and peace. Lucretia Bradshaw may have portrayed a young Venus, with Mrs Prince as "Spring," singing and dancing with her nymphs.

The Generous Choice, a comedy with a Spanish setting by novice playwright Francis Manning, was the second new production at Lincoln's Inn Fields in February. The play offers the familiar hustle of intrigue among four dons and four young women, "A Woman of Intrigue," and a maidservant. Although no actors' names are given, the two ladies (who enter in breeches) were roles probably intended for Bracegirdle and Elizabeth Bowman. The text calls for only two musical events, songs performed in the first and final acts.

The first song is, unusually for contemporary comedies, sung offstage "at some distance."[141]

> Custom, alas! doth partial prove,
> Nor gives us equal measure:
> To Maids it is a Pain to Love,
> But 'tis to Men a pleasure.
> ....
> Then equal Laws let *Custom* find,
> Nor either Sex oppress:
> More freedom give to Womankind,
> Or give to Mankind less.[142]

Taking direct issue with the double standard for men and women, this song leads Don Bernardo offstage to Donna Olivia, who has dressed as a man and traveled to Valencia in pursuit of Don Philip, who had "enjoyed" and abandoned her. Bernardo is naturally disturbed to hear Olivia's story, since Don Philip is engaged to his sister.

The second song is performed near the beginning of the fifth act. Dramatically, it is neatly symmetrical to the first, being sung for Don Philip by a servant onstage,

---

[141] A setting of this text by John Barrett survives, however it is not clear (since Barrett otherwise worked exclusively for DL) whether it was written for the premiere or simply resetting a favored poem. Its title line makes no mention of the play. See Hunter 5 (309). An uninspired later setting by a Mr Turner entitled "The Maid's Complaint," also exists.

[142] Francis Manning, *The Generous Choice* (London, 1700), pp. 5–6.

and expressing his sentiments, as the first did hers. The song represents an important transition between his callous past actions and his final "generous choice."

> Beauty is not what I pray,
>   I ask no shining Graces;
> Celia has another way,
>   Without the Tricks of Faces.
> So our Humours still agree,
> Kind Heav'n, it is enough for me ...[143]

The two songs, in addition to giving Donna Olivia and Don Philip importance in the eyes and ears of the audience, suggest their compatibility. At the end of the play, the reformed rake vows to relinquish his engagement and marry Donna Olivia—after much dueling among their male relatives and a confrontation between the two ladies themselves, in which they draw and "Fight awkerdly."[144]

In February the Patent Company staged Colley Cibber's latest tragedy, a very different work from *Xerxes*. *The Tragical History of King Richard III*, in which Cibber played the title character, was based on Shakespeare, like Betterton's well-received version of *King Henry IV*.[145] Cibber's first act, showing the death of Henry VI, ran afoul of the censoring pen of the Master of the Revels.[146] It contains virtually no interpolated music; the only exceptions are trumpet cues for a march and an alarm (with drums) in Act IV.

The Patent Company reserved its musical forces for John Oldmixon's pastoral dramatick opera *The Grove; or, Love's Paradice*, also in February. The masques and musical entertainments, with their agricultural laborers, and gods Pan and Ceres, are reminiscent of the Dryden–Henry Purcell *King Arthur*, while other passages suggest more recent productions, *Phaeton* and the rival house's *Rinaldo and Armida* (the relationships between these works are discussed in Chapter Two).

Given their collegiality, it is no surprise that Oldmixon appears to follow John Dennis rather than Motteux as his model, though he does not eschew suggestive musical dialogues. In his preface, Oldmixon writes:

> This Play is neither Translation nor Paraphrase [like *Amintas*]; ... the Story is entirely new; ... 'twas at first intended for a Pastoral, tho in the last three Acts, the Dignity of the Characters rais'd it into the form of a Tragedy, ...

---

[143] Ibid., p. 38.

[144] Ibid., p. 45. The dueling ladies owe something to Dryden's *Marriage à la Mode*.

[145] For more on Cibber and other adaptations, see Christopher Spencer, ed., *Five Restoration Adaptations of Shakespeare* (Urbana, Illinois, 1965).

[146] See Timothy J. Viator and William J. Burling, eds, *The Plays of Colley Cibber*, vol. 1 (London, 2001).

As to what relates to the composition, no man ever consulted the meaning of Words more than Mr *Purcel* has done, and he has succeeded too well with the Publick, to want the applause of his Author.[147]

Earlier, Oldmixon complains that the last Act had been cut in the interests of time, which created confusion, and "if what he had writ had been spoken, everything wou'd have appear'd clear and natural." Perusal of the printed version, however, makes the cuts understandable. Previous acts are generally brief and full of music, while in Act V there are ten solid pages of dialogue before the final brief masque of Cupid and Hymen. Oldmixon varied the pattern from *Amintas*, no longer having the musical sections at the end of each act. This compounds the problem, since the Act IV entertainment falls near its beginning, leaving a very long stretch without any music.

As with *Massaniello*, the songs may well have been more popular than the show. Walsh published a book of songs from *The Grove* and many of them also appeared as single sheets. A full score of the opera survives in GB-Lcm 988. While comparison of the printed text with the score reveals some minor omissions (the first song in Act I), additions (the dialogue for a satyr and a nymph, perhaps added by another hand to spice things up), and emendations, the two are remarkably consistent. Several of the songs, left quite bare in the printed songsheets, acquire additional charm when reunited with their instrumental accompaniments. All of the singers are featured: Pate, Freeman, Lindsey, and Erwin with bass-baritone Marcellus Laroon (Pan, Hymen) in place of the absent Richard Leveridge. Daniel Purcell rose to the occasion with lively trumpet sonatas and graceful verses. The final grand chorus, reworked from his 1698 Ode for St Cecilia's Day, is indeed, as an anonymous pencil noted on the manuscript, "very good."[148]

Yet quality, as measured by later critics, is no guarantee of contemporary success. The last play Congreve wrote for the theater, his most famous comedy, *The Way of the World*, premiered at Lincoln's Inn Fields in March 1700. Despite an excellent cast, featuring Bracegirdle as the sparkling Millamant, it did not equal the success of Congreve's previous two plays. Within the same month *The Way of the World* gave way to the more prolific Pix's *The Beau Defeated*, which proved another comedy of limited success. Nearly all of the surviving music for *The Way of the World* was composed by Eccles, including a unique set of act tunes and one of his most dramatically striking songs for Mary Hodgson, "Love's but the

---

[147] Oldmixon, *The Grove; or, Love's Paradice. An Opera* (London, 1700), unpaginated, italics reversed.

[148] See Humphreys, *Daniel Purcell*, catalogue no. 119. Daniel Purcell seems to have gotten plenty of use out of his ode. At a York Buildings concert in December, a benefit evening he shared with John Pate, the advertised program was "a consort of Musick with the last St Cecilia's Song." *London Stage* vol. 1, p. 520.

frailty of the mind," placed at the heart of the play in Act III.[149] Other musical events included a typical drinking song and the entertainment of dancing arranged by the aging would-be seductress Lady Wishfort, both in Act IV, as well as the conventional final dance.

Eccles's instrumental pieces for the play include a light-hearted overture in D major and lively act tunes in closely related keys, none of which is remarkable.[150] The other contemporary surviving instrumental piece attributed to Congreve's play is a country dance published in Walsh's *Theater Musick* in 1700,[151] which was probably used in the final scene. Downes again praised Bracegirdle's performance but noted "not the Success the Company Expected."[152] It was successful enough to be revived.[153]

Two songs by Eccles from Pix's less sophisticated comedy *The Beau Defeated* were printed after the play's premiere.[154] "Delia tir'd Strephon with her Flame" was sung in the middle of the second act by John Bowman in character as Sir John Roverhead, the title role. In Pix's earlier comedy *The Innocent Mistress* (June 1697), Bowman as the con-man Spendall sang "At dead of night when wrapped in sleep" to impress a similar audience of ladies.

Roverhead's song introduces and then imitates a dialogue between the aged, amorous Delia and the youthful, disgusted Strephon. In their exchanges, the old woman's words usually verge on recitative while Strephon continues more tunefully. Eccles sets four of the song's eight quatrains, ending with a series of angry repetitions ("Delia may to the Devil go"). Presumably the enjoyment lay in Bowman's comic performance.

In his first appearance onstage, Bowman uses a snatch of song, "She threw by her knotting in haste," as an exit line. Like some of the musical quotations in Drury Lane comedies, this makes a playful reference to one of the company's earlier productions, Dilke's *The Lover's Luck* (Winter 1695). In the earlier comedy, Bowman played Goosandelo, who wrote and performed the ridiculous song "Rich Mines of Hot Love."[155]

---

[149] See Kathryn Lowerre, "Music and Meaning in Congreve's *The Way of the World*," RECTR 15 (2000): 24–52.

[150] Like those for *Measure for Measure*, the only known copies of the overture and act tunes for *The Way of the World* are housed in Chicago's Newberry Library. Unlike his songs, many sets of Eccles's act tunes are hard to come by.

[151] Price notes another dance printed in the 1718 edition of *The Dancing Master* (*Music in the Restoration Theatre*, p. 233), but it was probably written for a revival.

[152] Downes, *Roscius Anglicanus*, pp. 94–5.

[153] Hume, "A Revival of *The Way of the World* in December 1701 or January 1702," *Theatre Notebook* 26 (1971): 30–6.

[154] "Delia tir'd Strephon with her Flame," sung by John Bowman, appeared in a songsheet by Thomas Cross, and the other, "Relieve, the fair Belinda said," in Eccles's 1704 *Collection*.

[155] The lines he sings are from the second stanza.

Locating Eccles's second song within Pix's play is more difficult. Onstage characters call for the conventional final song and dance at the end of Act V, which, we are told, will be performed by landlady Mrs Fidget (Elizabeth Willis), and Toby, a servant. However, the sentiments of the text are much more appropriate to an exchange between Lady Landsworth (Bracegirdle) and a maid, Betty in Act I. Lady Landsworth, a wealthy widow married against her will at a very young age, shares the sentiments of the singer, though it's unlikely she sang herself.[156]

> Relieve the fair Belinda said,
> Relieve ye Gods a Lover's Pain,
> Relieve a poor unhappy Maid
> By faithless Vows to Love betray'd; ...
> Till fifteen, Parents we obey;
> Then Lovers sigh and Moan,
> And leave us not, till they convey,
> With am'rous Sighs our Hearts away
> So that there ne'er our own.
> How wretched are we Women grown;
> Our Hearts and Wills are ne'er our own.

Eccles's lovely A minor setting divides the text into three sections, the first more lyrical and ornamented, the second and third syllabic and declamatory. Although the range is fairly wide, the song is not particularly difficult, and it is impossible to deduce which among the company's singers might have performed it, though Hodgson and Willis are plausible candidates.

Drury Lane also had a new spring comedy, *The Reform'd Wife*, a surprise success by a first-time author. Three songs by Daniel Purcell are associated with the production, and two were printed in the play text. Again, though said to be sung in character, the songsheets name professional singers. The first song, "Corinna with a graceful Air," was written for Cleremont to sing to the hypochondriac Lady Dainty, whom he is wooing: "Such Charms adorn the Sickly fair./ We scarce can wish her well" (7). The text is read aloud in the first act, and then sung to Lady Dainty from behind the scenes (supposedly by Cleremont) in Act II, as she consults with her doctor, apothecary, astrologer, and so on about being tastefully and aristocratically unwell (13). The second song is requested by Clarinda as she walks with her cousin Sylvia, thinking of the soldier she loves. According to Walsh's songsheet, this was sung by Mrs Erwin (this season's featured soprano), rather than by Diana Temple (Sylvia).

The third song, "Sabina has a thousand charms," performed by Mr Bourdon, uses an amusing text also set by John Blow (in *Amphion Anglicus*, without reference to the play). Apparently those who fall in love with the beautiful Sabina are cured as soon as she opens her mouth! This does not seem like a suitable number for

---

[156] If Bracegirdle had sung this song, presumably Eccles would have noted it.

the "bridal song" in Act V, though it would fit well between the first and second acts, setting up the first entrance of Lady Dainty, whose speeches would definitely dissuade a less determined lover than Cleremont.

Once Astrea, the less-than-perfectly faithful wife of the title, has been sufficiently reformed, Lady Dainty and Cleremont enter, "Follow'd by the Dr. and Attendants with Musick, Dancers, &c." Over Lady Dainty's objections to the "primitive Barbarism" of the celebration, Cleremont offers the remedy of music, "A Bridal Song, and after it a Mimick Dance" (42). Like vulgar good health, Lady Dainty must learn to appreciate music properly.

Lincoln's Inn Fields followed *The Beau Defeated* with a very different work, Thomas Southerne's new tragedy *The Fate of Capua*, described by Downes as "better to Read then Act."[157] It is set in Capua, where rival factions support the opposing interests of Rome and Carthage. In the first act, the wily Pacuvius plays upon the feelings of a pro-Carthage mob and saves the Capuan senators from execution, although Roman citizens of Capua have been put to death.

After this grim scene, the play shifts to the noble Virginius's house, where his wife Favonia is at work with her women. To further contrast with the uproar in the senate, the domestic scene opens with the performance of a pair of songs.

>   *A Song written by a Lady.*
> WHAT's Beauty? Bright *Favonia*, tell.
> The Mistress of it knows it well.
> 'Tis not Colour, 'tis not Feature,
> Easie Fashion, nor good Nature:
> . . . .
> Not yielding Lips, or wishing Eyes:
> But she is handsom who denies.
>   *A Song in Answer written by a Gentleman.*
> WHAT Beauty is, let *Strephon* tell,
> Who oft has try'd it, knows it well:
> . . . .
> Not Youth, not Shape, not Air, not Eyes,
> She only charms me who complies.[158]

Although no music for the first song is known, a setting by Eccles for the second, sung by Mary Hodgson, appeared in the anthology *Mercurius Musicus*.[159] It is a simple, lilting triple-meter air over an unfigured bass. Given the shared

---

[157] Downes, *Roscius Anglicanus*, p. 94.

[158] Thomas Southerne, *The Fate of Capua. A Tragedy* (London, 1700), pp. 18–19, italics reversed.

[159] The publication of "What's Beauty? bright *Favonia*, tell" in a musical periodical for January–February 1700 creates apparent dating problems; however, issue dates often precede actual publication. The January–February 1700 *Mercurius Musicus* was

meter and some identical rhymes, it is possible that the songs used the same music.[160] The pairing of the real Favonia (in love with her husband's friend) with an imaginary Strephon and the debate between complying and denying become significant as the plot unfolds.

The act tunes for Southerne's play, composed by Lenton, are cursory. Although the tunes are in the minor mode, it is hard to imagine that the jig after Act I or the hornpipe after Act II are supposed to have any connection with the events onstage, unlike some of Lenton's later sets of act tunes.

Drury Lane's major production for the spring months was a revised version of Fletcher's comedy *The Pilgrim* combined with Dryden's *The Secular Masque*, which may have been inspired by the earlier combination at Lincoln's Inn Fields of *Measure for Measure* with "Entertainments of Musick." Dryden's prologue and epilogue are unremittingly bitter, linking stage reformers railing against lewdness with attacks on the monarchy. Dryden's death occurred during the initial run.

Fletcher's comedy, revised by Vanbrugh, still presents a very different society than contemporary comedies. This is not the town and the drawing room, but a wider world in which pilgrims travel, beggars appear at the door, and giving (rather than consumption of services and goods) is enacted. Music appears in many of the usual places, in a mad house in Act III (24), in a snatch of a ballad sung by the heroine while pretending to be mad in Act IV (28), and twice in Act V, both as "strange Musick" in a pleasant grove where the hero remembers his beloved (37), and "Solemn Musick" for a ritual offering of penance. The penitential ceremony is overseen by the Governor of Segovia (40), who will eventually invite all to celebrate with the masque by "the late great Poet of our Age" (42).

In addition to the masque, prologue, and epilogue, Dryden also contributed a mad dialogue between "a Scholar and his Mistress, who being Cross'd by their Friends, fell Mad for one another; and now meet in Bedlam" (43–6). The lovers enter at separate doors, "each held by a Keeper," before breaking free and running to each other. The staging provided suggests it was performed as the scenes were changed between the play and the masque. John Barrett's act music, published in *Harmonia Anglicana*, contains only the usual number of tunes, mostly Continental dances (allemande, courant, gavotte, minuet), with no additions to cover the transition.[161]

---

not advertised until the end of April, while in 1701 the January–February issue was not advertised until the end of March (Day and Murrie, *English Song-Books*, 120, 125).

[160] A recent example of paired songs using the same tune (a minuet), the first "If you will love me, be free in expressing it," can be found in Durfey's *Don Quixote*, Part II (UC, 1694).

[161] They are also all in E major, whereas the masque begins in D major. A brief symphony in A major would make the transition easy, but there is no evidence in the printed text or manuscript score that there was any music prior to Janus's "Chronos, Chronos, mend thy pace."

A partial score of the masque was copied into GB-Lbl Add. MS 29378, which otherwise consists entirely of music by Eccles. Although the Daniel Purcell music appears to be in the same hand, it is also from a later season than the other works. The printed songs from the masque are all Purcell's, except for a single song written by Gottfried Finger for Mary Anne Campion to sing as Venus—a role she probably played in *The Judgment of Paris* competition as well. The music for the masque was likely divided between Purcell and Finger. The remainder of the music (and the mad dialogue) does not seem to have survived—regrettably, given the charm of Finger's seductive and memorable song "Calms appear where storms are past," which would be quoted and referred to in later productions.

The other singers named in the songsheets are Freeman as solemn Janus, Pate as laughing Momus, and Mrs Erwin as the spirited Diana (with obbligato trumpets). Their solos, particularly Erwin's, bear some similarity to those written for them in *The Grove*, and some of the costumes and scenery, particularly for Diana's attendants, could be easily transferred. *The Secular Masque* continued to appear with *The Pilgrim* during the 1699–1700 season, but when *The Pilgrim* was revived in subsequent years it featured other musical attractions.[162]

The new summer comedy at Drury Lane, David Craufurd's *Courtship A-la-mode*, would have made sense at the Lincoln's Inn Fields playhouse, since several scenes take place in Lincoln's Inn Walks and a character plans to buy a house there—lines which probably got a laugh not originally intended when performed at Drury Lane. In his preface, Craufurd makes no bones about problems encountered pre-production.

> Finding that six or seven people cou'd not perform what was design'd for fifteen, I was oblig'd to remove it after so many sham Rehearsals, and in two days it got footing upon the other Stage. Where 'twas immediately cast to best Advantage, and Plai'd in less than twenty days. How far it answer'd their labours, I leave to be judg'd by themselves.[163]

There is no evidence Craufurd's comedy was any loss to Lincoln's Inn Fields, but had the play been performed there, it seems likely some musical numbers might have taken a different form.

With the exception of a song by the witty Flora, "Occasion's swift, and bald behind," in the first act, the musical events are huddled into the last act of the play, and half of them are inserted for the benefit of the comedians Penkethman and Bullock. Penkethman, as the foolish university student Dick, has already executed one of his usual routines, singing and dancing awkwardly in an attempt to court a lady (III, 27). At the resolution of Act V (50), with three couples happily

---

[162] Once the turning century was no longer topical, the well-known concluding couplets may have been too stark a reminder: "Thy Wars brought nothing about;/ Thy Lovers were all untrue./ 'Tis well an Old Age is out,/ And time to begin a New" (54).

[163] David Craufurd, *Courtship A-la-mode* (London, 1700), unpaginated.

married and their old relations resigned to it, Dick insists on singing "a Comical Song" before "Mr. Chorus" comes in to help celebrate. Not to be outdone, Willie (Bullock), the Scottish footman, must do a Scottish dance, though he must accept a violin instead of a bagpipe as accompaniment. Afterwards, presumably the professional singers and dancers come in for a song and a "Figure dance."

Composer William Croft wrote an attractive set of act music for Craufurd's play, including a substantial overture more Italian than French in its antecedents. It was one of the first sets of instrumental music to be published in John Walsh's new series, *Harmonia Anglicana*. Despite the author's ethnicity, and the prominent character of Willie, only one of the tunes is a "Scotch Tune." That Drury Lane could mount a play with such a large cast this late in the season suggests that both Drury Lane and Lincoln's Inn Fields were anxious to keep playing into the summer of 1700 as long as they possibly could.[164]

Revivals, 1699–1700

The Patent Company revived several old stock plays during this season, but they are difficult to connect with any new music. These included Durfey's song-filled comedy *The Marriage-Hater Match'd*; as so often happened, the originators of many of the roles were at Lincoln's Inn Fields. The song "Awake, awake unhappy Man" (in the August 1699 *Mercurius Musicus*) composed by Gottfried Finger for Durfey's tragedy *Bussy d'Ambois* may be the first musical evidence of the composer's move to Drury Lane from Lincoln's Inn Fields following his return from the Continent.

Once again, very little is known about revivals at Lincoln's Inn Fields. The company revived Betterton's Molière-based stock comedy *The Amorous Widow* in December. From the printed text, it seems to have been an ideal production for bringing in all the latest dance numbers, with dances at the ends of Acts III, IV, and V. They also successfully revived Betterton's version of *King Henry the Fourth*, Shakespeare with minor emendations,[165] featuring Betterton as Falstaff. There are two sets of contemporary act tunes associated with *Henry the Fourth*, one by James Paisible and one by William Corbett, but it is unlikely either was used at this time.[166] A revival of the third part of Shakespeare's trilogy, *Henry V*, may have taken place around this time, evidenced by Eccles's hearty "Two-part SONG in the

---

[164] This year, both plays (drolls) and 'musick-meetings' were banned at Bartholomew Fair, limiting summer opportunities for comic performers like Penkethman and Elizabeth Willis. See Rosenfeld, *London Fairs*, pp. 1, 14, 109.

[165] Milhous and Hume note it "should be considered a players' quarto." "Attribution Problems in English Drama, 1660–1700," *Harvard Library Bulletin* 31 (1983): 19.

[166] In Walsh's *Harmonia Anglicana*, advertised in August 1703, Corbett's tunes are described as "Play'd all the time of the Publick Act in *Oxford*." Corbett was presumably asked to provide new music the summer that Betterton's company performed there. An earlier set of tunes by Paisible ("in the Comedy call'd the Humors of Sr Iohn Falstaff")

Play call'd Harry the fifth" beginning "Fill, fill all the glasses," presumably sung by or for Pistol and the remnants of Falstaff's gang.[167]

In February, Lincoln's Inn Fields brought back Congreve's *The Mourning Bride*, advertising it with dancing, "[The Moorish] Entry perform'd by [The Little] Boy,"[168] and in June, his *Love for Love*.[169] Congreve's past successes were presumably staged at other times as well.

Spring and summer revivals of dramatick operas at Drury Lane include the usual favorites, both old (*Dioclesian*, *The Tempest* "with some Additional Entertainments") and new (*The Island Princess*). At least once, they brought back Vanbrugh's comedy *The Relapse*, and Farquhar's *Trip to the Jubilee* (as it was most popularly referred to) continued going strong throughout the season, into July. *The History of Hengist, The Saxon King of Kent* performed at Drury Lane in June may have been an adaptation of Thomas Middleton's early seventeenth-century play. Middleton's version includes several musical events, including conventional temple and banquet scenes, but without further evidence it is impossible to know what might have been performed.

In early July, the two companies appear to have gone head to head with music-laden benefit nights. Lincoln's Inn Fields offered Durfey's *The Comical History of Don Quixote*, "both Parts being made into one by the Author," for the benefit of a family "in great distress," featuring a laundry list of added attractions: "With a new Entry by the little Boy, being his last time of Dancing before he goes to France: Also Mrs Elford's new Entry, never performed but once; and Miss Evan's Jigg and Irish Dance: With several new Comical Dances, compos'd and perform'd by Monsieur L'Sac and others. Together with a new Pastoral Dialogue, by Mr George [Gouge] and Mrs Haynes; and variety of other Singing."[170] Much of the attraction would be to see Anne Bracegirdle and John Bowman performing the roles of Marcella and Cardenio, and singing their signature songs, "I burn, I Burn" and "Let the dreadful Engines."[171]

The Patent Company benefit was a more conventional one for actress Anne Oldfield, offering *The Pilgrim* and *Secular Masque* with "Entertainments of Singing and Dancing between the Acts and in particular, a new Entry Compos'd by the late Mr Eaglesfield, and perform'd by Mr Weaver, Mr Cottin, and Miss

---

were advertised in December 1701 and probably written for Dennis's comedy *The Comicall Gallant; or, The Amours of Sir John Falstaff* (PC, 1700–1701).

[167] Hunter 5 (71).

[168] *London Stage* vol. 1, p. 524.

[169] See *Theatrical Documents*, no. 1646. This was a benefit for "poor English Slaves" abroad. A similar benefit production of *The Tempest* was held at DL.

[170] *London Stage* vol. 1, pp. 530–31.

[171] Without a performance score, one can only hypothesize which songs were kept and which were cut, although Bracegirdle and Bowman's signature songs were doubtless included. Bracegirdle's singing and acting in the new version is complimented in Downes, *Roscius Anglicanus*, pp. 93–4.

Campion. A Scotch Song with the Dance of the Bonny Highlander; never done but once before on the English Stage."[172]

Conclusion

Productions from the 1697–98 season demonstrate both Lincoln's Inn Fields' vitality in the face of continuing competition from the Drury Lane company and the number of musical performers it had available. The success of *Europe's Revels* probably played a part in the company's decision to mount the even more musically ambitious *Rinaldo and Armida* in the following season.

Looking back in 1702 on the competition between the theaters in their first seasons, one of the speakers in *A Comparison Between the Two Stages* observes:

> *Oronoko*, *Æsop*, and *Relapse* are masterpieces, and subsisted *Drury-lane* House, the first two or three Years: *The Mourning Bride*, *Sham Doctor*, and the *Provok'd Wife* kept up the *other* at the same time: And of latter Years there have been now and then a Play worth seeing.[173]

His comment is preceded by a list of about forty plays from the 1695–98 seasons—nearly all "damned."[174]

The 1698–99 season marked a balance in the competition between the two companies. Driving their rivals out of business and thus controlling the London theater market was no longer conceivable for Lincoln's Inn Fields, given the Patent Company's increasingly successful seasons, capped by its immensely profitable production of *The Island Princess*. Betterton and his company had gambled on musical tragedies like *Rinaldo and Armida* and *Xerxes* and lost—prompting the return to, and further growth of, more diverse bills in the following seasons. The Patent Company had gambled too; gambled and won with *The Island Princess*, only to lose on *Massaniello*. There were few other new productions at either theater, and those which are known offer little of interest musically.

In the following season Lincoln's Inn Fields once again lost competitive ground. Like *Rinaldo and Armida*, Congreve's *The Way of the World* was a success, but it could not match the runaway popularity of Farquhar's *The Constant Couple*. Both houses did fairly well with the combination of revised play and masque, with big-name authors (Shakespeare, Dryden), but Drury Lane's gamble on another dramatick opera, *The Grove*, proved a mistake.

Overall, music for new productions and the number of known new productions began to wane after these seasons. The decline in music is visible in the tragedies, but even in comedies musical insertions become increasingly less specific. In the

---

[172] *London Stage* vol. 1, p. 531.
[173] *A Comparison between the Two Stages*, pp. 32–3.
[174] Ibid., pp. 24–32.

ensuing seasons we begin to see clearer separation into main pieces and afterpieces, with the increasing additions (or documentation of additions) of entertainments of music and dancing no longer attached to the production.

Chapter Five
Power Shift, 1700–1703

The first seasons of the new century were difficult ones for both companies. Their musical rivalry continued through new dramatick opera productions and competing guest artists, as well as the usual round of music in plays. The increasing use of newspaper advertisements reveals more details about featured numbers and performers, particularly for benefit nights and special events staged at the theaters.

Context

These years were marked by a series of royal deaths. The 1700–1701 season began badly when the theaters closed in mourning following the death of Princess Anne's only surviving child, the Duke of Gloucester.[1] Several theater composers and poets active at court had written pieces for and about the juvenile duke. The international political situation became quite tense in September 1701 when Louis XIV officially recognized James Francis Edward Stuart as King James III of England, Scotland, and Ireland upon the death of his father, James II. In Britain, news of the deposed king's death produced a stream of elegies from anonymous Jacobite sympathizers and angry reactions from Williamites. Six months later, William III's horse took its famous stumble. Recent ill health exacerbated William's injuries, and he died on 7 March 1702. A flood of elegies followed, and once again the theaters were closed.

The transition from William to Anne was generally smooth, despite the resumption of military activities on the Continent. After Britain entered the war of the Spanish Succession under Marlborough, it celebrated a series of small victories, but the most effectively propagandized event was the naval campaign led by Admiral Rooke and the Duke of Ormond, James Butler. Although the British did not capture their goal, Cadiz, they captured the Spanish silver fleet in Vigo Bay in September 1702. The queen declared a public thanksgiving, celebrated in London on 12 November.[2] Ormond and his duchess were patrons of poets and playwrights (among them Dennis, Dryden, and Durfey), and commendatory poems and songs promptly appeared. Durfey's "Scotch" song "Then welcome from Vigo," sung by

---

[1] *Theatrical Documents*, no. 1649. They were closed for six weeks, August through mid-September.

[2] Luttrell, *State Affairs*, vol. 5, p. 232.

Leveridge, was no doubt heard at Drury Lane, where both Durfey and Steele made a point of including patriotic music and speeches in their plays.

In the autumn of 1700 Lincoln's Inn Fields ceased functioning as an actors' cooperative when the Lord Chamberlain intervened to appoint Thomas Betterton as official manager.[3] In November, he took additional steps to reform the theaters by forbidding women in vizard masks, often worn by prostitutes, to enter.[4] The Lord Chamberlain's efforts do not seem to have been successful, since Queen Anne's 1704 proclamation "against vice and immorality in the theatre" particularly mentions vizard masks, and it was not until June 1704 that John Bowman performed the new ballad "The Misses' Lamentation for want of their Vizard Masks in the Playhouse."

Legal harassment of the actors continued. In November 1700 John Hodgson was fined for profanity and three others were cited in December.[5] In the same month the Grand Jury of Middlesex complained that plays acted in both houses were debauched and a bad influence on the youth of the city.[6] Plays and "Musickbooths" were again forbidden at Bartholomew Fair.[7]

In mid-February 1702, prior to William's death, the Lincoln's Inn Fields company was indicted. At trial the entire company was found guilty of using "Profane, Vicious, & immoral Expressions" in performing *Love for Love*, *The Anatomist*, and *The Provok'd Wife*.[8] The acquittal of Patent Company performers for similar sins (in *Volpone*, *The Humour of the Age*, and *Sir Courtly Nice*) must have rubbed salt into the wound.[9] In early March both theaters were closed and only permitted to reopen after Queen Anne's coronation on 23 April.[10]

Fortunately the 1702–1703 season permitted both companies to recover, although their respective weaknesses, financial and otherwise, were clear. Plans to reunite them began to be seriously considered.

---

[3] Milhous observes "The move was most unusual and bespeaks the inability of the members of the cooperative to come to any workable agreement." Milhous, *Thomas Betterton*, p. 115.

[4] *Theatrical Documents*, no. 1657.

[5] Ibid., nos. 1658 and 1661.

[6] Ibid., no. 1659.

[7] Ibid., nos. 1639, 1645, 1648, 1650, 1667 and 1668. The ban was repeated in following seasons.

[8] For excerpts of a legal report on the trial see *Theatrical Documents*, no. 1685.

[9] Ibid., no. 1683.

[10] As announced in *The Post-Boy* for 10–12 March 1702. *Theatrical Documents*, no. 1687.

Musical Assets

Actor-singers

Among the actor-singers, Dogget, the immensely popular but touchy comedian who had left Lincoln's Inn Fields in the spring of 1696, renegotiated a contract sometime in the autumn of 1700.[11] The Patent Company continued to be well served with male actors who could sing and dance in comic roles, including Cibber, Penkethman, and, in his rakish mode, Wilks. Of course, comic singing didn't have to sound pretty to be enthusiastically received. As Cibber would later recall, "no *Italian Eunuch* was more applauded than when I sung in *Sir Courtly* [*Nice*],"[12] and he continued to write singing bits for himself into his comedies.

The Patent Company continued to cultivate its crop of young actress-singers, such as Margaret Mills and dancing comedienne Jane Lucas. Since appearing in *The Female Wits* in 1696, Lucas had acquired a series of popular supporting roles, often with musical dialogues, where her vocal and physical talents could be displayed. She performed an epilogue c.1700 in which she states "Y'have seen me Dance, and ye have heard me Sing,/ But now I'm put upon another thing;/ By way of *Epilogue* ..." and concludes "We'll sing the last new Dialogue instead."[13] Similar to Elizabeth Willis at Lincoln's Inn Fields, she did not play leads, but was an important utility player.

Singers

Among the companies' male singers, tenor-countertenor John Pate continued to be heavily used in dramatick operas and comedies at Drury Lane. Francis Hughes and Marcellus Laroon were added to the vocal ranks by the end of the previous season (1699–1700). However, the Patent Company was not always so lucky. John Freeman, after being very active in musical works such as Oldmixon's *The Grove* and Durfey's *Massaniello*, obtained a position at the Chapel Royal in December 1700 and presumably left the stage shortly thereafter. Singer-composer Richard Leveridge left London for Dublin in 1699 and would not return until 1702, another loss to its singing forces. Foreign artists were also in the rotation: a mysterious 'Signior Mancini' from the Spanish court performed at Drury Lane in January 1701 before returning to the Continent.[14]

At Lincoln's Inn Fields, Mr Gouge had been a significant part of musical productions during the previous seasons, yet there is no record of him appearing during this period, although a few songsheets naming him as performer cannot

---

[11] *Theatrical Documents*, no. 1651.
[12] Cibber, *Apology*, vol. 1, p. 224.
[13] Danchin, *Prologues and Epilogues of the Restoration 1660–1700*, Part 3, vol. 5, pp. 561–3 (B518).
[14] M&H *London Stage*, p. 18.

be dated or assigned to specific productions. The company acquired the services of tenor Richard Elford, who both sang and composed, although a series of increasingly prestigious chapel jobs would draw much of his time.[15]

Lincoln's Inn Fields also attempted to hire singers of the same magnitude as their dance attractions. John Abell, the famous (and debt-ridden) Scottish vocalist, toyed with the management at both houses.[16] It seems neither house would agree to his demands, and instead Abell continued to promote his own concerts at Richmond Wells, Hampstead Wells, and other venues, with limited success.

Women singers at Drury Lane included Mary Lindsey, Mrs Shaw, and the youthful Mary Anne Campion. Campion's professional relationship with young composer John Weldon led to tremendous exposure as a singer at York Buildings and in other venues during this period, while Mrs Erwin, so prominent in the productions of the previous seasons, seems to have disappeared, though scanty performance records are no certain guide. Campion was also increasingly featured as a dance attraction, executing many of the functions previously assigned to Letitia Cross.

Lincoln's Inn Fields maintained the essential services of Mary Hodgson, whose concert activities at York Buildings and elsewhere are increasingly well documented during this period. She frequently sang with performers from the other house. These joint concert appearances, featuring singers and sometimes composers from both houses prefigure the collaborative performances and concert series that became a significant part of the later 1703–1705 seasons, discussed in Chapter Six.

While developing their English singers, both companies also made an effort to obtain headliners from the Continent. Soprano Margarita de l'Epine sang between the acts of the pastoral *The Fickle Shepherdess* in the spring of 1703, possibly at the premiere (a receipt for her services is dated 27 May 1703).[17] De l'Epine (c.1680–1746) was initially extremely popular and patronized by the nobility (notoriously the Earl of Nottingham) for her singing of Italian songs and arias, settled in London, and eventually married the composer Pepusch.[18] Joanna

---

[15] Elford, who sang at Durham Cathedral before coming to London, sang at St Paul's from March 1700, at St George's Chapel, Windsor from December 1701 and entered the Chapel Royal choir in August 1702. Elford has sometimes been described as a countertenor, but Baldwin and Wilson point to his tenor partbook, preserved at Durham Cathedral. DNB vol. 18, p. 32.

[16] In the summer of 1698, recently returned from the Continent, he entered negotiations with Drury Lane. See Linda Merians, "John Abell's Return to England," *Music and Letters* 66 (1985): 241–4. In January 1701 Congreve complained "tho' he has received £300 of the money belonging to the new Play-house has not yet sung and is full of … shifting tricks." *Theatrical Documents*, no. 1662.

[17] *Theatrical Documents*, no. 1718.

[18] See D.F. Cook, "Françoise Marguérite de l'Epine: The Italian Lady?" *Theatre Notebook* 35 (1981): 58–73, 104–113.

Maria Lindelheim, known as 'the Baroness,' also appeared at Drury Lane as an added attraction. She and violinist Gasparo Visconti ('Gasperini') may have first performed at York Buildings concerts in November and December 1702.[19] Like de l'Epine, she settled in London, and she married the cellist-impresario Nicola Haym. A third soprano singer of Italian repertoire, Maria Margarita Gallia, sang at Lincoln's Inn Fields in June 1703, accompanied by Giuseppe Fedeli Saggione.[20]

It is worth noting that de l'Epine was paid by Elizabeth Barry, demonstrating Barry's executive power at Lincoln's Inn Fields, and that she received twenty guineas (£21s) for "one days Singing." In comparison, Dogget, the company's most popular comedian, was making three pounds a week plus yearly benefit nights, and the lowest-ranked singers and actors might be contracted for twenty pounds a year. Although star singers drew audiences, regularly sustaining such expense was problematic, and such marked inequities in pay were bound to foster resentment.

Dancers

From newspaper accounts, we know that Colley Cibber's comedy *Love Makes a Man* was performed in December 1700 with "a French Scaramouche Dance betwixt the second and third Acts," which was interrupted by an audience member throwing oranges.[21] This is one of the earliest specific accounts of dancing in the theaters after 1695 which is not drawn from a play text (*Dr. Faustus*, *Brutus of Alba*, and *Natural Magic* had all included Harlequin or Scaramouche dances).[22]

Novelties appeared in the spring, usually accompanying the revival of old stock plays, like Ben Jonson's *The Alchymist* at Drury Lane with "several new Entertainments of Dancing, by the famous Youth, under Nine Years of Age, newly arrived from the Opera at Paris."[23] At Lincoln's Inn Fields, Anthony l'Abbé was advertised with a revival of *Circe*, and musical entertainments from *The Mad Lover* and *Acis and Galatea* in June 1701.[24] L'Abbé is the only dancer officially listed as part of the Lincoln's Inn Fields company in 1700–1701, and had a contract with

---

[19] M&H *London Stage*, pp. 78–9. Milhous and Hume suggest that the "Italian Gentlewoman" whose singing is advertised was de l'Epine, but Baldwin and Wilson note that de l'Epine sang with Greber during her early years in London, while "the Baroness" sang with Gasperini.

[20] M&H *London Stage*, p. 103.

[21] M&H *London Stage*, pp. 13–14.

[22] For more on Scaramouche and Harlequin dances on the London stage, see Jennifer Thorp, "From Scaramouche to Harlequin: Dances 'in grotesque characters' on the London stage," in *Stages 'Adorned with ev'ry Grace'* (Ashgate, forthcoming).

[23] M&H *London Stage*, p. 24.

[24] Ibid., p. 32.

Betterton that ran until June 1703.²⁵ In January 1703 Drury Lane gained its own French master, Philippe Du Ruel, advertised, for those in the know, as a student of Louis Pécour, the famous French dancer and choreographer.²⁶

In late 1701, Lincoln's Inn Fields brought over Marie-Thérèse Perdou de Subligny (Madame Subligny), also from the Paris Opéra, to add to its list of star attractions. In subsequent seasons her dancing would be imitated by "the Devonshire Girl" (Mrs Mosse), a new addition to Drury Lane. The following year Charles Fairbank, son of a Patent Company actor, signed on with Lincoln's Inn Fields. Of the actress-singer-dancers, Jane Lucas continued at Drury Lane, where Margaret Bicknell joined her, while Mrs Prince continued at Lincoln's Inn Fields. There was also a small host of dancers, French and English, who appeared briefly at either or both theaters.

Joseph Sorin, dancing master at Lincoln's Inn Fields at the beginning of the decade, began making appearances at Drury Lane during these seasons. Choreographer John Weaver, famous for his treatise and later work in pantomime, also apparently moved between Lincoln's Inn Fields and Drury Lane.

As with other kinds of entertainment, newspaper advertisements describing dancing at Drury Lane become much more frequent, beginning in the summer of 1702. Sometimes favorite performers are promised (Jane Lucas, Mary Anne Campion) and sometimes specific dances (Tollet's Ground) or kinds of dances (comic, character) are named. In August 1702 the advertisements become very descriptive, for example: "A Dance between two French-Men and two French-Women, and other Dances. And Monsieur Serene [Sorin] and another Person [Richard Baxter?] lately arrived in England, will perform a Night Scene by a Harlequin and a Scaramouch, after the Italian manner."²⁷ The "Night Scene" was popular enough to be advertised again that autumn.

There is evidence of equally elaborate dancing at Lincoln's Inn Fields in December 1702 with a revival of Wycherley's stock comedy *The Country Wife*, including a "Mad-Man's Dance," "A new Dance perform'd by 16 Persons in Grotesq; Habits, in which a Black will perform Variety of Postures to Admiration," and "Mr Weaver will perform *Roger a Coverley* as it was done Originally after the Yorkshire Manner."²⁸ Although the evidence is limited, the variety of serious and comic dances described by dance scholars (those representative of nations, occupations, or celebrations; those featuring grotesque/*commedia dell'arte*

---

[25] M&H *Theatrical Documents*, no. 1750. Like others circa 1703, he complained of Betterton's management.

[26] See, for example, M&H *London Stage*, p. 85 (2 January 1703).

[27] M&H *London Stage*, p. 65. Other entertainments included Mr Clench of Barnet's imitations of an organ and a pack of hounds (among other things) and vaulting.

[28] M&H *London Stage*, p. 84.

characters; and specialty dances with props) were already an important part of the evening's entertainment at both theaters.[29]

Instrumental Music and Composers

As in previous seasons, instrumental special attractions were typically used to supplement performances of stock plays. As with singers, there was special cachet in being (or seeming to be) of Italian origin. Italian violinist Nicola Cosimi played seven concerts at Lincoln's Inn Fields before 21 July 1702 (when he was paid for them).[30] Violinist Gasparini [Gasparo Visconti], billed as "lately arriv'd from Rome," performed "several Entertainments of Musick by himself, and in Consort with others" at Drury Lane during a revival of Shadwell's *The Lancashire Witches* in December 1702.[31] Afterwards Gasparini appeared regularly at Drury Lane, performing "entertainments" of his own composing, "Italian sonatas," and, in November and December 1702, "new Sonatas for the Violin lately brought from Rome, Compos'd by the Great Arcangelo Corelli."[32]

In September 1700 the Lincoln's Inn Fields company staged Shadwell's *The Virtuoso* with an entertainment of music "by the famous Monsieur le Rich, lately arrived from the Court of Poland."[33] Francis (or François) La Rich (Le Rich), a bass player, had been a member of the King's Musick in the 1680s, played concerts in 1697 and departed to the Continent in the spring of 1698.[34]

Violinist Thomas Deane was presumably Lincoln's Inn Fields' answer to the Patent Company violinists, although the lack of newspaper advertisements from Betterton's company limits the evidence. Deane appeared in the list of performers at a benefit concert at York Buildings in March 1701. The following summer he performed in a series of concerts at the Hampstead Wells resort, including one featuring Eccles's instrumental music for the Queen's Coronation, Weldon's songs for his consort at York Buildings, and his own "Entertainment on the Violin."[35] He may have composed the instrumental music for Oldmixon's *The Governour of Cyprus* (LIF, January 1703), although there are enough contemporary Thomas Dean(e)s to make the ascription uncertain.

---

[29] See, for example, Moira Goff, "'Actions, Manners, and Passions': entr'acte dancing on the London stage, 1700–1737," *Early Music* 26/2 (1998): 213–28.

[30] M&H *London Stage*, p. 64.

[31] Ibid., p. 83.

[32] Ibid., pp. 48, 51. From December 1702 to December 1703 Gasperini was advertised with performances of 22 different plays, both to enliven stock plays (*Volpone*, *The Rover*) and revivals of recent comedies (*The Constant Couple*, *The Funeral*, *Tunbridge Walks*).

[33] M&H *London Stage*, p. 8.

[34] *Biographical Dictionary*, s.v. "La Rich, Francis." Music by Le Rich is copied in GB-Lbl Add. MS 35043 with music for stage works from the 1690s.

[35] M&H *London Stage*, pp. 60, 62, 64.

Eccles made less substantial musical contributions to theatrical productions after being named Master of the King's Musick. In addition to performance and administrative duties, the position required him to compose odes for court occasions. Eccles also must have devoted a significant portion of his time to composing the music for Congreve's masque *The Judgment of Paris*, part of a high-profile competition sponsored by "several persons of quality" which pitted his compositional skills against Finger, Daniel Purcell, and Weldon.[36] In Eccles's work for Lincoln's Inn Fields the scant number of new productions known is matched by the limited amount of music that survives.

John Lenton became Lincoln's Inn Fields' most reliable source of instrumental music, documented in the many sets of his tunes published in Walsh's *Harmonia Anglicana*. He was as prolific as Finger at instrumental music, but does not seem to have tried to compete with Eccles in songwriting. Lenton was not a drawing card such as the young lion John Weldon or the popular composer-performer Richard Leveridge. Violinist William Corbett would later write act music for Granville's dramatick opera *The British Enchanters* (1706), but he appears, from available evidence, to have composed for Lincoln's Inn Fields only occasionally.

The burden of providing most of the vocal music continued to rest on Eccles, but his 1704 *Collection of Songs* preserves only a few examples, particularly a new mad song for Bracegirdle in *The Fickle Shepherdess* and vocal selections from spectacular musical scenes in *The Fair Penitent*. The Patent Company's more varied array of composers and composer-performers wound up working to their advantage, by leaving room for the new. Lincoln's Inn Fields suffered from too much stability in personnel—both actors and musical talent.

Drury Lane management maintained its ties to the Purcell–Blow contingent of composers: Daniel Purcell, Croft, and Clarke, and continued to receive the occasional set of instrumental music from Paisible. They also acquired the services of Gottfried Finger, who turned out numerous sets of act tunes as well as contributing to major musical productions, including dramatick operas and Dryden's *Secular Masque*. When Finger left England, after the judges in *The Judgment of Paris* competition slighted his entry, act tunes for Drury Lane begin to appear from organist John Barrett, yet another of Blow's former students, who also contributed vocal music. If Finger had left Lincoln's Inn Fields out of a sense of competition with Eccles, at Drury Lane Daniel Purcell did the majority of the vocal composition. As before, while they were doubtless glad to have him, Finger seems to have been replaceable.

---

[36] Organized by Charles Montagu, Lord Halifax and supported by other members of the nobility "for the Encouragement of MUSICK." Franck also set Congreve's libretto. Weldon won. For more on *The Judgment of Paris*, see Richard Platt's preface to the facsimile edition of Eccles's published score, in *Music for London Entertainment 1660–1800*, Series C, vol. 1 (Tunbridge Wells, 1984), and the essays in *Stages 'Adorned with ev'ry Grace'* (Ashgate, forthcoming) by Olive Baldwin and Thelma Wilson, Matthew Roberson, and Robert Rawson.

Just as singers did, instrumentalists collaborated and appeared together on the ever-growing concert circuit, as well as appearing at the theaters. While John Weldon organized and played in concerts with performers from both theaters (Richard Elford, Mary Hodgson, Mary Lindsey, and Mary Anne Campion) he appears to have been recruited by the Patent Company during the summer of 1702, when they first advertised "some of Mr Weldon's new Songs" during a revival of *Oroonoko*,[37] and then included songs by him in 1702–1703 comedies by Cibber, Estcourt, and Centlivre. Raphael Courteville, who had written a song for the original production of *Oroonoko*, occasionally contributed a song sung between the acts, but none associated with any specific production.

Competing Claims: The 1700–1701 Season

During this season there is another clear case of direct musical competition between dramatick opera productions: *The Mad Lover*, *The Rival Queens*, and *The Virgin Prophetess*.[38] The earlier competition between *Rinaldo and Armida* and *The Island Princess* was not conclusive, and their popularity made similar operatic productions attractive propositions, despite the extra rehearsal time and financial outlay involved.

Other signs of direct competition are not hard to find. In 1700–1701 there were five plays by Shakespeare performed in later seventeenth-century versions by authors such as Nahum Tate and Thomas Shadwell, resulting in several evenings of Shakespeare vs. Shakespeare. When Lincoln's Inn Fields mounted George Granville's new version of *The Merchant of Venice*, *The Jew of Venice*, in January, the Patent Company performed Shadwell's versions of *The Tempest* and *Timon of Athens*. Later in the spring it turned to Ben Jonson's comedies, while Lincoln's Inn Fields staged three new tragedies.

New Productions

The 1700–1701 season began in mid-October at Drury Lane with performances of Susanna Carroll Centlivre's tragedy *The Perjur'd Husband*. The late start was due to the closing of the theaters after the death of Princess Anne's son. Casting suggests Centlivre's play was not part of the regular autumn season. The Lincoln's Inn Fields company staged nothing of note until late November, when it revived Shakespeare's *Henry VIII*, presumably another lightly adapted version of Shakespeare prepared by Betterton. Its new productions have only conjectural dates. Although Lincoln's Inn Fields offered little for the autumn, as shown in

---

[37] M&H *London Stage*, p. 63.

[38] Noted by Milhous and Hume in their introduction to the 1700–1701 season in the new *London Stage*, p. 2.

Table 5.1, during the winter months both companies mounted representative new productions in three genres: comedy, tragedy, and dramatick opera.

Table 5.1 New productions during the 1700–1701 season

	New works for the Patent Company		New works at Lincoln's Inn Fields	
AUTUMN	*The Perjur'd Husband*	Tragedy		
	Love at a Loss	Comedy		
WINTER	*Love Makes a Man*	Comedy	*The Ambitious Stepmother*	Tragedy
			The Jew of Venice	Comedy
			The Mad Lover + Acis and Galatea	[Dramatick Opera] + Masque
	The Unhappy Penitent	Tragedy	*The Ladies Visiting Day*	Comedy
	Alexander the Great	[Dramatick Opera]		
SPRING			[*The Stage Coach*	Farce]
	The Humour of the Age	Comedy	*The Double Distress*	Tragedy
			The Czar of Muscovy	Tragedy
			Love's Victim	Tragedy
	Sir Harry Wildair	Comedy		
	The Virgin Prophetess	Dramatick Opera		
	The Bath	Comedy		
SUMMER			*The Gentleman Cully*	Comedy

In the spring, the companies took diverging paths: Lincoln's Inn Fields played to its acting strengths with new serious works, while the Patent Company emphasized comedy and finished the season with another spectacular dramatick opera. As would become typical in future seasons, suites of instrumental music from the new productions at Drury Lane, composed by William Croft, Daniel Purcell or, most often, by Gottfried Finger, were quickly issued by John Walsh in his series *Harmonia Anglicana*. As with newspaper advertisements, Lincoln's Inn Fields lagged behind its rival, and its productions do not appear regularly in the Walsh series until 1703.

A few additional productions may have been mounted this season, leaving little trace. As in earlier seasons, these 'lost plays' are known only by inference.[39] Three songs survive attributed to *The Self-Conceit; or, The Mother Made a Property*. Two were set by Eccles, one sung by Elizabeth Bowman "Oh! the mighty pow'r of Love," and one by Mary Hodgson, "When first to bright Maria's Charms"; and one set by John Church, sung by John Bowman, "Come, come Phillis, never sigh nor mourn."[40] All were engraved by Thomas Cross; the songs by Eccles were also printed by Walsh and appear in his 1704 *Collection*. Mrs Bowman's song was popular enough to be included in Durfey's *Wit & Mirth* (1706).[41] Although the dating to this season is purely conjectural, from the songs, one might hypothesize a Dilke-like comedy, with the Bowmans playing characters involved in romantic intrigue and Hodgson's song featured in a concert scene.

Centlivre's *The Perjur'd Husband; or, The Adventures of Venice* makes good use of musical scenes to emphasize the exotic setting, Venice during Carnival. The husband of the title, the Savoyard Count Bassino, finds himself in a classic fix: "Married to *Placentia*, and in Love with *Aurelia*," who is already betrothed. Bassino's friend Armando tries to intervene, Placentia follows him to Venice in disguise, and things end conspicuously badly. Some lighter moments are provided by a foppish Frenchman, who regularly "enters singing," in semi-successful amorous intrigues. His dialogue with a pert maid (Jane Lucas) makes comprehensive use of the comedy cliché using music and dancing as metaphors for sex.[42] Centlivre's next four plays, performed at both houses, are all comic.

Act I opens with a masquerade ball featuring a "Spanish Entry," presumably of the type l'Abbé had made popular at court and onstage during recent seasons. This is paralleled at the opening of Act V when Bassino throws his own masked ball, featuring "An Entry of three Men, and three Women of several Nations." All the musical events Centlivre calls for, both the dancing scenes and a short song

---

[39] Price hypothesizes a production, *Love's Stratagem*, on the basis of a set of act tunes by Paisible published in *Harmonia Anglicana*, of uncertain date. They are probably not the tunes for Centlivre's comedy *Love's Contrivance* (PC, 1703).

[40] The Cross songsheets can be found in US–DLC.

[41] Thus it is the only song that appears in Day and Murrie's catalogue.

[42] S. Carroll [Centlivre], *The Perjur'd Husband; or, The Adventures of Venice, A Tragedy* (London, 1700), 31.

also performed at Bassino's party, are eminently practicable and well integrated. No music associated with the play is known, and pre-existing dance music was probably used. Centlivre's preface and the cast list suggest that this production got short shrift (lacking "good Actors, and a full Town,") but did, she insists, garner applause.[43]

Having disposed of Centlivre's tragedy, the Patent Company proceeded with comedies by familiar authors: Catharine Trotter's *Love at a Loss; or, The Most Votes Carry It* and Colley Cibber's *Love Makes a Man*. As in her serious plays, Trotter makes very little reference to musical numbers within her play text. The only music called for is an unspecified song at the end of Act II and an equally unspecified dance in the traditional slot in Act V. However, close examination of Trotter's text reveals another use of music: actor Robert Wilks, playing Beaumine, regularly sings quotations from pre-existing songs. Trotter's quotations for Wilks as Beaumine are often carefully specified—and borrowed from John Bowman's repertoire.

Significantly, many of Beaumine's singing moments occur in scenes like those between Congreve's Mirabell and Millamant. In Trotter's comedy, it is song rather than poetry which the lovers (and others) trade back and forth. Trotter likely had Congreve's *The Way of the World* in mind—not to mention his other plays—while writing her comedy,[44] but she also had Dryden at her elbow.

Beaumine uses song both to torment Lesbia, whom he will eventually agree to marry, and to flirt madly with the coquette Miranda: "When present we'll love, when absent agree;/ I think not of Iris, nor Iris of me," lines from Henry Purcell's "For Iris I sigh" from Dryden's 1690 comedy *Amphitryon*. Beaumine also quotes songs from 1690s comedies by Congreve and Durfey. In the final act, Beaumine quotes "Sound a parley, ye Fair, and Surrender," the rousing duet for Cupid and the Cold Genius (Bowman again) from Dryden's dramatick opera *King Arthur*, regularly revived by the Patent Company. Like much of Purcell's vocal music, it was available in print,[45] and the "Frost Scene" featuring the Cold Genius was often performed as an excerpt.

Similarly, there is a later advertisement for a performance of Southerne's *Oroonoko*, during which singers would perform the musical dialogue "Fair Iris and her swain," another song from *Amphitryon*.[46] Even when they were not staging complete works with music by the late, great Mr Purcell, the Patent Company appears to have kept his music in near-constant circulation.

There was plenty of music involved in the performance of Colley Cibber's new comedy, *Love Makes a Man; or, The Fop's Fortune*, but the play text is

---

[43] [Centlivre], *The Perjur'd Husband*, unpaginated.

[44] Paula R. Backscheider, "Stretching the Form: Catharine Trotter Cockburn and Other Failures," *Theater Journal* 47 (1995): 443–58, p. 449.

[45] "Sound a parley" was printed in the first book of *Orpheus Britannicus* (London, 1698).

[46] M&H *London Stage*, pp. 106–7.

disappointingly vague about musical events. The three surviving songs, "For Rurall and Sincerer Joys," "Thou gay, thou cruel, cruel Maid" and "Ofelia's Aire, her Meen, her Face," were all included in Walsh's *A Collection of the Choicest Songs and Dialogues* (Hunter 5), but are not found in the play text.[47] Any or all of them may have been sung in the dinner/seduction scene in Act IV, marked "Musick here" and "A SONG here" (50, 51), although textual hints suggest they may have been performed earlier as part of the marriage masque referred to at the end of Act II (32), before the scholarly hero Carlos (Wilks again) and his love Angellina (Diana Temple) run away from her arranged marriage with his foolish brother Clodio.

All three songs were set by Daniel Purcell in G minor, a key suitable to the complementary pastoral and romantic texts. They feature the professional 'concert' singers (Mrs Shaw, James Bowen and Francis Hughes), which suggests a unified entertainment. In addition, a newspaper reports that a "French Scaramouche Dance betwixt the second and third Acts" was performed on the play's third night (and possibly earlier).[48] Though it is hard to connect this comic dance with the serious songs, the foolish Francophile Clodio is constantly expressing himself with French music and dance. It might also ease the abrupt change into place. Act III suddenly opens in Lisbon.

Cibber clearly wrote the part of Clodio—who loses Angellina and his inheritance but emerges with a bride and money—for himself. Clodio sings snippets of French songs in character, leads in a procession of "hautboys" while singing, and guides the company in a "Dance *ala Mode D'Angleterre*" at the end of the play. Fellow comedian Penkethman as Don Lewis also whistles, sings and dances while he fences. The most obvious quotation occurs in the second act, when Carlos's servant Sancho sings "Ban. Ban, Cac-caliban" while drunk—a reference to *The Tempest*, revived at Drury Lane the following month.

Competing against Cibber's comedy was Nicholas Rowe's first tragedy, *The Ambitious Step-mother.* The prologue complains once again about the use of variety acts like Mr Clinch of Barnet, and the need to rely on "farce, song, and dance." The epilogue, spoken by Bracegirdle, is friendly to music, though still manifesting concern:

> Musick in vain, supports with Friendly aid
> Her Sister Poetry's declining head.
> Show but a Mimick Ape, or *French* Buffoon,
> You to the other House in Shoals are gone,
> And leave us here to Tune our Crowds alone.
> Must *Shakespear*, *Fletcher*, and laborious *Ben*,

---

[47] "Thou gay, thou cruel, cruel Maid" also appeared in Purcell's *Collection of New Songs*, published by Walsh in May 1701. Baldwin and Wilson, personal communication.

[48] Reported as part of the orange-throwing incident. M&H *London Stage*, pp. 13–14.

Be left for *Scaramouch* and *Harlaquin*?[49]

With an all-star cast, Downes comments that it "answer'd the Companies expectation."[50] Proof of the play's popularity can be seen in the speedily issued second edition (1702).[51]

The first musical number takes place at the beginning of Act III when the ingénue Cleone (Elizabeth Bowman) is "discover'd lying on a Bank of Flowers," accompanied by a song, "Upon a shady Bank repos'd," closely reflecting both her emotional and physical state. A second musical interlude occurs at the end of Act III, and consists of an equally conventional temple scene with a "HYMN to the Sun," performed by the chief celebrant Magas (John Bowman) and a chorus of priests in the presence of all the principal characters.

The act music by John Lenton appeared in Walsh's *Harmonia Anglicana*, the first set of act tunes from a Lincoln's Inn Fields production to be included.[52] They were first advertised near the beginning of February 1701, presumably about six weeks after the play's premiere.[53] Lenton would compose act tunes for all of Rowe's plays for Lincoln's Inn Fields.

Another winter production at Lincoln's Inn Fields, George Granville's comedy *The Jew of Venice*, based on Shakespeare's *The Merchant of Venice*, was printed by late January 1701. In the prologue, "The Ghosts of Shakespear and Dryden arise Crown'd with Lawrel." Their dialogue consists of mutual compliment, predictable denigration of modern tastes,[54] and lavish praise of Granville's work. Shakespeare's comic characters are cut; instead, Dogget played the title role, although the substantial amount of Shakespeare's text that Granville kept makes it difficult to believe that his 1701 Shylock was purely comic. Bracegirdle played Portia.

The sole significant musical event in the play is the *Masque of Peleus and Thetis*, inserted in Act II, in a new scene added by Granville. It is performed during

---

[49] Rowe, *The Ambitious Step-mother. A Tragedy* (London, 1701), p. 80, lines 22–28, italics reversed.

[50] Downes, *Roscius Anglicanus*, p. 95.

[51] The new edition supposedly contains "a New SCENE," though Milhous and Hume find no evidence of this, and includes author attributions for the songs: B. Stote and William Shippen, presumably friends of Rowe's.

[52] The E minor tunes display the usual variety of dance types (hornpipe, gavotte, and jig) with "Scotch" and "Slow" airs. No settings for the vocal music are known.

[53] See Price, *Theater Music*, Appendix II, "A List of Sets of Act Music published by John Walsh 1701–1710," p. 238.

[54] This includes a passage spoken by Dryden insisting that the modern audiences are deaf to nature (Shakespeare's works) and love (Dryden's), with an emphatic Dennis-like attack on narcissism and homosexuality (here conflated): "*Strephon* for *Strephon* sighs; and *Sapho* dies,/ Shot to the Soul by brighter *Sapho*'s Eyes:/ No Wonder then their wand'ring Passions roam …" (lines 20–22).

a banquet at Antonio's house at which he, Gratiano, Bassanio, and Shylock are all present. Masque characters include Prometheus, his friend the hero Peleus; the nymph Thetis; and Jupiter, descending from the skies on his eagle. In addition to the four principal roles there are indications for choruses and passages of instrumental music. The masque ends traditionally "with Variety of Dances." The names of the performers are not given, and without the music, it is difficult to hypothesize which singers may have been cast, although Mary Hodgson seems a likely Thetis.

Just as the famous masque of Orpheus in Settle's *The Empress of Morocco* or *The Rape of Europa* in Rochester's *Valentinian*, *Peleus and Thetis* has clear allegorical connections to the drama in which it appears. Prometheus is Antonio, bound to torment, whose friend Peleus (Bassanio) proves the instrument of his salvation, through his beloved Thetis (Portia). Jupiter, like Shylock, is forced to concede when he is not willing to pay the price for what he wants. In both masque and play, love and friendship triumph over lust (greed) and hate; Jupiter releases Prometheus from his chains. The masque *Peleus and Thetis* can be added to the list of classical masques performed at Lincoln's Inn Fields, including *Hercules* and *Ixion*. The masque text in the Folger Shakespeare Library, which does not list the author but notes that the masque was "Set to Musick by Mr. *Eccles*," was probably printed for distribution at the theater, like other editions of musical entertainments.[55]

A much lighter example of the masque appeared as part of Lincoln's Inn Fields' next production. *The Mad Lover* was a dramatick opera conceived along the lines of *The Island Princess* or *The Indian Queen*. Like Motteux's earlier work, it featured a few major musical entertainments, of which the final masque was the longest and quite independent. The masque, *Acis and Galatea*, featured Anne Bracegirdle, John and Elizabeth Bowman performing music by Eccles. It became one of the long-running successes, and was often featured as an afterpiece.[56]

Altogether, the surviving music for *The Mad Lover* and *Acis and Galatea* is of very uneven quality. Although Eccles wrote the music for both, the lack of a full musical score makes it difficult to compare with the Patent Company's dramatick operas. The printed musical numbers are often far shorter and disappointingly formula based when compared with those for *Rinaldo and Armida*. Excerpts from the masques and martial welcome appeared in the periodical *Mercurius Musicus*

---

[55] Folger PR 3539 L4 P4 1701. Granville's masque appears in all subsequent editions of the play except his 1732 collected works, where it appears with his poems. The 1732 play text reads "Here to be a complete Concert of Vocal and Instrumental Musick, after the *Italian* Manner."

[56] Milhous and Hume have also hypothesized that, like *Europe's Revels*, *Acis & Galatea* may have been presented at court before its appearance on the public stage. M&H *London Stage*, pp. 16–17.

(many are also included in Eccles's 1704 *Collection*), and his act music appeared in *Harmonia Anglicana*.[57]

If the musical entertainment and masques occurred in Acts II, III, and V as indicated, Motteux must have restructured Fletcher's play. In the original, in which the valiant general Memnon is unmanned by the sight of a beautiful princess, Memnon is welcomed home from war in the first act, not the second, and there is a mock funeral with dead march in Act III. The masque of Orpheus, with which Memnon's friends attempt to restore his sense of perspective about love and duty, takes place in Act IV, while the fifth act includes a musical invocation to the goddess Venus, the goddess's reply, and a martial song performed to humor Memnon's madness.

The surviving songs from the "Martial Welcome" in Act II are nearly all in the martial key of D major, suitable for the "warlike symphony" which introduced them, undoubtedly including trumpets. The Act II entertainment featured the professional singers, particularly Mr Cook and Mary Hodgson, and the songs are more elaborate than those in the masques that follow. The most striking song is Cook's rousing "When the whole World amaz'd," another musical picture of the field of war, which requires agility and power. The following duet for the boy and girl, "Let gentle Notes succeed your Noise," provided the usual contrast, followed by Hodgson's elegant pastoral air, "Let all be gay, let Pleasure Reign."[58] The dance of mariners, "Their Mistresses with them, and *African* Slaves," which precedes the grand chorus, recalls both the popularity of sailors' dances in comedies and the exoticized dance of summer in Motteux's Masque of the Seasons ("Enter an *African* Lady, with Slaves who dance with Timbrels. A *Negro* Lord makes love to her" [42]).

The *Masque of Wine and Love* in Act III featured the actor-singers Bracegirdle, John Bowman, and Dogget supplemented by singer John Wiltshire.[59] Here Bracegirdle plays Cupid, Bacchus's traditional opponent, doubtless in a fetching costume. As in earlier masques, the choruses and instrumental music, including a "humorous Symphony, expressing the reeling of Drunkards" and a dance of "four Drunkards, and four Women to whom they make Love," were not printed and no source for them is known. However, the central portion of the masque, the solo for Cupid and the following duet and dialogue survive.

---

[57] A modern edition of the *Harmonia Anglicana* tunes has been published by Dr Peter Holman in the Restoration Theatre Suites series (St Albans, 1998).

[58] When printed in *Mercurius Musicus,* the second line "Peace and *Memnon* cheer the Plain" was altered to "Peace and *William* cheer the Plain," a nod to England's military monarch. The original text was used in Eccles's 1704 *Collection*.

[59] Musical versions of this standard topos appeared in many productions, including the dramatick opera *Dioclesian*, with music by Henry Purcell. The best known is probably the masque of Cupid and Bacchus in Shadwell's *Timon of Athens* (revived 1695), also set by Purcell.

Bracegirdle's solo "Cease of Cupid to complain," opens like a chaconne, though the ground bass breaks pattern after the second repetition. Like the instrumental chaconne Eccles wrote for the third act of *Rinaldo and Armida*, the air is in G minor, the subject is love, and Cupid is present.[60] The rival claims of Cupid and Bacchus (Wiltshire) are united in the brief duet which follows, which sounds like a rollicking country dance: "Appear, jolly Lovers [Topers], to cooe [Drink] laugh and toy./ And rais'd with hot Love [brisk Wine] give a Taste of your Joy." A typical Motteux bawdy musical dialogue follows it: "Now, Women, I Scorn you; brisk Wine's my Delight." Musically static, the dialogue rolls along on the strength of its performers and broad humor: a drunken gentleman (Bowman) debating with a "Woman of the Town" (Dogget). Dogget as a 'beauty' holding out for marriage against a lascivious Bowman, intent on drinking and dalliance, would have made for quite a show—a smart competitive response to the popularity of similar dialogues featuring Pate and Leveridge.

The final musical entertainment in *The Mad Lover* starred Bracegirdle as Acis and the two Bowmans as Galatea and Polyphemus.[61] An interrupted onstage wedding featured Dogget as the clownish groom and Elizabeth Willis as the country bride, a role she was still playing in 1723.

A song for Acis, when his anger at Galatea's supposed betrayal precipitates an energetic display of musical insanity, is the highlight of the masque. As in "I burn, I burn, my brain consumes to ashes" (*Don Quixote*, UC, 1694), Eccles writes a brief declamatory opening followed by some simple scalar passagework, here on the word "rave."

> Must a Faithful Lover go
> Scorn'd, and Banish'd like a Foe!
> Oh let me Rave, Dispair, Dispair,
> Curse, curse my Fate, yet bless the Fair:
> For, oh! in spight of her Disdain
>   I still must love and hug my Chain.
> Yet why shou'd Love my Heart molest
>   When Hate her Soul possess?
> Revenge or Scorn shou'd rule my Brest,
>   When such a Swain she blesses.
> Then I'll no more to Coyness sue,

---

[60] Two different printed versions of the continuo part exist. The version in Eccles's *Collection* alters the simple notes of the first (accompanied by strings in the stage production) to something more suitable for keyboard. Several songs in Eccles's *Collection* have additional bass figures and other details not found in other printed sources, presumably supplied by Eccles himself.

[61] No music for Polyphemus (Bowman) was published, and many of his lines are marked as cut in performance. Surviving songs for Bowman after c.1700 are predominantly comic, although Eccles still writes a high g♭ for him in the dialogue with Dogget.

> Faith, and constant Love, Adieu!
> Farewell, Dotage, fond Disease!
> Welcome Freedom, welcome Ease!
>> I'll Rove, and I'll Range,
>> I'll Love, and I'll Change,
>> Ev'ry Hour, ev'ry Place,
>> Ev'ry Fair, ev'ry Face.
> I'll vow, and protest, I'll swear and Deceive
> All, all who like me are so mad to believe.

Throughout the first half of the piece, fluid shifts of meter keeps the listener's sense of pulse constantly off balance. The song is constructed as a grand crescendo and accelerando as the conflicting ideas of love and hate (and Eccles's warring duple and triple meter) are welded into Acis's mad dance of unending infidelity (Figure 5.1). Eccles effectively uses the simplest materials, as in the surprisingly satisfying stepwise descent down the octave for "All, all who like me are so mad to believe," emphasizing the inevitability of disillusionment. Like Hamlet, Acis is only mad "north-north-west".

The forthrightly comic portions of the musical entertainments seem to have been the most popular, though Acis's mad song would prove a favorite source for song quotation. In July 1701 a revival of Charles Davenant's *Circe* was advertised with music from *The Mad Lover*, "particularly *The Wedding* and the dialogue between Dogget and Boman," and from 1703 to 1705 *Acis and Galatea* was performed at least seven times together with new and stock comedies. The duet between Bowman and Dogget also appears separately, described as "That celebrated Dialogue ... *A Drunken Officer and a Town Miss*."[62]

The Patent Company's response to *The Mad Lover* was a musical version of *The Rival Queens*. Another stock play revised into a dramatick opera, *Alexander the Great*, premiered near the end of February. The lead characters, Alexander and his rival royal wives, Roxana and Statira, were utterly familiar to London audiences. As discussed in Chapter Two, *The Rival Queens* was often revived, alluded to and quoted (reverentially or mockingly) in prologues and other plays (for example, Farquhar's *The Constant Couple*).

For this new opera the compositional responsibilities were again shared between composers. The manuscript score indicates the music for Acts II and IV was Gottfried Finger's, and that for Acts III and V was Daniel Purcell's, although Finger also contributed a "Symphony for Four Flutes" (including bass) to the final act.[63] Finger's suite of act music was published in *Harmonia Anglicana* and Purcell's setting of the solo and instrumental sections of the opening scene in

---

[62] M&H *London Stage*, pp. 175 and 206.

[63] "The Musick in the Opera of the Rivall Queens" is included together with music for *Circe*, Leveridge's music for *Macbeth*, Finger's music for *The Virgin Prophetess*, and Purcell's setting of the *Judgment of Paris* in GB-Cfm MU MS 87.

Figure 5.1 J. Eccles, "Must then a faithful lover go" from *Acis and Galatea*. From Eccles, *A Collection of Songs*, pp. 86–7.

Figure 5.1   Concluded

Act V (sung in the original play) also appeared in print. While the text includes lines for the ghosts of both Statira's parents, the printed title line suggests that everything was sung by Pate ("in the OPERA").[64] In the music manuscript, pencilled annotations indicate that Darius and Statira were sung by Mr Teno[65] and Margaret Mills.[66]

The blocks of music in manuscript can be inserted into Lee's play relatively easily and, as a practical matter, would not appear to require any complex coordination between musical performers and the speaking cast. Finger's preludium for three trumpets, kettledrum, and strings presumably belongs to the opening of Act II, "Noise of Trumpets sounding far off," anticipating a properly martial welcome for the returning Alexander. Daniel Purcell's Act III music calls for only a single trumpet and strings, and the text "Welcome, welcome Glorious Day" suggests that this music, the most extended and elaborate series of solos,[67] follows Alexander's parting command "All Revel out the day" at the end of the act. It is also directly copied from Purcell's 1698 birthday ode for Princess (later Queen) Anne, which explains some of the textual insistence on "this blest day" and an occasional slip where the copyist forgot to change a feminine pronoun.[68] Daniel Purcell had already composed some music for a 'straight' version of the play: a "Symphony for Alexander the Great" appears in a collection of theater music from c.1695–7.[69] He may have written very little that was new in 1701, reinforcing the idea that the operatic *Alexander* was a hastily assembled competitive response to *The Mad Lover*.

Finger's short series of symphonies (with oboes), solos, and chorus for Act IV would also fit at the end of the act, as the text is all about Alexander's ultimately

---

[64] The settings of "Is innocence so void of cares" and "She walks as she dreams" were part of Daniel Purcell's 1701 *Collection* (D&M 1836) and later part of Walsh's *Collection of Choicest Songs & Dialogues*. See Hunter 5 (106, 267), where the two pages are numbered separately.

[65] A minor singer. See Baldwin and Wilson's "Notes on the Songs" in Richard Leveridge, *Complete Songs*, no. 168, where he is tentatively identified as 'Stephen Tenoe.'

[66] In Cfm MU MS 87, ff. 69v–73 (viewed in 1998). Pate, who had apparently been abroad in 1700, may have taken over from Teno when he returned, or alternatively, the singers' names in pencil may represent a later cast. All of those named (see below) were active for several years after 1701. Pate died early in 1704.

[67] Pencilled notes suggest Mary Lindsey ['Lind'] sang the first solo, Francis Hughes ['Hews'] the next three (in alto and tenor clefs) beginning with "An Universal Smile," Marcellus Laroon the bass solo, "Charming Majestick but not proud," and ending with a final solo "See see the Virtues" for Hughes.

[68] See Cfm MU MS 87, ff. 53v–65v for the section of *Alexander the Great* and Lcm 989 for the birthday ode. The *Alexander* copy omits the reprise of the first chorus "Welcome, welcome happy day" at the end, and scores the ground "now sooth our Joy" for two violins, countertenor, and continuo instead of the two flutes indicated in the GB-Lcm manuscript.

[69] See Lbl Add. MS 35043, f. 36v.

unsuccessful rush to save Statira from Roxana's vengeance. The fifth act music begins remarkably true to Lee's text, while the flute music and invocation of Morpheus were probably heard at the end of the act, when the poisoned and dying Alexander ends one of his speeches with "O let me sleep." Although it does not seem to have become a regular production, as an 'instant dramatick opera' *Alexander the Great* holds together quite well. However, its popularity may have been affected by the lack of the comic element so prevalent in *The Mad Lover* and in Drury Lane's last great dramatick opera success, *The Island Princess*.[70]

The Lincoln's Inn Fields company probably premiered William Burnaby's *The Ladies Visiting Day*, a bustling comedy with a large cast, in January. The central character as far as music is concerned is Lady Lovetoy (Barry), in whose honor all of the musical numbers are performed. A fickle and fashion mad character, her exotic whims make her lover Courtine seek her favor in a variety of foreign costumes and present her with outlandish gifts.[71]

Surviving music for *The Ladies Visiting Day* includes all three songs in the text but none of the instrumental pieces. The songs were set not by Eccles, but by Mr Curco[72] and Mr Gillier, whose collection of songs was printed in London in 1698.[73] They provide a clear demonstration of the varying levels of compositional talent available.

The first musical event is a song in the middle of Act II, performed by a "Turkish Boy" sent by Courtine to entertain Lady Lovetoy. The boy has been coached to sing a song, "Your Eyes, *Belinda*, you disarm," composed by Courtine (actually by Curco). Lady Lovetoy, like Vanbrugh's Lady Fancyfull (*The Provok'd Wife*), does not object, certain "I am the Subject." However she does not acknowledge the implied criticism of her in the lyric ("Giddy! Vain! … Fickle Fair") any more than Lady Fancyfull did under similar circumstances.

---

[70] The song "Phillis talk not more of Passion," attributed to Daniel Purcell and said to have been sung "in Alexander the Great," uses the same text as a song written 15 years earlier by Henry (D&M 2689), but is quite different.

[71] Courtine complains, "Her Rooms are Japan, and her Dress Indian; Her Equipage are all Monsters; The Coachman and his Horses are of a Country, both *Turks* (*Flanders* are too common), the rest of her Train are a motly Crowd of Blacks, Tawny, Olives, Philamots and pale Blews! In short, she's for any thing that come from beyond Sea" (p. 10). In short, Lady Lovetoy has become the embodiment of the British mercantile empire. She early declares her fondness for a "Tawny Face," and after tricking her into marriage Courtine swears to "lie in the Sun a whole Summer for an Olive Complexion" (p. 51). [Burnaby], *The Ladies Visiting-Day. A Comedy* (London, 1701).

[72] A bass singer who had been part of James II's Catholic Chapel in the 1680s and apparently sang at LIF, perhaps as one of their chorus basses. The only printed songs associated with him, "Let us revel and roar" and "Wine does wonders," are for two and three voices, not solos. As a singer-composer, he was no Richard Leveridge.

[73] Baldwin and Wilson note that this was probably *not* the better-known French composer Jean-Claude Gillier. See their *Monthly Mask*, note to no. 22.

Figure 5.2　Mr Gillier, "For mighty Love's unerring Dart" in *The Ladies Visiting Day*

The next song, "For mighty Love's unerring Dart," was originally performed at the end of Act IV, following another exotic musical entertainment. Lady Lovetoy, languishing on a couch, orders her maid "bid the Moors come and Dance to me, and the Bantam Woman Sing, for Musick is the food to Love, and while it sooths the pain indulges the Disease—" (15):

> For mighty Love's unerring Dart
>   No remedy is found,
> The Balm to cure a Lovers Smart,
>   Is to inlarge the Wound.
> We all the soft Destroyer prove
>   And Triumph in his Chains,
> But Oh! when Kind how wou'd he move,
>   Who Pleases when he Pains.

Gillier's setting of "For mighty Loves unerring dart," sung by Mary Hodgson, presumably in exotic costume, is a small triumph. One of its most striking touches is the use of the ascending chromatic fourth in the melody. It appears twice at the end of the song, "*who pleases* when he pains" (Figure 5.2). Another passage of chromatic motion in the melody occurs at the earlier phrase, "the balm to cure a lover's smart" (measures 10–14). In the earlier passage, the relationship between voice and continuo is a pungent series of dissonances (tritones), which become consonant ("pleasing") thirds in the final phrase.

Gillier's second song, "Chloe [Cloe] is divinely fair," sung by Mrs Haynes, closes the final act of the comedy, where it is introduced as music by "some Fidlers [who] have follow'd my Lady *Lovetoy*, and are going to Play" (51). While Gillier's musical setting is as conventional as his song's position in the play, unlike Vanbrugh's final song in *The Provok'd Wife*, it is an unconditional celebration. Burnaby is far more tolerant of Lady Lovetoy's affectations, musical and otherwise, than Vanbrugh of Lady Fancyfull's.

Drury Lane's next new play, Trotter's *The Unhappy Penitent*, is consistent with her earlier tragedies, and with tragedies performed at both theaters this season, in including relatively little music. In Act III King Charles VIII of France calls for a concert to entertain both the princess he's engaged to (who loves someone else) and the noblewoman he's interested in. All we learn of the music comes from the king's speech: "Musick can all the Passions calm, or raise, / And whilst it melts, and kindles you to love,/ I'll watch your Eyes ..." (19). Daniel Purcell's instrumental music for the tragedy includes a lengthy chaconne, an air and a hornpipe in A minor as well as the usual overture and act tunes in C minor. It is likely the pieces in A were heard as the first and second music, rather than during the concert, although the chaconne would be highly suitable for conveying a French king's love.

The spring productions at Lincoln's Inn Fields are of limited interest: virtually no music from them survives, and very little is called for in the play texts. At Drury Lane, in contrast, spring productions made the most of the company's musical assets, including music-laden comedies and a second, original (or more original) dramatick opera, *The Virgin Prophetess*.

The afterpiece *The Stage Coach*, a farce that included a new song delivered by the ever-popular Dogget, "Let's sing of Stage-Coaches," probably premiered during this time.[74] Dogget's ditty follows the model of "A Soldier and a Sailor" (in *Love for Love*) and was also set by Eccles, including plenty of opportunities for gesture and vocal imitation of the coachman calling to his team.

In March the Lincoln's Inn Fields company mounted two new serious plays by the prolific Pix, *The Double Distress* and *The Czar of Muscovy*, in suitably exotic settings. The prologue to *The Double Distress* includes yet another lament about the inability of plays to please without music. While Pix calls for "solemn Musick" in the second act, and places a temple scene with a "Hymn to Apollo" and "Antick Dances" in Act III, only the first violin parts for the act tunes, probably by Eccles, survive.[75] *The Czar of Muscovy* featured a single musical event, a temple scene in the grand style with processions, candles, flowers, and a musical invocation by the chief priest, following the marriage of the imposter Demetrius. The only other music occurs at the end of this first scene: as Demetrius, his bride, and their escort leave the stage "plaid out by Wind Musick."[76] Although Londoners had been wildly curious to see Peter the Great during his 1698 visit, they were less enthusiastic about Pix's Russians.

In April the company premiered Gildon's new tragedy *Love's Victim; or, The Queen of Wales*. Gildon's prologue objects to tragedies with exotic settings ("*Greece, France, Italy*, and *Spain;/* Nay distant *China*, and remote *Japan./* In sooty *Afric* too ...") and promises "To show *Domestic* Virtue."[77] Despite this promise, his heroine spends the entire play shipwrecked in Bayonne, where she and her children are abused by the local monarchs. John Bowman played the chief Druid, who attempts to restrain his royal masters, but there is no indication that he sang in any of the numerous temple scenes.

Where Lincoln's Inn Fields offered a series of tragedies, the Patent Company presented a string of new comedies, including Thomas Baker's *The Humour of the Age*, Farquhar's *Sir Harry Wildair*, and Durfey's *The Bath; or The Western Lass*, which was an enormous hit for Susanna Verbruggen as the country miss of the title. Typical of Durfey's comedies, *The Bath* was also filled to the brim with musical numbers.

Baker's *The Humour of the Age* is a tangle of intrigues set in a boarding house. As in Cibber's earlier comedy *Loves Makes a Man*, the three published songs by

---

[74] It has been attributed to Farquhar, possibly assisted by Motteux. See *The Works of George Farquhar*, ed. Shirley Strum Kenny (Oxford, 1988), vol. 2, p. 318.

[75] For more on the surviving music, see *Music Productions LIF*, pp. 481–2.

[76] Mary Pix, *The Czar of Muscovy* (London, 1701), p. 6.

[77] Charles Gildon, *Love's Victim; or, The Queen of Wales* (London 1701), prologue lines 16–18, 26.

Figure 5.3   Purcell, "Tis done, tis done the pointed arrow's in my heart" in *The Humour of the Age*.

Figure 5.3   Concluded

Daniel Purcell attributed to the play do not appear in the printed text.[78] A generic "Song" is called for by the "Airy Lady" Lucia in the middle of Act III, and Act V concludes with "An Entertainment," presumably the "Song and a Dance" mentioned and postponed two pages earlier. The instrumental music by Finger includes seven pieces in G minor, with a jig in D minor, perhaps the final dance, but it is harder to assign a song to the finale.

Purcell's "Tis done, tis done the pointed arrow's in my heart," sung by Mrs Shaw, would make dramatic sense in the scene with Lucia and her maid, when she contemplates the "confusion" caused by love. The bright B-flat major song opens with a typical series of declamatory statements (Figure 5.3), adds some modest passages of figuration and finishes with a simpler second section, "Hence dull content," based on a triadic motive, very appropriate to Lucia's character and situation.

The other two songs pose greater problems. In 1700–1701 a great deal of music was being written and published for the Patent Company, but the coordination between originators, copyists, and printers was not entirely smooth. Recent Patent Company productions reveal a cluster of plays with unspecified songs in the printed text. A similar cluster can be seen in the first full season, and in later seasons it is most often Drury Lane that fails to specify vocal pieces.[79]

"Fixt on ye fair Miranda's Eies," sung by James Bowen, could be a reference to the character Miranda in the comedy, a discarded mistress being wooed by a fatuous Middlesex judge, Judge Goose—doubtless a dig at those participating in the legal harassment of the players—and could conceivably have been inserted into one of their scenes together, or the final entertainment. The third song, "Beneath a gloomy Shade, for unhappy Lovers made," is hard to place. In length, structure, and style it resembles Purcell's songs for Pate from *Alexander the Great*—even referring to the "mournfull Flutes"—but this pastoral lament would be an incongruous lead-in for an apparently happy ending.

Although no musical events except a final dance are called for in the text, Farquhar's comedy *Sir Harry Wildair*, sequel to the wildly popular *The Constant Couple*, is not without music. Sir Harry (Wilks again) is still singing fragments of his mocking minuet, "tall al de rall," and the play is full of contemporary musical references, particularly to dancing.

In the passage below, Sir Harry attempts to reconcile with his not-so-dead bride Angelica (Jane Rogers), ending her double masquerade as both his younger brother and her own ghost:

> Don't be angry, my Dear; ... Had you but sent me Word of your coming, I had got three or four Speeches out of *Oroonoko* and the *Mourning Bride* upon this

---

[78] Like other songs from this season, these appeared in Purcell's 1701 *Collection* and were used in Walsh's *Choicest Songs & Dialogues*.

[79] These observations are based on my database of musical events in printed play and dramatick opera texts.

occasion, that wou'd have charm'd your very Heart. But we'll do as well as we can; I'll have the Musick from both Houses; *Pawlet* and *Locket* shall contrive for our Taste; we'll charm our Ears with *Abell*'s Voice; feast our Eyes with one another; and thus, with all our Senses tun'd to Love, we'll hurl off our Cloaths, leap into Bed, and there—[80]

Note Sir Harry's height of extravagance includes hiring the musicians from both theaters (plus catering) and paying singer John Abell's astronomical fees for a private concert.

With the summer season approaching, concert venues were opening along the river and at the spas and pleasure gardens. The best musicians, like the senior actors, presumably followed 'the quality' out of town to their summer retreats. Spring comedies often anticipated this move by shifting scenes to the country.

Durfey's *The Bath; or, The Western Lass* follows his usual formula, with a large cast of widely different social standing and dialects and an assortment of jingling songs. The most common sound-motif in the play, the hunting horn, and the emphasis on hunting songs and rustic musical dialogues, reflect the country setting.[81] A madman, Hairbrain, contributes the opening song and sings snatches of other pieces throughout the play—Durfey also gave the Restoration stage its most famous musical madman, Lyonel, in *A Fool's Preferment* in 1688.[82] In the end, Gillian (Susanna Verbruggen), the western lass and an heiress, winds up with Crab (Cibber). Crab turns out not to be a country fellow after all, but insists he still loves all country things. Their musical dialogue, "Where oxen do low," set to a simple tune by Daniel Purcell, confirms their compatibility.[83]

The musical dialogue at the beginning of the fifth act is the typical titillating type, staging a series of exchanges from flirtatious to physical between a "Countrey Girl of Thirteen Years Old" (Jane Lucas) and "a Town-Beau" (Mr Bourdon). Structurally it resembles the dialogue written by Motteux for Pix's *The Deceiver Deceiv'd* (LIF, November 1697), to which Durfey also contributed a dialogue, opening with a two-verse song for the young woman, printed separately, and then continuing in the usual short sections alternating between singers, ending with the girl's challenge to "catch me if you can." Unusually, the music appears to have

---

[80] Farquhar, *Sir Harry Wildair: Being the Sequel of the Trip to the Jubilee* (London, 1701), p. 46.

[81] The hunting song in Act III and act music do not appear to have survived. The lack of a suite in *Harmonia Anglicana* is curious, as is the cursory reference in Act V "Enter Crab with a Musician who Sings, and Exit" (43), as Durfey is usually quite informative about musical events.

[82] See Amanda Eubanks Winkler, *O Let Us Howle Some Heavy Note*, pp. 151–8 and Curtis Price, *Henry Purcell and the London Stage*, pp. 155–60.

[83] The singers' attribution in D&M 3846 (Mrs. Harris & Mr. Pierson) is based on the 1706 edition of *Wit & Mirth*. As dialogues were popular pieces for entr'acte and other performances, this does not mean they were the original performers.

been written by two different composers, Jeremiah Clarke and Samuel Akeroyde. As the songsheet for the dialogue portion states "the Tune by Mr. Akeroyde," rather than "set by" him, one suspects that Durfey was creating another contrafactum.[84]

The Virgin Prophetess; or, The Fate of Troy, in development for at least a year, was doubtless meant to end the season in a spectacular fashion.[85] Unfortunately, it proved a spectacular failure. The libretto contains predictably elaborate scenic descriptions, sounding much like author Elkanah Settle's designs for the Lord Mayor's Day processions, with ranks of interlocking scenes and arches, pyramids and statues.[86] Settle's heroine Cassandra is an uncomfortable and inconsistent melding of the classical prophetess-princess with the Christian mage and sorceress, busily harassing the guilty lovers Paris and Helen in besieged Troy. As in other, more popular dramatick operas, the musical numbers in *The Virgin Prophetess* cover all possible bases, from ritual choruses, pastoral ensembles, and a grand chaconne to low comedy and bawdy musical dialogues.

The fifth act Bacchanalian dialogue printed in *The Musical Entertainments in the Virgin Prophetess* (1701), "Dull Fool I defie thee,/ The Bottle's my Joy," was not included in the libretto or either of the manuscript scores,[87] and seems like a last-minute addition. The other comic dialogues, "A Dialogue between a Child and her Mother, sung between the Acts [I and II]" and "A Dialogue between a Mother and a Daughter" in Act III, are also missing from the score and may have been set by another composer. Further discussion of this dramatick opera can be found in Chapter Two.

Audiences largely unfriendly to *The Virgin Prophetess* were more receptive to the results of the competition between composers to set Congreve's masque *The Judgment of Paris*. Staged at the Dorset Garden theater, the musical settings by Eccles, Finger, Daniel Purcell, and Weldon, were heard successively from March through May, and then all together in June. There were also regularly scheduled concerts at York Buildings and additional concerts at Dorset Garden, such as John Abell's "Performance of Musick in English, Italian and French" on 21 May. Finger's opera was competing against a strong array of musically sophisticated alternatives. As for *The Judgment*, the junior competitor, Weldon, was acclaimed the victor by the aristocratic judges, with Eccles second, Purcell third, and Finger a disappointing fourth.[88] Writing of the event years later, Roger North observes "I will not suppose, as some did, that making interest as for favour, and partiallity influenced those determinations; but it is certein, that the community of the masters were not of the same opinion with them [the judges]. And so instead of

---

[84] Hunter 5 (208) in Lbl G.151a.

[85] A contract for painting the scenery was signed by Robert Robinson and several PC actors in March 1700. See *Theatrical Documents*, no. 1627.

[86] For discussion of the scenery and scene painter, see Sybil Rosenfeld, *A Short History of Scene Design in Great Britain* (Oxford, 1973), pp. 57–8.

[87] See GB-Cfm Mu MS 87, GB-Lcm MS 862.

[88] See note 32.

incouraging the endeavours of all, the happy victor onely was pleased and all the rest were discontented."[89] This disappointment seems to have pushed Finger back to the Continent.

The summer months, as usual, were largely given over to revivals, with casts drawn from the junior members of each company. In August the last new play of the season, Charles Johnson's comedy *The Gentleman Cully* was given short shrift by the actors at Lincoln's Inn Fields and an even shorter run by audiences. There is no music of any kind indicated in the printed play; unusual for a comedy, and not even act tunes survive—assuming any were written.

Revivals, 1700–1701

As previously mentioned, the increasing use of newspaper advertisements by the Patent Company during this season provides much more information about revived productions. Revivals give insight into the musical performances heard as part of an evening's entertainment, as well as some of the clearest instances of competitive practices using music and music-related performances like dancing.

In September the Lincoln's Inn Fields company staged Thomas Shadwell's *The Virtuoso*, with an entertainment of music "by the famous Monsieur le Rich, lately arrived from the Court of Poland" for the benefit of two actors.[90] The musical entertainment may have preceded or followed the play, or have been inserted in it, probably during the final act. The 1704 edition of Shadwell's comedy contains two musical interludes. The first is the fourth act song, "How wretched is the Slave to Love," (first set by Francis Forcer for the 1676 premiere), which offers the witty young characters a chance to practice their repartee, and the second a fifth act masquerade, in which the men and women onstage dance a bourée and a courante, followed by an "Entry of *Scaramouchi* and Clowns."[91]

Drury Lane anticipated the February premiere of its new dramatick opera *Alexander the Great* and counteracted Lincoln's Inn Fields' *The Mad Lover* with an assortment of earlier operas: *Dioclesian* (November and December), *The Island Princess* (December and January), *The Indian Queen* (January), *The Tempest* (January and February), and *King Arthur* (likewise). The three apparently most popular were each revived again in the spring months prior to the next new opera, *The Virgin Prophetess*. Having these major works in the repertoire kept a wide range of Henry Purcell's songs and ensembles current. This accounts, at least in part, for their presence in new anthologies like *Wit and Mirth*. It also demonstrates that the Patent Company maintained control of its Purcellian musical property.

Throughout the new year, the companies continued to produce plays by Shakespeare, including *Henry VIII* and *King Lear* at Lincoln's Inn Fields and *Timon of Athens* at Drury Lane. History plays, tragedies, and romances were popular, and

---

[89] *Roger North's* The Musical Grammarian *1728*, ed. Chan and Kassler, p. 267.
[90] M&H *London Stage*, p. 8.
[91] Thomas Shadwell, *The Virtuoso* (London, 1704), p. 65.

Betterton's Othello and Falstaff were particularly admired. The Patent Company also returned to its stock of comedies by Ben Jonson.

There is scant evidence of the works performed at Lincoln's Inn Fields during the summer season. In June the company revived Charles Davenant's *Circe* "with music from *The Mad Lover*," a dialogue, and dancing featuring Anthony L'Abbé. The "Martial Welcome" of Mars and Bellona and the "Masque of Wine and Love" may have been substituted for two of the masques in the original text of *Circe*, or presented as an afterpiece.[92] In August, the Patent Company offered Elkanah Settle's *The Empress of Morocco* (1675), advertised "with the original Mask set to new Music."[93] There is no record of who may have rewritten the music, originally by Matthew Locke. While Daniel Purcell would seem the obvious candidate, he would certainly have advertised himself and used the music again—anonymity suggests a young or amateur composer.

Comedy vs. Tragedy: The 1701–1702 Season

As in the 1699–1700 and 1700–1701 seasons, there are many known revivals, heavily outweighing the number of new productions, which slowed to a trickle compared with the flood during the first full seasons of competition (1695–97). While Betterton had been given managerial power within the Lincoln's Inn Fields company, both companies found managing their performers and their audiences challenging—all difficulties were exacerbated by the mandatory closing of the theaters after the death of William III.

New Productions

William III's death closed the theaters during the months when the Patent Company typically mounted a series of musical shows, building to a final flourish in June. Even in this truncated season, serious plays predominate at Lincoln's Inn Fields and comic ones at Drury Lane (Table 5.2).

---

[92] Price gives a sympathetic reading of Davenant's text and its many musical interludes (only one of which seems to have been set by Henry Purcell) in *Henry Purcell and the London Stage*, pp. 97–105. It is possible that the LIF company had access to Purcell's music for *Circe*, although when performing Purcell's music, they usually advertised the fact.

[93] M&H *London Stage*, p. 33.

Table 5.2 New productions during the 1701–1702 season

	New works for the Patent Company		**New works at Lincoln's Inn Fields**	
AUTUMN			*Antiochus the Great*	Tragedy
			Altemira	Tragedy
WINTER	*The Funeral*	Comedy	*Tamerlane*	Tragedy
	The Comical Gallant [*Falstaff*]	Comedy		
	The Generous Conqueror	Tragedy		
	The Modish Husband	Comedy		
	The False Friend	Comedy		
	The Inconstant	Comedy		
SPRING	[King William dies 8 March, theaters closed until April 24]			
SUMMER	*The Faithful Bride of Granada*	Tragedy	*The Beau's Duel*	Comedy

In November 1701 Lincoln's Inn Fields premiered *Antiochus the Great* by Jane Wiseman. Having previously encouraged "Ariadne," the anonymous author of *The Unnatural Mother*, and Mary Pix, Elizabeth Barry once again supported a woman playwright. Wiseman's play is another exotic erotic thriller with similarities to Manley's *The Royal Mischief*. The conventional Act III entertainment, a musical dialogue and dance, occurs during a banquet in masquerade being held by Babylonian royalty. The pastoral dialogue, between a young girl and a shepherd, is very like Motteux's, though the lyrics, "I vow I think I'm grown a Woman/ Have charms enough, to please a Man," are credited to Gildon. Like many similar interludes, it is unmistakably cued to a London audience's tastes, not ancient

Babylon's.⁹⁴ The other musical event falls in the middle of Act IV, when the Egyptian prince Ormades, unhappy in love and soon to be a casualty, is discovered "Lying on a Couch; ... soft Musick Playing" (23).

December began with the premiere of Nicholas Rowe's new tragedy *Tamerlane*, the second of three tragedies by Rowe performed in successive seasons. A transparent political allegory of William III and Louis XIV, in later years *Tamerlane* was performed annually on the anniversary of William's landing in England in 1688.⁹⁵ In Rowe's version of history, the noble Tamerlane (Betterton) captures the Grecian prince Moneses; Selima, daughter of Turkish emperor Bajazet (Bracegirdle); and finally Bajazet himself. Tamerlane is forgiving, modest, and staunchly military, while Bajazet is a seething mass of lusts, given to vain shows and gratuitous cruelty. Among other crimes, Bajazet has raped and married Arpasia (Barry), the princess betrothed to Moneses. Most of the play involves Bajazet's cruel schemes—he eventually succeeds in having Moneses murdered—with the women characters torn in the usual way between love and duty.

Fitting the martial backdrop of the play, the conquest of Asia, there are numerous flourishes of trumpets, and a "symphony of warlike music" opens the second scene of Act II, as Tamerlane processes into his tent with his officers, soldiers, and attendants. Lenton's suite of instrumental music appeared in *Harmonia Anglicana*, and has some unusual features: an interestingly varied symphony in place of the usual French overture and a closer-than-usual connection between the types of tunes (trumpet "round o", slow air, march) and the action of the scenes which precede and follow them.⁹⁶

The only vocal music called for is of a familiar type. Shortly after the beginning of Act IV the scene draws, "discovers Arpasia lying on a Couch," and the song "To Thee, oh! gentle Sleep, alone," a tribute to sleep's restorative powers, however grim one's waking circumstances, is sung (see Chapter Two). The songsheet reveals that Mary Hodgson was the featured singer, and singer-composer Richard Elford wrote the music.

The new plays at Drury Lane premiered during the winter months, during which Lincoln's Inn Fields apparently mounted no new productions, although the 'lost' play *The Royal Captive*, known only from another suite of music by Lenton published in *Harmonia Anglicana*, would help to fill the gap.⁹⁷ The Patent Company had the good fortune to end the calendar year with Richard Steele's *The Funeral*, which became immensely popular, despite criticism of its moral

---

⁹⁴ No music for the play is known to survive.

⁹⁵ In Act III, Tamerlane discovers and personally prevents an assassination attempt against himself. Rowe's play clearly references the 1696 plots, using anti-Catholic rhetoric.

⁹⁶ For more on this including excerpts, see *Music Productions LIF*, pp. 554–7.

⁹⁷ See Price, "Eight 'Lost' Restoration Plays," p. 302. In their revised *London Stage*, Milhous and Hume follow Price in assigning this play to DL, but there is no evidence Lenton ever composed for the PC.

tone and improbable action.[98] Thus in December and January 1701–1702, London audiences in search of new shows had a choice between the heroic (*Tamerlane*) and the comic (*Funeral*) at the usual theaters. Neither production was lavish in its use of music, but what there was, was good.

Although Sullen in *A Comparison Between the Two Stages* hopes the performance of *The Funeral* will not be too long, "I don't remember much Singing and Dancing in it" (140), he is being sarcastic. The printed text includes a number of musical events, with pairs of songs in Acts II and IV, and a multi-sectional entertainment at the end of Act V.[99] Once again Daniel Purcell supplied all the songs, generally simple and tuneful, while fellow organist William Croft provided the act music, which includes a pair of very violin-tutorial airs and a grand chaconne, to be followed by the overture and briefer act tunes ("Scotch" and slow airs, a jig), all in bright F major.

Pleasantly irreverent, Steele's comedy deserves its popularity. In it, Lord Brumpton pretends to be dead and then witnesses the reactions of his young widow, disinherited son, and two young wards. Existing conventions ensured the presence of songs in the printed text of virtually all comedies, but the number of songs and specificity of their description in Steele's suggests that Steele placed importance on them. *The Funeral* features several amusing twists on conventional musical insertions, and his songs are always in pairs, where the witty romance of one song (or one character's performance of it) is undercut by a parodic or contrasting one.

Mr Campley is a typical Wilks hero, witty and worldly wise, with a pronounced tendency to sing and dance, often quoting his own or Congreve's songs.[100] The first song in *The Funeral* is supposed to be a poem written by him and given to his elderly cousin Mrs Fardingale (played in drag). Although the set-up ("a gallant writing verses for his lady') was old hat, this scene was particularly objected to in *A Comparison Between the Two Stages*, due to the circumstances:

> First *Sharlot* and *Harriot*, under the same Roof, and at the Moment of his [Lord Brumpton's] death, are openly drolling and raillying [sic] each other about their Sweethearts; bnt [sic] that is not enough, presently *Fardingale*, a Servant in the House, comes in with a Song, and squeals it to the Lute, while *Campley's* Hat serves for a Desk to lay it on: Is not this an odd Prologue to a Funeral? … the old woman not singing it to their Minds, *Campley,* who is a Gentleman of Sense and Manners, is desired to sing it; he presently does it without any excuse or regard

---

[98] See *Comparison Between the Two Stages*, pp. 146–71.

[99] The author of the *Comparison* also draws attention to a scene in Steele's play very similar to one in Burnaby's *The Ladies Visiting-Day* (LIF, 1701). See Strum Kenny, ed., *The Plays of Richard Steele*, pp. 3–4 and also M&H *London Stage*, pp. 46–7.

[100] In Act II, sc. iii he quotes "Cynthia frowns whene'er I woo her," a song set by Henry Purcell from Congreve's *The Double Dealer*, which was revived at LIF in 1698–99 and possibly more recently. It had also been reprinted in *Orpheus Britannicus* (1698), making it familiar to amateur music lovers.

Figure 5.4   D. Purcell, "Let not Love on me bestow" in *The Funeral*

to the sad occasion ... and no sooner is that over, but he Gallants her with his Love in an Air of the greatest levity, and she hears him with all the Pleasure he cou'd desire![101]

While Fardingale's performance of it is ridiculous, "Let not Love on me bestow" is Campley's creation, and when Lady Sharlot recites it or Campley himself sings it,[102] we are meant to take it more seriously.

> Let not Love on me bestow
> Soft Distress, and tender Woe;
> I know none but substantial Blisses,
> Eager Glances, solid Kisses;
> I know not what the Lovers feign,
> Of finer Pleasure mix'd with Pain,
> Then prethee give me Gentle Boy,
> None of thy Grief but all thy Joy.

Daniel Purcell's simple setting is charming and memorable (Figure 5.4); aided no doubt by frequent repetition due to the popularity of Steele's comedy, it became part of the select repertoire of theater songs which show up in later plays as quotations.

While the first song is closely tied into the action of the play, the later songs are more detached. The impromptu mini-concert in Act IV marks the usual musical pause for breath amid the action of the plot, and a chance to show off popular young singer-actress Mary Anne Campion (perhaps dressed as a boy, per the play text). "Ye Minutes bring the happy Hour," is a courtly love song supposedly written by the other young male lead, Lord Hardy. However, this is immediately undercut by the servant Trim's (Penkethman's) parodic song of love for a cookmaid, beginning "Cynderaxa Kind and Good,/ Has all my Heart and Stomach too" and sung to the accompaniment of the percussive tongs in place of the lute.[103]

Up-to-date cultural references in the spoken dialogue include mockery of the Prize Musick competition of the previous season and of Italian music, a frequent feature of prologues and epilogues spoken by Penkethman. Here he is in character as Trim:

---

[101] *A Comparison Between the Two Stages*, pp. 151–2.

[102] Price includes a brief section on "Reading of Songs" but consigns the use of this device in Steele and Burnaby's plays to an endnote (*Music in the Restoration Theatre*, pp. 27 and 255–6, note 54). Although this practice is found in earlier seventeenth-century plays, Burnaby and Steele's use of it during these seasons is pronounced, compared with their contemporaries.

[103] The similarity between the name of Trim's lady love and the passionate Lyndaraxa in Dryden's *The Conquest of Granada* is probably not mere coincidence.

Pulling off his Hat and Bowing.] Your very Humble Servant Good Mr. *Campley,* Ay, this is Poetry, this is a Song indeed? Faith I'll Set it, and Sing it my self—Pray Pay to Mr. *William Trim*—so far in recitatiro[104]—Three Hundred, [*singing ridiculously*—] Hun—dred—Hundred—Hundred thrice repeated, because 'tis Three Hundred Pounds, I Love repetitions in Musick, where there's a good reason for it, Po—unds after the *Italian* Manner—If they'd bring me such Sensible words as these, I'd Out-strip all your Composers, for the Musick Prize—.[105]

Music as cultural capital, indeed.

There is also an excellent part for Jane Lucas as Mademoiselle d'Epingle, the 'French' seamstress. During the following seasons, Lucas's name appears frequently in the advertised dancing at Drury Lane, and her character is featured, with an unnamed French dancer, in the dance at the beginning of the Act V entertainment.

The texts of the two songs in the final entertainment, seen side by side on the page, might seem designed to promote emotional whiplash in the audience, but Purcell's settings of Steele's poems actually complement each other. Both songs open with a held note (pedal) D in the bass, but where the first, "On Yonder Bed supinely laid/ Behold thy Lov'd Expecting Maid," features a descending line in D minor imitating the reclining beloved, the second, with its triadic ascending line in D major, "Arise, great Dead, for Arms renown'd," reflects the image of the text. However delightful the joys of romance, Steele's message is clear. The relative age of the singers may have also been intentionally suggestive: young Bowen sings of love, while the mature Pate sings of arms. The seemingly incongruous combination of songs thus sets up Lord Brumpton's final speech, in which he advises men to "have always inclinations proper for the Stage of Life you're in."[106]

The song for Pate, with its fulsome praise of William III, is reminiscent of the odes inserted in 1696 productions. This patriotic paean to the king's military prowess probably served multiple functions, both as a compliment to William III, from whom Steele sought preferment, and, if assumptions that Steele seeded the opening night audience with fellow soldiers are correct,[107] as a means of ensuring a rousing endorsement from the military. The combination of Pate's voice and trumpet obbligato in Purcell's vigorous composition would ensure that no one sat on their hands at the end of the show.

---

[104] Recte *recitativo*.

[105] Steele, *The Funeral* (London, 1701), p. 22. This bit of business was objected to by Critick: "But why payable to the Man? ... if honest *Trim* had kept the Money, no common Law in *England* cou'd ha' taken it out of his Hands." *A Comparison Between the Two Stages*, pp. 164–5.

[106] Steele, *The Funeral*, p. 79.

[107] Strum Kenny, *Plays of Richard Steele*, p. 383.

The only serious play staged at Drury Lane this season, Bevill Higgons's *The Generous Conqueror*, was not a success, partly on its merits (or lack of) and partly due to the Jacobite 'design' many audience members and critics detected in characters and plot. If this was the best of the tragedies offered the Patent Company this season, one shudders to think what they refused.

Like Alexander the Great, the passions of Higgons's King Almerick can be profoundly swayed by music, and a concert scene in Act III shows him listening to both "martial" and "soft" music alternately. In the concert scene, Higgons slavishly follows convention, as Critic observes: "the Dialogue between the *King* and *Mal*[espine] is very good; but even here he runs into the same error with his Brethren, he introduces Musick in the midst of the hurry and hottest part of the whole Play. The Author makes it as pertinent as he can, by pretending it is to compose the King's vexations; and so the Musick shall divert us tell [*sic*] the next Act begins" (108–9). *A Comparison Between the Stages* informs us that the martial music in Act III was "an Entertainment of Trumpet musick" (134) but does not specify the softer sounds. Instrumental selections from the previous season's dramatick opera *Alexander the Great* could easily have been used here, and at the opening of Act V for the "Consorts of Musick, Shouts and Acclamations at distance" (58).

The only vocal music in the play is a sexually suggestive musical dialogue between 'Damon' and 'Flavia' performed before the princess Cimene and her confidante in Act II. It too came in for its share of abuse by Critic: "Oh Mr. *Collyer*, Mr. *Collyer*! What a relapse is here since thy Reformation!" (93). Although less explicit than many bawdy dialogues in recent dramatick operas and tragedies, presumably this one (composer and music unknown) was intended to perform the same function, entertaining the more salaciously inclined members of the audience and providing some light relief to the heavy scenes surrounding it.

William Burnaby's next comedy, *The Modish Husband*, also premiered at Drury Lane, where it did not fare well despite a strong cast. Burnaby follows his usual formula, with two songs in the early acts and music at the end of Act V, although here the typical reconciling dance seems especially unconvincing. Music, particularly song, is once again a clear indicator of social class, common sense, and sexual interest

The awkward son, Harry (Bullock), doesn't have a suitable song to serenade a lady with—he knows only ballad tunes like "Chevy Chase". His attempt to acquire more suitable repertoire from Sir Lively (William Bowen, *not* a singer) aptly illustrates the marketplace for music,[108] as a commodity and as a tool for the advancement of one's own ends.

> Har. —but stay, I must reform my Voice a little, to Sing under her window like a Ballad-singer won't do—I must find out some body to teach me a Song—Egad!

---

[108] William Burnaby, *The Modish Husband* (London, 1702), pp. 28–9. In Durfey's *The Virtuous Wife* (1679), John Bowman played Crotchett, a singing master with a similarly untalented pupil.

here comes one that looks like the Head of a Base Viol [a figurehead, bearded?], he must certainly understand Musick, I'll try   (*Enter Sir* Lively)
Pray Sir are you a Singing Master?
S.L. (*aside*)   A Singing Master! this fellows a Fool, I'll humour him—ay! Sir, I am a Singing Master.
Har.   That's lucky faith! Well, Friend, can you teach me a pretty Love Song?
Sr L.   Ay, Sir, if you'll pay me for't.
Har.   The Devil's in this Court, there's nothing done without a Bribe—Come, Sir, here's your Money first, for you look indeed too much like a Courtier to Trust.
Sr L.   Very well, Sir, wou'd you have a merry Song or a melancholy one?
Har.   No! a pox o' your merry Songs, and your Melancholy one's—I must have a Soft, Tender, Melting, Sighing, Despairing, Dying, Confounding Song! to charm her as she lyes in Bed.
Sr L.   Well, Sir, I have one.
Har.   Come on then.
Sr L.   Ha! hum! ha!—
Har.   I hate that damn'd putting of one's mouth in tune—learn me to sing all at once.
S.L.   Very well, but now I think on't you must proceed methodically, and learn your Notes first.
Har.   My Notes!—(*aside.*) what a Devil are they! I have no Notes about me but Taylors Bills, and I'm sure there's no Musick in them—well, come begin, Sir.
Sr L.   Speak after me—la! la! la!
Har.   La! la! la!
Sr L.   Sol! la! me! fa! fa!
Har.   fa! fa! fa! what a pox is the meaning of all this, I shall sooner learn to fiddle than sing, by this fa! fa! I'll e'en stick to the old *English* way of singing—Over Hills and high Mountains—ay! there's some sence in this, and so good b'ye to ye, fa! fa! with a pox!   (*Exit* Har.)[109]

Solfege jokes (do-re-mi-fa-sol-la) never get old.

The superficially more elegant songs performed for Ladies Cringe and Promise while they wait for, or flirt with, the "not too sincere" Lionel (Wilks) are vaguely pastoral invitations to *carpe diem*. I have found no setting for "Irene, Fair and Young," but the second song, "See, see where she lyes, Love and Ruin in her Eyes" (35–6), was set by Daniel Purcell and performed by Mary Lindsey. It appeared in the final installment of the periodical *Mercurius Musicus* for 1701.[110] As Lionel, Wilks merely echoes the final line "Opportunity is Merit" and proceeds to make the most of his opportunity with Lady Cringe.

---

[109]   *Love's Labor's Lost*, V, ii, 99. See also Penkethman's prologue to Durfey's *Massaniello* (PC, 1699) in Chapter Four.

[110]   D&M 2888.

Although Vanbrugh's *The False Friend* was named a comedy on the title page, the onstage death of the 'false friend,' Don John (Cibber, whose illness cut short the initial run), made at least one contemporary critic object to the designation.[111] The printed text is particularly uninformative, and it includes no musical events. The suite of instrumental music "by a Person of Quality" (thought to be William, Lord Byron) consists of the usual dances in B-flat major. However, the overture ends with a slow coda in minor, marked with the sign for *tremolo*, a special effect—the musical suggestion of uneasiness may be deliberate.[112]

In the Patent Company's next offering, *The Inconstant*, like Farquhar's other comedies, the precise connection between the printed songs and the play text is sometimes unclear. Unlike Sir Harry Wildair, this rakish young gentleman played by Wilks (Mirabel) is not given to singing himself. Instead, he calls for others to perform, as in Act V when invited to sing by the scheming Lamorce, who is about to have her bullies strongarm him. Here, music is an ill-timed distraction. The "new song" Mirabel requests, possibly one just heard at the playhouse where he and Lamorce picked each other up, is indicated only by the first two words: "Prethee Phillis."[113]

The other extended musical scene is also one in which a woman uses music to manipulate a man, though in a far more comic fashion. At the end of Act II, the "whimsical Lady" Bisarre (Susanna Verbruggen) calls for a fiddler and physically forces her would-be lover, the somewhat awkward Captain Duratete (Bullock) to dance a minuet, drink, and sing, until he's forced to feign a sprain to avoid performing a jig. Even the heroine, Orinda, has trouble keeping up with her friend Bisarre, and in this scene she's unstoppable.[114]

Daniel Purcell composed all the music conclusively connected to Farquhar's play, including the suite in *Harmonia Anglicana*, with its two minuets. Both text and composer for the song "Since Celia 'tis not in our Power" appear at the end of the play, and the song was probably performed at its conclusion.[115] There is no indication of a final dance, and while suggestive, the song does celebrate the union of a couple. The final song and lack of indication for a dance are increasingly common in 1702–1703 productions, perhaps a sign that the professional dancers'

---

[111] *A Comparison between the Two Stages*, p. 180.

[112] For the attribution, see Price, *Music in the Restoration Theatre*, p. 167. Repeated eighth-notes in the first violin part of the overture's coda are marked with a wavy line above them. This indication is also seen in Eccles's music for *Rinaldo and Armida* and Henry Purcell's music for the 'Frost Scene' in *King Arthur*. See Chapter Two, note 117.

[113] I have found no exact match, but it is possible to find appropriate contemporary songs such as "Prithee Celia" (John Weldon) or "Prithee Silvia" (William Richardson). Name shifts between play text and song text are not unusual (for example, "Fair Belinda" vs. "Fair Celinda" in *She Ventures and He Wins*).

[114] Farquhar, *The Inconstant; or, The Way to Win Him* (London, 1702), pp. 24–6.

[115] The songsheet is reproduced in Shirley Strum Kenny's edition of Farquhar's plays.

performances between and within the earlier acts had overtaken the practice of having the cast dance together.

James Paisible's "Ayre's in the Comedy call'd the Humors of Sr Iohn Falstaf" are most likely the incidental music for John Dennis's *The Comical Gallant; or, The Amours of Sir John Falstaffe*, a new version of Shakespeare's *The Merry Wives of Windsor*.[116] Paisible's suite includes an impressive passacaglia, which probably served as the first music. Within the printed play, there is no music called for until Act V, with its masque of fairies tormenting the jealous husband Ford in disguise—an ensemble which one imagines sounded very similar to the scene in which the fairies torment the drunken poet in *The Fairy Queen*. Individual musical numbers from the Henry Purcell dramatick opera were often added musical attractions, and in the following season, an act from the opera was advertised as part of a gala evening at Drury Lane.[117]

Lincoln's Inn Fields seems not to have mounted any new productions in 1702 prior to the king's death and the closing of the theaters in March. The companies were permitted to resume acting following Queen Anne's coronation on 23 April, but the Lincoln's Inn Fields company played only revivals until June, when it premiered Susanna Centlivre's comedy *The Beau's Duel; or, A Soldier for the Ladies*. Unlike her first tragedy for Drury Lane, Centlivre's second play was sufficiently well received to be revived the following October with a new prologue and epilogue, and a "Whimsical Song" by Pack, who played the fortune hunter Ogle. The most musical character is the pretentious Sir William Mode, written for John Bowman.

In courting the heroine Clarinda, Sir William arranges for a morning serenade in Act I. His 'French' valet announces the instruments "here be de Fidle, de Hautbois, de Courtel [bassoon], and Base Vial" (5) and Sir William congratulates himself on his strategy "[to] wake her in the Morning with harmonious Music" (6). Once he finishes congratulating himself and orders the musicians to play, the effect is not what he intended: "Ah! merciful Apollo, what a hideous Noise you make; there's a Sound fitter to storm a Breach with, than approach a Lady's Slumbers. Play some soft Air, a Concert of Flutes ..." When the musicians presumably oblige (the oboe players perhaps switching instruments), the stage directions indicate that "While the Music plays he uses a great many odd Postures" (6). Sir William's

---

[116] In my dissertation I followed Price's assumption that Paisible's tunes were written for a revival of Shakespeare's *King Henry IV* in January 1700 (Price, *Music in the Restoration Theatre*, pp. 186–7), but I now agree with William J. Burling. All other sets of act music in the third collection of Walsh's *Harmonia Anglicana* were from new productions mounted during 1701–1702, and there is no record of Paisible providing act music for or even performing at LIF, whereas he consistently composed and performed for the PC. Use of the play's secondary title and the substitution of "Humors" for "Amours" are similar to other sets. For a transcription of the passacaglia, see *Music Productions LIF*, appendix B, pp. 788–97.

[117] M&H *London Stage*, pp. 87–8.

second attempt, a morning concert for his friends in Act II, is quite ruined when the "incomparable" Mr Quaver burns his mouth with chocolate and can't sing as scheduled (14). The only other musical events are a snatch of drunken, misogynistic song from Toper, and the last scene, where Sir William, rejected, resolves to stick to music and forget about women, eschewing the final dance.

Unlike Centlivre's comedy, William Taverner's tragedy *The Faithful Bride of Granada* was not published until 1704, and its performance date is open to question. The publication of act tunes by Daniel Purcell from the play in August 1702 suggests a premiere earlier in the spring or summer,[118] and the epilogue supports this hypothesis, with its emphasis on stage reform, hoping "A vertuous Queen with her bright glorious Court,/ Shall give the Muse her Theme, and shall the Muse support" (lines 16–7). Musically and dramatically speaking the play has little to recommend it, being an exotic gumbo of the usual ingredients: racial and ethnic conflict, a secret marriage, a manipulative villain, and vengeful widow. Act III includes the requisite musical event, in this case a temple (mosque) scene with "Solemn Musick, Drums, Trumpets" (23).

Revivals, 1701–1702

Despite the short and difficult season, newspaper advertisements provide some significant data about revivals and the musical additions to each evening's main production. Milhous has argued that at this time "distinctions between theatres and fairs vanish," particularly at Drury Lane, but even at Betterton's house.[119] It is worth noting that this theatrical crossover goes both ways: performers like Dogget, Penkethman, and Elizabeth Willis were offering many of the same comic and musical attractions at the fairs as they did at the theaters. In late summer, the Patent Company emphasized the performance of stock comedies appropriate to the season (Ben Jonson's *Bartholomew Fair*, Shadwell's *Bury Fair*). Benefits for specific performers were held in July; plays with specially advertised dance additions were prevalent in August.

During this season we also have increasing evidence of crossover between concert and theater venues. John Abell and dancing-master Mr Isaac's scholars performed in a concert at Drury Lane on 2 May.[120] On 22 June Lincoln's Inn Fields performed *Oedipus* for soprano Mary Hodgson's benefit. Over the summer, she appeared in London concerts, and Eccles's music for the Queen's Coronation was

---

[118] M&H *London Stage*, pp. 119–20.

[119] Judith Milhous writes: "Both managements had to resort to extra features, first to entice non-theatregoers, then in the hopes of retaining the interest of unsophisticated patrons ... Lincoln's Inn Fields has to meet the competition, and so we find 'Vaulting on the Manag'd Horse' in the intervals of *The Country-Wife*." *Thomas Betterton*, pp. 77–8.

[120] For more on Isaac and his aristocratic pupils, see Jennifer Thorp, "'So Great a Master as Mr Isaac': an exemplary dancing-master of late Stuart London," *Early Music* 35 (2007): 435–46.

performed together with songs by John Weldon and a violin "entertainment" by Thomas Deane at Hampstead Wells.[121] Drury Lane also took advantage of the concert scene, combining a stock tragedy with sophisticated music on July 7, when they performed Southerne's *Oroonoko* (PC, 1695) together with "some of Mr. Weldon's new Songs, perform'd in his last Consort," dances, and "new Musick set to Flutes" by the Banisters. However, the bill also appealed to broader tastes by adding vaulting and a new comic epilogue by Penkethman.[122]

Significant evidence of revivals comes from lawsuits. At Drury Lane, actors were prosecuted for performances of Baker's *The Humour of the Age*, the previous season's success, and John Crowne's *Sir Courtly Nice*. Lincoln's Inn Fields presumably revived the popular comedies *Love for Love*, *The Anatomist*, and *The Provok'd Wife*, all premiered during the first two seasons of competition, as they are mentioned in a February 1702 indictment. Robert Hume has also made a convincing case for a revival of *The Way of the World* at the very end of 1701 or the beginning of 1702, with the additional attraction of French dancer Madame Subligny, visiting from the Paris Opéra.[123]

Published music provides evidence of another revival, of the history play *Edward III*. First performed in 1690, its dedication signed by actor-playwright William Mountfort, its revival is known only from printed music by Paisible, a new set of act tunes printed in *Harmonia Anglicana*, circa 1702. The play could have been revived this season or early during the following one, probably at Drury Lane, because of Paisible's connection with the company there.[124]

The Balance Shifts: The 1702–1703 Season

The 1702–1703 season shows some recovery from the previous season, with a substantial increase in the number of new productions at each house, although neither company attempted a new dramatick opera production this year. Prologues and epilogues consistently comment deprecatingly about audiences showing favoritism for music, dance, and foreign performers over British actors, as in this excerpt from Granville's epilogue to *As You Find It*, a spring comedy:

---

[121] M&H *London Stage*, p. 64.

[122] M&H *London Stage*, p. 63.

[123] See Hume's "A Revival of *The Way of the World* in December 1701 or January 1702," *Theatre Notebook* 26 (1971): 30–35.

[124] The order of productions in *Harmonia Anglicana* is not conclusive, but suggests the spring of 1702. Milhous and Hume conclude "probably an adaptation ... possibly by [John] Bancroft; staged by Mountfort." See "Attribution Problems" no. 16, pp. 13–14.

> ... in vain we write,
> Unless the Musick and the Dance invite.
> Sure in Expence, uncertain of Success,
> But drest and but adorn'd for Sacrifice.
> Well had it been if as we fetch from *France*
> And *Italy* their Mode of Song and Dance,
> Our sturdy *Britains* wou'd have borrow'd Sense.[125]

In new plays, and especially in revivals, the Patent Company made use of every possible combination of audience favorites, usually noted with some specificity in its newspaper advertisements. Milhous and Hume estimate that it advertised "something like 40 percent" of its performances in the *Daily Courant*.[126] Records for Lincoln's Inn Fields are less comprehensive.

New Productions

After another slow start, Lincoln's Inn Fields made a strong showing musically, utilizing extensive amounts of song and dance in its productions, much of which survive.[127] The Patent Company, too, mounted several comedies with significant amounts of music, both new and in quotation.

The Patent Company began the season (Table 5.3) with a variety show similar to Motteux's *The Novelty* (LIF, 1697), featuring acts from some of Colley Cibber's old work (*Richard III*, *Woman's Wit*) plus scenes from Vanbrugh's *Aesop*. Unlike Motteux's *The Novelty* (LIF, 1697) no published version is known.

Table 5.3 New productions during the 1702–1703 season

	New works for the Patent Company		New works at Lincoln's Inn Fields
AUTUMN	*The Medley*	One-Acts	
	All for the Better	Comedy	

---

[125] Charles Boyle, *As You Find It* (London, 1703), [69], lines 7–13, italics reversed.

[126] The *Courant*, London's first daily newspaper, began its run in March 1702. See M&H *London Stage*, pp. 3, 38, 68.

[127] Milhous and Hume note a published revision of *The Tragedy of King Saul*, which promises "Poetical Interludes of Ghosts, furies &c. which the Publisher has taken care should be set to Musick by the best Hands." (*London Stage*, 73). One wonders if publisher Henry Playford was recycling Henry Purcell's trio "In guilty night" (a musical scene between Saul and the Witch of Endor) which he had published in *Harmonia Sacra*.

	New works for the Patent Company		New works at Lincoln's Inn Fields	
WINTER	*She Wou'd and She Wou'd Not*	Comedy		
	The Patriot	Tragedy		
	The Twin Rivals	Comedy	*The Stolen Heiress*	Comedy
	Tunbridge-Walks	Comedy	*The Governour of Cyprus*	Tragedy
			Love Betray'd	Comedy
SPRING	*The Old Mode and the New*	Comedy	*The Fair Penitent*	Tragedy
	The Fair Example	Comedy	*As You Find It*	Comedy
			The Fickle Shepherdess	Pastoral
SUMMER	*Love's Contrivance*	Comedy		
	Vice Reclaim'd	Comedy		

Its next new work, Francis Manning's *All for the Better*, made the onstage connection between music and masculine power inescapable. All the musical events in Manning's Spanish comedy are instigated by the male lead, Don Alphonso, whether roistering through the streets with his companions, playing soothing music and a seductive song to the woman he's kidnapped, and plans to ravish, or in later acts calling for a song to soothe his own melancholy and entertaining his guests with a musical dialogue. Don Alphonso was played not by Wilks, who would seem the obvious choice, but by Benjamin Husbands.

Although Manning's text indicates that the first two songs were set by Daniel Purcell and the final dialogue, between a cupid and a girl, composed by John Barrett, I have found none extant. Jeremiah Clarke's act music, all in the uncommon key of F minor, was printed in *Harmonia Anglicana*. Keyboard versions of several of the tunes also appeared in the third book of Walsh's pedagogical series *The Harpsichord Master*.[128]

---

[128] See Price, *Music in the Restoration Theatre*, pp. 146–7 for concordances.

During November all of London, the queen, and the court were celebrating the naval victory at Vigo, although I have not uncovered any record of specific celebratory productions at the playhouses, nor any surviving texts or music beyond the occasional song. At the end of November Drury Lane mounted Cibber's latest comic effort, *She Wou'd and She Wou'd Not*, featuring Susanna Verbruggen in masculine drag. From a musical point of view, there is little to recommend it, although it hints at Cibber's habit of improvising comic song wherever he felt appropriate. Playing a heavy father, he hums as he locks his daughter up.

There is also one particularly apt bit of scripted quotation. The cross-dressing heroine Hypatia, impersonating her lover, goes to meet her lover's fiancée Rosaura. Rosaura is determined to ensure that 'he' not want her as a bride (enabling her to elope with the man she loves). Planning to be "impossible," Rosara sings "I'll Rove, and I'll Range, &c." and Hypatia joins in "I'll Love, and I'll Change—" (34), easily recognized lines from Acis's mad song "Must then a faithful Lover go" (*Acis and Galatea*, LIF, 1701). The musical quotation confirms the female bond between the characters, and it is especially appropriate since Hypatia is, like Bracegirdle as Acis, a woman playing a man's role.

Cibber baldly inserts the Act V music, "Sir, the Play-house Musick are come" (73), and the cast enjoy an unspecified entertainment. This is the most likely place for John Weldon's popular song "Celia my heart has often Rang'd," performed by Mary Anne Campion.[129] Paisible's last set of act tunes for a Drury Lane production, nearly all dances, was written for *She Wou'd and She Wou'd Not*. Unlike *Love's Last Shift*, for which Paisible also composed music, it was not a great success.

The Patent Company's sole serious play this season, Gildon's *The Patriot; or, The Italian Conspiracy*, was dedicated to Queen Anne, and the author promised "nothing unfit for the greatest, and the Chastest Ear."[130] In place of the conventional Act III concert scene found in any number of tragedies, Gildon simply has a character remark of the hero (Wilks), lying prostrate in a grove, "Time was, when the loud Trumpet, and the Drum,/ The Groans of dying Foes, the Victors Shouts,/ Were his Delight; now Melancholly Airs,/ And lonely Grotto's are his only Pleasure" (22). Neither type of music occurs within the action of the play, though Daniel Purcell's act tunes in C minor lean toward the latter.

The Patent Company's next new production, Farquhar's comedy *The Twin Rivals*, is remarkable for its lack of music in any form: musical numbers within the play text, printed songs attributed to it, even musical quotations or references. In her edition of Farquhar's works, Shirley Strum Kenny notes that this was unusual, but she does not connect Farquhar's professed desire to present a "moral and sharply original piece"[131] with the absence of songs. As in tragedy, eliminating music from the dramatic action was one way for a playwright to indicate high seriousness and

---

[129] Printed in the December 1702 *Monthly Mask*. See Baldwin and Wilson's notes to no. 4, where they list additional sources.

[130] Gildon, *The Patriot; or, The Italian Conspiracy* (London, 1702), unpaginated.

[131] Strum Kenny, *Works of George Farquhar*, vol. 1, p. 484.

moral intent to audiences and critics. By eliminating characters like beaux, cullies, and coquets, he has also eliminated many of the characters who would sing or demand to be sung to. Farquhar's purely unmusical comedy did have the usual complement of act tunes, composed by Croft, which were published in the usual outlet, *Harmonia Anglicana*. Presumably Farquhar's play was not accompanied by dancing between every act, with added comic and mad songs, like a recent revival of Durfey's *The Bath*.

Towards the end of December, Susanna Centlivre's new comedy, *The Stolen Heiress; or, The Salamanca Doctor Outplotted*, made its first appearance at Lincoln's Inn Fields. No music or dancing is indicated in the play text until the final page, "Enter Larich [a Sicilian Lord] Singing," but a song "designed to be Sung by Mr. *Dogget*" was printed following the dedication. Dogget portrayed Sancho, "A Pedant bred at Salamanca, designed by Larich a Husband for Lavinia [his daughter]." The song may have been sung in Act II when Sancho, eager to display his knowledge of the world, demonstrates how men of different natures (gamesters, beaux, country squires, etc.) wear their hats.[132]

Another song, "Celia's bright Beauties all others transcend," with words and music by Edward Keen,[133] was published as "Sung by Mrs. Willis in the Play call'd The Heires or the Sallamanca Docter." Since Willis was an active musical member of the company in 1702, but is not listed among the cast, it seems likely that this generic homage to Celia was sung between the acts, as Willis did on 29 December for a revival of *The Country Wife*.

The first new production of 1703 at Lincoln's Inn Fields was John Oldmixon's tragedy *The Governour of Cyprus*.[134] Oldmixon's tragedy opens with a pair of musical scenes, but—like Pix's *The Czar of Muscovy*—after this initial musical outburst introducing heroine and villain, no further interludes follow. Oldmixon juxtaposes the familiar trope of the female character listening to a song performed by her trusted servant in a private, retired location with a male-ordered serenade, complete with a company of onstage musicians.[135] In Oldmixon's tragedy, as in Manning's *All for the Better*, the serenade is clearly a form of masculine persecution.

---

[132] Susanna Centlivre, *The Stolen Heiress; or, The Salamance Doctor Outplotted* (London, 1703), p. 22.

[133] Another entrepreneurial composer, Keen was known as "the first Promoter of the Musical Entertainments in Sommerset House Garden." *The London Stage* vol. 1, p. 511.

[134] This premiere date, like many others, is based on publication. The premiere may have taken place in mid-December (one month prior to its publication), when no productions at LIF are known.

[135] In his discussion of "Grove Scenes," Price notes that they are quite common in early Restoration plays, and contrasts their atmosphere of "fantasy" with the comedy serenade, the "most common 'realistic' vehicle for music." *Music in the Restoration Theatre*, pp. 44–5. Here we have both in quick succession—and the text of the musical dialogue is certainly a fantasy of the Governor's.

In Act I the scene opens to reveal Lucinda (Elizabeth Bowman) "lying on a Bank of Flowers, a Grove near it," listening to a song apparently performed by her servant Zarma. The song "When *Sylvia* runs to Woods and Groves" presumably represents Zarma's opinions (or her limited repertoire) more than those of her mistress, warning "While Young, 'tis Foolish to be Coy." Dialogue reveals that Lucinda fears she has become an object of adulterous interest to the wicked Governor, who killed his first wife in order to marry the villainous Issamenea. She, in turn, was previously married to Jopano, Lucinda's brother, captured by the Turks and presumed dead. As in stock tragedies, the absent spouse still lives, and his return sets the plot in motion.

Once the audience has been enlightened by the women's dialogue, the Governor enters with his "Musick," and physically prevents Lucinda from leaving, saying:

> Why Fly'st while I pursue thee with a Song?
> Begin, you Men of Art, your Tuneful Strains;
> Let the soft Zephirs from the Citron Groves
> Disperse their evening Sweets,[136]

The musical dialogue, "Since tis to Sin, so very sweet," begins with the male singer and asserts that Nature trumps honor and duty. Lucinda does not find the argument convincing, but that does not prevent the Governor from pursuing her further. His power over the island, though not over Lucinda (yet) is shown in miniature with his serenade. As his attentions continue, Issamenea becomes furiously jealous; murder and madness ensue after Jopano's return.

While the songs do not seem to have been printed, Thomas Cross engraved the act music, composed by Thomas Deane—possibly the violin virtuoso who regularly performed at Lincoln's Inn Fields. This seems to be an attempt by Cross to compete with Walsh's *Harmonia Anglicana*, and the Royal College of Music copy is interleaved with closely contemporary act music from Walsh's successful series. Deane's tunes include a set of divisions over a ground, of the sort common in collections of violin "lessons" like those of Nicola Matteis.[137] Like earlier chaconnes and passacaglias, this is a lengthy concert-type piece, presumably played during the first and second music.[138] The tunes (all in the pastoral key of F major) are labeled by type (minuet, scotch air, sarabande, hornpipe) and include

---

[136] Some instructions (and possibly attributions) were accidentally cut from the 1703 edition of the text as the prompt at the bottom of page 3 does not match the text at the top of page 4, where the dialogue begins.

[137] See, for example, the fourth part of Nicola Matteis's *Ayrs for the Violin*, fascimile edition (Ridgewood, N.J., 1966).

[138] "A New Set of Tunes in four Parts, In the Governour of Cyprus Acted at the New Theater, and Composed by Thomas Deane of Worcester." For a transcription of the ground, see *Music Productions LIF*, appendix B, pp. 798–801.

some scattered tempo indications and dynamic contrasts (a series of echo effects, *forte/piano*).

William Burnaby's comedy *Love Betray'd; or, The Agreeable Disappointment*, a barely recognizable revision of Shakespeare's *Twelfth Night*,[139] premiered in January. The tone of Burnaby's preface is particularly defensive; he blames the production's ill success on the absence of the masque in the final act, which was never set to music. Eccles's songs for the actress-singers performing in character and the act music written for it survive.

Bracegirdle's character (Viola/Caesario) sings Eccles's first song in order to entertain her duke at the beginning of Act II.

> SCENE opens, and discovers *Moreno* on a Couch, *Caesario* kneeling by—
> Caesario sings.
> I.
> If I hear *Orinda* Swear,
>   She cures my jealous Smart;
> The Treachery becomes the Fair,
>   And doubly fires my Heart.
> II.
> Beauty's Strength and Treasure,
>   In Falsehood still remain;
> She gives the greatest Pleasure,
>   That gives the greatest Pain.

The song is followed by "Soft Musick, after which, *Moreno* rises" and speaks the famous first lines of Shakespeare's *Twelfth Night*.

For Mrs Prince, Eccles provided "Chloe found Love," a charming but relentlessly regular triple-time air, suitable for the merry Emilia as she twits proud Villaretta on having fallen in love with Caesario/Viola in the middle of Act III. What is most noteworthy is not the use of Bracegirdle and Prince singing in character but the lack of songs we might expect for other performers. Although Dogget was back at Lincoln's Inn Fields, playing the clownish Taquilet, he does not sing.[140]

This production also presents a minor musical puzzle, as two contemporary settings survive of the song "Love in her Bosom end my Care." The piece is titled "The Marriage Song" on one songsheet and attributed to Burnaby's *Love Betray'd* by both. One was composed by William Corbett (who wrote the act music), engraved by Thomas Cross, and sung by tenor John Davis. The other was composed by John Weldon, printed by John Walsh in the *Monthly Mask*, and sung

---

[139] Burnaby indicates in the 1703 edition which lines are his and which Shakespeare's (the difference is readily audible).

[140] Shakespeare's clown, Feste, sings some of his best-known songs in *Twelfth Night*: "O Mistress mine," "Come away Death," and "When that I was and a little tine boy."

by Mary Hodgson.¹⁴¹ The song is not given in the 1703 text, but it would make the most sense either in or in place of the masque meant to follow the marriage of Villaretta and Sebastian.¹⁴² Of the two settings, Corbett's is the more interesting, though Weldon is far better known as a song composer.¹⁴³

Despite the relative wealth of musical sources for *Love Betray'd*, questions remain. Why didn't Eccles set the Act V masque? As the company had several more musical works in development, it may well have decided that Burnaby's masque was not worth the time and money needed to compose and rehearse it. Since Burnaby did not publish the text, one cannot judge its merits.

Drury Lane responded to Lincoln's Inn Fields' new productions with a musical comedy of its own, Thomas Baker's *Tunbridge Walks; or, The Yeoman of Kent*, another spa comedy like Durfey's *The Bath* (PC, spring 1701). A solid success, it was revived throughout the summer and during the following seasons. Baker's play differs from his earlier comedy, taking the fondness for song quotation to new heights, as three different characters sing recognizable phrases from earlier Patent Company productions: *The Richmond Heiress*, *The Secular Masque*, and *The Funeral*.¹⁴⁴

In Baker's comedy, Robert Wilks and Susanna Verbruggen play a brother–sister pair, Reynard and Hillaria, who live by their wits. Woodcock, the yeoman of the title, is the solid British sort we expect. The cast also includes Mr Maiden (Bullock) who has a formidable assortment of feminine accomplishments to his credit including playing the guitar, wax-work, filigree, painting on glass, and millinery. Their musical interactions are naturally indicative of their characters.

Woodcock speaks slightingly of town amusements, though he seems very well versed in them. He condemns going to hear "a parcel of *Italian* Eunuchs, like so many Cats, squawll out somewhat you don't understand" (Act I, 4–5) and the Subscription Musick concerts, featuring "*French* Buffoons skipping over to run away" with English money (Act III, 28). He has raised his daughter Belinda (Jane Rodgers) in the country, for "I'le be Sworn Dancing Masters, Singing Masters, and such followers o'the Women, make greater Havock among Maidenheads in *London*" and proposes having "Beaus, Fidlers, Dancing-Masters, Poets, and Players, knockt o'the Head as they do useless Puppies," (Act II, 24, 25).

---

¹⁴¹ See Baldwin and Wilson, *Monthly Mask*, no. 19. *Love Betray'd* was revived in March 1705 as a benefit night for actors George Pack and Lucretia Bradshaw, advertised with singing by Hodgson.

¹⁴² It's also possible Burnaby was engaged in some recycling. His earlier comedy *The Reform'd Wife* (PC, 1700) included a "Bridal Song" in the final entertainment, not printed in the text.

¹⁴³ For more on these two settings and the composers' compositional choices, see *Music Productions LIF*, pp. 585–7.

¹⁴⁴ For more on the use of quotation in this comedy, see my essay "'Quotation is the sincerest form of …?':Signature Songs as Intertheatrical References" in *Stages 'Adorn'd with ev'ry Grace'* (Ashgate, forthcoming).

Yet under his anti-theatrical, xenophobic, and patriarchal prejudices, the Kentish Yeoman must have a sneaking fondness for music, since it is he who arranges the Act V musical entertainment, and he is sufficiently versed in London's dissolute culture (or at least Drury Lane's most successful comedies) to chastise his daughter thus: "I know very well you are for a Beau; ... that wou'd make you believe your Eyes are a pair of Flamboys, and Cringe to you with Bits of Love-Songs, in a Damn'd Couuter-Tenor [sic] Voice—(*Singing*) *Then prithee, prithee give me gentle Boy*—" (Act III, 32). The quotation is particularly appropriate, since it is the song Wilks's character used to woo Rodgers's character in Steele's *The Funeral* (PC, 1701). Penkethman's Squib, a tailor pretending to be a military officer, is equally ridiculous: singing as if he's Venus in Dryden's *Secular Masque* (PC, 1700): "Take me, take me, while you may,/ *Venus* comes not ev'ry Day" (Act IV, 42).

The witty siblings Reynard and Hillaria are naturally well versed in music, and can trim their tunes to match or manipulate their audiences. Reynard can sing both a ballad-style song to ingratiate himself with Woodcock (Act IV, 47), and Purcell's intricate mad song "Behold the Man that with Gigantick Might" (from *The Richmond Heiress*) to convince Belinda's flirtatious maid Lucy (Jane Lucas) that he is quite "confounded in all his senses2 (Act III, 33). The serious Loveworth, in turn, demonstrates that he can handle the lively Hillaria, 'curing' her melancholy by singing and dancing a minuet, which she imitates. After further verbal sparring, "Both sing and go out in the Minuet Step" (Act IV, 44). This provides another chance for Susanna Verbruggen to dance in character (as in Farquhar's *The Inconstant*), while the reconciliation between the lovers is physically and musically demonstrated.

The last musical character, Mr Maiden, is a special case, quite beyond anything seen at either theater thus far.

> *Enter* Mr. Maiden *with Musick.*
> *Maid.* Ladies, I have brought a fine Singer, that came down last night to Entertain you with a new Composure; one that's mightily admir'd at the *Small-Coal Musick Meeting.*[145]
> SONG.
> *[While the Song's Performing,* Maiden *uses a Fan, a Pocket Lookinglass, &c.]*
> If moving softness can subdue,
> See, Nymphs, a Swain more soft than you:
>   We Patch, and we Paint,
>   We're Sick, and we Faint,
> To the Vapours, and Spleen we pretend;
>   We play with a Fan,

---

[145] Referring to the private concerts held by coal dealer Thomas Britton above his warehouse in Clerkenwell. See Curtis Price, "The Small-Coal Cult," *Musical Times* 119 (1978): 1032–4.

> We Squeak, and we Skream,
> We're Women, meer Women i'th'end.
>   Your Airs we defie,
>   Your Beauty deny,
> Be as Gay, and as Fine as you can;
>   Ye Nymphs, have a care,
>   Be more Nice, and more Fair,
> Or your Lovers in time we may gain.
>
> *Goodf. [Mrs. Goodfellow]*   Mr. Maiden is the most useful Person in such a publick Place, and distinguishes himself so obligingly by promoting ev'ry Diversion.
> *Maid.*   Oh, Madam, I am Master of the Ceremonies here: appoint all the Dancing, Summon the Ladies, and Manage the Musick; tho' really, these Fidlers are such a parcel of idle, scoundrel Fellows, one has more trouble in keeping 'em together, than Mr. Rich has in governing the *Drury-lane Players*.
>
> ...
>
> ... I love mightily to go abroad in Women's Clothes: I was dress'd up last Winter in my Lady *Fussock's* Cherry-colour Damask, sat a whole Play in the Front-Seat of the Box.[146]

More so than any other character in Baker's plays, many of whom are performing roles as well as being performed by Drury Lane's actors, Mr Maiden is emblematic of the degree to which gender and gentility are performative.[147]

Rather than Durfey or Steele, Colley Cibber's *Love Makes a Man* seems to have been Baker's model for the fifth act, with its silly musical procession of Captain (tailor) Squib and his blushing bride (former barmaid). Like Cibber's *She Wou'd and She Wou'd Not*, there is an unspecified "Entertainment suitable to a Rural Marriage" in Act V, which sounds like a counter-attraction to the wedding scene in Lincoln's Inn Fields' *Acis and Galatea*. The finale of Baker's comedy may well have included some of the special attractions advertised with it after its premiere: singing, dancing, and instrumental novelties.

The new productions for March were a classic face-off between a Drury Lane comedy, *The Old Mode and the New; or, Country Miss with her Furbeloe,* and a Lincoln's Inn Fields tragedy, *The Fair Penitent*, though the 'old' playwright Durfey was writing for the young company at Drury Lane and the 'new' success,

---

[146] Thomas Baker, *Tunbridge Walks; or, The Yeoman of Kent* (London, 1703), pp. 20–21.

[147] Historian Mark. S. Dawson, in his reading of the plays of this period including Baker's, concludes that the figure of the fop reflects more concern over acquired gentility, "effeminacy" of manner and taste rather than fear of homosexual activities. Dawson, *Gentility and the Comic Theatre of Late Stuart London* (Cambridge, 2005), particularly chapter 8, "Suspect Sexuality and the Fop." Mr Maiden's earlier comment that "a Gentleman took a fancy to me, and left me an Estate" (Act I, 7) seems deliberately ambiguous, and is, as we discover, a falsehood.

Rowe, for the older actors at Lincoln's Inn Fields. The prologue to Baker's *Tunbridge Walks*, spoken by Penkethman, alludes cheekily to the usual division of genres: "Let others be with Tragick Lawrel's Crown'd,/ Where undisturb'd the Heroe struts around,/ And Empty Boxes Eccho to the Sound./ Plays are design'd for Mirth ..." (lines 13–16).

Although other comedies, combined with plenty of entr'acte entertainments, worked well for Drury Lane this season, Durfey's play was not a success. He claims in his dedication that it was "receiv'd with general Liking by both Houses," but he blames some faulty performances and audience members who were "expecting other sort of flashy Entertainment, would not let 'em mind the opening." Durfey employs many of his usual tricks, including patriotic speeches referring to recent military and naval victories (Act II, 23) and self-referential dialogue, when honest Queenlove promises not to court Lucia either "in *Tom Sternbold*'s grave Sonnets, nor in *Tom Durfey*'s airy ones, being equally unskill'd in both" (Act I, 2).

The plot centers around the elderly Sir Fumbler Oldmode, who loves the customs of Queen Elizabeth I's reign; his young second wife who humors him but likes his adult son; two French and Hispanophile intriguers; and the country miss of the title, Oldmode's niece. There are two musical scenes called for in the printed text. The first is a concert scene in Act II which opens with an instrumental sonata and continues with a formal, patriotic song in two movements ("The Infant Blooming Spring appears") in praise of Britain and Queen Anne.[148]

The "Musical Diversions" with "comical singing and dancing" which conclude Act V (64) feature a song performed by Leveridge, "Celladon when Spring came on," a racy pastoral ditty in which Silvia is convinced to avoid becoming an old maid. Like many Durfey songs, the melody is borrowed, this time from one of Henry Purcell's airs in *Bonduca* (revived in 1699 and possibly more recently). It survives in numerous printed versions. The other existing song attributed to *The Old Mode and the New* is "A new Health to Prince Eugene, a Triumphant Ode upon his returne to Vienna,"[149] commenting on military affairs on the Continent. Despite this high-sounding title, like "Celladon," it is a very simple, strophic piece. Whether Leveridge sang Durfey's ode between the acts or back in Act II with the patriotic speeches is uncertain. In both cases, Durfey's music seems designed for a masculine audience, accompanied by plenty of alcohol.

It is hard to imagine a greater contrast (within 1703 parameters) than that between Durfey's comedy and the tragedy at Lincoln's Inn Fields. Nicholas Rowe's *The Fair Penitent* was an important production on several counts, though it was not immediately obvious it would become a staple of the later eighteenth-century repertoire. Another adaptation of an early seventeenth-century work, Rowe's tragedy included two significant musical sections: a festive entertainment for the wedding of the noble Altamont and guilty Calista (Barry), including a teasing song

---

[148] Although listed in Day and Murrie (D&M 1814), the copy referenced is from a late edition of Durfey's *Wit & Mirth*, without music.

[149] D&M 3541, copy viewed GB-Lbl G.151a (song 160).

"Ah stay! ah turn! ah whither would you fly" (poem by Congreve, sung by Mary Hodgson), and an eerie two-part song (sung by Davis and Cook) for the Gothic scene of horror which opens Act V as Calista mourns by the bier of her murdered lover, Lothario. Both scenes were set to music by John Eccles.[150]

The opening of Act V has attracted a great deal of critical attention; however, the music for this scene is often ignored or misrepresented. Rowe may have been inspired by Ravenscroft's musical tragedy *The Italian Husband* (LIF, 1697), which has a similar scene for the guilty wife. It probably also owes something to the opening of Act V in Motteux's *The Island Princess* (PC, 1698) where:

> The Curtain slowly rises to mournful Musick, and discovers a Prison, *Quisara* lying on the Floor, all in White, reading by the Light of a Lamp; her Women in Black, some, Standing, others Kneeling by her, and Weeping: The Bell Tolls sometime before she speaks. (V, 32)

Rowe's heroine is revealed in a similar fashion,

> SCENE is a Room hung with Black; on one side, *Lothario's* Body on a Bier; on the other, a Table with a Skull and other Bones, a Book, and a Lamp on it. *Calista* is discover'd on a Couch in Black, her hair hanging loose and disordered; After Musick and a Song, she rises and comes forward.
> SONG
> I.
> Hear, you Midnight Phantoms, hear,
> You who pale and wan appear,
> ....
> From the Charnel, and the Tomb,
> Hither haste ye, hither come.
> ....
> See the Sexton with his Spade,
> See the Grave already made;
> Listen, Fair one, to thy Knell,
> This Musick is thy passing Bell.[151]

Eccles's music for this scene was often titled "The Passing Bell" in music manuscripts and copied into later collections of music.[152] Most of the music for Rowe's play was published promptly: Congreve's song in the March 1703 *Monthly Mask* (available five days after the play opened), Lenton's act music in *Harmonia*

---

[150] This production and its use of music are discussed in further detail in *Music Productions LIF*, pp. 601–22.

[151] Rowe, *The Fair Penitent* (London, 1703), pp. 52–53.

[152] The most interesting of these is the mid-eighteenth-century volume of theater music, GB-Lcm Music MS 2232.

Anglicana at the end of the month, and the two-part song as a single. Both songs were later used in multiple Walsh collections.[153]

Where *The Fair Penitent* highlighted Barry as tragic heroine, the next premiere featured Bracegirdle as musical comedienne. In *As You Find It* the rakish Hartley, a philandering husband with designs on the beautiful Orinda (Bracegirdle), is finally tricked into seducing his own wife (disguised) and promises to mend his ways. In Act I Orinda and her friend Eugenia discuss the follies of society and particularly of men. Eugenia offers a song recently written by a gentleman of her acquaintance as evidence and asks Orinda to sing it. After demurring, she performs "*Sabina*'s Haughty as she's Fair,"—but cruelty will conquer where affection will not.[154]

This second song, "He that has whom he lov'd possest," was sung by Mary Hodgson as part of a musical entertainment hosted by the country squire Sir Abel Single (Dogget) at the end of Act II. As several musicians enter, and several things occur onstage while the music is playing, it seems likely that some instrumental pieces were performed in addition to Eccles's song, though none are mentioned. The song text is the piteous plaint of a lover scorned by the haughty Celia, who resolves to "cure" her by good nature and flattery until she "to be perverse grow[s] kind." Eccles's setting takes advantage of Hodgson's vocal dexterity and power in the middle register. Like many of Eccles's songs from this season it was promptly printed in Walsh's *Monthly Mask* and appeared in the composer's 1704 *Collection*.[155]

An overture and act tunes for *As You Find It*, composed by William Corbett, appeared in *Harmonia Anglicana*. As the overture and first four tunes are all in G minor, while the final three are in G major, it seems likely that, as elsewhere, the preliminary music actually appears at the end of the group. The order of tunes suits this placement, as the witty discussion at the end of Act I would then be followed by an elegant air, and the second act entertainment of the bluff Sir Abel by a robust hornpipe.

The Patent Company's latest comedy, *The Fair Example*, written by comedian Richard Estcourt, provides virtually no information about the music performed with it. Instead, Estcourt's mocking dedication to Christopher Rich comments on musical conventions, specifically, the chaconne as the second music before the curtain, and mocks those who support their criticism with classical tags: "Song, that's Mrs. *Tofts* ... Dance, that Mr. De *Ruel* and his Wife, which Aristotle says are absolutely necessary."[156] Estcourt's text simply indicates an "entertainment" before the final short speech by Springlove (Colley Cibber), who has failed to seduce

---

[153] See Hunter 5 (159, 74) *Choicest Songs & Dialogues*; 8–11 (5, 48) Eccles's *Collection*; and 33 (95), a collection of uncertain date, possibly issued in 1710. Note that the musical setting of Congreve's lyric changes to "Stay, Ah stay, ah Turn."

[154] Although the play text states it was set by Eccles, I have not located a copy.

[155] See Baldwin and Wilson, *Monthly Mask*, no. 20.

[156] Estcourt, *The Fair Example; or, The Modish Citizens* (London, 1706), unpaginated, italics reversed.

Lucia, virtuous wife of Sir Rice-ap-Adam, an old Welsh knight. The only music associated with the production is a song by John Weldon, "Sung by Mrs Campion in the Play call'd the Fair Example." A typically tuneful piece in two contrasting sections with Italianate ornamentation presumably suited to Campion's voice, the message of the text fits the conclusion of the play: Mirtillo thought love "was but a Jest" but found "his Joys are false his pain too true."[157]

Song and comedy are central to the prologue spoken by Betterton before Boyle's *As You Find It* in spring 1703, which takes audiences to task in a familiar manner:

> ... to our Neighbours Joy th'exactest Play
> Must to a long and well writ Bill give Way,
> Or to th'Immortal *Trip* must yield the Day
> Tho' our *French* Heels, and our *Italian* Voice,
> Show the Judicious Niceness of our Choice;
> Show, when put to't, that We on play our Parts,
> And know the Way to win true *British* Hearts.
> But still we hope your Judgements soon may mend,[158]

Although productions at Lincoln's Inn Fields often met with critical acclaim, the theater at Drury Lane—thanks in no small part to its comedies and its rival musical attractions, including singers, dancers, and the Italian violinist Gasparini—was perceived as the popular success.

The anonymous *The Fickle Shepherdess* marked a return to the pastoral mode, which had recently experienced an onstage revival with Congreve's *The Judgment of Paris* and Motteux's *Acis and Galatea*.[159] Milhous and Hume tentatively assign its premiere to April; however, the musical evidence suggests it may have been several weeks later.[160] A performance in late May provides the first documentation of soprano Margarita de l'Epine singing at Lincoln's Inn Fields. Doubtless with past successes in mind, *The Fickle Shepherdess* included a starring role for Bracegirdle as a musical shepherd (again) who is driven mad by love (again), as well as roles for nearly all of the company's actresses.

The story involves twins, Amintas (Bracegirdle) and Amarillis, who are in love with siblings, Urania and Damon (Elizabeth Bowman in breeches), the children of the high priest of Ceres. The unhappy couples have been cursed, and in attempting

---

[157] This is the first song in Weldon's *Third Book of Songs,* published by Walsh in May 1703. Copy used, GB-Lbl G.301(song 1), with alternate title page.

[158] [Boyle], *As You Find It* (London, 1703), [69].

[159] For more on contemporary uses of the pastoral mode see Timothy Neufeldt, "Music, Magic, and Morality: Stage Reform and the Pastoral Mode," in *Stages 'Adorn'd with ev'ry Grace'* (Ashgate, forthcoming).

[160] M&H *London Stage*, p. 95. In 1703, Walsh's *Monthly Mask* generally printed songs from LIF soon after the play's premiere. The song from *The Fickle Shepherdess* did not appear until June, after a song from *As You Find It.*

Figure 5.5　J. Eccles, "Fie Amarillis, cease to Grieve" in *The Fickle Shepherdess*. From Eccles, *A Collection of Songs*, p. 42

to solve the riddle of "the impossible dowry" Amintas has gone mad. In a separate strand of plot the fickle shepherdess Clorinda (Barry) must choose between Alexis and Damon. Based on Thomas Randolph's pastoral *Amyntas* (Whitehall, c.1632), the anonymous author reduced five acts to three and eliminated the original songs and dances (by a group of fairies in Act IV). Amintas had appeared onstage recently and unsuccessfully in Oldmixon's *Amintas* (PC, 1698).

The first musical interlude takes place as rival suitors Damon and Alexis come with nymphs and swains to "Pipe and Dance before *Clorinda*."[161] A similar interlude takes place near the end of Act II, when Amintas's father, in disguise as a physician, instructs the revelers to "charm [Amintas] with some Musick ... put his Sense in Tune."[162] Once again, music frames an invitation to gaze upon the beautiful sleeping actress (here in a male role). The unspecified "Songs and Dances" are followed by a private prayer to Apollo, god of music and medicine, so it is not harmony alone which restores Amintas's wits. The last such celebration takes place, predictably, at the end of Act III, where there are "Songs and Dances" in honor of the happy answers to the riddle-curses which result in everyone being successfully paired off.

While these interludes are only generally noted, each act also contains a single vocal piece about which the author gives considerably more information. The first solo song, "Fie Amarillis, cease to Grieve," features some of Eccles's most beautiful vocal writing, though only the first verse is set (Figure 5.5).[163] As with his other more developed songs, often those for Hodgson, Eccles takes care to vary the written-out repetitions rather than repeating them mechanically.[164] There are more fluid shifts in harmony and generally lighter support from the bass, avoiding the frequent chains of first-inversion chords doubling the vocal line. Despite its beauty and sense, Amarillis rejects this musical advice and continues her hopeless adoration.

It should be noted that both "Fie Amarillis" and "Haste, give me wings" are far more substantial and musically interesting than the songs Eccles wrote for *Love Betray'd*, suggesting where his priorities lay. "Fie Amarillis" was sung by a professional vocalist, as "Cloe found Love" was not, but the difference between "If I hear Orinda swear" and "Haste, give me wings," both composed for Bracegirdle, is considerable.

Bracegirdle's mad song, "Haste give me wings," falls toward the middle of the play, near the beginning of the second act. Like most characters of the period, Amintas is classically mad, referring to Pegasus, Cytherea, the Hesperides, Venus,

---

[161] *The Fickle Shepherdess* (London, 1703), p. 8.

[162] Ibid., p. 28.

[163] As printed in the June 1703 *Monthly Mask* and in Eccles's *Collection* the following year.

[164] For a transcription with additional commentary, see *Music Productions LIF*, pp. 592–5.

Helen, Charon, Hades, and Proserpine, adding Neptune to the catalogue in his song:

> Haste, give me Wings and let me fly,
> That I may mount the starry Sky,
> And there, of all the Gods enquire
> How I may squench my fierce Desire:
> See where the charming Nymph does lie,
> Oh! Give her to me, or I die.
> I'll mount above and rescue my Sire,
> And I'll tumble the Tyrant down,
> He shall not dare to Embrace my Fair,
> Tho' graced with th'Imperial Crown.
> See! See! Neptune with his wat'ry Train,
> Come, come, ye Tritons, come all all around,
> Come Plunge me in the watery Main,
> And all my Flames confound.

There are minor but significant changes in the song text printed in Eccles's *Collection* from that in the play, given above.[165] Dramatically and musically mercurial, the song explores a range of emotions and suitably irrational ideas, coloring them with a characteristic variety of meters and motives. Eccles's song begins with a brilliant, breathless series of sequences, a clear vocal depiction of haste.[166]

Drury Lane finished its season with two comedies, Susanna Centlivre's adaptation of Molière, *Love's Contrivance, or Le Medecin malgre Lui* [*sic*], and Richard Wilkinson's *Vice Reclaim'd; or, The Passionate Mistress*. Both authors thanked Robert Wilks for his efforts, in their prefaces, and his characters are the prime movers in each drama.

The prologue to Centlivre's play comments "Courtiers in Com'dy place their chief Delight,/ 'Cause Love's the proper Bus'ness of the Night./ The Clown for Pastoral his half Crown bestows,/ But t'other House by sad Experience knows,/ This polish'd Town produces few of those" (lines 20–24), suggesting that performances of *The Fickle Shepherdess* in May were not a success. According to Centlivre, *Love's Contrivance* was a surprise hit, and it returned during the following seasons. Centlivre makes some use of casual singing in character, as the servant Martin and the would-be lively Sir Toby both sing—Martin's music is unspecified, Sir Toby's a minuet song, once again with clear sexual implications.

---

[165] See *Music Productions LIF*, pp. 596–8.

[166] Similar to Eccles's "I'll hurry, hurry thee hence" in *Justice Buisy* (LIF, 1699). See Amanda Eubanks Winkler's essay on musical eroticism in *The Fickle Shepherdess* in *Stages 'Adorn'd with ev'ry Grace'* (Ashgate, forthcoming). Included in Evelyn Tubb and Anthony Rooley's *Bewitching Bracegirdle* recordings.

However, little of the comedy's vocal music can be identified, and the sources for instrumental music are confused.[167]

Within the play, there are two formal musical events, both in Act V. The first occurs as obstinate Selfwill (Bullock) plans for his daughter Lucinda's wedding: "I spoke to some of the Singers in the Play-house to be ready if I sent for them" (53). Mrs Shaw duly enters, and Selfwill asks her to sing "some of your newest Entertainments" (Centlivre's text does not reveal what they were). When she does, he gives her five guineas, which seems suspiciously high—as if Mrs. Shaw were "the Italian lady." The specifically named performer, combined with vagueness about what was performed, is reminiscent of *The Female Wits* (PC, 1696).

The final musical numbers fall at the end of the act. The play text presents a song sung by Leveridge, "Sue to Celia for the Favour," and implies there is also a dance, though it is not clear if Leveridge's song accompanies the dance or supplants it. Its elaborate runs on "to" ("She is *to* herself most kind") suggest parody of Italian arias "English'd" and once again Leveridge's performance sits oddly with the supposed reconciliation and reformation marking the end of the comedy. Weldon's setting appeared both in his *Third Book of Songs* (May 1703), as sung by Laroon, and in Walsh's *Monthly Mask* (September 1704) as sung by Leveridge at the theater, suggesting that Centlivre or someone else involved with the production borrowed a recent song from a concert for use in the play.[168]

One of the most striking things about Wilkinson's *Vice Reclaim'd*, like Trotter's *Love at a Loss* (PC, 1701) is the sheer amount of musical quotation in the printed text. Several roles for Wilks and Bullock use quotation, but Wilkinson's references are spread throughout the comedy, and rather than referring to past Patent Company successes (as Baker did in *Tunbridge Walks*), Wilkinson's quotations are largely from very popular non-Drury Lane productions like *The Judgment of Paris* and *Acis and Galatea*. The quotations reinforce character types, as Wilks, playing the rakish Wilding, sings tags asserting masculine prerogative ("I'll rove and I'll range") while Bullock, playing the cuckold Fondle, is left with comically inappropriate and even emasculating vocal tags, as he channels *Don Quixote*'s mad Marcella, created by rival star Anne Bracegirdle, ("Bring me daggers, poyson, fire,") when he discovers he has been duped.

Aside from its use of quotation, Wilkinson's comedy includes a conventional song scene in Act II in which one of the young heroines, Annabella, sings to her friend Lucia—a prayer for peace that is promptly overheard by their two gallants. No music survives, and the text does pose some questions, since Jane Rodgers (Annabella) did not typically sing, though in spoken dialogue she mentions her lack of voice self-deprecatingly (12). In Act IV, Sir Feeble Goodwill (a merry old

---

[167] The tenor part to a set of act tunes (printed in *Harmonia Anglicana*) "Mr D. Purcell Tenor in Love's Contrivance" can be seen in GB-Lcm XXIX .A.11. This is actually the tenor part to *The Inconstant* (noted by Smith, *Bibliography of John Walsh*, entry 81), but the erroneous heading suggests that tunes were also printed for *Love's Contrivance*.

[168] For the music, see Baldwin and Wilson, *Monthly Mask*, no. 80.

gentleman) arranges for a "Dance of five Quakers" as part of his scheme to woo the wealthy widow Purelight.

The comedy concludes using Drury Lane's current fifth act formula: an obligatory dance and song sung by Leveridge, "You laugh to see me fond appear."[169] Although the play text says Leveridge also composed the song, Walsh's *Monthly Mask of Vocal Music* credits it to Daniel Purcell, and it is convincingly Purcellian.[170] While musically apt, the text could not be more inappropriate for a marriage celebration, concluding "As both have Hundreds done before,/ Each other we caress,/ Impartial she, no Man love's more,/ Nor I no Woman less" (62). Given such musical encouragement, it is hard not to be cynical about Wilding's final speech, in which he claims to be reformed, following the bright sun of Annabella's virtue. Suns do set, after all.

Revivals, 1702–1703

The most significant musical revival this season was the Shakespeare–Middleton–Davenant *Macbeth* at Drury Lane in November. Provided with new music by Richard Leveridge, this version of the work (with some adaptation) was to hold the stage for decades to come. Leveridge had been active as a song composer for over five years, but his music for *Macbeth* expands to include string ensemble, chorus, and soloists. Leveridge's compositional choices are often similar to Eccles's, as in the musical setting of the line "We should rejoice when good kings bleed," with its imitative melismas on "rejoice." An enlightening comparison between the two versions, their text, and music, has been made by Amanda Eubanks Winkler in her recent edition of the music for both settings.[171]

Leveridge's music is included in Cfm Mus Mss 87 with dramatick operas performed during 1701 and 1702. In the *Macbeth* music at least two layers of singers' names are indicated, one of which Baldwin and Wilson presume to be for the original production, including Leveridge, Laroon, Lindsey, Mills, and Shaw, all regular singers at Drury Lane.[172] The exception is Richard Elford, who wrote music and performed songs at the Lincoln's Inn Fields theater, but may have sung in the chorus for *Macbeth* as an act of friendship. A performance is confirmed for 21 November, and again on 17 June, the advertisement suggesting that several performances had taken place in the meantime. Drury Lane also continued to revive Shadwell's *The Lancashire Witches* this winter, and regularly revived

---

[169] This song is not identified in the title line as having been sung in the play, and thus there is no reference to the play in Hunter. It also appeared in the July 1703 *Monthly Mask*, Baldwin and Wilson, no. 30.

[170] See Baldwin and Wilson, *Monthly Mask*, no. 32.

[171] Eubanks Winkler, *Music for Macbeth*, in *Recent Researches in the Music of the Baroque Era* 133 (Middleton, Wisconsin, 2004).

[172] See Baldwin and Wilson's "Notes on the Songs," in Richard Leveridge, *The Complete Songs (with the music in* Macbeth*)*, no. 168.

favorites from past seasons, like Vanbrugh's *The Relapse*, as well as farces such as Behn's *The Emperor of the Moon* and Pix's *The Spanish Wives*.[173]

The autumn season at Lincoln's Inn Fields included revivals of plays by Shakespeare, Jonson, and Cowley, plus Fletcher and Rowley's *The Maid in the Mill*, with new songs.[174] Although it is tempting to assume that Lincoln's Inn Fields mounted a competitive production of *Macbeth* with Eccles's music, the only production confirmed for November 1702 was another stock comedy. December 1702 began with revivals of Beaumont and Fletcher's *The Scornful Lady*, Dryden's *The Indian Emperor* with Motteux's *Acis and Galatea*, and Wycherley's *The Country Wife*, with a host of special musical insertions, including "The Chimney Sweeper's Dialogue," "The Turkey-Cock Music," and "The Mad-Man's Dance." As mentioned at the beginning of this chapter, both houses advertised numerous entertainments of dancing at this time, particularly during the benefit season.

At Drury Lane in January 1703 Joanna Maria Lindelheim, 'the Baroness,' sang in French and Italian as part of the musical entertainments in a varied evening which also included Vanbrugh's short farce *The Country House* and singing by Leveridge, Hughes, and Laroon (no rival sopranos), plus French dancing by Du Ruel and Mary Anne Campion. Lindelheim sang Italian songs by Venetian Giuseppe Saggione, who would also write songs for Maria Gallia to sing at York Buildings.

In April 1703 the Patent Company began advertising violin sonatas, performed and in some cases composed by Gasparo Visconti ('Gasperini'), also offering pieces by Paisible and other members of the musick, paired with revivals of stock plays and many other attractions.[175] In June, Lincoln's Inn Fields advertises "several Italian Trumpet Sonatas, being intirely new" combined with dancing and songs by Henry Purcell during a revival of a stock comedy.[176]

In June, Drury Lane presented new or recent comedies like *Love's Contrivance* and *Tunbridge Walks* in alternation with older tragedies, with sonatas by Gasperini and dancing by Du Ruel. We have an unusually complete picture of revivals at Lincoln's Inn Fields. The first week in June the company returned to tragedies by Nathaniel Lee, *The Rival Queens* and *Theodosius*, with musical entertainments.[177] *The Rival Queens* included singing in Italian by soprano Maria Margarita Gallia,

---

[173] Information for these productions is drawn from Milhous and Hume's *London Stage*.

[174] This production, missed by Avery in the first edition of *The London Stage*, has been included in Milhous and Hume. For additional details about the songs and their links to an October 1702 performance, see Kathryn Lowerre, "Musical Evidence for an Early Eighteenth-Century Revival of *The Maid in the Mill* at Lincoln's Inn Fields," *Theatre Notebook* 54 (2000): 86–97.

[175] See M&H *London Stage*, pp. 97–105.

[176] Ibid., pp. 105–6.

[177] Although at this time *Theodosius* was advertised with "music by the best Masters," in February 1704 it was revived again and advertised "With the Original Musical

"lately arriv'd from Italy" and ready to emulate Margarita de l'Epine's success on stage and in concert. The last known production of the season was *The Villain*, with fashionable new music ("Italian Trumpet Sonatas"), as well as old favorites such as "Purcell's celebrated Trumpet Song, *The Fife and Harmony of War*" and "The *Mad Song* in *Don Quixote*." All of the productions in June advertised entertainments of dancing with a variety of styles and subjects, by performers including Monsieur l'Abbé, Mr and Miss Prince, Mrs Elford, Mr Fairbank, and Mr Godwin.[178]

Conclusion

The 1700–1701 season marked a crisis point for theater operations in London, as both houses were closed for an extended period in the early autumn and shortly afterwards the new Lord Chamberlain was forced or persuaded to step in and take the management of the Lincoln's Inn Fields theater away from the actors' cooperative and assign it to Betterton exclusively. The season of 1701–1702, with its frequent interruptions and closings, was also challenging for both companies.

The absence of Motteux from the list of authors writing for the Lincoln's Inn Fields company after 1701 is notable, considering the important role his works had played during the company's earlier seasons. If Shirley Strum Kenny's hypotheses about the co-authorship and premiere of *The Stage-Coach* are correct, Motteux returned to Lincoln's Inn Fields following *The Island Princess*, and had a hand in the company's two most marked successes of the 1700–1701 season, *The Stage-Coach* and *Acis and Galatea*. Both were short comic pieces making good use of the popular Dogget; works which in later seasons were combined with a variety of main pieces and concert programs. The company continued to revive his *The Loves of Mars and Venus*, and the advertisements for the *The Fickle Shepherdess* suggest that it was the result of a search for other "novelties," to replace Motteux's usual contributions.

There is an increasing amount of musical evidence from these seasons, but it becomes much harder to pin down. Unspecified Act V entertainments, seen occasionally in 1690s play texts, are perceptibly more common from 1702 to 1703, at both houses. The inception of Walsh's *Monthly Mask* series in November 1702 documents the range of songs performed in concerts and at the theater, including many not named as part of any specific production, though created and performed by theater regulars, and sung "at the Theater."[179]

Entertainments" (M&H *London Stage*, p. 144). Price details the music written for the 1680 premiere in *Henry Purcell and the London Stage*, pp. 30–37.

[178] M&H *London Stage*, pp. 103–5.

[179] See, for example, Raphael Courteville's "To touch your heart," "Sung by Mr. Hughs at the Theater in Drury-Lane" from January 1703. Baldwin and Wilson, *Monthly Mask*, no. 8.

From 1695 through 1700–1701 virtually every theater season included one or more dramatick opera premieres. Yet the following seasons have none, although popular dramatick operas like *The Island Princess* continued to be revived. Instead, concert series and events such as the "Subscription Musick" (featuring short dramatic works and scenes from dramatick operas like *King Arthur*) assumed greater and greater prominence.

The operas staged at Lincoln's Inn Fields in 1700 and 1701, *The Mad Lover* and *Measure for Measure* with *Dido and Aeneas*, were reusing older material, rather than attempting to create original works. Regardless of the Patent Company's past successes with opera, it was the comedies that kept the company afloat, despite attempts at both types of dramatick opera, the newly written and the adapted. *The Virgin Prophetess* was clearly a disappointment, although it did have an interesting afterlife, inspiring a famously elaborate droll at Bartholomew Fair.[180] At this point, opera essentially goes into re-runs, until *Arsinoe, Queen of Cyprus* appears in January 1705, heralding a new age of Italian (or almost Italian) opera.

---

[180] *The Siege of Troy, A Dramatick performance. Presented in Mrs. Mynn's Booth ... during the Time of the present Bartholomew-Fair. Containing A Description of all the Scenes, Machines and Movements, with the whole Decoration of the Play, and Particulars of the Entertainment* (London, 1707). It promises entertainment "in no ways Inferiour even to any one *Opera* yet seen in either of the *Royal Theaters*." Several scenes and special effects are taken directly from *The Virgin Prophetess*, including complicated constructions such as ten elephants, canopied and castled, each bearing ten people (*The Siege of Troy*, p. 7; *The Virgin Prophetess*, p. 5). See Sybil Rosenfeld, *The Theatre of the London Fairs in the Eighteenth Century* (Cambridge, 1960), pp. 19–20, 140–41, 161–6.

Chapter Six
Realignment, 1703–1705

The final seasons of competition between the Patent Company and Lincoln's Inn Fields produced relatively few new productions, but provide considerable evidence regarding the musical practices in the theaters and the musical tastes of their audiences. In 1705, two new operatic productions laid the ground for subsequent seasons of competition between Rich's Patent Company and Sir John Vanbrugh's new theater in the Haymarket.

Context

During these seasons unrest in the theaters paralleled political uneasiness, as the initial enthusiasm for Queen Anne began inevitably to turn. Debates over occasional conformity and the proposed union of England with Scotland dragged on.[1] In December 1703, the "Scotch plot," another Jacobite conspiracy, was made public in the House of Lords. According to Narcissus Luttrell, in March 1704 Parliament was still investigating and ordering the prosecution of persons involved. The House of Lords addressed the queen regarding the Scottish succession on 1 April and shortly thereafter the Scottish parliament agreed to consider it as well.[2]

On 21 April a Scottish gentleman, David Lindsay, was arraigned and charged with high treason for his part in the plot. He was quickly found guilty and sentenced to death. His wife petitioned the queen for a pardon, offering a confession in exchange for clemency, and Lindsay was reprieved at Tyburn on 11 May.[3]

Although they had long been popular, the craze for "Scotch" songs and dances was quite pronounced at Lincoln's Inn Fields during the spring of 1704. Similar "Scotch" offerings had been made at Drury Lane during the previous season, but the advertisements for spring 1704 feature Italian and French music and dancing. The regular recurrence of "Scotch" entertainments at Lincoln's Inn Fields in

---

[1] 'Occasional conformity' was the practice of attending Church of England services periodically in order to remain eligible for civic or military employment and to vote. Presbyterians (Dissenters) would be fined for attending other services. See Defoe's famous satire *The Shortest Way with the Dissenters*.

[2] Although the crowns were united, the countries and parliaments were not. While the Scottish parliament never declared an alternative (non-Hanoverian) line of succession, there was the potential that it might.

[3] These events can be found in Luttrell, *State Affairs*, vol. 5, pp. 407–9, 415–19, and 423.

April 1704 certainly reflects their popularity and the tendency to repeat theatrical offerings from week to week—but Scotland was also highly topical.[4]

Moral issues related to the theaters were raised again after the "great storm" of 26 November 1703, when Drury Lane staged *Macbeth* with Leveridge's music. The actors were accused by Jeremy Collier of mocking "the Voice of an angry Heaven," making it "a Jest at the Play House: Macbeth with his Lightning and thunder the Entertainment of the Day, and the mention of Chimnies blown down, clapt by the Audience with an unusual Length of Pleasure and Approbation."[5] Collier was not just objecting to cavalier attitudes towards meteorological display and property damage. The bishop of Bath and his wife were among those killed during the storm.[6] It was seen as a sign by proponents of the Societies for the Reformation of Manners that England had failed in its needed moral revolution.[7]

In response, the Lord Chamberlain moved to tighten the controls on representation in the theaters. In January 1704 he issued orders to both companies and to the Master of the Revels, reiterating once again that "all plays (old and new), songs, prologues, and epilogues" had to be licensed before being performed.[8] These orders were followed by a public proclamation from the queen "against vice and immorality in the theatre."[9]

In August 1704, London's inhabitants were more cheerful following the Duke of Marlborough's famous victory over the French and Bavarians at Blenheim, announced to Drury Lane audiences in the prologue to a revival of Behn's farce *The Emperor of the Moon*.[10] The same summer, Admiral Rooke captured Gibraltar, and although the occupying English made themselves unpopular with the Spanish by looting the city, it still inspired celebratory poems and a comedy by Dennis.

Late in the spring of 1705 the Lincoln's Inn Fields company moved to the newly finished Queen's Theatre in the Haymarket, designed by Sir John Vanbrugh and initially managed by him with William Congreve. When Vanbrugh took over the Lincoln's Inn Fields company in the spring, he apparently cherished the idea of reuniting it with the other company.[11] However, his self-serving proposals were roundly rejected both by Rich and by the actors at Drury Lane.[12] During the 1703–1705 seasons Christopher Rich manifested understandable annoyance

---

[4] Milhous draws attention to the production of *The Albion Queens* (DL, March 1704) and the care taken to get the play (originally *Mary Queen of Scotland*) sufficiently rewritten to pass the censor. *Thomas Betterton*, p. 180.

[5] Excerpt in M&H *London Stage*, p. 130.

[6] W.A. Speck, *The Birth of Britain* (Blackwell, 1994), p. 58.

[7] Ibid., p. 58.

[8] Summarized in *Theatrical Documents*, nos. 1753, 1754.

[9] *Theatrical Documents*, no. 1755.

[10] M&H *London Stage*, p. 176.

[11] What can be gleaned from newspapers and other sources is presented in *Theatrical Documents*, nos. 1782, 1789, 1792, 1793, 1797–1799.

[12] *Theatrical Documents*, nos. 1812–1815.

over Vanbrugh's plans for the new theater, which would eliminate his practical advantage in controlling both Drury Lane and the larger Dorset Garden theater.

Musical Assets

It was unclear during this period in what form the two companies would continue to exist or in which theaters they would perform. A financial plan for a reunited company provides some economic perspective on the relationship between musicians, composers, actors, and other theater personnel at both houses, and on what Vanbrugh hoped to accomplish at his new theater.[13]

According to the plan, John Eccles, as "master to oversee ye music," would receive £40 per annum. For vocal music, Leveridge was to receive the same amount as "Master to teach." Eccles and Leveridge are logical choices, but it is interesting that Vanbrugh selected one master from each company. Most actors' salaries are given as two figures (management presumably hoping for the lower one), but the music masters' salaries are equivalent to the salaries of the lowest-paid male actors (twice as much as the barbers). They are roughly one-quarter to one-third of the salaries of leading actors like Wilks, Powell, Barry, Bracegirdle, and Betterton (who also received extra "to teach").

The plan includes singers associated with both houses, all of them English. Their salaries are similarly modest: Hughes and Cook, Lindsey and Mills all at £20 and Mary Hodgson at £30, plus additional singers as needed. The budget for dancers is considerably larger, listing Anthony l'Abbé as master (£60), with Du Ruel, Mrs Elford, and Mrs Mayers at £40, Rene Cherrier at £30, and Miss Mosse (the Devonshire Girl) and Miss Evans at £20. In addition, both singers and dancers were to receive a certain sum every time they performed. Unfortunately, the instrumental musicians are estimated as a group: "twenty musicians allowing 20s. per week to each for 40 weeks."[14] As for composition, after summing up the totals for players, dancers, singers, under officers,[15] "rent, candles, managers," and the musick (the instrumental ensemble), the planners put aside a round sum "remaining for incidentals, as scenes, cloaths, printing, new plays, coals &

---

[13] Transcriptions of Public Record Office documents from M&H *London Stage*, pp. 94–5. Also see Milhous, "The Date and Import of the Financial Plan for a United Theatre Company in P.R.O. LC 7/3," *Maske und Kothurn* 21 (1975): 81–8.

[14] According to a contemporary document (composer J.S. Kusser's commonplace book), "The best musicians are paid one pound for each performance, less important musicians are paid ten shillings and the least important are paid five shillings." Translated in Harold E. Samuel, "A German Musician comes to London in 1704," *Musical Times* 122 (1986): 591–3 (p. 591). This suggests that the hypothetical musicians above (at 20s per week) were not getting top fees, and only performing four or five times a week, perhaps at a slightly lower rate since it was regular employment rather than a single concert.

[15] Such as the prompter, doorkeepers, wardrobe keeper, carpenters, dressers, etc.

compositions of music &c." Although music is last on the list, it is among the non-personnel items considered essential, like scenery and heating.

This document is usually referred to as evidence of a rapprochement between the two companies,[16] and there is musical evidence of company collegiality and increased interaction as well. Dancers, singers, instrumentalists, and composers from both companies collaborated on concerts, including the Subscription Musick concert series in 1703–1704, for which performances were divided equally between the two theaters. Just as contemporary theater evenings were more musical than might be expected by later standards, these concert evenings were more theatrical, including scenes and short dramatic and musical works.[17]

Although Eccles and Daniel Purcell continued to compose for their respective companies, many composers from earlier seasons were less involved. Jeremiah Clarke wrote songs for soprano Mary Hodgson to sing at Lincoln's Inn Fields for the premiere of *Love at First Sight*, and during the 1704 revivals of *Madam Fickle* and *Timon of Athens*; however, there is no record of music by him at Drury Lane after November 1702, except in a Subscription Musick concert. These final seasons were also marked by the increasing prominence of foreign composers (below).

Actor-singers

Many of the actor-singers appearing at both theaters in 1703–1705 were familiar favorites from earlier seasons, including Dogget, who continued switching between companies, and Bracegirdle. However, the following changes are worth noting.

George Pack, who had begun at Lincoln's Inn Fields some three seasons earlier, was gradually acquiring status as a singer of humorous and racy songs and undertaking some comic roles, eventually playing alongside Bracegirdle. Like Dogget, he could sing and dance as well as act, and like John Bowman, he also dabbled in composition.

Midway through the 1704–1705 season, Letitia Cross returned to the stage. Although she now had to compete with the vocal and visual attractions of Catherine Tofts (below), in short order she landed at least one good new comic role and the second female lead in one of the most successful musical productions of the 1695–1705 decade, the opera *Arsinoe*.

---

[16] As Milhous writes, "the intense competition [Colley Cibber] described in the late 1690s should not be generalized: by 1702 the theatres had learned to live and let live." Milhous, *Thomas Betterton*, p. 188.

[17] The Subscription Musick concerts were not part of the regular theatrical season (admittance only by special subscribers' tickets, managed separately).

Singers

Plays from these seasons are often non-specific about musical numbers intended to be performed in them ("A song and a dance"). However, there are a number of contemporary songs printed for John Walsh or engraved by Thomas Cross which explicitly state in their title line "sung at the new Theater" or "sung at the Theatre Royall" which feature the latest singers like Mr Cook (bass), John Davis (tenor), and Francis Hughes (countertenor) as well as old favorites like Mary Hodgson. While these songs cannot be conclusively linked to a specific production, they were doubtless heard either within or between the acts, or during one of the increasingly frequent concert evenings. From 1702–1703, many were published in Walsh's new series *The Monthly Mask of Vocal Musick*, now available in a facsimile edition.[18]

The singer most often advertised as appearing with a play or other production was Richard Leveridge. He was frequently paired with Mary Anne Campion (until her retirement in spring 1704) and sometimes with Mary Lindsey, but most often appeared solo. Sometimes his repertoire was mentioned: "the best stage songs," "a song by the late Mr Henry Purcell," or "a comical dialogue from *The Island Princess*." In December 1704, in conjunction with the ninth performance of Cibber's popular new comedy *The Careless Husband*, newspapers touted the return of Letitia Cross, singing a new musical dialogue with Leveridge.[19] In addition to Leveridge, advertisements puffed Hughes, another "new boy," and most of all, soprano Margarita de l'Epine. All of the star singers appearing at Drury Lane (de l'Epine, Leveridge, Tofts) got a nice bonus after singing at court for the entertainment of the English-supported claimant to the Spanish throne in December 1703. James Paisible wrote a suite of instrumental music for the occasion, "Musick Perform'd before her Majesty and the new King of Spain."[20]

The most prominent English singer during these seasons was, without a doubt, soprano Catherine Tofts. Colley Cibber would later recall, "whatever Defect the fashionably Skilful might find in her manner, she had, in the general Sense of her Spectators, Charms that few of the most learned Singers ever arrive at. The Beauty of her fine proportion'd Figure, and exquisitely sweet, silver Tone of her Voice, with that peculiar rapid Swiftness of her Throat, were Perfections not to be imitated by Art or Labour."[21] She apparently performed on a limited basis,

---

[18] *The Monthly Mask of Vocal Music 1702–1711*, ed. Olive Baldwin and Thelma Wilson (Aldershot, 2007).

[19] M&H *London Stage*, p. 200. The announcement may have been premature. On 2 January 1705 another performance of *The Careless Lover* was advertised with a new pastoral dialogue performed by Leveridge and Cross "Being the first time of her Appearance on the Stage these 5 Years." M&H *London Stage*, p. 202.

[20] See M&H *London Stage* pp. 134–5. Paisible's music was published by Walsh in *Harmonia Anglicana*.

[21] Cibber, *Apology*, ed. Lowe, vol. 2, pp. 54–5.

in conjunction with high-status events like the Subscription Musick concerts, in which she sang in both Italian and English, and the opera *Arsinoe*. Tofts acquired some notoriety for her rivalry with de l'Epine,[22] although the two made at least one joint appearance, during the initial performance of *Arsinoe*, in which Tofts played the title character, and de l'Epine was advertised as singing "before the Beginning and after the Ending of the Opera ... several Entertainments of Singing in Italian and English." However, this appears to be the only overlap, and subsequently de l'Epine sang on other nights.

Foreign singers were more frequently advertised in the theaters and at York Buildings and other concert venues than in the previous seasons. De l'Epine had been a featured performer at Lincoln's Inn Fields during 1702–1703, but by January 1704 she had a contract with Rich at Drury Lane. In addition to de l'Epine, Gallia, and the "Baroness," 1703–1705 audiences heard the mysterious Ziuliana de Celotte (Celotti) and "Signior Olsii, lately come from Italy." Olsii may have been a castrato, like Clemente (Clementine) and Fideli, who sang in concerts and at Drury Lane, or the great Nicolini, who ravished audiences after his arrival in late 1705. Signior Olsii later sang "several Italian Songs with the Trumpet and other Instruments, accompany'd by Mr Dupare [Dieupart]" in a concert at York Buildings on 18 May 1704.[23] English-born singers were not forgotten, however, and the careers of both Marcellus Laroon and Francis Hughes flourished during this period.

Dancers

Featured dancers continued to be key attractions for new productions, and especially for revivals. Newspaper advertisements placed by the Patent Company are the best source of information about the terpsichorean pleasures audience members might expect.

Like the other entertainments offered at the theaters, the dance numbers advertised reveal a wide variety of performers and acts to suit all tastes. The dances included everything from courtly French dances for a large ensemble ("a new Chaconne composed by Monsieur Cherrier, and perform'd by him and 6 others") to comic solos ("the Country Farmer's Daughter") and duos ("A French Peasant and his Wife").[24] Dances featuring *commedia dell'arte* characters like Scaramouche and Harlequin were often featured.[25]

---

[22] Tofts had to apologize for her former servant throwing oranges at de l'Epine singing during a revival of *The Chances* on 5 February 1704. See M&H *London Stage*, p. 144.

[23] M&H *London Stage*, p. 167.

[24] Ibid., pp. 146, 187, 189, 202, 170, 172.

[25] See, for example, the "Comical Entertainment in a Tavern between Scaramouch, Harlaquin and Punchanello" performed frequently during the 1703–1704 season, M&H *London Stage,* pp. 123, 129, 133, 137–8, 143, 162.

Just one example of the popularity and profitability of theater-related dance publications can be found in Walsh's January 1705 advertising of *A Collection of the most celebrated Jigs, Lancashire Horn-pipes, Scotch and Highland Lilts, Northern Frisks, and Cheshire Rounds. Together with several excellent new Stage Dances by Mr. Duruel, Mr. Cherier, Mr. Cotine and others, being all High Dances, fitted to the Humours of most Countries and People*.[26] The French masters listed were regular performers at Drury Lane, while "lilts" and "frisks" were danced by popular English performers like Mrs Mosse, "the Devonshire Girl." Similar Scottish and Irish dances were performed by Elizabeth Willis's daughters at Lincoln's Inn Fields. While a great many dancers were advertised during these seasons, Mrs Mosse and Monsieur Du Ruel, who both arrived in 1702–1703, were the most frequently mentioned.

Composers

During these seasons audiences heard works by a number of song composers, including Richard Elford, Mr Hickes,[27] Littleton Ramondon, William Robart, and John Wilford. At the same time, several experienced theater composers, including the previously prolific Paisible and Clarke, seem to have been more active in concert venues than on the stage. In 1705 a concert of patriotic music, "in Praise of the Success of her Majesty's Forces,"[28] featured Clarke and William Croft, who were both increasingly involved with sacred music and received a joint appointment as organists for the Chapel Royal in 1704. Royal duties may also have affected Elford, who appears to have sung less during these seasons following his chapel appointment, although he continued to compose songs performed by his singing colleagues Davis and Hodgson.

In January 1704, Walsh began publishing a monthly series of solos and sonatas for the violin, including works "performed at the theatre" by Gasperini and Thomas Deane.[29] Like the concert song, these sonatas mark the repertoire overlap between the theaters and concert rooms at York Buildings and Richmond Wells.

Foreign composers, many of them German, came to make their way in London, including the Pepusch brothers (Gottfried and Johann Christoph), and Johann Sigismund Kusser. Like Haydn many years later, Kusser kept a commonplace book where he noted items of interest and importance, providing an invaluable bit of musical history and amusing commentary on the contemporary London theater and concert scene.

Kusser, of Hungarian parentage, had studied with Lully in Paris, worked as *kapellmeister* at German courts, traveled to Italy to recruit singers, and toured with

---

[26] See Smith, *Bibliography*, no. 164.
[27] First name unknown. Baldwin and Wilson note two possibilities. *Monthly Mask*, notes to no. 45.
[28] M&H, *London Stage*, pp. 205–6.
[29] For more on the series, see *Music Productions LIF*, pp. 644–9.

an opera company. Familiar with international opera styles, he arrived in London on 25 December 1704. His commonplace book records thirty-three instructions for succeeding in London from fellow-composer Jakob Greber. Many are worth quoting:

> 3. Present yourself to Sr Ritsch [Rich]; he has the big theatre.
> 4. If he doesn't want to give you enough, go to Sr Patterdon [Betterton], who has the little theatre, and say: Ritsch offers such and such an amount, even though it is not true, for these two theatres compete against each other.
> 5. If neither of these two is willing to make a contract ["subscription"], Halifax or Nottingham will.
> 6. Before signing the contract, let a trustworthy friend translate it, so that you will not be cheated.
> 7. At the signing of the contract, announce that you cannot remain longer than about six weeks.
> ....
> 15. Associate cordially with the musicians, but without great familiarity; seldom go drinking with them ...
> 16. Don't let them make a controversy of you. They are masters at this.
> 17. Prepare yourself with music to fit their taste—no pathos certainly, and short, short recitatives.
> ....
> 19. Devote yourself to the English language, and sing an English aria from time to time. That pleases them very much.
> 20. Praise the deceased Purcell to the skies and say there has never been the like of him.[30]

It was excellent advice, and many of the foreign singers, composers, dancers, and instrumentalists who came to London conducted themselves—by wit or instruction—along these lines.

An important development among the composers was the staging of violinist-composer Thomas Clayton's Italian-style opera *Arsinoe* at Drury Lane, rather than at the new Haymarket theater. In October 1704 both *Arsinoe* and an opera by Daniel Purcell, *Orlando Furioso*, were said to be in preparation, "both ... to be perform'd by the best Artists eminent both for Vocal and Instrumental Musick at the Opening of the House."[31] *Arsinoe*'s success at Drury Lane made the lost production doubly wounding. Daniel Purcell seems not to have finished his opera.

---

[30] For all 33 of Greber's instructions see Harold Samuel, "A German Musician comes to London," pp. 591–3.

[31] In *The Diverting Post* 28 October 1704. See *Theatrical Documents*, no. 1782.

Cellist-composer Charles Dieupart, part of the Patent Company since the 1702–1703 season,[32] was apparently instrumental in helping Clayton get his opera staged in 1705. He was also involved in the production of Motteux's 1704 *Britain's Happiness*, an all-sung 'interlude' described as "design'd ... for an Introduction to an Opera, ... call'd The Loves of *Europe*."[33] Although he is not known to have contributed music to any spoken plays in 1703–1705, his part in these all-sung works foreshadows the important role he would play in operatic productions during later seasons.

Librettists

With fewer and fewer new productions staged, the role of the writer shrank accordingly. During these seasons, Motteux was a free agent, usually creating comic and operatic successes for Drury Lane, like *The Mountebank* and *Britain's Happiness*. The English translation of the libretto for one of the most significant musical-dramatic works from these seasons, Clayton's opera *Arsinoe*, is also attributed to him.

Competition and Collaboration: The 1703–1704 Season

Descriptions of the offerings at both theaters, particularly for Lincoln's Inn Fields, are considerably more detailed for the 1703–1704 and following seasons than for earlier ones. While relatively few new productions were mounted, the combination and recombination of stock plays and masques, together with the overlapping offerings of new dances, songs, and instrumental music alongside old favorites, meant that the evening's entertainment changed frequently.

New Productions

Surveying the season in Table 6.1, it is striking that there were so few premieres at Drury Lane, and the new productions mounted there seem reactionary. Steele's *The Lying Lover* debuted after Lincoln's Inn Fields' new autumn comedies; *Love the Leveller* appears to have been patched together to combat the popularity of *Abra Mule*—indeed, the only excuse for this mishmash of a play; while *The Albion Queens* was presumably a response to Lincoln's Inn Fields' successful winter tragedies. Different musical settings of Motteux's "entertainment of vocal musick after the manner of an opera," *Britain's Happiness*, were performed as part of the

---

[32] He had also organized or participated in a concert held at LIF in February 1702, but there is no suggestion that he was attached to the company there. See M&H *London Stage*, p. 55.

[33] Letter to the reader in Motteux, *Britain's Happiness, A Musical Interlude* (London, 1704), unpaginated.

Subscription Musick, a concert series which divided its performances between the two theaters and featured performers from both.

Table 6.1 New productions during the 1703–1704 season

	New works for the Patent Company		**New works at Lincoln's Inn Fields**	
AUTUMN			Marry, or Do Worse	Comedy
			The Different Widows	Comedy
WINTER	The Lying Lover	Comedy		
	Love the Leveller	Tragicomedy	Abra Mule	Tragedy
	[Britain's Happiness	Entertainment][a]	Liberty Asserted	Tragedy
SPRING	The Albion Queens	Tragedy	[Britain's Happiness	Entertainment]
			Love at First Sight	Comedy
			[Squire Trelooby	Farce]
			The Rival Brothers	Tragedy
SUMMER			Wit of a Woman	Farce

Note: [a] Performances of *Britain's Happiness* and *Squire Trelooby* were not part of the regular theater season, but part of the Subscription Musick concert series. They had many ties to both theater companies and are discussed below.

The first known new production for the 1703–1704 season was William Walker's rustic comedy *Marry, or do Worse*, at Lincoln's Inn Fields. Walker had previously written *Victorious Love*, a vehicle for Letitia Cross (PC, 1698). In the preface to his play, Walker complains that his work was shortchanged of "Time and Rehearsals." Dramatically, the play moves quickly, using stock characters, including the witty servant Snap who "enters singing" (what, is not specified), disguised as his master (Act IV, 54). Walker marks conventional spaces for musical numbers, in the first case for a loud instrumental serenade from the "Magisterially Drunk" rake Manley and his hired fiddlers at the beginning of Act V (59), and in the second for a wedding scene at the conclusion of the play (Act V, 72). The comments of the characters—who are not the would-be expert listeners of Pix and Dilke's plays—give no hint of what they heard, an old-fashioned ballad or the latest French minuet. No surviving music is attributed to this play. It may well have reused music already written, given Walker's complaints.

Walker's feeble effort was followed by Mary Pix's latest comedy, *The Different Widows; or, Intrigue a la Mode*. Surprisingly, given Pix's frequent and effective use of music in her earlier comedies, it calls for little music. Again, the fifth act closes with an entertainment of "Musick, Songs, and Dances after that" celebrating a series of masked weddings which have paired off the widows, the maid, and the requisite virtuous young lady. Lack of attention to the music may reflect the absence from the cast of Lincoln's Inn Fields' principal players—another play which did not get the company's full support.

After an autumn of nothing but revivals at Drury Lane, at the end of November, the first Subscription Musick concert was held there. The *Daily Courant* for 30 November 1703 promised a very special event:

> At the Theatre Royal in Drury-Lane ... will be presented an Extraordinary Consort of Vocal and Instrumental Musick by Subscription; In which Mrs Tofts performs several Songs in Italian and English, accompany'd by the best Masters in England. With Danceing by Monsieur Labbe and others. None to be admitted into the Pit or Boxes but by the Subscribers Tickets, which are deliver'd out at White's Chocolate House in St. James's Street. The Boxes on the Stage and the Galleries are for the Benefit of the Actors. Beginning exactly at Five a clock.[34]

While feted English soprano Catherine Tofts sang regularly as part of this series, there is no evidence that she became part of the regular productions at either house until she appeared in the title role in Thomas Clayton's opera *Arsinoe* in January 1705. Famed dancer-choreographer Anthony l'Abbé had been a featured dancer at Lincoln's Inn Fields during the previous seasons, but had left when his contract expired in June.[35]

Although singer-composer John Abell had been mounting concerts for his own benefit by subscription during 1702 (with limited success), this 1703–1704 series would involve many more performers and both theaters. The idea of a regular, high-status concert series at the theaters may have been inspired by the Prize Musick Competition in 1700–1701 as well as the regular consorts of music by

---

[34] M&H *London Stage*, pp. 130–31.
[35] See *Theatrical Documents*, no. 1750. L'Abbé complained of mistreatment by Betterton, but he danced at LIF as part of the concert series and at least one other time during 1704–1705, as did his students.

various performers and composers at sites like York Buildings. The Subscription Musick organizers may have been influenced by the desire to 'encourage English music': later that spring two different musical settings of a patriotic entertainment by Motteux, *Britain's Happiness*, were heard at Drury Lane and Lincoln's Inn Fields.

The Subscription Musick always had a dramatic component. During the winter of 1704 it included two performances of John Weldon's setting of Congreve's masque *The Judgment of Paris*, winner of the 1701 prize, with Catherine Tofts as Pallas. Later Subscription Musick performances included the farce *Squire Trelooby*, while the surviving program for a 'straight' concert is heavily theatrical (and Purcellian), with ensemble and chorus scenes from *Bonduca*, *The Fairy Queen*, and *King Arthur* alternating with songs from Tofts and dances as well as an ode "on the Glorious Beginning of Her Majesty's Reign" by Daniel Purcell.[36] While there seems to have been considerable overlap between this and the performance at court before royal Spanish visitors on 30 December (see Musical Assets, this chapter), there is no mention made of Paisible's music.

Pierre Danchin draws attention to the epilogue (quoted below) and another piece printed with it which attacks High-Church Tories and urges the Hanoverian succession. The epilogue proper is less political, though supporting Archduke Charles as prospective king of Spain and, of course, England's Queen, Anne.

> Your Country's Friends, you love the Native Strains
> Of Musick here, where *England*'s Genius reigns.
> In other Walls, tho' Harmony be found,
> You know 'tis foreign, and disdain the Sound:
> Who haunt new Consorts, Faction wou'd create,
> And are Dissenters in *Apollo*'s State:
> They shun our Stages, where he keeps his Court,
> And to some gloomy Meeting-house Resort.[37]

Rather than referring to Lincoln's Inn Fields, as Danchin suggests, these lines refer more generally to concert venues like York Buildings, Chelsea College, and Hampstead. Unlike the court performance on 30 December, there is no mention of Margarita de l'Epine, Greber, or Gasperini being involved with the Subscription Musick. This suggests some 'native vs. foreign' competitiveness, although many of the dancers for the Subscription Musick were French and Tofts regularly sang in Italian. The composers and singers mentioned in advertisements for the Subscription Musick were all English, regardless of the theater at which they performed.

---

[36] M&H *London Stage*, pp. 136–7.
[37] Danchin, *Prologues and Epilogues of the Eighteenth Century*. Part I: 1701–1720, vol. 1, p. 172.

There is a pronounced contrast between the two Lincoln's Inn Fields comedies and the first new Patent Company comedy this season. From a musical point of view, Steele's second comedy, *The Lying Lover*, has much in common with *The Funeral*, his first. Steele fills his comedy with musical events in virtually every act and ends it with a patriotic song, this time making the popular connection between Queen Anne and Queen Elizabeth. Rather than post-mortem hypocrisy, Steele presents the aftermath of drinking and dueling in serious terms, as his title character wakes up in jail believing he killed his friend. While all ends happily, critics have been dismissive of its didacticism and audiences were unenthusiastic. *The Lying Lover* ran for a respectable six nights, but unlike *The Funeral* there is no evidence that it was revived in later seasons. *The Lying Lover* has been called "Steele's only stage failure" but it has much to recommend it musically,[38] and is discussed in greater detail in Chapter One.

New year productions at Lincoln's Inn Fields commenced with Joseph Trapp's tragedy-with-a-happy-ending, *Abra Mule; or, Love and Empire*, one of the company's few solid successes this season. It received considerable contemporary acclaim as a vehicle for Anne Bracegirdle. *Abra Mule* is set in Constantinople, with Bracegirdle portraying the virtuous title character, a slave desired by nearly all the male characters. Abra Mule is sold into the emperor's seraglio just prior to the beginning of the first act, and her attachment to the noble Pyrrhus is threatened at every turn.

Since the 1698–99 season, the evidence of the printed texts suggests that productions identified as tragedies had become increasingly modest in their use of music. Tragedies at Lincoln's Inn Fields remained slightly more likely to use music and to include more musical events than those staged at Drury Lane; however, the small number of new tragedies premiered during these seasons makes the evidence less than conclusive. It certainly suggests a drawing away from musical events within the dramatic structure, and this general trend can easily be seen in the post-1705 tragedies of Rowe.

The prologue promises that the author, relying on his own powers, has not stooped to any dramatic tricks, and it is surprisingly accurate about the music:

> ... 'tis pure Tragedy which he prepares,
> With no relieving Interval of Farce.
> Nay, but one Song; his Numbers rarely chime,
> Nor bless the Gall'ries with the Sweets of Rhime.
> Few Actors are to fall, no Ghosts to rise;
> No Fustian roars, nor mimick Lightning flies; [39]

---

[38] See Shirley Strum Kenny, *The Plays of Richard Steele* (Oxford, 1971), p. 105.

[39] Joseph Trapp, *Abra-Mule* (London, 1704), prologue, lines 13–18.

If Trapp takes after any earlier Lincoln's Inn Fields productions, it is the exotic splendor of Manley's *The Royal Mischief* and the musically conservative tragedies of Congreve, Gildon, and Otway.

Virtually all of the music associated with the production survives: instrumental music by John Lenton, published in *Harmonia Anglicana*, and the song by Benjamin Short (possibly another violinist). The overture is charming, and both it and what appear to have been the act tunes are in the appropriately solemn and sweet key of C minor. The presumed first and second music are in F major, including a courtly minuet and gracious sarabande, ending with a lively jig.[40]

Despite the best efforts of Pyrrhus and his friend the Kistler Aga, Superintendant of the seraglio, in Act III the emperor becomes curious about his beautiful new acquisition and orders Abra Mule brought to "the pleasant Grotto near the Palace," where like Jove he "enjoys the Sweets of Love."[41] The following act (Act IV) opens in the pleasant grotto. The emperor's brother enters and hides to "listen to the Sultan's Courtship," having already made advances to Abra Mule himself. He is followed by the Kistler Aga and Abra Mule:

> Enter Eunuchs with six Women of the *Seraglio*: The *Kistler* places them with *Abra*. Then enter *Mahomet*, and seats himself.
> *A Symphony of soft Musick; after which this Song.*
> Happy Monarch, who with Beauty
>   Tiresome Cares of State beguiles;
> Whose Fair Subjects pay their Duty
>   In Consenting Looks and Smiles:
> Who from the noisy Battle comes,
> From the shrill Trumpet's Clangor, and the thund'ring Drums;
> With Love's soft Accents to compose
>   His Passion, ruffled by his Foes.
> And happy she whose Eyes can dart
>   A killing shaft to reach his Heart:
> For sure more Glory can no Female have,
> Than She whose Charms this Conqu'ror can enslave:
> Who the World's Lord her fighting Captive views,
> And in their mighty Monarch all Mankind subdues.
> [After the Song, the Sultan rises, and singles out *Abra*: Eunuchs go off with the rest of the Women: The *Kistler* retires to a Corner of the Stage.[42]

Following the song, the emperor questions Abra Mule's downcast looks and promises her whatever she asks—she of course immediately asks to be dismissed

---

[40] For more on the instrumental music, including excerpts, see *Music Productions LIF*, pp. 706–7 and 823–6.

[41] *Abra Mule*, p. 35.

[42] Ibid., p. 37, italics reversed.

from court. The scene continues with some classic Bracegirdle special pleading, repeatedly kneeling and insisting that she prizes her "Honour" above all. Moved, the emperor swears to marry her and make her his empress, then sends her away.

The song "Happy Monarch, who with Beauty" survives in a single songsheet[43] revealing its composer, and performer Mr Cook. A recent acquisition by the Lincoln's Inn Fields company, at this time Cook was performing extensively between acts and in concerts.

As it is printed in the play text, the song spends eight lines celebrating the emperor, the "Happy Monarch" who can escape the cares of military action and diplomacy with his "Fair Subjects," and then six lines addressing the "happy she" who can charm the monarch. However, Short did not set the final four lines, ending instead with "a killing shaft to reach his heart." Short's setting emphasizes the martial far more than the seductive, and begins briskly for a song following a "soft symphony."[44] The words "a killing shaft" are repeated no less than seven times, but this is pure musical hyperbole: in *Abra Mule*, despite a great deal of threatened violence, when the emperor is deposed, he is merely led away to prison.

Two weeks after the successful premiere of *Abra Mule*, Drury Lane mounted *Love the Leveller; or, The Pretty Purchase*, a tragicomedy by "G.B." The setting is said to be ancient Crete, but the chocolate house scene in Act V explodes the pretense, utterly unconvincing even by contemporary standards.[45] In the comic portion of the play, the non-noble Sordico is asked to pimp his wife to a lord, and she resists. In Act II, Sordico has a "singing-man" visit and sing him a song, which apparently makes him feel better about prostituting his wife, though we are not told which song has that Collier-like power. On the serious side, the duchess Semorin provides two musical entertainments to divert Princess Constantia, who is in love with the heroic but only recently ennobled Andramont, making the caste-conscious members of the Cretan court and royal family furious. The first entertainment is apparently a masque, "The SCENE Draws, and Discovers *Venus* sitting on a Couch, and Four Cupids standing round her. An Entertainment of Musick and Dancing" (Act II, 19, italics reversed), and the second an unspecified song and dance (Act V, 60). These musical numbers could easily have been recycled from previous productions, and only a song by Leveridge has even a

---

[43] A Thomas Cross, junior, songsheet from the Rowe Music Library, King's College, Cambridge. Although the songsheet gives the vocal line in treble clef, it does not rise above f#^{II} and would not cross the bass line if transposed down an octave.

[44] For more about this song and a transcription, see *Music Productions LIF*, pp. 700–706.

[45] The author insists that the murderous, hypocritical priests of "Senphan" are not meant to suggest any "Christian Brotherhood" despite clear reference to the Gunpowder Plot.

tentative connection to the play.[46] The author's benefit was on the second night, and the play retired into well-deserved oblivion.

The next new production staged at Lincoln's Inn Fields, *Liberty Asserted*, was a serious play by John Dennis, again with instrumental music by Lenton. In Dennis's play, military conflicts in Canada between the Iroquois nations, the French, and the English are largely reduced to heroic individual maneuvers—Elizabeth Barry playing a Huron princess captured by the Iroquois, but eventually reunited with the long-absent father of her child, now the governor of "new France." Although set in the same key as the tunes for *Abra Mule*, Lenton's music for *Liberty Asserted* provides an interesting contrast. The two overtures are perceptibly different and instead of an exotic sarabande and courtly minuet, the *Liberty Asserted* set includes a more robust assortment of tunes: two jigs, a hornpipe, a rigaudon (a folk-like French dance), a "Trumpet Aire" in C major and a "Scotch Malancholly Aire."[47]

John Banks's tragedy *The Albion Queens*, a revision of his twenty-year-old play *The Island Queens*, premiered two weeks after Dennis's tragedy. It went head to head with the Lincoln's Inn Fields production on several evenings, until both companies began to alternate their new tragedies with performances of stock comedies. If, like *Love the Leveller*, this was another Patent Company attempt to compete against its rival's new production, it was far more successful.

In romanticizing the conflict between Elizabeth I and Mary Queen of Scots, Banks manages to present a sympathetic vision of both Queen Anne's great-grandmother and the English queen to whom Anne was so often compared by English panegyrists, although Mary Stuart, as usual, gets the lion's share of sympathy. Like Dennis's *Liberty Asserted*, Banks's tragedy uses music sparingly. Only two scenes in the play call for music, the reconciliation scene at the end of Act III, featuring "Harmony of Drums and Trumpets" as the two queens (friends for the moment) are acclaimed by all, and a scene in the middle of the final act, as Mary prepares for execution. Printer Richard Wellington published a prompter's copy, revealing how many lines in advance it was necessary to get "Soft Musick ready with Flutes" (57) before the scene opens, revealing the Queen of Scots (Anne Oldfield) kneeling upstage. The music is doubtless meant to heighten the pathos of this scene, as well as providing time for the audience to gaze at the actress in this attractive posture,[48] and it is particularly poignant within the context of the previous musical scene. At the end of Act III, Elizabeth I had promised her newly

---

[46] The song, "Whilst health and blooming youth combine," with the heading "A SONG in the Play call'd the Leveller Sung by Mr Leveridge," appeared in Walsh's *Monthly Mask* for December 1710.

[47] The addition of "melancholy" to the title is a necessary indication of mood, since on the page, except for the mode, the piece looks as lively as any of the composer's other "Scotch" airs.

[48] See Jean Marsden, *Fatal Desire*, pp. 66–8, particularly her analysis of Edward Young's account of Lady Jane Grey, and the "ideal male fantasy" of the beautiful woman spied on at prayer.

reconciled cousin the restoration of all her royal prerogatives, and instructed "Soft Musick Sound, where e're she wakes or sleeps,/ Music as Sweet, Harmonious, and as still/ As does this soft and gentle Bosom fill" (Act III, 36).

The act music by John Barrett offers some evidence of the production having been hastily revised and mounted. As published in *Harmonia Anglicana*, the three-part overture is in the incongruously bright key of D major, with fanfare-like opening and closing sections, whereas all of the shorter pieces, which would be used between the acts or in the first and second music, are in C minor, which certainly seems more appropriate to the play but is harmonically distant from the key of the overture. This suggests that the overture and the tunes were written for different occasions. Curtis Price notes a concordance between one of the tunes and the 1702 anthology *The Harpsichord Master*, which supports the idea that Barrett was reworking earlier material.[49] Given the limited remuneration for music, it should not be surprising how often composers' theater pieces were used and reused in (or borrowed from) other publications.

New productions for February and March 1704 also included another of the increasingly frequent subscription concerts, this time featuring a musical entertainment by Motteux titled *Britain's Happiness*. The advertised performance at Drury Lane in February used music composed by John Weldon (vocal) and Charles Dieupart (instrumental), while attendees in March at the Lincoln's Inn Fields performance heard music by Leveridge.

In his letter to the reader Motteux relates how the text came to be set twice:

> This Interlude was long since design'd only for an Introduction to an Opera, which, if ever finish'd, may be call'd, The Loves of *Europe*, every Act shewing the manner of a different Nation, in their Addresses to the Fair Sex. But some Persons of Quality who did not know that Mr *Leveridge*, had set this Part of it to Musick, having engaged Mr *Weldon* to put Notes to it; I am oblig'd to let it appear without the rest. There is room indeed in this for Great Musick, but much more for Humour, and every Passion in those that were to follow. I could wish they might have appeared all together, but 'tis the desire of those Persons, to whom I must submit, that this should be perform'd in the mean time. They will at least have the satisfaction of Hearing fine Music, and observing how the same Words may be admirably set i[n] a different manner, when two Masters exert their Genius, to please and to excel.[50]

Despite the disclaimers in the prologue, where Motteux insists that the two settings were made by accident, it's hard not to wonder if this was Motteux's answer to Congreve's *The Judgment of Paris*.

---

[49] See Price, *Music in the Restoration Theatre*, p. 145.

[50] Motteux, *Britain's Happiness. A Musical Interlude. Perform'd at both the Theatres Being Part of the Entertainment Subscrib'd for by the Nobility* (London, 1704), unpaginated, italics reversed.

Britain's Happiness compares favorably with earlier Motteux efforts, from *The Taking of Namur* to *Acis and Galatea*. While the interlude contains some typical "Motteuxisms," on the whole the gods Pallas and Neptune are treated much more seriously than, say, Mars and Venus. It opens with a "Prospect of Dover-Castle and the Sea"—an unusually specific setting, and one quite appropriate to Motteux's joint projects of emphasizing Queen Anne's dominion on the seas and her power overseas.

In many ways *Britain's Happiness* resembles *Europe's Revels* (LIF, 1697) in miniature, explicitly celebrating the sovereign in a way the other masques and interludes, like those in *The Island Princess*, do not. Here Motteux places more emphasis on the choruses and (at least on the page) ensemble numbers rather than on solos. As in *Europe's Revels*, a "Dance of several Nations" demonstrates the English ruler's international power and is followed by the rustic songs and dances of the simple folk of England, here both sailors and "clowns" (rustics), each with his lass. *Britain's Happiness* lacks a conventional Motteux salacious-comic dialogue. Instead, the musical dialogue between Neptune and Pallas is cast as a debate between Passion (Neptune's rage) and Reason, as Neptune must be reconciled to Queen Anne's power over his domain. In the end the god of the sea acknowledges her just claims and the interlude closes with a grand chorus.

Three songs by Weldon were printed in Walsh's *Monthly Mask of Vocal Music*, "as sung in the Subscription Musick," providing information about the cast not listed elsewhere. Although Motteux's libretto describes the first song as a solo, Weldon set the verse "Happy *Britains*, seated here" as a two-part song, which, according to the libretto, is echoed by a chorus. A solo by tenor John Davis, "The Welfare of All on blest *ANNA* depends," is the second movement of the following three-part piece for two officers who sing "with Glasses in their Hands." A song for Dogget is part of the rustic English entertainment following the dance of several nations. His song "Just coming from Sea/ Our Spouses and we," uses simple melodic sequences and includes a calling pattern ("Hey, hey, hey, hey, hey my brave boys") like previous songs for Dogget. This comic song for a sailor fit audience tastes. A setting of this verse by Leveridge also survives, the only music known from his version of the entertainment.[51]

Other spring premieres at Lincoln's Inn Fields included David Craufurd's comedy *Love at First Sight*, and the farce *Squire Trelooby*, a collaboration between Congreve, Vanbrugh, and William Walsh. While the prologue claims "He 'as larded his supply [of wit], with Song and Dance" (line 9), Craufurd's comedy is of limited interest musically. Rambunctious Hector Single sings snatches of drinking songs at the end of the first act (with "Violons and Hooboys at some Distance") and the third ("The Smiles of the Glass/ Invite our Approach"), dancing and singing until his companions join in. In Act V the witty Melissa (Mrs Prince) sings at least

---

[51] Printed as part of a collection in 1709, probably available as a songsheet previously, see Hunter 56 (5). Weldon's setting was included by Walsh in a collection of sea songs in 1720 (Hunter 109).

one line, "Just so the Panting Shepherd lay," to mock her lover Courtly and Hector chimes in with the "Fal—ara tal dal" from his drinking song. At the end of Act IV the old reprobate Sir John Single, Hector's father, calls for a song and dance (unspecified) to keep his drunken son entertained, and the play ends, inevitably, with "one Dance before we go to Dinner." The only extant music, "The rosy morn looks blith and gay," a simple "Scotch" song sung by Hodgson and composed by Clarke, may have been performed in Act IV.

In contrast to Craufurd's effort, *Squire Trelooby* contains some hilariously funny and up-to-date scenes of music making. An adaptation of Molière's *Monsieur de Pourceaugnac*, the contemporary play text is the translation not by the Kit-Cat Club collaborators but by another gentleman. In the printed version, music and dancing occurs at the end of every act—Italian at the end of Act I, French at the end of Act II, and "several Masks &c." (presumably English) at the end of Act III.

In the first act the very confused Squire Trelooby has been placed in the care of physicians by a London "friend."

> Mr. *Gellier* and another Musician (habited like Physicians *à la grotesque*, follow'd by eight Buffoon-Dancers) sing the following words in *Italian*, with Instrumental Musick.[52]
> *The 2 Musicians sitting down on Chairs on each side the Squire.*
> 2. *Musicians.*
> BON di, Bon di, Bon di,   [*They rise and*
> Non vi lasciate uccidere,   [*bow to him.*
> Dal Dolor Melanconico,
> Noi vi faremo ridere,
> Col nostro Canto harmonico,
>   Sol' per guarirvi
>   Siamo venuti qui,
> Bon di, Bon di, Bon di.   [*They rise and bow to him.*

This is followed by solos for each, "Altro non è la pazzia" and "Su, cantate, ballate, ridete." In the printed edition, the Italian song is followed by a (fairly accurate) rhymed English translation, "lest some People shou'd think there's more matter in't than really there is."[53] At the very end of the act the musicians and dancers encircle the squire, singing to him like Italian mountebanks, attempting

---

[52] Mr Gellier is almost certainly London theater composer Mr Gillier, but as previously noted, not the better-known Jean-Claude Gillier. In the original Molière *comédie-ballet*, Lully played one of the doctors. John S. Powell, *Music and Theatre in France, 1600–1680* (Oxford, 2000), p. 405.

[53] Without text repetitions, the translation reads: Good morrow, Sir, Kill not your self with Grief, Nor be cast down with Sorrow. We're come to your Relief, With Bagpipe and with Fief, Good Morrow, Sir, Good Morrow. After this duet, the first musician (still

to make him take one of the apothecary's treatments—he escapes, "taking up the Chair he sits upon, …. to defend his Posteriors."

The singers at the end of Act II are "Councellors Musicians, one whereof speaks slow, and the other very fast, attended by two Attorneys and two Apparitors." They sing in French, "La Polygamie est un cas," in a manner which perfectly prefigures W. S. Gilbert, particularly *Trial by Jury*, with its catalog of famous legal authors (original English "translation" below):

> *1. Councellor drawling his Words, sings.*
> Poly—gamy is a Crime, a—Crime of Death Ca—pable.
> Poly—gamy is a Crime, a—Crime that is Hang—able.
> *2. Councellor precipitating his Words, sings.*
> The Case is plain,
> And you in vain,
> The Fact maintain!   [*Staring on Trel.*
> Search all Reports,
> And Rules of Courts,
>   Commentators,
>   Legislators,
>   And Glossators.
> Ulpian, and Papinian,
> Tribonian, and Justinian,
>   John Imolus,
>   And Bartholus,
> Cook, Plowden, and Keeble,
> Who in Law are not feeble—[54]
>   Search all their Common-places—
> Polygamy's a Tyburn-Case, a Case to make wry Faces—
> *[He mimicks a Man hanging to Trel.*

Alas, no music for *Squire Trelooby* is known to survive. As part of the Subscription Musick, it was first performed with "select comedians from both houses" (including Dogget, Bracegirdle, Betterton, Cibber, Penkethman), together with singing by Tofts, Leveridge, and Lindsey, and dancing by the French masters (L'Abbé, Du Ruel, Cherrier) and others. Later in the spring and summer the farce was performed with Eccles's music for the Queen's birthday and "Henry Purcell's

---

singing) orders Trelooby not to be melancholy. The second prescribes singing, dancing, laughing—and drinking and smoking. *Squire Trelooby* (London, 1704), pp. 23–5.

[54] Cook is Sir Edward Coke (1552–1634) the famous jurist, referred to in several contemporary comedies. Notes on the song can be found in Montague Summers' edition of Congreve's *Works* (New York, 1964), vol. 3, pp. 224–5. Original text, *Squire Trelooby* (London, 1704), pp. 43–5.

Figure 6.1   J. Eccles, "In vain malicious Fate contrives" in *The Rival Brothers*

The Four Seasons," a masque from Act IV of *The Fairy Queen*, during benefit nights for Bracegirdle and another actress.[55]

In the midst of its spring comedies, Lincoln's Inn Fields did not neglect serious plays. The anonymous *The Rival Brothers; or, A Fatal Secret*, probably performed this spring, uses the same basic plot as Otway's popular 1680 tragedy *The Orphan*. Two brothers love the same woman, Victoria. One marries her secretly and, through deception, the other spends her wedding night with her, committing incest as well as fornication. When the truth is revealed the results are self-banishment, death by broken heart, and suicide.

The only musical event called for in the text is a conventional pastoral entertainment ("A Dance of Sheppards and Nymphs," 27) during a banquet at the end of the second act, before the fatal night. However, Elizabeth Willis performed a song in *The Rival Brothers*, "In vain malicious Fate contrives/ To make a Wretch of him that loves." Willis probably played either Sylvia or Lucy, attendants to the lead female characters. The text of the song ("in Love I cou'd out rival Anthony") resembles a speech given by the secret husband, Theodor, at the end of Act I, when he insists on the power of love to combat "malicious Fortune" (14). If not performed during the Act II banquet scene, Eccles's song would make dramatic sense inserted here. It is more vocally elaborate than most songs written for Willis (Figure 6.1), and if the singer's name is not an error on engraver Thomas Cross's part, it would be interesting to know why it was not given to a professional singer, either Hodgson (who often sang 'male' texts) or Davis.

Lincoln's Inn Fields' usual summer comedy was William Walker's *The Wit of a Woman*. The farce, performed with Dryden's tragedy *The Spanish Fryar*, seems Walker's most successful dramatic effort: the action is lively, and the overwrought pastoral dialogue between the servants Flash and Liddy, parodying the "Road of Courtship" between genteel lovers (4) was doubtless played for all it was worth. Walker's farce is not lavish in its use of music. The song Liddy sings to amuse her mistress in Act II, "Love is a pretty, pretty Thing," sounds like the usual sweet tune for Mrs Prince or Elizabeth Willis. There is instrumental music and a dance by house guests in Act III, during which the hero and heroine sneak away to be married. During the summer Drury Lane revived some of its older farces, *The Fond Husband* and *The Emperor of the Moon*, possibly to counteract *Squire Trelooby* and Walker's new show.

Revivals, 1703–1704

Records of numerous revivals at both theaters exist for the 1703–1704 season, particularly for the spring and summer months. These were usually advertised with a great deal of additional music and several dance numbers.

In September 1703 Lincoln's Inn Fields opened their new season with a series of revivals, mainly plays over twenty years old. Bills promised new prologues

---

[55] M&H *London Stage*, pp. 167, 169.

and epilogues, singing and dancing. At the end of October, the company revived Congreve's *The Double Dealer*, with music by "Signior Olsii, lately come from Italy."

The Patent Company resumed acting on 6 October, after performing at Bath while the queen was there. Throughout the season, they kept up a brisk rotation of their successes from earlier in the decade: *Oroonoko*, *Love's Last Shift*, *Love Makes a Man*, *The Relapse*, *The Funeral*, *The Pilgrim*, *The Constant Couple*, and the recent comic hit *Tunbridge Walks*.

A song from Shadwell's *Timon of Athens*, "Alas here lies the poor Alonzo slain," composed by Clarke and sung by Mary Hodgson, was printed in *The Monthly Mask of Vocal Music* for January 1704.[56] The timing of the song's appearance in print, together with Hodgson's performance, indicates that it was performed at Lincoln's Inn Fields on 27 January, although Clarke had previously composed for the rival theater. *Timon of Athens* was performed at Drury Lane the following month, advertised with singing by Leveridge, and had been regularly revived by them using "the Original Masque, set to Musick by the late Mr Henry Purcell."[57]

Macbeth, with the music by Leveridge, was regularly revived at Drury Lane, consistently advertised with his music and him performing. In 1704 the production seems to have included a new song by Daniel Purcell, "Cease, gentle swain, thy am'rous suit forbear," published in the February *Monthly Mask of Vocal Musick*. Any connection between the song text and the play would be a stretch. It was likely sung before or after the performance or between the acts.

Near the end of January, the Lincoln's Inn Fields company offered the amazing triple bill of *The Anatomist* and *The Loves of Mars and Venus* together with *Dido and Aeneas*, perhaps as an afterpiece. Recombining the successful double production of November 1696 with the Tate–Purcell piece which had been shaped into a similarly structured relationship with Gildon's *Measure for Measure* in February 1700 would have resulted in a heavily musical evening. Although the tragedy of Dido seems to contrast rather oddly with the comic atmosphere created by the other works, the combination of light-hearted musical acts with tragedies—like Elizabeth Willis's comic songs at a production of Lee's *Caesar Borgia* in June 1704 or a comic dialogue in *Othello* in February—was not unheard of.

On 6 February, both companies contributed to a gala performance of Dryden's *All for Love* at court in honor of the queen's birthday, including musical dialogues sung by Leveridge and Hodgson from *King Arthur* and *The Lover's Luck* (LIF, 1695), and dancing by l'Abbé, Miss Campion, Cherrier, Du Ruel, Mrs Elford, and Mrs

---

[56] While Hodgson appeared in concerts with DL performers and sang songs by composers like Weldon who were associated with the rival house, there is no evidence that she sang there after the UC split, whereas her important musical role in most productions at LIF is well documented.

[57] It was advertised several times from 1703 to 1705. See M&H *London Stage*, pp. 102, 132, 198, 206.

Mayers, concluding with a "Grand Spanish Dance" for six.[58] Drury Lane was quick to capitalize on this, the next day promising audiences the same dances "perform'd yesterday before Her Majesty at St. James's."[59] Additional musical highlights for this month included another appearance of *The Anatomist* paired with *The Loves of Mars and Venus* (a benefit for John Bowman) and Nahum Tate's *A Duke and No Duke* with *Acis and Galatea* "and the other Musical Entertainments that were perform'd in *The Mad Lovers* [sic]."[60] Drury Lane promised new Italian songs composed by Greber for Margarita de l'Epine and a new sonata performed by Gasperini.

The Patent Company continued to revive old favorites, often with singing by Leveridge and 'comick' or 'grotesque' dancing. March and April productions at Lincoln's Inn Fields included their new tragedy successes, *Liberty Asserted* and *Abra Mule*, alternating with considerably more shopworn comedies.[61] The schedule of productions from April 1704 continues to be dominated by revivals, although it is interesting that, for the dates we know the productions at both theaters, they often seem to be in generic competition, placing tragedy against tragedy and comedy against comedy. The only innovations at either house are in the musical entertainments: an unusual seven-man consort of "Hautboys, Flutes, and German Horns" composed and performed by Johann Christoph Pepusch and his brother Gottfried. The consort appeared throughout the month with performances of *The Cautious Coxcomb*, *Tamerlane*, *The Anatomist*, and *She Wou'd if She Cou'd*.

Fletcher and Rowley's *The Maid in the Mill* is first listed at Lincoln's Inn Fields during this month, but, as previously mentioned, it had probably been performed in the autumn of 1702. In April 1704 the play was advertised with a "Scotch Song in Praise of a Highland Laird; and follow'd by a *Grand Dance* of the Laird and his Highland Attendance [sic]; with several other *Scotch Dances* and Songs in and between the Acts."[62] The play was revived again in July 1704, "made into a Farce of three Acts," accompanied with three dialogues, including the perennially popular "Now Women I scorn you," with Bowman and Dogget (in drag), and "Hark you Madam" from *Love's a Jest* (now eight years old).[63]

The "Scotch" songs and dances regularly advertised at Lincoln's Inn Fields in March and April always appeared on nights a stock comedy was being performed. Dryden's *The Spanish Fryar* was advertised with singing by John Bowman (the perennially popular "Let the dreadful engines of eternal will" from *Don Quixote*), Willis (a "Scotch" song, perhaps "Ken you who comes here, the Laird of aw the

---

[58] Full program in M&H *London Stage*, pp. 145–6.
[59] Ibid., p. 146.
[60] Ibid., p. 147.
[61] The act tunes by William Gorton for Fletcher's *The Humorous Lieutenant* are probably from a DL revival (summer 1697). See Price, *Music in the Restoration Theatre*, pp. 178–9. No extant music is associated with the 1704 LIF revival.
[62] M&H *London Stage*, p. 164.
[63] Ibid., p. 175.

Clan"), Hodgson, Davis, and Cook, as well as dancing between the acts.[64] Two pieces of music by Eccles are attributed to this play: a chorus, "Look down ye blest above" (preserved in manuscript), and a song for Mary Hodgson, "Silvia how cou'd you e're mistrust," printed in his 1704 *Collection*. Since the play was a stock piece, and the repertoire copied in GB-Lbl Add. MS 29378 written before 1700, only the song could have been composed for this revival, although both pieces of music may have been used in 1704.[65] Another stock play revived this month, for which an Eccles song of uncertain date exists, was Etherege's *She Wou'd if She Could*. A song in Act V, "To little or no purpose I spent many days," sung by Bracegirdle, is included in Eccles's *Collection*.

May 1704 saw more revivals—Shadwell, Shakespeare, Dryden—and the return of *Squire Trelooby*. Amongst the revivals, Shadwell's *Don John; or, The Libertine Destroy'd* offers the most numerous opportunities for music making. The first act includes two serenades with fiddlers, and in the second Don John calls the musicians onstage to sing his epithalamium, celebrating his seven marriages, "When with one my stomach is cloy'd,/Another shall soon be enjoy'd." In Act III, two Spanish ladies privately sing a protest against the sexual double standard, and in the fourth, an extended pastoral scene calls for a "symphony of rustic music" with songs and dances. Act V calls for a chorus of devils as the wicked Don descends to hell in fire and thunder. The "proper Musick and Dances" performed at Lincoln's Inn Fields probably included Eccles's two-part song "What's Love, 'tis all o're a deceit," which uses the same gastronomical metaphor as the Don does—Celia is informed she's no feast, just "a slender disert." Eccles clothes these rakish sentiments in bright C major and a rollicking 6/4 meter, concluding with a typical drinking song pattern.

John Wilford's song "In vain I hope to find relief" may also have been performed, possibly during one of the Act I serenades. Wilford's portentous, highly ornamented call to "pale Tyrant" Death (Figure 6.2) could be sung ironically, intended to manipulate its female auditor into giving way (Don John's song), or as a serious evocation of hopeless passion (Don Octavio's). The swift changes in meter in the later sections of the piece suggest a mad song.

Other numbers in *The Libertine* at Lincoln's Inn Fields may well have been recycled using similar ones from other previous productions. The advertisement does not suggest that either the original music by William Turner or Henry Purcell's music for the 1695 Drury Lane revival were heard. At the end of the month, the Patent Company advertised *The Libertine Destroy'd* to be performed with Henry Purcell's original music, a move which, like their revival of Shadwell's *Timon of Athens* with Purcell's masque, seems clearly competitive.

During this season there were no new dramatick operas composed for the theaters. Even more unusually, there were no revivals staged until 9 June, when Drury Lane offered Shadwell's *Psyche*, featuring the original music by Matthew Locke, the "chief

---

[64] On 29 April 1704. See M&H *London Stage*, p. 165.

[65] Price discusses the extant music for Dryden's play (including pieces by Eccles) in *Henry Purcell and the London Stage*, pp. 86–9.

Figure 6.2   J. Wilford, "In vain I hope to find relief" from *The Libertine*

Characters" sung by Leveridge, and dancing by Cherrier, Du Ruel, and La Forrest: "the first Performance of an Opera this Year."[66]

More complete descriptions of the entertainments offered at Lincoln's Inn Fields become available for the summer of 1704. Elizabeth Willis's name is especially prominent,[67] as are those of the dancers Clark, Evans, and Fairbank. Even first-rank players like John Bowman and Thomas Dogget occasionally appear to sing a song—sometimes together, a certain crowd pleaser. Several advertisements promise comic songs by Dogget, Willis (imitating an old woman or a "turkey-cock"), and Bowman—at the end of the summer Dogget and Willis would take their material to Bartholomew Fair.

Final Flings: The 1704–1705 Season

During the autumn and winter, as the regular season began and benefit productions ceased, newspaper advertisements describing musical entertainments at Drury Lane are fairly common though often unspecific ("several entertainments of music and dancing"), while those at Lincoln's Inn Fields are sketchy. Whether this represented an actual reduction or change in the type of such entertainments from the summer offerings cannot be definitely determined, although during the regular season the special attractions of French dancers and Italian singers may have taken the place of some of the native talents touted during the summer.

As in the previous season, revivals with various "entertainments" of music and dancing predominated at Lincoln's Inn Fields, though they continued their previous season's string of successful new farces with *The Metamorphosis*. Again the Patent Company was slow to stage new productions. Although it began acting in September, audiences were regaled for three months with a judicious mixture of stock favorites, some (like Richard Brome's *The Northern Lass*) quite old.

New Productions

During the winter months, Drury Lane had another new comedy by Cibber to compete with Rowe's first (and only) attempt at comedy. Rich and his company scored a coup when they acquired Clayton's English-language Italian-style opera *Arsinoe*, originally intended for the new Haymarket theater, which over time proved a stunning success.

The season began more conventionally with new plays at Lincoln's Inn Fields, as shown in Table 6.2. John Corey's farce *The Metamorphosis* was staged in October, and appears to have been fairly well liked. Taking his cue from the summer shows, Corey took care to include a great deal of music in an emphatically comic vein, and

---

[66] M&H, *London Stage*, p. 170.
[67] She appears to have had a surprising two benefits (one 30 June and one 24 July), both shared with "Mr Short." M&H *London Stage*, pp. 172, 174. There were several Shorts at LIF.

to fulfill the promise of his prologue to keep it short! An excerpt from what must have been a high point of the production was printed in the *Monthly Mask of Vocal Music* for November 1704. Titled simply "The Conjurer's SONG" in Walsh's periodical, "Hail Powers beneath! Whose Influence imparts" is Eccles's setting of the first verse of a song parodying the musical incantations of tragedy and dramatick opera.

Table 6.2 New productions during the 1704–1705 season

	New works for the Patent Company		New works at Lincoln's Inn Fields and the Haymarket	
AUTUMN			*The Metamorphosis*	Farce
			Zelmane	Tragedy
			The Biter	Comedy
WINTER	*The Careless Husband*	Comedy		
	Arsinoe	Opera	*The Gamester*	Comedy
	Farewel Folly + *The Mountebank*	Comedy + Interlude		
	Gibraltar	Comedy		
SPRING	*The Quacks*	Comedy		
			[*Gli Amori d'Ergasto*	Italian opera][a]
	The Tender Husband	Comedy	*The Consultation*	Farce
			The Conquest of Spain	Tragedy
SUMMER			*The Cares of Love*	Comedy

Note: ᵃ In brackets because the LIF company did not perform in the opera, though Anne Bracegirdle spoke Congreve's epilogue for the production.

Corey's farce is built around the character Sir Credulous Mammon, who bears a strong family resemblance to Sir Nicholas Gimcrack (*The Virtuoso*) and Foresight (*Love for Love*). This gullible gentleman is manipulated by the sharper Trickwell, "a Pretender to Astrology." In Act I, Sir Credulous visits the astrologer's house, where Trickwell's assistant shows him various enchanted objects, including an "Astrascope," a magical telescope wherein Nickum pretends to see events abroad. In Muscovy, he claims, the Czar and Prince Alexander are "in their Wast-coats and Drawers, hard at Work with the Shipwrights" (7). This is no more than anyone could glean from international reports in the newspapers, but Sir Credulous is extremely impressed.

The wonders of the Astrascope are matched by the Otocausticon, which allows the wearer to hear things at a distance and which Nickum kindly allows Sir Credulous to test himself. Hidden from his view Nickum laughs, explaining "That comes from the Playhouse at *Drury Lane*," then "squalls," explaining "That's an *Italian* Singer, mightily in Vogue at a Consort in *York-Buildings*," and finally cues some offstage assistants for "Drums and Trumpets" which, he explains, is the noise of "The Confederate Army drawn out to Storm *Landau*" (8).

When Trickwell finally makes his appearance as "the great Alcantara," he promises Sir Credulous "a Taste of my Art," conjuring up spirits to perform a musical entertainment, including a dance and a song by bass Mr Cook, a parody of musical incantation scenes in serious productions. The most famous example was (and is) the often reprinted "Conjurer's Song" from *The Indian Queen*, "You twice ten hundred Deities," set by Henry Purcell. Purcell's song was strongly identified with performer Richard Leveridge, star of the rival house. Cook had a varied repertoire of songs of his own, but in this piece he had the opportunity to 'out-Leveridge Leveridge.'

> Hail Powers beneath! Whose Influence imparts,
>   The Knowledge of Infernal Arts;
> By whose un-erring Gifts we move,
>   To alter the Decrees above:
> Whether on Earth, or Seas, or Air,
>   The Mighty Miracle we dare …

The second verse refers to the sorceress Medea's transformation of age into youth, and the final verse concludes:

> Henbane, and Hemlock did the Charmer use,
>   Steep'd in Nocturnal Dews,
> With Herbs that cover'd the Deceas'd Abodes,
> The Blood of Vipers, Ravens, and of Toads;
>   And I the same Ingredients chuse,

>Oh let them not their Virtues lose;
>But the same Cause the same Effect precede,
>While I attempt as bold a Deed,
>Invoke your Help, and your Assistance crave,
>To shape into a Gentleman, a slave.[68]

Despite the conventionally gruesome lyrics, the song is definitely not supposed to scare anyone. In Eccles's setting of the first verse, a bombastic declamatory opening precedes a bouncy triple-meter air: "Whether on Earth, on Seas," etc. While it occasionally dips into minor mode, the song is predominantly in bright major, emphasizing its humor.[69] The final lines refer to Alcantara's agreement to transform Sir Credulous's servant Roger into his neighbor Old Traffick, a wealthy merchant. Roger (as Traffick) will then give his master, Credulous, Traffick's beautiful daughter in marriage.

The dance that followed was undoubtedly also a comic parody, probably a grotesque dance with deliberately awkward gestures. The "spirits" are supposed to be men from the stews of London, not airy beings. There is another potentially parodic moment when the servant Roger, drunk, enters singing "She's but a Woman, what care I" (Act V, 53), lines from Henry Purcell's song "Take not a Woman's Anger Ill," originally sung by Leveridge in *The Rival Sisters* (PC, 1695).

Leveridge sang virtually every night at Drury Lane during the 1703–1704 season, and this looks like an attempt by Lincoln's Inn Fields to match the Patent Company's comic quotations and imitations of Bracegirdle and Bowman. The musical scene is dramatically superfluous, but its comedic elements worked on at least two levels, mocking the fondness of the gullible for threadbare theatrical enchantments and Leveridge's usual 'lines' in performance. In the final scene Old Traffick graciously forgives Sir Credulous and invites him to "a small Entertainment" along with the young lovers. What sort of "Musick" was performed is not specified. As in other recent productions, a selection of the latest vocal or instrumental music, with one or two favorite pieces (perhaps more Purcell), would have been included.

Corey's farce was followed in November by an unsuccessful play attributed to Mary Pix, *Zelmane; or, The Corinthian Queen*, a politically timely example of a proud but virtuous and forgiving monarch. Barring some conventional language and a single trumpet call, there is no music indicated in the printed text, even in scenes which would usually require it; as when Princess Antimora muses alone at the opening of Act III.

Nicholas Rowe's sole attempt at comedy, *The Biter*, premiered at the end of November. Despite an all-star cast and songs by John Eccles, including a musical

---

[68] [John Corey], *The Metamorphosis: or, The Old Lover Out-witted. A Farce* (London, 1704), pp. 14–15.

[69] For the music (first verse only), see Baldwin and Wilson, *The Monthly Mask of Vocal Music*, no. 88.

dialogue featuring Anne Bracegirdle, it failed to win over its audiences.[70] Soon the company was alternating it with revivals of the previous season's hit, *Abra Mule*.

The 'biter' (spoofer) of the title is the uncouth Squire Pinch (actor-singer George Pack), whose obstreperous pursuit of amusement is curtailed by the witty Mariana (Bracegirdle) and the East India merchant Sir Timothy Tallapoy (Betterton). Tallapoy is the father of the woman Pinch is supposed to be marrying, and interested in Mariana himself. Compared with more recent comedies, *The Biter* suggests a return to the musical practices of the early seasons of competition. It is discussed at greater length in Chapter One.

In December, the Patent Company had a new comedy of its own from Colley Cibber, one of its most reliable actor-playwrights. In Cibber's *The Careless Husband* Wilks played the male lead as the constantly straying Sir Charles Easy. However, he is only once indicated as singing, and there is only one musical event noted. The epilogue complains stridently about music, particularly the Subscription Musick concerts:

> We're still in Fears (as you of late from *France*)
> Of the Despotick Power of Song and Dance:
> For while Subscription, like a Tyrant reigns,
> Nature's Neglected, and the *Stage* in Chains.[71]

Although no musical entertainments were advertised with it during its opening performances, by the eighth day it was accompanied by dancing by Monsieur Cherrier and instrumental music by Paisible and Bannister. By January the usual rotation of performance attractions added vocal music as well, both English and Italian, despite its caustic epilogue.

Cibber's comedy concludes, as so many recent Patent Company productions do, with a song performed by Leveridge. Set in a series of short contrasting sections by Daniel Purcell and published in *The Monthly Mask*, in this case the song, "Sabina with an Angel's Face," seems particularly out of tune with Cibber's message of reform, unlike the masque concluding *Love's Last Shift* (revived during the previous season). The too proud Sabina, rejecting her lovers, is cursed by Cupid; thus she'll age twice as fast as normal and die alone. Yet Sir Charles Easy is supposedly converted to chaste love of his wife, and to abandon his conquests, many of whom are present. Though the play was popular, audiences must have highlighted different elements of the performance: some of Sir Charles's earlier scenes and Leveridge's song are not the voice of "sentimental reform."[72]

In January 1705, Christopher Rich and the company at Drury Lane mounted the opera *Arsinoe*, leaving the Lincoln's Inn Fields company to stage a series of revivals

---

[70] Downes notes after six days "it Sicken'd and Expir'd." *Roscius Anglicanus*, p. 95.

[71] Cibber, *The Careless Husband. A Comedy* (London, 1705), epilogue lines 7–10, italics reversed.

[72] Hume, *The Development of English Drama*, p. 469.

with a patchwork of musical entertainments. The music for the opera "after the *Italian* manner" was composed by English violinist Thomas Clayton, the libretto translated from the Italian by Motteux. It has often been said that Clayton's work was "stolen" by Christopher Rich, since an opera by Clayton had been mentioned in the *Diverting Post* on 28 October 1704 as one of two operas which would be premiered in the new Haymarket Theater when it opened.[73] However, according to Clayton, "I was not able to bring my Opera of *Arsinoe* to be so much as heard, but by the Mediation of Mr. *Dupar* [Dieupart], who, for half the Profit, which came to two hundred Pounds, bustled through that Affair for me."[74] Presumably John Eccles started writing his own opera, *Semele*, similarly combining an English libretto (by Congreve) and Italianate music, around this time.[75]

The title role was sung by English soprano Catherine Tofts, the star of the Subscription Musick concert series, now at the height of her popularity. She was supported by the Patent Company's leading singers, Francis Hughes as her love interest, General Ormondo; Letitia Cross as Princess Dorisbe, "a Pretender to the Crown of *Cyprus*, in Love with *Ormondo*"; Leveridge as captain of the queen's guards, also in love with Dorisbe; with Mary Lindsey and a Mr Good playing servants.[76]

Like *The Island Princess*, *Arsinoe* was a tremendous success with contemporary audiences, although panned by most critics and historians.[77] Milhous describes Christopher Rich's decision to stage *Arsinoe* as "an experiment both cautious and daring: he minimized his [financial] outlay as much as possible, and buttressed the innovation with familiar adjuncts [dancing and singing]."[78] Although there were none of the Cecil B. De Mille tableaux and extensive use of machines found in dramatick operas like *The World in the Moon* or *The Virgin Prophetess*, Rich did invest money in his lead singer (Tofts was never cheap) and in elegant new

---

[73] Milhous and Hume, *Theatrical Documents*, no. 1782.

[74] From the preface to *The Passion of Sappho, and Feast of Alexander. Set to Musick by Mr. Thomas Clayton* (London, 1711), [iii–iv]. Quoted in "Thomas Clayton and the Introduction of Italian Opera to England," *Philological Quarterly* 77 (1998): 171–86, p. 172.

[75] For more on Eccles's *Semele*, see the edition by Richard Platt in the *Musica Britannica* series, which borrows the overture from *Rinaldo and Armida*. A recording of the recent student performance under the direction of Anthony Rooley at Florida State University is available commercially.

[76] The cast in the libretto lists "Mr. Cook or Mr. Good" in the role of Delbo; however, printed songs make it clear that Good got the part. Cook was a regular performer at LIF, and it's possible the managers there opposed his participation.

[77] McGeary has argued for a more generous evaluation both of Clayton's work and of its apparent change of venue in "Thomas Clayton and the Introduction of Italian Opera to England."

[78] Milhous, *Thomas Betterton*, p. 195.

scenery designed by James Thornhill.[79] As Milhous notes, *Arsinoe*'s popularity is not exclusively attributable to novelty, though it was the first all-sung opera in English, with Italian style recitatives and *da capo* arias. However, it is not only the additional entertainments of singing and dancing (Monsieur Du Ruel, of course) that the original audiences would have found familiar.

The lead characters, Queen Arsinoe and her general Ormondo (secretly prince of Athens), may seem laughably undeveloped to a modern reader, and the situations in which they find themselves incredibly implausible,[80] but the conventions of contemporary tragedy meant that London audiences were completely familiar with these types and the stock dramatic situations that led to distrust, jealousy, imprisonment, mortal peril, and—as in some productions of our own time—the quick resolution of a happy ending. For a contemporary audience, the libretto needed to do no more than convey the bare bones of the plot in a kind of dramatic shorthand, and let the performers and the music carry the moment.

Beyond the familiar elements of the serious plot, *Arsinoe* contained some very conventional crowd-pleasing numbers, like the comic musical dialogue "Delbo, if thou wilt not Woe [woo] me," for the buffoon Delbo and Nerina, Arsinoe's old nurse. Comic nurse characters are a staple of seventeenth-century dramatic works throughout Europe, but the most likely resonance for an English audience would be the very similar role Mary Lindsey had sung in Durfey's comedy *The Campaigners*.

Other scenes were immediately visually familiar. *Arsinoe* includes not one but two scenes in which the audience and male characters are invited to gaze on the heroine, first "sleeping in a Garden. The Time Night, the Moon shining" (1) as she is threatened by an assassin, and then reclining on a couch in her royal apartment (10), tormented by love. It can be no coincidence that of the four extant set designs sketched by Sir James Thornhill, two are for these scenes. They are part of the tradition of such scenes in contemporary tragedy, scenes often played with music,[81] and particularly prevalent during the previous decade.[82] Notably, it

---

[79] All four sketches are reproduced in Sybil Rosenfeld's *Georgian Scene Painters and Scene Painting* (Cambridge, 1981): opposite p. 82. Although highly decorative, they do not include elaborate multi-level scenes of the type described by Settle in *The World in the Moon* (PC, 1697). See Rosenfeld, pp. 71–2.

[80] See Fiske, *English Theatre Music*, pp. 32–3.

[81] See the discussion of discovery scenes in Chapter Two. There are additional moments when Arsinoe pauses (and poses) for effect.

[82] See Marsden, *Fatal Desire*, pp. 79, 98–9. Marsden's comments also illustrate one example of the 'drama in shorthand' effect of *Arsinoe*. She observes "Each play establishes the sexualized heroine as the visual object early in the action" (70). *Arsinoe*, like Congreve's *The Mourning Bride*, does this from the rise of the curtain. With the usual lack of verisimilitude in opera, Ormondo sees her and sings two short arias without waking her up.

is Arsinoe's life and her rule that are endangered—unlike many tragic heroines, her chastity never appears directly threatened.

Another familiar element was the masque-like entertainment in Act III. The final scene includes an extensive choral epithalamium for Ormondo and Arsinoe that, McGeary argues, comes from the dramatick opera tradition rather than that of Italy.[83] Afterwards, Dorisbe makes a last attempt to break up the royal couple by publicly stabbing herself, but is saved (unlike Dennis's Armida). Arsinoe forgives her, Feraspe's love converts her and the quartet of leads (Tofts, Cross, Hughes, and Leveridge) sing happily about living in the realm of love, pastoral sentiments echoed by all voices in the final grand chorus.

Arsinoe was performed sixteen times during its first season, and regularly revived thereafter. A work this popular naturally generated many musical publications. Sixteen of the songs were quickly released as part of Walsh's *Monthly Mask of Vocal Music*,[84] while David Hunter documents nine separate issues of song books for *Arsinoe* printed between 1706 and 1714.[85] A full score of the opera also exists, including all of the recitatives and choral sections which were, as usual, not printed.[86] Musically, *Arsinoe* is not the "execrable performance" it has been called,[87] but it is uneven overall and even within single numbers. For example, in the duet for Arsinoe and Ormondo in Act II, "Doubtful Heart, O tell me why" begins as a graceful triple-meter air, and the setting of the line "If to Love you will not bend," with its reiteration of the same pitch (no bending) could be dramatically effective. However the repetitive melismas that immediately follow (on "whether") seem thrown in just to be "Italian." The very Italianate rage aria for Dorisbe which precedes it, "Assist ye Furies from the Deep/ Revenge, Revenge prepare," accompanied by agitated violins, is more consistently successful. It must have been interesting for 1705 audiences to see Letitia Cross raging rather than coquettish or seductive.

While promoting an elite taste for 'English'd' Italian opera, the Patent Company management had not lost sight of more earthy possibilities, as its schedule for January includes a series of robust stock comedies as well as the return of its most recent comic success, Cibber's *Careless Husband*, and a new farce from Motteux, *Farewel Folly; or, The Younger the Wiser*, presented with a "musical interlude," *The Mountebank; or, The Humours of the Fair*. Indeed, *Farewel Folly* was performed more often than *Arsinoe* until the spring months, when Drury Lane traditionally performed dramatick operas.

Given his previous work, it is no surprise that Motteux's farce is well provided with musical events (ten, in a three-act play), even without the added interlude.

---

[83] McGeary, "Thomas Clayton and the Introduction of Italian Opera," p. 175.
[84] See Baldwin and Wilson, *Monthly Mask*, for these songs.
[85] Hunter 12, 12a, 26, 29, 30, 31 (all 1706); 78a, 78b (1711); 90 (1714).
[86] Lbl Egerton 3664, microfilm available.
[87] In Sir John Hawkins, *A General History of the Science and Practice of Music,* rev. edition (London, 1875), vol. 2, p. 810.

Motteux seems to have drawn on the songwriting talents of several of the Patent Company composers: Daniel Purcell, Leveridge, and Weldon. All the songs and dances are familiar, and many play off the talents (and previous roles) of the cast. In *Farewel Folly*, Colley Cibber as "Mimick, a player" gets to impersonate "a Woman, a Bully, and a Frenchman," and many of the musical moments come from his scenes, as when he enters "dancing to the Musick, in a Foppish French Dress, with some Fiddles with him" (47) and begins to sing a French drinking song, like Baldernoe in *A Plot and No Plot* or Clodio in *Love Makes a Man*. The final musical number, "Gay Hoboys, the Dragoons Delight"(57–8), with its choreographed drinking scene ("Rest Your Flask—Poise your Flask—Open your Mouth ..."), chorus, and dance, with oboe consort and drums, is the deluxe version of the "Posture-Dance in Imitation of Soldiers exercise" in *The Cornish Comedy* (PC, 1696) and the Grenadiers' exercise in *Europe's Revels* (LIF, 1697).

The Mountebank is reminiscent of Durfey, with its rustic characters crowding into the fair for a variety of reasons, mostly to do with 'sport,' as described in their songs. Leveridge has the largest role, as a Doctor Dulcamara-like figure who can cure anything.[88] One of the songs, "Here are People and Sports" showing "Dr Leverigo and his merry Andrew Pinkanello" performing, was issued as an illustrated broadside (Figure 6.3), a relatively rare depiction of these two performers singing. Weldon's song "From grave Lessons and Restraint" (later retitled "on a Lady Rambling in May Fare") had apparently been sung by Lucretia Bradshaw in some of the subscription concerts the previous spring.[89] Presumably these spring performances included the rest of the entertainment,[90] as the Subscription Musick series had previously included short dramatic works (like Motteux's *Britain's Happiness* and *Squire Trelooby*) as well as all kinds of musical performances.

Sometime during these disappointing winter months the Lincoln's Inn Fields company brought out Susanna Centlivre's comedy *The Gamester*, which was a great success. In Centlivre's play, the gamester Valere must be reformed before he can marry the beautiful Angelica (Bracegirdle). Among the cast of characters—gamblers, gentlemen, ladies, a milliner and a pawnbroker—is the "Marquis of Hazard, a supposed French Marquis," in truth a former footman returned from abroad. Like Sir William Mode in Centlivre's earlier play, Hazard sings to seduce. His song in Act II, "In vain You sable Weeds put on" (19), to the widowed coquette Lady Wealthy, is a piece of hyperbolic flattery. The second song, printed on the

---

[88] Ben Jonson's *Volpone*, with its mountebank scene, was a stock play with documented revivals at DL every season from 1699 to 1705. Doctor Dulcamara is a character in Donizetti's comic opera *L'Elisir d'Amore*.

[89] This song was printed by both Walsh and Cross, in multiple versions. It was also used by Sir John Hawkins as a musical example in his *History of Music*. See Hunter 5 (399), also Baldwin and Wilson, *Monthly Mask*, no. 65, from May 1704.

[90] Milhous and Hume note a probable Subscription Musick performance on 26 April 1705, but nothing is known about the performers and their material. M&H *London Stage*, p. 164.

Figure 6.3   "Here are People and Sports" in *The Mountebank*

same page, "Fair *Celia*, she is nice and coy," is addressed to the gamester Valere "when he has won Money," (presumably in Act III after he wins a small fortune), and probably sung by his servant Hector (George Pack).

In Centlivre's comedy it is the servants, rather than the gentlemen, who are the musical ones. Hector quotes a snatch of the country dialogue from Motteux's *Europe's Revels* (31), whereas, earlier in the scene, Valere insists "There's no Music like the Chink of Gold—… sweeter in my Ear—than all the *Margaretta*'s in *Europe*—" (31). This is clearly a reference to the singers Margarita de l'Epine and Maria Margarita Gallia, and no compliment—while de l'Epine had sung at Lincoln's Inn Fields during the spring of 1703, by January 1704 she was at Drury Lane and she performed there regularly in 1705.

Lenton's act music for Centlivre's play appeared in *Harmonia Anglicana*, but the songs called for in the play text have not been recovered. The act music, all in G minor, includes a curious "Bass Minuet," with the bass line carrying the melody. The other tunes include Lenton's usual airs, jigs, and a hornpipe. The play seems to have been moderately successful, and was performed several times at the Queen's Theatre after the initial production.

In February John Dennis hoped that his *Gibraltar; or, The Spanish Adventure* would satisfy the current taste for "low Comedy" and benefit from topicality, namely the recent taking of Gibraltar by the English. There are some potentially amusing scenes featuring international characters, for example when French and Spanish lieutenants are convinced they need to adopt the other's dress, wig, and manner. To be French, one must always sing and dance, however inappropriate the circumstances (Act II, 19–20). Dennis plays up the maritime element with a drunken sailor singing in Act III and, at the end of Act V, a celebration very reminiscent of Motteux's *Britain's Happiness*. It begins with a musical dialogue between an importunate English mariner and a resisting Spanish shepherdess, and concludes with a chorus of dancing seamen: "In the soft Field of Love; or the rough Field of War,/ There's no resisting an *English* Tar" (70, italics reversed). Despite the patriotic sentiments which would work so well for later productions up through Gilbert and Sullivan, Dennis's play was not a hit.

The last new production at Drury Lane prior to the opening of the Haymarket theater was Owen Swiney's *The Quacks; or, Love's the Physician*. Like many recent comic successes (*Love's Contrivance*, *Squire Trelooby*) it was based on Molière, in this case *L'Amour Médecin*. The prologue is acid about Lincoln's Inn Fields' "Tatter'd Monarchs, and their Aged Queens!" (line 24). Some of the animosity is due to the trouble Swiney had getting his play past the Lord Chamberlain.[91] In the play, lovesick Lucinda is 'cured' when her father is persuaded to consult her lover in disguise as a doctor. The music indicated included a song, "To gentle Strephon tell your grief," to amuse Lucinda at the beginning of Act III (composed by Leveridge and published in Walsh's *Monthly Mask*), and the inevitable "Entertainment of Singing and Dancing" (no further details) at the end of it. Even the newspaper

---

[91] See Milhous, *Thomas Betterton*, p. 197.

advertisements for the performances are general, promising music and dancing by "the best Performers."[92]

The new theater in the Haymarket made its grand opening with an all-sung Italian pastoral, *Gli Amori d'Ergasto*. Although the popularity of singers performing Italian arias and of the opera *Arsinoe* was undeniable, it is hard to imagine that any critical observer (inside or out of the theater) seriously thought *Ergasto* would be a hit. Pastoral interludes in larger works had been well received, but the recent fully pastoral productions, Oldmixon's *Amintas* (PC, 1698) and *The Fickle Shepherdess* (LIF, 1703) had been a disaster and only a marginal success, respectively, while Congreve's *The Judgment of Paris* (the "Prize Musick") was, in every respect of performance and production, an exceptional work.

Ergasto's extremely undramatic alternation of two shepherd–nymph pairs, though offering scenes in both hopeful and despondent moods, had nothing to match the melodrama of *Arsinoe*, and it was only performed five times. Although Italian arias were popular in concerts and as entr'acte music, there was (and is) a very appreciable difference between a few lyrics sung in Italian and an entire production in a largely unfamiliar language. Liking to hear "Nessun dorma" does not automatically mean enjoying—or attending—even one act of Puccini's opera *Turandot* (which is considerably more dramatic).

Jakob Greber (Italianized to "Giacomo" on the *Ergasto* title page and elsewhere) served as accompanist and composer for Margarita de l'Epine's successful concerts and playhouse appearances from June 1703, but his was hardly a name to conjure with. Similarly, while there is little conclusive evidence about the singers who performed *Ergasto*, there is a general consensus that they did not shine. De l'Epine, because of her association with Greber, seems very likely, as does "the Baroness" Johanna Maria Lindelheim.[93] Another recently arrived Italian singer who may have been included was Juliana Celotti, who sang at Lincoln's Inn Fields in February.

Without the score, it is impossible to know whether the roles of the shepherds as well as the nymphs may have been sung by women—it is known that de l'Epine sang male roles in several later operas.[94] The printed libretto does show that virtually all the solo songs and duets were in *da capo* form, following Italian conventions, while the exit arias (sung as a character prepares to leave the stage) do not indicate the usual return to 'the head.' The English verse translation, presumably by Motteux, is not ungraceful.

Whatever its merits may have been, by the third week of April, *Ergasto* was being performed with a short farce, *The Consultation*, presumably based, like

---

[92] M&H *London Stage*, pp. 218–19.

[93] See Price, "The Critical Decade for English Music Drama," p. 53.

[94] No music for the 1705 London production is known. Six years later, a revised version of *Ergasto* was performed in Vienna, for which a score survives. I have not had the opportunity to compare the Vienna score with the London libretto.

Swiney's *The Quacks*, on Molière's comedy.[95] The advertisement for 24 April also suggests a substitution for one of the female sopranos in the original cast, as it states that the role of the shepherdess Licori will be sung by "the new Italian Boy"— possibly stepping up from the role of Cupid, who only sang the prologue.[96]

Regarding the Queen's Theatre's disastrous opening month, Downes insists "had they Open'd the House at first, with a good new *English* Opera, or a new Play; they wou'd have preserv'd the Favour of Court and City, and gain'd Reputation and Profit."[97] It is here that Eccles and Congreve's opera *Semele*, with its excellent English libretto and charming English–Italian music could have saved the day, had both the score and all the necessary performers been available.[98]

After a turbulent April, each company had another play by a proven playwright in reserve for later: Steele's comedy *The Tender Husband* and Pix's tragedy *The Conquest of Spain*. However, the new Queen's Theatre company largely had to rely on revivals using summer gimmicks like an all-female cast in *Love for Love*.

The Tender Husband matches Steele's earlier comedies with its emphasis on music and use of familiar Steele tricks like reading song lyrics aloud before performing them. All three songs from *The Tender Husband* appeared in Walsh's *Monthly Mask*, two by Daniel Purcell in the April and May 1705 issues, and a third, "Sett and Sung" by Littleton Ramondon, in May 1706.[99] The printed text for *The Tender Husband* also provides record of an interesting substitution, wherein a lengthy and militantly patriotic song, similar in type to those Steele had included in his earlier comedies, was replaced by a short love song more conventionally suited to its dramatic setting, a serenading scene.

The musical events in *The Tender Husband* center on two characters, the coquettish Mrs Clerimont (Letitia Cross) and her brother-in-law, the witty Captain Clerimont (Wilks). Like Cross herself, Mrs Clerimont has spent time abroad and she returns convinced of the superiority of all things French. She finally appears at the beginning of the third act, and soon has her 'spinet master' perform a song for her. The song, "With Study'd Airs, and practis'd Smiles,/ *Flavia* my Ravish'd Heart beguiles," was first performed by its composer, Ramondon, and the text was read aloud. However, Steele does not stop there, as Mrs Clerimont reprises the song in two different manners: hummed "a la françoise" and sung like an "insensible" Englishwoman with a cold (Act III, I, lines 76–96).

---

[95] Apparently never printed, no copy of the text is known to survive.

[96] M&H, *London Stage*, p. 223.

[97] Downes, *Roscius Anglicanus*, p. 100 (48).

[98] *Semele* was apparently not ready for rehearsal until January 1707. See Price, "The Critical Decade," p. 61 and *Theatrical Documents*, no. 1888.

[99] The act music by John Barrett, in *Harmonia Anglicana*, is lost. The music for the songs (in three quite different keys), can be seen in Baldwin and Wilson's edition (*Monthly Mask*, nos. 101, 105 and 144). The apparent delay in publication of Ramondon's song may be due to a desire to keep it for his own repertoire, or time needed to establish a relationship with Walsh. Ramondon's first song in the *Monthly Mask* appeared in April 1706.

When Captain Clerimont enters shortly thereafter, he is quickly reminded of a promise to teach his sister-in-law three dance steps (coupés: basically a rising step, with many possible variations). Wilks and Cross dance together in character, and then Cross invites Penkethman (as the country booby, Humphrey Gubbin) to dance with her. As in the previous musical encounter, Cross transforms an artful musical event (an elaborate song, French courtly dance) into broad comedy.

In the fourth act, the music is all the Captain's. The first piece heard is the serenading song that replaced Steele's planned patriotic entertainment. Sung by countertenor Francis Hughes, "Why lovely Charmer, tell me why,/ So very kind and yet so shy,"[100] Daniel Purcell's setting, though always remaining in the plaintive key of E minor, moves from declaiming the text over a slow-moving bass line to a more energetic and tuneful conclusion, constantly repeating. "I cannot love thee less or more."

Later, having made his way (in disguise) into the home of his intended, the captain has a servant sing "While gentle Parthenissa walks."[101] With its jaunty dotted-rhythm musical motives and exaggerated poetry, "A thousand Shafts around her fly,/ A thousand Swains unheeded Dye," manages to be both touching and comic. As the audience knows, "Parthenissa" is the name chosen for herself by the young lady (known as "Biddy" to her unromantic family).[102] Naturally, Captain Clerimont's musical wooing is completely successful and the play ends with the usual final dance.

Martial music, though cut from Steele's comedy, does make an appearance at Lincoln's Inn Fields. Mary Pix's *The Conquest of Spain*, like Dennis's *Gibraltar*, was probably intended to take advantage of recent interest in the Spanish peninsula, though the play is set during the time of the Moorish Conquest. The topical connection would have been reinforced for contemporary audiences if the "several Tunes of Victory" (29), played during the beginning of Act III, included recognizable pieces from the celebrations following the capture of Gibraltar (or the victory at Blenheim) the previous summer. Pix indicates no other music beyond trumpet calls, and no surviving music is associated with Pix's *Conquest*.

In the late summer, with the company back at Lincoln's Inn Fields, first-time author A. Chaves's comedy *The Cares of Love* ran at least three nights. Musical cues of any sort (song, dance, quotation) are surprisingly absent from the printed text, although the epilogue "As it ought to have been Spoken" savagely mocks *Arsinoe*, which Drury Lane continued to perform through 10 July. In addition to speaking

---

[100] For some reason the generic "lovely Charmer" was replaced with the name "Belvidera" when the song was printed, though both "Parthenissa" (and the words printed in Steele's text) would fit.

[101] This performer, referred to as "the Boy" by Walsh, is identified by Baldwin and Wilson as Henry Holcombe. See their *Monthly Mask*, notes to no. 101.

[102] Captain Clerimont sympathizes with her plight, censuring the "insupportable Tyranny of Parents, to fix Names on helpless Infants, which they must blush at all their Lives after!" (Act II, ii, lines 240–42).

the usual couplets, the performer (unnamed) is instructed to sing "in Imitation of the Opera," quoting some of the least-inspired and dramatically incongruous lines (rivals singing at swordpoint, a sung letter).[103] Making fun of singers and songs in prologues was nothing new, though the best-documented and funniest examples of it, performed by comedians Jo Haynes and William Penkethman, had been heard at Drury Lane. It would be worth knowing why Chaves's epilogue did not get performed at Lincoln's Inn Fields, as it seems a perfectly logical extension of competitive practice. Perhaps Vanbrugh did not want to permit any potentially damaging attacks on operas per se at the same time as he hoped to stage more such productions at the Haymarket.

Revivals, 1704–1705

Scanning the advertisements for plays and concerts during this period, one notices many more revivals of Henry Purcell's music, ranging from favorite songs to entire productions, like Drury Lane's *Timon of Athens*, featuring Purcell's masque, performed 6 December 1704.[104] In *The Rise of Musical Classics in Eighteenth-Century England*, historian William Weber has insightful things to say about the ways in which Purcell and his music were used during the later eighteenth century. However, his brief account of the early years of the century fails to take notice of several points. Weber states that "Purcell's theatre music returned to the London stage during the crisis triggered by the arrival of Italian opera in England,"[105] but it had never really left.

Henry Purcell's "native genius" was often set up in opposition to imported talents by critics concerned about theatrical continuity and national pride long before 1710. His music was also performed by "the enemy" (foreign musicians). Following the advice of Jakob Greber (as noted by Kusser), foreign musicians in London at the turn of the century found it politic to at least pay lip service to the glories of Purcell.[106] Many concerts by foreign musicians included Henry Purcell's music, often alongside Italian sonatas and arias. On Thursday, 20 April 1704 a benefit concert for Maria Gallia featured:

---

[103] Chaves, *The Cares of Love; or, A Night's Adventure. A Comedy* (London, 1705), [53].

[104] M&H, *London Stage*, p. 198.

[105] William Weber, *The Rise of Musical Classics in Eighteenth-Century England: A Study in Canon, Ritual, and Ideology* (Oxford, 1992), p. 90. Weber mentions the 1704 revival of *Dido and Aeneas* at LIF, along with a spate of other Purcell revivals at DL, but seems unaware of its performance in 1700 (91). He briefly lists songs often performed from the 1710s to the 1750s but does not consider Purcell songs performed throughout the first decade of the century.

[106] See Musical Assets, this chapter.

Vocal and Instrumental Musick, composed by that great Italian Master Seignior Gioseppe Saggion. With several Sonatas with Flutes and Hautboys, and likewise a Sonata with two Flutes, by Mr Paisible and Mr Banister. And several Songs in Italian with Flutes and Hautboys, by Seigniora Maria Margarita Gallia, who never Sung in any publick Consort in England but once. The whole being entirely new composed and accompanied by Seignior Gioseppe Saggion. And likewise several songs in English, composed by the late Famous Mr Henry Purcell.[107]

Margarita de l'Epine also sang Purcell's songs,[108] as did the leading English singers like Hodgson, Leveridge, and Tofts. *The London Stage* provides plenty of evidence that Purcell's theater music continued to be used onstage in scenes, solo songs, and entire productions between 1695 and 1710.

During the 1704–1705 season, the Patent Company continued the pattern of the previous season, showing if anything an even greater reliance on old stock plays (Brome, Dryden, Howard, Shadwell) and performing their new favorites (Baker, Cibber, Farquhar, Southerne) a bit less frequently. Many autumn advertisements promise "entertainments of singing and dancing" but do not specify who or what. Richard Leveridge is not advertised as singing until November.

More information is often provided about dancing. For exceptional shows like Behn's farce *The Emperor of the Moon* and Lacy's *Sawny the Scot*, elaborate dance descriptions were given. For Behn, this meant 'grotesque' dancing by Punchanello and a Harlequin dance by Monsieur Cherrier;[109] for Lacy, the "Devonshire Girl" performing Scotch and Irish dances.[110] A similar division can be seen in the November productions of Otway's tragedy *Venice Preserv'd* (dancing by the Du Ruels and Cherrier) and Brome's comedy *The Northern Lass* (dancing by Bicknell, Lucas, and Mosse for the women, and La Forest and Cottine for the men).[111] Margaret Bicknell and Jane Lucas were also cast in the play. This is not to say that the Du Ruels did not appear with comedies, for they did, but the divisions are often suggestive.

In November 1704 the Lincoln's Inn Fields company featured revivals of tragedies by Lee, *Sophonisba; or, Hannibal's Overthrow*, and Shakespeare, *Othello*. A festival of bloody rants and supernatural horrors, *Sophonisba* includes a long prophecy scene like that parodied in *The Metamorphosis*.[112] Betterton's *Henry IV* was also performed, probably with William Corbett's music, written for summer performances at Oxford. In December, Drury Lane answered with

---

[107] M&H *London Stage*, p. 162.
[108] Ibid., pp. 168, 169, 171, 173.
[109] Ibid., p. 202.
[110] Ibid., p. 173.
[111] Ibid., pp. 192–3.
[112] Price discusses the musical events, particularly the "extravagant" conjuration scene, in *Henry Purcell and the London Stage*, pp. 58–9.

Shadwell's *Timon of Athens*, including the masque by Henry Purcell featuring Leveridge as Bacchus.[113]

In late December and early January Lincoln's Inn Fields revived last season's successful *Abra Mule* and Etherege's endlessly popular *The Man of Mode* against Drury Lane's new comedy *The Careless Husband*. The Lincoln's Inn Fields shows were advertised with dancing "By the famous Mlle de la Val, lately arriv'd in England."[114] She was the last of the series of French dancers who had appeared with the Lincoln's Inn Fields company (L'Abbé, Balon, Subligny) during this decade. De la Val continued to appear throughout the spring season. Her performances were linked to revivals of *The Amorous Widow*, *Othello*, *Don Sebastian*, and *The Virtuoso*.

Lincoln's Inn Fields continued with revivals against the Patent Company's new opera, *Arsinoe*. On 9 February, *The Man of Mode* was accompanied by singing "In Italian by Signiora Ziuliana de Celotte; All the Instrumental and Vocal Musick compos'd by that eminent Master Sigismond Cousser [Kusser], both lately arriv'd in England."[115] Kusser and de Celotte may have been intended to offset the popularity of the "Englished" Italian opera with new music from the Continent, or to fill the space of Margarita de l'Epine. De l'Epine returned to sing at Drury Lane in December, where she continued to appear through March, in alternation with Leveridge and "the new boy."[116] As records for Lincoln's Inn Fields remain scant in comparison to those for Drury Lane, it is impossible to tell whether Signora de Celotte made further appearances in competition with the better-known soprano.

In March, Lincoln's Inn Fields revived Burnaby's *Love Betray'd, or the Agreeable Disappointment* as a benefit for actor-singer George Pack and actress Lucretia Bradshaw. Other plays known to have been staged there during this month were all benefits, while Drury Lane continued showing *Arsinoe* alternating with works by Dryden, Etherege, and Vanbrugh. On 29 March 1705 the Lincoln's Inn Fields company staged Shadwell's *The Virtuoso* together with Motteux's masque *Acis and Galatea* and entertainments of dancing. Advertisements solemnly stated it was "the last time of Acting at this House."[117] Like many farewell performances, it was not quite as final as it sounded.

In April the Patent Company focused on music and comedy, bringing back *Arsinoe*, Leveridge's musical *Macbeth*, and Behn's *Emperor of the Moon* (featuring Ramondon's first stage appearance) together with older stock plays. It ended the month with *Love's Last Shift*, promising "several Entertainments of Singing by Mr Leveridge, Mr Hughs, Mrs Lindsey, and the new Boy. Particularly the Frost Musick in the 4th [recte 3rd] Act of *King Arthur*, Compos'd by the late Mr Henry Purcel, … And several Serious and Grotesque Dances by Monsieur du Ruel, Mrs

---

[113] M&H *London Stage*, p. 198.
[114] Ibid., p. 199.
[115] Ibid., p. 210.
[116] See note 86.
[117] M&H *London Stage*, p. 219.

du Ruel, Monsieur Cherrier, and Mrs Moss."[118] Lincoln's Inn Fields responded in kind with Motteux's *The Loves of Mars and Venus* and Durfey's *Don Quixote*.

In May, the two companies staged Dryden's *Amphitryon* in close succession, Drury Lane leading off. While Henry Purcell's songs and a set of act music for the musical play had been published and were thus accessible to anyone, it is not clear whether one company or both had access to the full score.[119] Drury Lane's advertisement guaranteed "all the Songs set by the late Mr Henry Purcell," plus dancing by Letitia Cross, while Lincoln's Inn Fields similarly promised "The Vocal Musick set by the late Mr Henry Purcell, with several Entertainments of Dancing."[120] Drury Lane performed it at least twice in May, while the documented Lincoln's Inn Fields performances were in May and again in July. Because records are incomplete, it may well have been performed more often.

Although, as Milhous notes, by June the two companies seem to have been performing on alternate nights, in April and May they often went head to head.[121] This summer change may simply be a practical reaction to a dwindling potential audience. The summer repertoire was, for the most part, very old stock comedies with a leavening of Shakespeare tragedies with, at Drury Lane, an occasional performance of *Arsinoe*. Interestingly, the one night in June that the two companies both performed (9 June), they offered different Dryden plays. Both Dryden's plays and Henry Purcell's music remained performance territory worth claiming and holding.

Conclusion

These final seasons demonstrate that, musically speaking, new productions employing traditional takes on comedy could not match the popularity of their predecessors. At Lincoln's Inn Fields, the failure of *The Biter* with its traditional musical numbers by Eccles—particularly the comic dialogue performed by Bracegirdle and Pack—must have been an unpleasant surprise. At Drury Lane, Steele's *The Lying Lover* and *The Tender Husband* (considerably more popular in the seasons after its premiere) met with similarly limited enthusiasm even though they included numbers for Letitia Cross singing and dancing and sprightly songs of courtship by Daniel Purcell. Of the six new serious plays mounted during these two seasons, Lincoln's Inn Fields staged five, including the only real success, Trapp's *Abra Mule*.

---

[118] Ibid., p. 225.

[119] The score in the Fitzwilliam Museum, Cambridge is an early copy, not Purcell's own. In 1705, the Patent Company may have had the composer's score and LIF the Cambridge manuscript or a similar copy.

[120] M&H *London Stage*, p. 226.

[121] Milhous, *Thomas Betterton*, p. 200.

The stress and cost of mounting new productions during these uncertain seasons probably limited the company managers' interest in making such efforts. Thanks to the competition for audiences during the previous eight years, both companies had a modest stock of well-received plays that they could revive successfully, beginning with Congreve's *Love for Love* and Cibber's *Love's Last Shift*.

Innovations were most often found in the increasingly well-documented traffic of musical entertainments between court, concert rooms, and the theaters rather than in new productions. Series like the Subscription Musick sought to present an elite entertainment in public spaces, while other concerts brought court and theater music to dancing schools and spas. During these last seasons the newspaper record begins to document repertoires of vocal music, dancing, and even instrumental music in a way that allows us a more three-dimensional appreciation of the world of performance in which turn-of-the-century actors, musicians, and audiences operated.

The comic song remained one sure crowd pleaser. Such songs were widely advertised in these final years, with older musical dialogues, like the older comedies, being regularly revived. For theater songs performed during these seasons, both comic and serious, the key source is Walsh's *Monthly Mask*, which demonstrates an increasing proportion of songs sung "at the theater" (often specifying which theater) but unassociated with any particular play. The performers ranged from old favorites like Leveridge and Hodgson to younger singers, such as Tofts and Hughes, who were featured in the experiments with Italian opera during the following seasons.

Epilogue

As has been shown, despite political and military conflict with other European nations, the London theaters were far from isolated. Musicians from France, Germany, Italy, and even farther afield traveled to London to make their way in the thriving metropolis.

The seasons following the construction of the Queen's Theater in the Haymarket were marked by Vanbrugh's attempts to control his new company and develop an audience for opera. English opera productions such as Granville's *The British Enchanters*, featuring Betterton, Barry, and Bracegirdle with music by Eccles and Corbett, demonstrated that the English model could still win favor with London theater goers.

The Italian opera productions in London during the years leading up to the arrival of Handel in 1711 have been the focus of several music historians. Curtis Price identified 1700–1710 as the "critical decade for music drama," specifically, opera. I would argue that the success of Clayton's English-language Italian-style opera *Arsinoe* built on the musical and dramatic practices of the Drury Lane and Lincoln's Inn Fields companies in ways that can only be appreciated by a closer look at all types of theatrical performances during the 1695–1705 decade.

Productions which succeeded during this decade found the "sweet spot" between tradition and innovation. Just as there is more to the music of this decade than Henry Purcell, there is more to the drama than the plays of Congreve and Steele. The continuous process of change in musical and theatrical practices meant that seemingly new developments remained inextricably interconnected with the lively, interactive theatrical culture that produced them. Although audience and critical favorites would change with time, debates over the importance of performers and the expressive powers of speech, dance, and song in relation to drama continued. Later polemics regarding the proper use of music in plays, in operas, and in society at large sprang from the discourse of turn-of-the-century critics and authors.

In addition, productions originally staged during the 1695–1705 decade made significant additions to the popular culture repertoire of the mid and later eighteenth century. This decade produced a cornucopia of theater songs which circulated in a variety of printed forms, from broadsheets to numerous printed collections, both with and without music. Its productions were precursors to and frequent musical resources for the later ballad operas and pantomimes, and furnished future companies with several of their stock plays.

The range of musical and dramatic references in a well-known later eighteenth-century work like *The Beggar's Opera* should come as no surprise, given the range of music performed before or within these earlier productions, and their fondness for allusion to and quotation from other works, not only on the literary level but on the musical one as well. The persistence of the music and songs from 1695–1705 productions is remarkable. In addition to revivals of the plays themselves, they became part of the cultural fabric. Song texts such as "Mortals learn your lives to measure" and "To Thee, oh! gentle Sleep, alone" were still being recomposed as glees and rounds at the end of the eighteenth century.

Appendix 1
Glossary of Musical Terms and Concepts

Act tunes, act music: Short instrumental pieces played between the acts of a dramatic production. "Act music" can also include by inference the first and second music played before the production begins, and the overture that follows the prologue.

Aria, da capo aria: Italian term for a song, often implying something more elaborate (operatic) than the English 'song.' The da capo aria is in the musical-textual form AB(A), where the repeat of the opening section (A) is indicated by the instruction "da capo" (from the head).

Bar [see Measure]

Cadence: The close at the end of a section of music or an entire piece. Composers could use a variety of harmonic patterns to create a feeling of finality.

Castrato: A male singer who had surgery before completing puberty, retaining his high voice. Castrati grew to adult size (and lung power) but without secondary sex characteristics linked to testosterone. Castrati had sung in Catholic churches in Italy since the Renaissance. During the seventeenth century they were increasingly used in opera performances and found in musical establishments—court, sacred, and civic—throughout Europe.

Catch: A popular form of music making, in which all voices sing the same tune and text at intervals (a "round" like "Row, row, row your boat"). While catches could have any type of text and varying degrees of musical difficulty, many were bawdy and easy enough to sing while drinking.

Chaconne: A dance and variation form often used by French opera composer Jean-Baptiste Lully. Chaconnes typically use a repeating chord progression, heard in the continuo part.

Chords: Group of notes which are played (sounded) simultaneously. The basic harmonic building blocks of a piece. The notes can be rearranged (inverted) in various combinations.

Chromatic: Music using tones from outside the key of a piece, indicated by special signs (accidentals). Chromatic music destabilizes the sense of key (the musical "center").

Clef: Symbol placed at the beginning of each musical line indicating the pitches associated with the lines and spaces shown. Continuo parts and the lowest male voices were written in bass clef, high voices and instruments were often written in treble clef. Composers also used other clefs between these two extremes.

Continuo: "Continuous" instrumental accompaniment, usually with a keyboard (like harpsichord) or a plucked-string instrument (lute or theorbo), often assisted by a bowed instrument (bass viol) to bring out the bass line. In written music, the continuo parts sometimes use "figured bass" (see below) but always rely on the skill of the performers to decide what notes should be played above the bass line and how they are played. This is similar to what a jazz pianist today might do with a standard—each time the piece is performed, it's recognizable but different.

Contrafactum: The setting of a new text to existing music. Thomas Durfey often took popular tunes (vocal or instrumental) and wrote new words to go with them.

Counterpoint: The practice of writing music with multiple independent lines which are all important (e.g., a Bach fugue) rather than a melody and simple accompaniment. This complex music was the subject of treatises and academic study. Popular music (then and now) rarely involves much counterpoint.

Countertenor [see Voice types]

Dance suite: A set of dances typically including the allemande, courante, sarabande, and gigue, but which can also include other dances such as the hornpipe, minuet, rigadoun, etc. Most dances are in binary form (AABB). An exception is the rondo (Rondeau, "round o", see below).

Dialogue: A vocal piece for two or more singers in which they alternate singing different phrases (conflict) before coming together in a chorus at the end (resolution).

Diatonic: Music which uses only the notes in the scale of its original key. Opposite of chromatic.

Dissonance: Generally speaking, a harsh or clashing sound, which according to harmonic rules should resolve to a pleasing, consonant one.

Divisions: The practice of "dividing" the long notes of a melody or bass line into many smaller ones (not all the same as the original note). Divisions both varied the musical material and made it trickier to play.

Dynamics: Written indications regarding volume level, usually very basic: soft (Italian *piano*) and loud (*forte*). More elaborate dynamic markings occur in later music.

Figured bass: A bass part which includes numbers written over the notes (indicating musical intervals) and other signs instructing the player which chords or harmonies should be played with the bass line.

Flute: Usually a high, relatively soft woodwind instrument associated with pastoral and romantic situations. References to flutes during this period usually refer not to the modern flute (held horizontally) but to the instruments called recorders today, held vertically.

Fugue: A piece in which an opening theme (subject) is worked out in several voices according to the rules of counterpoint. German composers were famous for their fugues.

Ground bass: A continuously repeated pattern of notes in the lowest-sounding part, over which the upper parts change. To keep the music interesting, composers sometimes varied the ground bass after several repetitions. Some specific four-note descending bass patterns were known as "lament basses," a convention borrowed from Italian opera.

Harmony, harmonic language: Harmony includes both chords and the sequences of chords (chord progressions) used. Harmonic language refers to the chord choices made by the composer from the vocabulary of possible chords (simple vs. complex, or consonant vs. dissonant).

Harpsichord: A keyboard instrument, like a piano, but typically smaller and with a "brighter" sound. The difference in sound is due to its construction: touching a key on the harpsichord results in plucking strings inside the instrument, whereas the piano key results in hammering strings (longer and thicker ones).

Hautboy [see Oboe]

Hornpipe: In the late seventeenth century the hornpipe was simply a lively dance form, without its later association with the sea. Many hornpipes were written by Henry Purcell, John Lenton, and others for decidedly non-nautical plays.

Imitation, imitative: A musical technique in which a tune or motive is heard in different voices or parts at staggered intervals. Unlike a catch or round, imitation does not have to be exact (identical).

Instruments: Many of the instruments still used in Western music today were part of the theater ensemble (the Musick), including woodwinds (flutes/recorders, oboes), bowed string instruments (violins, viols), brass (trumpet), and percussion (drums).

Inversion [see Chord]

Jig: An energetic dance, also (earlier definition) a short comic performance which is sung and danced.

Key: A system used to refer to pieces of music by the "key note" where it comes to rest at the end of the piece and the groups of notes associated with it. A piece ending on F is said to be in the key of F, either major or minor (see Mode, below). Music theorists and composers often assigned moods or meanings to specific keys, some of which were practical: D major was associated with celebration and was one of the keys in which trumpets could play easily.

Lute: A plucked stringed instrument (somewhat like the "newer" guitar), popular among amateurs and virtuosos since the Renaissance and most suited for performance in intimate settings. Used both as a solo instrument and as accompaniment, particularly for songs.

Measure [also "bar"]: Shortest unit of musical meter, indicated by vertical bar lines. A piece of less than 24 measures is very short, one of over 100 relatively long. However, the amount of time taken to play a measure is not fixed and depends on the tempo.

Melisma: A section of melody in which many notes are sung to one word or syllable. See Text-setting.

Meter: Like poetic meter, musical meter establishes regular patterns and groupings. As in poems, musical pieces can begin with an unaccented "pickup" before the first strong beat, duple-meter works in groups of two or four, and triple meter in threes. Compound meters combine groups on different levels. The most common modern compound is 6/8 time, in which each measure contains two large beats with three sub-beats ("Greensleeves").

Minuet: A simple and elegant social dance in triple meter from France, danced by aristocrats (and their emulators) across Europe.

Mode (major/minor): The scale (and chords) used in a piece of music. The third note in a major scale is higher than that in the minor, producing a brighter sound. According to Roger North, pieces in the major mode were associated with "triumph, mirth, and felicity," pieces in the minor mode with "sorrow and dejection" (*Roger North's* The Musicall Grammarian 1728, p. 170).

Motive: In music, a short theme or phrase that can be easily distinguished.

Oboe: A relatively new instrument. Made of wood, its sound is produced by blowing through a reed. Seventeenth-century oboes could be harsher sounding than modern ones. They were often associated with the military and with outdoor (rather than indoor) music.

Ornaments, ornamentation: Small embellishments applied to (or the practice of embellishing) a piece of music. These could be simple, like a quick added note or two, to "spice up" a tune, or more complex, involving significant changes in rhythm, range, melodic contour, etc. As with fashions in clothing, debates over "good taste" often warn of the dangers of inappropriate or badly applied ornaments.

Overture, French overture: A substantial piece of instrumental music. As with dances, the most common form came to England from France. The typical French overture opens with a stately, fanfare-like section followed by a faster, lighter section in which different groups of instruments pass a motive from one group to another (imitation). English composers had been writing "French" overtures for decades by 1695, and it is debatable whether they thought of them as French— unlike French dance forms, which definitely kept their national association.

Passacaglia: Similar to a chaconne (see above). Usually a set of variations over a ground bass.

Petite reprise ("little repetition"): A popular musical device in which the composer uses a sign to indicate that the last few measures of a piece of music should be repeated, providing a sense of closure, similar to the closing couplets spoken at the ends of acts.

Range: The range signifies all the notes used in a musical line, from lowest to highest. Voice types (and specific singers) can often be surmised from the range and tessitura (see below) of pieces, even when they are not identified.

Recitative: Vocal music which attempts to follow the patterns of speech. Typically less tuneful than other kinds of vocal music.

Ritornello, "ritornell": A short instrumental section of music which returns throughout (in whole or in part) after contrasting (often solo) sections.

Rondeau, "Round O": A musical form in which the opening section (refrain) alternates with other sections and returns at the end. Can be instrumental or vocal.

Sarabande: Originally a dance-song from Spain and Latin America, transformed by French musicians into a stately dance in triple meter, emphasizing the second beat of the measure (da-**dah**-da).

Scale: A sequence of consecutive notes which define a key or mode.

Score, full score, and parts: A full score shows all the music written, with each voice type and instrument given its own line of music. Vocal music was often published with just the voice part and the bass line. The relationship of musical score to parts is roughly equivalent to the relationship between a prompter's copy and actors' individual parts.

Scotch Snap: A rhythmic pattern in which the beat is divided into a short, accented first note and a longer second one (in music notation, usually a sixteenth note followed by a dotted eighth note). The reverse of the usual "dotted rhythm" pattern, long–short.

Sequence: Taking a motive or short section of music and immediately repeating it multiple times at higher or lower pitches, so it is still recognizable but sounds different. Common in Italian music of the period.

Seventh chords: Most chords used in this repertoire consist of triads (three notes). More complex and more dissonant seventh chords contain four notes, the top one being the interval called a seventh from the root of the chord. They become common later.

Slur: In this context, the smooth movement from one note to another sung on the same syllable, often with a "sighing" effect (moving from a higher note to a lower one). Not derogatory!

Solmization: A centuries-old mnemonic practice of assigning syllables to pitches, indicating where larger (whole step) and smaller (half step) intervals are found, helping singers to read music they have not heard. The song "Do-re-mi" from Rodgers and Hammerstein's *The Sound of Music* incorporates all the modern syllables and pitches for a major scale (do-re-mi-fa-sol-la-ti-do). During the seventeenth century, solmization was taught in patterns of six (ut-re-mi-fa-sol-la) and used in theoretical writing about music as well as for practical purposes.

Sonata: A piece of instrumental music, typically in several contrasting sections, often featuring a solo instrument with continuo (like Corelli's violin sonatas) or small instrumental ensemble.

Spinet: A small keyboard instrument related to the harpsichord.

Suspension: A note in a chord which is held (suspended) while the other notes change. This typically creates a dissonance (see above) against the new chord.

Symphony: A section of instrumental music, usually quite short. It may be separate or combined (for example, "A Song with a Symphony"), always including instruments other than continuo, sometimes indicated in the text ("symphony with flutes," etc.). Not to be confused with large-scale instrumental works by later composers like Mozart or Beethoven. A symphony in London c.1700 would last three or four minutes at the most.

Tempo: The speed at which a piece of music should be played or sung. Most music from this period does not include the Italian tempo markings (allegro, andante, etc.) that became common later and are still used in classical music.

Tessitura: Tessitura is the pitch area where a musical line is most often found, and helps distinguish different singers and voice types. For example, a song for a soprano could have a wide range (from very low to very high) but its tessitura might fall near the bottom of the range (i.e., include mostly low notes).

Tetrachord: A four-note group. See ground bass.

Text-setting: Relationship between the words of a song and the music written to sing it. The most common settings (syllabic) provide one note for each syllable of text (for example, most nursery songs, hymns, many folk and popular songs). More musically elaborate settings (melismatic) indicate many notes should be sung on a single syllable. This can make a very short poem into a very long song.

Theorbo: A large, plucked-string instrument related to the lute (above), but with additional long bass strings, usually used to play continuo parts.

Triad: A group of three notes, the most common type of chord, containing two pairs of thirds (for example, pitches C and E, E and G). Can be major or minor.

Variations: A musical form in which a theme or melody is repeated several times, but altering the original theme each time (by ornamenting it with added notes, changing the harmonies played with it, etc.)

Viols, bass viol: Bowed string instruments with frets (for finger positions, like a guitar), held in the player's lap or between the legs. The bass viol was the largest and lowest-sounding viol and frequently used in France and Germany as a solo instrument. Treble and tenor viols would play with the bass in a traditional English viol consort, but in theater music the higher string parts were played by violins.

Voice types: In descending order from highest-sounding to lowest-sounding they are soprano, alto, tenor, baritone, bass. Soprano and alto parts are typically sung by women or young boys. A countertenor is an adult male voice able to sing in the alto and even into soprano range.

Appendix 2
Composers Active in the London Theaters, 1695–1705

Name[a] & Dates	Primary Instrument	Training/Background	Court Positions	Theater Companies[b]	Selected Publications[c]
AKEROYDE, SAMUEL [Ackeroyde, Akeroyd] (fl.1684–1706)	Violin		Private Musick	PC, LIF, (UC)	*New Songs in DQ III, MercM, New Songs in Massaniello, W&M*
BARRETT, JOHN (c.1676–1719)	Keyboard (organ)	Chapel Royal chorister		PC, LIF	*Theater Musick, MercM, HA, Harpsichord Master (1702), MM*
Berenclow, Mr (fl.1689–1704)				LIF	*MercM, W&M, MM*
Blow, John (1649–1708)	Keyboard (organ)	Chapel Royal chorister	Master of Children, organist, composer at Chapel Royal; organist at Westminster Abbey	PC, (UC)	*MercM, DM, Theater Musick, Amphion Anglicus (1700), W&M, New Catches (1702)*
Byron, William, Lord (1668/9–1736)		Private study	Gentleman of the Bedchamber to Prince George	PC	*HA*
Church, John (1674–1741)	Voice (tenor)	Chorister at St John's College, Oxford	Chapel Royal choir and lay vicar at Westminster from 1697, master of choristers at Westminster from 1704	PC	*W&M*
CLARKE, JEREMIAH (c.1674–1707)	Keyboard (organ)	Chapel Royal chorister	Chapel Royal Gentleman from 1700 and organist from 1704 (position shared with Croft), later Master of Choristers	PC, LIF	*Songs in The World in the Moon, Theater Musick, MercM, W&M, HA, Harpsichord Master (1702), New Catches (1702), MM*

Name[a] & Dates	Primary Instrument	Training/ Background	Court Positions	Theater Companies[b]	Selected Publications[c]
Clayton, Thomas (1673–1725)	Violin	Italy	Private Musick	PC	MM
Corbett, William (1680–1748)	Violin		After 1709	LIF	HA, MM
Courteville, Raphael (fl.1675–c.1735)	Keyboard (organ)	Possibly Chapel Royal chorister		PC	DM, ThM, New Songs in DQ III, MercM, MM
CROFT, WILLIAM (1678–1727)	Keyboard (organ)	Chapel Royal chorister	Chapel Royal Gentleman from 1700 and organist from 1704 (position shared with DP)	PC, LIF[d]	MercM, HA, Harpsichord Master (1702), Six Sonatas for Two Flutes
Curco, Mr (fl.1687–1700)	Voice		James II's Catholic Chapel	LIF	
Deane, Thomas	Violin, or unknown[e]			LIF	
Dieupart, Charles	Violoncello			PC	
Draghi, Giovanni Baptista (c.1640–1708)	Keyboard	Italy (Venice?)	James II's Catholic Chapel	LIF, (UC)	W&M

Name[a] & Dates	Primary Instrument	Training/Background	Court Positions	Theater Companies[b]	Selected Publications[c]
ECCLES, JOHN (1668–1735)	Violin		Private Musick, from 1700 Master of the Musick	LIF, (UC)	*DM, ThM, Songs in Mars & Venus, Theater Musick, MercM, HA, Judgment of Paris, Lessons for the Harpsichord, MM, Collection of Songs* (1704)
Eccles, Solomon (1649–1710)	Bass viol		Private Musick	LIF, (UC)	*W&M*
ELFORD, RICHARD (c.1676–1714)	Voice (tenor-countertenor)	Lincoln Cathedral chorister, Durham Cathedral choir	Chapel Royal and Westminster Abbey choirs from 1702, patronized by Queen Anne	LIF	*MercM, MM*
FINGER, GOTTFRIED (c.1660–1730)	Bass viol	Moravia, family musicians	James II's Catholic Chapel	LIF, PC	*ThM, Songs in Mars & Venus, Theater Musick, MercM, HA, Six Sonatas for Two Violins*
Forcer, Francis (1649–1705)	Organ	Durham Cathedral chorister		LIF, (UC)	
Francisco, Mr [Goodsens?]	Bass viol, violoncello		Later Chapel Royal and Private Musick	LIF	*MM*
FRANCK, JOHANN WOLFGANG (1644–c.1710)	Keyboard?	Germany: Wittenberg University, Ansbach, Hamburg; Italy		PC	*ThM*

Name[a] & Dates	Primary Instrument	Training/ Background	Court Positions	Theater Companies[b]	Selected Publications[c]
Gillier, Mr				LIF	*Collection of New Songs* (1698), *MM*
Gorton, William (d.1711)	Violin, organ		Private Musick	PC	*Choice Collection of New Ayres* (date?), *A View of the First Rudiments of Music* (1704)
Gouge, Mr (fl.1698–1730?)	Voice (baritone)			LIF	*MercM*
Greber, Jakob (d.1731)	Keyboard	Italy		PC, LIF	
Hart, Philip (1674?–1749)	Keyboard (organ)			LIF	*MM, Fugues and Lessons* (1704)
Hickes, Mr	Keyboard (organ)			LIF	*MM*
Isham [Isum], John (c.1680–1726)	Keyboard (organ)			LIF	*MM*
Keen, Edward				LIF	
Keller, J. Gottfried (d.1704)	Keyboard (harpsichord)		1699 sonatas dedicated to Princess Anne	PC	*A Compleat Method for Attaining to Play Thorough Bass* (1705)

Name[a] & Dates	Primary Instrument	Training/ Background	Court Positions	Theater Companies[b]	Selected Publications[c]
King, Robert (c.1660–1726)	Violin		Private Musick, composer	PC	*ThM, Theater Musick, MercM, W&M*
Kusser [Cousser], Johann Sigismund (1660–1727)		France: study with Lully in Paris	Later master of music for Her Majesty in Ireland	LIF	*MM*
La Rich, Francis (fl.1685–1700?)	Bass viol		Private Musick under James II	LIF	
Lenton, John (1656–1719)	Violin[f]		Private Musick, performer and composer, later Groom of the Chapel Royal	LIF	*Harmonia Anglicana*
Leveridge, Richard (1670–1758)	Voice (bass)			PC	*New Book of Songs* (1697), *Second Book of Songs* (1699), *New Songs in Massaniello, MercM, W&M*
Matteis, Nicola (d.1700?)	Violin	Italy: Naples		PC	*Collection of New Songs* (1696), *Collection of New Songs* (1699), *MercM,*
Morgan, Thomas (d.1699)	Keyboard (organ)	Ireland		PC	*New Songs in DQ III, Collection of New Songs* (1697), *Theater Musick, MercM,*

Name[a] & Dates	Primary Instrument	Training/ Background	Court Positions	Theater Companies[b]	Selected Publications[c]
PAISIBLE, JAMES (c.1656–1721)	Recorder (also bass violin)	France	Court positions under Charles II and James II; service to James II in exile and then to Princess (and Queen) Anne	PC, (UC)	HA, Six Sonatas for Two Flutes, Court and Country Dances (1704), additional court dance pieces
Pepusch, Johann Christoph (1667–1752)	Keyboard	Prussia		LIF, PC	
PURCELL, DANIEL (c.1664–1717)	Keyboard (organ)	Chapel Royal chorister		PC	ThM, Songs in Brutus of Alba, Songs in The World in the Moon, Songs in Phaeton, MercM, Theater Musick, Six Sonatas for Violin and Flute, New Songs in Massaniello, Collection of New Songs (1700), Songs in The Grove (1700), Collection of New Songs (1701), HA, Judgment of Paris, Lessons for the Harpsichord

Name[a] & Dates	Primary Instrument	Training/ Background	Court Positions	Theater Companies[b]	Selected Publications[c]
PURCELL, HENRY (1659–1695)	Keyboard (organ)	Chapel Royal chorister	Keeper of instruments, composer for King's Musick, organist at Chapel Royal and Westminster Abbey	PC, (UC)	*DM, ThM, Songs in The Indian Queen, Songs in Bonduca, New Songs in DQ III, Ayres for the Theatre* (1697), *Orpheus Britannicus* (1698, 1702), *MercM, New Catches* (1702), *MM*
Ramondon, Littleton (1684–after 1715)	Voice (Baritone)			PC	*MM*
Robart, William	Voice			LIF	*Collection of Songs* (1699), *MercM*
Saggione, Giuseppe Fedeli (fl.1680–1733)	Trombone?	Italy: Venice		LIF	
Short, Benjamin	Violin?			LIF	
Tollett, Thomas (d.1696?)	Violin	Ireland	Private Musick	LIF, (UC)	*W&M*
Visconti, Gasparo (1683–c.1713)	Violin	Italy, studies with Arcangelo Corelli		DL	*Solos for a Violin* (1703), *Airs for Two Flutes* (1703)

Name[a] & Dates	Primary Instrument	Training/ Background	Court Positions	Theater Companies[b]	Selected Publications[c]
Weldon, John (1676–1736)	Keyboard (organ)	Eton College chorister, studies with Henry Purcell	Gentleman of the Chapel Royal from 1701, later organist and composer there	PC	MercM, Collection of New Songs (1702), Third Book of Songs (1703)
Whichello, Abiell (1683–1747)	Keyboard (harpsichord, organ)			LIF	MM, Lessons for the Harpsichord (1702)
White, E. [Edmund?]	Keyboard (organ)			LIF	MM
Wilford, John	Voice			LIF	MercM, MM
Williams, William (1675–1701)	Violin	Probably Westminster Abbey chorister	Private Musick	PC, LIF?	ThM, Six Sonatas for Violins and Flutes (1703)

Notes: [a] Names of composers who regularly wrote for the theaters (contributing to five or more named productions) are distinguished by small capital letters.

[b] The theater companies indicated here are for the 1695–1705 decade, LIF (including Queen's Theatre productions) and PC (Drury Lane and Dorset Garden). UC indicates that they previously composed music for the United Company.

[c] Publications from this decade, presented in roughly chronological order. Abbreviated titles used for individual publications, with the following abbreviations for popular series: DM = Deliciae Musicae, HA = Harmonia Anglicana, MercM = Mercurius Musicus, MM = The Monthly Mask of Vocal Music, ThM = Thesaurus Musicus, W&M = Wit & Mirth [up to 1705]. For more on specific composers' publications within and beyond the 1695–1705 decade, see BUCEM, RISM, and Grove Music Online. For full titles of songbooks, see D&M. Publication dates are included for works with general titles ("A Collection …"), but not for songbooks associated with specific, datable production premieres or published over a range of years.

[d] One song, in Durfey's Intrigues at Versailles.

e The Thomas Deane who played the violin at LIF and in concerts may not have been the Thomas Deane of Worcester who wrote the music for *The Governour of Cyprus*.

f Sir John Hawkins claims Lenton played the flute (*General History of the Science and Practice of Music*, vol. 2, pp. 770–71) but it was certainly not his principal instrument. In the warrant enrolling Lenton as a member of the King's Private Musick he is specifically described as "a musician for the violin." Andrew Ashbee, *Records of English Court Music*, vol. 1, p. 195.

Selected Bibliography

Manuscript Sources

Fitzwilliam Museum

Mu MS 87
Mu MS 642

British Library

Add. MS 12219,
Add. MS 15318 facsimile edition, *The Island Princess*, intro. Curtis A. Price and Robert D. Hume. In *Music for London Entertainments 1660–1800* series C, volume 2 (Tunbridge Wells: Richard Macnutt, 1985).
Add. MS 24889
Add. MS 29378
Add. MS 30934
Add. MS 31449
Add. MS 31813
Add. MS 35043

Royal College of Music

MS 862
MS 988
MS 1144
MS 1172 facsimile edition, *Instrumental Music for London Theatres, 1690–1699*, intro. Curtis Price. In *Music for London Entertainment, 1660–1800* Series A vol. 3 (Withyham: Richard Macnutt, 1987).

Bodleian Library

Tenbury MS 1175
Tenbury MS 1232
Tenbury MS 1266

Yale University

Filmer MSS 9, 12

Printed Primary Sources

Unless otherwise indicated, all play texts are from the first printing, available via EEBO or ECCO and are not listed here. Bibliographic information for printed song collections can be found in D&M or in Hunter. Bibliographic references for individual printed songs are given in footnotes.

Baldwin, Olive and Thelma Wilson, *The Monthly Mask of Vocal Music, 1702–1711: A Facsimile Edition* (Aldershot: Ashgate, 2007).
Bray, Thomas, *Country Dances: Being A Composition Entirely New; And The whole Cast Different from all that have yet been publish'd; with Bass and Treble to each Dance* (London, 1699).
Cibber, Colley, *An Apology for the Life of Mr. Colley Cibber*, ed. Robert W. Lowe (2 vols, London: John C. Nimmo, 1889).
Collier, Jeremy, *A Short View of the Immorality and Prophaneness of the English Stage: A Critical Edition*, ed. Benjamin Hellinger (New York and London: Garland Publishing, 1987).
Congreve, William, *Works*, ed. Montague Summers (New York: Russell & Russell, 1964).
A Comparison Between the Two Stages, with an Examen of The Generous Conqueror (London, 1702).
Danchin, Pierre, ed., *The Prologues and Epilogues of the Restoration, 1660–1700, Part III: 1691–1700*, vol. 5 (Nancy: Presses Universitaires de Nancy, 1985).
——, *Prologues and epilogues of the eighteenth century. Part I: 1701–1720*, vol. 1 (Nancy: Presses Universitaires de Nancy, 1990).
The Second Part of the Dancing Master, printed for H. Playford (London, 1698).
Dennis, John, *The Musical Entertainments in the Tragedy of Rinaldo and Armida*, in C.H. Wilkinson (ed.), *Theatre Miscellany: Six Pieces connected with the Seventeenth-Century Stage* (Oxford: Basil Blackwell, 1953), pp. 97–116.
Downes, John, *Roscius Anglicanus*, eds Judith Milhous and Robert D. Hume (London: Society for Theatre Research, 1987).
Durfey, Thomas, *Wit and Mirth; or, Pills to Purge Melancholy* (London, 1700).
Eccles, John, *The Judgment of Paris*, facsimile edition, intro. Richard Platt, *Music for London Entertainment 1660–1800*, Series C, vol. 1 (Tunbridge Wells: Richard Macnutt, 1984).
Evelyn, John, *The Diary of John Evelyn*, ed. E.S. de Beer (London: Clarendon Press, 1955).
Farquhar, George, *The Works of George Farquhar*, ed. Shirley Strum Kenny (2 vols, Oxford: Clarendon Press, 1988).
Gildon, Charles, *The Life of Mr. Thomas Betterton* (London, 1710).
Leveridge, Richard, *Richard Leveridge: The Complete Songs (with the music in* Macbeth*)*, intro. Olive Baldwin and Thelma Wilson, *Music for London Entertainment 1660–1800*, Series A, vol. 6 (London: Stainer & Bell, 1997).

Luttrell, Narcissus, *A Brief Historical Relation of State Affairs from September 1678 to April 1714* (6 vols, Oxford, 1857).
Motteux, Pierre, *The Gentleman's Journal, Or The Monthly Miscellany. By Way of Letter To A Gentleman in the Country. Consisting of News, History, Philosophy, Poetry, Musick, Translations, &c.* (London, 1692–94).
——, *The Rape of Europa by Jupiter (1694) and Acis and Galatea (1701)*, facsimile edition, ed. Lucyle Hook, The Augustan Reprint Society Publication 208 (Los Angeles: William Andrews Clark Memorial Library, 1981).
Settle, Elkanah, *Glory's Resurrection; Being The Triumphs of London Revived* (London, 1698).
Steele, Richard, *The Plays of Richard Steele*, ed. Shirley Strum Kenny (Oxford: Clarendon Press, 1971).
Viator, Timothy J. and William J. Burling, eds, *The Plays of Colley Cibber*, vol. 1 (London: Associated University Presses, 2001)
Winkler, Amanda Eubanks, *Music for Macbeth*, in *Recent Researches in the Music of the Baroque Era* 133 (Middleton, Wisconsin: AR Editions, 2004).

Secondary Sources

Backscheider, Paula R., "Stretching the Form: Catharine Trotter Cockburn and Other Failures," *Theater Journal* 47 (1995): 443–58.
Baldwin, Olive and Thelma Wilson, "The Music for Durfey's *Cinthia and Endimion*," *Theatre Notebook* 41/2 (1987): 70–4.
——, *Richard Leveridge: The Complete Songs (with the music in* Macbeth*)* in *Music for London Entertainment, 1660–1800* Series A vol. 6 (London: Stainer & Bell, 1997).
Barstow, Robert, "The Theatre Music of Daniel Purcell" (Ph.D. diss., Ohio State University, 1968).
Bartley, J.O., *Teague, Shenkin, and Sawney: Being an Historical Study of the Earliest Irish, Welsh, and Scottish Characters in English Plays* (Cork: Cork University Press, 1954).
Baskervill, Charles Read, *The Elizabethan Jig and Related Song Drama* (Chicago: University of Chicago Press, 1929).
Bucholz, R.O., *The Augustan Court: Queen Anne and the Decline of Court Culture* (Stanford: Stanford University Press, 1997).
Burden, Michael, ed., *Performing the Music of Henry Purcell* (Oxford: Clarendon Press, 1996).
Burling, William J., *A Checklist of New Plays and Entertainments on the London Stage, 1700–1737* (Rutherford, N.J.: Fairleigh Dickinson University Press, 1993).
Bray, Thomas, *Thomas Bray's Country Dances 1699*, eds Christine Helwig and Marshall Barron (New Haven: Playford Consort Publications, 1988).

Cook, D.F., "Françoise Marguérite de l'Epine: The Italian Lady?" *Theatre Notebook* 35 (1981): 58–73, 104–13.

Dawson, Mark S. *Gentility and the Comic Theatre of Late Stuart London* (Cambridge: Cambridge University Press, 2005).

Day, Cyrus Lawrence and Eleanore Boswell Murrie, *English Song-Books, 1651–1702* (London: The Bibliographical Society, 1940).

Downes, John, *Roscius Anglicanus*, eds Judith Milhous and Robert D. Hume (London: Society for Theatre Research, 1987).

Duffin, Ross W., *Shakespeare's Songbook* (New York: W.W. Norton, 2004).

Farquhar, George, *The Works of George Farquhar*, ed. Shirley Strum Kenny, 2 vols (Oxford: Clarendon Press, 1988).

Fiske, Roger, *English Theatre Music in the Eighteenth Century*, 2nd edition (London: Oxford University Press, 1986).

Freeman, Lisa, *Character's Theater: Genre and Identity on the Eighteenth-Century English Stage* (Philadelphia: University of Pennsylvania Press, 2002).

Goff, Moira, "'Actions, Manners, and Passions': Entr'acte Dancing on the London Stage, 1700–1737," *Early Music* 26/2 (1998): 213–28.

Hawkins, Sir John, *A General History of the Science and Practice of Music*, rev. edition (London: Novello, Ewer & Co., 1875).

Highfill Jr., Philip H., Kalman A. Burnim and Edward A. Langhans, *A Biographical Dictionary of Actors, Actresses, Musicians, Dancers, Managers & Other Stage Personnel in London, 1660–1800* (16 vols, Carbondale: Southern Illinois University Press, 1973–93).

Holland, Peter, *The Ornament of Action: Text and Performance in Restoration Comedy* (Cambridge: Cambridge University Press, 1979).

Holman, Peter, *Four and Twenty Fiddlers: The Violin at the English Court, 1540–1690* (Oxford: Clarendon Press, 1993).

——, "Purcell's Orchestra," *Musical Times* 137 (1996): 17–23.

Howe, Elizabeth, *The First English Actresses: Women and Drama 1660–1700* (Cambridge: Cambridge University Press, 1992).

Hughes, Derek, *English Drama, 1660–1700* (Oxford: Clarendon Press, 1996).

Hume, Robert D., *The Development of English Drama in the Late Seventeenth Century* (Oxford: Clarendon Press, 1976).

——, "Jeremy Collier and the Future of the London Theater in 1698," *Studies in Philology* 96/4 (1999): 480–511.

——, "The Politics of Opera in Late Seventeenth-Century London," *Cambridge Opera Journal* 10 (1998): 15–43.

——, "A Revival of *The Way of the World* in December 1701 or January 1702," *Theatre Notebook* 26 (1971): 30–36.

Hume, Robert D., ed., *The London Theatre World, 1660–1800* (Carbondale: Southern Illinois University Press, 1980).

Humphreys, Mark, "Daniel Purcell: A Biography and Thematic Catalogue" (D.Phil. diss., New College, Oxford, 2004).

Hunter, David, "George Frideric Handel as Victim: Composer–Publisher Relations and the Discourse of Musicology," in David Crawford and G. Grayson Wagstaff, eds, *Encomium Musicae: Essays in Memory of Robert J. Snow* (Hillsdale, New York: Pendragon Press, 2002), 663–91.

———, *Opera and Song Books Published in England, 1703–1726: A Descriptive Bibliography* (London: Bibliographical Society, 1997).

Jordan, R., "Richard Norton and the Theatre at Southwick," *Theatre Notebook* 38 (1984): 105–15.

Kephart, Carolyn, "Thomas Durfey's *Cinthia and Endimion*: A Reconsideration," *Theatre Notebook* 39 (1985): 134–9.

Knapp, J. Merrill, "Eighteenth-Century Opera in London before Handel, 1705–1710" in Shirley Strum Kenny, ed., *British Theatre and the Other Arts, 1660–1800*, (Washington, D.C.: Folger Shakespeare Library, 1984).

Koon, Helene, *Colley Cibber: A Biography* (Lexington: University Press of Kentucky, 1986).

Lincoln, Stoddard, "John Eccles: Last of a Tradition" (Ph.D. diss., Oxford University, 1963).

The London Stage, 1660–1800. Part 1 (1660–1700), ed. William Van Lennep, Emmet L. Avery, and Arthur H. Scouten. Part 2 (1700–1729), ed. Emmett L. Avery (Carbondale, Illinois: Southern Illinois University Press, 1965, 1960).

Lowerre, Kathryn, "Dramatick Opera and Theatrical Reform: Dennis's *Rinaldo and Armida* and Motteux's *The Island Princess*," *Theatre Notebook* 59 (2005): 23–40.

———, "Music and Meaning in Congreve's *The Way of the World*," *Restoration and Eighteenth-Century Theatre Research* 15/1 (2000): 24–52.

Luckett, Richard, "Exotic but Rational Entertainments: the English Dramatick Operas," in Marie Axton and Raymond Williams, eds, *English Drama Forms and Development* (Cambridge: Cambridge University Press, 1977).

Luttrell, Narcissus, *A Brief Historical Relation of State Affairs, from September 1678 to April 1714* (6 vols, Oxford: University Press, 1857).

Marsden, Jean I., *Fatal Desire: Women, Sexuality, and the English Stage, 1660–1720* (Ithaca and London: Cornell University Press, 2006).

McGeary, Thomas, "Thomas Clayton and the Introduction of Italian Opera to England," *Philological Quarterly* 77 (1998): 171–86.

Milhous, Judith, "The Multimedia Spectacular on the Restoration Stage," in Shirley Strum Kenny, ed., *British Theatre and the Other Arts, 1660–1800* (Washington, D.C.: Folger Books, 1984), pp. 41–66.

———, *Thomas Betterton and the Management of Lincoln's Inn Fields, 1695–1708* (Carbondale and Edwardsville: Southern Illinois University Press, 1979).

Milhous, Judith and Robert D. Hume, "Dating Play Premières from Publication Data, 1660–1700," *Harvard Library Bulletin* 25 (1974): 374–405.

———, "New Documents about the London Theatre 1685–1711," *Harvard Library Bulletin* 36 (1988): 248–74.

——, *A Register of English Theatrical Documents, 1660–1737* (2 vols, Carbondale and Edwardsville: Southern Illinois University Press, 1991), vol. 1, 1660–1714.

——, "Theatrical Politics at Drury Lane: New Light on Letitia Cross, Jane Rogers, and Anne Oldfield," *Bulletin of Research in the Humanities* 85 (1992): 412–29.

——, eds, *Vice Chamberlain Coke's Theatrical Papers, 1706–1715* (Carbondale and Edwardsville: Southern Illinois University Press, 1982).

Moore, Robert Etheridge, *Henry Purcell and the Restoration Theatre* (Cambridge, Mass.: Harvard University Press, 1961).

Muller, Frans, "Flying Dragons and Dancing Chairs at Dorset Garden: Staging *Dioclesian*," *Theatre Notebook* 47/2 (1993): 80–95.

Neufeldt, Timothy, "The Social and Political Aspects of the Pastoral Mode in Musico-dramatic Works; London, 1695–1728" (Ph.D. diss., University of Toronto, 2006).

Novak, Maximilian, "The Closing of Lincoln's Inn Fields Theatre in 1695," *Restoration and Eighteenth-Century Theatre Research* 14 (1975): 51–2.

Noyes, Robert Gale, "Conventions of Song in Restoration Tragedy," *PMLA* 53 (1938): 162–88.

Pinnock, Andrew, "Play into Opera: Purcell's *The Indian Queen*," *Early Music* 18/1 (1990): 3–21.

Plank, Steven E., "'And Now about the Cauldron Sing': Music and the Supernatural on the Restoration Stage," *Early Music* 18/3 (1990): 392–407.

Price, Curtis A., "The Critical Decade for English Music Drama, 1700–1710," *Harvard Library Bulletin* 26 (1978): 38–76.

——, *Henry Purcell and the London Stage* (Cambridge: Cambridge University Press, 1984).

——, "Restoration Stage Fiddlers and Their Music," *Early Music* 7/3 (1979): 315–22.

——, *Music in the Restoration Theatre* (Ann Arbor: UMI Research Press, 1979).

——, "The Small-Coal Cult," *Musical Times* 119 (1978): 1032–34.

Roberson, Matthew, "Of Priests, Fiends, Fops, and Fools: John Bowman's Song Performances on the London Stage, 1677–1701" (Ph.D. Diss., Florida State University, 2006).

Rosenfeld, Sybil, *Georgian Scene Painters and Scene Painting* (Cambridge: Cambridge University Press, 1981).

——, *A Short History of Scene Design in Great Britain* (Oxford: Basil Blackwell, 1973).

——, *The Theatre of the London Fairs in the Eighteenth Century* (Cambridge: Cambridge University Press, 1960).

Samuel, Harold E., "A German Musician comes to London in 1704," *Musical Times* 122 (1986): 591–3.

Savage, Roger, "'Even the Music between the Acts…'—John Dennis, Johann Adolph Scheibe and the Rethinking of Incidental Music, 1698/1738," in John

Thomson, ed., *Books and Bibliography… Essays in Commemoration of Don McKenzie* (Wellington: Victoria University Press, 1998).

——, "The Theatre Music" in Michael Burden ed., *The Purcell Companion* (Portland, Ore.: Amadeus Press, 1994).

Sawkins, Lionel, "Trembleurs and Cold People: How Should They Shiver?" in Michael Burden, ed., *Performing the Music of Henry Purcell* (Oxford: Clarendon Press, 1996).

Semmens, Richard, "Dancing and Dance Music in Purcell's Operas," in Michael Burden ed., *Performing the Music of Henry Purcell* (Oxford: Clarendon Press, 1996).

Shay, Robert and Robert Thompson, *Purcell Manuscripts: The Principal Musical Sources* (Cambridge: Cambridge University Press, 2000).

Simpson, Claude M., *The British Broadside Ballad and Its Music* (New Brunswick, N.J.: Rutgers University Press, 1966).

Speck, W.A., *The Birth of Britain: A New Nation, 1700–1710* (Oxford: Blackwell, 1994).

Spitzer, John and Neal Zaslaw, *The Birth of the Orchestra: History of an Institution, 1650–1815* (Oxford: Oxford University Press, 2004).

Sternfeld, F.W., *Music in Shakespearean Tragedy* (London: Routledge and Kegan Paul, 1963).

Thomas, David and Arnold Hare, compilers, *Restoration and Georgian England, 1660–1800*, ed. David Thomas (Cambridge: Cambridge University Press, 1989).

Thorp, Jennifer, "Dance in Late 17th-century London: Priestly Muddles," *Early Music* 26/2 (1998): 198–210.

——, "'So Great a Master as Mr Isaac': an Exemplary Dancing-master of Late Stuart London," *Early Music* 35 (2007): 435–46.

Thorp, Willard, ed., *Songs from the Restoration Theater* (Princeton: Princeton University Press, 1934 [repr. Da Capo Press, 1970]).

Weber, William, *The Rise of Musical Classics in Eighteenth-Century England: A Study in Canon, Ritual, and Ideology* (Oxford: Clarendon Press, 1992).

Winkler, Amanda Eubanks, *O Let Us Howle Some Heavy Note: Music for Witches, the Melancholic, and the Mad on the Seventeenth-Century English Stage* (Bloomington and Indianapolis: Indiana University Press, 2006).

Winn, James A., "Heroic Song: A Proposal for a Revised History of English Theater and Opera, 1656–1711," *Eighteenth-Century Studies* 30 (1996): 113–37.

Index of Persons

L'Abbé, Anthony 201–2, 237, 267, 273, 294, 326, 331, 339, 348, 351, 371
Abell, John 266, 291–2, 305, 339
Akeroyde, Samuel 45, 145, 203, 235, 239, 292
Allinson, Maria 183, 200, 231
Anne, Queen (Princess) of England 143, 147, 174, 178, 190, 216, 221–2, 243, 263–4, 269, 271, 283, 304, 309, 316, 329, 340–1, 344–6, 348
Ayliff, Mrs 46, 127–8, 150, 153, 156, 170, 191, 201, 211

Baker, Thomas 27, 287, 306, 313–5, 323, 370
Balon, Jean 201–2, 237, 371
Banks, John 71, 78, 148–50, 344
Barrett, John 72, 171, 250–1, 257, 270, 308, 345, 367
Barry, Elizabeth 8, 55, 70, 83, 125, 141, 158, 164, 172, 178–9, 206–7, 240, 267, 284, 295–6, 316–8, 321, 331, 344, 375
Beaumont, Francis 65, 80, 190, 225, 325
Behn, Aphra 35, 37, 42, 60, 139, 145, 153, 325, 330, 370–71
Betterton, Thomas 7–8, 46, 55–60, 81, 83, 89, 125–6, 129, 134, 147–8, 158, 164, 187, 201, 215, 249, 252, 259, 261, 264, 268–9, 271, 294, 296, 305, 319, 326, 331, 336, 339, 348, 359, 370, 375
Bicknell, Margaret 24, 268, 370
Blow, John 3, 13, 128, 143–5, 195, 255, 270
Bourdon, Mr 255, 291
Bowen, James (Jemmy) 45, 104–5, 127, 135, 139, 144–6, 152, 159, 161, 176, 200, 220, 232, 275, 290, 300
Bowen, William 144, 301

Bowman, Elizabeth 53–4, 81, 125, 158, 172–3, 179–82, 185, 199, 209, 211, 216–7, 250–1, 254, 260, 273, 276–7, 279, 311, 319
Bowman, John 1, 19, 26–7, 30, 44, 47, 52–3, 63, 114, 125, 133, 134, 147, 158, 160, 166, 170, 172–3, 179–82, 185, 191, 199, 209, 211, 214, 216–7, 248, 250–1, 254, 264, 273–4, 276–80, 287, 301, 304, 332, 352, 355, 358
Boyle, Charles 76, 307, 319
Boyle, Roger 76, 164
Bracegirdle, Anne 8, 19, 22, 28, 30, 44, 47–853, 56–60, 63, 70, 76, 81, 83, 109, 112, 125–6, 131, 133, 141, 144, 147, 150–1, 154, 156–7, 160, 170, 172, 178–9, 181, 193, 199, 207, 214, 229–30, 236, 240, 242, 250–1, 253–5, 260, 270, 275–9, 296, 309, 312, 318–19, 321–3, 331–2, 341–3, 348, 350, 353, 356, 358–9, 363, 372, 375
Bradshaw, Lucretia 45, 54, 251, 313, 363, 371
Bray, Thomas 129–30, 201
Brome, Richard 355, 370
Bullock, William 63, 183, 199, 231, 258–9, 301, 303, 313, 323
Burnaby, William 284–6, 297, 299, 301, 312–13, 371
Butler, James, Duke of Ormond 222, 263
Byron, William, Lord 178, 303

Campion, Mary Anne 22, 24, 104–105, 127, 171, 187, 200–201, 220, 222, 232, 239, 258, 261, 266, 268, 271, 299, 309, 319, 325, 333, 351
Celotti, Ziuliana 334, 366

Centlivre, Susanna 76, 80, 271, 273–4, 304–5, 310, 322–3, 363–5
Charles II, King of England 7, 13, 124, 128, 139, 159
Cherrier, Rene 10, 331, 334, 348, 351, 355, 359, 370–2
Church, John 127, 135, 168, 188, 273
Cibber, Colley 17, 22, 35–7, 42–3, 56, 61–3, 66, 70–73, 79, 81, 125, 130, 139, 152–3, 158, 163, 166–7, 171, 174, 177–80, 199, 221, 232–3, 237, 252, 265, 267, 271, 274–5, 287, 291, 303, 307, 309, 315, 318, 332–3, 348, 355, 359, 362–3, 370, 373
Cibber, Katherine Shore 127, 177–8, 206
Clarke, Jeremiah 3, 43, 64, 92, 128, 145, 161, 164, 166, 171, 176, 189–92, 203, 208, 222, 231, 250, 270, 292, 308, 332, 335, 347, 351
Clementine, Signior 201, 237, 334
Collier, Jeremy 196–8, 220–1, 225, 236, 330, 343
Congreve, William 2, 4, 11, 13, 17, 25–6, 44, 69–70, 130–136, 139, 155, 166, 170, 178, 193, 198, 202–3, 207, 216, 240–241, 253–4, 260–261, 266, 270, 274, 292, 297, 317–9, 330, 340–342, 345–6, 348, 351, 356, 360–361, 366–7, 373, 375
Cook, Mr 57–8, 60, 278, 317, 331, 333, 343, 353, 357, 360
Corbett, William 13, 167, 259, 270, 312–13, 318, 370, 375
Corelli, Arcangelo 3, 129, 269
Corey, John 248, 355–8
Cottin(e), Mr. 260, 370
Courteville, Raphael 128, 145–7, 203, 225–6, 271, 326
Cousser see Kusser
Craufurd, David 258–9, 346–7
Croft, William 3, 61–3, 182, 259, 270, 273, 297, 310, 335
Cross, Letitia 21–2, 24, 35–6, 41, 45, 63, 76, 91, 126, 128, 130, 135, 139, 142, 144–7, 152–5, 159–61, 163, 166–9, 174, 176, 178, 187–9, 191, 193, 200, 206, 208, 222, 266, 332–3, 338, 360, 362, 367–8, 372
Cross, Thomas 6, 13, 29, 36, 41–2, 53, 139, 147, 153, 166, 176, 178, 185, 216, 222–3, 227, 229–32, 239, 241, 244, 254, 273, 311–12, 333, 343, 350, 363
Crowne, John 27, 71, 77, 215, 222, 229, 306
Curco, Mr 127, 148, 230, 284

Davenant, Charles 88, 96, 113, 280, 294
Davenant, William 7, 89, 191, 324
Davis, John 57–60, 312, 317, 333, 335, 346, 350, 353
Deane, Thomas 13, 269, 306, 311, 335
Dennis, John 10–11, 65, 68, 72, 77–8, 84, 88, 96–7, 99–109, 112–9, 129, 183, 198, 204, 223, 226, 230–231, 237, 244–5, 252, 260, 263, 276, 304, 330, 344, 362, 365, 368
Dieupart, Charles 334, 337, 345, 360
Dilke, Thomas 43–4, 85, 129, 147, 163, 172–5, 216–20, 254, 273, 339
Dogget, Thomas 8, 19, 27, 35, 51, 63, 125–6, 130–131, 133, 147, 155–6, 158–9, 170, 174, 176–9, 199, 265, 267, 276, 278–80, 287, 305, 310, 312, 318, 326, 332, 346, 348, 352, 355
Downes, John 88, 148, 150, 160, 201–2, 207, 214, 229, 254, 256, 260, 276, 359, 367
Draghi, Giovanni Baptista 128, 158
Drake, James 183, 185
Dryden, John 7, 24, 44, 52, 78, 88, 100, 106, 132, 134, 139, 145, 147, 150, 156, 163–4, 167, 190, 196, 204, 206, 214–15, 221, 225–6, 241, 252, 257, 261, 263, 270, 274, 276, 299, 314, 325, 350–353, 370–372
Durfey, Thomas 19–20, 23–4, 26–8, 52, 63, 66, 68, 71, 76, 79, 81, 92, 113, 118, 125, 130, 136, 142, 144, 153, 156–7, 159, 164, 166, 175–7, 179, 181–3, 189–90, 197–8, 204, 214, 217, 221, 229, 231, 233, 237–9, 243, 257, 259–60, 263–5, 273–4,

Index od Persons 403

287, 291–2, 301–2, 310, 313, 315–16, 361, 363, 372
Du Ruel, Eleanor 370–371
Du Ruel, Philippe 268, 325, 331, 335, 348, 351, 355, 361, 370–371–9

Eccles, John 3, 11, 13, 20, 22–3, 29–35, 43–7, 52–5, 57–60, 63–4, 72, 85, 87, 96, 102–4, 107–116, 119, 126, 128–9, 131–4, 136–7, 139, 141, 144, 147–51, 156–60, 166, 170, 172–5, 179, 181–2, 185–6, 191–2, 203, 206, 208, 210–211, 214, 218, 220, 224–5, 229–31, 241–2, 259, 253–6, 258–9, 269–70, 273, 277–81, 284, 287, 292, 303, 305, 312–13, 317–18, 321–2, 324–5, 331–2, 348–50, 353, 356, 358, 360, 367, 372, 375
Eccles, Solomon 203, 243
Edwards, Thomas 37, 41, 127, 143, 168–9, 188
Elford, Mrs 10, 260, 326, 331, 351
Elford, Richard 73–5, 266, 271, 296, 324, 335
Elizabeth I, Queen of England 316, 341, 344
l'Epine, Margarita de 202, 266–7, 319, 326, 333–4, 340, 352, 365–6, 370–371
Erwin, Mrs 93, 227, 245, 253, 255, 258, 266
Estcourt, Richard 9–10, 271, 318 –19

Fairbank, Charles 268, 326, 355
Farquhar, George 4, 18, 23–5, 81, 230–231, 243, 260–261, 280, 287, 290–291, 303, 309–310, 314, 370
Fideli, Signior 201, 334
Filmer, Edward 85–6, 90, 166, 175, 185
Finger, Gottfried 6, 12–1326, 46–51, 84, 92, 95, 128, 131, 133–4, 145, 151, 157–9, 170, 173, 178, 202–3, 226, 250, 258–9, 270, 273, 280, 283, 290, 292–3
Fletcher, John 7, 65, 80, 95, 142, 151, 160, 190–1, 225–6, 231, 240, 257, 275, 278, 325, 352

Forcer, Francis 186, 202–3, 207, 293
Franck, Johann Wolfgang 37–40, 153, 270
Freeman, John (singer) 37, 104–5, 126–7, 135, 143, 145, 158, 169, 176–7, 187, 191, 193, 200, 206, 208, 220, 223, 232,238–9, 244, 253, 258, 265

Gallia, Maria Margherita 201–2, 267, 325, 334, 365, 369–70
Gasperini *see* Visconti, Gasparo
Gildon, Charles 37, 41, 65, 68, 71–2, 79, 96–100, 103–6, 112–19, 128, 153, 169, 198, 220, 248–50, 287, 295, 309, 342, 351
Gillier, Mr 283–5, 347
Gorton, William 191, 352
Gouge, Mr 105, 107, 230, 241–2, 250, 260, 265
Gould, Robert 76, 143
Granville, George 46, 88, 150–1, 214–15, 270–271, 276–7, 306, 375
Greber, Jakob 267, 336, 340, 352, 366–7, 369

Harris, Joseph 20, 171, 235
Haynes, Joseph (Jo) 27, 154, 161, 168, 174, 188, 230, 369
Haynes, Mrs. 230, 260, 286
Higgons, Bevill 76, 301
Hodgson, John 45, 127, 264
Hodgson, Mary 31, 45, 47–8, 51, 53, 57–60, 74, 99, 127, 136, 147, 159, 163, 170, 173, 179, 186, 191, 201, 209, 211, 226, 230, 241, 250–1, 253, 255–6, 266, 271, 273, 277–8, 286, 296, 305, 313, 317–18, 321, 331–3, 335, 347, 350–353, 370, 373
Hopkins, Charles 77, 136, 139, 207, 242–3
Hughes, Francis 265, 275, 283, 325, 331, 333–4, 360–362, 368, 373

James II, former King of England 7, 123–4, 128, 159, 243, 263, 284
Jonson, Ben 3, 175, 267, 271, 294, 305, 325, 363

Keen, Edward 310
Killigrew, Charles 124, 198

King, Robert 164, 231
Kusser, Johann Sigismund 331, 335, 369, 371

La Rich, Francis 269, 293
Laroche, James (Jemmy) 45, 53–4, 109, 151, 158, 181, 213
Laroon, Marcellus 253, 265, 283, 323–5, 334
Lee, Michael 42–3, 170, 191, 209
Lee, Nathaniel 81–84, 113, 150, 163, 240, 283–4, 325, 351, 370
Lenton, John 3, 57, 72–3, 128, 163–4, 195, 203, 214, 220, 226, 250, 257, 270, 276, 296, 317, 342, 344, 365
Leveridge, Richard 37, 41, 61–2, 64, 76, 91, 116, 127, 135, 144–6, 155, 161, 163, 166, 169–71, 174, 176–8, 183–4, 187–8, 191, 200, 203, 208, 216, 231–2, 236–9, 241, 244, 251, 253, 264–5, 270, 279–80, 283–4, 316, 323–5, 330–331, 333, 343, 345–6, 348, 351–2, 354, 357–60, 362–3, 365, 370–371, 373
Lindelheim, Joanna Maria "the Baroness" 267, 325, 366
Lindsey, Mary 104, 127, 171, 176, 200, 205–6, 208, 216, 220, 222, 227, 232, 253, 266, 271, 283, 302, 324, 331, 333, 348, 360–361, 371
Louis XIV, King of France 52, 123, 170, 195, 212, 263, 296
Lucas, Jane 21–2, 24, 125, 130, 166–7, 187, 191, 200, 265, 268, 273, 291, 300, 314, 370
Lully, Jean-Baptiste 3, 10, 70, 96, 100–101, 104, 114, 129, 230, 335, 347

Magnus, Mr and his pupil, "Magnus's Boy," 105, 201, 220, 232
Manley, Delarivier 27, 153–4, 158–60, 164, 166–7, 207, 295, 342
Manning, Francis 251, 308–10
Mary II, Queen of England 71, 123, 145
Matteis, Nicola 222, 311
Mills, Margaret 206, 231, 265, 283, 324, 331

Molière, Jean-Baptiste 238, 259, 322, 347, 365–7
Morgan, Thomas 128, 142, 145, 164, 203, 205–6, 208, 226, 231
Mosse, Mrs "The Devonshire Girl" 268, 331, 335, 370
Motteux, Pierre Antoine (Peter A.) 5, 13, 22, 24, 27, 36, 41, 42–56, 57–8, 60, 63, 68–9, 76, 87–90, 95, 116–19, 126, 129–31, 139, 142, 152–5, 159–60, 166, 170, 175, 185, 189–90, 192–3, 196–8, 200, 204, 208–12, 214, 221, 226, 230–231, 233–6, 252, 277–9, 287, 291, 295, 307, 317, 319, 325–6, 337, 340, 345–6, 360, 362–3, 365–6, 371–2
Mountfort, Susanna *see* Verbruggen, Susanna Mountfort

North, Roger 12, 17–18, 20, 42, 67, 197, 292–3
Norton, Richard 77, 154–5

Oldfield, Anne 128, 260, 344
Oldmixon, John 23, 52, 54–5, 65, 92–4, 97, 100, 129, 155, 185, 204, 223, 227, 241, 252–3, 265, 269, 310, 321, 366
Olsii, Giuseppe 332, 348
Ormond, Duke of *see* Butler, James
Otway, Thomas 66, 84, 163, 342, 350, 370

Pack, George 56–7, 304, 313, 332, 359, 365, 371–2
Pate, John 46, 76, 104–5, 116, 123–4, 127–8, 133–4, 136, 167, 193, 200, 205, 220, 232, 236, 238–9, 243–4, 253, 258, 265, 279, 283, 290, 300
Paisible, James 13, 128, 146, 152, 154, 259, 270, 273, 304, 306, 309, 325, 333, 335, 340, 359, 370
Penkethman, William 41, 63, 174, 183, 199, 231,235–8, 245, 258–9, 265, 275, 299, 302, 305–6, 314, 316, 348, 368–9
Pepusch, Johann Christoph 266, 335, 352
Perrin, Anne 158, 166, 170, 173, 201, 211
Philips, William 76, 80, 221–2

Pix, Mary 27, 76–7, 79, 157, 159–63, 166, 180, 185–6, 193, 205, 208, 213, 216, 223, 235, 240–241, 253–5, 287, 291, 295, 310, 325, 339, 358, 367–8
Powell, George 3, 8, 41, 130, 142, 161, 167–8, 205–6, 215, 230, 331
Prince, Joseph 129, 326
Prince, Miss & Mrs 24, 172–3, 199, 214, 251, 268, 311, 326, 346, 350
Purcell, Daniel 1, 3, 35, 41, 46, 61–2, 84, 91–2, 96, 103–4, 107, 128–9, 132, 135, 145, 152–5, 159–62, 168–9, 171, 174–7, 189, 192, 200, 203, 216, 222–3, 226–8, 231–2, 238, 243, 245–7, 250, 253, 255, 258, 270, 273, 275, 280, 283–6, 288–92, 294, 297–300, 302–3, 305, 308–9, 323–4, 332, 336, 340, 351, 359, 363, 367–8, 372
Purcell, Henry 3–6, 10, 19, 24, 46, 60, 66–7, 71–2, 76, 80–81, 84–5, 87, 91–2, 96, 103–4, 114, 119, 123, 126, 128–32, 134–5, 139, 142–7, 155, 160, 163, 167, 177–8, 192, 203, 206, 221, 226, 232–4, 240–1, 243, 248–50, 252, 270, 274–5, 278, 291, 293–4, 297, 303–4, 307, 314, 316, 324–6, 333, 336, 348, 351, 353, 357–8, 369–72, 375

Quinault, Philippe 70, 96–7, 220, 230

Ramondon, Littleton 29, 335, 367, 371
Ravenscroft, Edward 46, 79, 86–7, 104, 170, 208, 213, 215–16, 317
Reading, John 43, 46, 48, 53, 123–4, 127, 134, 136, 147–8, 170, 201
Rich, Christopher 7, 9–10, 13, 56, 130, 144, 161, 175, 187, 203, 315, 318, 329–30, 334, 336, 355, 359–60
Richardson, Vaughan 195, 231
Robart, William 335
Rowe, Nicholas 23, 56–60, 61, 63, 71–2, 74, 80, 275–6, 296, 315–17, 341, 355, 358

Saggione, Giuseppe Fedeli 267, 325

Scott, Thomas 79, 131, 141–2, 160
Settle, Elkanah 21, 77, 79, 94–5, 118, 130, 151, 187–9, 239, 277, 292, 294, 361
Shadwell, Thomas 12, 51, 71, 79–80, 88, 139, 190, 269, 271, 278, 293, 305, 324, 351, 353, 370–371
Shakespeare, William 7, 60, 65, 76, 139, 157, 163, 191–2, 196, 248, 252, 259, 261, 271, 276, 293, 304, 312, 324–5, 353, 370, 372
Shaw, Mrs 266, 275, 290, 323–4
Short, Benjamin 342–3, 355
Sorin, Joseph 55, 129, 205, 268
Southerne, Thomas 72, 131, 145–7, 153, 172, 226, 256–7, 274, 306, 370
Steele, Richard 21, 56, 60–63, 264, 296–300, 314–15, 337, 341, 367–8, 372, 375
Subligny, Marie-Thérèse Perdou de 268, 306, 371
Swiney, Owen 365–7

Tasso, Torquato 70, 100, 106, 116, 223, 230
Tate, Nahum 145, 233, 271, 351–2
Temple, Diana 41, 93, 130, 176, 200, 236, 255, 275
Thornhill, Sir John 361
Tofts, Catherine 318, 332–4, 339–40, 348, 360–362, 370, 373
Tollett, Thomas 128, 148, 164, 203, 226
Trapp, Joseph 80, 341–2, 372
Trotter, Catharine 78, 81, 152, 166, 216, 221, 235, 274, 286, 323

Vanbrugh, John 37, 125, 130, 171, 174, 179–81, 185, 198–202, 215, 226, 241, 257, 260, 284–6, 303, 307, 325, 329–31, 346, 369, 371, 375
Verbruggen, John 56, 126, 168, 244
Verbruggen, Susanna Mountfort 126, 145, 159, 161, 287, 291, 303, 309, 313–14
Visconti, Gasparo "Gasperini" 267, 269, 325, 335, 340, 352

Walker, William 78, 84, 221–3, 230, 338–9, 350
Walsh, John 6, 10, 13, 29, 57, 61–2, 72, 103, 106–7, 109–10, 140, 171, 178, 189, 220, 223, 227, 230–231, 239–41, 244–5, 253–5, 259, 270, 273, 275–6, 283, 290, 304, 308, 311–12, 318–19, 323–4, 326, 333, 335, 344, 346, 356, 362–3, 365, 367–8, 373
Weaver, John 260, 268
Weldon, John 3, 195, 266, 269–71, 292, 303, 306, 309, 312–13, 319, 323, 340, 345–6, 351, 363
Wilford, John 335, 353–4
Wilks, Robert 26, 61–3, 81, 200, 243, 265, 274–5, 290, 297, 302, 308–9, 313–14, 322–3, 331, 359, 367
Wilkinson, Richard 322–3
William III 45, 123–4, 129, 170, 175, 177, 195–6, 202 211–12, 233, 263–4, 278, 294–6, 300
William, Duke of Gloucester 191, 263
Williams, William 163, 209, 231
Willis, Elizabeth 24, 53, 126, 169, 171, 179, 191, 199, 209, 235, 251, 255, 259, 265, 279, 305, 310, 335, 350–352, 355
Wiltshire, John 191, 201, 209, 250–251, 278–9
Wiseman, Jane 70, 76, 80, 295

Index of Productions

Titles of new productions are given in bold. Revivals of musical interest are in plain text. Plays commonly referred to by a protagonist's name are indexed by that name: for example, *King Lear* and *Don Quixote* instead of *The True and Ancient History of King Lear* and *The Comical History of Don Quixote*. Revived plays without new music, mentioned only in passing, are not indexed.

Abdelazer; or, The Moor's Revenge 139, 153, 186
Abra Mule; or, Love and Empire 80, 337–8, 341–4, 352, 359, 368, 371–2
Achilles; or, Iphigenia in Aulis 242, 245–7
Acis and Galatea 19, 22, 55, 76, 107, 251, 267, 272, 277, 279–81, 309, 315, 319, 323, 325–6, 346, 352, 371
Aeneas and Dido see *Dido and Aeneas*
Aesop 126, 165, 174–5, 191, 193, 307
Aesop, Part II 165, 175
Agnes de Castro 78, 140, 152
Albion Queens; or, The Death of Mary Queen of Scotland, The 330, 337–8, 344–5
Alexander the Great (dramatick opera based on *The Rival Queens*) 84, 92, 174, 271–2, 280–284, 290, 293, 301
All for the Better; or, The Infallible Cure 308, 310
All for Love; or, The World Well Lost 164, 351
Altemira 76, 295
Amalasont, Queen of the Goths 227–8
Ambitious Step-mother, The 71, 272, 275–6
Amintas 23, 97, 100, 223, 227, 252–3, 321, 366
Amorous Widow; or, The Wanton Wife 259, 371

Amphitryon; or, The Two Sosias 52, 274, 372
Anatomist; or, The Sham Doctor, The 46–7, 165, 170, 213, 216, 264, 306, 351–2
Antiochus the Great 70, 76, 80, 295–6
Arsinoe, Queen of Cyprus 176, 327, 332, 334, 336–7, 339, 355–6, 359–62, 366, 368, 371–2, 375
As You Find It 306–308, 318–19

Bath; or the Western Lass, The 20, 272, 287, 291–2, 310, 313
Beau Defeated; or, The Lucky Younger Brother 242, 253–6
Beau's Duel; or, A Soldier for the Ladies, The 295, 304–305
Beauty in Distress 69, 198, 205, 221
Biter, The 23, 56–61, 356, 358–9, 372
Boadicea; Queen of Britain 77, 186, 203–204, 207–208
Bonduca; or, The British Heroine 76, 85, 88, 90–91, 103–104, 117, 130, 140, 142–3, 164, 168, 186, 208, 241, 243, 316, 340
Britain's Happiness 210, 337–8, 340, 345–6, 363, 365
Brutus of Alba; or, Augusta's Triumph 66–7, 78–9, 85, 92, 101, 104, 113, 118, 126, 130, 155, 165, 168–70, 187, 190, 205, 220, 267
Bussy d'Ambois 259

Caligula 71, 77, 80, 96, 205, 215–16, 221–2
Campaigners; or, The Pleasant Adventures at Brussels 221–2, 361
Careless Husband, The 333, 356, 359, 362, 371
Cares of Love; or, A Night's Adventures, The 356, 368–9
Cinthia and Endimion; or, The Loves of the Deities 24, 52, 67, 92, 118, 165, 174–7, 181, 187, 189, 191, 206
Circe 88, 96, 113, 117, 267, 280, 294
City Bride; or, The Merry Cuckold, The 20, 141, 158, 235
City Lady; or, Folly Reclaim'd, The 85, 158, 165, 172–4, 191, 207
Comical Gallant; or, The Amours of Sir John Falstaff 295, 304
Comical History of Don Quixote see *Don Quixote*
Committee; or, The Faithful Irishman, The 156, 225
Conquest of Granada by the Spaniards, The 139, 147, 299
Conquest of Spain, The 356, 367–8
Constant Couple; or, A Trip to the Jubilee, The 23, 81, 242–4, 260–1, 269, 280, 287, 351
Consultation, The 356, 366
Cornish Comedy, The 21, 93, 141, 147, 161, 190, 193, 212, 363
Country House, The 204, 215, 325
Country-Wake, The 141, 155, 158
Country Wife, The 268, 305, 310, 325
Courtship A-la-mode 242, 258–9
Cure for Jealousie, A 25, 242, 248
Cyrus the Great; or, The Tragedy of Love 71, 76, 78–9, 85, 109, 140, 148–50, 191
Czar of Muscovy, The 272, 287, 310

Deceiver Deceived, The 204, 208, 213–14, 291
Dido and Aeneas 6, 130, 139, 233, 248–51, 327, 351, 369
Different Widows; or, Intrigue All-A-Mode, The 338–9

Dioclesian 12, 66, 95, 104, 113, 130, 168, 187, 190, 226, 231, 260, 278, 293
Dr. Faustus 24, 35, 55, 190, 205, 267
Don John; or, The Libertine Destroy'd 71, 190, 353–4
Don Quixote, The Comical History of, Parts I & II 19, 28, 71, 103, 144, 150, 154, 161, 197–8, 238, 257, 260, 279, 323, 326, 352, 372
Don Quixote, The Comical History of, Part III 140, 142, 144–5, 197–8, 238
Don Sebastian; King of Portugal 190, 371
Double Dealer, The 44, 198, 240, 297, 351
Double Distress, The 77, 79, 272, 287

Edward III, King 306
Emperor of the Moon, The 325, 330, 350, 370–1
Empress of Morocco, The 79, 239, 277, 294
Europe's Revels for the Peace of Ryswick 159, 191, 196, 201, 204, 208–13, 251, 261, 277, 346, 363, 365

Fair Example; or, The Modish Citizens, The 9–10, 308, 318–19
Fair Penitent, The 63, 80, 270, 308, 316–18
Fairy Queen, The 46, 60, 88–9, 91, 129–30, 168, 186, 188, 249, 304, 340, 350
Faithful Bride of Granada, The 71, 295, 305
False Friend; or, The Fate of Disobedience, The (LIF, 1699) 227, 240
False Friend, The (DL, 1702) 295, 303
Famous History of the Rise and Fall of Massaniello, The see *Massaniello*
Farewel Folly; or, The Younger the Wiser 356, 362–3
Fatal Discovery; or, Loves in Ruins, The 2, 79–81, 205, 215
Fatal Friendship, The 205, 216, 221
Fate of Capua, The 172, 242, 256–7
Feign'd Friendship; or, The Mad Reformer 25, 227, 239–40, 248

Female Wits; or, The Triumvirate of Poets at Rehearsal 27, 130, 160, 164–7, 187, 265, 323
Fickle Shepherdess, The 19, 23, 266, 270, 307, 319–22, 326, 366
Fond Husband; or, The Plotting Sisters, The 190–1, 350
Fox, The see *Volpone*
Friendship Improv'd; or, The Female Warriour 242–3
Funeral; or, Grief A-la-mode, The 21, 61, 66, 269, 295–300, 313–14, 341, 351

Gamester, The 356, 363, 365
Generous Choice, The 242, 251–2
Generous Conqueror; or, The Timely Discovery, The 22, 72, 76, 295, 301
Generous Enemies; or, The Ridiculous Lovers, The 163
Gentleman Cully, The 272, 293
Gibraltar; or, The Spanish Adventure 356, 365, 368
Gli Amori d'Ergasto 356, 366–7
Governour of Cyprus, The 13, 269, 308, 310–11
Grove; or, Love's Paradice, The 92–5, 104, 155, 174, 241–2, 244, 252–3, 258, 261, 265

Hamlet, Prince of Denmark 20, 79, 139, 280
Henry the Fourth; with the Humours of Sir John Falstaff 252, 259, 370
Henry V 259
Henry VIII 271, 293
Hercules 19, 43, 52–4, 87, 101, 185, 277
Heroick Love 204, 214
History of Hengist, The Saxon King of Kent, The 260
Humorous Lieutenant, The 191, 352
Humour of the Age, The 264, 272, 287–90, 306
Husband His Own Cuckold, The 141, 155–8

Ibrahim, The Thirteenth Emperor of the Turks 76, 141, 159–60, 216
Imposture Defeated; or, A Trick to Cheat the Devil 19, 130, 203–207, 213, 215, 230
Inconstant; or, The Way to Win Him, The 24, 295, 303–304, 314, 323
Indian Queen, The (dramatick opera) 78, 85, 90–92, 95–6, 128, 130, 132, 134–6, 156, 160–1, 164, 186–7, 190, 192, 223, 226, 232, 277, 293, 357
Innocent Mistress, The 27, 165, 185–7, 192–3, 203, 254
Intrigues at Versailles, The 125, 165, 181–3, 196–7, 204, 217, 221
Iphigenia 77, 97, 242, 244–5
Island Princess, The (dramatick opera) 21–2, 67, 76, 91, 95–6, 116, 118, 130, 200–201, 204, 216, 226–7, 230–4, 236–7, 239, 244, 260–261, 271, 277, 284, 293, 317, 326–7, 333, 344, 346, 360
Italian Husband, The 79–80, 86–7, 104, 204, 208, 213–14, 317
Ixion 87, 213, 215, 277

Jew of Venice, The 271–2, 276–7
Judgment of Paris, The 170, 258, 270, 280, 292, 319, 323, 340, 345, 366
Justice Buisy; or, The Gentleman Quack 23, 227, 229–30, 322

King Arthur; or, The British Worthy 24, 88–9, 91, 106, 109, 112, 114, 118–9, 128, 130, 167–8, 206, 221, 223, 226, 230, 252, 274, 293, 303, 327, 340, 351, 371

Ladies Visiting Day, The 272, 284–6, 297
Lancashire Witches; or, Teague O'Divelly, The 79, 190, 269, 324
Libertine, The and *Libertine Destroy'd, The* see *Don John*
Liberty Asserted 338, 344, 352
Lost Lover, The 27, 141, 153–4
Love and a Bottle 18, 25, 227, 230
Love and Riches Reconcil'd 227, 235
Love at a Loss; or, The Most Votes Carry It 81, 272, 274, 323

Love at First Sight 26, 330, 336, 344–5
Love Betray'd; or, The Agreeable Disappointment 308, 312–13, 321, 371
Love for Love 17, 20, 25, 126, 131–6, 140–141, 147, 152, 158, 166, 178, 190, 192, 207, 216, 249, 260, 264, 287, 306, 357, 367, 373
Love for Money 23, 26, 231, 243
Love Makes a Man; or, The Fop's Fortune 13, 43, 267, 272, 274–5, 315, 363
Love the Leveller; or, The Pretty Purchase 337–8, 343–4
Love without Interest; or, The Man Too Hard for the Master 227, 235–6
Love's a Jest 22, 42–6, 52–3, 95, 141, 155, 160, 204, 352
Love's Contrivance; or, Le Medicin malgre Luy 80, 273, 308, 322–3, 325, 365
Love's a Lottery, and a Woman the Prize 227, 235
Love's Last Shift; or, The Fool in Fashion 17, 22, 25, 35–40, 46, 64, 140, 152–3, 171, 190, 193, 309, 351, 359, 371, 373
Love's Victim; or, The Queen of Wales 272, 287
Lover's Luck, The 43–4, 58, 128, 140, 147–9, 152, 163–4, 175, 203, 254, 351
Loves of Aeneas and Dido see *Dido and Aeneas*
Loves of Mars and Venus, The 24, 42, 46–54, 68, 90, 101, 103–4, 109, 126, 165–6, 170, 175, 190, 192, 197, 204, 220, 235, 251, 326, 351, 372
Lying Lover; or, The Lady's Friendship 56, 60–64, 337–8, 341, 372

Macbeth 78–9, 84, 150, 191–2, 251, 280, 324–5, 330, 351, 371
Mad Lover, The (dramatick opera) 95, 112, 267, 271–2, 277–80, 283–4, 293–4, 327, 352
Madam Fickle; or, the Witty False One 190–191, 332

Maid in the Mill, The 46, 325, 352
Maid's Tragedy, The 80, 225
Maiden Queen, The see *Secret Love*
Man of Mode; or, Sir Fopling Flutter, The 28–30, 241, 371
Marriage-Hater Match'd, The 259
Marry, or Do Worse 338–9
Masque of Hercules see *Hercules*
Masque of Peleus and Thetis 276–7
Massaniello 21, 66, 68, 76, 79, 81, 86, 92, 96, 103, 113, 204, 227, 237–9, 245, 253, 261, 265, 302
Match at Bedlam, The 166
Measure for Measure; or, Beauty the Best Advocate 242, 248–51, 254, 257, 327, 351
Medley, The 307
Metamorphosis; or, The Old Lover Outwitted 355–8, 370
Mock-Marriage, The 131, 140–2, 203
Modish Husband, The 295, 301–302
Monsieur Raggou; or, The Old Troop 164
Mountebank; or, The Humours of the Fair, The 337, 356, 362–364
Mourning Bride, The 69–70, 165–6, 178, 193, 202, 216, 260–1, 290, 361
Music for the Peace of Ryswick 195, 203–4, 208–9; see also *Europe's Revels*
Mustapha, Son of Solyman the Magnificent 164

Neglected Virtue; or, The Unhappy Conqueror 27–8, 71, 141, 154
Northern Lass; or, The Nest of Fools, The 355, 370
Novelty; or, Every Act a Play, The 42, 52–56, 64, 129, 165–6, 175, 185, 189–90, 192, 307

Oedipus, King of Thebes 113, 150, 163, 240, 305
Old Batchelor, The 131, 139
Old Mode and the New; or, Country Miss with her Fourbelow, The 308, 315–16

Oroonoko 72, 131, 139–40, 145–7, 152–3, 190, 193, 226, 271, 274, 290, 306, 351
Othello, Moor of Venice 139, 163, 294, 351, 370–71

Patriot; or, The Italian Conspiracy, The 308–9
Pausanias, The Betrayer of His Country 77, 141, 154–5
Perjur'd Husband, The 76, 80, 271–4
Phaeton 68, 79, 86, 96–107, 112–17, 200, 205, 220–222, 230, 252
Philaster; or, Love Lies a Bleeding 85, 141, 151–2
Pilgrim, The 171, 242, 257–8, 260, 351
Plot and No Plot, A 165, 183–5, 363
Pretenders; or, The Town Unmask'd, The 203, 205, 216–19
Princess of Parma, The 227, 236–7, 240
Prophetess; or, the History of Dioclesian, The see *Dioclesian*
Provok'd Wife, The 125–6, 165, 179–83, 185, 192, 198–9, 217, 261, 264, 284, 286, 306
Psyche 51, 88, 187, 190, 203, 353
Pyrrhus, Kng of Epirus 131–2, 136–9, 141, 150, 207

Quacks; or, Love's the Physician, The 356, 365, 367
Queen Catharine; or, The Ruines of Love 205, 223

Rape of Europa, The 277
Reform'd Wife, The 242, 255, 313
Relapse; or, Virtue in Danger, The 37, 165, 171, 181, 183, 193, 226, 260–261, 325, 351
Revengeful Queen, The 76, 80, 86, 205, 221–2
Richard III, The Tragical History of 66, 242, 252, 307
Richmond Heiress, The 19, 27, 156, 313–14
Rinaldo and Armida 10–11, 65, 67–8, 72, 78, 80, 84, 86, 88, 92, 96–118, 191, 223, 226–7, 230–3, 237, 244, 252, 261, 271, 277, 279, 303, 360, 362
Rival Brothers, The 338, 349–50
Rival Queens; or, The Death of Alexander the Great, The (play) 81–84, 215, 223, 240, 280, 325
Rival Queens, The (dramatick opera) see *Alexander the Great*
Rival Sisters; or, The Violence of Love, The 72, 76, 85, 140, 143–4, 146, 178, 358
Roman Bride's Revenge, The 71–2, 85, 96–7, 165, 169–70
Royal Captive, The 296
Royal Mischief, The 85, 127, 141, 158–9, 207, 295, 342

Secret Love; or, The Maiden Queen 203, 226
Secular Masque, The 204, 214, 241–2, 257–8, 260, 270, 313–14
Self Conceit; or, The Mother Made a Property, The 273
Sham Lawyer; or, The Lucky Extravagant 165, 183, 185
She Ventures and He Wins 19, 23, 30–7, 140–1, 147–8, 150, 159, 206, 303
She Wou'd, and She Wou'd Not; or, The Kind Impostor 308–9, 315
She Wou'd if She Cou'd 352–3
She-Gallants, The 46, 140, 150–1, 186, 239
Sir Courtly Nice; or, It Cannot Be 264–5, 306
Sir Harry Wildair; Being the Sequel of the Trip to the Jubilee 23–4, 272, 287, 290–91
Sophonisba; or, Hannibal's Overthrow 370
Spanish Fryar; or, The Double Discovery, The 164, 350, 352
Spanish Wives, The 141, 157, 161–3, 166, 185, 205, 241, 325
Squire Trelooby 338, 340, 346–8, 350, 353, 363, 365
Stage Coach, The 272, 287, 326
Stolen Heiress; or, The Salamanca Doctor Outplotted, The 308, 310

Subscription Musick (various) 3, 313, 327, 332, 334, 338–40, 346, 348, 359–60, 363, 373
Surpriz'd Lovers, The 166

Tamerlane 72–5, 295–7, 352
Taming of the Shrew see *Sauny the Scot*
Tender Husband; or, The Accomplish'd Fools, The 356, 367–8, 372
Tempest, The 12, 88, 139, 187, 190, 226, 260, 271, 275, 293
Theodosius; or, The Force of Love 81, 325
Timoleon; or, The Revolution 76, 165, 177
Timon of Athens; or, The Man-Hater 80, 190, 271, 278, 293, 332, 351, 353, 369, 371
Triumphs of Virtue, The 165, 178–9
Troilus and Cressida; or, Truth Found Too Late 139, 224–5
Tunbridge Walks; or, The Yeoman of Kent 27, 269, 308, 313–16, 323, 325, 351,
Twin Rivals, The 308–309

Unhappy Kindness; or, A Fruitless Revenge, The 79–80, 141, 160
Unhappy Penitent, The 272, 286
Unnatural Brother, The 53, 85, 165–6, 175, 185
Unnatural Mother, The 77–9, 86, 204, 206–207, 295

Venice Preserv'd; or, A Plot Discover'd 84, 370

Vice Reclaim'd; or, The Passionate Mistress 308, 322–4
Victorious Love 78, 84, 86, 205, 221–3, 230, 338
Villain, The 10, 241, 249, 326
Virgin Prophetess; or, The Fate of Troy, The 6, 12, 92–6, 101, 104, 271–2, 280, 287, 292–3, 327, 360
Virtuoso, The 269, 293, 357, 371
Virtuous Wife; or, Good Luck at Last, The 164, 221, 301
Volpone; or, The Fox 3, 264, 269, 363

Way of the World, The 2, 132, 242, 250, 253–4, 261, 274, 306
Wheel of Fortune, The 235
Wife for Any Man 166
Wit of a Woman, The 338, 350
Woman's Wit; or, The Lady in Fashion 165, 177–8, 307
Women Will Have Their Wills 241–2
World in the Moon, The 21–2, 67, 77, 92, 95, 104, 118, 165, 187–9, 193, 220, 360–61

Xerxes 70–71, 73, 79, 86, 106, 227, 232–4, 252, 261

Young Coquet, The 227
Younger Brother; or, The Amorous Jilt, The 35, 37, 41–2, 141, 153, 203

Zelmane; or, The Corinthian Queen 356, 358